BY THE EDITORS OF CONSUMER GUIDE®

ELITE CARS

An Exciting Look at the Most Expensive, Exotic, and Elegant Cars in the World

Beekman House

New York

CONTENTS

Library of Congress Catalog Card Number: 79-67185

This edition published by:
Beekman House
A Division of Crown Publishers, Inc.
One Park Avenue
New York, N.Y. 10016

Photo Credits

Andy Lightbody; Aston Martin Lagonda Inc.; Avanti Motor Corporation; BMW of North America, Inc.; Bozell & Jacobs Inc., Brownell & Staff, Detroit, MI; California Custom Coach; Clenet; Continental Motors, LaGrange, IL; DeLorean Motor Company; Duesenberg Brothers, Inc.; Excalibur Automobile Corporation; Jaguar Rover Triumph Inc.; Joe Marchetti, International Auto Ltd , Chicago, IL; Joseph Molina; Lotus North America Inc.; Mark Grody Associates; Maserati Automobiles Inc.; Mel Winer; Mercedes-Benz of North America Inc.; Porsche + Audi, Volkswagen of America, Inc.; Rolls-Royce Motors Inc.; Scala/O'Brien Porsche + Audi Inc., Chicago, IL; Southeastern Replicars Inc.; Stutz Motor Car of America Inc.

3

INTRODUCTION

The spirit of the great cars can still be felt in the annals of automotive history. You already know their names: Hispano-Suiza, Isotta-Fraschini, Packard, Peerless, Pierce-Arrow, Franklin, Marmon, and more. You might not have actually driven a car like these, but you might have seen pictures of restored examples and maybe have even come close enough to touch such an auto at a museum or classic-car show.

There is something about such cars that sets them apart from other cars. Perhaps it's the distinctive styling that catches your eye. Perhaps it's the aura of quality. It might be the simple fact you don't see cars like these anymore. But you know when you see one that you're looking at something special, something superior.

This book is all about cars that are rare, unusual, and expensive: The elite cars.

At the turn of the century, all automobiles were, in a sense, elite cars. In the early years of motoring the automobile was little more than a cantankerous, unreliable, mechanical novelty. To many people, the sight and sound of one of these contraptions sputtering and clattering its way down the street was at once wondrous and ridiculous. Most onlookers thought the automobile was an impractical plaything for the rich. Others, though, were fascinated by automobiles and dreamed about them.

Those early cars were the odd mechanical dreams of a new generation of tinkerers and inventors. The first cars were rather like home-built experiments and, as a result, were very scarce and very expensive. A price of $2,500 in 1905 for a Ford Model K might not sound like much today, but in that year, the same money would have bought several strong horses or even a large, comfortable house. After all, those were the years of penny candy, the dime novel, and two-dollar shoes.

It was the well-to-do folk who bought those early cars. They were the only people who could. Automobiles were both costly and rare in those days because they were hand-built. Each one was a unique creation, constructed with the care and patience of a da Vinci painting. It took weeks or even months to build a single car. The work was done by artisans who had come from the blacksmith and carriage trades.

All that changed in 1909, when Henry Ford set up the first mass production automobile assembly line. Suddenly, cars were neither uncommon nor extraordinary. Soon, the average wage earner could afford to own one. In 1925, the price of the Model T roadster had fallen to just $250. By then, the whole nation was on wheels. The automobile had ceased to be a toy for the idle rich; it had become an important necessity

of daily living for millions.

But even as the automobile became more commonplace, there were still those affluent people who yearned for cars that were unusual and better than those everyone else was driving. And such wealthy customers could afford to own the very best. In the 1920s and '30s, this elite clientele kept the smaller auto makers and specialist coachbuilders in business. These people were the patrons of the automotive art. And the artists of that period built cars that have become the "classics" of today. It was the age of the Great Gatsby. And in the midst of the Depression the fact that there were those who could own such elite cars kept the dream alive for those who couldn't.

Today, of course, society and cars are much different. The automobile industry has grown into a multimillion-dollar international business. Automotive design no longer reflects the taste of the privileged class. Mass production and mass marketing have made cars more and more alike. But even in today's world of compromises there are still a few very special cars that carry on the tradition of uncompromising excellence inherited from the past. More than any other, these are the cars that catch our eye and our imagination; they are the cars we can dream about.

We call them elite cars for

several reasons. First, all of them are limited-production automobiles and most are largely hand-built to suit each customer's individual taste. Therefore, they are unique and relatively scarce. Of the cars presented here the Mercedes-Benz 300TD wagon has the highest annual production rate. But only about 11,000 of them are made each year; that's about one-fifth the number of cars Chevrolet builds in a *week*. Some elite cars, like the Aston-Martin V-8 or the Rolls-Royce Camargue, are only produced by the handful each year. And two of the elite cars covered in the following pages aren't even being made yet. The DeLorean DMC-12 and the Duesenberg sedan described here are prototypes and are not yet available for sale.

By the laws of supply and demand, limited production means a high price, and that's the second reason these are elite cars. Not everyone can afford to buy one. The least expensive model in this select group, the American-made Intermeccanica Speedster, is priced at about $11,000. From there prices rapidly climb to $100,000 and more.

The third reason these cars deserve the name elite is their distinctiveness. All of them are unusual in at least one aspect of styling, mechanical design, or both. This is what makes an elite car so obviously different from the mass-production

look-alike vehicles we're all familiar with. And a more diverse group of automobiles you'll hardly ever find. For example, the Lotus Esprit, Maserati Merak, and Ferrari 308GTB are all mid-engine sports cars. Their levels of acceleration, speed, and handling are so high that only a few drivers are likely to have the skill needed to utilize such capabilities to their fullest. Another group of elite cars are the so-called "neoclassics." These cars have specially built 1930s-style bodywork, but make use of ordinary production-car chassis and drivetrain components. Cars like the Clenet and Panther J-72 offer styling that evokes memories of the great classics. The neoclassics appeal to those who missed out on the chance to own one of the originals, or who simply prefer vintage styling combined with the advantages of a modern, reliable chassis and running gear.

Some of our selected cars, such as the Avanti II and Jaguar XJ12, have become classics in their own time. They are not copies of anything; they are original, contemporary masterpieces.

And there are elite cars which are so unusual as to defy all categories. Is the Corvette America only a four-door sedan version of "America's only true sports car," or is it still a sports car? Is the Stutz Blackhawk coupe simply a customized

Pontiac, or is it a worthy modern successor to the famous 1930s Blackhawk? Is the Excalibur merely an inexact replica of the fabulous 1928 Mercedes SS, or has it become something more than the most successful "replicar" ever made?

One thing is for sure: The owner of any of these cars is not likely to see another one just like it every day. These are very exclusive automobiles. For most of us, they will remain in the realm of fantasy and dreams. We may never actually drive or get close to one of these cars, but we can imagine what it's like to own one.

And that is the purpose of this book. In these pages, you'll discover what it's actually like to drive and live with these cars. Of course, the owner of the futuristic $75,000 Lagonda would probably be wealthy enough to afford to own another less exotic car for everyday chores. But what if he had to use the Lagonda as his only car? How practical is this, or any of the other elite cars, in actual use? The answers vary with each car. But you may be surprised to find that these automobiles are not entirely frivolous, even though they are often bought as playthings by the rich and famous.

The following group of cars is not ordinary. Get set to shift your imagination into high gear. That's really all the equipment you need for touring—and enjoying—the world of elite cars.

ASTON MARTIN V~8

Historically, the name Aston Martin goes back to 1914, Lionel Martin, Robert Bamford, and the Aston Clinton hill climb. The 1.5-liter Astons of the 1930s are some of the nicest small Classics around. But the history of Aston Martin as a real force in the automobile world begins in 1947, when Sir David Brown, of David Brown Tractors, bought the firm. Brown's hobby was racing, and under his leadership Astons won Le Mans and the World Manufacturers Championship in 1959. Brown also produced a long line of big, fast touring cars which are the only postwar British GT's that are recognized as Milestone cars, along with Ferrari,

Mercedes-Benz, and Maserati GT's of the '50s. Yet the company suffered financial problems in the 1960s despite the excellence of its cars.

In 1974 Aston Martin was bought by Peter Sprague, an American; and George Minden, a Canadian. They rescued the company from bankruptcy, and production has since risen to six cars a week. Aston Martin now

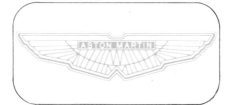

builds three variations on the GT theme (the V-8 coupe, Vantage coupe, and Volante convertible), plus the incredible Lagonda sedan. All are collectors items bought by enthusiasts who have at least $50,000 to spend.

The current Aston Martin V-8 Coupe design appeared in 1967 as the DBS, powered by a six-cylinder engine which was based on a 30-year-old design. The Aston's styling bore an unfortunate resemblance to Ford's Mustang of the same year. The Mustang body went out of production in 1970, but the Aston is still being made. The passé long-hood, short-deck design provides almost no trunk space and severely limits

Opposite: Introduced in 1967, the Aston Martin V-8 is beginning to look dated. Above left: A very British driving position features full instrumentation, but the steering wheel sits too close for comfort.

Above right: The Coupe's interior dimensions are like those of a mid-1960s "pony car" and room is just as limited. Below: The Vantage sports front and rear spoilers to match its higher performance.

visibility. As a result the body is not very space efficient and the styling is beginning to look dated.

In 1963 Tadek Merak, Aston Martin's chief engineer, began work on a 4.8-liter V-8 to replace the six. This engine finally appeared in the DBS in 1968. A 5340cc version came to the U.S. market two years later. Originally intended as a 5-liter racing engine, the Aston V-8 is made of aluminum, including the block. It has chain-driven, double overhead camshafts on each bank of cylinders; four Weber carburetors, and a plethora of high-performance internal niceties. All of this makes it a nightmare to service—almost as

irritating as Jaguar's equally complex V-12, one of the most difficult engines to keep properly tuned. If you aren't friends with a trained mechanic, this isn't the car for you.

The standard transmission is an excellent ZF five-speed; a Chrysler Torqueflite three-speed automatic is optional. As you might expect, the V-8's fuel economy is not good, no matter which transmission you choose— 10 miles per gallon is the most you'll ever see. On the road it's quickly apparent that this big engine produces a lot of power even though Aston doesn't quote a horsepower figure for the V-8. Driving an Aston is like piloting a late-1960s muscle car. It may

not handle all that well, and it's not very comfortable, but it's fast: 0-60 mph in less than six seconds; 0-100 in 13 seconds; and, amazingly, 0-100-0 in 19 seconds.

The Aston Martin is one of the few cars equipped with a De Dion-type independent rear suspension on coil springs. The front suspension is also independent by wishbones and coil springs. Even with this sophisticated suspension, however, the ride of the Aston V-8 Coupe is harsh thanks to the very stiff springs and limited suspension travel.

The chassis is a simple platform type, with a 102-inch wheelbase (four inches longer than a Corvette's). The aluminum body of the Coupe stretches out to 183 inches, and is 52 inches high. The car weighs 3,800 pounds, roughly the same as a Camaro or Firebird.

And it feels like an American sporty car when driven—too much so. The present Aston Martin has been in production for so long that, by today's standards, it has an almost "vintage" feel, just like the equally long-lived Camaro. The handling exhibits classic understeer. Front-end plowing is a fact of life with the Aston Martin, though the extravagant horsepower lets you balance the car on the throttle to create an artificially neutral feel. The Aston Martin's steering has too much heft to it, and the brakes and clutch demand more effort than most people are used to. On a tight winding road, you really have to work hard to drive fast. The brakes are huge power-assisted Girling vented discs at all four wheels and they stop the car cleanly and quickly. But pedal effort is high despite the power assist. The clutch also feels heavy and it chatters. The shifter is stiff and notchy. All in all, driving an Aston Martin is really too much work.

The interior is pure British luxury car. The two front buckets and tiny rear seats are upholstered in top-grade Connolly leather as are the door panels and shift console. The carpets, trim, and interior hardware are all made of high quality materials. A full complement of British-made gauges is set into a woodgrain dash panel. The wheels are beautiful alloy jobs, cast by Aston Martin. They carry Pirelli 255/70VR-15 tires.

Unfortunately, the headroom is insufficient for an average-size person, the steering wheel is

positioned too close to the driver for comfort, and the fat C-pillars restrict rear vision. Front seat legroom is excellent, but the

rear seat is best reserved for Munchkins.

Aston Martin also makes a convertible version of its V-8

Coupe. Called the Volante, it's identical with the coupe in its every feature, save the folding soft top.

For those who always want just a little bit more, Aston Martin offers the Vantage. This is basically a V-8 Coupe equipped with a performance package that adds Koni shock absorbers, low-profile Pirelli tires, special bucket seats and dashboard trim, driving lights, and a fiberglass front spoiler under the bumper. The Konis and Pirellis make the already-stiff suspension really rock hard. This means a bad pothole could break the spoiler which has minimal ground clearance anyway. The special seats are harder to get into than the stock versions. The Vantage is for looking at, not driving. Priced at almost $65,000, it is a very expensive piece of old-school sculpture indeed.

Opposite top: The Volante is a convertible version of the V-8 Coupe, but is identical with it in most other respects. Opposite bottom: There's luxury open-air motoring for two in the Volante; its rear seat isn't big enough for normal-sized people. Below: With the top down, the Volante looks sleeker and more modern than its Coupe sibling. Lower left: Aston's complex all-aluminum V-8 is based on a would-be racing engine and is a mechanic's nightmare to service. Lower right: The Volante's rear-end styling is neat and clean.

ASTON MARTIN V-8 COUPE/VOLANTE CONVERTIBLE MAJOR SPECIFICATIONS

Manufacturer/Importer:
Aston Martin Lagonda
14 Weyman Avenue,
New Rochelle, NY 10805
Body type—2-door, 4-passenger coupe/convertible

Wheelbase, in./cm—102.7/260
Overall length, in./cm—183.7/466
Overall width, in./cm—72/183
Overall height, in./cm—52.3/133
Track, front, in./cm—59/150
Track, rear, in./cm—59/150
Curb weight, lb./kg—3800/1710
Engine type—water-cooled dohc V-8
Hp @ rpm—NA
Displacement, cu. in./cc—326/5340

Carburetion—four 2-bbl Weber
Transmission—5-speed manual (3-speed automatic optional)
Brakes front/rear—ventilated disc/ventilated disc
Fuel Economy, normal driving—8-10 mpg
Est. top speed—160 mph
Approx. price—$48,000-73,000

Specifications for U.S. market model unless otherwise noted.

AUBURN SPEEDSTER

California Custom Coach builds one of the best of the new breed of replicars. Unlike neoclassics such as the Clenet or Excalibur, which have old-fashioned styling but are not exact replicas of any particular model, the CCC Speedster is an authentic duplicate of a 1935 Auburn 851 Speedster. Indeed, the molds for the CCC car's fiberglass bodywork were taken from a real Auburn Speedster; it would be possible to authentically restore an original Auburn by using CCC pieces. The CCC Speedster is a fascinating mixture of old and new.

The huge body is 191 inches long, 76 inches wide, and seemingly a mile high. It's made up of a hood that looks as long as the bow of a yacht, bulging fenders, exterior exhaust pipes, headlight nacelles which resemble punctuation marks, and the winged Auburn mascot leading the way. Yet driving all this is not rapture. The V-shaped windshield directs a strong blast of air back onto the passengers, quickly destroying

Opposite page, clockwise from upper left: Auburn Speedster hood sports authentic mascot; dash uses modern instruments; from any angle, an impressive automobile. Above, clockwise from upper right: Note the modern, wide tires; with top up, cockpit feels cramped; exhaust pipes are only for looks; interior has classic tuck-and-roll upholstery.

hairdos, and eventually good moods. Put the top up, and you'll feel like you're riding in a suitcase, because the cockpit is so cramped. The ineffective side curtains must be removed and stored in the trunk. They cannot simply be rolled down. Luggage space is nearly nonexistent.

The car's ride and handling are surprisingly old-fashioned, too. You'll experience a great deal of understeer, a harsh ride, and lots of tire squeal even on gentle bends. Braking is no more than adequate for modern highways. The steering system transmits lots of road feel. But there are modern touches, that make this a much better car than the original Auburn. The chassis for the CCC car comes from a full-size Ford sedan, along with its 400 cubic-inch V-8, three-speed automatic transmission, air conditioning, and AM/FM stereo cassette deck. Therefore, mechanical parts and service are available right around any corner. And the car *goes.* Such a big V-8 in a car that weighs 3,200 pounds makes for

AUBURN SPEEDSTER

acceleration better than that of most modern passenger cars.

Construction quality of the CCC Speedster is superb. The fiberglass bodywork is flawless, as is the lacquer paint job. All the trim is made of chrome-plated brass or stainless steel. The classic tuck-and-roll upholstery is genuine Connolly leather.

A car like the CCC Speedster is surprisingly inexpensive to own. Nothing on the body can ever rust, and the Ford chassis can be expected to cover 100,000 miles easily before needing any major attention. The running costs of this flamboyant replicar are actually less than those of a conventional Mercedes-Benz or Rolls-Royce sedan of the same price.

Prior to 1979, California Custom Coach sold the Auburn Speedster as a do-it-yourself kit. The car became so popular, however, that the company recently began production of complete machines, and that's the only way you can buy one nowadays. A two-seater, complete and ready to run, costs $37,500. A similar 2 + 2 version, made by fitting a second seat into the space where the folding top would ordinarily be stored, sells for $42,000.

A CCC Speedster is not a car you can push like a Ferrari, though at fast highway speeds it's perfectly happy. The Speedster's real forte is making grand entrances. Glide up to the curb and doormen fight to assist

you; restaurant prices will immediately double should the *maître de* see you pull into the parking lot. Much more than any new Mercedes or Rolls-Royce, the CCC Speedster shouts "money!" Tell people the real price and they won't believe you. They want it to cost at least $100,000.

The car has looks that will turn all heads, it out-performs most new cars, its body is virtually unbreakable, its price is not outlandish, and it is sure to appreciate in value. More than any other elite car, the CCC Auburn Speedster captures the spirit of motoring's extravagant past. If you're not worried about where that $38,000 will come from, and don't mind a little wind in your face, buy one now.

AUBURN SPEEDSTER MAJOR SPECIFICATIONS

Manufacturer/Importer:
California Custom Coach
1285 East Colorado Boulevard,
Pasadena, CA 91106
Body type—2-door, 2-passenger roadster

Wheelbase, in./cm—127/323
Overall length, in./cm—191/485
Overall width, in./cm—70/178
Overall height, in./cm—58/147
Track, front, in./cm—63/160
Track, rear, in./cm—65/165
Curb weight, lb./kg—3200/1400
Engine type—water-cooled ohv V-8

Hp @ rpm—159 @ 3400
Displacement, cu. in./cc—400/6555
Carburetion—one 2-bbl
Transmission—3-speed automatic
Brakes front/rear—disc/drum
Fuel Economy, normal driving—12 mpg
Est. top speed—110 mph
Approx. price—$37,500

Specifications for U.S. market model unless otherwise noted.

It's pretty hard to find a car of any price that doesn't look a bit like something else. In these days of mass production, mass marketing, and intense competition between the giant auto companies, most cars end up looking pretty much alike. The small, specialist builders strive for something different and often the result is styling that's so different it's ugly. But, there's one modern car that's both beautiful and totally unlike any other: the Avanti.

The original Avanti was designed for Studebaker a few years before that company stopped making cars. Bob Andrews, Tom Kellogg and John Ebstein were stylists working for Raymond Loewy in 1961. Working in secret and almost around-the-clock, the four of

them took just two weeks to design what would turn out to be one of the all-time modern classics. The subtle curvaceousness of the Avanti body makes one of the great visual statements of our time. The Smithsonian Institution apparently agrees because several years ago an Avanti was on display there for a long time.

The Avanti was produced by Studebaker for only a little over a year. When the company consolidated its car production in Canada in 1964, the Avanti was dropped from the line-up and seemed destined for oblivion.

Then, a pair of irrepressible Studebaker dealers, Nate Altman and Leo Newman, bought the rights to the Avanti name along with the tooling for the car and the old Studebaker factory in South Bend, Indiana. Newman and Altman reworked the Avanti's chassis but wisely left the body styling alone. In 1966 Altman and Newman started producing the Avanti II.

The Avanti II for 1980 costs $17,670, which is a bargain for what you get. One thing you get is that stylish Loewy body, painstakingly handcrafted in fiberglass. If Corvette or Lotus is your idea of a good fiberglass finish, take a look at the Avanti's impressive and impeccable bodywork. The Molded Fiber Glass Company makes both Corvette and Avanti

AVANTI II

bodies, but construction quality on the Avanti II is superior.

The chassis of the Avanti II is derived from the 1962 Studebaker Lark Wagonaire station wagon. Rear suspension consists of a rigid axle, upper control arms, and leaf springs. The front suspension is independent by means of coil springs and wishbones. There are anti-roll bars front and rear. This chassis design means the Avanti II doesn't handle especially well. A great deal of understeer is the predominant handling characteristic. The Avanti II is not a car you'd want to race over a winding road, but it is perfectly satisfactory for everyday driving. As compensation for the dull handling, the Avanti II has a surprisingly soft, comfortable ride.

In order to meet federal emissions requirements, Avanti Motors buys its engines already certified from General Motors. The Corvette L-48, a 350 cubic-inch V-8 from Chevrolet, is the only engine offered. This is teamed along with the excellent three-speed Turbo Hydra-matic 400 transmission. The big V-8 and low-restriction mufflers combine to produce a roar that brings back memories of the '60s "muscle cars." Helped by the Avanti's moderate weight (3,570 pounds), this reliable, popular and easily serviced engine produces excellent quarter-mile times of around 17 seconds at 85 mph. The 0-60 mph time is about nine seconds, and the car has a top speed of 120 mph. In more normal driving, the Avanti II will return between 15 and 20 mpg. The front-disc, rear-drum brake system stops the car impressively with no noticeable fade, noise, or chatter.

The Avanti II is strictly custom-built. Avanti Motors starts to construct your car only after you order it. Almost any color, upholstery material or option can be included to suit each

Below: There's hardly a straight line anywhere on the Avanti's subtly curvaceous body which still looks striking after more than 15 years. Opposite page, left: The Avanti's interior can be upholstered in the customer's choice of materials. Opposite right: Modern instrument panel was inspired by aircraft cockpit design and is largely unchanged from Loewy's original.

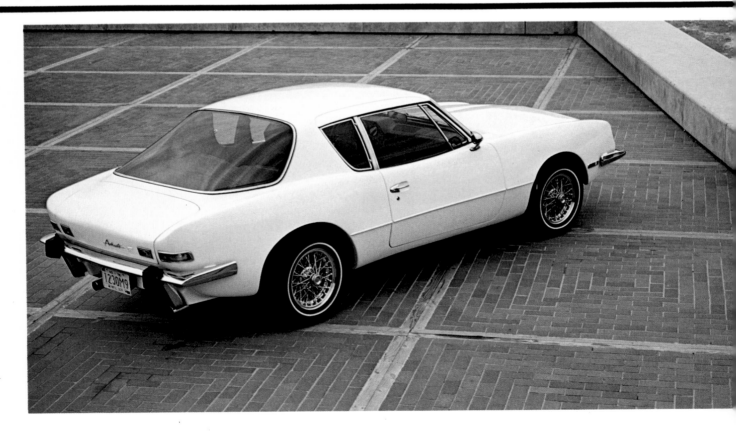

customer's individual tastes. The standard paint chart lists hundreds of colors and the factory upholstery book contains everything from velours that would be embarrassing in Mae West's living room to leathers that are too expensive even for Rolls-Royce to use. If you can't find what you want at the factory, Avanti Motors will upholster the car in any yard good, no matter how bizarre, which the customer cares to supply. Some owners match their living room couch, a favorite dress, or a pair of custom-made Texas boots.

Standard equipment includes an AM/FM/CB radio with retractable antenna; power brakes, steering and windows; automatic transmission; air conditioning; and a futuristic bucket-seat interior which is basically the same as Loewy's original Studebaker design, and still among the nicest on any 1980 car. The seats are comfortable; and there's excellent headroom (at least in front), and plenty of hip room, shoulder room, and legroom. What the Avanti's body lacks is luggage space, but there's still more room here than in the similar-size Camaro/Firebird. And the Avanti has a handy hatch that lets you reach into the trunk from inside the car.

Avanti Motors has never built more than 400 cars a year, and the waiting list is usually long. Yet, people stand in line to buy Avantis for a number of reasons. Because of the custom-built nature of the car, buyers are assured of getting exactly what they order. Because of the outstanding craftsmanship, they'll get one of the most carefully assembled and finished cars in the world. Because of the unique body, they'll get a car that's sure to be noticed. And because so few cars are made each year, used Avantis have a very high resale value.

Most of all, Avanti owners belong to an exclusive group. They like being treated as part of a big family by the charming and hard-working craftsmen at Avanti Motors. Avanti doesn't advertise, there are few dealers, and you have to wait six to nine months just to take delivery. But many Avanti II buyers are already on their second or third Avanti, while others habitually bring their older models back to the South Bend factory to be reconditioned. So, the Avanti II is not only an unusual car; for the owners it's a way of life.

AVANTI II MAJOR SPECIFICATIONS

Manufacturer/Importer:
Avanti Motor Corp.
765 South Lafayette Boulevard,
South Bend, IN 46634
Body type—2-door, 4-passenger coupe
Wheelbase, in./cm—109/277

Overall length, in./cm—197.8/502
Overall width, in./cm—70.4/179
Overall height, in./cm—54.4/138
Track, front, in./cm—57.3/146
Track, rear, in./cm—56.6/144
Curb weight, lb./kg—3570/1619
Engine type—Chevrolet water-cooled ohv V-8
Hp @ rpm—185 hp @ 4000 rpm

Displacement, cu. in./cc—350/5736
Carburetion—one 2-bbl
Transmission—3-speed automatic
Brakes front/rear—ventilated disc/drum
Fuel Economy, normal driving—15-20 mpg
Est. top speed—120 mph
Approx. price—$17,670

Specifications for U.S. market model unless otherwise noted.

BENTLEY T~2

In the glory days of the 1920s, when diamond heir Woolf Barnato financed W.O. Bentley's automotive fantasies, Bentley was *the* name in sporting motorcars. Even today, there is nothing on the road to compare with a demanding late-1920s Vanden Plas tourer on the 3-liter or 4.5-liter Bentley chassis. In the '30s, after Bentley was purchased by Rolls-Royce, the Derby-built 4/14 made its debut. It is one of the nicest small cars ever built, particularly the ones with bodies by Gurney Nutting. And the Bentley Continental Mulliner Flying Spur from the 1950s is certainly one of the most delectable postwar coupes.

Then there's the current Bentley T-series, which has been in production for over a decade. In a word, the current Bentley is dull. The mystical element that made the Bentleys of old so special has been lost, probably forever. It's significant that, although the Bentley T-2 and the Rolls-Royce Silver Shadow are identical except for their grilles, the Bentley is nowhere near as popular as the Rolls. Bentley sells only 30 cars a year in the United States.

Sales of the same machine with a Rolls-Royce grille average around 1,100 units.

The standard Bentley four-door sedan is a variation on the Rolls-Royce Silver Shadow; the Bentley two-door coupe and convertible are the same as the Rolls-Royce Corniche. All three Bentleys are built with a modern unitized body/chassis that's much more rigid than any classic Bentley frame. This chassis has

Opposite page: The Bentley looks like a Rolls-Royce Silver Shadow because that's what it is; only the grille and badges are different. Above: The latest T-2 features this two-tone paint treatment similar to that used on the Bentleys of yesteryear; the square-cut styling is simple but conservative; note rear seat headrests.

a 120-inch wheelbase. But in relation to the wheelbase the body is short—only 207 inches in overall length. In American car parlance, the Bentley has a "full-size" wheelbase and a "compact" length. This lack of overhang gives the car a stubby, awkward appearance, something like a Volvo 144 with rounded fenders and Checker Marathon headlights. Even die-hard Bentley fans find it difficult to get excited about the T-2's styling.

Mechanically, the Bentley is conservative. A conventional independent suspension with coil springs and unequal-length A-arms is used at the front. The rear suspension is fully independent, with trailing arms and coil springs. The Bentley

suspension is tuned to maximize comfort rather than cornering ability. A T-2 has a much softer ride than Mercedes-Benz's 6.9, and leans dizzyingly in hard cornering.

The Bentley is softer than the Mercedes in other ways, too. The T-2's standard four-wheel disc brakes are adequate, but not outstanding. The rack-and-pinion steering is accurate; but the power assist—basically the same as that of big General Motors cars—is too light. All in all, the Bentley is about a decade behind the times in chassis design. It simply can't be driven quickly with any sort of confidence, and it feels clumsy at low speeds. We'd expect to get something more

than this for our $65,000.

The Bentley's automatic transmission does make soft, almost imperceptible shifts, mostly because the General Motors three-speed Hydra-matic is one of the best transmissions of its type. The Bentley is also fitted with an electronic gear selector, which further softens manual shifts with the automatic. Bentley's obvious aim is to build a quiet, comfortable owner-driven luxury car for conservative drivers—not the kind of automobile Bentley used to build. These days, when even Chevrolet offers what could be called European-style ride and handling, the too-soft Bentley is an expensive anachronism.

The current Rolls-Royce Bentley engine has been in

production since 1958. It's essentially a light, oversize version of the famous General Motors small block V-8, which was introduced in 1955. As used in the Bentley, this engine displaces 412 cubic inches. Only the full-size Cadillac of '78 and earlier, and the Excalibur, have larger engines. Not surprisingly, the Environmental Protection Agency's estimate of 10 miles per gallon for the Bentley is the lowest of any passenger vehicle sold in the United States, including the big four-wheel-drive Chevy Blazers and Ford Broncos. The Bentley's fuel economy is hampered by its weight of some 5,000 pounds. Its serviceability is complicated by an old-style tiny hood. The underhood view of a Bentley is

enough to give even a master mechanic claustrophobia.

Oh, but the Bentley T-2 is one of the most comfortable sedans in the world. Real woodgrain trim covers the dash, the window sills, and the center console. Connolly leather is used for the upholstery, in a choice of muted shades like gray, tan, blue, and dark red. The front seats are upright chairs that provide plenty of legroom, knee room, headroom, and hip room. However, the back seat is small. Thick C-pillars restrict rear vision. The old-fashioned British steering wheel and column shifter look appropriate, considering the Bentley's stodgy feel and styling.

David Plastow, the exuberant young man who heads

Rolls-Royce, has taken his friend Bill Mitchell's advice and has begun painting his cars in contrasting colors like a Bentley from the 1920s, or Mitchell's own Bentley-inspired Caprice Classic.

The difference between a 1929 Bentley 3-liter and a '29 Chevrolet is vast. An old Chevy can't be judged by Bentley standards. But the styling and engineering of other makes have improved dramatically in the past two decades, while the Bentley design has changed little. So, by today's standards, the Bentley isn't as good a car now as it was 20 years ago. A Chevrolet Caprice can do almost everything a T-2 can do, and for $50,000 less. The Bentley T-2 is years behind the times.

The T-2's Rolls-Royce heritage is evident from any angle; grille costs less to make than a Rolls's.

BENTLEY T-2 MAJOR SPECIFICATIONS

Manufacturer/Importer:
Rolls-Royce Motors
Century Road, Paramus, NJ 07652
Body type—4-door, 5-passenger sedan
Wheelbase, in./cm—120.1/305
Overall length, in./cm—207.5/527
Overall width, in./cm—71.8/182
Overall height, in./cm—59.8/152
Track, front, in./cm—60/152

Track, rear, in./cm—59.6/151
Curb weight, lb./kg—4930/2218
Engine type—water-cooled ohv V-8
Hp (a rpm—N A
Displacement, cu. in./cc—412/6750
Carburetion—two 1-bbl SU

Transmission—3-speed automatic
Brakes front/rear—ventilated
    disc/ventilated disc
Fuel Economy, normal driving—10 mpg
Est. top speed—118 mph
Approx. price—$65,000

Specifications for U.S. market model unless otherwise noted.

BMW 633CSi

BMW introduced the 630CSi in 1977 as a replacement for the 3.0CS, which had been one of the most popular GT cars of its era. The 3.0CS and its predecessor, the 2800CS, are collector's items today—worth more now than they were when new. The 633CSi, a big-bore version of the 630CSi introduced two years ago, clearly has the potential to become a collector's car: Many experts consider it to be one of the great automobiles of our time.

Like the 3.0CS, the 633CSi doesn't appear impressive on the specifications sheet. The 633CSi gearbox is a four-speed, non-overdrive unit connected to a 3.45:1 final drive—short by modern standards. The engine is a 3210cc single-overhead-cam six, which is rated at only 177 horsepower at 5500 rpm. This

mildly-tuned engine uses Bosch L-Jetronic fuel-injection, but little else about it is remarkable.

The specs of the 633CSi chassis are nothing to get excited about either. The 103.4-inch-wheelbase unitized body/chassis uses a relatively simple four-wheel independent suspension made up of

MacPherson struts at the front and semi-trailing arms with coil springs at the rear. Four-wheel disc brakes are standard, as are alloy wheels and Michelin XDX 195/70VR-14 tires. (Those wheels, incidentally, are rare and expensive BBS Mahle Motorsport wheels that cost nearly $300 each.) Simple though it may be, this chassis works flawlessly.

The BMW 633CSi is one of the most delightful driver's cars available at any price. The steering is remarkably precise, the shifter is properly located in relation to the pedals, seat, and steering wheel, and is a pleasure to use. The driving position was obviously designed for a full-size person who needs lots of elbow room.

All BMWs handle well, the 633CSi especially so. The car is slightly nose-heavy—56 percent of its 3,430-pound weight is carried on the front wheels. As a result, there's some understeer in tight, low-speed corners taken too fast. Driven intelligently, though, the car feels perfectly neutral. During hard braking, the car's nose dips alarmingly: There's not enough anti-drive built into the chassis. But the

brakes pull the car down to a clean stop quickly and safely.

Styling is not one of the things BMW does well. Many people say they think the 633CSi is funny-looking. The large greenhouse, sharply pointed nose, short rear deck, and BMW's trademark grille "nostrils" are a

few of the reasons.

However, the 633CSi really shines inside. The smooth leather bucket seats are comfortable, but slippery, so some buyers choose the optional cloth upholstery instead. The seats can be adjusted in a variety of ways. The driving position is excellent, and the thin

Above left: Fuel-injected sohc six-cylinder engine looks crowded under the hood. Above right: Heating and air conditioning controls are on angled section of dash to right of wheel. Below

left: Rear passenger compartment is a little cramped. Below right: Front seat accommodations are excellent despite slippery leather seating surfaces; cloth is optional.

roof pillars and large windows make for uncommonly good visibility in all directions. The only complaint we have about the interior is that the 633's steering wheel, like those of other BMW models, is set a bit too high.

Options used to be a problem for buyers of the 630CSi. The car's $26,000 price did not include a radio, for example. Standard on the 633CSi are: an AM/FM stereo cassette unit; air conditioning; power steering, brakes, and windows; metallic paint; and leather upholstery. That list of equipment is more in keeping with BMW's first-cabin prices.

The 633CSi is a wonderful grand touring car. Its performance is virtually identical with that of a Ferrari 308GTB—0 to 60 mph in 10 seconds, 130 mph top speed—but the feeling of the BMW is much more relaxed, civilized.

The BMW is quiet, comfortable, reliable, and capable of carrying four passengers in extraordinary luxury. Its nearest competition in price and performance is probably the Mercedes-Benz 450SLC, a car of completely different character but having the same unbreakable feel. Judged by any standard, the 633CSi is one of the great cars of our time. It is built in small numbers, so its exclusivity almost assures it will be a collector's item 20 years from now.

BMW 633CSi MAJOR SPECIFICATIONS

Manufacturer/Importer:
BMW of North America
Montvale, NJ 07645
Body type—2-door, 4-passenger coupe
Wheelbase, in./cm—103.4/262
Overall length, in./cm—192.7/489

Carburetion—Bosch L-Jetronic fuel injection
Transmission—4-speed manual (3-speed automatic optional)
Brakes front/rear—ventilated disc/ventilated disc
Fuel Economy, normal driving—13 mpg
Est. top speed—134 mph
Approx. price—$28,000

Overall width, in./cm—67.9/172
Overall height, in./cm—53.7/136
Track, front, in./cm—56.0/142
Track, rear, in./cm—58.0/147
Curb weight, lb./kg—3430/1543
Engine type—water-cooled sohc inline six
Hp (a rpm—177 (a 5500 rpm
Displacement, cu. in./cc—196/3210

Specifications for U.S. market model unless otherwise noted.

The San Remo Dorado is one of a new crop of custom-built American convertibles which have popped up since the last production Eldorado convertible was built in 1976. The San Remo conversion is based on the new, front-wheel-drive Eldorado, and both the design and workmanship of the finished product are exquisite. Which is just as well for, at $34,500, the San Remo isn't cheap. You have to wonder why—if an Eldorado already costs $14,000—it should cost more than twice that much just to cut the top off. Similar conversions on other cars, like Thunderbirds, and Mark Vs, add less than $10,000 to the price of the standard car. The only conclusion you can draw is that Cadillac dealers who handle the San Remo are collecting a handsome profit, indeed.

The first step in converting the Eldorado into a San Remo is to reinforce the unitized body/chassis with extra frame rails which are welded on all the way around the perimeter of the chassis. With the chassis thus strengthened, the roof is snipped off. The convertible top

CADILLAC SAN REMO

mechanism is specially made for the San Remo, but Cadillac hardware and materials are used for the trim and the latching mechanism.

As a distinguishing touch, a chrome cap is added to the Eldorado grille. Genuine knock-off wire wheels, wide whitewall tires, and hand-rubbed lacquer paint complete the exterior work.

On the inside, the stock front seats are reupholstered in Connolly leather. The rear seat and door panels are covered to match. The result is an interior even more luxurious than that of the stock Eldorado.
Everything else in the San Remo is taken straight from the Eldorado, right down to the optional diesel V-8.

Driving a San Remo is just about like driving a stock Eldorado. The convertible conversion adds only 80 pounds to the Eldorado's 3,800 pound curb weight, and since the wheelbase is unaltered, performance and handling of the two cars are similar. The strengthened frame seems to compensate adequately for the loss of torsional rigidity from removing the roof.

Opposite, clockwise from top: San Remo's conversion looks like a factory-built Eldorado convertible; except for the lack of a roof, rear-end styling is unchanged from stock; grille features a wide chrome cap. Below, clockwise from lower left: Eldorado dashboard is retained intact; interior is re-trimmed in Connolly leather; convertible top steals very little space from the rear compartment.

CADILLAC SAN REMO

While the San Remo is a typically American car that prefers smooth freeways to rough corners, it performs well in the sort of lazy, open road driving for which it is intended. Acceleration is adequate with the Eldorado's standard 350 cubic-inch small block V-8 in 170-horsepower gasoline form, though the optional 120-hp diesel version of this power plant delivers pretty anemic acceleration. The four-wheel disc brakes perform as well as the brakes on almost any car made in America, and the variable-ratio GM power steering unit is superior to most other assisted steering systems in the amount of road feel transmitted to the driver. Some experimenting with aftermarket shock absorbers, anti-sway bars, and tires can upgrade the Eldorado's dynamic qualities so that the car actually justifies the "American Mercedes" label General Motors likes to use.

Justifying an Eldorado convertible that costs over twice as much as the standard model, however, may be difficult for some buyers. Curiously enough, the biggest problem with the San Remo, in view of its exclusivity and price, is that it doesn't draw much attention because the conversion looks like the sort of thing Cadillac would build if it made an Eldorado convertible. Even knowledgeable car buffs look at the San Remo and think of it as a production Eldorado. Later, they do a double-take and it hits them—Cadillac doesn't make a convertible!

CADILLAC/SAN REMO CONVERTIBLE MAJOR SPECIFICATIONS

Manufacturer/Importer:
Coach Design Group
31344 Via Colinas,
Westlake Village, CA 91361
Body type—2-door, 4-passenger, convertible

Wheelbase, in./cm—114/289
Overall length, in./cm—204/518
Overall width, in./cm—71.4/182
Overall height, in./cm—54.2/138
Track, front, in./cm—59.3/150
Track, rear, in./cm—60.5/154
Curb weight, lb./kg—3880/1746
Engine type—water-cooled ohv V-8
Hp (a rpm—170 (a 4200 (DIN)

Displacement, cu. in./cc—350/5735
Carburetion—electronic fuel injection
Transmission—3-speed automatic
Brakes front/rear—ventilated
        disc/ventilated disc
Fuel Economy, normal driving—14 mpg
Est. top speed—115 mph
Approx. price—$34,500

Specifications for U.S. market model unless otherwise noted.

One of the nice things about fiberglass is that just about anybody can cut and paste his way to a custom body. Many handy people have played around with the fiberglass bodies of Corvettes. They usually do so to make an old-fashioned Corvette body look sleeker, racier or more modern than stock. And they usually leave the chassis alone.

Then there are the folks from California Custom Coach. They decided to add 30 inches and two doors to a stock Corvette, creating a limited-production Corvette four-door sedan. The result, named the Corvette America, resembles a giant hot dog. A chopped-up Corvette that can carry a party of four will cost you: doubling the doors more than doubles the price, to

$39,500. The Corvette America is the answer to a question nobody asked.

Here's how the thing comes into being. A new Corvette is cut in half behind the seats, and 30 inches of stock Corvette frame rail are welded in. Four new doors, smaller than the original two, are built up from Chevrolet inner components and CCC fiberglass skins. The

CORVETTE AMERICA

CORVETTE AMERICA

window glass is stock Corvette, modified to fit. A second targa-style roll bar is added as a B-pillar, and a second set of stock Corvette bucket seats is added in the rear, along with matching carpets and door panels. A second set of stock Corvette moonroofs finishes the job.

The end product looks like a factory-fresh Corvette four-door sedan, 215 inches long, riding a 128-inch wheelbase. The conversion leaves all the Corvette's weaknesses either unchanged or worse. These include poor visibility, poor handling, poor bucket seats, which provide no lateral support, minimal luggage space, anemic

Below: Conversion of the Corvette to this four-door sedan accentuates the standard car's flowing lines. Bottom: The long wheelbase makes the car look like an ungainly caricature

CORVETTE AMERICA MAJOR SPECIFICATIONS

Manufacturer/Importer:
Design America
1285 East Colorado Boulevard,
Pasadena, CA 91106
Body type—4-door, 4-passenger sedan
Wheelbase, in./cm—128/325

Overall length, in./cm—215/546
Overall width, in./cm—69/175
Overall height, in./cm—49/124
Track, front, in./cm—58.7/149
Track, rear, in./cm—59.5/151
Curb weight, lb./kg—3874/1743
Engine type—water-cooled ohv V-8
Hp @ rpm—225 @ 5200
Displacement, cu. in./cc—350/5736

Carburetion—one 4-bbl
Transmission—4-speed manual (3-speed automatic optional)
Brakes front/rear—ventilated disc/ventilated disc
Fuel Economy, normal driving—13 mpg
Est. top speed—120 mph
Approx. price—$39,500

Specifications for U.S. market model unless otherwise noted.

acceleration, an assortment of squeaks and rattles, and little suspension travel.

The four-door understeers even more than the two-door, but its ride is softer, because of the longer wheelbase. Ground clearance is a serious problem on rough roads and steep driveways. And because the four-door weighs considerably more than the stock two-door

car, the Corvette America's acceleration is worse than stock, even with the "hot" 225-horsepower L-82 V-8.

In the process of adding the extra doors, CCC must take the stock Corvette apart, and then repaint the entire car. This gives the company an opportunity to make one improvement. The Corvette America is much better finished throughout than a stock

Corvette, with flawless paint and upholstery. However, the moonroofs still leak, and there are twice as many of them to let water drip on twice as many shoulders.

CCC expects to build and sell 20 four-door Corvettes a month. That just goes to show that you can sell almost anything in the U.S.A., especially if it's made of plastic.

Clockwise from upper right: From the front and rear, the America looks like a stock Corvette; access to rear is reasonable; targa-style roof provides needed body rigidity.

Alain Clenet is generally acknowledged even by his competitors to have started the current revival in "neoclassic" exotic cars. A neoclassic, like the CCC Auburn Speedster, isn't a true replica of any particular classic car. Instead, a neoclassic merely evokes the '30s look by means of certain styling cliches associated with classic cars—styling fillips like outside exhaust pipes, upright grille, long hood, separate fenders and headlights, and wire wheels. Brooks Stevens, of Excalibur fame, created the first of these cars over 15 years ago, but no one thought to challenge him in this small

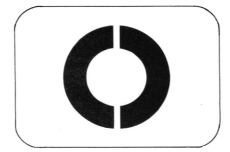

market until Clenet. Now there are well over a dozen neoclassics available, and more are on the drawing boards all over the country. Sad to say, some of these companies, eager to cash in on this new boom market, are under-financed. As a

result, their cars are ill-conceived and overpriced. Only Excalibur, Clenet, and a few other companies seem likely to stand the test of time.

Alain Clenet is a flamboyant Frenchman who once worked as a stylist at American Motors before deciding to start a car company of his own. Through thoughtful design, careful attention to detail, and perfect timing, he's become a highly successful builder of neoclassic cars.

His Clenet Roadster is a curious amalgam of parts that would make a purist blanch. The Clenet's 120-inch wheelbase chassis is taken from the Lincoln

CLENET

Continental Mark V. The Mark V's drivetrain is also used, including the stock 351 cubic-inch small block V-8 engine: three-speed automatic transmission; and front-disc, rear-drum braking system. From a mechanical point of view, one of the secrets to Clenet's success as a car builder is that he doesn't tamper with the stock components. The chassis is already tuned for the soft ride which Clenet buyers prefer. The brakes are more than adequate to the job of bringing the car's 3,900-pound mass to a halt, since they were designed for the Mark V which weighs 50 percent more than the Clenet. Use of production-car components means the Clenet can be serviced easily at Lincoln dealers coast-to-coast. The engine and transmission have already been proven quite reliable in the Lincoln, so for Clenet owners, service intervals should be relatively long.

Unlike Brooks Stevens' Excalibur, which uses an original body design built by the Excalibur factory, the Clenet uses a modified version of a body taken from a production car. This saves time and money for Clenet, who would otherwise have to bother with engineering such necessities as roll-up windows, a properly fitting top, and a dashboard with functional controls. It's the same rationale that led old-time hot-rodders to drop a Model T body onto a '32 Ford frame. The Clenet's body is based on one of the smallest of production cars, the MG Midget. Actually, the Clenet uses just the MG's cockpit and trunk (placed well back on the Mark V chassis), and not its hood or front fenders. Since the Midget is comfortable only for people five feet nine and under, the Clenet's passenger accommodations are similarly limited.

Few people would pay Clenet's $65,000 asking price if the car only looked and felt like

Opposite: The Clenet's non-functional exhaust pipes and upright grille are similar to the Excalibur's; the long air horns really work. Below: Underneath the 1930's styling is an MG body and a Continental chassis. Lower left: Wood rub strips add a decorative touch to the rear decklid; Lower right: and to the running boards.

an elongated Midget. So Clenet dresses up the interior of his Roadster by replacing virtually all the stock MG fittings with higher-quality materials and parts of the sort expected in this class. A set of padded bucket seats upholstered in Connolly leather replaces the MG's thinly padded seats. The door panels are trimmed in matching leather, of course. The carpet is Wilton lamb's wool, direct from England. Clenet substitutes a dashboard made of black walnut

for the MG's metal one. A padded leather steering wheel is used in place of the standard MG wheel. Still, it's hard to forget the humble origins of the Clenet's body, especially since the tight cockpit means that when shifting you can easily jab your passenger in the ribs.

On the outside, Clenet adds a curvaceous rear deck which hides a foot locker's worth of luggage space—more than what is provided by the stock Midget, or the Mark V for that matter.

Capping the rear deck is an outside spare tire perched above an authentic-looking split bumper that might have come from any '30s sports car.

But most of the effort on the car's bodywork goes into the area ahead of the firewall. The Clenet features an old-fashioned hood, which must be one of the longest ever made. In the vintage manner, it opens from the sides by means of a long piano hinge which runs along the top of the hood. Punched

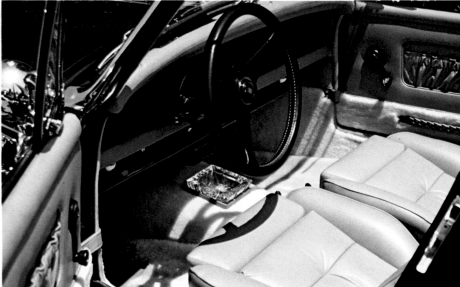

into its sides are more louvres than any American hot rodder ever stamped into the fenders of a '32 Ford. The front of the car is a veritable beehive of visual activity. The squared-off radiator shell is flanked by two huge headlights; two equally large driving lights; and a pair of long, chrome-plated air horns. All these elements make the car impressive-looking, if overly busy. This front end, by the way, is very similar to that of the Excalibur—driving lights, air horns, and all. Along its sides, the Clenet features gracefully sweeping fenders that might have been inspired by a Bugatti; chromed, non-functional exhaust pipes styled to evoke the SSK Mercedes (or to imitate the Excalibur); and wire wheels that come directly from the Mark V.

What sets the Clenet's derivative exterior styling apart from that of other neoclassics is the high quality of assembly. Evidence of careful attention to detail is found by close inspection of the car's lacquer paint; its chrome work; and the fit of its body panels, hand-formed fenders, and hood. Unlike some other high-ticket neoclassics, the Clenet looks like it might actually be worth its price.

What you're paying for, of course, is the view from inside.

The sight of that long hood stretching out proudly into the distance is worth the price of admission. You're also paying for the reactions you'll get from onlookers who stop and stare as you drive by. The Clenet isn't quiet, comfortable or especially practical. But it is well built.

Like most neoclassic cars, Alain Clenet's 1930s-style Roadster is fast becoming a status symbol among those in the upper tax brackets. In view of its $65,000 price tag, mixed assortment of production car components and nostalgic looks, the Clenet seems to prove the whole can be greater than the sum of its parts.

Opposite page, clockwise from upper right: The Clenet's cozy interior is upholstered in Connolly leather; dash features walnut veneer and padded leather steering wheel; MG vent windows are retained; note wide rear fenders and outside spare tire. Below: The long hood and sweeping fenders take up half the Clenet's overall length.

CLENET ROADSTER MAJOR SPECIFICATIONS

Manufacturer/Importer:
Clenet Coachworks
495 South Fairview Avenue, Santa
    Barbara, CA 93017
Body type—2-door, 2-passenger roadster

Wheelbase, in./cm—120.4/306
Overall length, in./cm—192/488
Overall width, in./cm—73.6/187
Overall height, in./cm—57/145
Track, front, in./cm—62.9/160
Track, rear, in./cm—62.6/159
Curb weight, lb./kg—3908/1772
Engine type—Ford water-cooled ohv V-8

Hp @ rpm—135 @ 3400
Displacement, cu. in./cc—351/5732
Carburetion—one 2-bbl Ford
Transmission—3-speed automatic
Brakes front/rear—ventilated disc/drum
Fuel Economy, normal driving—12 mpg
Est. top speed—120 mph
Approx. price—$65,000

Specifications for U.S. market model unless otherwise noted.

DeLOREAN DMC-12

The first DeLorean DMC-12 was originally scheduled to be delivered to a dealer in June 1979. That dealer is still waiting. If you find a DeLorean for sale within the next two years, be sure to snap it up. Should the DMC-12 reach production, which most experts think is unlikely, there won't be many built. Each one will instantly become a collector's item, like the Tucker Torpedo, the Edsel Citation, and the Bricklin coupe.

The concept of the DeLorean is beautiful, but the reality is something else. John Z. DeLorean has projected a production run of 30,000 DMC-12s over the next five years, each car to be priced at roughly $17,000. The bodies are to be built in South America, the engines in France, the chassis in England; and final assembly is to take place in Northern Ireland. To build the cars, DeLorean has borrowed $93 million, including $67 million from the government of Northern Ireland. For that same $93 million, he could have bought a controlling interest in American

Opposite page, top: The DeLorean's gullwing doors in full flight. Lower left: Note flying buttress roof styling. Lower right: Safety-conscious interior has knee pad and provision for air bags. At top: *DeLorean uses larger tires and wheels at the rear for better stability. Below: A narrow false grille and built-in under-bumper chin spoiler.*

Motors, a company with two dozen factories and established sales of 400,000 vehicles a year.

Bill Collins, the engineer who created the 1978 General Motors B-body cars, designed the DeLorean. The 95-inch-wheelbase chassis is made from a fiberglass sandwich, which consists of two layers of fiberglass cloth over a urethane core. It's not unlike the fiberglass chassis that Colin Chapman designed for his first Lotus Elite in 1957. To this unusual chassis, Collins added a conventional independent front suspension. The rear suspension is similar: independent A-arms connected by an anti-roll bar. Disc brakes of 11.5 inches are used at all four wheels.

The DeLorean is planned around a single-overhead-cam Renault V-6 engine of 2673cc displacement, mounted at the rear, like the Porsche 911. A four-speed Renault transaxle, taken from the front-wheel-drive R30 sedan, is used. Extremely poor weight distribution of 62.5 percent on the rear wheels—even worse than the

DeLOREAN DMC-12

911—means that the DeLorean would be undriveable if it were not for the big Pirelli P7 tires used at the rear. These tires are 265/50VR-16s. In front narrower 195/50VR-15 tires are used. All are mounted on turbo-finned alloy wheels.

One of the high points of the DMC-12 is its body, designed by the Italian genius Georgetto Giugiaro. It looks very much like Giugiaro's Maserati Merak and Lamborghini Espada, but has gull-wing doors like the Bricklin's. The body material is satin-finish stainless steel. DeLorean's theory is: It's cheaper to build a car of stainless steel because you don't have to paint it, and

of course, it won't rust. The drawback is that it can't be repaired; if your DMC-12 were ever damaged, you'd have to replace the entire fender, door, or whatever. Safety bumpers, said to provide protection from impact at up to 10 miles an hour (twice the U.S. government's current standard), are used front and back.

Giugiaro's design for the DMC-12 interior is the best part of the car. The interior is built to accommodate large persons. Collins is six-foot-four, so the twin bucket seats of the car he designed are extremely comfortable for people of all sizes. There's plenty of legroom.

The large instruments are located in just the right places. The DeLorean is planned for the use of air bags; these are concealed in the padded steering wheel and dashboard. There's also a padded knee bar which is blended into the doors to be as attractive as it is functional.

The biggest drawback of the DMC-12 will most likely be dismal performance. The Renault V-6 is rated at only 120 horsepower, and the car weighs 2,200 pounds. The DMC-12 will be substantially slower than the Corvettes and Porsches with which it will have to compete in price. And the small Renault six isn't the quietest or most reliable engine in the world.

Chapman, who probably knows more about building this type of limited-production sports car than almost anyone else, has been hired to refine the DMC-12 and Lotus will produce chassis components, so there's a slim chance the design will be significantly improved before it reaches production. At the moment, no one outside the DeLorean Motor Company has driven the prototype enough to have a true idea of what the production car will be like.

By using factories in England and Ireland to supply DMC-12 parts, John Z. DeLorean might become an important person in the British motor industry. British Leyland (now known as Jaguar Rover Triumph in the U.S.) is looking for a new president, and a lot of people are betting that DeLorean will get the job. At that time, Lotus and the DeLorean Motor Company could become BL subsidiaries. Such a relationship might be good for the British auto company, and could give DeLorean the manpower he'll need to turn an untested idea into a real car.

DE LOREAN DMC-12 MAJOR SPECIFICATIONS

Manufacturer/Importer:
DeLorean Motor Corporation
100 West Long Lake Road
Bloomfield Hills, MI 48013
Body type—2-door, 2-passenger rear-engine coupe
Wheelbase, in./cm—94.9/241
Overall length, in./cm—165.4/420
Overall width, in./cm—73/185
Overall height, in./cm—46/117
Track, front, in./cm—63.5/161

Track, rear, in./cm—59.8/152
Curb weight, lb./kg—2200/990
Engine type—Renault water-cooled dohc V-6
Hp @ rpm—120 @ 5500 rpm
Displacement, cu. in./cc—163/2673
Carburetion—Bosch K-Jetronic fuel injection
Transmission—4-speed manual
Brakes front/rear—disc/disc
Fuel Economy, normal driving—20 mpg (est.)
Est. top speed—120 mph
Approx. price—NA

Specifications for U.S. market model unless otherwise noted.

DUESENBERG

The Duesenberg brothers, Fred and August, were among the most celebrated craftsmen in the history of the American automobile. They were authentic folk geniuses, even to people who didn't know anything about cars. Those who grew up with the legendary Duesenberg cars of the '30s recognized them as some of the best automobiles ever built. The expression "It's a Duesie" did not start with car collectors.

Today, of course, the Duesenberg "J" and "SJ" models are prized by collectors whose enthusiasm for the marque has pushed prices for pristine specimens to astronomical levels. The original Duesenbergs were limited-production cars with prices that were high for the Depression era. But even the

Duesenberg brothers would be amazed by how much some people are willing to pay for one of their cars today: Figures as high as $150,000 are not uncommon.

Now come Harlan and Kenneth Duesenberg, nephews of the renowned brothers, eager to cash in on the fame and fortune of their uncles' cars. The nephews have linked up with Robert Peterson of the Lehman-Peterson Company (which builds hearses, ambulances and stretch-wheelbase limousines, including the armor-plated limousines used by the White House). Peterson and the Duesenbergs have formed a company called Duesenberg Brothers, Inc. They plan to market a new Duesenberg four-door sedan which they dub

the "Renaissance of 'The World's Finest Motor Car.' "

But the proposed rebirth of Duesenberg as a make may turn out to be nothing more than another stillborn dream car. So far, only one prototype has been built and no one outside the company has yet driven it. If the car is produced, it will be built in very small numbers. If you want one you'll need a key to Fort Knox: The reincarnated Duesie will sell for about as much as one of the classic originals does today.

The new Duesenberg is designed around a Cadillac frame with the wheelbase stretched to 133 inches, halfway between the 121-inch wheelbase of the Sedan de Ville and the 144-inch wheelbase of the Fleetwood limousine. The chassis layout is typical for a big car, and also very conventional. The rear suspension consists of a well located live axle, controlled by four separate trailing arms and carried on coil springs. An automatic load leveler system completes the rear end layout. The independent front suspension is a General Motors-type design having coil springs, unequal-length A-arms, and an anti-sway bar. The power steering unit, disc brakes (one per wheel) and "high performance" 3.08:1 rear axle ratio are also taken from the GM parts shelves, as is the V-8 engine. This is Cadillac's 425 cubic-inch power plant which is rated at 195 hp and 320 foot-pounds of torque. It's fitted with the Bendix electronic fuel-injection system used by Cadillac. Fuel injection generally helps driveability and gas mileage, but the system is sophisticated and not as easy to repair as a carburetor. GM's three-speed Hydra-matic, one of the best automatic transmissions in the world, is retained from the De Ville.

With this proprietary chassis and running gear the "World's Finest Motor Car" is likely to be as strong, unbreakable, and safe handling as its Cadillac parent. The quoted weight for the Duesenberg is 4,500 pounds—about 250 pounds more than a Fleetwood Brougham—so acceleration and braking performance should be similar to a Cadillac's. So should the ride, which, no doubt, will be very soft and what most potential Duesenberg buyers will want.

Of course, all these GM mechanical components can be purchased as a Cadillac for less than $15,000 and wrapped up with more luxury options than King Tut ever dreamed of. By contrast, the new Duesenberg is slated to cost a breathtaking

$100,000. Since even Cadillacs, not to mention Dodge Diplomats, can be had with leather upholstery, the Duesenberg's wool carpets, and mahogany instrument panel are the only other touches of elegance offered which are not on the De Ville's option list. Even the Duesenberg's wire wheels can be ordered on the GM car, for one-seventh the price. And there are some surprising omissions from the Duesie's option sheet: For example, a sunroof will not be available.

Most ultra-expensive limited-production cars feature eye-catching, if not always beautiful, styling to justify their high prices. Usually the styling is

the main reason, aside from exclusivity, that the customer is willing to spend the extra money for such a car, especially if it doesn't have original, sophisticated, or high-performance mechanicals. Unfortunately, the Duesenberg is about as eye-catching as a Ford Granada. The lines of the boxy, slab-sided steel body are naive and awkward. The rear end treatment is plain and uninteresting. The front styling is pretentious. A vertical Lincoln Continental-like grille, flanked by stacked quad headlights, is half-hidden behind a "bow-tie" bumper meant to evoke the curvaceous bumper shape that became a trademark of Uncle

DUESENBERG MAJOR SPECIFICATIONS

Manufacturer/Importer:
Duesenberg Brothers
888 Tower Road, Mundelein, IL 60060
Body type—4-door, 5-passenger sedan
Wheelbase, in./cm—133/338
Overall length, in./cm—233/592
Overall width, in./cm—79/207
Overall height, in./cm—57.4/146
Track, front, in./cm—61.7/157

Track, rear, in./cm—60.7/154
Curb weight, lb./kg—4500/2059
Engine type—Cadillac water-cooled ohv V-8
Hp @ rpm—195 @ 3800
Displacement, cu. in./cc—425/6964
Carburetion—electronic fuel injection
Transmission—3-speed automatic
Brakes front/rear—disc/disc
Fuel Economy, normal driving—14 mpg
Est. top speed—110 mph
Approx. price—$100,000

Fred's Model J. Putting this bumper on what looks like a customized Lincoln front end is not the epitome of good taste. When it comes to styling and style, the Duesenberg underwhelms.

Fifty years ago the SJ Duesenberg featured outside exhaust pipes and a rotary supercharger that boosted performance of the legendary straight-eight engine. Not to be outdone by its ancestor, the "Renaissance" model can be equipped with *two* turbochargers which Peterson claims will squeeze 650 hp from the Cadillac V-8. This may be true; but, as all too many neophyte engine builders have discovered, to their customers' subsequent sorrow, achieving engine durability with a turbocharger installation requires long and careful development work.

Prospective Duesenberg customers should hope this has been done before ordering a car so equipped, if it ever goes on sale.

The new Duesenberg will probably sell well in Saudi Arabia and other oil-rich nations. But it's not a very practical proposition in America. A Mercedes-Benz 450SEL is more economical and offers the Duesie's prestige value for less than half the price. A Cadillac Fleetwood is about as large as the Duesenberg, and you could buy seven Fleetwoods for what you'd pay for one Duesenberg. Either the Mercedes or the Cadillac will give you pride of ownership. But driving a Duesenberg may just make you feel embarrassed about owning a car that has a name of such illustrious heritage tacked onto what is essentially a rebodied Cadillac.

Given the economics of the automobile industry today, it is probably unrealistic to expect Harlan and Kenneth Duesenberg to produce a modern version of their uncles' legendary machines, or to duplicate the engineering excellence and sheer brute strength that went into those cars. The nephews are not the craftsmen their uncles were; they are salesmen. This "Renaissance" car could have turned out a lot worse. It could also have been a lot better. Builders like Alain Clenet and Brooks Stevens have already shown that by using off-the-shelf components it is possible to create cars of distinction and elegance, cars that are becoming legends in their own time. Perhaps the biggest disappointment in the new Duesenberg is that it fails to carry on the legend of its name.

Opposite: The Duesie's plush interior features a split front bench seat. Above: In profile, the car looks like a larger-than-life Cadillac; note the heavy rear quarter pillars. Below: The traditional Duesenberg "bow-tie" front bumper is the main styling feature of the otherwise bland front-end design.

EXCALIBUR

Run-of-the-mill movie actors and actresses 10 years ago drove Rolls-Royces or Ferraris. Big box-office stars and studio executives owned custom-built Excaliburs. That's still true today, even though the $28,000 Excalibur is losing some of its prestige to more expensive automotive toys like the Clenet. Among the natives of Tinseltown the Excalibur is known as the "Santa Monica Maverick" because you can't cross the

street without having to dodge one.

The Excalibur, the original "neoclassic" car, was designed in 1962 and put into production in 1964. The Excalibur company was a gift from automotive stylist Brooks Stevens to his sons. Stevens is independently wealthy (a classic car museum is one of his other hobbies) and is a gifted industrial designer. In 1962, Stevens was on retainer to Studebaker when that company had a marketing agreement with

Clockwise from upper right: Rakish Excalibur has side-mount spares, real wire wheels, and an authentic convertible top complete with side curtains; current front-end styling bears only slight resemblance to Mercedes SSK which served as Stevens's inspiration; vintage styling dictates a narrow body sitting atop frame rails which makes for cramped seating.

Mercedes-Benz to handle Mercedes sales in the United States. "What would happen," asked Stevens, "if we made a replica of the Mercedes-Benz SSK and mounted it on a Studebaker chassis?" The result thrilled neither Mercedes nor Studebaker, but Stevens walked away from his first auto show with about three dozen orders for his Excalibur SS. He financed the setup of a small car-building factory in Milwaukee,

and the rest is history.

After Studebaker went out of the car business in 1966, Stevens modified the Excalibur chassis to accept a Corvette's V-8 engine and chassis components. As the Corvette grew, so did the Excalibur. It now has Corvette independent front and rear suspension with power-assisted disc brakes all around, and is powered by a massive 454 cubic-inch V-8 from a Chevrolet truck. Corvette

hasn't been available with an engine this large for years, but Stevens is somehow still able to wangle big-blocks out of General Motors for the Excalibur Series III. These huge engines are rated at only 215 horsepower, but they produce an awesome 350 foot-pounds of torque—some 70 foot-pounds more than the Corvette's L-82 power plant. Fuel economy is only about 11 miles per gallon, but Excalibur owners don't seem to care.

EXCALIBUR

The latest Excalibur doesn't really look like a 1929 Mercedes: The car has evolved into a distinctive style of its own. On a 112-inch wheelbase, the Stevenses build a mostly-fiberglass shell—body, fenders, and removable top—with aluminum and stainless steel trim, including the hood, grille, and extravagant exterior exhaust pipes. Genuine wire wheels (including two side-mounted spares), quadruple air horns, and built-in driving lights give the exterior that final touch of '20s class. The use of Volkswagen turn signals and taillights, however, diminish the total effect.

Inside, the Excalibur is horribly cramped. The leather-upholstered front and rear bucket seats are set on top of the frame rails, so there's very little foot room. The car's cutaway doors make you feel like you'll go tumbling out every time the car goes into a turn, and the low windshield does nothing to keep the wind out of the face of a six-footer. Attachment of the fiberglass top, a two-man chore, means that tall people have to stay home—there's no room for them in the car. Since the car is essentially a Corvette with an old-style body, things like air conditioning, power accessories, and an engine-turned dashboard full of expensive gauges are standard.

The car's performance is exhilarating. At 4,350 pounds, the four-passenger Excalibur weighs 800 pounds more than a two-passenger Corvette, but its engine is 100 cubic inches larger and delivers more power and torque. Incredible as it may seem, the old-fashioned Excalibur can out-perform a Corvette up to 100 miles an hour, even though aerodynamics favor the 'Vette. Excalibur's top speed is over 120 mph. And 0.8 G braking—with perfect control—is easy to achieve. The car performs in a way that no 1929 Mercedes ever did. The long wheelbase improves both ride and handling. You can steer with the throttle.

Driving an Excalibur is a joy. First, you tend to forget the uncomfortable seating as soon as you start the engine. The big Chevrolet V-8 pumps out a cacaphony that surely equals the roar of the famous supercharged SSK Mercedes in volume, if not in pitch. A touch of your toe to the accelerator pedal can make the tires squeal in any gear at any speed. The wind, engine noise, and exposed driving position combine to make 55 mph feel like 155. The car has no trunk; the engine, tied to those outside pipes, is virtually impossible to service; and the weather protection is a joke. But grocery bags will fit in the back seat, Chevy engines run forever, and it never rains in Santa Monica.

If you want to know what it's like to be a Hollywood VIP, drive an Excalibur. Little kids holler and wave, teenagers beep the horn and want to race, and everybody stops and stares. Get yourself a set of California license plates and a $30 haircut, and all onlookers east of Pasadena will think you're a movie mogul. The name "Excalibur" means that instant celebrity status can be yours for $27,600.

EXCALIBUR MAJOR SPECIFICATIONS

Manufacturer/Importer:
Excalibur Automotive Corporation
1735 S. 106th Street,
Milwaukee, WI 53214
Body type—2-door, 4-passenger
    roadster/phaeton
Wheelbase, in./cm—112/284
Overall length, in./cm—175/444
Overall width, in./cm—72/183
Overall height, in./cm—58/147
Track, front, in./cm—62.5/159

Track, rear, in./cm—62.5/159
Curb weight, lb./kg—4350/1973
Engine type—Chevrolet water-cooled ohv V-8
Hp (a rpm—215 (a 4000
Displacement, cu. in./cc—454/7440
Carburetion—one 4-bbl
Transmission—3-speed automatic
Brakes front/rear—ventilated
    disc/ventilated disc
Fuel Economy, normal driving—11 mpg
Est. top speed—120 mph
Approx. price—$27,600

Specifications for U.S. market model unless otherwise noted.

FERRARI 308GTB

In the world of elite cars, the Ferrari 308GTB stands out. It's not the biggest, the fastest, the most comfortable, or the most expensive of such cars. But the Ferrari is so well balanced it can be driven, and driven hard, with great pleasure. Everything about it works with nearly perfect precision, and no one part overshadows any other. If you have $36,000 to spend for a two-passenger car, the Ferrari 308GTB is one the serious driver should consider.

Pininfarina has styled most of the classic Ferraris over the years, including this one. The 308GTB is obviously a descendant of the Dino 246, but has a curvy sensuality all its own. Crafted in aluminum, this Ferrari has a light, rounded look that is very different from the

angular motifs used by Georgetto Giugiaro for his Maserati and Lamborghini designs. Giugiaro is a genius, but Pininfarina's cars have a timeless elegance that the

younger designer has not matched.

The 308GTB is small. Built on a 92-inch wheelbase, it's 172 inches long and 44 inches high. The short, sharply sloping hood offers excellent visibility to the front, but rear vision is poor due to the "flying buttress" roof design. As for luggage space, forget it. The hood covers the spare tire and radiator, and the engine is positioned behind the seats, so any luggage, preferably soft bags, must be stored in a small carpeted bin behind the rear wheels. Ferrari owners travel light, but fast.

They also travel in comfort. The car's genuine leather seats are stylish and provide very good support. The leather-wrapped steering wheel is in just the right position. Also, the pedals are properly located

FERRARI 308GTB

for easy heel-and-toe gear changes. The Ferrari 308GTB's brushed chrome instrument panel contains nine gauges and nearly a dozen warning lights. They're all located so the driver can see them without having to peek around the spokes of the steering wheel.

All Ferraris have an unusual five-speed gearshift design, much like that of racing cars. Instead of using a shift lever that sticks up from a rubber boot like those of most cars, the Ferrari has a lever that projects from a chrome-plated gate. The driver guides the lever from one gear to the next through the gate's precise paths. The Ferrari has one of the best shifters in the world—it's light, quick, and positive.

The engine is a 2926cc V-8

Above: GTB borrows some styling details from its predecessor, the Dino 246GT. Below left: The interior is very comfortable for two lucky people. Below right: Note unusual slotted gearshift.

Opposite page, clockwise from left: Alloy wheels are standard, engine access is difficult; squat rear-end appearance suggests high performance.

with double overhead camshafts and four Weber carburetors. It's rated at 205 horsepower. In the 308GTB, the powerplant is mounted transversely, and inaccessibly, under a cover between the twin roof buttresses. You wouldn't want to be the mechanic who has to work on this jewel of an engine. It's as hard to get at as the power-plant in a mid-engine Fiat X1/9,

and three times as complicated. Just a simple spark plug change is a $100 operation. When in tune, the engine can run superbly, winding up to its 7400 rpm redline with the marvelous whirring of cams and gears. The low-speed acceleration isn't breathtaking (0-60 mph in 10 seconds; 0-100 in 23 seconds), but the 140 mph top speed can be reached more

quickly in the 308GTB than in almost any other car. This engine and gearbox are intended for flat-out cruising, not Friday night drags. But such performance doesn't come cheap—10 miles per gallon is about all you can get.

The Ferrari 308GTB chassis is outstanding. It has independent suspension, unequal-length A-arms front and rear, vented front and rear disc brakes, and Michelin XWX 205/70VR-14 tires on alloy wheels. It's all attached to a stiff, tubular space frame. About 58 percent of the car's 3,110 pounds rests on the rear wheels, but you'd never know it from the driver's seat. The 308-GTB feels neutral at all times. You can drive it at breakneck speeds over some of the worst roads around, then get out and walk away nonchalantly as though you'd done nothing special. But later, you'll catch yourself smiling.

And the 308GTB manages to combine this remarkable handling and steering feel with a soft ride that should be the envy of every Rolls-Royce owner. This Ferrari is proof that you can have great handling without compromising ride or steering feel; excellent acceleration without compromising top speed; and an aerodynamic body design without compromising interior comfort.

A Ferrari, however, isn't made for fetching groceries. It's designed for transporting two people (one of them, no doubt, wealthy) in style and comfort across autostradas or sinuous mountain roads about as fast as it's possible to go in anything less than a racing car. The 308GTB seems to be the best car that Ferrari has ever built for this admittedly limited purpose, which makes it one of the best Grand Turismo machines in the world. It might be difficult to get out of second gear without exceeding the national speed limit, but you can't hold that against the car.

FERRARI 308GTB MAJOR SPECIFICATIONS

Manufacturer/Importer:
Modern Classic Motors
3225 Mill Street, Reno, NV 89510
Body type—2-door, 2-passenger
   mid-engine coupe
Wheelbase, in./cm—92.1/234
Overall length, in./cm—172.4/438
Overall width, in./cm—67.7/172
Overall height, in./cm—44.1/112
Track, front, in./cm—57.5/146

Track, rear, in./cm—57.5/146
Curb weight, lb./kg—3110/1399
Engine type—water-cooled dohc V-8
Hp @ rpm—205 @ 6600
Displacement, cu. in./cc—178.5/2926
Carburetion—four 2-bbl Weber
Transmission—5-speed amnual
Brakes front/rear—ventilated
   disc/ventilated disc
Fuel Economy, normal driving—10 mpg
Est. top speed—140 mph
Approx. price—$36,000

Specifications for U.S. market model unless otherwise noted.

The Intermeccanica name has been around for about two decades. For most of those years, the company was headquartered in Turin, Italy, and was under the aegis of Frank Reisner. Intermeccanica produced a series of beautifully built hybrid sports cars in the 1960s and into the '70s. These cars used American V-8s and hand-built chassis. The Apollo, Omega, Torino, and Indra were the names applied to what was basically the same car. Any of these variations is prized as a collector's item today. Intermeccanica is now located in Los Angeles and Tony Baumgartner is the man in charge, but the firm is still building collector's items.

The Intermeccanica Speedster is the company's latest offering and represents a departure from the kind of cars Intermeccanica made in Italy. The Speedster is a replicar, nearly identical with the Porsche Speedster of which it is a reproduction. And in

INTERMECCANICA SPEEDSTER

some ways, the copy is better than the real thing. For instance, Intermeccanica's Speedster has a body made of fiberglass (the Porsche's was steel), so there's no worry about rust.

Intermeccanica duplicates the Porsche original line-for-line and inch-for-inch. A Porsche-like box-section perimeter frame with an 82-inch wheelbase is used. At the front is the familiar Volkswagen Beetle front suspension, complete with torsion bars. The rear suspension is VW, too: the infamous swing-axle independent design with trailing arms and torsion bars. Intermeccanica uses a 1584cc version of the Beetle's horizontally opposed four-cylinder engine, rated at 50 horsepower, and fitted with twin Solex carburetors. Skinny 5.60x15-inch tires on four-inch rims contribute to the original Speedster look on the outside. The car even uses old-fashioned drum brakes just like the ones Porsche used.

Opposite: About the only thing you won't find on this very authentic replica is a Porsche nameplate. Below, clockwise from upper left: Dies for Intermeccanica's body were made on an original Speedster; the familiar bathtub shape; dash features modern instruments in place of original-style units; snug bucket seats help when cornering.

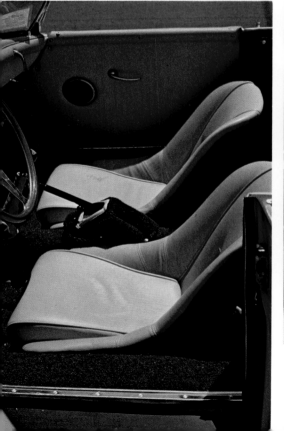

INTERMECCANICA SPEEDSTER

The fiberglass body molds for the replica were formed on a genuine Porsche Speedster, so the Intermeccanica's beautifully finished bathtub is virtually indistinguishable from the original. The same cut-down windshield, the same funny body-color bumpers, and the same muffin pan shape are all perfectly duplicated. The same goes for the interior. The Intermeccanica has leather bucket seats, a convertible top, side curtains, and dashboard that are just like those of the 1954 Porsche. The only interior change is a beautiful wood-rimmed Nardi steering wheel, which replaces the old-fashioned white plastic Porsche wheel. Since many owners of the early Porsche Speedsters often substituted better-looking steering wheels, this change doesn't detract from the replica's air of authenticity.

The original Speedster weighed 1,800 pounds and couldn't top 100 miles per hour unless a lot of work was done to the engine to improve its meager power output. The Intermeccanica Speedster weighs 1,580 pounds and has a claimed top speed of 110 mph. Fuel consumption is a miserly 28 miles per gallon—about what you'd expect from a modestly powered, lightweight, low-slung roadster. The original Speedster was notorious for its tail-heavy handling, and the modern version is no different. Since it has 59 percent of its weight on the rear wheels, and has narrow tires, the replica exhibits really frightening oversteer even at moderate speeds. If you enjoy opposite-lock cornering, however, you'll have a lot of fun driving this car.

The Intermeccanica's price is $10,250, which seems like a lot of money for what is essentially a fiberglass-bodied Volkswagen. But at current prices, the replica costs far less than a genuine restored Porsche Speedster. The Intermeccanica version also has the advantage of using parts that are cheaper than the genuine Porsche pieces. The resale value of the replica is likely to remain high even after you've enjoyed the car for a few years. It even delivers good gas mileage, and not many elite cars can do that. If the 50-hp engine doesn't produce enough performance for you, Intermeccanica will install a turbocharger to raise the output 50 percent. Also available is a Weber-carbureted 1640cc engine with racing exhaust. Depending on which of these engine options you order, the car's price can go as high as $14,800.

The original Porsche Speedster was popular partly because it was so easy to modify. If you buy the Intermeccanica Speedster, you can do what owners of the original Porsche did. Usually they added wider tires and wheels, disc brakes, a modified suspension, a roll bar, a souped-up engine, and a transmission with altered gear ratios. The Intermeccanica replica invites that same kind of modification. And a replica can't be more authentic than that.

INTERMECCANICA SPEEDSTER MAJOR SPECIFICATIONS

Manufacturer/Importer:
Automobili Intermeccanica
2421 South Susan Street,
Santa Ana, CA, 92704
Body type—2-door, 2-passenger rear-engine roadster
Wheelbase, in./cm—82.7/210
Overall length, in./cm—148/376
Overall width, in./cm—61/155
Overall height, in./cm—53/135

Track, front, in./cm—51.6/131
Track, rear, in./cm—53.2/135
Curb weight, lb./kg—1580/711
Engine type—Volkswagen air-cooled ohv flat four
Hp @ rpm—50 @ 4000 (DIN)
Displacement, cu. in./cc—97/1584
Carburetion—two 1-bbl Solex
Transmission—4-speed manual
Brakes front/rear—drum/drum
Fuel Economy, normal driving—28 mpg
Est. top speed—110 mph
Approx. price—$10,250

Specifications for U.S. market model unless otherwise noted.

JAGUAR XJ12L &XJ~S

The Jaguar XJ12L may be the best sedan in the world, and one of the two or three best cars of any type currently available. At $22,000 it's also a relative bargain among luxury cars. The Jaguar lists for about half the price of a Mercedes-Benz 6.9 and one-third the price of the least expensive Rolls-Royce.

To some people the Jaguar is not only prettier, quieter, faster, and more comfortable than those other two luxury sedans, but is also a lot more fun to drive. It will out-handle and out-brake many sports cars and will accelerate with a Ferrari up to 140 mph. It will cover freeway miles with incredible ease and carry four people plus their luggage with insouciant grace. It

is a car that can be quiet and genteel when driven at 55 mph, and be entertaining and lively when taken down a twisting road. Owners seem to love both the sedate and sporting side of this competent automobile.

The Jaguar's ability to stir such passions may be the reason XJ12 owners put up with

the car's reliability problems. Jaguar has earned an unfortunate reputation in the U.S. for poor quality control. The current XJ sedans are better built than any previous Jaguar, but they're still not put together as well as a $5,000 Chevrolet. Most failures that occur are relatively minor ones. They usually involve the electrical system or the Jaguar's complex engine, which demands regular, thorough, and frequent maintenance. If you live near a Jaguar mechanic who can keep your car running properly, all you'll probably worry about is finding the money for parts and labor. Considering the excellence of the car's basic design and its versatile nature, most owners seem willing to pay that price.

The XJ sedan was introduced in 1968 as the XJ6, using Jaguar's venerable double-overhead-cam six-cylinder engine. In 1971, a 12-cylinder engine, displacing 326 cubic inches (5343 cc), was dropped into the XJ6 engine bay to produce the XJ12. Both cars were mildly face-lifted in 1973, and were given longer wheelbases and an "L" suffix designation to become the Series II XJ6L and XJ12L. The cars have since gone through another round of changes including a taller greenhouse, minor mechanical modifications, and additional standard equipment. These cars were introduced in mid-1979 as the Series III models.

The XJ sedan was the last Jaguar styled by Sir William Lyons, the company's founder, who had designed every car he ever sold. Like all Jaguars, the XJ has nearly timeless styling. In its latest Series III guise the car looks as fresh and modern today as it did in 1969. The lines of the tightly drawn body suggest a kind of rippling musculature; yet the styling is pretty without being cute or trendy.

The styling changes made to the Series III cars are subtle, and, if anything, enhance the original design. The most noticeable differences between the Series III and the earlier cars are the new model's lower beltline; higher roofline; and larger windshield, side windows, and rear window. The interior is practical yet luxurious, and shows just how good the body design still is. The larger windows and the thin roof pillars provide excellent visibility all around. There's plenty of headroom, legroom and shoulder room for the largest of passengers. The big thin-rimmed steering wheel is well placed for drivers of all sizes, and features telescopic adjustment. This, along with the multi-adjustable seats, allows anyone to find a

Below left: Front end of XJ Series III sedans has new deeper, wraparound front bumpers.
Below right: The seats are as comfortable as they look; center armrest on console conceals

storage bin. Opposite: Latest Series III XJ features taller greenhouse, more upright rear window, wraparound rear bumpers, and revised taillights, but the lines are still classic.

comfortable driving position. Instruments are grouped conveniently in front of the driver. They are set in a genuine polished-wood dashboard, which is typically British in character and lends an aura of old-world charm to the elegantly understated interior furnishings. These include leather upholstery, wool carpets, and hardware made of stainless steel. The front bucket seats are exceptionally comfortable. The bench seat in back is also comfortable and is contoured to accommodate two full-size adults; three people can ride back there with little discomfort. For long hours of interstate travel, the XJ sedan provides a roomy and restful environment. By actual measurement the XJ12L's noise levels at 70 mph are lower than those of a BMW

733i or Mercedes 450SEL. The Jaguar is a perfect example of what happens when a brilliant original design is carefully refined for a decade.

Surprisingly, the XJ12L has a 112.8-inch wheelbase and 200-inch overall length, which make it a compact car by American standards. The unitized body/chassis is unusually strong. But the Jaguar, having a curb weight of about 4,300 pounds, is heavy for its size.

The suspension is independent at both ends. Coil springs, an anti-sway bar, and wishbones are used at the front. At the rear the suspension consists of wishbones, upper half-shafts which act as trailing arms, lower radius arms, and two coil springs for each wheel. In the British tradition the steering system is a power-assisted

rack-and-pinion unit. The brakes are huge vented discs all around—11.2 inches in diameter at the front and 10.4 inches at the rear. Wide tires, size 205/70 VR-15, provide terrific grip during braking and play a big part in helping the suspension deliver handling and roadholding, which are outstanding for a heavy sedan. In fact, the XJ12L will out-corner all but a handful of sports cars, and without the harsh ride that's usually the price paid for good handling. That suspension soaks up the worst bumps and potholes with ease; yet the XJ12L's ride does not have the pitching motion found in many American luxury cars. In short, the XJ12L strikes a beautiful balance between ride, handling, and roadholding.

And there's no compromise in performance. The Jaguar's V-12

JAGUAR XJ12/XJ6 MAJOR SPECIFICATIONS

Manufacturer/Importer:
Jaguar Rover Triumph Inc.
600 Willow Tree Road,
Leonia, NJ 07605
Body type—4-door, 5-passenger sedan
Wheelbase, in./cm—112.8/286
Overall length, in./cm—200.5/509
Overall width, in./cm—69.8/177

Overall height, in./cm—54.1/137
Track, front, in./cm—58.2/148
Track, rear, in./cm—58.8/149
Curb weight, lb./kg—4334/1950 (XJ12)
    4068/1830 (XJ6)
Engine type—water-cooled sohc V-12 (XJ12)
    water-cooled dohc inline six (XJ6)
Hp @ rpm—244 @ 5250 (XJ12) 176 @ 4750 (XJ6)
Displacement, cu. in./cc—326/5343 (XJ12)
    258/4235 (XJ6)

Carburetion—Lucas-Bosch fuel injection
Transmission—3-speed automatic
Brakes front/rear—ventilated disc/disc
Fuel Economy, normal driving—15 mpg
Est. top speed—130 (XJ12), 120 (XJ6)
Approx. price—$25,000 (XJ12), $19.000 (XJ6)

(Specifications are the same for the XJ12 and XJ6 unless otherwise indicated)

Specifications for U.S. market model unless otherwise noted.

engine may be a nightmare to look at, but when it's working well it will pump out 244 horsepower and propel the XJ12L through the quarter-mile at almost 90 mph in about 17 seconds. And that sprint is achieved with the GM-built three-speed Hydra-matic transmission (the only gearbox offered on U.S. specification XJ12s) left to its own devices. In 1980, this is considered muscle-car performance, but few muscle-cars can touch the Jaguar's ability to sustain 130 mph for hours on end. In more normal everyday driving the car will return at least 15 miles per gallon. By luxury-car, GT-car or sports-car standards, the Jaguar delivers impressive performance.

Most comments about the XJ12L can also be applied to its stablemate, the XJ6L. This car uses the XJ12L's body and chassis, but is powered by the six-cylinder "XK" series engine which has powered every production Jaguar since the famed XK-120 of 1948. The "XK" power plant is perhaps the most long-lived engine still in production; in its latest 4.2-liter form, it benefits from the additional refinement of Bosch fuel injection, which appeared on U.S. cars in 1978. Compared with the XJ12L, the six-cylinder Jaguar is about 10 mph slower in top speed (though still capable of reaching 120 mph), about one second slower through the quarter-mile, and around 2 mpg more thrifty. The six-cylinder engine also weighs less than the twelve.

As long as you can find someone to repair it, owning an XJ6L or XJ12L makes a lot of sense. Because customer demand for Jaguars has always been greater than the supply, these cars tend to appreciate in value rather than depreciate. Most important, perhaps, is the

Jaguar's poised and polished behavior on the road. Driving an XJ sedan at 100 mph is almost as safe as sitting in a parked Volkswagen. Jaguar owners may complain about parts, service, and reliability; but few of them complain about the car itself.

Automotive pundits have dubbed the Jaguar XJ "The Best Sedan in the World" for so long that they've retired the trophy. Even in the world of elite cars, the Jaguar XJ sedans are cars that can be all things to all people.

The XJ-S is the first Jaguar designed by a committee. If only the XJ-S wore a nameplate other than "Jaguar" perhaps the car wouldn't be such a disappointment to die-hard enthusiasts.

Every Jaguar model for 40 years, including the current XJ sedan series, was styled by Sir William Lyons, the company's founder, who is now retired. He never received the degree of acclaim given to Pininfarina or Giugiaro, but Sir William can be regarded as one of the master stylists of the post-war period. The XJ-S began life in the early '60s as a study by Sir William's long-time associate, the late Malcolm Sayer. But the two men were not able to complete the work themselves. Instead, Sayer's original design was turned over to marketeers within the vast British Leyland combine. What had begun as a cleanly styled two-plus-two was subjected to numerous compromises and last-minute fiddling by men who lacked Sir William's keen eye for graceful line and form.

As a result, when the XJ-S appeared in 1976 its styling turned out to be an unhappy marriage of Sayer's original ideas and late '60s styling clichés. The XJ-S has, for example, the C-pillar flying buttresses of the Ferrari 250LM;

the greenhouse line of the Lotus Europa; the long-hood, short-deck silhouette popularized by the Ford Mustang; and the shallow grille and pug nose of the MG-B. Taken altogether, the styling of the XJ-S is a visual Mulligan's stew.

The XJ-S can be thought of as a sporty version of the XJ12L sedan, with which it shares drivetrain components and basic chassis layout. Like the Camaro/Firebird (based on the old Nova platform), the XJ-S costs more than the equivalent sedan—about $3,000 more. As is usually the case with sporty coupes based on sedan components, the higher price of the XJ-S is reflected mostly in its bodyshell, which is less practical and less commodious than that of the XJ12L.

In contrast to its clumsy styling, the XJ-S' chassis is well-executed. Its 102-inch wheelbase is some 10 inches shorter than the XJ sedan's, and the coupe's 192-inch overall length is eight inches less. The XJ-S is also a full six inches lower than the sedan. This takes its toll in reduced headroom, especially for back seat passengers.

The best part about the XJ-S is the marvelous 326 cubic-inch V-12 engine. This single-overhead-cam power-plant delivers smooth, effortless power over an extremely wide rpm band. Rated at 244 horsepower, this engine is one of the most powerful you can buy. In spite of the XJ-S' near 4,000-pound curb weight the engine has enough muscle to take the car up to a top speed of about 125 miles per hour. Acceleration is brisk, as shown by the quarter-mile time of 16 seconds at 90 miles per hour. Performance might be even more impressive were it not for the standard equipment

Top: U.S.-specification XJ-S features heavier bumpers than European model and quad headlights instead of single halogen units; front-end styling looks like wide MG-B. Below left:

Businesslike dash has unusual vertical-reading engine gauges. Below right: Front seats are comfortable but when the doors are closed, side windows are too close to occupants' heads.

automatic transmission, the only one available for the XJ-S in federal form. Like the XJ12, the XJ-S uses the three-speed Turbo Hydra-matic 400 transmission from General Motors, although shift point settings are suitably revised to match the torque curve of the Jaguar V-12 engine. The GM automatic downshifts more readily under part-throttle load than the old Borg-Warner box previously used. But the XJ-S has a tall 3.07:1 final drive ratio. The result is acceleration that's brisk but not blinding, at least up to 60 mph. Gas mileage is a bit extravagant—10 miles per gallon in normal driving—in these days of short gas supplies and long lines at the pumps.

The XJ-S features all-independent suspension and four-wheel disc brakes, again taken from the XJ12. The suspension has relatively firm springs and shock absorbers, so high-speed cruising is very stable and sure-footed. Thanks to generous wheel travel, the ride is also good. It's resilient and poised over the worst of roads, and the chassis handles dips and bumps with aplomb. The steering and brakes are both power-assisted—too much so for some tastes. The steering also lacks adequate feel. But once you get used to the steering's featherweight effort, the XJ-S can be thrown around

corners with a gusto that belies its hefty size and weight.

What a pity, then, that the interior appointments belie the car's $25,000 price tag. Unlike the XJ12's interior, which employs high quality materials appropriate for a luxury/touring sedan in the "Olde English" tradition, the XJ-S interior lacks visual appeal, and seems cheap by comparison. The dashboard is a run-of-the-mill hodge-podge of dials, knobs, and switches in odd shapes and sizes. Nothing seems to have been designed to harmonize either visually or functionally. Even the steering wheel is a skinny two-spoke affair that would look more at home in a Pinto than in what is supposed to be a top-notch luxury GT.

Visibility in the XJ-S isn't a

strong point either. The small rear window and flying-buttress roof styling restrict rear three-quarter vision. The long hood and low roofline limit over-the-road vision to the front.

Despite its considerable exterior bulk, the XJ-S is no more than a two-passenger car. Its trunk is cube-shaped but small—barely adequate for two people's luggage. The back seats are best used for additional luggage space since passengers will not be happy there for longer than short jaunts around town. Front seat accommodation is good but the extreme inward curvature of the side windows puts glass too close to the heads of front seat occupants.

The XJ-S was intended to fill a gap as the sporty model in Jaguar's line-up when the legendary E-type was phased out a few years ago. Rather than create another true sports car, however, Jaguar chose instead to enter the broader and more lucrative luxury GT market. But the XJ-S is neither sports car nor GT. Think of the XJ-S as a "boulevardier," a two-door version of the XJ12 sedan, or Jaguar's Mustang. The XJ-S is a competent performer although it is no better than the sedan on which it is based. The coupe's styling is the product of a corporate approach to design that may be acceptable in a mass-produced economy car but seems strangely inappropriate for a Jaguar.

The awkward, undistinguished styling of the XJ-S is evidence that an era in Jaguar history has ended. The XJ-S could have been a great car had Sir William Lyons been involved with its design from start to finish. But the styling of XJ-S is not the product of Sir William's mind alone. That single fact makes the XJ-S a Jaguar in name only.

JAGUAR XJ-S MAJOR SPECIFICATIONS

Body type—2-door, 2-passenger 2 + 2 coupe
Wheelbase, in./cm—102/259
Overall length, in./cm—192.25/469
Overall width, in./cm—70.6/179
Overall height, in./cm—47.8/121
Track, front, in./cm—58.6/148
Track, rear, in./cm—58.6/148

Curb weight, lb./kg—3936/1771
Engine type—water-cooled sohc V-12
Hp @ rpm—244 @ 5250
Displacement, cu. in./cc—326/5343
Carburetion—Lucas-Bosch fuel injection
Transmission—3-speed automatic
Brakes front/rear—ventilated disc/disc
Fuel Economy, normal driving—10 mpg
Est. top speed—125 mph
Approx. price—$25,000

Specifications for U.S. market model unless otherwise noted.

LAGONDA

Lagonda, one of the grandest names in British motor car history, is being revived for a new production car by Aston Martin. (The last production Lagonda was a four-door version of the Aston DB4 and was built up to 1963.) The new Lagonda is based on the chassis and drivetrain of the Aston Martin V-8 Coupe, but it's a completely different automobile. The Aston is virtually a vintage car; the Lagonda is one of the most technically advanced automobiles in the world.

This new Lagonda started out in 1976 as a styling exercise by William Towns, an Aston Martin designer. It was then tested in prototype form for three years. Production is now under way, and Aston Martin expects to produce one Lagonda a week.

The car's futuristic body is striking. Reminiscent of the extremely angular creations of Georgetto Giugiaro, Towns' four-door sedan has one of the lowest drag coefficients (under 0.40) of any sedan in production. (The single-seat Lola T333 Can-Am racing car, one of the sleekest around, has a drag coefficient of 0.50.) With its long, long hood, pointed nose, large greenhouse, and chopped-off rear deck, the Lagonda looks like it's doing 100 mph just sitting at the curb. That's a

cliché, but appropriate for this car.

The interior is also futuristic: It resembles part of the bridge on the starship *Enterprise*. The single-spoke steering wheel is covered with soft Connolly leather to match the four bucket seats, the door panels, and the center console. Stereo speakers are built into each door. Plush carpeting and all the usual amenities—electrically powered seats, windows and door locks; power assist on all controls; standard air conditioning, and AM/FM stereo—make the Lagonda's interior one of the most comfortable places in the world of automobiles.

The dashboard of the Lagonda is built by National Semiconductor in California (owned by Peter Sprague, Aston Martin director). It contains a

computer to process all data on engine operation, trip time and distance, and fuel consumption. The dash also features touch-sensitive switches, digital readouts, graphic displays, and fine functional styling. None of this electronic technology is especially innovative for this computerized age, but this is the

first time that it's been made to work successfully in the hot, vibrating environment of an automobile.

Mechanically, the Lagonda is an Aston Martin V-8 with an extra foot added to the wheelbase. It uses the Aston's independent front suspension, De Dion rear suspension,

Chrysler Torqueflite automatic transmission, and a 5.3-liter V-8. The Lagonda weighs 4,400 pounds, nearly 500 pounds more than an Aston Martin V-8 Coupe; however, its aerodynamic body is so much more slippery than the old-fashioned Aston's that the Lagonda is actually quicker and faster than the

LAGONDA MAJOR SPECIFICATIONS

Manufacturer/Importer:
Aston Martin Lagonda
14 Weyman Avenue,
New Rochelle, NY 10805
Body type—4-door, 4-passenger sedan
Wheelbase, in./cm—114/290
Overall length, in./cm—207.9/528
Overall width, in./cm—70/178
Overall height, in./cm—50.9/129
Track, front, in./cm—58.2/148

Track, rear, in./cm—59.1/150
Curb weight, lb./kg—4400/2000
Engine type—water-cooled dohc V-8
Hp @ rpm—NA
Displacement, cu. in./cc—326/5340
Carburetion—four 2-bbl Weber
Transmission—3-speed automatic
Brakes front/rear—ventilated
      disc/ventilated disc
Fuel Economy, normal driving—12 mpg
Est. top speed—140 mph
Approx. price—$75,000

Specifications for U.S. market model unless otherwise noted.

Opposite: The Lagonda's futuristic styling makes it one of the most aerodynamically efficient sedans in the world. Above, top: Britain's William Towns styled the wedge-shaped body, not Italy's Giugiaro. Above left: The digital instrument display is dazzling.

Coupe. It even gets better mileage—about 12 mpg.

Driving the Lagonda is pure pleasure. It handles much better than the Aston V-8 Coupe, and its steering feel is superb. Braking is sure and controlled. And there's enough horsepower available to out-accelerate almost any car in the world up to 120 mph. The Lagonda even has adequate luggage room for four weekend travelers. The big V-8 power plant is complicated to repair, but much more accessible than the engine of the Aston Martin V-8 Coupe.

The Lagonda, even though priced at $75,000, can be considered as a bargain in today's elite car market. It's everything the Rolls-Royce should be and isn't: fast, quiet, luxurious, comfortable, beautiful, and technologically advanced. The Lagonda is certainly one of the most unusual sedans ever built. But then, when you pay 75 grand for a set of wheels, you expect something extraordinary.

LOTUS ESPRIT & ELITE/ECLAT

Colin Chapman, of Lotus fame, built his reputation as a designer on the success of his racing cars. When he turned to designing road cars in the late '50s it was only natural that they turned out looking and driving much like his race cars. Early Lotus production models were tiny, lightweight machines built for speed and cornering, not for comfort and durability. The word "fragile" came to be synonymous with the name Lotus. Perhaps the best example of these early Lotus road cars is the Lotus Seven. This was very much like a Formula Two racer, equipped with cycle fenders and two seats. The Seven stayed in production without major change for over 20 years and, like every Lotus model introduced since, won a loyal enthusiast following. Chapman's cars obviously appealed to a great many frustrated Mario Andrettis willing to give up creature comforts in exchange for race car-like handling.

Today's Lotus models are more refined, and construction quality has been improved in recent years. The newer cars also have more of the amenities expected in a modern sports car than their predecessors had. But the new Lotuses still offer what Lotuses always have—handling and roadholding which are better than that of almost any other production car.

Lotus currently offers a three-model lineup. All three—the Esprit, the Elite, and the

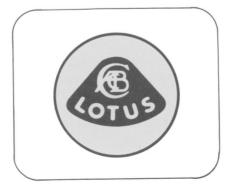

Eclat—share the same engine and chassis layout.

Of these models the Esprit is probably the most interesting. Back in the '60s Chapman offered a sleek but uncomfortable sports car (even by Lotus standards) called the Europa. This used a production Renault sedan engine placed amidships in the chassis behind the seats. For the Turin Auto Show in 1972, Italian stylist Georgetto Giugiaro gave the Europa chassis a new wedge-shaped body. Chapman was enchanted with this design study, and so were the show crowds. Three years later, at the Paris Auto Show, a production version of Giugiaro's design was shown. This car had only a few minor revisions to make it more suitable for series production. Giugiaro even suggested the name Esprit—and it stuck. Rarely has a one-off show car been put into production with so few changes.

Opposite: Lotus Esprit is based on Giugiaro show car; latest S2 models feature front spoiler and revised exterior trim. Above, clockwise from upper right: unusual curved instrument pod puts all dials and controls within easy view; the Esprit looks low, wide, and purposeful with its huge taillights and chunky lines; Esprit has a true wedge shape, sharply-raked windshield, and fastback roof.

At about that same time, 1972, Chapman entered into an agreement with Jensen by which Lotus would supply its new 2.0-liter double-overhead-cam four-cylinder engine for use in the soon-to-be-announced Jensen-Healey two-seat roadster. The original plan was that Lotus would first gain production experience with the new engine, and eventually would put two of these blocks together to form a 4.0-liter V-8 for use in a new Lotus GT car. The energy crisis of 1973 changed Chapman's mind about offering a big V-8 in a Lotus. After all, such an engine might seem too thirsty, and therefore be unsaleable, in the aftermath of a fuel shortage. As a result, the Esprit was designed around the lightweight, 1973cc four, now rated at 140 horsepower in U.S.-legal form. This engine also powers the larger Elite and Eclat models.

The Esprit's chassis is an improved version of the Europa's design. This is basically Chapman's patented "backbone" chassis first used in the Elan roadster of the early '60s. The backbone is fabricated of sheet steel and forms a rigid spine that runs longitudinally along almost the entire length of the car. At either end of the backbone is a Y-shaped extension. The front suspension and steering gear are attached to the front extension. At the rear the Y carries the rear suspension and the engine, which is mounted longitudinally ahead of the rear wheels. The transaxle consists of the differential and manual five-speed gearbox as used in the now-discontinued Citroen SM. The SM, of course, was a front-engine, front-wheel-drive car. But since its Maserati-built engine rode ahead of the front wheels, the SM's transaxle suits the mid-engine Esprit's engine/transmission layout.

Chapman is generally acknowledged to be one of the leading suspension designers in the world. Lotus cars have always been famous for handling, and the Esprit reflects Chapman's latest thinking on suspension design. By using surprisingly ordinary bits and pieces, Chapman has combined nimble handling and light, precise steering with a supple ride. The Esprit's front suspension is taken from the European Opel Ascona sedan and consists of A-arms, transverse lower links, and an anti-roll bar plus tube shocks and coil springs. The rear suspension uses the patented Chapman Strut which first appeared in the late '50s. The Chapman Strut is similar in design to a McPherson strut, and consists of a shock strut around which a coil spring is concentrically mounted. The rear suspension also uses the transaxle's half-shafts as upper control arms in conjunction with lower lateral arms and trailing arms. It's a lightweight, positively-located independent rear suspension. The basic geometry has worked successfully on Lotus racing and sports cars for nearly 25 years. Rounding out the Esprit's chassis specifications are four-wheel disc brakes, and Dunlop Super Sport tires mounted on wide Speedline alloy wheels (14x6 inches front, 14x7 inches rear).

This carefully developed chassis gives the Esprit delightfully neutral handling in transient maneuvers. Because of its 96-inch wheelbase and 167-inch overall length, the spritely Esprit can be flung into corners like a tiny Formula car. The ride, considering the short wheelbase, is surprisingly comfortable and well cushioned over smooth highways and bumpy byways alike. The Esprit does not sacrifice ride comfort for its good handling.

Unfortunately, there are some sacrifices in other aspects of the car's design. The free-revving engine, although powerful for a 2.0-liter, just doesn't have enough muscle to move the Esprit's 2,444 pounds very quickly. Although the Esprit will do 0-60 in slightly less than 10 seconds and has a top speed of about 120 miles per hour, there are many cars which are much quicker than this and cost much less than the Esprit's $25,900. Because it's overworked, the little engine only returns about 15 miles per gallon. That isn't very good mileage these days, especially for such a small displacement powerplant, albeit a highly tuned one.

Then there's the matter of room—or rather the lack of it. The Esprit ostensibly has a front luggage compartment. But this space is filled by the spare tire,

radiator, and fluid reservoirs, so it's practically useless. A small number of soft bags can be carried at the rear in a fiberglass tray which doubles as the engine cover. But beware of what you stow there because

that area gets toasty warm from engine heat.

The passengers get toasty warm too. Uninsulated pipes from the front-mounted radiator run through the central backbone where they transmit a lot of heat

into the cockpit. To make matters worse, the Esprit has almost no ventilation other than by opening the windows and air conditioning is not available. The large, severely raked windshield, one of Giugiaro's characteristic styling features, also lets in a lot of heat on sunny days. The Esprit may well be the world's sportiest sauna.

There are other problems with the interior, too. The central tunnel formed by the backbone chassis is tall and wide so driver and passenger feel separated and very cramped. The bucket seats are only lightly padded, too thin to be very comfortable at the end of a long day's drive. The Espirit looks squat and low because it is: Its overall height is only 43.7 inches. This makes entry and exit difficult, not to mention restricting headroom severely for anyone taller than five feet ten. The pedals are small and set too close together. A normal-size American male can easily push any two of them at once, a feat (no pun intended) which can be embarrassing if you hit the brake when you really want just the clutch. The parking brake can gouge your leg because the

Opposite top: Elite is a four-seat GT with squared-off hatchback roofline. Center: The Elite's wedge shape was created by Lotus. Bottom: Eclat is similar to Elite, except for fastback roof.

Above: U.S.-model Eclat has heavy front bumpers. Below left: Elite/Eclat dashboard is well thought out. Below right: Rear seat headroom in Eclat is very limited.

LOTUS ESPRIT & ELITE/ECLAT

lever is mounted on the driver's door sill right in harm's way.

For those who want a somewhat bigger car that can carry up to four passengers yet still deliver that famous lightning-quick Lotus handling there's the hatchback Elite and its fastback cousin, the Eclat. These cars share suspension design and hardware with the Esprit, as well as its 2.0-liter engine and five-speed transmission. But the Elite/Eclat are one size larger than the Esprit and use a front-engine/rear-drive layout. Their unitized body/chassis is made entirely of fiberglass. Chapman used a fiberglass monocoque body for his original 1957 Elite coupe, but abandoned fiberglass for many years because that car was criticized for being too flimsy. Since then,

fiberglass molding techniques have become much more sophisticated. So, Chapman decided to try fiberglass again for the new Elite and Eclat. Chapman even added a new wrinkle. Instead of painting the bodies after they come out of the molds, Lotus sprays paint into the molds before the liquid fiberglass is poured. The paint is thus impregnated in the fiberglass. This means that, with a little polish, most minor scratches can be rubbed out without using touch-up paint on the body surface.

The Eclat is a fastback two-plus-two available with an optional automatic transmission in place of the standard manual gearbox. The Elite is basically the same car but has a squared-off hatchback roofline and a liftgate in place of the

Eclat's sloping roof and normal trunk. Both cars weigh about 2,400 pounds and have an overall length of 179 inches on a wheelbase of 98 inches. Like the Esprit, the Elite/Eclat are not really very fast. But they do offer slightly more room than the Esprit, and are therefore slightly more comfortable. They can be equipped with creature comforts not available on the mid-engine car (like air conditioning). Either one costs close to $29,000, roughly the price of a Mercedes 450SL, a Porsche 928 or a BMW 633CSi.

Pat Bedard of *Car and Driver* once wrote that "Lotuses shed parts like Alsatians shed hair." In the past, Lotus owners have probably said things less kind than that. Lotus takes such comments seriously and is concerned about its reputation for poor quality control and flimsy construction. The workers at Hethel are now putting the cars together better than ever before. And the factory has recently set up its own exclusive U.S. distributorship in an attempt to improve parts availability and dealer service. Such problems cannot be solved overnight, of course, so if durability, reliability and easy maintenance are important considerations for you, don't even look at a Lotus.

But a lot of people do look at Lotuses and buy them. The main reason is handling. Any Lotus is more fun to drive over a twisty road than almost any other car. Unfortunately, Chapman's cars are not very practical for everyday use. In view of Lotus' poor reliability record you wouldn't want to depend on one as your only car anyway. But if you love to go around corners like the Mario Andretti you know you are, then you and a Lotus were made for each other. Colin Chapman wouldn't have it any other way.

LOTUS ESPRIT MAJOR SPECIFICATIONS

Manufacturer/Importer:
Lotus Cars of America
2649 South Bayshore Drive,
Miami, FL 33133
Body type—2-door, 2-passenger mid-engine coupe
Wheelbase, in./cm—96/244
Overall length, in./cm—167.7/426
Overall width, in./cm—73.3/186
Overall height, in./cm—43.7/111
Track, front, in./cm—59.5/151
Track, rear, in./cm—60.5/154
Curb weight, lb./kg—2444/1100
Engine type—water-cooled dohc inline-four
Hp @ rpm—140 @ 6500
Displacement, cu. in./cc—120.4/1973
Carburetion—two 1-bbl Zenith
Transmission—5-speed manual
Brakes front/rear—disc/drum
Fuel Economy, normal driving—15 mpg
Est. top speed—135 mph
Approx. price—$25,900

LOTUS ELITE/ECLAT MAJOR SPECIFICATIONS

Body type—2-door, 4-passenger hatchback coupe/fastback coupe
Wheelbase, in./cm—97.7/248
Overall length, in./cm—179.7/456
Overall width, in./cm—71.5/182
Overall height, in./cm—47.3/120
Track, front, in./cm—58.5/149
Track, rear, in./cm—59/150
Curb weight, lb/kg—2430/1093
Engine type—water-cooled dohc inline-four
Hp @ rpm—140 @ 5800
Displacement, cu. in./cc—120.4/1973
Carburetion—two 1-bbl Stromberg
Transmission—5-speed manual (3-speed automatic optional)
Brakes front/rear—disc/drum
Fuel Economy, normal driving—15 mpg
Est. top speed—120 mph
Approx. price—$29,600/28,500

Specifications for U.S. market model unless otherwise noted.

MASERATI MERAK/QUATTROPORTE

Over the past decade, Officine Alfiere Maserati S.p.A. has had more ups and downs than a roller coaster. Originally founded in 1926 by the five Maserati brothers from Bologna (who later went on to start OSCA), the firm was purchased in the 1930's by the Orsi family conglomerate. In 1968, the Orsis sold Maserati to Citroen. But when the fuel shortage of 1973 hit, the French automaker's sales temporarily declined. For a time, Citroen (and therefore, Maserati) seemed destined for bankruptcy. Fortunately, Peugeot purchased Citroen in 1974. But Peugeot didn't want to bother with running Maserati. So, for another two years Maserati struggled along with financial help from

the Italian government until Alejandro de Tomaso came to the rescue in 1978 and bought Maserati for a ridiculously low price.

Part of the cast in this corporate soap opera is the Maserati Merak. The Merak's

history is much shorter, but almost as checkered, as the company's. In 1971, Maserati introduced its first mid-engine car, the Bora. The Bora used Maserati's famous 5.0-liter double-overhead-cam V-8, an engine designed in the mid-1950s that has powered many Maserati street and racing machines. The Bora's body was styled by Georgetto Giugiaro.

At about the time the Bora debuted, Citroen gave Maserati the task of building the engine for the now-discontinued Citroen SM. This engine was a 2.6-liter V-6, and Maserati was able to build more engines than Citroen needed for the slow-selling SM. And thus the Merak was born. Maserati had actually planned to use the V-6 in the Bora body anyway because the company wanted to field a competitor for the Ferrari Dino 308s. The Merak also originally used Citroen's hydraulic braking system and the complete SM dashboard. Nowadays, the Merak is available with a smaller version of the same V-6 engine. Its 2.0-liter displacement allows the car to qualify for a lower tax bracket in Europe. The Merak SS has the 3.0-liter version of this engine and this is the car now imported to the U.S. As part of his revitalization program, de Tomaso has replaced most of the Merak's other Citroen components with new Maserati-designed pieces.

De Tomaso will also need to revitalize the faith of Maserati owners in their cars. Maserati has the worst reputation for reliability among Italian exotic cars. The average Maserati spends a lot of time in the shop, waiting for hard-to-get parts. Whether the Merak will be any more reliable than previous Maseratis remains to be seen. But if you worry about trouble-free motoring, owning a Maserati could mean a lot of sleepless nights.

As a dream car, however, the Merak SS is hard to beat. Even though the Giugiaro design has been around for nearly a decade, the Merak still looks fresh, muscular, and racy. Compared to the Merak, a Ferrari 308GTB seems almost delicate and feminine in appearance. The Merak's styling does have a few quirks, however. The Bora was a true fastback with fixed rear quarter windows and a large sloping backlight. The Merak keeps the same roofline, but uses a small rear window placed vertically behind the seats, and it has no rear quarter windows at all. The result is a flying buttress roofline that seems perfectly acceptable until you realize that,

except for styling, the two "basket handles" serve no purpose at all. For the American market the Merak also grows bigger, rubber-covered bumpers and side marker lights, neither of which is required in Europe.

The chassis specifications of the Merak SS look good on paper, but on the road, chassis behavior is less than expected. Of course, the Merak has all-independent suspension, huge four-wheel vented disc brakes, rack-and-pinion steering, a five-speed transmission (overdrive on the top two gears), and huge Pirelli tires on alloy wheels. But the suspension has only limited vertical wheel travel and little compliance control, so the ride is bouncy and jerky over rough roads, and stiff and uncomfortable on smooth freeways. There's no anti-dive control under hard braking, so, even though the brakes themselves work well enough, you hesitate to use them strongly. The steering is very heavy for a car that has more than half its weight on the rear wheels. The transmission, because of its remote shift linkage, is difficult to shift. It's easy to grind the gears. Others may watch with envy as you drive by, but they don't know the trouble you're having getting into third.

The best part of the Merak is the Citroen/Maserati engine, which is a jewel. It features double overhead cams on each bank of cylinders, an aluminum alloy block and heads with shrunk-in wet liners, hemispherical combustion chambers, and three Weber carburetors. In U.S. trim, Maserati rates this V-6 at 182 horsepower at 6000 rpm (40 hp less than the European version) and maximum torque is 185 foot-pounds. Maximum speed is a claimed 155 miles per hour, which seems a bit optimistic.

The true top speed is probably more like 135 mph. The EPA says the Merak SS returns a miserable 10 miles per gallon on high-octane fuel.

Miserable is also the word for the Merak's space utilization. The front-mounted radiator takes up most of the space under the front trunk lid, although soft luggage can be stored behind the front seats on a pair of miniature "plus-2" jump seats. Merak owners will learn to travel light. Most of them will also be small. Cockpit space—especially headroom and legroom—is at a premium, even though the car rides on a 102-inch wheelbase and has an overall length of 180 inches. Owners would also do well to develop a sixth sense about traffic. Because of the small windows, the Merak's visibility to the sides and rear is poor, and this only aggravates the cramped feeling of the cockpit.

There was a time when the mid-engined layout, used so successfully in racing cars, seemed like the best way to achieve balanced handling and roadholding in production sports cars. But this configuration usually means compromises in passenger comfort, noise level, luggage space, serviceability and visibility, all of which outweigh the slightly better weight distribution achieved. The Merak SS offers proof that, in a street machine, it's still better to put the horse before the cart.

The story behind the development of the Maserati Quattroporte is a perfect example of the intrigue that surrounds Alejandro de Tomaso. In the early '70s De Tomaso Automobili had plenty of money for new projects. De Tomaso is not hesitant about borrowing someone else's good idea and adapting it to his own ends. So

Top: Large wheel openings and squat, flowing contours. Center left: Rear view shows Merak's small vertical back window and useless "basket handle" roof struts. Center right: Quattroporte styling is heavy-looking and goes along with the car's hefty curb weight. Bottom left: From this angle, Maserati's four-door looks vaguely like a squared-off Jaguar XJ; note "character line" along the flanks. Bottom right: There's high-performance luxury for four.

he came up with a four-door sedan, powered by a Ford 351 cubic-inch V-8, and called the result the Deauville. In looks, size, chassis layout, suspension design, and general concept, the Deauville is an unabashed copy of the Jaguar XJ12. Next, De Tomaso had Georgetto Giugiaro design a two-door coupe, called the Longchamp. This car used a chassis similar to the Deauville's. The Longchamp is an unabashed copy of the Mercedes 450SL.

By the mid-'70s, Maserati was in financial trouble. The Italian government decided to sell its interest in the company to De Tomaso. De Tomaso made minor changes to the Maserati Merak and Khamsin, and phased out the mid-engine Bora. By means of a simple engine swap, De Tomaso turned the Ford-powered Longchamp coupe into the Maserati Kyalami. Now, a similar engine transplant has been given to the Deauville sedan to create the new Maserati Quattroporte. In this

case, however, the surgery is more extensive: The Quattroporte's body is another new Giugiaro design. When it comes to making new cars out of old, Alejandro de Tomaso is a master of disguises.

On the other hand, the new De Tomaso/Maserati models, and especially the Quattroporte, are very desirable cars. The Quattroporte is 196 inches long on a 110-inch wheelbase—about the same size as a Jaguar XJ12. The unitized body/chassis is made of steel. Equipped with all its standard luxury items, the car weighs a hefty 4,650 pounds. Mechanically, the Quattroporte is as interesting as any sedan in the world. Both the front and the rear suspension are independent; the car uses four-wheel disc brakes; and the tires are oversize 215/70VR-15s, mounted on 7x15-inch steel wheels.

The Maserati V-8 engine is a 25-year-old design, but is still one of the more complex production engines. It has

hemispherical combustion chambers, alloy block and heads, double overhead camshafts on each bank of cylinders (with a 90-degree angle between banks), and four Weber carburetors. The 4136cc version is rated at 288 horsepower. In the Quattroporte, the engine is coupled to a three-speed GM Hydra-matic as used in the Deauville. (No manual transmission is available.) This engine/transmission combination produces a top speed of 143 mph and delivers 17 miles per gallon when the heavy Quattroporte is driven with restraint.

The Quattroporte interior is a not-too-subtle amalgam of Maserati, De Tomaso, and other proprietary parts. Surprisingly, all the parts blend well enough together to create a pleasing overall effect. The car has four leather-covered bucket seats, a center console, a complete set of round white-on-black instruments, lots of rocker switches, a dashboard covered in brushed aluminum, and a padded four-spoke steering wheel.

Driving the Quattroporte is surprisingly pleasant, too, considering the car's thoroughly mixed parentage. It has more than adequate performance; excellent brakes; good visibility (except where the heavy C-pillars create blind spots); and the kind of gentle, predictable handling for which Maserati has always been famous.

Despite its awkward styling, borrowed chassis, and me-too concept, the Maserati Quattroporte is a very well-done high-performance sedan that sells for $50,000. But it's not as well-done as the Jaguar XJ12, which offers equal performance and more elegant styling for half the price.

MASERATI MERAK SS MAJOR SPECIFICATIONS

Manufacturer/Importer:
Maserati Automobiles
Box 8786, Baltimore, MD 21240
Body type—2-door, 2+2 mid-engine coupe
Wheelbase, in./cm—102.3/260
Overall length, in./cm—180/457
Overall width, in./cm—69.6/177
Overall height, in./cm—44.6/113
Track, front, in./cm—58/147
Track, rear, in./cm—58/147
Curb weight, lb/kg—3185/1433
Engine type—water-cooled four-cam V-6
Hp (a rpm—182 (a 6000
Displacement, cu. in./cc—181/2965
Carburetion—three 2-bbl Weber
Transmission—5-speed manual
Brakes front/rear—ventilated
  disc/ventilated disc
Fuel Economy, normal driving—10 mpg
Est. top speed—155
Approx. price—$31,000

MASERATI QUATTROPORTE MAJOR SPECIFICATIONS

Body type—4-door, 4-passenger sedan
Wheelbase, in./cm—110.2/280
Overall length, in./cm—196/498
Overall width, in./cm—70.4/179
Overall height, in./cm—53.1/135
Track, front, in./cm—60.0/152
Track, rear, in./cm—60.0/152
Curb weight, lb./kg—4650/2093
Engine type—water-cooled dohc V-8
Hp (a rpm—288 (a 5200
Displacement, cu. in./cc—253/4136
Carburetion—four 2-bbl. Weber
Transmission—3-speed automatic
Brakes front/rear—ventilated
  disc/ventilated disc
Fuel Economy, normal driving—17 mpg
Est. top speed—143 mph
Approx. price—$50,000

Specifications for U.S. market model unless otherwise noted.

What defines an elite car? The Mercedes 300TD would seem to qualify, since its base price is $22,000. But this Mercedes has a top speed of only 97 miles an hour. The interior is mostly covered in vinyl and is not at all fancy for a car in this price range. In appearance, the 300TD is about as bland as any compact car. Yet the 300TD is exclusive—only 2,900 are to be made available for the U.S. market each year in 1979 and 1980. Already there's a waiting list that's months long. So, the 300TD is an elite car on the basis of its high price and limited availability. It's also the only station wagon in this select group—the first wagon ever built by the Mercedes factory. What makes this station wagon even

more unusual is that it's powered by a diesel engine. In short, the 300TD is one of the most unlikely elite cars ever made.

In Germany, there are five versions of the "T" series station wagon, which has been in production since early 1978 at the Mercedes factory in Bremen. For the home market, Mercedes offers 2.3-, 2.5-, and 2.8-liter gasoline engine models, plus a 2.4-liter diesel version. For the U.S. market, however, the only model offered is powered by the 3.0-liter, five-cylinder diesel engine used in the 300D sedan. Apparently, Mercedes-Benz of North America figures the typical American station wagon buyer is mainly interested in good mileage, and the 77-horsepower

diesel five delivers the second-best fuel economy of any Mercedes engine. Curiously, the low-output diesel makes the 300TD less than practical as a carrier of big loads. The diesel engine also brings with it a disadvantage for owners in some parts of the country where diesel filling stations are hard to find.

The 300TD wagon is based on the smaller of two Mercedes body shells: the W123 body as used for the 240D, 280E and 300D sedans, and the 300CD and 280CE coupes. Like the sedans, the wagon rides a 110-inch wheelbase and is 190 inches long. Most of the wagon's other dimensions are shared with the sedan; however, the wagon is actually a half-inch lower if you don't count its

MERCEDES~BENZ 300TD & 450SLC

MERCEDES-BENZ 300TD & 450SLC

built-in roof rack. The wagon is also equipped like the 300D sedan: individual front bucket seats, center console, climate control system, and four-speed Daimler-Benz automatic transmission with floor-mounted selector. Curb weight is about 3,800 pounds, which is more than 300 pounds heavier than the sedan's. Nevertheless, the wagon actually records a slightly higher top speed than the 300D sedan (about 8 mph faster, in fact, mostly because the wagon body has better aerodynamics.)

Since the 300TD is so much like the sedans, it's no surprise to find the wagon performs like them, too. The 300TD's ride is surprisingly smooth and compliant for a station wagon. Mercedes uses hydropneumatic struts in the wagon to supplement the semi-trailing arms, coil springs, and anti-roll bar of the rear suspension,

Above: The first factory-built Mercedes-Benz station wagon is available only with a diesel engine for the American market; luggage rack bolts directly onto roof-mounted attachment points.

Below left: 300TD interior is almost identical with that of the smaller Mercedes sedans. Below right: Rear door opens high on gas struts to reveal a roomy and usefully shaped load area.

MERCEDES-BENZ 300TD MAJOR SPECIFICATIONS

Manufacturer/Importer:
Mercedes-Benz of North America
One Mercedes Drive, Montvale, NJ 07645
Body type—4-door, 5-passenger station wagon
Wheelbase, in./cm—110/279

Overall length, in./cm—190.9/485
Overall width, in./cm—70.3/178
Overall height, in./cm—57.9/147
Track, front, in./cm—58.6/149
Track, rear, in./cm—57.2/145
Curb weight, lb./kg—3780/1715
Engine type—water-cooled ohv inline 5-cylinder diesel

Hp @ rpm—77 @ 4000
Displacement, cu. in./cc—183/2998
Carburetion—Bosch fuel injection
Transmission—4-speed automatic
Brakes front/rear—disc/disc
Fuel Economy, normal driving—25 mpg
Est. top speed—90 mph
Approx. price—$22,000

Specifications for U.S. market model unless otherwise noted.

which is borrowed from the sedan. The struts incorporate an automatic leveling control that senses when the rear end sags under heavy load and automatically corrects the rear ride height. This rear suspension design allows Mercedes to use spring rates that are somewhat soft for a wagon, and this is what makes the ride so good.

Handling is characterized by mild understeer that most drivers will find reassuring if it becomes necessary to back off the throttle after entering a corner too quickly. Roadholding is also good for a two-ton car, despite the 195/70SR-14 radial tires, which are a bit narrow for the weight of the car. The brakes are power-assisted four-wheel discs, and in the customary Mercedes manner, the 300TD stops swiftly and controllably. Mercedes' advertising boasts that before it could be a station wagon, the 300TD first had to perform like a Mercedes. The exemplary road manners of the 300TD indicate the company reached its goal.

The 300TD also performs its role as a wagon very well. With the rear seat in place, the car has 29.6 cubic feet of luggage space. Another 16.3 cubic feet of space is available by folding down both sections of the rear seat. The 300TD's back seat is split off-center. This arrangement allows long loads—like skis, surfboards and tall candelabra—to be carried along with a third passenger. Loading or unloading the cargo area is easy because the rear "door" extends down to bumper level, and lifts up high on gas-filled struts.

The new Mercedes wagon is about the same size as a Ford Fairmont wagon. But the German car weighs 700 pounds more than the American one, and the 300TD's diesel engine is considerably less powerful than the Ford engine. As a result, the Mercedes gets only about one extra mile per gallon compared to the Fairmont,

according to the EPA. For carrying really heavy loads, the Mercedes is limited by its anemic engine. Drivers will have to allow extra time when entering freeways or passing on two-lane roads because acceleration is leisurely even without a load. Most 300TD owners, however, probably won't worry about this. They'll use their wagons mainly for hauling around cases of Chateau Rothschild or for making quick trips to Neiman-Marcus.

Most elite cars are virtually hand-built and have distinctive styling that's not always practical. The Mercedes 300TD is built in a factory and has bland styling that's very practical. Yet the Mercedes wagon belongs in the elite car class, mostly because it is first and foremost a Mercedes. As such, the 300TD has that special mystique that seems to surround every car that wears the three-pointed star. So if you've always wanted the status of a Mercedes and the practicality of a station wagon combined in one car, head for your nearest Mercedes dealer and get in line. The wait will be worth it.

Judged as a full line of automobiles, the Mercedes-Benz range contains some of the best cars in the world. From the small diesel to the fabulous 6.9 sedan (now sold only in Europe), every Mercedes is built to last a lifetime. This makes any one of their cars a good long-term investment. The secret of Mercedes' reputation for reliability is incredible attention to engineering detail and execution. Mercedes designs and builds cars with a precision and thoroughness that would drive most other car makers crazy.

Nowhere is the Mercedes philosophy of building cars more evident than in the 450SLC, Stuttgart's competitor for the Jaguar XJ-S and BMW 633CSi. The 450SLC has been in production without major change

for some eight years, yet it is still totally contemporary. The only aspect of its design that dates the 450SLC, as indeed it dates most other pre-1973 designs, is size. In an increasingly energy-conscious era, a four-passenger two-plus-two coupe which weighs 3,900 pounds and returns only 15 miles per gallon is almost antisocial.

Like its BMW and Jaguar rivals, the 450SLC is based on a sedan, in this case the Mercedes 450SEL. These cars share most suspension parts and Mercedes' excellent 4.5-liter V-8. Mercedes' V-8 is a very straightforward single-overhead-cam design with a cast-iron block, aluminum heads and Bosch electronic fuel injection. In American, trim the engine is rated at 180 horsepower produced at a relatively low 4800 rpm. By European standards, this is a low-output engine, considering its displacement.

Mercedes does not offer a manual transmission on any of its cars sold in the U.S. except for the 240D. Therefore, the 450SLC is available only with a three-speed automatic transmission which is similar in design to the GM Turbo Hydra-matic. Unlike American automatics, however, the M-B gearbox shifts much more decisively, especially on full-throttle upshifts and on kickdown to a lower gear. Shifts are also more noticeable with the Mercedes unit although it changes gears smoothly and without jerkiness. The ratios of this gearbox are matched perfectly to the torque curve of the big, slow-turning V-8 engine.

All Mercedes cars use a similar all-independent suspension system: unequal-length A-arms, anti-sway bar, and coil springs in the front; semi-trailing arms, anti-sway bar, and coil springs in the rear. What's remarkable about the Mercedes chassis is the generous amount of wheel travel

Above: Mercedes 450SLC is a four-passenger version of shorter-wheelbase 450SL; rear quarter pillar louvres and window treatment influenced styling of 1979 Ford Mustang. Opposite, top: The alloy wheels cost extra but the prestige of the three-pointed star is standard equipment.
Opposite bottom: Inside, the steering wheel is too large, but instruments and controls are well laid out.

provided, plus firm spring and shock absorber control. The result is surprisingly little body lean in corners and a supple ride over any type of road. In fact, a 450SLC can be driven over rough roads at speeds that would have a typical American car crashing on its bump stops. The SLC's suspension behaves competently and predictably, even in the worst of conditions.

The 450SLC uses disc brakes all around, nestled inside 6.5x14-inch alloy wheels wearing 205/70 HR-14 Michelin XVS tires. These tires work well with the SLC's suspension. The car will record high lateral "G" figures on the skid pad and high deceleration rates when braking.

The SLC's body is essentially an enlongated version of the 450SL two-seater. In profile the stretched wheelbase of the otherwise unchanged SL gives the SLC the look of a dachshund. No one would describe this car as pretty, but like all Mercedes cars, the styling of the SLC has an air of purposefulness and aggressiveness about it.

The driving feel of the 450SLC is also typically Mercedes. The nonadjustable steering wheel seems too large, the dashboard seems too high and the seats feel rock hard. The power-assisted steering requires more effort than in most other cars and so do the brakes. All the minor controls have a similar heavy feel. The seatbelts are positioned so that the shoulder straps cut into the tops of the shoulders of occupants over six feet tall.

But after a long spell of high-speed, cross-country driving, your impressions of the 450SLC probably will change from negative to positive. The seats that felt so hard initially prove to be comfortable after a long drive. There's no muscle ache or fatigue even after hours of sitting in these seats. The big wheel and heavy steering, which seemed so clumsy at first,

MERCEDES-BENZ 450SLC MAJOR SPECIFICATIONS

Manufacturer/Importer:
Mercedes-Benz of North America
One Mercedes Drive, Montvale, NJ 07645
Body type—2-door, 4-passenger coupe
Wheelbase, in./cm—111/282
Overall length, in./cm—196.4/499
Overall width, in./cm—70.4/179
Overall height, in./cm—52.4/133

Track, front, in./cm—57.2/145
Track, rear, in./cm—56.7/144
Curb weight, lb./kg—3795/1707
Engine type—water-cooled dohc V-8
Hp @ rpm—180 @ 4800
Displacement, cu. in./cc—276/4520
Carburetion—Bosch fuel injection
Transmission—3-speed automatic
Brakes front/rear—ventilated disc/ventilated disc
Fuel Economy, normal driving—12 mpg
Est. top speed—125 mph
Approx. price—$34,760

Specifications for U.S. market model unless otherwise noted.

transmit exactly the right feel of what the front wheels are doing at all times. This makes for relaxed long-haul driving and imparts a sense of confidence and stability on Interstates and back roads alike. The minor controls and accessories, which seemed confusing at first, turn out to be so thoughtfully arranged that after a while you begin to operate the various knobs and switches almost without thinking. About the only interior change anyone could reasonably demand is an adjustable steering wheel, preferably of the tilt-and-telescope variety. To this, Mercedes engineers would

probably answer in typically Teutonic fashion, "What, after we've spent 10 years determining *precisely* the correct steering wheel position?"

In fact, it's precision that makes the 450SLC, or any other Mercedes, worth its high initial price. If you like your mechanical contrivances to be trouble-free year in and year out, this precision—the thoroughness of Mercedes engineering and the high quality of assembly—may cause you to forget some of the 450SLC's shortcomings. For example, in acceleration and top speed the SLC is slower than a Pontiac Trans Am. The SLC lacks

sufficient luggage space for its four passengers' belongings. The engine requires a master's degree in mechanical engineering to repair. A Mercedes exhaust pipe costs $500, and that's just one of the cheaper parts.

Yet, it's that bank-vault solidity—that precision—which is so characteristic of every Mercedes that makes anyone who ever bought one a Mercedes owner for life. Simply stated, a Mercedes works—every day, consistently, for a lifetime. And in today's "throw away" society that quality makes Mercedes-Benz cars very special indeed.

PANTHER J~72 & DeVILLE

Panther Westwinds is one of the pioneer firms in the replicar field. For eight years, Panther has been building and selling a pair of fascinating cars, both based on Jaguar running gear. The J-72 roadster and the DeVille sedan are very different from most American-made neoclassics. Panther uses the finest materials and mechanical parts. The coachwork is exceptionally well built and well finished. Both cars sell for a moderate price compared with the prices of some other neoclassics. No modified MG Midget bodies or cheap fiberglass construction techniques would be acceptable at Panther.

The J-72 roadster was the first car conceived and built by Bob Jankel, the company's founder. The J-72 is still available and features styling borrowed from the classic SS-100 roadster, the forerunner of today's Jaguar.

The J-72's ladder-type frame is welded together out of square steel tubing and has a wheelbase of 111 inches. The chassis is engineered to accept an independent front suspension made up mostly of current proprietary Jaguar parts—conventional A-arms, coil springs, and an anti-sway bar. At the rear, Panther uses a heavy Salisbury rigid axle (equipped with limited-slip differential) mounted on coil springs, and located by trailing arms and a Panhard rod. The front brakes are discs, the rears are drums. Traditional knock-off wire wheels carry 225/70VR-15 tires and also add an authentic styling touch. This chassis design is similar to that used for the Jaguar XK-150, but has been refined by engineering experience gained in the 20

years since that car was built.

The engine is pure Jaguar. Panther uses the tried-and-true 4.2-liter version of the famous XK six, rated at 190 horsepower. This engine, which was very advanced for its time when introduced in 1948, still provides smooth, effortless performance that's a match for more recent engine designs. The XK powerplant uses seven main bearings, double overhead camshafts, hemispherical combustion chambers, aluminum alloy head, and twin SU carburetors. Panther wisely couples this engine to Jaguar's own four-speed manual transmission, complete with overdrive. The happy result, in a car that weighs only 2,500 pounds, is a top speed of 115 miles per hour (limited by the poor aerodynamics of the car's vintage styling), and 0-to-60 acceleration in under 10 seconds. The J-72 will get through the quarter mile in 17 seconds at about 90 mph. Combined with the competent chassis, this engine makes the J-72 fun to drive. Gas mileage, considering the performance, is a reasonable 15 miles per gallon.

The J-72's roadster body is handcrafted and made entirely of aluminum. Since the XK engine is much wider than the 3.5-liter six that powered the original SS-100, a large scoop is mounted on either side of the hood. Other styling deviations from the original SS-100 include the J-72's fat tires (wide even by modern standards), which necessitate the wide fenders, and the oversize turn signal/parking lights. The headlamp shells are big enough to house the P-100 Lucas lights that graced the original SS-100,

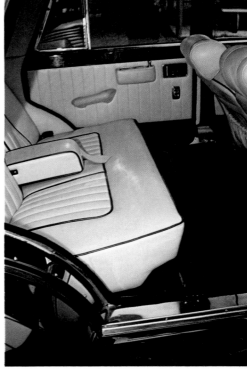

Opposite top: The DeVille's interior has a host of modern amenities. Opposite bottom: Upright styling and a long wheelbase mean lots of room in the DeVille's rear compartment. This page, clockwise from top: It looks like a scaled-down replica, but the DeVille is still a big car; grille shape emulates Bugatti's famous horseshoe; the DeVille carries a separate, free-standing trunk just like a 1930's touring sedan; underneath the center-hinged bonnet, a modern Jaguar engine.

but on the J-72 smaller, modern sealed-beam units are used. Otherwise, the styling of the J-72 appears very authentic, right down to the hood louvres, expanded-mesh grille, body-mounted outside gas tank, and exterior spare tire. It's the kind of car a schoolboy might have doodled in 1935: low, racy, and very sleek.

Panther Westwinds is noted for its quality of construction. The body of the $35,000 J-72 features flawless hand-formed aluminum construction, carefully applied metallic paint, sliding side windows made of acrylic, and an authentic-looking snap-down top. The interior has leather seats and the dashboard is filled with a complete set of engine gauges. Indeed, the whole car is put together as well as anyone could want.

The J-72 isn't a literal replica of the SS-100, since the car uses some modern hardware and design concepts, especially on the interior. But the J-72 does recall the excitement of driving in a bygone age.

Panther also makes the DeVille. It's a much larger car and a more ambitious undertaking than the J-72. The DeVille is meant to be a loose copy of the Bugatti Royale, scaled down to about three-quarter size. Like the J-72, the DeVille is built on a ladder-type, steel-tube frame and uses mostly Jaguar mechanical components. The DeVille has a very long (142-inch) wheelbase, but because of its 30s-style body, the DeVille has little overhang. Overall length is only 204 inches, not much more than an American compact.

The DeVille's engine is Jaguar's fuel-injected 326 cubic-inch V-12 coupled to the General Motors Turbo 400 Hydra-matic transmission—the same drive train Jaguar fits to the XJ12 sedan. In the 4,400-pound DeVille, this combination gives a claimed top speed of 128 mph. Acceleration is as impressive as the XJ12's. The quarter mile can be covered in about 17 seconds at 90 mph, and that's a lot faster than any Bugatti Royale.

The DeVille uses a modified version of the XJ sedan's independent suspension. At the front, A-arms, an anti-roll bar, and coil springs are used; at the rear are trailing links, and two springs and two shock absorbers per wheel. Jaguar also donates the all-disc braking system,

limited-slip differential, 6x15-inch steel wheels, and 235/70VR-15 tires. It's no surprise that the DeVille handles, brakes and stops just as well as the competent XJ12 sedan. Of course, the upright Bugatti-style bodywork of the DeVille isn't as aerodynamically efficient as the sedan's, and this limits top speed. But the DeVille performs in an uncanny manner for a large car with such old-fashioned looks.

The DeVille really doesn't look much like a Bugatti Royale. The styling bears only a slight resemblance to Royale Number

411111, the Coupe de Ville now in Harrah's Automobile Collection in Las Vegas. An imaginative person can tell where Bob Jankel received his inspiration. But when you compare the actual cars—or even a pair of photos—side by side, there's simply no comparison. For one thing, the DeVille is a much smaller car, so the proportions on the Henri Binder original have had to be modified. And the DeVille is a four-door sedan; not one of the six Royales built in the late '20s and early '30s used this body style.

Obviously, a Bugatti purist isn't going to be interested in a Panther DeVille. The prospective DeVille customer will be more intrigued with the idea of having an elegant '30s-style body plus the advantages of a thoroughly modern chassis and interior. And if the DeVille's chassis is pure Jaguar, its interior is pure Panther Westwinds. Before Panther started building complete cars, it specialized in creating custom interiors for Rolls-Royce. It's no surprise, then, that the DeVille's interior is superbly crafted with the best materials and is lovingly finished by skilled artisans. The DeVille has four very comfortable leather bucket seats, lots of burled walnut veneer on the dashboard and door sills, and a four-spoke steering wheel much like that of a real Bugatti. But the interior uses a lot of modern components like instruments and recessed interior door handles. Air conditioning, a stereo tape deck, a rear-compartment television, and power windows are just some of the contemporary concessions to comfort found in the DeVille.

The $92,000 DeVille is a curious anomaly. On the one hand, it's superbly built and finished, and it drives as nicely as Jaguar's XJ12 sedan, which is saying a lot. On the other hand, the DeVille has a delicate aluminum body that you won't want to park near crowds or in crowded parking lots, its gas mileage is only about 10 miles per gallon, and luggage space is extremely limited. The flamboyant styling attracts plenty of attention, which is not a plus for those who value anonymity. But for what it is, the DeVille is an excellent car.

Opposite top: Its body, tires, and fenders are wider than the original, but in appearance, the Panther J-72 pays tribute in almost every other way to the first Jaguar, the SS-100 roadster. Opposite bottom: What a beautiful way to go touring; the J-72's body-mounted outside gas tank and rear-mounted spare tire are features of true vintage styling. Above: Low, racy, and sleek, the J-72's graceful elegance is enhanced by long, sweeping fenders and wire-spoked wheels; note the tie-down strap for the louvred bonnet and the low-cut doors curving down from the cowl line.

PANTHER J-72 MAJOR SPECIFICATIONS

Manufacturer/Importer:
Panther Westwinds
Canada Road, Byfleet, Surrey, England
Body type—2-door, 2-passenger roadster
Wheelbase, in./cm—111/282
Overall length, in./cm—165/419
Overall width, in./cm—68.5/174
Overall height, in./cm—49/124
Track, front, in./cm—58.5/149
Track, rear, in./cm—58.5/149
Curb weight, lb./kg—2576/1166
Engine type—water-cooled dohc inline-six
Hp @ rpm—190 @ 5000 (DIN)
Displacement, cu. in./cc—258/4235
Carburetion—two 1-bbl SU
Transmission—4-speed manual
Brakes front/rear—disc/drum
Fuel Economy, normal driving—15 mpg
Est. top speed—115 mph
Approx. price—$35,000

PANTHER DeVILLE MAJOR SPECIFICATIONS

Body type—4-door, 4-passenger sedan
Wheelbase, in./cm—142/361
Overall length, in./cm—204/519
Overall width, in./cm—71/180
Overall height, in./cm—61/155
Track, front, in./cm—58/147
Track, rear, in./cm—58/147
Curb weight, lb./kg—4360/1973
Engine type—Jaguar water-cooled sohc V-12
Hp @ rpm—244 @ 5250
Displacement, cu. in./cc—326/5343
Carburetion—Lucas-Bosch Fuel injection
Transmission—3-speed automatic
Brakes front/rear—disc/disc
Fuel Economy, normal driving—10 mpg
Est. top speed—128 mph
Approx. price—$92,000

Specifications for U.S. market model unless otherwise noted.

PORSCHE 928 & 930 TURBO

There are few car fans as dedicated as Porsche fans. The tail-heavy coupes they have admired have always seemed strange to enthusiasts not caught up in the Porsche mystique. But the new 928 is a Porsche anybody can love. You don't need stringback driving gloves, a tweed cap, and a passion for high-performance driving to appreciate that the 928 is the best Porsche ever, and one of the best GT coupes you can buy. It's already the favorite of many who know cars, and it's virtually guaranteed to be an important collector's item 10 years from now.

Many people are attracted to the 928 by its looks. Tony Lapine, who used to work for William L. "Bill" Mitchell in General Motors Styling, and who was a good racing driver in his day, is now the chief stylist at Porsche. Like Mitchell, Lapine is a kind of "designer's designer" whose work contains many subtle visual references to other cars. There are traces of the Camaro and Firebird, Corvette Stingray, Opel GT, AMC Pacer, Ferrari Daytona, Maserati Merak, Lamborghini Miura, and Datsun 280-Z in the Porsche 928, as well as similarities to its sibling, the 924, and the long-lived 911.

Unlike so many pretty cars, function in the 928 hasn't been sacrificed to styling. The long doors open wide for easy entry, and even six-foot-tall drivers will find plenty of room inside. The hip-hugging bucket seats have fore-aft and height adjustment plus reclining backrests, so it's easy to find a comfortable driving position. The thick-rimmed steering wheel, with its three broad, padded spokes, also adjusts up-and-down. In many cars with this feature the instruments can be partially obscured by the wheel rim in some positions. The 928 overcomes this problem with an instrument cluster that tilts with the wheel. This means the instruments can always be clearly seen since their alignment remains constant relative to the steering wheel, no matter what its position.

There are other thoughtful touches like this in the 928's

Opposite: Porsche's 928 has one of those pure shapes that look as though it was carved from a single piece of marble. Above, clockwise from far right: Interior features wide, sweeping center console and armrests integrated with ends of dash; body-colored bumpers contribute to clean rear-end styling with its rounded rear quarter contours; in profile the 928's curvaceous lines are set off by squared wheel arches and unusual alloy wheels.

interior. For instance, the two small rear seats fold flat to make an unobstructed load floor nearly five feet long and four feet wide. This area is accessible through a hatchback which opens up the whole back of the car from the central roll bar/roof pillar down to the back bumper. The relationship between the heavily padded shifter and the steering wheel is good. Minor controls are all conveniently located, clearly labeled and easy to use. Among these is a lever for adjusting headlight aim hydraulically from inside the car. This allows the driver to compensate for the effects of a "nose up-tail down" attitude when carrying heavy loads in the rear. The foot

pedals are spaced correctly for heel-and-toe gear changes. The armrests (which conceal the air conditioning ducts and stereo speakers) are designed to blend into the outer edges of the dashboard. The glove box is of a useful size, and there's a small package shelf under the dash on the passenger's side. About the only jarring note is the optional checked upholstery fabric done in an "op art" pattern. It's completely out of character with the rest of the materials used in this eminently understated interior.

There's nothing understated about the 928's chassis, however. Porsche spent some $80 million on its development and it shares no parts with any

other Porsche model. The 928 has a short wheelbase of 98.4 inches and an overall length of 175.1 inches. The bodyshell is made of steel, welded into a single unit with the frame. The doors, front fenders, and hood are made of aluminum and are not structurally part of the unit body/chassis. The design of the independent front suspension is conventional: upper A-arms, lower trailing arms, and coil springs. The rear suspension is also independent: upper transverse arms, lower trailing arms, and coil springs. What makes the rear layout unusual is that the differential is mounted directly to the chassis and is integral with the transmission. Buyers can choose from either

Porsche's own five-speed manual gearbox or a Mercedes-built three-speed automatic. The driveshaft is long, thin, and flexible, and connects the rear-mounted transmission and the front-mounted engine. The single-overhead-cam all-aluminum V-8 uses Bosch fuel injection to turn out 219 horsepower from its 4474 cc displacement.

For a 3,285-pound car with a tall 2.75:1 final drive ratio, the 928 is surprisingly fast. Quarter-mile times are about 15 seconds at over 90 mph, and the 0-60 sprint takes just seven seconds. Top speed is around 145 miles per hour which makes the 928 one of the fastest cars available on the U.S. market. Amazingly, gas mileage, considering the performance available, is good: 16 miles per gallon is possible in everyday driving. The 928 stops as well as it goes. Vented disc brakes, 11 inches in diameter, are mounted at each wheel. Cast alloy wheels of 16-inch diameter are used and were styled by Lapine. The 928 offers astounding ride, handling, and braking, due in part to its standard equipment Pirelli P7 tires, size 225/50VR-16. The P7 is considered by many to be the "state of the art" in performance tire development. But the ultimate in anything never comes cheap, and a set of four P7's costs about $1,500. Worse, these tires usually last only about 15,000 miles because their soft, grippy rubber compound wears out relatively fast. But these tires give the 928 excellent handling, superb grip (the car recorded .81G on the skid pad), plus a soft ride.

Over the years, Porsche's 911 series built up a loyal enthusiastic following as Porsche continually refined the car to eliminate the inherent disadvantages of its rear-engine design. The 911 gradually evolved into a car with a character all its own, a car with impeccable, all-around performance. The new 928 already has impeccable performance. But its character is completely different from the 911's, one with undeniable appeal to an even broader range of drivers. The 928 seems destined to win a whole new band of enthusiasts to the Porsche camp.

The Porsche 930 Turbo looks like the most outrageously customized 911 you've ever seen. It has fat rear fenders, a curious rubber-edged wing on the tail, and gigantic tires. The stock Porsche 911 is known for its tricky handling because 58 percent of its weight rests on the rear wheels. The standard rear-mounted flat-six engine has enough power to send the 911 into sudden, and sometimes uncontrollable, oversteer in tight corners taken at speed. Despite the changes Porsche has made over the years to tame the 911's handling vices, this car still demands an alert and sensitive driver.

You'd expect the handling of the 930 Turbo to be even worse, since it has even more horsepower pushing the already twitchy chassis. And you'd be wrong.

The 930 Turbo looks like a 911, but it is a completely different car mechanically. That's why it's not called the 911 Turbo.

Compared to the stock 911, the 930 has a much meaner appearance, primarily because its front and rear fenders are made much wider in order to cover much wider tires and wheels. These fender bulges make the 930 over six inches wider than the normal 911. The track is also six inches wider. The 911 uses 15x6-inch wheels and 185/70-section tires all around. But the 930 comes with giant 16x7-inch wheels on the front and 16x8s on the rear. Porsche specifies Pirelli's new super-sticky P7 performance tire for the 930, size 205/55VR-16 on the front and 225/55VR-16 on the rear. The 930's weight distribution is even worse than the 911's—64 percent is on the rear wheels—because the Turbo engine is heavier than the 911's. So, Porsche uses tires and wheels that are wider at the rear than at the front to compensate for the rear end weight bias and because the 930's speed potential is considerably higher than the 911's.

Since it's designed to go like a race car, Porsche uses a lot of race car technology for the 930's chassis. The four-wheel disc brakes are the same as those used in the over-200 mph 917 racer that Mark Donohue and George Follmer drove when they dominated the Can-Am series in the early '70s. The MacPherson-strut front suspension and independent rear suspension are similar to the design of the 935 Group 5 racer. For the 930, both suspensions have been modified to produce low-speed understeer. But if you take a corner at too high a speed and then lift off the accelerator you may find yourself leaving the road backwards.

The heart of the 930 is its turbocharged engine. This 3299cc single-overhead-cam flat six has Bosch fuel injection and a Porsche-developed turbocharger, which is limited to just under 12 pounds of boost between 4000 and 5500 rpm. Porsche's powerplant is rated at 261 horsepower, which translates to about 1.3 horsepower for each of its 201 cubic inches.

The 930's performance is, as the British say, shattering. Accelerating from rest to 60 mph is accomplished in less than five

Clockwise from top: It may look like a customized 911, but the 930 Turbo is a completely different car; the "whale-tail" spoiler and huge rear tires distinguish the 930 from lesser Porsches; this is about the only view other drivers get of Stuttgart's slingshot; sticky P7 tires give phenomenal cornering grip; the cockpit is reserved for serious driver only.

seconds, and it takes about 12 seconds to reach 100 mph from a dead stop. The quarter mile is covered in a blistering 13.7 seconds at 105 mph. The amazing thing about the Turbo engine is the great amount of torque it produces over a very wide rpm band. The generous spread of torque allows the 930 to make do with a four-speed gearbox on which the top two gears are overdrive ratios. This high gearing means the 930 can reach a top speed of 165 mph. Needless to say, such speed is of academic interest in any country.

The Turbo engine's wide torque curve also gives the 930 a curiously split personality. The engine idles smoothly at 500 rpm, it starts easily from cold, and it pulls strongly from as low as 1000 rpm in any gear. The turbocharger whirling at 90,000 rpm even helps keep exhaust noise lower than in the 911. Driven gently, the 930 Turbo is as docile and sober as Dr. Jekyll. But mash down on the throttle in any gear and Mr. Hyde emerges. Careless use of the accelerator will leave two intermittent black rubber streaks on the road as the rear suspension skitters and hops. At speeds above 90 mph, the 930 wobbles uncertainly. The huge "whale tail" rear spoiler helps keep the rear pair of P7s glued to the road, but the front end is particularly susceptible to aerodynamic lift. The 930 is also not very stable in gusty crosswinds—another well-known disadvantage of a rear-engine layout. In short, the 930 is not an easy car to drive fast.

There are other things this car is not. At about 15 miles per gallon, the 930 is hardly an economy car. The short wheelbase makes for a very choppy ride so the 930 is not a car for driving on bumpy roads. And although the steering feels too light at high speeds, it takes Popeye the Sailor Man to maneuver this Porsche in a parking lot. The brake and clutch pedals require a lot of effort, too, so the 930 is not a car for 98-pound weaklings. The shift lever has that classic Porsche feel—rather like a spoon in a bowl of tapioca. On the other hand, the combination of those big ventilated disc brakes and sticky P7s bring the 930 to a halt in short order.

The 930 interior, like the car's road manners, is a mixture of the sublime and the ridiculous. The pedals and the padded steering wheel are both uncomfortably offset towards the center of the car because the front wheel arches take up space in the front floor area. But the seats are superbly shaped Recaro-like buckets that are very comfortable and hold you in place during hard cornering. The dashboard and the five large instrument dials are clearly visible through the steering wheel. And the interior is attractive and lovingly finished.

Servicing the 930's engine is not a task for amateurs, but then the 930 is not in any way an amateur's car. This is not a car for daily transportation. The 930 Turbo is a professional machine that demands a dedicated professional owner/driver.

Unhappily, you'll need to be dedicated if you want to own one of these cars. The 930 will be withdrawn from the U.S. market after 1979, although the Turbo will continue to be sold in Europe, until it is eventually replaced by the turbocharged version of the 928.

So if you can find a new 930 Turbo, or even a low-mileage used one, snap it up fast. This car is likely to become a collector's item very soon and for a very good reason. In an age of increasingly bland cars, the 930 is an outrageous reminder that once there were high-performance cars—when gas was cheap and the air was cleaner.

PORSCHE 928 MAJOR SPECIFICATIONS

Manufacturer/Importer
Volkswagen of America
Englewood Cliffs, NJ 07632
Body type—2-door, 2-passenger coupe
Wheelbase, in./cm—98.4/250
Overall length, in./cm—175.1/445
Overall width, in./cm—72.3/184
Overall height, in./cm—51.7/131
Track, front, in./cm—61.1/155
Track, rear, in./cm—60.2/153
Curb weight, lb./kg—3285/1478
Engine type—water-cooled sohc V-8
Hp @ rpm—219 @ 5250
Displacement, cu. in./cc—273/4474
Carburetion—Bosch K-Jetronic fuel
    injection
Transmission—5-speed manual (3-speed
    automatic optional)
Brakes front/rear—ventilated
    disc/ventilated disc
Fuel Economy, normal driving—16 mpg
Est. top speed—145 mph
Approx. price—$30,000

PORSCHE 930 TURBO MAJOR SPECIFICATIONS

Body type—2-door, 4-passenger
    rear-engine coupe
Wheelbase, in./cm—89.4/227
Overall length, in./cm—169/429
Overall width, in./cm—69.9/178
Overall height, in./cm—52.3/133
Track, front, in./cm—56.4/143
Track, rear, in./cm—59.1/150
Curb weight, lb./kg—2855/1285
Engine type—air-cooled sohc
    turbocharged flat-six
Hp @ rpm—261 @ 5500
Displacement, cu. in./cc—201/3299
Carburetion—Bosch K-Jetronic fuel
    injection
Transmission—4-speed manual
Brakes front/rear—ventilated
    disc/ventilated disc
Fuel Economy, normal driving—15 mpg
Est. top speed—165 mph
Approx. price—$38,500

Specifications for U.S. market model unless otherwise noted.

ROLLS-ROYCE

Nowhere is the decline of the British motor industry more evident than at Rolls-Royce. Up until about 20 years ago many automobile connoisseurs agreed with the company's advertising, which proclaimed Rolls-Royce as "the best car in the world." But today most experts believe that Mercedes-Benz, Jaguar, Lagonda, BMW, and even Cadillac build luxury cars that are at least the equal of Rolls-Royce in craftsmanship, durability, and elegance. In fact, since Rolls introduced the Silver Shadow line in 1966, the general level of automotive excellence has risen to the point where many lower-priced cars now approach the Rolls in ride,

roadholding, handling, body design, and luxury.

Many people don't realize that Rolls-Royce makes only 3,600

cars each year, one-third of which come to America. By comparison, Mercedes-Benz sells almost 50,000 cars a year in the United States alone, and that's only 10 percent of its total production. Over the years the Rolls-Royce company has grown to include an aircraft engine division, which got into such financial trouble that in 1973 the future of Rolls-Royce as an auto maker was threatened. To save the car side of the business the British government split off the aircraft engine division, and the car-making operations were consolidated that year as Rolls-Royce Motors Limited. This firm remains hugely profitable today, despite the low annual production rate. Even during the height of the first "energy crisis" in the fall of 1973, Rolls-Royce waiting lists were longer than ever. Even in times of economic uncertainty there are affluent people who remain relatively unaffected by forces like inflation and fluctuating monetary exchange rates. These people have always been, and probably always will be, Rolls-Royce customers. But other manufacturers are challenging Rolls-Royce's supremacy in the upper-echelon market as never before. What R-R now needs most, perhaps, is a replacement for the aging Silver Shadow.

The Silver Shadow has always been controversial for a Rolls-Royce. When it was announced, most automotive writers compared it unfavorably to the Silver Cloud range it replaced. Fourteen years ago the Shadow was considered a dull car, and today it seems even more lackluster when compared with those competitors designed and introduced since 1966. The styling of the Silver Shadow bears an unfortunate resemblance to the Volvo 264 or the Checker Marathon. Of course, the Rolls buyer prefers, and therefore expects, a car with conservative, dignified lines. But take away the traditional "cathedral" radiator grille and "Spirit of Ecstacy" hood ornament, and the Shadow would go almost unnoticed. So, for $65,000, the Silver Shadow buyer gets a car with somewhat dated styling that's distinguished, but hardly distinctive. Visibility isn't very good either, since the car has a high beltline, small windows, and thick rear quarter pillars. The dashboard and steering wheel seem to intrude on forward vision; they and the large headrests on all four seats produce a feeling of claustrophobia for driver and passengers alike.

The Silver Shadow uses a unitized body/chassis with a long 120.1-inch wheelbase. The upright styling dictates short front and rear overhang, so the car's overall length is a relatively compact 207 inches—almost the same as the Cadillac Seville or Mercedes 450SEL.

Mechanically, the Silver Shadow isn't at all innovative.

The 412 cubic-inch V-8 engine is made largely of aluminum alloy, and its design is essentially that of the 1955 Chevrolet "small block" engine; the main difference between the Rolls and the Chevy power plants is the larger displacement of the Rolls unit. Rolls-Royce has been using this engine

virtually unchanged since 1958. It has no overhead cams, fuel-injection or any other technically interesting details; just old-fashioned pushrods and two single-barrel carburetors. This engine, which could come from any GM car, is coupled to a transmission that actually does come from GM: The Shadow's three-speed Hydra-matic unit is virtually identical with that used in any garden-variety Malibu. The Shadow's 5,000-pound curb weight, host of power-robbing accessories, big V-8 engine, and automatic transmission combine to limit the car's mileage figure to a bare 10 miles per gallon of increasingly expensive gasoline. That might not be a financial consideration for Rolls-Royce's clientele, but it's a concern for anyone who's had to wait in long lines to fill up.

The Silver Shadow's all-independent suspension employs coil springs, anti-sway bars, and control arms at each wheel. Lower wishbones at the front, and semi-trailing arms at the rear, complete the suspension layout. Disc brakes are used all around. The Shadow's steering system is a powered rack-and-pinion unit. which was adopted in 1978 with the introduction of the current Silver Shadow II models. The idea was to increase road feel through the steering wheel for handling response that would be

Opposite top: Rolls-Royce styling has always been conservative yet elegant. Opposite bottom: The R-R mystique is best symbolized by the famous cathedral grille and "Flying Lady" *mascot. Above: The latest American-market Silver Shadow II is slightly longer than the European model. Below: A full-length character line gives the Corniche convertible a slightly sportier look.*

ROLLS-ROYCE SILVER SHADOW MAJOR SPECIFICATIONS

Manufacturer/Importer:
Rolls-Royce Motors
Century Road, Paramus, NJ 07652
Body type—4-door, 4-passenger sedan
Wheelbase, in./cm—120.1/305
Overall length, in./cm—207.5/527
Overall width, in./cm—71.8/182
Overall height, in./cm—59.8/152
Track, front, in./cm—60/152
Track, rear, in./cm—59.6/151
Curb weight, lb./kg—4930/2218
Engine type—water-cooled ohv V-8
Hp @ rpm—NA
Displacement, cu. in./cc—412/6750
Carburetion—two 1-bbl SU
Transmission—3-speed automatic
Brakes front/rear—ventilated
    disc/ventilated disc
Fuel Economy, normal driving—10 mpg
Est. top speed—118 mph
Approx. price—$65,000
Specifications for U.S. market model unless otherwise noted.

Above: The ultra-exclusive Camargue displays its massive-looking prow; the styling was created mainly by Italy's Pininfarina. Below left: Camargue dash is festooned with black-finish switches and dials set against a wood veneer background; gauge at the right is an outside thermometer. Below right: Camargue offers only minimal legroom for rear seat passengers.

a closer match for Mercedes and Jaguar steering systems. The ultimate cornering power of a Rolls-Royce still isn't any higher than that of a Chevrolet Caprice, but the Shadow's steering no longer feels as vague and overassisted as it did before. Handling is surprisingly good for such a tall, heavy car having a high roll center. The "Roller" does roll somewhat on tight turns, but the car's main handling trait is gentle under-steer that's predictable and safe.

Braking is excellent for a car of this size and weight. Unlike the Mercedes-Benz automatic transmission, which shifts cleanly but noticeably, the Rolls-Royce automatic is set up for slurred, unobtrusive gear changes. The transmission's syrupy upward shifts make for anemic acceleration (which, in keeping with the Rolls image, might be more flatteringly described as stately). By modern standards the Silver Shadow is quiet, but not as quiet as the old Phantom II. This is a result of the Shadow's unit body/chassis, which transmits more noise to the passenger compartment than a separate body and chassis. The ride, however, is better than that of any previous Rolls-Royce. The earlier cars had flexible frames, long wheelbases, and very heavy bodies; these made for a well-damped ride on smooth roads, but also produced uncontrolled flexing on rough roads. With its independent suspension, short wheelbase (for a Rolls) and more rigid construction, the Silver Shadow has a more composed and comfortable ride than earlier Rolls-Royces. The driver is hardly aware the suspension is working. The smoothness is upset on rough roads only by some mild pitching, due to the relatively short wheelbase.

Like the Jaguar XJ12 or Mercedes 6.9, the Rolls-Royce is a mechanic's nightmare. The hood opening is narrow and the engine bay is crowded with assorted pipes and hoses.

Major maintenance is complicated and parts prices are high. Typical examples are $200 for a simple head gasket and $1,000 for a muffler. But as the saying goes, "if you have to ask the price. . . ."

There is also a two-door version of the Shadow called the Corniche. It is available in either coupe or convertible body styles. The Corniche engine, chassis and interior are all lifted intact from the Shadow. However, the Corniche costs roughly $40,000 more than the four-door. It is not one of the great automotive bargains of our time.

At the very top of the Rolls-Royce price and exclusivity ladder is the Camargue coupe priced at an eye-popping $115,000, plus tax. Like other Rolls models, the Camargue's body is largely hand-built; this work is actually carried out by H.J. Mulliner/Park Ward, which survives as a subsidiary of Rolls-Royce after both firms were acquired by the company 20 years ago. The Camargue uses a slightly modified Silver Shadow chassis, so most of the car's additional cost stems from the fact that Rolls deliberately limits the Camargue's production. Even at the price, the company sells every one of these very exclusive cars it makes.

The Camargue's monocoque body shell is ungainly in appearance, even though Italy's master stylist Pininfarina did most of the design work. The body weighs some 200 pounds more than the standard sedan's, so the Camargue's performance is predictably less eager than that of its less expensive siblings. The Camargue is also lower than other Rolls models. This limits headroom both front and rear for people over six feet tall. Rear legroom is sparse. The rear quarter windows don't roll down because there's no room in the bodywork for the winding mechanism, nor do they swing out. But then, Rolls claims its fully automatic heating and air conditioning systems are the

most advanced in the world. Perhaps the company feels that with this complex climate controller on duty, Camargue owners don't need opening rear windows. Curiously, the same system is now fitted to all Silver Shadows and Corniches, which do have opening rear windows.

If any car can honestly be said to be worth $60,000 to over $100,000, then workmanship is what makes a Rolls-Royce worth its price. There are examples of painstaking attention to detail in every nook and cranny of a Rolls. Real wood veneers used on dashboard and door trim are carefully cut so that the grain is exactly symmetrical. The individual grain patterns for each car made are kept on file at the factory so replacement veneers can be cut and matched, if necessary, at a later date. Genuine Wilton wool carpets, Connolly leather hides, and stainless steel trim are expected in cars at this rarified price level, and Rolls-Royce continues to use these materials as it has for decades. The bodywork is perfection itself. The fit of all body panels and the mirror-like paint surface testify to the Rolls-Royce tradition of building cars in the unhurried old-world way.

Rolls-Royce is known to be working on a replacement for the Silver Shadow. Carrying the code-name "SZ," the new car, which could appear as early as 1981, is said to be smaller and lighter than the Silver Shadow though very similar in appearance. Whenever the "SZ" appears, the value of the current Silver Shadow and its derivatives as collectors' cars will no doubt rise, though it is difficult to predict just how quickly this might happen. When the Silver Shadow is discontinued, it will not be remembered as one of the great Rolls-Royces. Instead it will be remembered simply because it is a Rolls-Royce. There's no finer tribute than that in the world of elite cars.

Tom McBurnie and Ray Kinney, the designers of the Sceptre, seem to have a better feeling for late 1930s design than almost anybody since Gordon Buehrig, the man who designed the famous coffin-nose Cord 810. The Sceptre looks like it could have been built in 1939, instead of 1979. It stands as a landmark of Art Deco design. The Sceptre's styling has all the verve and panache that made so many 1930s cars the classics they are today.

The Sceptre is bigger than most of the '30s classics but bears a faint resemblance to the BMW 328 roadster, or to some of Pininfarina's Lancia and Alfa Romeo designs from that era. This is not to say that the Sceptre is an imitation of an old BMW or Lancia. It's an original work of art: beautiful, sophisticated, and tasteful. The Sceptre's styling recalls the transition period of automotive design that occurred just before the envelope body appeared. It was the age of streamlining, and

the Sceptre's lines are much like those of the late '30s Auburns and Cords. The fenders are separate from the body, the hood is long, the trunk is short, the cockpit compact. But these body panels are rounded and smooth instead of square-cut and sharp-edged. To many industrial designers this kind of transitional look between the separate body and fenders of the early '30s and the envelope body of the '40s represents some of the finest automobile styling ever produced.

SCEPTRE 6.6S

In light of its $50,000 price—considerably less than that of most other neoclassic cars—the Sceptre is surprisingly well made. Sceptre Motor Car Company uses a heavily modified Mercury Cougar chassis, along with the stock Cougar 351 cubic-inch V-8 engine and three-speed automatic transmission. The engine/transmission unit is moved back in the chassis two feet for better weight distribution. The wheelbase remains unaltered at 118 inches. A considerable amount of extra bracing is welded onto the chassis to provide additional stiffness. The box frame is reinforced with channel-section steel girders. Another 2x5-inch channel-section brace is welded on across the back of the chassis. The entire passenger compartment is ringed with 2x3-inch square steel tubing. Finally, a 20-gallon racing fuel cell is used in place of the stock gas tank. The Sceptre weighs about 3,100 pounds, a ton less than the Cougar. The Cougar's independent front suspension and live-axle rear suspension are revised to suit the Sceptre's lighter weight. Two shock absorbers are fitted to each wheel, and rear axle location is improved by use of both trailing arms and torque arms. The brakes are left unchanged; there are discs in front and drums in the rear. Since the Cougar's brakes were designed to stop a 4,500-pound car, they should have little trouble stopping the Sceptre. Completing the chassis

Opposite: A sloped, rounded nose and tear-drop fenders give the Sceptre the look of a 1930's car with ''streamlined'' styling. Below, clockwise from left: Interior room is limited because the main body structure comes from the MG Midget; the Sceptre manages to look like many classic cars and entirely original at the same time; flowing rear deck features embossed trunk lid.

specifications are seven-inch-wide wire wheels carrying GR70-15 Firestone tires. The Cougar's 65-inch front and rear track dimensions are retained.

Cars with 1930's styling have very little overhang compared with more modern designs. Sceptre, despite its compact overall length of just 188 inches, still seems very large. What makes it seem so big is its proportions. The front two-thirds of the car's length is all hood; only the rear third is used for the cockpit and trunk. This

makes the Sceptre's fiberglass body beautiful, but very inefficient in its use of space. That hood is longer than it needs to be: The excessive length is used just for styling effect. But then this kind of extravagant design is one of the hallmarks of late '30s cars.

The Sceptre may not be much on space utilization, but it's practical in other ways. The fiberglass body is a quarter-inch thick and finished in lacquer. The Sceptre uses large body panels, so repair bills could be high should one of them need

to be replaced due to accident damage. On the other hand, the Sceptre does have 5-mph impact-absorbing bumpers, side-guard door beams, and side marker lights. The extra-strength chassis and six-foot-long front end also contribute to occupant safety in the Sceptre.

As with other elite cars, the Sceptre's interior is upholstered in Connolly hide. The dashboard is filled with gauges and is covered with Brazilian walnut veneer. There's also a padded leather steering wheel. The Sceptre uses the windshield and top from the MG Midget.

The Sceptre cockpit is a marvelous place to be, even though the visibility is limited by the small windshield. Plan on filling up the 19.5-gallon fuel cell at the rate of one gallon every 16 miles. The Sceptre handles well, feeling surprisingly lithe and neutral in almost all conditions. The brakes provide sure, fade-free stops. The Mercury power steering is over-assisted and feels too light. But even though the steering requires four turns lock-to-lock, the Sceptre is still surprisingly easy to maneuver. It's no sports car, but the Sceptre certainly qualifies as a classically styled pre-war Grand Tourer, especially since its top speed is over 120 miles per hour.

If you're in the market for a neoclassic, the Sceptre deserves consideration. The whole point of a car like this is styling, and the Sceptre is one of the better-looking neoclassics. To some eyes it's even prettier than the Auburn Speedster replicars, or cars like the Clenet and Excalibur. The workmanship is beyond reproach, and the attention paid to safety is one example of the thoroughness with which the Sceptre is built. As a neoclassic the Sceptre has a lot of class.

SCEPTRE 6.6 MAJOR SPECIFICATIONS

Manufacturer/Importer:
Sceptre Motor Car Company
7242 Hollister Avenue, Goleta, CA 93017
Body type—2-door, 2-passenger roadster
Wheelbase in./cm—118.4/301
Overall length, in./cm—188.5/479
Overall width, in./cm—74.5/189
Overall height, in./cm—54/137
Track, front, in./cm—65/165

Track, rear, in./cm—65/165
Curb weight, lb./kg—3100/1395
Engine type—water-cooled ohv V-8
Hp @ rpm—168 @ 4000 (DIN)
Displacement, cu. in./cc—351/5732
Carburetion—one 4-bbl. Ford
Transmission—3-speed automatic
Brakes front/rear—disc/drum
Fuel Economy, normal driving—16 mpg
Est. top speed—128 mph
Approx. price—$50,000

Specifications for U.S. market model unless otherwise noted.

SILVER VOLT

Electric cars are all the rage these days. Almost every engineer in the country seems to have a grant from the Department of Energy to develop a ''near-term'' electric car. But the engineering, and therefore the usefulness, of most of these vehicles is fairly limited. The usual formula is to take the smallest car you can find, fill it up with batteries, and send it out to hum round the block. The Electric Auto Corporation has used just this approach for its new Silver Volt. This car has been described by a well-known car magazine as ''the most practical electric car yet.'' But that's misleading. The technology

does not currently (pun intended) exist to make the electric car a practical proposition for most motorists. Nor does technology allow manufacturers like EAC to sell electric cars at prices competitive with those of internal-combustion engine cars.

Nevertheless, the Silver Volt is here now. It starts life as a GM ''A-body'' station wagon. To disguise the body, EAC grafts a new, sharply pointed nose onto the front end and covers the rear quarter windows with a padded vinyl top. This top also helps to hide the batteries that fill up the cargo compartment. A set of ''futuristic'' Centerline spun aluminum

wheels and a blue-and-silver paint scheme are the finishing exterior touches.

In order to electrify the wagon (the prototype is a Buick Century; production won't start until calendar year 1980), EAC must remove everything under the hood and replace it with a bank of EFP TPX long-life batteries. This half-ton battery pack complements the equal-size battery pack located in the cargo area. Under the hood, EAC also finds room for a 50 kw (peak), 20 kw (continuous) electric motor with a transistorized controller. This motor is connected to a torque converter having an infinitely variable ratio. The rest

SILVER VOLT

of the drivetrain is stock GM, as is the chassis.

According to EAC, the top speed of this $14,500 rig is 70 miles per hour. At a constant speed of 50 mph, the Silver Volt can go for about 60 miles before it needs to be recharged. A quick charge, performed in less than an hour, restores 80 percent power. This procedure dramatically shortens the life of the expensive batteries if it is used too often. In practice, the Silver Volt must be recharged with a slow charge once every 60 miles. It takes eight hours to recharge the batteries this way, at a cost of less than a dollar at standard utility rates. Under this type of arduous use, however, conventional batteries only last for 300 to 500 discharge cycles. After that, the batteries must be replaced. For the Silver Volt, that amounts to a $1,000 expense.

There's another problem. In order to run the heater, air conditioning, and power steering and brakes, the Silver Volt is equipped with a two-cylinder gasoline engine that must operate at all times. Obviously, this little auxiliary engine doesn't use as much fuel as the V-6 engine of the stock Buick Century. But considering that the electric car's purchase price is

twice that of the Buick, and adding the cost of battery replacement every year or two, and utility charges, the Silver Volt doesn't make very good economic sense.

As a car, the Silver Volt doesn't make much sense either. The heavy batteries push the springs right down to the stops. The car doesn't brake, handle, or steer very well at all. With all that weight to pull around, the Silver Volt's little electric motor just isn't powerful enough to move this car as quickly as most traffic situations demand. And since most of the cargo area is filled with batteries, there's no room for anything except four people. You couldn't go anywhere you'd need luggage, anyway, because the range per charge is limited to only 60 miles.

The Silver Volt, like other electric cars, uses the best batteries now available. But today's batteries are too heavy, too expensive, too quickly drained, and too quickly used up to be of much use in a modern car.

Within the next decade, it's likely a new type of battery will be invented to solve all the problems of on-board electricity storage. At that point, the electric car will become practical. The only problem then will be finding a way to recharge millions of electric vehicles. This will place even heavier demands for electricity on utility companies, that in turn depend on dwindling, increasingly expensive supplies of fuel oil to turn their generators. The Silver Volt is called "pollution-free and cheap to run" by its manufacturers. That may be true, but the practical electric car is still some years away.

SILVER VOLT MAJOR SPECIFICATIONS

Manufacturer/Importer:
Electric Automobile Corporation
Troy, Michigan
Body type—4-door, 4-passenger
    station wagon
Wheelbase, in./cm—108/274
Overall length, in./cm—210/533
Overall width, in./cm—72/183
Overall height, in./cm—54/137
Track, front, in./cm—58.5/148
Track, rear, in./cm—57.8/147

Curb weight, lb./kg—4000/1800
Engine type—air-cooled electric,
    separately-excited field
Hp @ rpm—50 kW peak, 20 kW
    continuous
Displacement, cu. in./cc—NA
Carburetion—NA
Transmission—infinitely-variable torque
    converter
Brakes front/rear—disc/drum
Fuel Economy, normal driving—60 miles
    per charge @ 50 mph
Est. top speed—70 mph
Approx. price—$14,500

Specifications for U.S. market model unless otherwise noted.

Opposite: Based on a Buick Century station wagon, the Silver Volt's styling features a long, pointed nose and padded vinyl roof. Above:

Letters on the license plate are manufacturer's initials. Below: Battery-powered prototype is finished in "electric blue" paint scheme.

STUTZ SPEEDSTER

Dave Samuels, the head of Southeastern Replicars, runs one of the finest restoration shops in this country. For some years Samuels has been building Auburn Speedster replicars. He now offers what is easily the best replicar of its type, a reproduction of the 1928 Stutz Blackhawk boattail Speedster. Two things make Samuels' Stutz different from every other replica: The chassis isn't of modern design (the car uses a new Ford engine and transmission); and, although the body is made of fiberglass, it is an *exact* replica of the 1928 original in every detail. This is a unique way of building a replica. The Southeastern Replicars Stutz Blackhawk is not a modern car disguised as an old one: It is a genuinely new 1928 car.

Samuels starts with a set of custom-made channel-section frame rails of exactly the same measurements as the original Stutz components. The chassis has a 131-inch wheelbase, and the frame rails are eight inches deep, tapering to less than four inches at the ends. Samuels uses a rigid front axle carried on two half-elliptic leaf springs; a rigid rear axle on two half-elliptic leaf springs; lever-action hydraulic shock absorbers; and tall, narrow, 23-inch-diameter wire wheels fitted with original-type tires. Big drum

Opposite: The only way to tell this highly authentic replica from the original is to thump the body. Top left: Note the tall, narrow-section tires similar to those used by Stutz for the original. Top right: The Speedster's boattail design has become one of the symbols of classic late '20s styling. Above: The epitome of "jazz age" automobiles is preserved in every detail of this carefully crafted replica; it's a genuinely new 1928 car.

brakes of the kind originally specified by Stutz are used on each wheel. Each of these components, except the rear axle (taken from a Ford truck), has been fabricated from scratch so as to be almost identical with the components of the original.

Samuels uses a 300 cubic-inch six, rated at 117 horsepower and taken from a Ford truck. This powerplant is coupled to a three-speed manual transmission. The 1928 Stutz Blackhawk came with a straight-eight engine of 300 cubic inches, rated at 115 hp, or 125 hp with the optional high-compression head. In other words, Samuels fits a modern engine that has exactly the same size and power output as the 1928 Stutz engine. This concern for authenticity is typical of Samuels's approach to recreating this classic car.

The original Stutz Blackhawk Speedster is considered by many experts in the field of classic cars to have the best styling of any Stutz ever built. As one writer once put it: "One's inevitable first impression is 'Good Grief. What a gorgeous automobile!'" The Blackhawk dates from that era when stylists were beginning to experiment with streamlining, and the Stutz was one of the first cars to feature this kind of design. A character line runs rearward along the car's flanks from the

STUTZ SPEEDSTER

cowl, fading away into the rear bumper. The sharply pointed boattail rises from the flat plane at the end of the rear deck. The front fenders are of the separate cycle-type and have canvas skirts. The tall radiator rises proudly between two huge headlights. Gorgeous is the word, all right.

The Speedster replica is a line-for-line copy, almost impossible to differentiate from the original—for anyone but an expert, that is. The interior is also exactly like the original's, except for the contemporary instruments mounted in the old-fashioned dashboard. Even the steering wheel and foot pedals are reproductions. This attention to detail is simply unheard of at most replicar companies. It's no exaggeration

to say that the only way you can tell this isn't a real 1928 Stutz Blackhawk Speedster is to thump the body and thereby discover that it's made of fiberglass, or to raise the hood and recognize the Ford truck engine. Even some experts could mistake the Ford engine for the original 1928 single-overhead-cam straight-eight, which was considered to be a very advanced design for its time.

If a replicar should be a modern and authentic reproduction of an old design, then Dave Samuels's Stutz is probably the most authentic of any replicar. Driving Samuels's Stutz is just like driving the 50-year-old original. The frame flexes more than the suspension; brake performance and

acceleration are surprisingly good; and the handling has that "corners on rails" feel that writers were always talking about in the late 1920s. Since the original Stutz's engineering made that car drive so much better than other late '20s machines, it's no surprise that this exact copy really doesn't feel that old to drive either. The driving position is high, there's a lot of wind in the face, and the steering wheel is big and close. But for driving in today's traffic conditions, the performance is more than sufficient.

Dave Samuels's Stutz Blackhawk is a rare and fascinating piece of machinery and represents a marvelous way to spend $30,000. This really is an elite car in every sense of the word.

**STUTZ SPEEDSTER
MAJOR SPECIFICATIONS**

Manufacturer/Importer:
Southeastern Replicars
611 Commerce Drive, Largo FL 33540
Body type—2-door, 2-passenger roadster
Wheelbase, in./cm—131/333

Overall length, in./cm—185/470
Overall width, in./cm—69/175
Overall height, in./cm—70/178
Track, front, in./cm—65/165
Track, rear, in./cm—65/165
Curb weight, lb./kg—3500/1575
Engine type—water-cooled ohv inline-six
Hp @ rpm—117 @ 3000

Displacement, cu. in./cc—300/4916
Carburetion—one 2-bbl Ford
Transmission—3-speed manual
Brakes front/rear—drum/drum
Fuel Economy, normal driving—18 mpg
Est. top speed—116 mph
Approx. price—$29,000

Specifications for U.S. market model unless otherwise noted.

STUTZ BLACKHAWK

As a stylist, Virgil Exner became famous for putting tailfins on Chrysler Corporation products in the 1950s and early '60s. And while some of Exner's cars are considered handsome even today—the 1957 Chrysler 300C, for example—others definitely are not. Remember the Dodges of the early '60s with their split-level tailfins and soaring front grilles? After Exner retired as chief of styling at Chrysler, he started doodling around with concepts for contemporary versions of several famous-name cars. His idea was to create the styling these companies would offer if they were presently making cars. He drew up proposals for a new Duesenberg, a Mercer, a Jordan Playboy, and a Stutz, among others. They were all characterized by classic vertical grilles, sweeping fender lines, and "formal" rooflines.

A group of entrepreneurs from New York built a couple of Exner-styled Duesenberg sedan prototypes in the mid-'60s before they decided against going into production with that car. Then William O'Donnell, also from Manhattan, put Exner's Stutz coupe design into production. By keeping the price high and volume low, O'Donnell created a market for his Stutz Blackhawk among celebrities like Elvis Presley, Tommy Smothers, and Phyllis Diller. Production crept up to three dozen a year as the price doubled and redoubled. Today the Stutz continues as the mainstay of a certain Hollywood crowd. It is to the '70s what the Dual-Ghia was to

Frank Sinatra and his group in the '50s. That's no bad thing for a limited-production car to be.

During his years with Chrysler, Exner had frequently turned to Carrozzeria Ghia in Turin for show-car styling ideas. These design studies were always built on a Chrysler chassis (one of them, the Dodge Firearrow, eventually became the Dual-Ghia). The prototype Duesenberg sedan bodies were also built by Ghia, which now builds the Stutz. O'Donnell was able to make a better deal with Pontiac than with Chrysler, however, so the Stutz is built on a Pontiac Bonneville chassis. The 1980 version comes equipped with a 403 cubic-inch V-8 engine and General Motors three-speed Turbo Hydra-matic transmission. Since the Pontiac

chassis is left completely stock, the Stutz is not a car that will appeal to serious driving enthusiasts. The stock Bonneville chassis is not noted for the finesse with which it goes around corners or traverses bumpy roads. The Stutz weighs 4,500 pounds—half a ton more than the Pontiac. Since its engine produces only 185 horsepower, the Stutz provides only adequate performance. Fuel economy is a dismal 10 miles per gallon.

Stutz buyers don't care. They're shopping for exclusivity and prestige. O'Donnell obliges.

Opposite, clockwise from top: Newest addition to the Stutz line is the $107,000 Bearcat convertible; rear decklid embossed with spare tire is a Virgil Exner trademark; Bearcat's targa rollbar is fixed; interior features gold-plated hardware. This

page, clockwise from upper right: Stutz styling is contrived; front end resembles a Pontiac Grand Prix; note sedan's formal roof treatment and two-tone paint scheme; the dashboard comes straight from Pontiac.

A production rate of only three dozen cars a year means a limited clientele. And since the cheapest four-door sedan model costs about $70,000, only those to whom money is no object need apply for a test drive. The original fixed-roof Blackhawk coupe is now available with a removable hardtop as the $107,000 Bearcat convertible. There's also a special-order-only limousine model priced at $200,000.

The styling of the Stutz is garish and relies too heavily on excess ornamentation. The car has much too much front and rear overhang—a 224-inch overall length, and a 116-inch wheelbase. The stand-up grille divides a set of free-standing headlights, like those Exner used on the 1961-63 Imperial. The trunk lid has a fake spare tire bulge embossed on it, also like the '61 Imperial. Indeed, the Stutz looks like what the 1961 Imperial would have looked like if that car's styling hadn't been toned down by someone in Chrysler management who had a modicum of taste. Almost everything about the Stutz's styling is contrived—from the fake outside exhaust pipe which protrudes out the front fender, to the fake running boards which

open with the doors.

This flamboyant exterior is matched by an equally flamboyant interior. The seats are upholstered in super-soft Italian leather, the carpets are made of fur, and the interior hardware is plated in 24-carat gold. English walnut veneer is used on the dashboard, but most of the controls and gauges are stock Pontiac. The quality of the materials used and the way they are assembled are both excellent. The body is made of steel, not aluminum or fiberglass. Paint, chrome, and soft trim are all carefully applied.

One of the great truths of marketing is that it's not so

much what you sell as how you sell it. There have been many good cars that never sold well because the men involved were too busy to worry about selling them. On the other hand, William O'Donnell is one of the slickest salesmen in the car business. The Stutz is not mechanically interesting, nor is it particularly satisfying to drive. But by creating a demand for his cars, O'Donnell has been able to sell enough Stutzes to make a big profit. About the only thing O'Donnell hasn't done is to re-introduce tailfins. But if they ever make a comeback you can be sure his Stutz will have them first.

STUTZ BLACKHAWK MAJOR SPECIFICATIONS

Manufacturer/Importer:
Stutz Motor Car Corporation of
    America
Time-Life Building, Rockefeller
    Center, New York, NY 10020
Body type: 4-door, 4-passenger
    sedan

Wheelbase, in./cm—116/295
Overall length, in./cm—224/569
Overall width, in./cm—79/201
Overall height, in./cm—54/137
Track, front, in./cm—61.6/156
Track, rear, in./cm—61.1/155
Curb weight, lb./kg—4500/2041
Engine type—water-cooled ohv V-8
Hp @ rpm—185 @ 3600

Displacement, cu. in./cc—403/6605
Carburetion—one 4-bbl.
Transmission—3-speed automatic
Brakes front/rear—disc/drum
Fuel Economy, normal driving—10 mpg
Est. top speed—115 mph
Approx. price—$70,000

Specifications for U.S. market model unless otherwise noted.

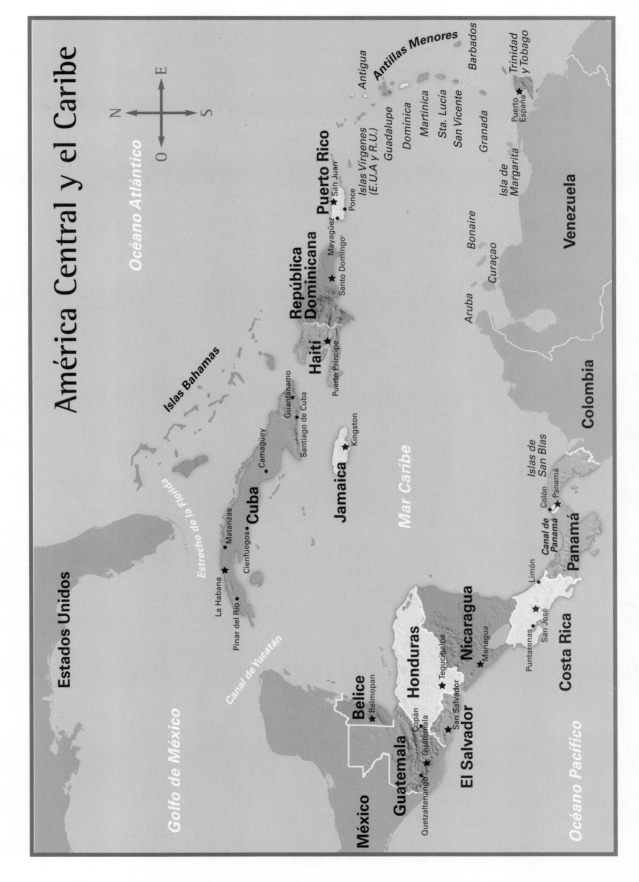

América Central y el Caribe

Estados Unidos

Golfo de México

Océano Atlántico

N — E / O — S

Estrecho de la Florida

Islas Bahamas

Canal de Yucatán

La Habana
Pinar del Río
Matanzas
Cienfuegos • Cuba
Camagüey
Santiago de Cuba
Guantánamo

Jamaica
Kingston

Mar Caribe

Haití
Puerto Príncipe

República Dominicana
Santo Domingo

Puerto Rico
Mayagüez ★ San Juan
Ponce

Islas Vírgenes
(E.U.A y R.U.)

Antigua

Antillas Menores

Guadalupe
Dominica
Martinica
Sta. Lucía
San Vicente
Granada
Barbados

Trinidad
y Tobago
Puerto ★
España

Isla de
Margarita

Aruba
Bonaire
Curaçao

Venezuela

Colombia

México

Belice
★ Belmopan

Guatemala
Copán •
Quetzaltenango ★ • Guatemala

El Salvador
★ San Salvador

Honduras
★ Tegucigalpa

Nicaragua
★ Managua

Costa Rica
Puntarenas •
San José

Limón

Panamá
Canal de
Panamá
Colón • Panamá

Islas de
San Blas

Océano Pacífico

AVENTURAS

Primer curso de lengua española

Philip Redwine Donley
Austin Community College

José Luis Benavides
California State University, Northridge

Solivia Márquez
Boston University

VISTA
HIGHER LEARNING

Boston, Massachusetts

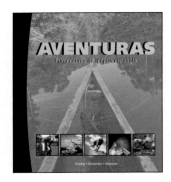

Publisher: José A. Blanco

Editorial Director: Denise St. Jean

Director of Operations: Stephen Pekich

Art Director: Linda Jurras

Staff Editors: Sabrina Celli, Gustavo Cinci, Deborah Coffey, Francisco de la Rosa, Sarah Kenney, Kristen Odlum, Paola Ríos Schaaf

Contributing Writers and Editors: Sharon Alexander, Janet Welsh Crossley, Kristin Gagne, Jane Johnson, Mary F. Lado, Lynne R. Lemley, Cherie Mitschke, Lourdes Murray, Nicolás Naranjo, Marcia Tugendhat

Senior Designer: Polo Barrera

Design Team: Anne Alvarez, Linde Gee

Photographer: Martin Bernetti

Production Team: María Eugenia Castaño, Oscar Díez, Mauricio Henao, Holly Kersey

Printed in the United States of America.

Student Text ISBN 1-932000-45-3
Instructor's Annotated Edition ISBN 1-932000-54-2

Library of Congress Card Number: 2002116925

3 4 5 6 7 8 9 VH 06 05 04

Introduction

Welcome to **AVENTURAS**. You are about to embark on an exciting adventure as you learn Spanish and explore the many diverse cultures of the Spanish-speaking world.

AVENTURAS is a new introductory Spanish program designed to provide you with an active learning experience. Its goal is to help you learn to communicate in Spanish in the real world. In light of this, here are some of the features you will encounter:

- Practical, high-frequency vocabulary for you to use in communicating in real-life situations

- Clear, concise grammar explanations that graphically highlight important concepts you need to learn

- Numerous guided activities to practice the vocabulary and grammar structures you are learning, so that you feel confident communicating in Spanish

- Abundant opportunities to interact in a variety of communicative situations with a classmate, in small groups, or with the whole class

- Systematic development of reading, writing, and listening skills that integrates learning strategies and a process approach

- Presentation of important cultural aspects of the daily lives of Spanish speakers and coverage of the entire Spanish-speaking world

- A complete set of print and technology ancillaries to make learning Spanish easier for you

In addition, **AVENTURAS** incorporates features unique to textbooks published by Vista Higher Learning that distinguish them from other college-level introductory Spanish textbooks:

- Original, user-friendly graphic design and layout that both support and facilitate language learning

- A visually dramatic and more cohesive way of integrating video with the student textbook

- An abundance of illustrations, photos, charts, and graphs, all specifically chosen or created to help you learn

- A highly structured, easy-to-navigate lesson organization

AVENTURAS has sixteen lessons, and each lesson is organized exactly in the same manner. In addition, a special **Aventuras en los países hispanos** section appears after every two lessons. To familiarize yourself with the textbook's organization and features, turn to page xii and take the **AVENTURAS**-at-a-glance tour.

table of contents

	PREPARACIÓN	**AVENTURAS**

table of contents

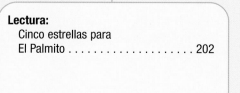

table of contents

	PREPARACIÓN	**AVENTURAS**

table of contents

Lesson Openers
outline the content and goals of each lesson.

4 El fin de semana

Communicative Goals

You will learn how to:
- talk about pastimes, weekend activities, and sports
- make plans and invitations
- say what you are going to do

PREPARACIÓN

pages 78-83
- Words related to pastimes and sports
- Places and activities in the city
- Word stress and accent marks

AVENTURAS

pages 84-87
- Don Francisco informs the students that they have an hour of free time. Inés and Javier decide to walk through the city. Maite and Álex go to a park.

GRAMÁTICA

pages 88-97
- Present tense of **ir**
- Present tense of stem-changing verbs
- Verbs with irregular **yo** forms

LECTURA

pages 98-99
- Newspaper article: *Guía para el fin de semana*

RECURSOS

These student supplements provide additional practice:
- Textbook Audio CD
- Workbook/Video Manual (WB/VM)
- Lab Manual (LM)
- Lab Audio CDs
- Video CD-ROM
- Interactive CD-ROM
- WB/VM/LM Answer Key

Lesson organization Each lesson's content is organized in major sections that are color-coded for easy navigation.

Recursos The **recursos** box provides a handy reference to program-specific ancillaries that reinforce and expand on the lesson's content.

Preparación
introduces meaningful vocabulary central to the lesson theme.

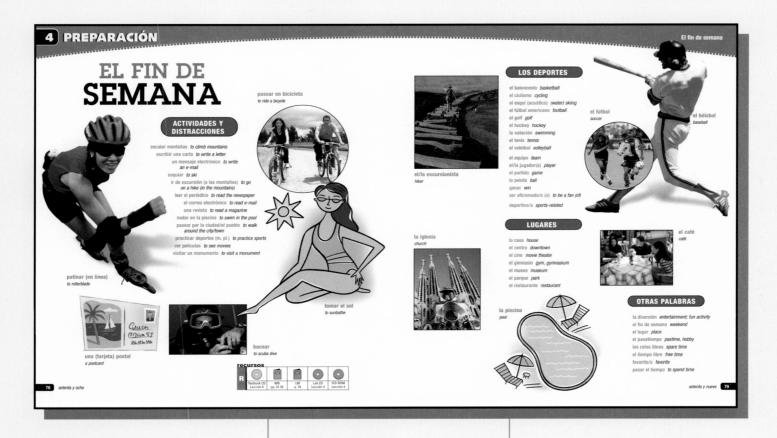

Art High-frequency vocabulary is presented with dynamic, full-color photos and illustrations.

Vocabulary Important theme-related vocabulary appears in easy-to-reference Spanish-English lists.

AVENTURAS-at-a-glance

Preparación
practices vocabulary in stages in a variety of contexts.

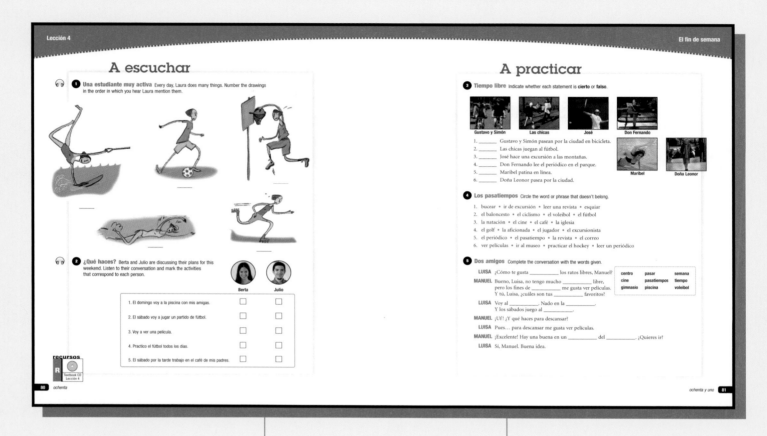

A escuchar Practice always begins with listening activities that allow you to recognize and understand the new vocabulary in real-life contexts, before you have to use it orally or in writing. Drawings and photos are often used to facilitate your comprehension.

A practicar Practice always continues with guided, meaningful activities that reinforce the new vocabulary in diverse and engaging formats.

Preparación

wraps up vocabulary practice with communicative activities.

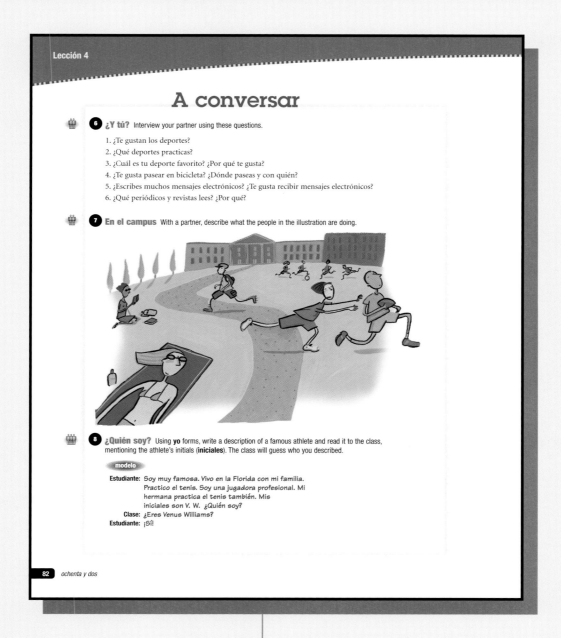

A conversar

6 **¿Y tú?** Interview your partner using these questions.

1. ¿Te gustan los deportes?
2. ¿Qué deportes practicas?
3. ¿Cuál es tu deporte favorito? ¿Por qué te gusta?
4. ¿Te gusta pasear en bicicleta? ¿Dónde paseas y con quién?
5. ¿Escribes muchos mensajes electrónicos? ¿Te gusta recibir mensajes electrónicos?
6. ¿Qué periódicos y revistas lees? ¿Por qué?

7 **En el campus** With a partner, describe what the people in the illustration are doing.

8 **¿Quién soy?** Using **yo** forms, write a description of a famous athlete and read it to the class, mentioning the athlete's initials (**iniciales**). The class will guess who you described.

modelo

Estudiante: Soy muy famosa. Vivo en la Florida con mi familia. Practico el tenis. Soy una jugadora profesional. Mi hermana practica el tenis también. Mis iniciales son V. W. ¿Quién soy?
Clase: ¿Eres Venus Williams?
Estudiante: ¡Sí!

A conversar This final set of activities gets you using the words and expressions creatively for self-expression in interactions with a partner, a small group, or the entire class.

Preparación

Pronunciación and *Ortografía* present the basics of Spanish pronunciation and spelling.

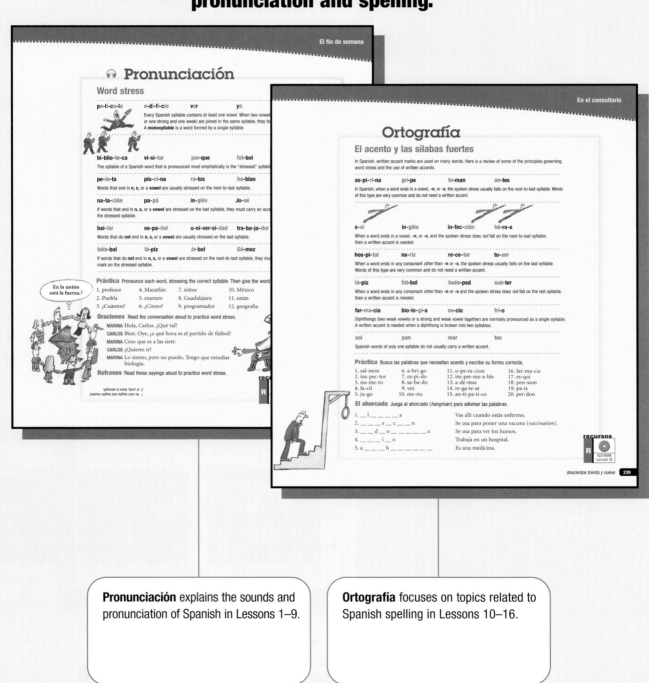

El fin de semana

🎧 Pronunciación

Word stress

pe-li-cu-la **e-di-fi-cio** **ver** **yo**

Every Spanish syllable contains at least one vowel. When two vowels or one strong and one weak) are joined in the same syllable, they fo A **monosyllable** is a word formed by a single syllable.

bi-blio-te-ca **vi-si-tar** **par-que** **fút-bol**

The syllable of a Spanish word that is pronounced most emphatically is the "stressed" syllable

pe-lo-ta **pis-ci-na** **ra-tos** **ha-blan**

Words that end in **n**, **s**, or a **vowel** are usually stressed on the next-to-last syllable.

na-ta-ción **pa-pá** **in-glés** **Jo-sé**

If words that end in **n**, **s**, or a **vowel** are stressed on the last syllable, they must carry an acce the stressed syllable.

bai-lar **es-pa-ñol** **u-ni-ver-si-dad** **tra-ba-ja-dor**

Words that do **not** end in **n**, **s**, or a **vowel** are usually stressed on the last syllable.

béis-bol **lá-piz** **ár-bol** **Gó-mez**

If words that do **not** end in **n**, **s**, or a **vowel** are stressed on the next-to-last syllable, they mu mark on the stressed syllable.

Práctica Pronounce each word, stressing the correct syllable. Then give the word

1. profesor	4. Mazatlán	7. niños	10. México
2. Puebla	5. examen	8. Guadalajara	11. están
3. ¿Cuántos?	6. ¿Cómo?	9. programador	12. geografía

Oraciones Read the conversation aloud to practice word stress.

MARINA Hola, Carlos. ¿Qué tal?

CARLOS Bien. Oye, ¿a qué hora es el partido de fútbol?

MARINA Creo que es a las siete.

CARLOS ¿Quieres ir?

MARINA Lo siento, pero no puedo. Tengo que estudiar biología.

Refranes Read these sayings aloud to practice word stress.

En la unión está la fuerza.²

¹ He who laughs last laughs loudest. ² In unity, there is strength.

En el consultorio

Ortografía

El acento y las sílabas fuertes

In Spanish, written accent marks are used on many words. Here is a review of some of the principles governing word stress and the use of written accents.

as-pi-ri-na **gri-pe** **to-man** **an-tes**

In Spanish, when a word ends in a vowel, **-n**, or **-s**, the spoken stress usually falls on the next-to-last syllable. Words of this type are very common and do not need a written accent.

a-sí **in-glés** **in-fec-ción** **hé-ro-e**

When a word ends in a vowel, **-n**, or **-s**, and the spoken stress does *not* fall on the next-to-last syllable, then a written accent is needed.

hos-pi-tal **na-ríz** **re-ce-tar** **to-ser**

When a word ends in any consonant *other* than **-n** or **-s**, the spoken stress usually falls on the last syllable. Words of this type are very common and do not need a written accent.

lá-piz **fút-bol** **hués-ped** **sué-ter**

When a word ends in any consonant *other* than **-n** or **-s** and the spoken stress does *not* fall on the last syllable, then a written accent is needed.

far-ma-cia **bio-lo-gí-a** **su-cio** **fri-o**

Diphthongs (two weak vowels or a strong and weak vowel together) are normally pronounced as a single syllable. A written accent is needed when a diphthong is broken into two syllables.

sol **pan** **mar** **tos**

Spanish words of only one syllable do not usually carry a written accent.

Práctica Busca las palabras que necesitan acento y escribe su forma correcta.

1. sal-mon	6. a-bri-go	11. o-pe-ra-cion	16. far-ma-cia
2. ins-pec-tor	7. ra-pi-do	12. im-per-me-a-ble	17. es-qui
3. nu-me-ro	8. sa-ba-do	13. a-de-mas	18. pen-sion
4. fa-cil	9. vez	14. re-ga-te-ar	19. pa-is
5. ju-go	10. me-nu	15. an-ti-pa-ti-co	20. per-don

El ahorcado Juega al ahorcado (*hangman*) para adivinar las palabras.

1. _ l _ _ _ _ _ a   Vas allí cuando estás enfermo.
2. _ _ _ _ e _ c _ _ _ n   Se usa para poner una vacuna (*vaccination*).
3. _ _ d _ o _ _ _ _ _ _ a   Se usa para ver los huesos.
4. _ _ _ _ i _ o   Trabaja en un hospital.
5. a _ _ _ _ b _ _ _ _ _ _ _ Es una medicina.

recursos

R ◉ ICD-ROM Lección 10

doscientos treinta y nueve **239**

Pronunciación explains the sounds and pronunciation of Spanish in Lessons 1–9.

Ortografía focuses on topics related to Spanish spelling in Lessons 10–16.

Aventuras
tells the story of four students traveling in Ecuador.

Personajes The photo-based conversations take place among a cast of recurring characters—four college students on vacation in Ecuador and the bus driver who accompanies them.

AVENTURAS Video The photo-based **Aventuras** conversations appear in the textbook's video program. To learn more about the video, turn to pages xxvi and xxvii in this at-a-glance tour.

Conversations Taken from the **AVENTURAS** video, the conversations re-enter vocabulary from **Preparación**. They also preview structures from the upcoming **Gramática** section in context <u>and</u> in a comprehensible way.

Expresiones útiles organizes new, active words and expressions by language function so you can focus on using them for real-life, practical purposes.

Aventuras

¿Qué piensas? reinforces the *Aventuras* conversations.

¿Qué piensas?

1 Ordenar Put the following events in order from 1 to 5.

_____ a. Álex y Maite deciden ir al parque.

_____ b. Álex y el joven juegan al fútbol.

_____ c. Maite y Álex vuelven al autobús.

_____ d. Maite decide escribir unas postales.

_____ e. El joven causa un accidente.

2 Pasatiempos Scan **Aventuras** and indicate which pastimes the characters mention. Then indicate whether you participate in each pastime.

ÁLEX

_____
_____
_____

MAITE

_____
_____
_____

3 Preguntas Get together with a partner and take turns asking each other these questions.

1. ¿Qué desean hacer Inés y Javier?
_____

2. ¿Cuáles son los deportes favoritos de Álex?
_____

3. ¿Qué desea hacer Maite en el parque?
_____

4. ¿Qué desea hacer Álex en el parque?
_____

5. ¿Qué deciden hacer Álex y Maite esta noche?
_____

6. ¿Cuáles son tus pasatiempos favoritos?
_____

7. ¿Cuáles son los pasatiempos favoritos de tu mejor (*best*) amigo/a?
_____

¿Qué piensas? provides guided exercises to check your understanding of the **Aventuras** conversations and communicative activities to allow you to react to them in a personalized way.

Aventuras

Exploración provides cultural information related to the *Aventuras* episode.

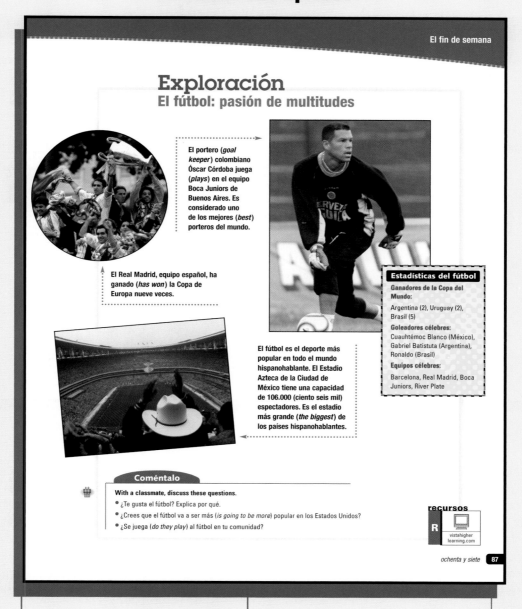

Exploración
El fútbol: pasión de multitudes

El portero (*goal keeper*) colombiano Óscar Córdoba juega (*plays*) en el equipo Boca Juniors de Buenos Aires. Es considerado uno de los mejores (*best*) porteros del mundo.

El Real Madrid, equipo español, ha ganado (*has won*) la Copa de Europa nueve veces.

El fútbol es el deporte más popular en todo el mundo hispanohablante. El Estadio Azteca de la Ciudad de México tiene una capacidad de 106.000 (ciento seis mil) espectadores. Es el estadio más grande (*the biggest*) de los países hispanohablantes.

Estadísticas del fútbol

Ganadores de la Copa del Mundo:
Argentina (2), Uruguay (2), Brasil (5)

Goleadores célebres:
Cuauhtémoc Blanco (México), Gabriel Batistuta (Argentina), Ronaldo (Brasil)

Equipos célebres:
Barcelona, Real Madrid, Boca Juniors, River Plate

Coméntalo

With a classmate, discuss these questions.

- ¿Te gusta el fútbol? Explica por qué.
- ¿Crees que el fútbol va a ser más (*is going to be more*) popular en los Estados Unidos?
- ¿Se juega (*do they play*) al fútbol en tu comunidad?

recursos

R · vistahigher learning.com

ochenta y siete **87**

Dynamic photos bring to life important facets of the cultural topic.

Photo captions expand on the cultural points, spotlighting important and intriguing facts.

Coméntalo gives you the opportunity to discuss and react to the cultural information.

Gramática

uses innovative design to support the learning of Spanish.

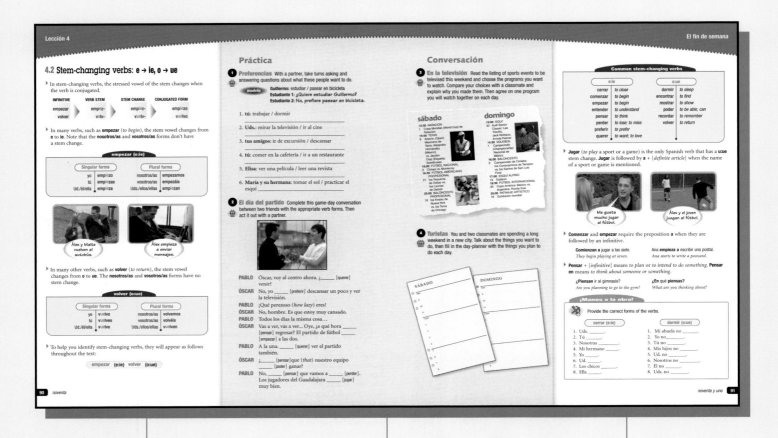

Text Format For each grammar point, the explanation and practice activities appear on one self-contained spread of two facing pages. Grammar explanations in the outside panels offer handy on-page support for the activities in the central, inside panels, providing you with immediate access to information essential to communication.

Charts and Diagrams Within the clear, easy-to-grasp grammar explanations, colorful, carefully designed charts and diagrams call out key grammatical structures and forms, as well as important related vocabulary.

Graphics-intensive Design Photos from the **AVENTURAS** Video Program consistently integrate the lesson's video episode and **Aventuras** section with the grammar explanations. There are also additional photos, drawings, and graphic devices, enlivening activities and heightening visual interest.

Gramática

provides varied types of directed and communicative practice.

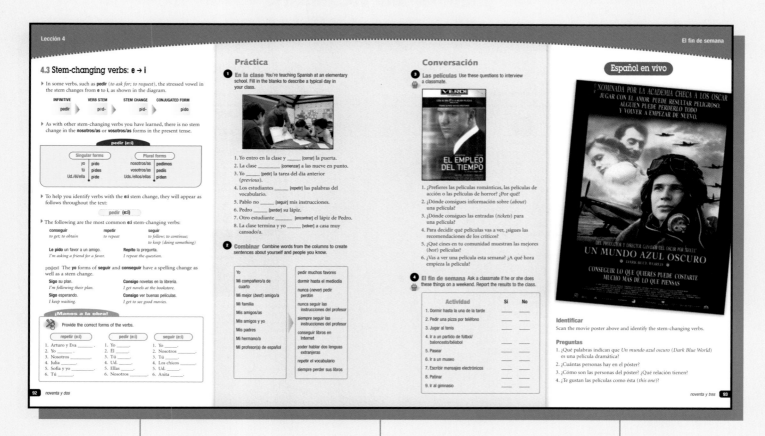

¡Manos a la obra! exercises are your first step in practicing each new grammar point. They get you working with the grammar point right away in simple, easy-to-understand formats.

Práctica activities provide a wide range of guided exercises in contexts that combine current and previously learned vocabulary with the current grammar point.

Español en vivo activities incorporate authentic documents, like advertisements and movie posters, into the grammar practice, highlighting the new grammar point in a real-life context.

Conversación offers opportunities for creative expression using the lesson's grammar and vocabulary. Activities take place with a partner, in small groups, or with the whole class.

Gramática

Ampliación develops language skills as it synthesizes the lesson's grammar and vocabulary.

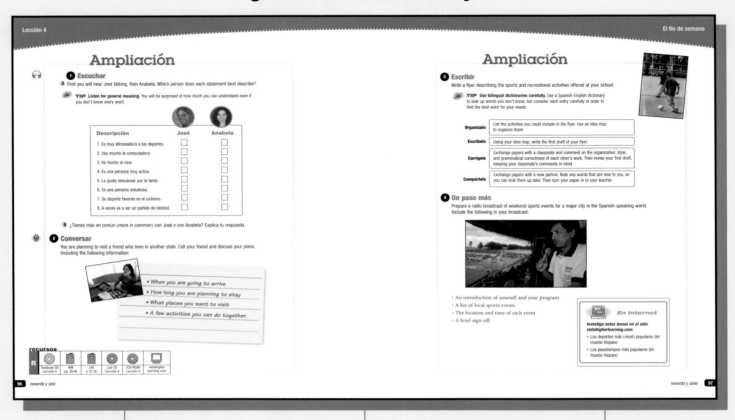

Escuchar uses a recorded conversation or narration to develop your listening skills in Spanish and checks your understanding of what you heard.

Tips present valuable on-the-spot listening and writing strategies to help you carry out the accompanying activities more easily and effectively.

Conversar focuses on developing your oral communication skills through realistic, practical role-plays and situations.

Escribir provides a writing topic and takes you step-by-step through the writing process, including planning, writing a first draft, peer review, and correcting your work.

Un paso más engages you in a project in which you research and create a tangible product such as a radio broadcast, a brochure, or a Web page.

En Internet lists relevant topics you can research on the Web.

Lectura

develops reading skills in the context of the lesson theme.

Antes de leer presents helpful reading strategies and pre-reading activities to build your reading abilities in Spanish.

Readings are specifically related to the lesson theme and recycle the vocabulary and grammar you have learned. Lessons 13 – 16 feature literary selections so you can experience reading works by well-known authors in Spanish.

Después de leer includes exercises to check your comprehension of the reading.

Coméntalo activities encourage you to discuss and to apply the material in the reading to your own life.

Vocabulario

summarizes all the active vocabulary in each lesson.

4 VOCABULARIO

Actividades

bucear	to scuba dive
escalar montañas (f. pl.)	to climb mountains
escribir una carta	to write a letter
un mensaje electrónico	an e-mail message
una (tarjeta) postal	a postcard
esquiar	to ski
ganar	to win
ir de excursión (a las montañas)	to go for a hike (in the mountains)
leer el correo electrónico	to read e-mail
un periódico	a newspaper
una revista	a magazine
nadar	to swim
pasar el tiempo	to spend time
pasear en bicicleta	to ride a bicycle
pasear por la ciudad/el pueblo	to walk around the city/town
patinar (en línea)	to skate (in-line)
practicar deportes (m. pl.)	to play sports
ser aficionado/a (a)	to be a fan (of)
tomar el sol	to sunbathe
ver películas (f. pl.)	to see movies
visitar un monumento	to visit a monument
la diversión	fun activity; entertainment
el/la excursionista	hiker
el fin de semana	weekend
el pasatiempo	pastime, hobby
los ratos libres	spare time
el tiempo libre	free time

Deportes

el baloncesto	basketball
el béisbol	baseball
el ciclismo	cycling
el equipo	team
el esquí (acuático)	(water) skiing
el fútbol	soccer
el fútbol americano	football
el golf	golf
el hockey	hockey
el/la jugador(a)	player
la natación	swimming
el partido	game
la pelota	ball
el tenis	tennis
el voleibol	volleyball

Verbos

cerrar (e:ie)	to close
comenzar (e:ie)	to begin
conseguir (e:i)	to get; to obtain
dormir (o:ue)	to sleep
empezar (e:ie)	to begin
encontrar (o:ue)	to find
entender (e:ie)	to understand
hacer	to do; to make
ir	to go
jugar (u:ue)	to play
mostrar (o:ue)	to show
oír	to hear
pedir (e:i)	to ask for; to request
pensar (e:ie)	to think
pensar + inf.	to intend; to plan
pensar en	to think about
perder (e:ie)	to lose; to miss
poder (o:ue)	to be able to; can
poner	to put; to place
preferir (e:ie)	to prefer
querer (e:ie)	to want; to love
recordar (o:ue)	to remember
repetir (e:i)	to repeat
salir	to leave
seguir (e:i)	to follow; to continue
suponer	to suppose
traer	to bring
ver	to see
volver (o:ue)	to return

Adjetivos

deportivo/a	sports-related
favorito/a	favorite

Lugares

el café	café
la casa	house
el centro	downtown
el cine	movie theater
el gimnasio	gymnasium
la iglesia	church
el lugar	place
el museo	museum
el parque	park
la piscina	swimming pool
el restaurante	restaurant

Expresiones útiles	See page 85.

recursos

R | Lab CD Lección 4 | LM p. 24

Aventuras en los países hispanos
presents the nations of the Spanish-speaking world.

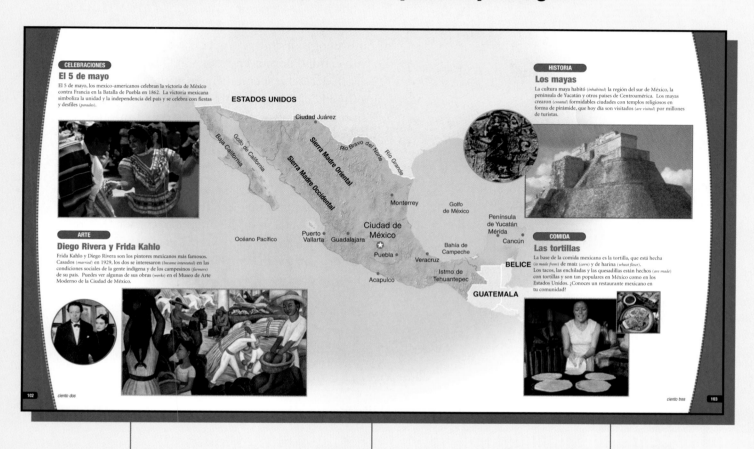

CELEBRACIONES

El 5 de mayo

El 5 de mayo, los mexico-americanos celebran la victoria de México contra Francia en la Batalla de Puebla en 1862. La victoria mexicana simboliza la unidad y la independencia del país y se celebra con fiestas y desfiles (*parades*).

ARTE

Diego Rivera y Frida Kahlo

Frida Kahlo y Diego Rivera son los pintores mexicanos más famosos. Casados (*married*) en 1929, los dos se interesaron (*became interested*) en las condiciones sociales de la gente indígena y de los campesinos (*farmers*) de su país. Puedes ver algunas de sus obras (*works*) en el Museo de Arte Moderno de la Ciudad de México.

HISTORIA

Los mayas

La cultura maya habitó (*inhabited*) la región del sur de México, la península de Yucatán y otros países de Centroamérica. Los mayas crearon (*created*) formidables ciudades con templos religiosos en forma de pirámide, que hoy día son visitados (*are visited*) por millones de turistas.

COMIDA

Las tortillas

La base de la comida mexicana es la tortilla, que está hecha (*is made from*) de maíz (*corn*) y de harina (*wheat flour*). Los tacos, las enchiladas y las quesadillas están hechos (*are made*) con tortillas y son tan populares en México como en los Estados Unidos. ¿Conoces un restaurante mexicano en tu comunidad?

ESTADOS UNIDOS
Ciudad Juárez
Baja California
Golfo de California
Sierra Madre Occidental
Sierra Madre Oriental
Río Bravo del Norte
Río Grande
Monterrey
Golfo de México
Península de Yucatán
Mérida
Cancún
Océano Pacífico
Puerto Vallarta
Guadalajara
Ciudad de México
Puebla
Veracruz
Bahía de Campeche
BELICE
Acapulco
Istmo de Tehuantepec
GUATEMALA

102   ciento dos

ciento tres   103

Opening page The opening page sets the scene for the section with a dramatic photo and statistics about the location.

Maps illustrate significant geographical sites and features and situate the country or area within its region and the world.

Photo captions Contemporary, eye-catching photos with captions explore key facets of the target location's culture such as history, fine arts, foods, celebrations, and traditions.

¿Qué aprendiste? activities check your understanding of key ideas.

En Internet suggests related topics for you to investigate further on the Web.

Video program

Fully integrated with your textbook, the **AVENTURAS** video contains fifteen episodes. The episodes present the adventures of four college students who are studying at the **Universidad de San Francisco** in Quito, Ecuador. They each decide to spend their vacation break on a bus tour of the Ecuadorian countryside with the ultimate goal of hiking up a volcano. The video, shot in various locations in Ecuador, tells their story and the story of Don Francisco, the tour bus driver who accompanies them.

The **Aventuras** section in each textbook lesson is actually an abbreviated version of the dramatic episode featured in the video. Therefore, each **Aventuras** section can be done before you see the corresponding video episode, after it, or as a section that stands alone in its own right.

The Cast

Here are the main characters you will meet when you watch the **AVENTURAS** video:

 From México, Alejandro (Álex) Morales Paredes

 From Ecuador, Inés Ayala Loor

 From Puerto Rico, Javier Gómez Lozano

 From Spain, María Teresa (Maite) Fuentes de Alba

 And, also from Ecuador, don Francisco Castillo Moreno

As you watch each video episode, you will first see a live segment in which the characters interact using vocabulary and grammar you are studying. As the video progresses, the live segments carefully combine new vocabulary and grammar with previously taught language. You will then see a **Resumen** section in which one of the main video characters recaps the live segment, emphasizing the grammar and vocabulary you are studying within the context of the episode's key events.

In addition, in most of the video episodes, there are brief pauses to allow the characters to reminisce about their home country. These flashbacks—montages of real-life images shot in Spain, Mexico, Puerto Rico, and various parts of Ecuador—connect the theme of the video to everyday life in various parts of the Spanish-speaking world.

Student Ancillaries

Textbook Audio CDs

Free-of-charge with each copy of **AVENTURAS**, the Textbook Audio CDs contain the audio recordings for the following activities in your textbook: the **A escuchar** exercises in each **Preparación** section, the **Pronunciación** exercises (Lessons 1–9), and the **Escuchar** activity in each **Ampliación** section.

Workbook/Video Manual

The Workbook activities provide additional practice of the vocabulary and grammar in each textbook lesson. The Video Manual includes previewing, viewing, and post-viewing activities to help you understand and explore each module of the **AVENTURAS** video.

Lab Manual

The Lab Manual activities for each textbook lesson focus on building your listening comprehension, speaking, and pronunciation skills in Spanish.

Web-SAM

Created in conjunction with Quia Corporation, the Web-SAM is the electronic version of the printed **AVENTURAS** Workbook, Lab Manual, and Video Manual. The Web-SAM delivers these components in their entirety on-line with automatic scoring, plus it includes the complete Lab Audio Program. The Web-SAM also offers instructors in-depth, easy-to-use tracking of students' scores by individual student, by class, by activity, and by lesson. Instructors can also customize the Web-SAM by editing existing exercises to create their own activities.

Lab Audio Program

The Lab Audio Program contains the recordings to be used in conjunction with the activities of the Lab Manual. It comes in two versions: 16 high-fidelity audio CDs or 1 audio CD-ROM containing compressed MP3 files that can be played in the CD-ROM drive of your computer.

Video Program

This text-specific video includes dramatic vignettes, cultural footage, and unique summary features that are fully integrated with the lessons in your textbook

Interactive CD-ROMs

Free-of-charge with each copy of **AVENTURAS**, these two dual-platform CD-ROMs provide useful reference tools and highly interactive, visually captivating multimedia materials and activities.

Video CD-ROM

Free-of-charge with each copy of **AVENTURAS**, the Video CD-ROM offers you the complete Video Program with videoscripts, note-taking capabilities, and enhanced navigation tools.

Web Site (vistahigherlearning.com)

The **AVENTURAS** Web site at **vistahigherlearning.com** supports you and your instructor with a wide range of online resources—cultural information and links, Internet activities, teaching suggestions, lesson plans, course syllabi, and more—that directly correlate to your textbook and go beyond it.

Pocket Dictionary & Language Guide

Free-of-charge with each copy of **AVENTURAS**, the Pocket Dictionary & Language Guide is a text-specific, portable reference for Spanish words and expressions, idioms, and more, that both complements and extends the vocabulary and other information presented in **AVENTURAS**.

Instructor Ancillaries

In addition to the student ancillaries, all of which are available to the instructor, the following supplements are also available.

Instructor's Annotated Edition
The Instructor's Annotated Edition (IAE) provides a wealth of information designed to support classroom teaching. The IAE contains answers to exercises over printed on the page, cultural and lexical information, suggestions for implementing and extending student activities, and cross-references to student and instructor ancillaries.

Instructor's Resource Manual
The Instructor's Resource Manual (IRM) offers materials that reinforce and expand on the lessons in the student text. It includes a supplementary reproducible list of vocabulary for each lesson, teaching suggestions and expansion activities for the **Gramática** sections and selected **Preparación** section in the student textbook, English equivalents of the **Aventuras** photo captions, tapescripts of the Lab Audio Program and Textbook Audio CDs, and the videoscript of the **AVENTURAS** Video Program.

Workbook/Lab Manual/Video Manual Answer Key
This component contains answer keys for all activities with discrete answers in the Workbook, Lab Manual, and Video Manual.

Testing Program with Audio CD
The Testing Program contains versions A and B of the following: a test for each of the textbook's 16 lessons, semester exams for Lessons 1–8 and 9–16, and quarter exams for Lessons 1–6, 7–11, and 12–16. All tests and exams include sections on listening comprehension, vocabulary, grammar, and communication. Listening scripts, answer keys, suggestions for oral tests, and an audio CD of the listening sections are also provided.

Test Files CD-ROM for Windows® and Macintosh®
This CD-ROM contains the tests, exams, listening scripts, and answer keys of the printed Testing Program as Microsoft Word® files.

Overhead Transparencies
The Overhead Transparencies include maps of the Spanish-speaking world, drawings to reinforce vocabulary presented in the textbook's **Preparación** sections, and other useful illustrations for presenting or practicing concepts such as telling time.

acknowledgments

On the behalf of its authors and editors, Vista Higher Learning expresses its sincere appreciation to the many college professors nationwide who reviewed the AVENTURAS manuscript. Their insights, ideas, and detailed comments were invaluable to the final product.

AVENTURAS Reviewers

Anna Adams
Muhlenberg College, PA

Lourdes Albuixech
Southern Illinois University, IL

Rosalinda S. Alemany
University of Lousiana at Lafayette, LA

Tom Alsop
Marian College, IN

Isabel Álvarez
University of Wisconsin-Oshkosh, WI

Hersilia Álvarez-Ruf
Hope College, MI

Catherine Angell
Austin Community College
Rio Grande Campus, TX

Mary Jo Arns-Radaj
Normandale Community College, MN

Ingetraut R. Baird
Anderson University, IN

Robert Baum
Arkansas State University, AK

Judy Berry-Bravo
Pittsburg State University, KS

Keith H. Brower
Salisbury University, MD

María Teresa Cabal-Krastel
University of Maryland-College Park, MD

Francisco Cabanillas
Bowling Green State University, OH

José A. Carmona
Daytona Beach Community College, FL

Marco Tulio Cedillo
Lynchburg College, VA

June Chatterjee
Contra Costa College, CA

Maritza Chinea-Thornberry
University of South Florida, FL

Anne Marie Chuckrey
Quinnipiac University, CT

Chyi Chung
Northwestern University, IL

Richard K. Curry
Texas A&M University, TX

Aida Dean
University of Richmond, VA

Ana María Díaz-Marcos
Dartmouth College, NH

Rocio de la Rosa Duncan
Rockhurst University, MO

Douglas Duno
Chaffey College, CA

Mark Ebel
Huntingdon College, AL

Barbara Eickmeyer
Coconino Community College, AZ

Otis Philip Elliott, Jr.
Southern University at Baton Rouge, LA

Francia Espinosa
Broome Community College, NY

Molly Falsetti
Smith College, MA

Claudia Ferman
University of Richmond, VA

April Fisher
Oregon State University, OR

Judith Friedemann
College of Southern Idaho, ID

Celerina J. García
New School University, NY

Raquel N. González
University of Michigan, MI

Gail González
Georgetown College, KY

Amy Gregory
University of Tennessee-Knoxville, TN

Carolyn J. Halstead
West Virginia State College, WV

Alexandra D. Henderson
Catawba College, NC

Danielle Holden
Oakton Community College, IL

Roberta Holtzman
Schoolcraft College, MI

Channing Horner
Northwest Missouri State University, MO

Diana R. Hossain
Manchester Community College, CT

Harriet Hutchinson
Bunker Hill Community College, MA

Elizabeth Janzen
Kansas State University, KS

Hilary Landwehr
Northtern Kentucky University, KY

Jeff Longwell
New Mexico State University, NM

Sergio Martínez
San Antonio College, TX

Adrian Pablo Massei
Furman University, SC

Marsha Mawhirter
Butler County Community College, KS

Kathryn Gene McConnell
Point Loma Nazarene University, CA

Rose McEwen
State University of New York College
at Geneseo, NY

Sandra Delgado Merrill
Central Missouri State University, MO

Nancy Taylor Minguez
Old Dominion University, VA

Edgar J. Montaño
John A. Logan College, IL

Eunice Doman Myers
Wichita State University, KS

Marcella Ochoa
Cornell College, IA

María de los Santos Onofre-Madrid
Angelo State University, TX

Keith Phillips
Moraine Valley Community College, IL

David Quintero
Seattle Central Community College, WA

Maria T. Quintero-Pi
Hillsborough Community College, FL

Karen L. Robinson
University of Nebraska at Omaha, NE

Fernando Sánchez-Gutiérrez
Illinois State University, IL

Theresa Ann Sears
University of North Carolina-
Greensboro, NC

Michele Shaul
Queens University of Charlotte, NC

Victor E. Slesinger
Palm Beach Community College, FL

Anita Smith
Pitt Community College, NC

Lidia C. Stahl
Southern Illinois University, IL

Kristi Steinbrecher
Coastal Carolina University, SC

Antoinette Tackkett
Coffeyville Community College, KS

Ralph F. Tarnasky
Aims Community College, CO

Edith Valladares
Central Piedmont Community College, NC

José L. Varela-Ibarra
Eastern Kentucky University, KY

Barry L. Velleman
Marquette University, WI

Marianne J. Verlinden
College of Charleston, SC

Gayle Fiedler Vierma
University of Southern California, CA

Gloria F. Waldman
York College, CUNY, NY

Julia Wescott
Canisius College, NY

Alexander P. Wolpe
Ohlone College, CA

Janice Wright
College of Charleston, SC

1 Hola, ¿qué tal?

RECURSOS

These student supplements provide additional practice:
- Textbook Audio CD
- Workbook/Video Manual (WB/VM)
- Lab Manual (LM)
- WB/VM/LM Answer Key
- Lab Audio CDs
- Video CD-ROM
- Interactive CD-ROM

HOLA, ¿QUÉ TAL?

SALUDOS Y DESPEDIDAS

Buenas noches. *Good evening; good night.*

Buenas tardes. *Good afternoon.*

Hasta la vista. *See you later.*

Hasta pronto. *See you soon.*

SEÑORA	Hola, señor Lara. ¿Cómo está usted?
SEÑOR	Muy bien, gracias. ¿Y usted, señora Salas?
SEÑORA	Bien, gracias.
SEÑOR	Hasta luego, señora Salas. Saludos al señor Salas.
SEÑORA	Adiós.

¿CÓMO ESTÁS?

¿Cómo estás? *(familiar) How are you?*

No muy bien. *Not very well.*

¿Qué pasa? *What's happening?; what's going on?*

JUANA	Hasta luego, Sofía.
SOFÍA	Chau, Juana. Nos vemos mañana.

CARLOS	¿Qué tal, Roberto?
ROBERTO	Regular. ¿Y tú?
CARLOS	Bien. ¿Qué hay de nuevo?
ROBERTO	Nada.

recursos

R	Textbook CD Lección 1	WB pp. 1-2	LM p. 1	Lab CD Lección 1	ICD-ROM Lección 1

PRESENTACIONES

¿Cómo se llama usted? *(formal) What's your name?*

Le presento a… *(form.) I would like to introduce (name) to you.*

Te presento a… *(fam.) I would like to introduce (name) to you.*

Éste es… *This is... (masculine)*

Ésta es… *This is... (feminine)*

LAURA	Buenos días. Me llamo Laura.
ESTEBAN	Buenos días. Me llamo Esteban. Mucho gusto.
LAURA	El gusto es mío. ¿De dónde eres?
ESTEBAN	Soy de los Estados Unidos, de Texas.

SUSANA	Leti, éste es el señor Garza.
LETICIA	Encantada.
SEÑOR GARZA	Igualmente. ¿De dónde es usted, señora?
LETICIA	Soy de Puerto Rico. ¿Y usted?
SEÑOR GARZA	De México.

¡Muchas gracias!

EXPRESIONES DE CORTESÍA

Por favor. *Please.*

De nada. *You're welcome.*

No hay de qué. *You're welcome.*

Lo siento. *I'm sorry.*

Muchas gracias. *Thank you very much; thanks a lot.*

A escuchar

1 **¿Lógico o ilógico?** Listen to each conversation and indicate whether the conversation is logical or illogical.

	Lógico	Ilógico
1.	___	✗
2.	___	✗
3.	✗	___
4.	✗	✗
5.	✗	___
6.	✗	___

2 **¡Hola!** Margarita is having an all-day party to celebrate her twentieth birthday.
Listen to the conversations and indicate whether each guest is arriving (**Llega**) or leaving (**Sale**).

	Llega	Sale
1. Ramiro	✗	___
2. Sra. Sánchez	___	✗
3. Luisa	✗	___
4. Vicente	___	✗
5. Profesor Lado	✗	___
6. Sr. Torres	✗	___

3 **Seleccionar** Listen to each question or statement, then choose the correct response.

1. a. Muy bien, gracias. b. Me llamo Graciela.
2. a. Lo siento. b. Mucho gusto.
3. a. Soy de Puerto Rico. b. No muy bien.
4. a. No hay de qué. b. Regular.
5. a. Mucho gusto. b. Hasta pronto.
6. a. Nada. b. Igualmente.
7. a. Me llamo Guillermo Montero. b. Muy bien, gracias.
8. a. Buenas tardes. ¿Cómo estás? b. El gusto es mío.

recursos

R | Textbook CD
Lección 1

A practicar

4 **Escoger** For each expression, write a word or phrase that expresses a similar idea.

> **modelo**
>
> ¿Cómo estás? _¿Qué tal?_

1. De nada. _No hay de qué._
2. Encantado. _____
3. Adiós. _Hasta la vista._
4. Te presento a Antonio. _____
5. ¿Qué hay de nuevo? _____
6. Mucho gusto. _____

5 **Ordenar** With a classmate, put this scrambled conversation in order. Then act it out.

—Muy bien, gracias. Soy Rosabel.

—Soy del Ecuador. ¿Y tú?

—Mucho gusto, Rosabel.

—Hola. Me llamo Carlos. ¿Cómo estás?

—Soy de la Argentina.

—Igualmente. ¿De dónde eres, Carlos?

CARLOS _Hola. Me llamo Carlos. ¿Como estás?_

ROSABEL _Muy bien, gracias. Soy Rosabel._

CARLOS _Mucho gusto, Rosabel._

ROSABEL _Igualmente. ¿De dónde eres, Carlos?_

CARLOS _Soy del Ecuador. ¿Y tú?_

ROSABEL _Soy de la Argentina._

6 **Cambiar** With a partner, correct the second part of each conversation to make it logical.

> **modelo**
>
> —¿Qué tal?
>
> —~~No hay de qué.~~ Bien. ¿Y tú?

1. —Hasta mañana, señora Ramírez. Saludos al señor Ramírez.
   —_Muy bien, gracias._ _____

2. —¿Qué hay de nuevo, Alberto?
   —_Me llamo Alberto. ¿Cómo te llamas tú?_ _____

3. —Miguel, ésta es la señorita Perales.
   —_No hay de qué, señorita._ _____

4. —¿De dónde eres, Antonio?
   —_Muy bien, gracias. ¿Y tú?_ _____

A conversar

 7 Diálogos With a partner, complete and act out these conversations.

DIÁLOGO 1

—Hola. Me llamo Teresa. ¿Cómo te llamas tú?

_____

—Soy de Puerto Rico. ¿Y tú?

_____

DIÁLOGO 2

_____

—Muy bien, gracias. ¿Y usted, señora López?

_____

—Hasta luego, señora. Saludos al señor López.

_____

 8 Conversaciones With a partner, make up a conversation in Spanish for each photo.

 9 Situaciones Work with two classmates to write and act out these situations.

1. As you leave class on the first day of school, you strike up a conversation with the two students who were sitting next to you. You find out each person's name and where he or she is from before you say goodbye.
2. You meet up with a friend and find out how he or she is doing. As you are talking, your friend Elena walks by. Introduce her to your friend.
3. You say hello to your parents' friends Sra. Sánchez and Sr. Rodríguez and find out how they are doing. As you say goodbye, you send greetings to Sra. Rodríguez.

🎧 Pronunciación

The Spanish alphabet

The Spanish alphabet consisted of 30 letters until 1994, when the **Real Academia Española** (*Royal Spanish Academy*) removed **ch** (**che**) and **ll** (**elle**). You may still see **ch** and **ll** listed as separate letters in reference works printed before 1994. Two Spanish letters, **ñ** (**eñe**) and **rr** (**erre**), don't appear in the English alphabet. The letters **k** (**ka**) and **w** (**doble ve**) are used only in words of foreign origin.

Letra	Nombre(s)	Ejemplos	Letra	Nombre(s)	Ejemplos
a	a	adiós	ñ	eñe	mañana
b	be	bien, problema	o	o	once
c	ce	cosa, cero	p	pe	profesor
d	de	diario, nada	q	cu	qué
e	e	estudiante	r	ere	regular, señora
f	efe	foto	rr	erre	carro
g	ge	gracias, Gerardo, regular	s	ese	señor
			t	te	tú
h	hache	hola	u	u	usted
i	i	igualmente	v	ve	vista, nuevo
j	jota	Javier	w	doble ve	walkman
k	ka, ca	kilómetro	x	equis	existir, México
l	ele	lápiz			
m	eme	mapa	y	i griega, ye	yo
n	ene	nacionalidad	z	zeta, ceta	zona

Práctica Spell these words aloud in Spanish.

1. nada
2. maleta
3. quince
4. muy
5. hombre
6. por favor
7. San Fernando
8. Estados Unidos
9. Puerto Rico
10. España
11. Javier
12. Ecuador
13. Maite
14. gracias
15. Nueva York

Oraciones Repeat these sentences after your instructor, then spell each word aloud.

1. Me llamo Carmen.
2. Hasta luego, señora Herrera.
3. ¿Qué tal, David?
4. Buenos días, Pedro.

Refranes Read these sayings aloud after your instructor.

Ver es creer.[1]

En boca cerrada no entran moscas.[2]

1 Seeing is believing. 2 Silence is golden.

recursos

R	Textbook CD Lección 1	LM p. 2	Lab CD Lección 1	ICD-ROM Lección 1

¡Todos a bordo!

Los cuatro estudiantes, don Francisco y la Sra. Ramos se reúnen (*meet*) en la universidad.

SRA. RAMOS Buenos días, chicos. Yo soy Isabel Ramos de la agencia Ecuatur.

DON FRANCISCO Y yo soy don Francisco, el conductor.

SRA. RAMOS Bueno, ¿quién es María Teresa Fuentes de Alba?

MAITE ¡Soy yo!

SRA. RAMOS Ah, bien. Aquí tienes los documentos de viaje.

MAITE Gracias.

SRA. RAMOS ¿Javier Gómez Lozano?

JAVIER Aquí... Soy yo.

JAVIER ¿Qué tal? Me llamo Javier.

ÁLEX Mucho gusto, Javier. Yo soy Álex. ¿De dónde eres?

JAVIER De Puerto Rico. ¿Y tú?

ÁLEX Yo soy de México.

DON FRANCISCO Bueno, chicos, ¡todos a bordo!

INÉS Con permiso.

recursos

| R | Video/VCD-ROM Lección 1 | VM pp. 169-170 | ICD-ROM Lección 1 |

Personajes

DON FRANCISCO

JAVIER

INÉS

ÁLEX

MAITE

SRA. RAMOS

SRA. RAMOS Y tú eres Inés Ayala Loor, ¿verdad?

INÉS Sí, yo soy Inés.

SRA. RAMOS Y tú eres Alejandro Morales Paredes, ¿no?

ÁLEX Sí, señora.

INÉS Hola. Soy Inés.

MAITE Encantada. Yo me llamo Maite. ¿De dónde eres?

INÉS Soy del Ecuador, de Portoviejo. ¿Y tú?

MAITE De España. Soy de Madrid, la capital. Oye, ¿qué hora es?

INÉS Son las diez y tres minutos.

ÁLEX Perdón.

DON FRANCISCO ¿Y los otros?

SRA. RAMOS Son todos.

DON FRANCISCO Está bien.

Expresiones útiles

Identifying yourself and others

¿Cómo se llama usted?
What's your name?
Yo soy don Francisco, el conductor.
I'm Don Francisco, the driver.

¿Cómo te llamas?
What's your name?
Me llamo Javier.
My name is Javier.

¿Quién es... ?
Who is... ?
Aquí... Soy yo.
Here... That's me.
Tú eres... , ¿verdad?/¿no?
You are... , right?/no?

Saying what time it is

¿Qué hora es?
What time is it?
Es la una. / Son las dos.
It's one o'clock. / It's two o'clock.
Son las diez y tres minutos.
It's 10:03.

Saying "excuse me"

Con permiso.
Pardon me; excuse me. (to request permission)
Perdón.
Pardon me; excuse me.
(to get someone's attention or to ask forgiveness)

When starting a trip

¡Todos a bordo!
All aboard!
¡Buen viaje!
Have a good trip!

Getting a friend's attention

Oye...
Listen...

¿Qué piensas?

1 **Completar** Complete this conversation.

INÉS   Hola. ¿Cómo te _____?

MAITE   _____ llamo _____.
¿Y _____?

INÉS   Inés. Mucho _____.

MAITE   _____ gusto _____ mío.

INÉS   ¿De dónde _____?

MAITE   _____ de _____.
¿Y _____?

INÉS   Del _____.

2 **¿Cierto o falso?** Indicate if each statement is **cierto** (*true*) or **falso** (*false*). Then correct the false statements.

Cierto   Falso

_____   _____   1. Javier y Álex son pasajeros (*passengers*). _____

_____   _____   2. Javier Gómez Lozano es el conductor. _____

_____   _____   3. Inés Ayala Loor es de la agencia Ecuatur. _____

_____   _____   4. Inés es del Ecuador. _____

_____   _____   5. Maite es de España. _____

_____   _____   6. Javier es de Puerto Rico. _____

_____   _____   7. Álex es del Ecuador. _____

3 **Conversar** Using these cues, have a conversation with someone you just met at an airport.

• Greet each other.

• Find out each other's names.

• Ask each other how you are feeling today.

• Find out where each of you is from.

• Wish each other a good trip and say goodbye.

Exploración
Los saludos

Daniel y Juan se dan un abrazo (*give each other a hug*).

El señor Rivas y la señora Casas se dan la mano (*shake hands*).

Rita le da un beso a su abuela (*kisses her grandmother*).

Observaciones

• **Darse la mano**
Hispanics generally shake hands when they meet for the first time.

• **El abrazo**
Hispanic men often greet men they know well with an **abrazo**—a quick hug and a pat on the back.

• **El beso**
Hispanic women often greet friends and loved ones with a brief kiss on one or both cheeks.

Coméntalo

With a classmate, discuss these questions.

- How do you greet a person you don't know well?
- How do you greet your friends?
- How do you greet your parents?

recursos

R | vistahigher learning.com

1.1 Nouns and articles

▸ Nouns identify people, animals, places, or things. All Spanish nouns have gender (masculine or feminine) and number (singular or plural).

▸ Most nouns that refer to males are masculine. Most nouns that refer to females are feminine.

Masculine		Feminine	
el hombre	the man	la mujer	the woman
el chico	the boy	la chica	the girl
el pasajero	the passenger	la pasajera	the passenger
el conductor	the driver	la conductora	the driver
el profesor	the teacher	la profesora	the teacher

| la chica | la pasajera | el chico | el conductor |

▸ Most nouns ending in **–o**, **–ma**, and **–s** are masculine. Most nouns ending in **–a**, **–ción**, and **–dad** are feminine.

Masculine		Feminine	
el cuaderno	the notebook	la cosa	the thing
el diario	the diary	la escuela	the school
el diccionario	the dictionary	la grabadora	the tape recorder
el número	the number	la maleta	the suitcase
el vídeo	the video	la mochila	the backpack
el problema	the problem	la palabra	the word
el programa	the program	la lección	the lesson
el autobús	the bus	la conversación	the conversation
el país	the country	la nacionalidad	the nationality

¡ojo! **El lápiz** (*pencil*), **el mapa** (*map*), and **el día** (*day*) are masculine. **La mano** (*hand*) is feminine.

▸ Some nouns have identical masculine and feminine forms. The definite article (**el** or **la**) indicates the gender of these words.

Masculine		Feminine	
el **turista**	the tourist	la **turista**	the tourist
el **joven**	the young man	la **joven**	the young woman
el **estudiante**	the student	la **estudiante**	the student

Práctica

1 **Singular y plural** Make the singular words plural and the plural words singular.

1. el turista _____ 6. el problema _____
2. la cosa _____ 7. unos hombres _____
3. la mujer _____ 8. unos diarios _____
4. la mochila _____ 9. un pasajero _____
5. los países _____ 10. una escuela _____

2 **Identificar** For each photo, provide the noun and the appropriate definite and indefinite articles.

modelo

las maletas, unas maletas

1. _____ 4. _____

2. _____ 5. _____

3. _____ 6. _____

Conversación

3 Clasificar With a partner, identify the photos in Spanish and supply the definite and indefinite articles. Then indicate whether the photos represent objects or persons.

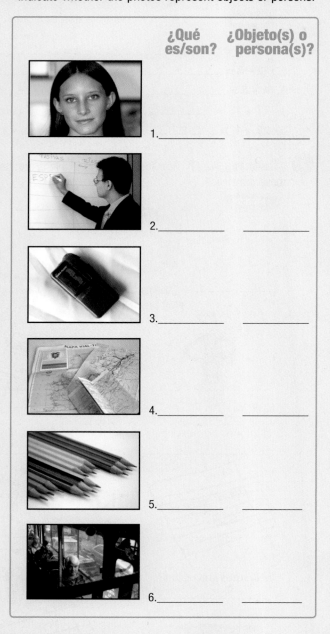

	¿Qué es/son?	¿Objeto(s) o persona(s)?
1.	___	___
2.	___	___
3.	___	___
4.	___	___
5.	___	___
6.	___	___

4 Charadas In groups, play a game of charades. Individually, think of two nouns for each charade—for example, a boy using a computer (**un chico; una computadora**). The first person to guess correctly acts out the next charade.

Plural of nouns

▶ Nouns that end in a vowel form the plural by adding **–s**. Nouns that end in a consonant add **–es**. Nouns that end in **–z** change the **–z** to **–c**, then add **–es**.

SINGULAR	PLURAL	SINGULAR	PLURAL
el chico	los chicos	el país	ls países
la palabra	las palabras	el lápiz	los lápices

¡ojo! When a singular noun has an accent mark on the last syllable, the accent is dropped from the plural form:

la lección → las lecciones   el autobús → los autobuses

▶ The masculine plural form may refer to a mixed-gender group.

1 pasajero + 2 pasajeras = 3 pasajeros

Spanish articles

Spanish has four forms that are equivalent to the English definite article *the*. Spanish also has four forms that are equivalent to the English indefinite article, which, according to context, may mean *a, an,* or *some*.

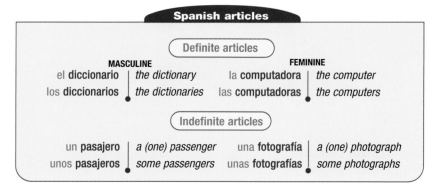

Spanish articles

Definite articles

MASCULINE		FEMININE	
el diccionario	the dictionary	la computadora	the computer
los diccionarios	the dictionaries	las computadoras	the computers

Indefinite articles

un pasajero	a (one) passenger	una fotografía	a (one) photograph
unos pasajeros	some passengers	unas fotografías	some photographs

¡Manos a la obra!

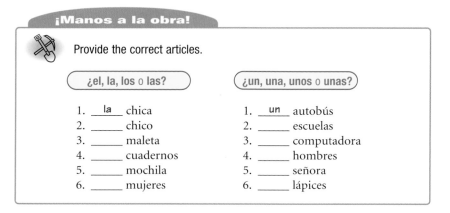

Provide the correct articles.

¿el, la, los o las?
1. __la__ chica
2. ____ chico
3. ____ maleta
4. ____ cuadernos
5. ____ mochila
6. ____ mujeres

¿un, una, unos o unas?
1. __un__ autobús
2. ____ escuelas
3. ____ computadora
4. ____ hombres
5. ____ señora
6. ____ lápices

1.2 Numbers 0-30

Numbers 0–30				
0 cero	6 seis	12 doce	18 dieciocho	24 veinticuatro
1 uno	7 siete	13 trece	19 diecinueve	25 veinticinco
2 dos	8 ocho	14 catorce	20 veinte	26 veintiséis
3 tres	9 nueve	15 quince	21 veintiuno	27 veintisiete
4 cuatro	10 diez	16 dieciséis	22 veintidós	28 veintiocho
5 cinco	11 once	17 diecisiete	23 veintitrés	29 veintinueve
				30 treinta

▸ Before a masculine noun, **uno** shortens to **un**. Before a feminine noun, **uno** changes to **una**.

un **hombre** → veintiún **hombres**

una **mujer** → veintiuna **mujeres**

▸ To ask *how many*, use **¿Cuántos?** with a masculine noun and **¿Cuántas?** with a feminine one. **Hay** means both *there is* and *there are*. Use **¿Hay…?** to ask *is/are there…?* Use **no hay** to express *there is/are not*.

—**¿Hay** chicas en la fotografía?
Are there girls in the picture?

—No, **no hay** chicas.
No, there aren't any girls.

—**¿Cuántos** chicos **hay?**
How many guys are there?

—**Hay** cuatro.
There are four.

¡ojo! The numbers **16–19** and **21–29** can also be written as three words, as in **diez y seis** and **veinte y uno**. **Uno** and **veintiuno** are used when counting (**uno, dos, tres… veinte, veintiuno, veintidós…**). They are also used after a noun, even if it is feminine (**la lección uno**).

¡Manos a la obra!

Provide the Spanish words for these numbers.

1.	7	siete	6.	15 _____	11.	30 _____	16.	10 _____
2.	16 _____		7.	21 _____	12.	4 _____	17.	2 _____
3.	29 _____		8.	9 _____	13.	12 _____	18.	5 _____
4.	1 _____		9.	23 _____	14.	28 _____	19.	22 _____
5.	0 _____		10.	11 _____	15.	14 _____	20.	13 _____

Práctica

1 **Matemáticas** Solve these math problems.

+ **más** − **menos** = **es (singular)/son (plural)**

modelo   **9 + 2 =** Nueve más dos son once.

1. **3 + 10 =** _____
2. **22 − 3 =** _____
3. **4 + 8 =** _____
4. **17 + 13 =** _____
5. **22 + 1 =** _____
6. **5 − 2 =** _____
7. **11 + 12 =** _____
8. **10 − 10 =** _____
9. **3 + 14 =** _____
10. **22 − 11 =** _____

2 **¿Cuántos hay?** How many persons or things are there in these drawings?

modelo

¿Cuántas maletas hay?
Hay cuatro maletas.

1. ¿Cuántos hombres hay?   4. ¿Cuántas fotografías hay?
_____

2. ¿Cuántos chicos hay?   5. ¿Cuántos turistas hay?
_____

3. ¿Cuántas conductoras hay? 6. ¿Cuántas chicas hay?
_____

Conversación

3 **Describir** Get together with a classmate and answer these questions about the photo.

1. ¿Cuántos conductores hay en la fotografía?

_____

2. ¿Cuántas mujeres hay?

_____

3. ¿Cuántos hombres hay?

_____

4. ¿Cuántos pasajeros hay?

_____

5. ¿Cuántos pasajeros son hombres?

_____

6. ¿Cuántos autobuses hay?

_____

4 **En la clase** With a classmate, take turns asking and answering these questions about your classroom.

1. ¿Cuántos estudiantes hay?
2. ¿Cuántos profesores hay?
3. ¿Cuántos hombres hay?
4. ¿Cuántas mujeres hay?
5. ¿Hay una computadora?
6. ¿Hay fotografías?
7. ¿Cuántos mapas hay?
8. ¿Hay diccionarios?
9. ¿Hay cuadernos?
10. ¿Cuántas grabadoras hay?
11. ¿Cuántas mochilas hay?
12. ¿Hay chicos?

Español en vivo

Libro de cuentos: $ 12

Oso con pijama: $ 15

Árbol de Navidad: $ 30

La felicidad: no tiene precio

Hay ciertas cosas que el dinero no puede comprar, para todo lo demás existe MasterCard.

Aceptada en más lugares de los que imaginas.

Identificar

Scan the advertisement above, find the places where numbers appear, and say the numbers out loud.

Preguntas

1. Fill in the prices of the following items:
   Teddy bear _____ Storybook _____ Christmas tree _____
2. What is the message of the advertisement?
3. Do you think it is effective? Why?

1.3 Present tense of ser (to be)

Subject Pronouns

Subject pronouns

	Singular		Plural	
FIRST PERSON	yo	*I*	nosotros	*we (masculine)*
			nosotras	*we (feminine)*
SECOND PERSON	tú	*you (familiar)*	vosotros	*you (masc., fam.)*
	usted (Ud.)	*you (formal)*	vosotras	*you (fem., fam.)*
			ustedes (Uds.)	*you (form.)*
THIRD PERSON	él	*he*	ellos	*they (masc.)*
	ella	*she*	ellas	*they (fem.)*

▶ A subject pronoun replaces the name or title of a person or thing and acts as the subject of a verb.

> Carlos **es estudiante.** → Él **es estudiante.**

▶ Spanish has two subject pronouns that mean *you* (singular). Use **tú** when talking to friends, family members, and small children. Use **usted** when talking to someone with whom you have a more formal relationship, such as an employer or a professor, or to someone who is older than you.

▶ **Usted** and **ustedes** are abbreviated **Ud.** and **Uds.**

¡**ojo!** In Latin America, **ustedes** and **Uds.** are used as the plural of both **tú** and **usted**. In Spain, **vosotros/as** is used as the plural of **tú**.

▶ **Nosotros**, **vosotros**, and **ellos** refer to a group of males or to a group of males and females. **Nosotras**, **vosotras**, and **ellas** refer only to groups of females.

nosotros, vosotros, ellos   nosotros, vosotros, ellos   nosotras, vosotras, ellas

▶ There is no Spanish equivalent of the English subject pronoun *it*.

—¿Qué es?   —Es una computadora.
What is it?   *It's a computer.*

Práctica

1 **¿Quién es?** With a partner, take turns asking who these people are and where they are from.

modelo

Estudiante 1: *¿Quién es?*
Estudiante 2: *Es Jennifer López.*

Estudiante 1: *¿De dónde es?*
Estudiante 2: *Es de Nueva York.*

Jennifer López / Nueva York

Martin Sheen / Ohio   **Sammy Sosa / La República Dominicana**

Gloria Estefan / Cuba   **Salma Hayek / México**

Shakira / Colombia   **Carlos Santana / México**

2 **¿Qué es?** Ask your partner what each object is and to whom it belongs.

modelo

Estudiante 1: *¿Qué es?*
Estudiante 2: *Es una grabadora.*
Estudiante 1: *¿De quién es?*
Estudiante 2: *Es del profesor.*

1.

3.

2.

4.

Conversación

3 **En el dormitorio** Using the items in the word bank, ask your partner questions about Susana's dorm room.

¿Quién?	¿De dónde?	¿Cuántos?
¿Qué?	¿De quién?	¿Cuántas?

4 **Personas famosas** Pretend to be a person from Spain, Mexico, Puerto Rico, Cuba, or the United States who is famous in one of these professions. Your classmates will try to guess who you are.

actor	actor
actriz	actress
deportista	athlete
escritor(a)	writer
cantante	singer
músico/a	musician

modelo

Estudiante 3: ¿Eres de Cuba?
Estudiante 1: Sí.
Estudiante 2: ¿Eres mujer?
Estudiante 1: No. Soy hombre.
Estudiante 3: ¿Eres músico?
Estudiante 1: No. Soy actor.
Estudiante 2: ¿Eres Andy García?
Estudiante 1: ¡Sí! ¡Sí!

Andy García

The present tense of ser

ser (to be)

Singular forms		Plural forms	
yo	**soy** (*I am*)	nosotros/as	**somos** (*we are*)
tú	**eres** (*you are*)	vosotros/as	**sois** (*you are*)
Ud./él/ella	**es** (*you are; he/she is*)	Uds./ellos/ellas	**son** (*you/they are*)

▶ Use **ser** to identify people and things.

—¿Quién **es** ella?
Who is she?

—**Es** Inés Ayala Loor.
She's Inés Ayala Loor.

—¿Qué **es**?
What is it?

—**Es** un mapa.
It's a map.

▶ Use **ser** to express possession, along with **de**. **De** combines with **el** to form the contraction **del**.[1] Note that Spanish doesn't use [*apostrophe*] + *s* to indicate possession.

—¿**De** quién **es**?
Whose is it?

—**Es** el diario **de** Maite.
It's Maite's diary.

—¿**De** quiénes **son**?
Whose are they?

—**Son** los lápices **del** chico.
They are the boy's pencils.

▶ Use **ser** to express origin, along with **de**.

—¿**De** dónde **es** Inés?
Where is Inés from?

—**Es del** Ecuador.
She's from Ecuador.

▶ Use **ser** to talk about someone's occupation.[2]

Don Francisco **es** conductor.
Don Francisco is a driver.

Isabel **es** profesora.
Isabel is a teacher.

---

[1] **De** does not form contractions with **la**, **los**, or **las**.
[2] Spanish does not use **un** or **una** after **ser** when mentioning a person's occupation, unless the occupation is accompanied by an adjective.

¡Manos a la obra!

Provide the correct subject pronouns in the first column, and the correct present forms of **ser** in the second column. The first item has been done for you.

1. Gabriel   <u>él</u>   <u>es</u>
2. Juan y yo   _____   _____
3. Óscar y Flora   _____   _____
4. Adriana   _____   _____
5. las turistas   _____   _____
6. el chico   _____   _____
7. los conductores   _____   _____
8. el señor y la señora Ruiz   _____   _____

1.4 Telling time

▶ Use numbers with the verb **ser** to tell time. To ask what time it is, use **¿Qué hora es?** To say what time it is, use **es la** with **una** and **son las** with other hours.

Es la una.

Son las cuatro.

▶ Express time from the hour to the half hour by adding minutes.

Son las dos **y diez**.

Son las ocho **y veinte**.

▶ Use **y cuarto** or **y quince** to say that it's fifteen minutes past the hour. Use **y media** or **y treinta** to say that it's thirty minutes past the hour.

Son las cuatro **y cuarto**.

Son las nueve **y media**.

Práctica

1 **Emparejar** Match each watch with the correct statement.

_____ _____ _____

_____ _____ _____

1. Son las ocho menos veinticinco de la mañana.
2. Es la una menos diez de la mañana.
3. Son las tres y cinco de la mañana.
4. Son las dos menos cuarto de la tarde.
5. Son las seis y media de la mañana.
6. Son las once y veinte de la noche.

2 **¿Qué hora es?** With a partner, answer the questions using the clocks as a guide.

modelo

Estudiante 1: Son las siete de la noche en Los Ángeles. ¿Qué hora es en San Antonio?
Estudiante 2: Son las nueve de la noche en San Antonio.

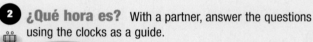

Miami   **San Antonio**   **Denver**   **Los Ángeles**

1. Son las cuatro en punto de la tarde en Los Ángeles. ¿Qué hora es en Miami? _____
2. Son las seis de la tarde en San Antonio. ¿Qué hora es en Denver? _____
3. Son las siete de la noche en Denver. ¿Qué hora es en Los Ángeles? _____
4. Son las dos y media de la tarde en Los Ángeles. ¿Qué hora es en Miami? _____
5. Son las once de la mañana en San Antonio. ¿Qué hora es en Los Ángeles? _____
6. Es la una de la tarde en Los Ángeles. ¿Qué hora es en San Antonio? _____

Conversación

3 **En la televisión** With a partner, take turns asking and answering questions about these television listings.

modelo

Estudiante 1: ¿A qué hora es el programa
Las computadoras?
Estudiante 2: Es a las nueve en punto de la noche.

TV Hoy
Programación

11:00 am	Telenovela: *Cuatro viajeros y un autobús*
12:00 pm	Película: *El cóndor* (drama)
2:00 pm	Telenovela: *Dos mujeres y dos hombres*
3:00 pm	Programa juvenil: *Fiesta*
3:30 pm	Telenovela: *¡Sí, sí, sí!*
4:00 pm	Telenovela: *El diario de la Sra. González*
5:00 pm	Telenovela: *Tres mujeres*
6:00 pm	Noticias
7:00 pm	Especial musical: *Música folklórica de México*
7:30 pm	La naturaleza: *Jardín secreto*
8:00 pm	Noticiero: *Veinticuatro horas*
9:00 pm	Documental: *Las computadoras*
10:00 pm	Telecomedia: *Don Paco y doña Tere*
11:00 pm	Película: *Pedro Páramo*

4 **Entrevista** Use the following questions to interview a classmate.

1. ¿Qué hora es?
2. ¿A qué hora es la clase de español?
3. ¿A qué hora es el programa *60 minutes?*
4. ¿A qué hora es el programa *Nightline?*
5. ¿Hay una fiesta el sábado (*on Saturday*)? ¿A qué hora es?
6. ¿Hay un concierto el sábado? ¿A qué hora es?

▶ To express time from the half-hour to the hour in Spanish, subtract minutes or a portion of an hour from the next hour.

Son las dos **menos cuarto.**   Son las once **menos quince.**

Son las nueve **menos diez.**   Son las ocho **menos cinco.**

Time-telling expressions

▶ Here are some useful phrases related to time-telling.

—**¿Qué hora es?**
What time is it?

—Son las cuatro **de la tarde.**
It's 4 p.m. (in the afternoon).

—Son las diez **de la noche.**
It's 10 p.m. (at night).

—**¿A qué hora es** la clase?
(At) what time is the class?

—La clase es **a la una.**
The class is at one o'clock.

—Son las nueve **de la mañana.**
It's 9 a.m. (in the morning).

—Es **el mediodía.**
It's noon.

—Es **la medianoche.**
It's midnight.

—La clase es **a las dos.**
The class is at two o'clock.

—La clase es a las ocho **en punto.**
The class is at 8 o'clock on the dot (sharp).

¡Manos a la obra!

Practice telling time by completing these sentences.
The first item has been done for you.

1. (1:00 a.m.) Es la ____una____ de la mañana.
2. (2:50 a.m.) Son las tres _____ diez de la mañana.
3. (4:15 p.m.) Son las cuatro y _____ de la tarde.
4. (8:30 p.m.) Son las ocho y _____ de la noche.
5. (9:15 a.m.) Son las nueve y quince de la _____.
6. (12:00 p.m.) Es el _____.
7. (6:00 a.m.) Son las seis de la _____.
8. (4:05 p.m.) Son las cuatro y cinco de la _____.
9. (12:00 a.m.) Es la _____.
10. (9:55 p.m.) Son las _____ menos cinco de la noche.

Ampliación

1 Escuchar

A Listen to the conversation between Srta. Martínez and a traveler. Then fill in the missing information on the form.

 TIP **Listen for words you know.** Listening for familiar words and phrases will help you follow a conversation.

Aero Tur

Número de pasajeros
1.

Nombre (first name) del pasajero
2.

Apellido (last name) del pasajero
3.

Destino
4.

Número de maletas
5.

B When does this conversation take place? How do you know?

2 Conversar

With two classmates, act out an interview between school newspaper reporters and a visiting **profesor de literatura.** After introducing themselves, the reporters should find out the following information.

- The professor's name
- Where the professor is from
- What time the professor's class starts
- How many students are in the class

recursos

| R | Textbook CD Lección 1 | WB pp. 3-8 | LM pp. 3-8 | Lab CD Lección 1 | ICD-ROM Lección 1 | vistahigher learning.com |

Ampliación

3 Escribir

Write a list of names, numbers, addresses, and websites that will help you in your study of Spanish. Use the plan below to guide you in your writing.

 TIP **Write in Spanish.** Use grammar and vocabulary that you know. Also, look at your textbook for examples of style, format, and expressions in Spanish.

Organízalo	Make a list of campus resources and contact information. Then explore web resources and jot down a few addresses.
Escríbelo	Using the material you have compiled, write the first draft of your list.
Corrígelo	Exchange papers with a classmate and comment on the organization, style, and grammatical correctness of each other's work. Then revise your first draft, keeping your classmate's comments in mind.
Compártelo	Share your list with two new classmates. If they found resources you didn't mention, add them to your list. Store your list with your other study aids.

4 Un paso más

Prepare a presentation about how Hispanic cultures have influenced an American city. Include the following in your presentation:

- An introduction of yourself in Spanish
- A general description of the city
- Examples of how Hispanic cultures have influenced the city
- Photos, drawings, and charts to make your presentation more interesting.

SAN ANTONIO

 En Internet

Investiga estos temas en el sitio vistahigherlearning.com.
- Ciudad de Nueva York
- Ciudad de Miami
- Ciudad de Los Ángeles

Antes de leer

Cognates are words that share similar meanings and spellings in two or more languages. The Spanish words **computadora**, **problema**, and **programa** are examples of cognates.

When you read in Spanish, look for cognates and use them to get the general meaning of what you're reading. But watch out for false cognates such as **librería**, which means *bookstore*, not *library*.

Laura, a university student, made a list of important names and numbers she needed to remember. Look for cognates while you read her list.

For now, read the phone numbers one digit at a time. The period (.) is called **punto** and the "at" symbol (@) is called **arroba.**

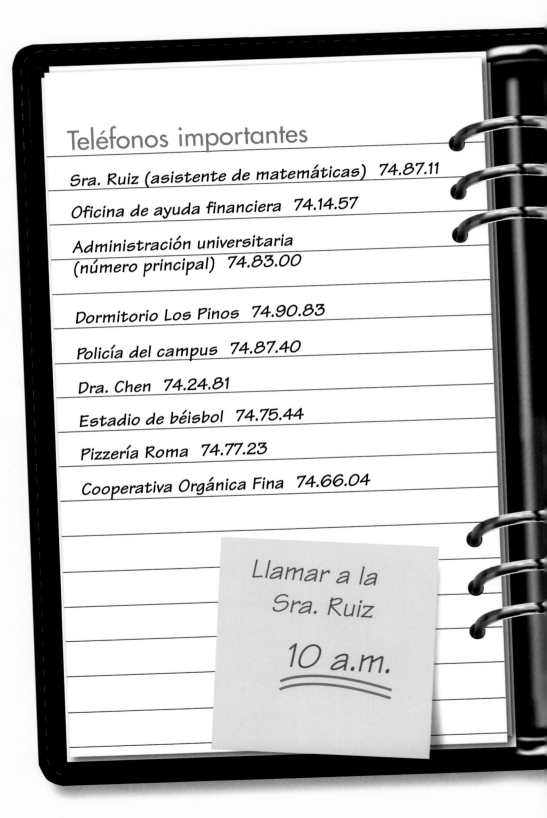

Teléfonos importantes

Sra. Ruiz (asistente de matemáticas) 74.87.11

Oficina de ayuda financiera 74.14.57

Administración universitaria
(número principal) 74.83.00

Dormitorio Los Pinos 74.90.83

Policía del campus 74.87.40

Dra. Chen 74.24.81

Estadio de béisbol 74.75.44

Pizzería Roma 74.77.23

Cooperativa Orgánica Fina 74.66.04

Llamar a la
Sra. Ruiz

10 a.m.

Direcciones electrónicas

Oficina de matemáticas
ofna@matematicas.unimetro.edu.pe

Profesora González
a.gonzalez@matematicas.unimetro.edu.pe

Farmacia
rx@farmaciagomez.com.pe

Gimnasio
informacion@gimnasio.unimetro.edu.pe

Después de leer

¿Comprendiste?

Indicate whether each statement is **cierto** (*true*) or **falso** (*false*).

Cierto   **Falso**

———— ———— 1. Professor González works in the math department.

———— ———— 2. If Laura wanted to get a student loan, she would call 74.83.00.

———— ———— 3. Laura never eats pizza.

———— ———— 4. If Laura needed to report a crime, she would dial 74.87.40.

———— ———— 5. To find out the price of organic apples, Laura would dial 74.66.04.

———— ———— 6. Laura would call 74.75.44 to get a baseball ticket.

Coméntalo

Think about the names, phone numbers, and e-mail addresses that Laura keeps in her address book. If you were preparing a similar address book, what names, telephone numbers, and e-mail addresses would you include?

recursos

R | vistahigher learning.com

Saludos

Hola.	Hello; hi.
Buenos días.	Good morning.
Buenas tardes.	Good afternoon.
Buenas noches.	Good evening; good night.

Despedidas

Adiós.	Goodbye.
Nos vemos.	See you.
Hasta luego.	See you later.
Hasta la vista.	See you later.
Hasta pronto.	See you soon.
Hasta mañana.	See you tomorrow.
Saludos a…	Greetings to…
Chau.	Bye.

¿Cómo está?

¿Cómo está usted?	How are you? (form.)
¿Cómo estás?	How are you? (fam.)
¿Qué hay de nuevo?	What's new?
¿Qué pasa?	What's happening?; what's going on?
¿Qué tal?	How are you?; how is it going?
(Muy) bien, gracias.	(Very) well, thanks.
Nada.	Nothing.
No muy bien.	Not very well.
Regular.	So-so; OK.

Expresiones de cortesía

De nada.	You're welcome.
Lo siento.	I'm sorry.
(Muchas) gracias.	Thank you (very much); thanks (a lot).
No hay de qué.	You're welcome.
Por favor.	Please.

Títulos

señor (Sr.)	Mr.; sir
señora (Sra.)	Mrs.; ma'am
señorita (Srta.)	Miss

Presentaciones

¿Cómo se llama usted?	What's your name? (form.)
¿Cómo te llamas (tú)?	What's your name? (fam.)
Me llamo…	My name is…
¿Y tú?	And you? (fam.)
¿Y Ud.?	And you? (form.)
Mucho gusto.	Pleased to meet you.
El gusto es mío.	The pleasure is mine.
Encantado/a.	Delighted; Pleased to meet you.
Igualmente.	Likewise.
Éste/ésta es…	This is…
Le presento a…	I would like to introduce you to… (form.)
Te presento a…	I would like to introduce you to… (fam.)

Países

Ecuador	Ecuador
España	Spain
Estados Unidos (EE.UU.)	United States
México	Mexico
Puerto Rico	Puerto Rico

Verbos

ser	to be

¿De dónde es?

¿De dónde es Ud.?	Where are you from? (form.)
¿De dónde eres?	Where are you from? (fam.)
Soy de…	I'm from …

Palabras adicionales

¿Cuánto(s)/a(s)?	How many?
¿De quién…?	Whose …? (sing.)
¿De quiénes…?	Whose …? (plural)
(No) Hay	There is (not); there are (not)

Sustantivos

el autobús	bus
la capital	capital city
la chica	girl
el chico	boy
la computadora	computer
la comunidad	community
el/la conductor(a)	chauffeur; driver
la conversación	conversation
la cosa	thing
el cuaderno	notebook
el día	day
el diario	diary
el diccionario	dictionary
la escuela	school
el/la estudiante	student
la foto(grafía)	photograph
la grabadora	tape recorder
el hombre	man
el/la joven	youth; young person
el lápiz	pencil
la lección	lesson
la maleta	suitcase
la mano	hand
el mapa	map
la mochila	backpack
la mujer	woman
la nacionalidad	nationality
el número	number
el país	country
la palabra	word
el/la pasajero/a	passenger
el problema	problem
el/la profesor(a)	teacher
el programa	program
el/la turista	tourist
el vídeo	video

Expresiones útiles	See page 9.
Numbers 0–30	See page 14.
Subject Pronouns	See page 16.
Time-telling expressions	See page 18.

recursos

| R | Lab CD Lección 1 | LM p. 6 |

2 Las clases

Communicative Goals

You will learn how to:
- talk about people, places, classes
- express likes and dislikes
- chat with a new friend
- talk about prices

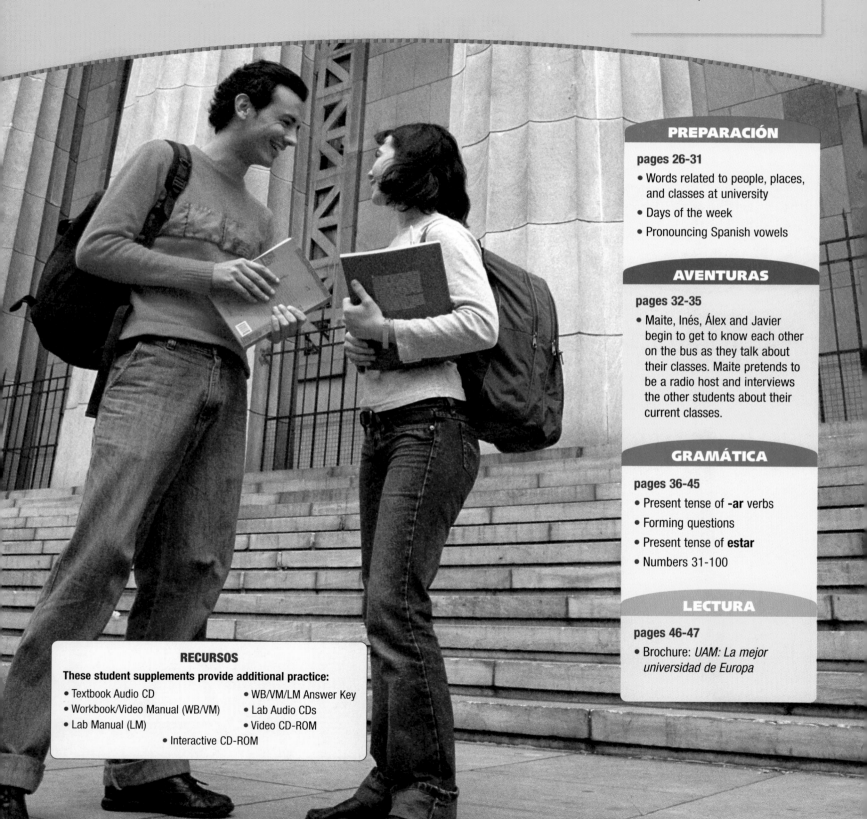

PREPARACIÓN

pages 26-31
- Words related to people, places, and classes at university
- Days of the week
- Pronouncing Spanish vowels

AVENTURAS

pages 32-35
- Maite, Inés, Álex and Javier begin to get to know each other on the bus as they talk about their classes. Maite pretends to be a radio host and interviews the other students about their current classes.

GRAMÁTICA

pages 36-45
- Present tense of **-ar** verbs
- Forming questions
- Present tense of **estar**
- Numbers 31-100

LECTURA

pages 46-47
- Brochure: *UAM: La mejor universidad de Europa*

RECURSOS

These student supplements provide additional practice:
- Textbook Audio CD
- Workbook/Video Manual (WB/VM)
- Lab Manual (LM)
- Interactive CD-ROM
- WB/VM/LM Answer Key
- Lab Audio CDs
- Video CD-ROM

LAS
CLASES

el laboratorio
laboratory

LUGARES

la cafetería *cafeteria*
la librería *bookstore*
la residencia estudiantil *dormitory*
la universidad *university*

el estadio
stadium

la biblioteca
library

LAS CLASES

la química
chemistry

la administración *business administration*
de empresas
el arte *art*
la biología *biology*
la clase *class*
la contabilidad *accounting*
los cursos *courses*
el español *Spanish*
la física *physics*
la historia *history*
el inglés *English*
las lenguas extranjeras *foreign languages*

las matemáticas *mathematics*
el periodismo *journalism*
la psicología *psychology*
la sociología *sociology*

la geografía
geography

la computación
computer science

recursos

R				
Textbook CD Lección 2	WB pp. 9-10	LM p. 7	Lab CD Lección 2	ICD-ROM Lección 2

EN LA CLASE

el borrador *eraser*
el examen *test; exam*
el horario *schedule*
la mesa *table*
el papel *paper*
la pizarra *blackboard*
la pluma *pen*
la prueba *test; quiz*
la puerta *door*
el semestre *semester*
la silla *chair*
la tarea *homework*
la tiza *chalk*
el trimestre *trimester; quarter*
la ventana *window*

el reloj
clock; watch

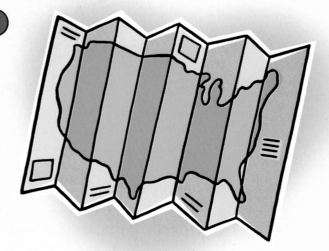

el mapa
map

el libro
book

el escritorio
desk

PERSONAS

el/la compañero/a de clase *classmate*
el/la compañero/a de cuarto *roommate*
el/la estudiante *student*

LOS DÍAS DE LA SEMANA

lunes *Monday*
martes *Tuesday*
miércoles *Wednesday*
jueves *Thursday*
viernes *Friday*
sábado *Saturday*
domingo *Sunday*

el día *day*
la semana *week*

Hoy es… *Today is…*

el profesor
teacher; professor

A escuchar

1 **Escuchar** Listen to Professor Morales talk about her Spanish classroom, then check the items she mentions.

1. puerta ❏
2. ventanas ❏
3. pizarra ❏
4. borrador ❏
5. tiza ❏
6. escritorios ❏

7. sillas ❏
8. libros ❏
9. plumas ❏
10. mochilas ❏
11. papel ❏
12. reloj ❏

2 **Mis clases** Listen and fill in the calendar with María's class schedule. Then complete the sentences below.

María

Estudiante	María	Semestre Nº 1		
lunes	martes	miércoles	jueves	viernes

AM / PM

1. Éste es el primer (*first*) _____ de María en la universidad.
2. El horario de María es de cuatro _____ .
3. La clase de _____ es el lunes a las diez y media de la mañana.
4. La clase de _____ es el martes a las dos y quince de la tarde.
5. La clase de periodismo es el _____ a las once de la mañana.
6. La clase de _____ es el jueves a las tres y media de la tarde.
7. María estudia (*studies*) en la _____ los viernes.

recursos

Textbook CD
Lección 2

A practicar

3 **Clasificar** Indicate whether each word is a **Persona**, **Objeto**, **Curso**, or **Lugar** (*place*).

	Persona	Objeto	Curso	Lugar
1. el periodismo	_____	_____	_____	_____
2. la residencia estudiantil	_____	_____	_____	_____
3. la estudiante	_____	_____	_____	_____
4. el estadio	_____	_____	_____	_____
5. la tiza	_____	_____	_____	_____
6. la contabilidad	_____	_____	_____	_____
7. la pluma	_____	_____	_____	_____
8. la compañera de clase	_____	_____	_____	_____

4 **Cursos** What is the subject matter of each class?

modelo
la cultura de España, los verbos
Es la clase de español.

1. los microbios, los animales
   _____

2. George Washington, Martin Luther King, Jr.
   _____

3. la geometría, la trigonometría
   _____

4. Frida Kahlo, Leonardo da Vinci
   _____

5. África, el río Amazonas
   _____

6. Freud, Jung
   _____

Frida Kahlo, famosa pintora (*painter*) mexicana.

El río Amazonas, en América del Sur.

5 **Analogías** Use these words to complete the analogies. Five words will not be used.

1. dos ←→ cuatro ⊜ martes ←→ _____
2. hoy ←→ mañana ⊜ viernes ←→ _____
3. EE.UU. ←→ mapa ⊜ hora ←→ _____
4. inglés ←→ lengua ⊜ miércoles ←→ _____
5. maleta ←→ pasajero/a ⊜ mochila ←→ _____
6. pluma ←→ papel ⊜ tiza ←→ _____
7. papel ←→ cuaderno ⊜ libro ←→ _____

biblioteca	pizarra	profesor(a)
jueves	semana	miércoles
estudiante	día	reloj
sábado	martes	domingo

A conversar

 6 **Horario** Create your own class schedule like the one below. Then discuss it with a classmate.

Manuel Domínguez

Estudiante	Manuel Domínguez		Semestre Nº 1	
lunes	**martes**	**miércoles**	**jueves**	**viernes**
8:30 biología Profesora Morales		8:30 biología		8:30 biología
10:15 inglés Profesor Herrera	9:45 historia Península Ibérica Profesora Cortés	10:15 inglés	9:45 historia	10:15 inglés
	12:45 psicología Profesor Blanco		12:45 psicología	
3:30 laboratorio (biología)		1:15 arte Profesor Pérez		1:15 arte
4:30 discusión (historia) biblioteca				

modelo

Estudiante 1: ¿Cuándo tomas (*when do you take*) biología?
Estudiante 2: Los lunes, miércoles y viernes tomo (I *take*) biología a las ocho y media de la mañana.
Estudiante 1: ¿Quién es el profesor?
Estudiante 2: Es la profesora Morales.

 7 **Entrevistas** Use these questions to interview two classmates. Then share the results of your interviews with the class.

1. ¿Cómo te llamas?
2. ¿Cómo estás hoy?
3. ¿De dónde eres?
4. ¿Cuántos cursos tomas?
5. ¿Cuándo tomas…?
6. ¿A qué hora es la clase de…?
7. ¿Quién es el/la profesor(a)?
8. ¿Qué hora es ahora (*now*)?

 8 **Nuevos amigos** You meet a new student in the cafeteria. Have a conversation based on the following cues.

- Greet your new acquaintance.
- Find out how he or she is doing.
- Ask where he or she is from.
- Compare class schedules.
- Say goodbye.

🎧 Pronunciación

Spanish vowels

a　　　**e**　　　**i**　　　**o**　　　**u**

Spanish vowels are never silent; they are always pronounced in a short, crisp way without the glide sounds used in English.

Álex　　　**clase**　　　**nada**　　　**encantada**

The letter **a** is pronounced like the *a* in *father,* but shorter.

el　　　**ene**　　　**mesa**　　　**elefante**

The letter **e** is pronounced like the *e* in *they,* but shorter.

Inés　　　**chica**　　　**tiza**　　　**señorita**

The letter **i** sounds like the *ee* in *beet,* but shorter.

hola　　　**con**　　　**libro**　　　**don Francisco**

The letter **o** is pronounced like the *o* in *tone,* but shorter.

uno　　　**regular**　　　**saludos**　　　**gusto**

The letter **u** sounds like the *oo* in *room,* but shorter.

Práctica Practice the vowels by saying the names of these places in Spain.

1. Madrid
2. Alicante
3. Tenerife
4. Toledo
5. Barcelona
6. Granada
7. Burgos
8. La Coruña

Oraciones Read the sentences aloud, focusing on the vowels.

1. Hola. Me llamo Ramiro Morgado.
2. Estudio arte en la Universidad de Salamanca.
3. Tomo también (*also*) literatura y contabilidad.
4. Ay, tengo clase en cinco minutos. ¡Nos vemos!

Refranes Practice the vowels by reading these sayings aloud.

Cada loco con su tema.[2]

Del dicho al hecho hay un gran trecho.[1]

recursos

R	Textbook CD Lección 2	LM p. 8	Lab CD Lección 2	ICD-ROM Lección 2

1 Easier said than done.
2 To each his own.

¿Qué clases tomas?

Maite, Inés, Javier y Álex hablan de las clases.

ÁLEX Hola Ricardo… Aquí estamos en la Mitad del Mundo. ¿Qué tal las clases en la UNAM?

MAITE Es exactamente como las fotos en los libros de geografía.

INÉS ¡Sí! ¿También tomas tú geografía?

MAITE Yo no. Yo tomo inglés y literatura. También tomo una clase de periodismo.

MAITE Muy buenos días. María Teresa Fuentes, de Radio Andina FM 93. Hoy estoy con estudiantes de la Universidad San Francisco de Quito. ¡A ver! La señorita que está cerca de la ventana… ¿Cómo te llamas y de dónde eres?

MAITE ¿En qué clase hay más chicos?

INÉS Bueno, eh… en la clase de historia.

MAITE ¿Y más chicas?

INÉS En la de sociología hay más chicas, casi un ochenta y cinco por ciento.

MAITE Y tú, joven, ¿cómo te llamas y de dónde eres?

JAVIER Me llamo Javier Gómez y soy de San Juan, Puerto Rico.

MAITE ¿Tomas muchas clases este semestre?

JAVIER Sí, tomo tres: historia y arte los lunes, miércoles y viernes, y computación los martes y jueves.

MAITE ¿Te gustan las computadoras, Javier?

JAVIER No me gustan nada. Me gusta mucho más el arte… y, sobre todo, me gusta dibujar.

ÁLEX ¿Cómo que no? ¿No te gustan las computadoras?

recursos

| R | Video/VCD-ROM Lección 2 | VM pp. 171-172 | ICD-ROM Lección 2 |

Personajes

JAVIER

INÉS

ÁLEX

MAITE

4

5

INÉS Hola. Me llamo Inés Ayala Loor y soy del Ecuador, de Portoviejo.

MAITE Encantada. ¿Qué clases tomas en la universidad?

INÉS Tomo geografía, inglés, historia, sociología y arte.

MAITE Tomas muchas clases, ¿no?

INÉS Pues sí, me gusta estudiar mucho.

9

10

ÁLEX Pero si son muy interesantes, hombre.

JAVIER Sí, ¡muy interesantes!

Expresiones útiles

Talking about classes

¿Qué tal las clases en la UNAM?
How are classes going at UNAM?

Tomas muchas clases, ¿no?
You're taking lots of classes, aren't you?

Pues sí.
Well, yes.

¿En qué clase hay más chicos?
In which class are there more guys?

En la clase de historia.
In history class.

Talking about likes/dislikes

¿Te gusta estudiar?
Do you like to study?

Sí, me gusta mucho. Pero también me gusta mirar la televisión.
Yes, I like it a lot. But I also like to watch television.

¿Te gustan las computadoras?
Do you like computers?

Sí, me gustan muchísimo.
Yes, I like them very much.

No, no me gustan nada.
No, I don't like them at all.

Talking about location

Aquí estamos en…
Here we are at/in…

¿Dónde está la señorita?
Where is the young woman?

Está cerca de la ventana.
She's near the window.

Expressing hesitation

A ver…
Let's see…

Bueno…
Well…

¿Qué piensas?

1 Escoger Choose the answer that best completes each sentence.

1. Maite toma (*is taking*) _____ en la universidad.
   a. geografía, inglés y periodismo   b. inglés, periodismo y arte
   c. periodismo, inglés y literatura

2. Inés toma sociología, geografía, _____ .
   a. inglés, historia y arte   b. periodismo, computación y arte
   c. historia, literatura y biología

3. Javier toma _____ clases este semestre.
   a. cuatro   b. tres
   c. dos

4. Javier toma historia y _____ los _____ .
   a. computación; martes y jueves   b. arte; lunes, martes y miércoles
   c. arte; lunes, miércoles y viernes

Inés

Javier   Maite

2 Completar These sentences are similar to things said in the **Aventuras** episode. Complete each sentence with the correct word(s).

1. Maite, Javier, Inés y yo estamos en _____ .

2. Hay fotos impresionantes de la Mitad del Mundo en los libros de _____.

3. Me llamo María Teresa Fuentes. Estoy aquí con estudiantes de _____.

4. Hay muchos chicos en _____.

5. No me gustan las computadoras. Me gusta más _____.

3 Conversar Use the following guidelines to have a conversation with a partner.

- Greet each other.
- Ask each other where you are from.
- Find out what each of you likes to study.
- Find out how many classes each of you is taking.
- Find out which classes each of you likes and dislikes.
- Say goodbye.

Exploración
Las universidades hispanas

Estadísticas universitarias

PRINCIPALES UNIVERSIDADES DEL MUNDO HISPANO	Número de estudiantes
1. Universidad Nacional Autónoma de México (México)	255.000
2. Universidad de Buenos Aires (Argentina)	206.700
3. Universidad Complutense de Madrid (España)	140.000
4. Universidad Autónoma de Santo Domingo (República Dominicana)	100.000

La Universidad de Salamanca, fundada en el siglo XIII (*thirteenth century*), es una de las universidades preeminentes de Europa. Ofrece muchos cursos y clases de español para extranjeros (*foreigners*).

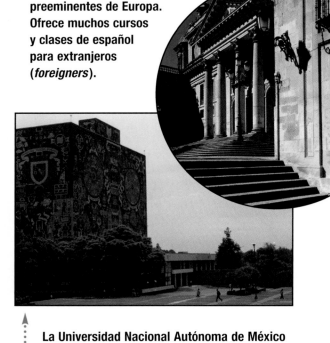

La Universidad Nacional Autónoma de México (UNAM), con unos 255.000 (doscientos cincuenta y cinco mil) estudiantes, es una de las más grandes del mundo (*biggest in the world*).

Fundada en 1821 (mil ochocientos veintiuno), la Universidad de Buenos Aires (UBA) es un importante centro de estudios sociales y científicos. La UBA ayudó (*helped*) en la formación de tres científicos que ganaron (*won*) el Premio Nobel.

Coméntalo

With a classmate, discuss the following questions.

- ¿Cuál (*which*) es la universidad más grande en tu ciudad (*city*) o estado (*state*)?
- ¿Te gustaría (*would you like*) estudiar español en Salamanca? (Sí, me gustaría… / No, no me gustaría…)

recursos

R

vistahigher learning.com

2.1 The present tense of regular –ar verbs

▸ To create the forms of regular verbs, drop the infinitive endings (**–ar,** **–er, –ir**). Then add the endings of the different subject pronouns. The chart below demonstrates how to conjugate regular **–ar** verbs.

estudiar (to study)

yo	estudi**o**	*I study*
tú	estudi**as**	*you (fam.) study*
Ud./él/ella	estudi**a**	*you (form.) study; he/she studies*
nosotros/as	estudi**amos**	*we study*
vosotros/as	estudi**áis**	*you (fam.) study*
Uds./ellos/ellas	estudi**an**	*you (form.)/they study*

¿Tomas muchas clases este semestre?

Sí, tomo tres.

Common –ar verbs

bailar	to dance	explicar	to explain
buscar	to look for	hablar	to talk; to speak
caminar	to walk	llegar	to arrive
cantar	to sing	llevar	to carry
comprar	to buy	mirar	to look (at); to watch
contestar	to answer	necesitar	to need
conversar	to talk	practicar	to practice
descansar	to rest	preguntar	to ask (a question)
desear	to want; to wish	preparar	to prepare
dibujar	to draw	regresar	to return
enseñar	to teach	terminar	to end; to finish
escuchar	to listen	tomar	to take; to drink
esperar	to wait (for); to hope	trabajar	to work
estudiar	to study	viajar	to travel

▸ The Spanish present tense can be translated in several ways. Note the following examples.

Ana **trabaja** en la cafetería.
Ana works in the cafeteria.
Ana is working in the cafeteria.
Ana does work in the cafeteria.

Paco **viaja** a Madrid mañana.
Paco travels to Madrid tomorrow.
Paco is traveling to Madrid tomorrow.
Paco does travel to Madrid tomorrow.

Práctica

1 **¿Te gusta… ?** Get together with a classmate and take turns asking each other if you like these activities.

¿Te gusta… ? *Do you like… ?*	▸	Sí, me gusta/No, no me gusta *Yes, I like/No, I don't like*

modelo
Estudiante 1: ¿Te gusta tomar el autobús?
Estudiante 2: Sí, me gusta tomar el autobús. No, no me gusta tomar el autobús.

	Sí	No
bailar	____	____
cantar	____	____
dibujar	____	____
estudiar	____	____
mirar la televisión	____	____
trabajar	____	____
viajar	____	____

2 **Completar** Complete the conversation with a partner.

Juan

Linda

JUAN ¡Hola, Linda! ¿Qué tal las clases?

LINDA Bien. _____ [tomar] tres clases: química, biología y computación. Y tú, ¿cuántas clases _____ [tomar]?

JUAN _____ [tomar] cuatro: sociología, biología, arte y literatura. Yo _____ [tomar] biología a las cuatro. ¿Y tú?

LINDA Lily, Alberto y yo _____ [tomar] biología a las diez.

JUAN ¿_____ [estudiar] ustedes mucho?

LINDA Sí, porque (*because*) hay muchos exámenes. Alberto y yo_____ [estudiar] dos horas juntos todos los días (*together every day*).

JUAN ¿Lily no_____ [estudiar] con ustedes?

LINDA No, ella _____ [estudiar] con su novio (*boyfriend*), Arturo.

Conversación

3 **Describir** With a partner, describe what the people in the photos are doing.

modelo

Manuela baila.

Manuela

Héctor

1. _____

Ernesto

3. _____

Mariana y Tina

2. _____

Mario y Celia

4. _____

4 **Entrevista** Use these questions to interview a classmate.

1. ¿Qué clases tomas?
2. ¿A qué hora terminan las clases?
3. ¿Qué llevas a la clase de español?
4. ¿Cuántas lenguas hablas?
5. ¿Estudias en la biblioteca o en la residencia estudiantil?
6. ¿Necesitas estudiar hoy para un examen?
7. ¿Miras mucho la televisión?
8. ¿Te gusta viajar? ¿Viajas mucho?
9. ¿Te gusta bailar? ¿Bailas salsa?
10. ¿Cuándo (*when*) descansas?
11. ¿Caminas a la clase de español?
12. ¿Te gusta conversar con tus amigos? ¿Conversan Uds. en español?

Using verbs in Spanish

▸ When two verbs are used together with no change of subject, the second verb is generally in the infinitive.

Deseo hablar con Maite.	**Necesito comprar** lápices.
I want to speak with Maite.	*I need to buy pencils.*

▸ To make a sentence negative, use **no** before the conjugated verb.

Yo **no** miro la televisión.	Ella **no** desea bailar.
I don't watch television.	*She doesn't want to dance.*

▸ Subject pronouns are often omitted because the verb endings indicate who the subject is.

¿Hablas español?

No, no hablo español.

▸ Subject pronouns are occasionally used for clarification.

—¿Qué enseñan **ellos**?	—**Él** enseña arte y **ella** enseña química.
What do they teach?	*He teaches art and she teaches chemistry.*

▸ Sometimes subject pronouns are used for emphasis.

—¿Quién desea trabajar hoy?	—**Yo** no deseo trabajar.
Who wants to work today?	*I don't want to work.*

¡Manos a la obra!

 Provide the present tense forms of the verbs.

1. ¿A qué hora ___regresan___ [regresar] Uds.?
2. Yo _____ [hablar] español.
3. Uds. _____ [desear] trabajar.
4. Elena y yo _____ [estudiar] mucho.
5. Mateo no _____ [bailar] muy bien.
6. Tú no _____ [trabajar] en la cafetería.
7. Yo no deseo _____ [estudiar].
8. Ellos _____ [cantar] muy bien.

2.2 Forming questions in Spanish

▶ You can form a question by raising the pitch of your voice at the end of a sentence. Be sure to use an upside-down question mark (¿) at the beginning of a question and a regular question mark (?) at the end.

¿Dibujas mucho?

Las computadoras son muy interesantes, ¿no?

Statement	Question
Uds. trabajan los sábados.	¿Uds. trabajan los sábados?
You work on Saturdays.	*Do you work on Saturdays?*
Miguel busca un mapa.	¿Miguel busca un mapa?
Miguel is looking for a map.	*Is Miguel looking for a map?*

▶ You can also form a question by putting the subject after the verb. The subject may even be placed at the end of the sentence.

Statement	Question
SUBJECT VERB	**VERB SUBJECT**
Uds. trabajan los sábados.	¿**Trabajan Uds.** los sábados?
You work on Saturdays.	*Do you work on Saturdays?*
SUBJECT VERB	**VERB SUBJECT**
Carlota regresa a las seis.	¿**Regresa** a las seis **Carlota?**
Carlota returns at six.	*Does Carlota return at six?*
SUBJECT VERB	**VERB SUBJECT**
La clase termina a las cinco.	¿**Termina** a las cinco **la clase?**
The class ends at five.	*Does the class end at five?*

▶ Questions can also be formed by adding ¿no? or ¿verdad? at the end of a statement.

Statement	Question
Uds. trabajan los sábados.	Uds. trabajan los sábados, ¿**verdad?**
You work on Saturdays.	*You work on Saturdays, right?*
Carlota regresa a las seis.	Carlota regresa a las seis, ¿**no?**
Carlota returns at six.	*Carlota returns at six, doesn't she?*
La clase termina a las cinco.	La clase termina a las cinco, ¿**no?**
The class ends at five.	*The class ends at five, doesn't it?*

Práctica

1 En el centro estudiantil Use the clues to ask questions about what's going on at the student center.

modelo

Ernesto / estudiar con Sara
¿Estudia Ernesto con Sara? /
¿Estudia con Sara Ernesto?

1. Sandra / hablar con su compañera de cuarto
_____
_____

2. La profesora Soto / buscar una mesa
_____
_____

3. Jaime / preparar la tarea
_____
_____

4. Jorge y Leticia / trabajar en la cafetería
_____
_____

5. Los chicos / escuchar música por la radio
_____
_____

2 Una conversación Irene and Manolo are chatting (quietly!) in the library. Complete their conversation with the appropriate questions.

IRENE _____
MANOLO Bien, gracias. _____
IRENE Muy bien. _____
MANOLO Son las nueve.
IRENE _____
MANOLO Estudio historia.
IRENE _____
MANOLO Porque hay un examen mañana.
IRENE _____
MANOLO Sí, me gusta mucho la clase.
IRENE _____
MANOLO El profesor Padilla enseña la clase.
IRENE _____
MANOLO No, no tomo psicología este semestre.

Conversación

3 Encuesta Change the phrases in the first column into questions and use them to survey two or three classmates. Then report the results of your survey to the class.

Actividades	Nombres
1. Estudiar contabilidad	_____
2. Tomar una clase de sociología	_____
3. Dibujar bien	_____
4. Cantar bien	_____
5. Bailar bien	_____
6. Escuchar jazz	_____
7. Necesitar comprar un reloj	_____
8. Tomar el autobús a la escuela	_____
9. Llevar una mochila a clase	_____
10. Desear viajar a España	_____

4 Entrevista Imagine that you are a reporter for the school newspaper. Use these questions and write three of your own to interview a classmate about student life.

1. ¿Dónde estudias? ¿Cuándo?
2. ¿Quién es tu profesor favorito?
3. ¿Cuántas clases tomas?
4. ¿Necesitas estudiar más (*more*)?
5. ¿Cómo llegas a la escuela?
6. ¿Trabajas? ¿Dónde?
7. ¿Qué programas miras en la televisión?
8. ¿_____?
9. ¿_____?
10. ¿_____?

Spanish interrogative words

▶ The following interrogative words are used to form questions in Spanish.

Interrogative words

¿Cómo?	How?	¿De dónde?	From where?
¿Cuál?, ¿Cuáles?	Which?; which one(s)?	¿Por qué?	Why?
¿Cuándo?	When?	¿Cuánto/a?	How much?
¿Qué?	What?; which?	¿Cuántos/as?	How many?
¿Dónde?	Where?	¿Quién?, ¿Quiénes?	Who?
¿Adónde?	Where (to)?		

▶ Use interrogative words in questions that require more than a simple *yes* or *no* answer. Interrogative words always carry a written accent mark.

¿Cuándo descansan Uds.?
When do you rest?

¿Adónde caminamos?
Where are we walking to?

¿Qué clases tomas?
What classes are you taking?

¿De dónde son ellos?
Where are they from?

▶ In questions that contain interrogative words, the pitch of your voice falls at the end of the sentence.

¿Cómo llegas a la escuela?
How do you get to school?

¿Por qué necesitas estudiar?
Why do you need to study?

¡Manos a la obra!

Make questions out of these statements. Use intonation in the first column and **¿no?** in the second.

Statement	Intonation	¿no?
1. Hablas inglés.	¿Hablas inglés?	Hablas inglés, ¿no?
2. Trabajamos mañana.	_____	_____
3. Uds. desean bailar.	_____	_____
4. Raúl estudia mucho.	_____	_____
5. Enseño a las nueve.	_____	_____
6. Luz mira la televisión.	_____	_____
7. Los chicos descansan.	_____	_____
8. Él prepara la prueba.	_____	_____
9. Tomamos el autobús.	_____	_____
10. Necesito una pluma.	_____	_____

2.3 The present tense of estar

▸ In Lesson 1, you learned how to conjugate and use the verb **ser** (*to be*). You will now learn a second verb which means *to be*, the verb **estar**.

▸ Although **estar** ends in **–ar**, it does not follow the pattern of regular **–ar** verbs. The **yo** form (**estoy**) is irregular. Also, all forms but the **yo** and **nosotros/as** forms have an accented **á**. As you will see, **ser** and **estar** are used in different ways.

estar (to be)

yo	estoy	*I am*
tú	estás	*you (fam.) are*
Ud./él/ella	está	*you (form.) are; he/she is*
nosotros/as	estamos	*we are*
vosotros/as	estáis	*you (fam.) are*
Uds./ellos/ellas	están	*you (form.)/they are*

Hola, Ricardo. Aquí estamos en la Mitad del Mundo.

Hoy estoy con estudiantes de la universidad.

Uses of ser and estar

Uses of estar	Uses of ser
LOCATION	**IDENTITY**
Estoy en el Ecuador.	Hola, soy Maite.
I am in Ecuador.	*Hello, I'm Maite.*
Inés está al lado de Javier.	
Inés is next to Javier.	**OCCUPATION**
	Soy estudiante.
HEALTH	*I'm a student.*
Álex está enfermo hoy.	
Álex is sick today.	**ORIGINS**
	¿Eres de España?
	Are you from Spain?
WELL-BEING	Sí, soy de España.
¿Cómo estás, Maite?	*Yes, I'm from Spain.*
How are you, Maite?	
Estoy muy bien, gracias.	**TIME-TELLING**
I'm very well, thank you.	Son las cuatro.
	It's four o'clock.

Práctica

1 **Completar** Complete this phone conversation between Daniela and her mother with the correct forms of **ser** or **estar**.

MAMÁ Hola, Daniela. ¿Cómo _____?

DANIELA Hola, mamá. _____ bien. ¿Dónde _____ papá? ¡Ya (*already*) _____ las ocho de la noche!

MAMÁ No _____ aquí. _____ en la oficina.

DANIELA Y Andrés y Margarita, ¿dónde _____ ellos?

MAMÁ _____ en el restaurante García con Martín.

DANIELA ¿Quién _____ Martín?

MAMÁ _____ un compañero de clase. _____ de México.

DANIELA Y el restaurante García, ¿dónde _____?

MAMÁ _____ cerca de la Plaza Mayor, en San Modesto.

DANIELA Gracias, mamá. Voy (*I'm going*) al restaurante. ¡Hasta pronto!

2 **¿Dónde está... ?** You are having trouble finding several things in the school bookstore. Look at the drawing and ask the clerk (your partner) where the items are located.

modelo

Estudiante 1: ¿Dónde están las mochilas?
Estudiante 2: Las mochilas están debajo de las computadoras.

Conversación

3 **¿Dónde estás... ?** Find out where your partner is at these times.

1. ¿Dónde estás los viernes al mediodía?
2. ¿Dónde estás los miércoles a las nueve y cuarto de la mañana?
3. ¿Dónde estás los lunes a las once y diez de la mañana?
4. ¿Dónde estás los jueves a las doce y media de la tarde?
5. ¿Dónde estás los viernes a las dos y veinticinco de la tarde?
6. ¿Dónde estás los martes a las cuatro menos diez de la tarde?
7. ¿Dónde estás los jueves a las seis menos cuarto de la tarde?
8. ¿Dónde estás los miércoles a las ocho y veinte de la noche?

4 **La Ciudad Universitaria** You and your partner are at the **Facultad de Bellas Artes** (School of Fine Arts). Take turns asking each other where other buildings on the campus map are located.

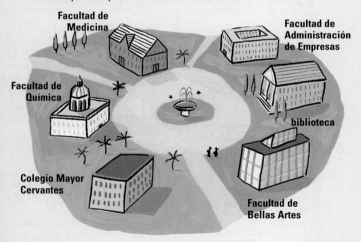

Facultad de Medicina
Facultad de Administración de Empresas
Facultad de Química
biblioteca
Colegio Mayor Cervantes
Facultad de Bellas Artes

1. ¿Está lejos la biblioteca de la Facultad (school) de Bellas Artes?
2. ¿Dónde está la Facultad de Medicina?
3. ¿Está la Facultad de Administración de Empresas a la derecha de la biblioteca?
4. ¿Dónde está el Colegio Mayor Cervantes?
5. ¿Está la Facultad de Administración de Empresas detrás del Colegio Mayor Cervantes?
6. ¿Dónde está la Facultad de Química?

Estar with prepositions of locations

Prepositions of location			
al lado de	next to; beside	delante de	in front of
a la derecha de	to the right of	detrás de	behind
a la izquierda de	to the left of	encima de	on top of
en	in; on; at	entre	between; among
cerca de	near	lejos de	far from
con	with	sobre	on; over
debajo de	below; under		

¡A ver! La señorita que está cerca de la ventana...

Aquí estoy con cuatro estudiantes de la universidad... ¡Qué aventura!

▶ **Estar** is often used with certain prepositions to describe the location of a person or an object.

La cafetería está **al lado de** la biblioteca.
The cafeteria is beside the library.

El estadio no está **lejos de** la librería.
The stadium isn't far from the bookstore.

Los libros están **encima del** escritorio.
The books are on top of the desk.

Estamos **entre** amigos.
We are among friends.

El laboratorio está **cerca de** la clase.
The lab is near the classroom.

Juan está **en** la biblioteca.
Juan is at the library.

Maribel está **delante de** José.
Maribel is in front of José.

El libro está **sobre** la mesa.
The book is on the table.

¡Manos a la obra!

Provide the present tense forms of **estar**.

1. Uds. __están__ en la clase.
2. José _____ en la biblioteca.
3. Yo _____ en el estadio.
4. Nosotras _____ en la cafetería.
5. Tú _____ en el laboratorio.
6. Elena _____ en la librería.
7. Ellas _____ en la clase.
8. Ana y yo _____ en la clase.
9. Ud. _____ en la biblioteca.
10. Javier y Maribel _____ en el estadio.
11. Nosotros _____ en la clase.
12. Yo _____ en el laboratorio.
13. Carmen y María _____ en la librería.
14. Tú _____ en la clase.

2.4 Numbers 31–100

Numbers 31–100

31 treinta y uno	37 treinta y siete	50 cincuenta
32 treinta y dos	38 treinta y ocho	60 sesenta
33 treinta y tres	39 treinta y nueve	70 setenta
34 treinta y cuatro	40 cuarenta	80 ochenta
35 treinta y cinco	41 cuarenta y uno	90 noventa
36 treinta y seis	42 cuarenta y dos	100 cien, ciento

¿En qué clase hay más chicas?

En la de sociología... casi un ochenta y cinco por ciento.

▶ The word **y** is used in most numbers from **31** through **99**.

Hay **ochenta y cinco** exámenes.
There are eighty-five exams.

Hay **cuarenta y dos** estudiantes.
There are forty-two students.

▶ With numbers that end in **uno** (31, 41, etc.), **uno** becomes **un** before a masculine noun and **una** before a feminine noun.

Hay **treinta y un** chicos.
There are thirty-one guys.

Hay **treinta y una** chicas.
There are thirty-one girls.

▶ **Cien** is used before nouns and in counting. The words **un**, **una**, and **uno** are never used before **cien** in Spanish. **Ciento** is used for numbers over one hundred.

—¿Cuántos libros hay?
How many books are there?

—Hay **cien** libros.
There are one hundred books.

—¿Cuántas sillas hay?
How many chairs are there?

—Hay **ciento diez** sillas.
There are one hundred ten chairs.

¡Manos a la obra!

Provide the word form of each number.

1. **56** cincuenta y seis
2. **31** _____
3. **84** _____
4. **99** _____
5. **43** _____
6. **68** _____
7. **72** _____
8. **35** _____
9. **87** _____
10. **59** _____
11. **100** _____
12. **61** _____
13. **96** _____
14. **74** _____
15. **42** _____

Práctica

1 **Baloncesto** Provide these basketball scores in Spanish.

OHIO STATE 85 MICHIGAN 74

DUKE 78 VIRGINIA 64

1. _____   4. _____

FLORIDA 100 FLORIDA STATE 92

KENTUCKY 63 TENNESSEE 57

2. _____   5. _____

STANFORD 58 UCLA 49

TEXAS 91 OKLAHOMA 86

3. _____   6. _____

2 **Números de teléfono** You are a telephone operator in Spain. Give the appropriate phone numbers and addresses when callers ask for them.

122   **MORALES – NAYA**

Morales Ballesteros, José Venerable Centenares, 22 ......(91) 944-6662
Morales Benito, Francisco Plaza Ahorro, 16 ....(91) 773-1216
Morales Borrego, Flora Mayor, 51 ....(91) 634-3211
Morales Calvo, Emilio Villafuerte, 49 ....(91) 472-2350
Morales Campos, María Josefa Toledo, 35 ....(91) 419-7660
Morales Cid, Pedro Rosal, 98 ....(91) 773-1382
Morales Conde, Ángel Alameda, 67 ....(91) 944-3915
Morales Crespo, José Pascual Fernando de la Peña, 13 ...(91) 634-7148
Morales de la Iglesia, Juliana Buenavista, 80 ....(91) 834-5238
Morales Fraile, María Rosa Plaza March, 74 ....(91) 834-3371

modelo

Estudiante 1: ¿Cuál es el número de teléfono de José Morales Ballesteros, por favor?

Estudiante 2: Es el noventa y uno, noventa y cuatro, cuatro, sesenta y seis, sesenta y dos.

Conversación *communication*

3 Precios (*prices*) With a partner, take turns asking how much the items in the ad cost.

modelo

Estudiante 1: Deseo comprar papel. ¿Cuánto cuesta (*how much does it cost*)?
Estudiante 2: Un paquete cuesta (*costs*) cuatro dólares y cuarenta y un centavos.

4 Entrevista Find out the telephone numbers and e-mail addresses of four classmates.

modelo

Estudiante 1: ¿Cuál es tu (*your*) número de teléfono?
Estudiante 2: Es el 6-35-19-51.
Estudiante 1: ¿Y tu dirección de correo electrónico (*e-mail address*)?
Estudiante 2: Es jota-Smith-arroba (*at*)-pe-ele-punto-e-de-u (*jsmith@pl.edu*).

Español en vivo

Below is the table of contents from a Latin American magazine.

CONTENIDO

59 Cuestionario
¿Dónde buscas el amor?

62 Encuesta
Entrevistamos a 100 estudiantes de la universidad para preguntarles cuáles son los cursos más importantes para su futuro profesional.

74 Rock en Español
Conversamos con la cantante mexicana Paulina Rubio sobre su nuevo álbum.

Identificar

Identify in Spanish the numbers used in the above document.

Preguntas

1. ¿Dónde buscas información sobre (*about*) tu futuro?
2. ¿En qué página está la información sobre la familia?
3. ¿Con quién conversan en la página 90?

Ampliación

1 Escuchar

A Listen to Armando and Julia's conversation. Then list the classes each person is taking.

 TIP Listen for cognates. Cognates are words that have similar spellings and meanings in two or more languages. Listening for cognates will help you increase your comprehension.

Armando

1. _____
2. _____
3. _____
4. _____
5. _____

Julia

1. _____
2. _____
3. _____
4. _____
5. _____

B ¿Cuántas clases toman Armando y Julia? ¿Cuántas clases tomas tú? ¿Qué clases te gustan y qué clases no te gustan?

2 Conversar

Greet a classmate, find out how he or she is, and get to know your classmate better by asking these questions.

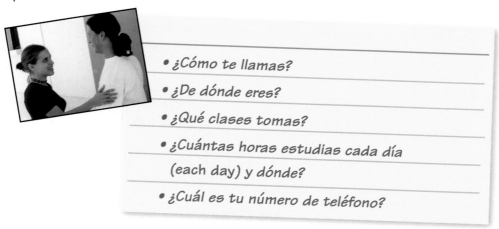

- *¿Cómo te llamas?*
- *¿De dónde eres?*
- *¿Qué clases tomas?*
- *¿Cuántas horas estudias cada día (each day) y dónde?*
- *¿Cuál es tu número de teléfono?*

recursos

Textbook CD Lección 2	WB pp. 11-18	LM pp. 9-12	Lab CD Lección 2	ICD-ROM Lección 2	vistahigher learning.com

R

Ampliación

③ Escribir

Write a description of yourself to post on a website in order to meet Spanish-speaking people.

 TIP Brainstorm. Spend ten to fifteen minutes writing down ideas about the topic you are going to write about. The more ideas you write down, the more you'll have to choose from later when you start to organize your thoughts.

Organízalo	Make a list of things you would like people to know about you, including your name, your major, where you go to school, what you're studying, where you work, and your likes and dislikes.
Escríbelo	Using the material you have compiled, write the first draft of your description.
Corrígelo	Exchange papers with a classmate and comment on the organization, style, and grammatical correctness of each other's work. Then revise your first draft, keeping your classmate's comments in mind.
Compártelo	Read your descriptions aloud in small groups. Point out the three best features of each description.

④ Un paso más

Create a poster that will encourage students to study in a university in a Spanish-speaking country. The poster might include these elements:

- A simple title
- Photos of university locations
- A campus map
- A short summary of the university's programs
- Photos of the town where the university is located.

 **En Internet**

Investiga estos temas en el sitio vistahigherlearning.com.

- Las universidades en España
- Las universidades en América Latina y en el Caribe

UNIVERSIDAD DE BARCELONA

El futuro en tus manos

Antes de leer

Examina el texto

Recognizing the format of a document can help you to predict its content. For instance, invitations and classified ads follow an easily identifiable format, which usually gives you a general idea of the information they contain. Glance at the document on this page and identify it based on its format.

Cognados

With a classmate, make a list of cognates in the text and guess their English meanings. What do the cognates reveal about the content of the document?

Piénsalo

If you guessed that this text is a brochure from a university, you are correct. You can now infer that the document contains information on courses, departments, and the university campus.

UAM

LA MEJOR UNIVERSIDAD DE EUROPA
Universidad Autónoma de Madrid

En el campus de la UAM hay ocho facultades:

- Ciencias
- Derecho
- Medicina
- Psicología
- Filosofía y Letras
- Ciencias Económicas y Empresariales
- Escuela Técnica Superior de Computación
- Facultad de Formación de Profesorado y Educación

Toma cursos de:

- Antropología Aplicada ·
Microbiología · Contabilidad
· Derecho Privado · Ecología
· Economía General ·
Filosofía Antigua · Física
General · Geografía ·
Historia Contemporánea ·
Computación · Literatura
Española · Matemáticas ·
Psicología Social · Química ·
Sociología ·

Después de leer

¿Comprendiste?

Indicate whether each statement is **cierto** (*true*) or **falso** (*false*).

Cierto	Falso	
———	———	1. La Universidad Autónoma de Madrid está en Europa.
———	———	2. En la UAM hay diez facultades.
———	———	3. Filosofía y Letras es un curso.
———	———	4. Es posible estudiar microbiología en la UAM.
———	———	5. Hay cursos de literatura china en la UAM.
———	———	6. Hay una facultad de psicología en la UAM.
———	———	7. En la UAM, las clases se inician en septiembre.
———	———	8. La UAM está en la carretera de Cantoblanco.

Preguntas

1. ¿Hay clases de contabilidad en la UAM?

_____

2. ¿Es posible estudiar medicina en la UAM?

_____

3. ¿En qué facultad hay clases de economía general?

_____

4. ¿En qué facultad hay clases de microbiología?

_____

5. ¿En qué facultad hay clases de literatura española?

_____

Coméntalo

Look at the ad of the Universidad Autónoma de Madrid and identify the courses taught there. Does your university offer the same courses? Are you taking any of those courses? Based on this ad, would you be interested in studying at the UAM? Why or why not?

mejor	*best*
derecho	*law*
carretera	*highway*

La clase y la universidad

el borrador	eraser
la clase	class
el/la compañero/a	classmate
de clase	
de cuarto	roommate
el escritorio	desk
el/la estudiante	student
el libro	book
el mapa	map
la mesa	table
el papel	paper
la pizarra	blackboard
la pluma	pen
el/la profesor(a)	professor; teacher
la puerta	door
el reloj	clock; watch
la silla	chair
la tiza	chalk
la ventana	window
la biblioteca	library
la cafetería	cafeteria
el estadio	stadium
el laboratorio	laboratory
la librería	bookstore
la residencia	dormitory
estudiantil	
la universidad	university
el curso	course
el examen	test; exam
el horario	schedule
la prueba	test; quiz
el semestre	semester
la tarea	homework
el trimestre	trimester; quarter

Verbos

bailar	to dance
buscar	to look for
caminar	to walk
cantar	to sing
comprar	to buy
contestar	to answer
conversar	to talk; to chat
descansar	to rest
desear	to want; to wish
dibujar	to draw
enseñar	to teach
escuchar	to listen
esperar	to wait (for); to hope
estar	to be
estudiar	to study
explicar	to explain
hablar	to talk; to speak
llegar	to arrive
llevar	to carry
mirar	to watch; to look (at)
necesitar	to need
practicar	to practice
preguntar	to ask (a question)
preparar	to prepare
regresar	to return
terminar	to end; to finish
tomar	to take; to drink
trabajar	to work
viajar	to travel

Los cursos

la administración de empresas	business administration
el arte	art
la biología	biology
la computación	computer science
la contabilidad	accounting
el español	Spanish
la física	physics
la geografía	geography
la historia	history
el inglés	English
las lenguas extranjeras	foreign languages
las matemáticas	mathematics
el periodismo	journalism
la psicología	psychology
la química	chemistry
la sociología	sociology

Los días de la semana	See page 27.
Expresiones útiles	See page 33.
Interrogative Words	See page 39.
Prepositions of location	See page 41.
Numbers 31-100	See page 42.

Palabras adicionales

¿dónde?	where?
¿cuál?, ¿cuáles?	which; which ones?
¿por qué?	why?
porque	because

recursos

| R | Lab CD Lección 2 | LM p. 12 |

AVENTURAS EN LOS PAÍSES HISPANOS

Todos los años *(every year)*, en el mes de junio, Nueva York organiza un gran desfile *(great parade)* en honor a los puertorriqueños.

ESTADOS UNIDOS

PAÍS DE HABLA ESPAÑOLA

Estados Unidos

Población de origen hispano: 34.540.000

País de origen de hispanos en EE.UU:

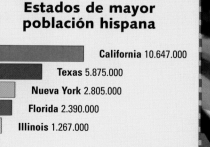

- 6,6% otros
- 9,6% Puerto Rico
- 4,3% Cuba
- 14,3% Centroamérica y Sudamérica
- 65,2% México

SOURCE: U.S. Census Bureau

Estados de mayor población hispana

- **California** 10.647.000
- **Texas** 5.875.000
- **Nueva York** 2.805.000
- **Florida** 2.390.000
- **Illinois** 1.267.000

SOURCE: U.S. Census Bureau

Ciudades de mayor población hispana

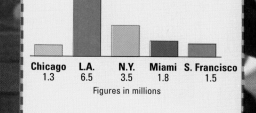

Chicago	L.A.	N.Y.	Miami	S. Francisco
1.3	6.5	3.5	1.8	1.5

Figures in millions

La Pequeña Habana

En Miami, el barrio conocido como *(neighborhood known as)* La Pequeña Habana fue establecido *(was established)* por cubanos que escaparon de *(escaped)* la dictadura de Fidel Castro.

CANADÁ

San Francisco

Los Ángeles

Las Vegas

San Diego

MÉXICO

Latinos famosos

Los estadounidenses de origen hispanoamericano contribuyen *(contribute)* en todos los niveles *(at all levels)* a la cultura y a la economía de los Estados Unidos.

Martin Sheen, actor, de origen salvadoreño

Ellen Ochoa, astronauta, de origen mexicano

Rosie Pérez, actriz, de origen puertorriqueño

Geraldo Rivera, periodista, de origen puertorriqueño

Historia

Influencia hispánica

La influencia de la cultura española es visible a través *(throughout)* de los Estados Unidos: desde California hasta la Florida.

Palacio de los Gobernadores (1610), Santa Fé, Nuevo México

Castillo de San Marcos (1565), San Agustín, Florida

Misión de San Xavier del Bac (1692), Tucson, Arizona

Comida

La comida mexicana

En casi todas las ciudades *(almost all cities)* de los Estados Unidos hay restaurantes mexicanos. Hoy día, los tacos y las quesadillas son tan populares como *(are as popular as)* las hamburguesas y las papas fritas *(french fries)*.

¿Qué aprendiste?

1 ¿Cierto o falso? Indicate whether the following statements are true or false, based on what you've learned about Latinos in the USA.

Cierto	Falso	
_____	_____	1. Los mexicanos son el grupo hispano más grande *(biggest)* de los EE.UU.
_____	_____	2. En Florida no hay muchas personas de origen hispano.
_____	_____	3. En Los Ángeles hay más de *(more than)* seis millones de latinos.
_____	_____	4. La Pequeña Habana está en la isla de Cuba.
_____	_____	5. Martin Sheen es un policía en Los Ángeles.
_____	_____	6. Gerardo Rivera es de origen hispano.
_____	_____	7. El Castillo de San Marcos está en Texas.
_____	_____	8. En Nuevo México hay muchos edificios antiguos *(old buildings)* de origen español.
_____	_____	9. Muchos puertorriqueños viven *(live)* en Nueva York.
_____	_____	10. A los estadounidenses, no les gustan los tacos.

2 Preguntas Answer the following questions.

1. ¿Hay muchos hispanos en tu *(your)* comunidad? ¿De dónde son?
2. ¿Quién es Ellen Ochoa?
3. ¿Dónde está el Palacio de Los Gobernadores?
4. ¿En qué ciudades de los Estados Unidos hay más habitantes hispanos?
5. ¿Dónde está la Pequeña Habana?
6. ¿Te gustan los restaurantes mexicanos? ¿Por qué?

En Internet

Busca más información sobre estos temas en el sitio vistahigherlearning.com. Presenta la información a tus compañeros/as de clase.

- El Día de los puertorriqueños
- La Pequeña Habana
- Rosie Pérez
- La ciudad de San Agustín en la Florida
- Las misiones españolas en California

3 La familia

Communicative Goals

You will learn how to:
- talk about your family
- describe people
- express ownership

RECURSOS

These student supplements provide additional practice:
- Textbook Audio CD
- Workbook/Video Manual (WB/VM)
- Lab Manual (LM)
- WB/VM/LM Answer Key
- Lab Audio CDs
- Video CD-ROM
- Interactive CD-ROM

LA FAMILIA

LA FAMILIA

el/la esposo/a *husband/wife*

el/la hermanastro/a *stepbrother/stepsister*

el/la hermano/a *brother/sister*

el/la hijastro/a *stepson/stepdaughter*

la madrastra *stepmother*

el/la medio/a hermano/a *half-brother/ half-sister*

el padrastro *stepfather*

los padres *parents*

el abuelo
grandfather

la abuela
grandmother

el padre
father

la madre
mother

LA FAMILIA EXTENDIDA

el/la cuñado/a *brother-in-law/sister-in-law*

el/la nieto/a *grandson/granddaughter*

la nuera *daughter-in-law*

los parientes *relatives*

el/la primo/a *cousin*

el/la sobrino/a *nephew/niece*

el/la suegro/a *father-in-law/mother-in-law*

el/la tío/a *uncle/aunt*

el yerno *son-in-law*

los hijos
sons; children

la hija
daughter

recursos

R	Textbook CD Lección 3	WB pp. 21-22	LM p. 13	Lab CD Lección 3	ICD-ROM Lección 3

el artista
artist

LAS PROFESIONES

el/la ingeniero/a *engineer*
el/la periodista *journalist*
el/la programador(a) *computer programmer*

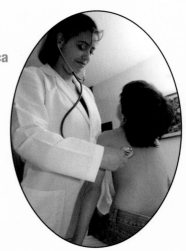

la médica
doctor

OTRAS PALABRAS

el/la amigo/a *friend*
la gente *people*
el/la muchacho/a *boy/girl*
la persona *person*

mi *my (sing.)*
mis *my (pl.)*

el niño
boy; child

la niña
girl

la novia
girlfriend

el novio
boyfriend

A escuchar

1 **Escuchar** Find Luisa Moya Sánchez on the family tree. Then listen to her statements and indicate whether they are **cierto** (*true*) or **falso** (*false*), based on her family tree.

Eduardo Sánchez Moreno

Sara García de Sánchez

Javier Moya Galán

Irene Sánchez de Moya

Adela Sánchez García

Pilar Sánchez de Donoso

Andrés Donoso Álvarez

Luisa Moya Sánchez

Miguel Moya Sánchez

Elena Donoso Sánchez

	Cierto	Falso		Cierto	Falso
1.	_____	_____	6.	_____	_____
2.	_____	_____	7.	_____	_____
3.	_____	_____	8.	_____	_____
4.	_____	_____	9.	_____	_____
5.	_____	_____	10.	_____	_____

2 **Emparejar** You will hear some definitions of vocabulary words. Provide the letter of the phrase that matches each definition.

1. a. Son mis padres.   b. Son mis abuelos.   c. Son mis suegros.
2. a. Es mi yerno.   b. Es mi sobrino.   c. Es mi cuñado.
3. a. Es un ingeniero.   b. Es una programadora.   c. Es una artista.
4. a. Es mi prima.   b. Es mi sobrina.   c. Es mi abuela.
5. a. Son mis nietos.   b. Son mis primos.   c. Son mis abuelos.
6. a. Es mi nieto.   b. Es mi tío.   c. Es mi hermano.

recursos

R
Textbook CD
Lección 3

A practicar

3 **Completar** Complete these sentences with the correct words.

1. Mi madre y mi padre son mis _____.
2. El padre de mi madre es mi _____.
3. Yo soy el _____ del hijo de mi hermana.
4. La esposa de mi hijo es mi _____.
5. Yo soy el _____ de los padres de mi esposa.
6. La hija de mi hermana es mi _____.
7. Mi hijo es el _____ de mi padre.
8. El esposo de mi hermana es mi _____.

4 **Profesiones** Complete the description of each photo.

1. Juanita Fuertes es

_____.

2. Héctor Ibarra es

_____.

3. Alberto Díaz es

_____.

4. Elena Vargas Soto es

_____.

5. Carlota López es

_____.

6. Irene González es

_____.

A conversar

5 **La familia Vargas** With a classmate, identify the members in the famiy tree by asking questions about how each family member is related to Graciela Vargas García.

modelo
Estudiante 1: ¿Quién es Beatriz Pardo de Vargas?
Estudiante 2: Es la abuela de Graciela.

David Vargas Olmedo
de Quito

Beatriz Pardo de Vargas
de Ibarra

Carlos Antonio López Ríos
de Cuenca

Lupe Vargas de López
de Quito

Juan Vargas Pardo
de Quito

María Susana García de Vargas
de Guayaquil

Ernesto López Vargas
de Loja

Ramón Vargas García
de Machala

Graciela Vargas García
de Machala

Now take turns asking each other these questions.

1. ¿Cómo se llama el tío de Graciela?
2. ¿De dónde es María Susana?
3. ¿Cómo se llama la hermana de Juan?
4. ¿De dónde es el yerno de David y Beatriz?
5. ¿Cómo se llama el sobrino de Lupe?
6. ¿De dónde es la abuela de Ernesto?

6 **¿Y tú?** With a classmate, take turns asking each other the following questions.

1. ¿Cuántas personas hay en tu familia?
2. ¿Cómo se llaman tus padres? ¿De dónde son?
3. ¿Cuántos hermanos tienes? ¿Cómo se llaman?
4. ¿Cuántos primos tienes? ¿Cuántos son niños y cuántos son adultos?
5. ¿Eres tío/a? ¿Cómo se llaman tus sobrinos/as? ¿Dónde estudian o trabajan?
6. ¿Tienes novio/a? ¿Tienes esposo/a? ¿Cómo se llama?

tengo *I have*	**tus** *your (fam., pl.)*
tienes *you (fam.) have*	**tu** *your (fam., sing.)*

🎧 Pronunciación

Diphthongs and linking

herma**no**   **ni**ñ**a**   **cu**ñ**ado**

In Spanish, **a**, **e**, and **o** are considered strong vowels. The weak vowels are **i** and **u**.

rui**do**   **par**i**entes**   **per**i**odista**

A diphthong is a combination of two weak vowels or of a strong vowel and a weak vowel.
Diphthongs are pronounced as a single syllable.

la abuela   **mi hijo**   **una clase excelente**

Two identical vowel sounds that appear together are pronounced like one long vowel.

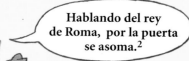

con Natalia   **sus sobrinos**   **las sillas**

Two identical consonants together sound like a single consonant.

es ingeniera   **mis abuelos**   **sus hijos**

A consonant at the end of a word is linked with the vowel at the beginning of the next word.

mi hermano   **su esposa**   **nuestro amigo**

A vowel at the end of a word is linked with the vowel at the beginning of the next word.

Práctica Say these words aloud, focusing on the diphthongs.

1. historia	5. residencia	9. lenguas
2. nieto	6. prueba	10. estudiar
3. parientes	7. puerta	11. izquierda
4. novia	8. ciencias	12. ecuatoriano

Oraciones Read these sentences aloud to practice diphthongs and linking words.

1. Hola. Me llamo Anita Amaral. Soy del Ecuador.
2. Somos seis en mi familia.
3. Tengo dos hermanos y una hermana.
4. Mi papá es del Ecuador y mi mamá es de España.

Refranes Read these sayings aloud to practice diphthongs and linking sounds.

Cuando una puerta se cierra, otra se abre.[1]

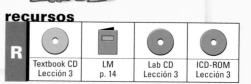

Hablando del rey de Roma, por la puerta se asoma.[2]

1 When one door closes, another opens.
2 Speak of the devil and he will appear.

recursos

R	Textbook CD Lección 3	LM p. 14	Lab CD Lección 3	ICD-ROM Lección 3

¿Es grande tu familia?

Los viajeros hablan de sus familias en el autobús.

MAITE Inés, ¿tienes una familia grande?

INÉS Pues, sí... mis papás, mis abuelos, cuatro hermanas y muchos tíos y primos.

INÉS Sólo tengo un hermano mayor, Pablo. Su esposa, Francesca, es médica. No es ecuatoriana, es italiana. Sus papás viven en Roma, creo. Vienen de visita cada año. Ah... y Pablo es periodista.

MAITE ¡Qué interesante!

INÉS ¿Y tú, Javier? ¿Tienes hermanos?

JAVIER No, pero aquí tengo unas fotos de mi familia.

INÉS ¡Ah! ¡Qué bien! ¡A ver!

INÉS ¿Y cómo es él?

JAVIER Es muy simpático. Él es viejo, pero es un hombre muy trabajador.

MAITE Oye, Javier, ¿qué dibujas?

JAVIER ¿Eh? ¿Quién? ¿Yo? ¡Nada!

MAITE ¡Venga! ¡No seas tonto!

MAITE Jaaavieeer... Oye, pero ¡qué bien dibujas!

JAVIER Este... pues...¡Sí! ¡Gracias!

recursos

| R | Video/VCD-ROM Lección 3 | VM pp. 173-174 | ICD-ROM Lección 3 |

Personajes

DON FRANCISCO **JAVIER** **INÉS** **ÁLEX** **MAITE**

4

JAVIER ¡Aquí están!

INÉS ¡Qué alto es tu papá! Y tu mamá, ¡qué bonita!

5

JAVIER Mira, aquí estoy yo. Y éste es mi abuelo. Es el padre de mi mamá.

INÉS ¿Cuántos años tiene tu abuelo?

JAVIER Noventa y dos.

9

MAITE Álex, mira, ¿te gusta?

ÁLEX Sí, mucho. ¡Es muy bonito!

10

DON FRANCISCO Epa, ¿qué pasa con Inés y Javier?

Talking about your family

¿Tienes una familia grande?
Do you have a large family?

Sí… mis papás, mis abuelos, cuatro hermanas y muchos tíos.
Yes, my parents, my grandparents, four sisters, and many (aunts and) uncles.

Sólo tengo un hermano mayor/menor.
I only have one older/younger brother.

¿Tienes hermanos?
Do you have siblings?

No, soy hijo único.
No, I'm an only (male) child.

Su esposa, Francesca, es médica.
His wife, Francesca, is a doctor.

No es ecuatoriana, es italiana.
She's not Ecuadorian; she's Italian.

Pablo es periodista.
Pablo is a journalist.

Es el padre de mi mamá.
He is my mother's father.

Describing people

¡Qué alto es tu papá!
Your father is so tall!

Y tu mamá, ¡qué bonita!
And your mother, how pretty!

¿Cómo es tu abuelo?
What is your grandfather like?

Es simpático.
He's nice.

Es viejo.
He's old.

Es un hombre muy trabajador.
He's a very hard-working man.

Saying how old people are

¿Cuántos años tienes?
How old are you?

¿Cuántos años tiene tu abuelo?
How old is your grandfather?

Noventa y dos.
Ninety-two.

¿Qué piensas?

1 **¿Cierto o falso?** Indicate whether each sentence is **cierto** or **falso.** Correct the false statements.

Cierto   Falso

_____ _____   1. Inés tiene una familia grande.

_____

_____ _____   2. Pablo, el hermano de Inés, es médico.

_____

_____ _____   3. La cuñada de Inés es italiana.

_____

_____ _____   4. Javier no tiene hermanos.

_____

_____ _____   5. El abuelo de Javier es muy perezoso (*lazy*).

_____

_____ _____   6. Javier habla del padre de su (*his*) padre.

_____

2 **Adivinar** Read these sentences and guess which video character is being described. Each name is used twice.

JAVIER   **INÉS**   **MAITE**

1. Tiene cuatro hermanas y muchos tíos y primos. _____
2. Su abuelo tiene noventa y dos años, pero es muy trabajador. _____
3. Ella dice que (*says that*) Javier dibuja muy bien. _____
4. Ella tiene muchas preguntas para (*for*) sus amigos. _____
5. Su mamá es muy bonita. _____
6. Su cuñada es médica. _____

3 **Sus familias** With a partner, use these questions to talk about your families.

• ¿Es grande o pequeña (*small*) tu (*your*) familia? ¿Cuántas personas hay en tu familia?

• ¿Tienes muchos tíos y primos? ¿Dónde viven?

• ¿Tienes un(a) tío/a o un(a) primo/a favorito/a? ¿Cómo es?

Exploración
La familia en el mundo hispano

En los países hispanos las personas usan doble apellido (*double last name*): uno del padre y el otro (*other*) de la madre. En la foto está Juan Antonio Moreno López con su esposa, María Eugenia Rojas de Moreno, y sus hijos Emilio Moreno Rojas y Ana Moreno Rojas.

En muchas familias hispanas, los abuelos y los tíos viven (*live*) en la misma casa (*same house*). En la foto, aparecen Osvaldo Marín Donoso y su (*his*) esposa Mónica, con sus (*their*) dos hijas, su yerno y sus cuatro nietos.

Muchos estudiantes universitarios viven (*live*) con sus padres durante sus estudios (*during their studies*). José Miguel López Betancourt, en la foto, asiste (*attends*) a la Universidad de Caracas y vive en casa con sus padres José Manuel y Laura.

Estadísticas de la familia

Tamaño medio (*average size*) de la familia

Colombia 5.2

México 5.0

Argentina 3.7

Uruguay 3.3

España 2.9

Estados Unidos 2.6

SOURCE: UN Secretariat

Coméntalo

With a classmate, discuss these questions.

- ¿Te gustaría vivir (*would you like to live*) con tu familia extendida? ¿Por qué sí o por qué no? (Sí, me gustaría… / No, no me gustaría…)

- ¿Te gustaría vivir con tus padres hasta (*until*) tu graduación de la universidad? ¿Por qué sí o por qué no?

recursos

R

vistahigher
learning.com

3.1 Descriptive adjectives

▶ Descriptive adjectives describe nouns. In Spanish, most adjectives agree in gender and number with the nouns or pronouns they describe.

▶ Adjectives that end in **–o** and **–or** have four forms.

Masculine	Feminine
el chico alto	la chica alta
los chicos altos	las chicas altas
el hombre trabajador	la mujer trabajadora
los hombres trabajadores	las mujeres trabajadoras

▶ Adjectives that end in **–e** or a consonant have the same masculine and feminine forms.

Masculine	Feminine
el chico inteligente	la chica inteligente
los chicos inteligentes	las chicas inteligentes
el chico joven	la chica joven
los chicos jóvenes	las chicas jóvenes

▶ Adjectives that refer to nouns of different genders use the masculine plural form.

Paco es alto. Ana es alta. → Paco y Ana son altos.

Common adjectives

alto/a	tall	gordo/a	fat	moreno/a	dark-haired
antipático/a	unpleasant	grande	large; great	mucho/a	much; many; a lot of
bajo/a	short	guapo/a	handsome		
bonito/a	pretty	importante	important	pelirrojo/a	red-haired
bueno/a	good	inteligente	intelligent	pequeño/a	small
delgado/a	thin; slender	interesante	interesting	rubio/a	blond
difícil	hard; difficult	joven	young	simpático/a	nice; likeable
fácil	easy	malo/a	bad	tonto/a	silly; foolish
feo/a	ugly	mismo/a	same	trabajador(a)	hard-working
				viejo/a	old

Adjectives of nationality

▶ Adjectives of nationality are formed like other descriptive adjectives. Note that adjectives of nationality that end in a consonant add **–a** to form the feminine.

Masculine	Feminine
Toño es mexicano.	Gloria es mexicana.
Ellos son mexicanos.	Ellas son mexicanas.
Héctor es español.	Sara es española.
Ellos son españoles.	Ellas son españolas.

Práctica

1 **Emparejar** Read the descriptions and match them with the photos.

1. __ Mateo es moreno.
2. __ Henri es francés.
3. __ Luisa es rubia.
4. __ Andrés hace el (*acts*) tonto.
5. __ Tanya es canadiense.
6. __ Raquel es pelirroja.

2 **Completar** Look at the photo of Amanda's family and imagine their personalities. Complete the sentences with appropriate adjectives.

1. Mi familia es _____.
2. Mis abuelos son _____. Mi abuelo es _____ y mi abuela es _____.
3. Mi padre se llama Julio. Él es _____.
4. Mi madre se llama Victoria. Ella es _____.
5. Mi hermana se llama Rosa. Ella es _____.
6. Y mi hermano Tomás es muy _____.

Conversación

3 **Describir** With a partner, take turns describing each photo. Tell your partner whether you agree (**Estoy de acuerdo**) or disagree (**No estoy de acuerdo**) with the descriptions.

modelo

Estudiante 1: Los Ángeles es muy bonita.
Estudiante 2: No estoy de acuerdo. Es muy fea.

Los Ángeles

El presidente Bush

La Torre (Tower) Sears

Britney Spears

Drew Carey

Santa Fe, Nuevo México

Nelly Furtado

4 **Anuncio personal** Write a personal ad that describes your ideal mate. Compare your ad with a classmate's.

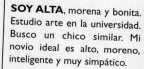

SOY ALTA, morena y bonita. Estudio arte en la universidad. Busco un chico similar. Mi novio ideal es alto, moreno, inteligente y muy simpático.

Some adjectives of nationality

alemán, alemana	German	francés, francesa	French
canadiense	Canadian	japonés, japonesa	Japanese
ecuatoriano/a	Ecuadorian	inglés, inglesa	English
español(a)	Spanish	mexicano/a	Mexican
estadounidense	from the United States	norteamericano/a	(North) American
		puertorriqueño/a	Puerto Rican

The position of adjectives

▶ Adjectives generally follow the nouns they modify.

La mujer **rubia** es de España.
The blond girl is from Spain.

¿Cómo se llama la mujer **ecuatoriana**?
What is the Ecuadorian woman's name?

¡ojo! Unlike descriptive adjectives, adjectives of quantity are placed before the modified noun.

Hay **muchos** estudiantes.
There are many students.

Hablo con **dos** turistas.
I am talking with two tourists.

▶ **Bueno/a** and **malo/a** can be placed before or after a noun. Before a masculine singular noun, the forms are shortened: **bueno → buen; malo → mal.**

José es un **buen** amigo.
José es un amigo **bueno**.

José is a great friend.

Hoy es un **mal** día.
Hoy es un día **malo**.

Today is a bad day.

▶ When **grande** appears before a singular noun, it is shortened to **gran**.

¡ojo! The adjective **grande** also changes its definition depending on its position: **gran** = *great*, but **grande** = *big, large*.

Mandela es un **gran** hombre.
Mandela is a great man.

La familia de Inés es **grande**.
Inés' family is large.

¡Manos a la obra!

 Provide the appropriate forms of the adjective **simpático** in the first column and **español** in the second.

1. Eres _simpático/a_ .
2. Yolanda es _____.
3. Nosotros somos _____.
4. Dolores y Pilar son _____.
5. Diego es _____.
6. Tomás y yo somos _____.
7. Ellas son _____.
8. La médica es _____.
9. Los niños son _____.
10. Él es _____.

1. Soy _español(a)_ .
2. Ángela es _____.
3. Los turistas son _____.
4. Nosotros somos _____.
5. El periodista es _____.
6. Ellos son _____.
7. Clara y Bárbara son _____.
8. Ella es _____.
9. Rafael y yo somos _____.
10. Luis es _____.

3.2 Possessive adjectives

▸ Possessive adjectives express ownership.

Forms of possessive adjectives

Singular forms	Plural forms	
mi	mis	my
tu	tus	your (fam.)
su	sus	his, her, its, your (form.)
nuestro/a	nuestros/as	our
vuestro/a	vuestros/as	your (fam.)
su	sus	their, its, your (form.)

¡ojo! Spanish possessive adjectives agree in number with the nouns they modify. **Nuestro** and **vuestro** agree in gender and number.

mi **primo**	mis **primos**		mi **tía**	mis **tías**
nuestro **tío**	nuestros **tíos**		nuestra **tía**	nuestras **tías**

▸ Possessive adjectives are placed before the nouns they modify.

¡Qué alto es tu papá! Y tu mamá, ¡qué bonita!

Éste es mi abuelo. Es el padre de mi mamá.

▸ **Su** and **sus** have multiple meanings (*your, his, her, their, its*). To avoid confusion, use this construction: [*article*] + [*noun*] + **de** + [*subject pronoun*].

	los parientes de él/ella	his/her relatives
sus **parientes**	los parientes de Ud./Uds.	your relatives
	los parientes de ellos/ellas	their relatives

¡Manos a la obra!

Provide the appropriate form of each possessive adjective.

1. Es __mi__ (*my*) libro.
2. _____ (*my*) familia es ecuatoriana.
3. _____ (*your, fam.*) esposo es italiano.
4. _____ (*our*) profesor es español.
5. Es _____ (*her*) reloj.
6. Es _____ (*your, fam.*) mochila.
7. Es _____ (*your, form.*) maleta.
8. _____ (*their*) sobrina es alemana.
9. _____ (*her*) primos son franceses.
10. _____ (*our*) primos son canadienses.
11. Son _____ (*their*) lápices.
12. _____ (*their*) nietos son japoneses.

Práctica

1 **Completar** Marta just took a photo of her family. Complete her description of the photo.

Ésta es una foto de _____ familia. Aquí están _____ abuelos. Son los padres de _____ papá. _____ casa (*home*) está en Miami.

Este hombre es _____ papá. Se llama David y es médico. _____ mamá se llama Rebeca; es periodista. _____ tía Silvia es la hermana de _____. Y aquí está _____ hermano Ramón. La esposa de _____ se llama Sonia. _____ hijos Javier y Sara son _____ sobrinos. Son muy simpáticos.

2 **¿Dónde está?** You can't remember where you put some of your belongings. Your partner will look at the pictures and remind you.

modelo

Estudiante 1: ¿Dónde está mi pluma?
Estudiante 2: Tu pluma está al lado de la computadora.

1.

2.

3.

4.

5.

6.

Conversación

3 Describir With a partner, describe these people and places.

modelo

La biblioteca de tu universidad
La biblioteca de mi universidad es muy grande.
Hay muchos libros en la biblioteca.

1. Tus padres
2. Tus abuelos
3. Tu mejor (*best*) amigo/a
4. Tu novio/a ideal
5. Tu universidad
6. La librería de tu universidad
7. Tu profesor(a) favorito/a
8. Tu clase de español

4 Tres fotos Choose one of the three family photos and describe the family as if it were your own. Your partner will guess which photo you are describing. Then switch roles.

Familia 1

Familia 2

Familia 3

Español en vivo

Gran chisme:
¡Mi niño tiene bigote!

¡La leche es
nuestra bebida favorita!
A mi hijo le gusta
por su excelente sabor.
Su vaso de leche diario
contiene vitaminas y minerales
esenciales para su crecimiento.
Y yo la tomo para que mis
huesos sean más fuertes
contra la osteoporosis.

¿Bebes leche?

Identificar

Scan the advertisement above, and identify the instances where possessive adjectives are used.

Preguntas

1. ¿Quiénes son las personas del anuncio (*advertisement*)?
2. ¿Qué beben (*do they drink*)?
3. ¿Por qué les gusta la leche?

3.3 Present tense of regular –er and –ir verbs

▶ In Lesson 2, you learned how to form the present tense of regular **–ar** verbs. You also learned about the importance of verb forms, which change to show who is performing the action. The chart below contains the forms of the regular **–ar** verb **trabajar**, which is conjugated just like **hablar, enseñar, comprar, estudiar,** and other **–ar** verbs you have learned. The chart also shows the forms of an **–er** verb and an **–ir** verb.

▶ **–Ar, –er,** and **–ir** verbs have very similar endings. Study the following chart to detect the patterns that make it easier for you to learn the forms of these verbs and to use them to communicate in Spanish.

Inés y Javier comen.

Maite escribe.

Present tense of –ar, –er, and –ir verbs

	trabajar	comer	escribir
	to work	*to eat*	*to write*
yo	trabajo	como	escribo
tú	trabajas	comes	escribes
Ud./él/ella	trabaja	come	escribe
nosotros/as	trabajamos	comemos	escribimos
vosotros/as	trabajáis	coméis	escribís
Uds./ellos/ellas	trabajan	comen	escriben

▶ The **yo** forms of all three types of verbs end in **–o.**

trabajo	como	escribo

▶ The endings for **–ar** verbs begin with **–a,** except for the **yo** form.

hablo	habla	habláis
hablas	hablamos	hablan

▶ The endings for **–er** verbs begin with **–e,** except for the **yo** form.

como	come	coméis
comes	comemos	comen

▶ **–Er** and **–ir** verbs have the exact same endings, except in the **nosotros/as** and **vosotros/as** forms.

nosotros	comemos	vosotros	coméis
	escribimos		escribís

Práctica

1 **Emparejar** Susana is describing her family. Complete each sentence with the correct verb form.

1. Mi familia y yo _____ [vivir] en Montevideo, Uruguay.

2. Mi hermano Alfredo es muy inteligente. Él _____ [asistir] a clases de lunes a viernes.

3. Los martes Alfredo y yo _____ [correr] en el parque.

4. Mis padres _____ [comer] mucho; son un poco gordos.

5. Yo _____ [creer] que (*that*) mis padres _____ [deber] comer menos.

2 **Completar** Juan is talking about what he and his friends do after school. Complete his sentences.

modelo

Yo __*corro*__ por (*for*) una hora.

1. Nosotros _____ en el restaurante.

3. Elena _____ en su diario.

2. Sofía y Eugenio _____ café.

4. Susana y Bárbara _____ unas fotos.

5. Cristina _____ en la biblioteca.

Conversación

3 **Entrevista** Use these questions to interview a classmate. Then report the results of your interview to the class.

1. ¿Dónde comes al mediodía? ¿Comes mucho?

2. ¿Debes comer más (*more*) o menos (*less*)?

3. ¿Dónde vives?

4. ¿Con quién vives?

5. ¿Cuándo asistes a tus clases?

6. ¿Cuál es tu clase favorita? ¿Por qué?

7. ¿Qué cursos debes tomar el próximo (*next*) semestre?

8. ¿Lees *The National Enquirer*? ¿Qué periódicos (*newspapers*) leen tus padres?

9. ¿Recibes muchos mensajes electrónicos (*e-mails*)? ¿De quién?

10. ¿Escribes poemas o cuentos (*stories*)?

4 **Encuesta** Walk around the class and ask your classmates if they do (or should do) the things mentioned on the questionnaire. Try to find at least two people for each item.

Actividad	Nombres
1. Asistir a conciertos de rock	_____
2. Correr todos los días (*every day*)	_____
3. Comprender chino	_____
4. Deber ser más (*more*) trabajador(a)	_____
5. Deber estudiar para (*for*) un examen	_____
6. Deber hablar más en la clase	_____
7. Abrir las ventanas cuando hace frío (*it's cold*)	_____
8. Deber mirar menos (*less*) la televisión	_____
9. Aprender contabilidad	_____
10. Creer que (*that*) la clase de español es fácil	_____
11. Vivir en una residencia estudiantil	_____
12. Deber leer más libros	_____

Common –er and –ir verbs

–er verbs		–ir verbs	
aprender	to learn	abrir	to open
beber	to drink	asistir (a)	to attend
comer	to eat	compartir	to share
comprender	to understand	decidir	to decide
correr	to run	describir	to describe
creer (en)	to believe (in)	escribir	to write
deber (+ inf.)	should, ought to; must	recibir	to receive
leer	to read	vivir	to live

Eugenio y Lilia **corren** en el parque.

Ramón **escribe** una carta.

¡Manos a la obra!

Provide the correct forms of the verbs below.

correr

1. Graciela ___corre___.
2. Tú _____.
3. Mi primo y yo _____.
4. Yo _____.
5. Mis hermanos _____.
6. Ud. _____.
7. Uds. _____.
8. La familia _____.
9. Marcos y yo _____.

abrir

1. Ellos ___abren___ la puerta.
2. Carolina _____ la maleta.
3. Yo _____ las ventanas.
4. Nosotras _____ los libros.
5. Ud. _____ el cuaderno.
6. Tú _____ la ventana.
7. Uds. _____ las maletas.
8. Él _____ el libro.
9. Los muchachos _____ los cuadernos.

aprender

1. Él ___aprende___ español.
2. Uds. _____ español.
3. Maribel y yo _____ inglés.
4. Tú _____ japonés.
5. Uds. _____ francés.
6. Mi hijo _____ chino.
7. Yo _____ alemán.
8. Ud. _____ inglés.
9. Nosotros _____ italiano.

3.4 Present tense of **tener** and **venir**

▸ The verbs **tener** (*to have*) and **venir** (*to come*) are frequently used. You will have to learn each form individually because most of the forms are irregular.

Present tense of *tener* and *venir*

	tener	venir
	to have	*to come*
yo	tengo	vengo
tú	tienes	vienes
Ud./él/ella	tiene	viene
nosotros/as	tenemos	venimos
vosotros/as	tenéis	venís
Uds./ellos/ellas	tienen	vienen

¿Tienes hermanos?

Sí, tengo cuatro hermanas y un hermano mayor.

▸ Note that the **yo** forms are irregular:

tengo   vengo

▸ The **nosotros** and **vosotros** forms are regular:

tenemos   venimos
tenéis   venís

▸ In the second person singular and the third person singular and plural forms, there is also an **e:ie** stem change.

INFINITIVE	VERB STEM		VERB FORM
tener	ten-	tú	tienes
		él/ella/Ud.	tiene
		ellos/ellas/Uds.	tienen
venir	ven-	tú	vienes
		él/ella/Ud.	viene
		ellos/ellas/Uds.	vienen

Práctica

1 **Completar** Complete the sentences with the forms of **tener** or **venir**.

1. Hoy nosotros _____ una reunión familiar.
2. Todos (*all*) mis parientes _____, excepto mi tío Ricardo.
3. Él no _____ porque vive en Guayaquil.
4. Mi prima Inés y su novio no _____ hasta las ocho porque ella _____ que trabajar.
5. En las fiestas mis sobrinos siempre (*always*) _____ ganas de cantar y bailar.
6. Después de (*after*) las fiestas, mi madre siempre dice que mis sobrinos son muy simpáticos. Creo que ella _____ razón.

2 **Describir** Describe these people using **tener** expressions.

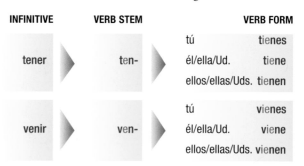

1. _____

2. _____

3. _____

4. _____

5. _____

6. _____

Conversación

3 **¿Sí o no?** With a partner, discuss whether these statements apply to you.

> **modelo**
>
> **Estudiante 1:** ¿Tiene tu madre cincuenta años?
> **Estudiante 2:** No, tiene cuarenta y dos años.

	Sí	No
1. Mi padre tiene 57 años.	____	____
2. Mis padres vienen mucho a la universidad.	____	____
3. Vengo a clase a la medianoche.	____	____
4. Tengo dos pruebas hoy.	____	____
5. Mis amigos vienen mucho a mi casa (*house*).	____	____
6. Tengo muchos problemas con mi novio/a.	____	____
7. Tengo sed.	____	____
8. Tengo miedo de comer sushi.	____	____
9. Tengo que estudiar los domingos.	____	____
10. Tengo una familia grande.	____	____

4 **Entrevista** Use these questions to interview a classmate.

1. ¿Cuántos años tienes? ¿Y tus hermanos?
2. ¿Cuándo vienes a la clase de español?
3. ¿Tienes que estudiar hoy? ¿Por qué?
4. ¿Siempre (*always*) tienes razón?
5. ¿Tienes muchas fiestas en tu casa (*house*)? ¿Quiénes vienen a tus fiestas?
6. ¿Tienes sueño? ¿Por qué?
7. ¿Qué tienes ganas de hacer (*what do you feel like doing*) el sábado?
8. ¿De qué tienes miedo? ¿Por qué?
9. ¿Cuándo vienen tus amigos a tu casa, apartamento o residencia estudiantil?

Expressions with **tener**

▶ In certain expressions, Spanish uses the construction **tener** + [*noun*] instead of **ser** or **estar** to express the English equivalent *to be* + [*adjective*].

Expressions with *tener*	
tener... años	*to be . . . years old*
tener (mucho) calor	*to be (very) hot*
tener (mucho) cuidado	*to be (very) careful*
tener (mucho) frío	*to be (very) cold*
tener (mucha) hambre	*to be (very) hungry*
tener (mucho) miedo	*to be (very) afraid/scared*
tener (mucha) prisa	*to be in a (big) hurry*
tener razón	*to be right*
no tener razón	*to be wrong*
tener (mucha) sed	*to be (very) thirsty*
tener (mucho) sueño	*to be (very) sleepy*
tener (mucha) suerte	*to be (very) lucky*

▶ To express an obligation, use **tener que** (*to have to*) + [*infinitive*].

> —¿**Tienes que** estudiar hoy?
> *Do you have to study today?*
>
> —**Sí, tengo que** estudiar física.
> *Yes, I have to study physics.*

▶ To ask people if they feel like doing something, use **tener ganas de** (*to feel like*) + [*infinitive*].

> —¿**Tienes ganas de** comer?
> *Do you feel like eating?*
>
> —No, **tengo ganas de** dormir.
> *No, I feel like sleeping.*

¡Manos a la obra!

Provide the appropriate forms of **tener** and **venir**.

tener

1. Ellos __tienen__ dos hermanos.
2. Yo _____ una hermana.
3. El artista _____ tres primos.
4. Nosotros _____ diez tíos.
5. Eva y Diana _____ un sobrino.
6. Ud. _____ cinco nietos.
7. Tú _____ dos hermanastras.
8. Uds. _____ cuatro hijos.
9. Ella _____ una hija.

venir

1. Mis padres __vienen__ de México.
2. Tú _____ de España.
3. Nosotras _____ de Cuba.
4. Pepe _____ de Italia.
5. Yo _____ de Francia.
6. Uds. _____ de Canadá.
7. Alfonso y yo _____ de Portugal.
8. Ellos _____ de Alemania.
9. Ud. _____ de Venezuela.

Ampliación

1 Escuchar

A Listen to Cristina and Laura's conversation. Then indicate who would make each statement.

 TIP Ask for repetition. You can ask someone to repeat by saying **¿Cómo?** (*What?*) or **¿Perdón?** (*Pardon me?*). You can ask your teacher to repeat by saying **Repítalo, por favor** (*Repeat it, please*). If you don't understand a recorded activity, simply replay it.

	Cristina	Laura
1. Mi novio habla sólo (*only*) del fútbol y del béisbol.	☐	☐
2. Tengo un novio muy interesante y simpático.	☐	☐
3. Mi novio es alto y moreno.	☐	☐
4. Mi novio trabaja mucho.	☐	☐
5. Mi amiga no tiene buena suerte con los muchachos.	☐	☐
6. El novio de mi amiga es un poco gordo, pero guapo.	☐	☐

B ¿Cómo son Laura y Cristina? ¿Cómo son sus novios? ¿Tienes novio/a? ¿Cómo es?

2 Conversar

You are taking a couple of friends to a reunion of your extended family. So that there won't be any surprises for your friends, you have a conversation with them to tell them about your relatives. During the conversation, your friends should find out about the following:

- Which family members are coming, including their names and their relationship to you
- What each family member is like
- How old each person is
- Where each person is from
- Where each person lives

recursos

R	Textbook CD Lección 3	WB pp. 23-30	LM pp. 15-17	Lab CD Lección 3	ICD-ROM Lección 3	vistahigher learning.com

Ampliación

3 Escribir

An e-mail friend wants to know about your family. Write a letter describing your family or an imaginary family.

 TIP **Use idea maps.** Idea maps help you group your information.

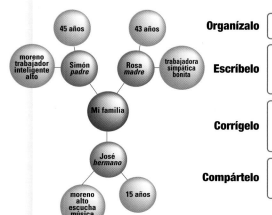

Organízalo — Use an idea map to help you list and organize information about your family.

Escríbelo — Using the material you have compiled, write the first draft of your letter. Use an appropriate greeting, such as **Querido/a** (*Dear*), and an appropriate closing, such as **Un abrazo** (*A hug*).

Corrígelo — Exchange papers with a classmate and comment on the organization, style, and grammatical correctness of each other's work. Then revise your first draft, keeping your classmate's comments in mind.

Compártelo — Read your letter aloud to a small group of classmates. Discuss how your families are similar (**semejantes**) and how they are different (**distintas**).

4 Un paso más

Create an illustrated family tree for your family and share it with the class. Your family tree might include these elements:

- A simple title
- A format that clearly shows the relationships between family members
- Photos of family members and their names, following Hispanic naming conventions
- A few adjectives that describe each family member.

 En Internet

Investiga estos temas en el sitio vistahigherlearning.com.

- La familia en las culturas hispanas
- La amistad (*friendship*) en las culturas hispanas

Antes de leer

You don't need to understand every word you read in Spanish. When you come across words you haven't learned, try to guess what they mean by looking at the context—the surrounding words and sentences. Look at this article about families and find a few words or phrases you don't know. Then guess what they mean, using the context as your guide.

Familias de todo tipo

◄ Hermana dedicada

Me llamo Isabel y tengo dieciocho años. Vivo con mi hermanito Daniel, mi padre Carlos y mi madre Estela. Estudio para programadora en la universidad. Soy muy buena para las computadoras. Por las tardes, le ayudo a Daniel a usar la computadora para hacer sus tareas. ¡Daniel aprende muy rápido!

Una madre ► orgullosa

Me llamo Ángela. Tengo dos hijos. Estoy muy orgullosa de ellos. La mayor se llama Lourdes y el menor José María. Lourdes tiene 18 años y José María tiene 15 años. Mis dos hijos son unos excelentes estudiantes. Lourdes toma clases de arquitectura y José María toma clases de italiano.

Primas futbolistas ►

Me llamo Roberto Sandoval. Mi hija se llama Mónica y es una aficionada al fútbol. Los sábados y domingos ella juega al fútbol con su prima Carolina y juntas ven todos los partidos de fútbol en la televisión. Mónica y Carolina desean jugar en el equipo nacional. ¡Qué honor... dos primas en el equipo nacional!

Después de leer

¿Comprendiste?

Look at the magazine article and see how the words and phrases in the first box are used in context. Then find their translations in the second box.

1. ayudo _____	a. the oldest
2. aficionada _____	b. producer
3. la mayor _____	c. proud
4. el menor _____	d. they watch
5. orgullosa _____	e. I help
6. único _____	f. the youngest
	g. only
	h. fan

Preguntas

1. ¿Cuántas personas hay en la familia de Isabel?

_____

2. ¿Con quién vive Luis?

_____

3. ¿Quiénes desean jugar en el equipo nacional?

_____

4. ¿Cuántos hijos tiene Ángela?

_____

Coméntalo

¿Es similar tu familia a las familias del artículo? En tu opinión, ¿son ideales las familias del artículo? ¿Cómo es la familia ideal?

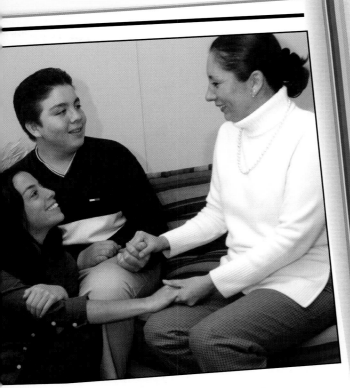

◀ Nieto único

Me llamo Luis y vivo con mi abuelo Artemio y mi abuela María. Soy su único nieto. No tengo hermanos ni primos. Mis abuelos trabajan mucho. Los fines de semana comemos con mis tías Carmen y Beatriz. Mis tías son muy cómicas.

MAYO DE 2003

juega	*plays*
jugar	*to play*
juntas	*together*
partidos	*games*
equipo	*team*
ven	*they watch*
ni	*nor*

recursos

R

vistahigher
learning.com

La familia

el/la abuelo/a	grandfather/grandmother
el/la cuñado/a	brother-in-law/sister-in-law
el/la esposo/a	husband/wife; spouse
la familia	family
el/la hermanastro/a	stepbrother/stepsister
el/la hermano/a	brother/sister
el/la hijastro/a	stepson/stepdaughter
el/la hijo/a	son/daughter
los hijos	children; sons
la madrastra	stepmother
la madre	mother
el/la medio/a hermano/a	half-brother/half-sister
el/la nieto/a	grandson/granddaughter
la nuera	daughter-in-law
el padrastro	stepfather
el padre	father
los padres	parents
los parientes	relatives
el/la primo/a	cousin
el/la sobrino/a	nephew/niece
el/la suegro/a	father-in-law/mother-in-law
el/la tío/a	uncle/aunt
el yerno	son-in-law

Otras personas

el/la amigo/a	friend
la gente	people
el/la muchacho/a	boy/girl
el/la niño/a	child; boy/girl
el/la novio/a	boyfriend/girlfriend
la persona	person

Adjetivos

alto/a	tall
antipático/a	unpleasant
bajo/a	short
bonito/a	pretty
buen, bueno/a	good
delgado/a	thin; slender
difícil	difficult; hard
fácil	easy
feo/a	ugly
gordo/a	fat
gran, grande	big, large; great
guapo/a	handsome; good-looking
importante	important
inteligente	intelligent
interesante	interesting
joven	young
mal, malo/a	bad
mismo/a	same
moreno/a	dark-haired
mucho/a	much; many; a lot of
pelirrojo/a	red-haired
pequeño/a	small
rubio/a	blond
simpático/a	nice; likeable
tonto/a	silly; foolish
trabajador(a)	hard-working
viejo/a	old

Profesiones

el/la artista	artist
el/la médico/a	doctor; physician
el/la ingeniero/a	engineer
el/la periodista	journalist
el/la programador(a)	computer programmer

Verbos

abrir	to open
aprender	to learn
asistir (a)	to attend
beber	to drink
comer	to eat
compartir	to share
comprender	to understand
correr	to run
creer (en)	to believe (in)
deber (+ inf.)	to have to; should
decidir	to decide
describir	to describe
escribir	to write
leer	to read
recibir	to receive
tener	to have
venir	to come
vivir	to live

Expressions with *tener*

tener… años	to be… years old
tener (mucho) calor	to be (very) hot
tener (mucho) cuidado	to be (very) careful
tener (mucho) frío	to be (very) cold
tener ganas de (+ inf.)	to feel like (doing something)
tener (mucha) hambre	to be (very) hungry
tener (mucho) miedo	to be (very) afraid/scared
tener (mucha) prisa	to be in a (big) hurry
tener que (+ inf.)	to have to (do something)
tener razón	to be right
no tener razón	to be wrong
tener (mucha) sed	to be (very) thirsty
tener (mucho) sueño	to be (very) sleepy
tener (mucha) suerte	to be (very) lucky

Expresiones útiles	See page 61.
Nationalities	See page 65.
Possessive adjectives	See page 66.

recursos

R | Lab CD Lección 3 | LM p. 18

4 El fin de semana

Communicative Goals

You will learn how to:
- talk about pastimes, weekend activities, and sports
- make plans and invitations
- say what you are going to do

RECURSOS

These student supplements provide additional practice:
- Textbook Audio CD
- Workbook/Video Manual (WB/VM)
- Lab Manual (LM)
- Lab Audio CDs
- Video CD-ROM
- Interactive CD-ROM
- WB/VM/LM Answer Key

EL FIN DE
SEMANA

pasear en bicicleta
to ride a bicycle

ACTIVIDADES Y DISTRACCIONES

escalar montañas *to climb mountains*

escribir una carta *to write a letter*

un mensaje electrónico *to write an e-mail*

esquiar *to ski*

ir de excursión (a las montañas) *to go on a hike (in the mountains)*

leer el periódico *to read the newspaper*

el correo electrónico *to read e-mail*

una revista *to read a magazine*

nadar en la piscina *to swim in the pool*

pasear por la ciudad/el pueblo *to walk around the city/town*

practicar deportes (m. pl.) *to practice sports*

ver películas *to see movies*

visitar un monumento *to visit a monument*

patinar (en línea)
to rollerblade

tomar el sol
to sunbathe

una (tarjeta) postal
a postcard

bucear
to scuba dive

recursos

R	Textbook CD Lección 4	WB pp. 31-32	LM p. 19	Lab CD Lección 4	ICD-ROM Lección 4

LOS DEPORTES

el **baloncesto** *basketball*
el **ciclismo** *cycling*
el **esquí (acuático)** *(water) skiing*
el **fútbol americano** *football*
el **golf** *golf*
el **hockey** *hockey*
la **natación** *swimming*
el **tenis** *tennis*
el **voleibol** *volleyball*

el **equipo** *team*
el/la **jugador(a)** *player*
el **partido** *game*
la **pelota** *ball*
ganar *win*
ser aficionado/a (a) *to be a fan (of)*

deportivo/a *sports-related*

el béisbol
baseball

el fútbol
soccer

el/la excursionista
hiker

LUGARES

la **casa** *house*
el **centro** *downtown*
el **cine** *movie theater*
el **gimnasio** *gym, gymnasium*
el **museo** *museum*
el **parque** *park*
el **restaurante** *restaurant*

la iglesia
church

la piscina
pool

el café
café

OTRAS PALABRAS

la **diversión** *entertainment; fun activity*
el **fin de semana** *weekend*
el **lugar** *place*
el **pasatiempo** *pastime, hobby*
los **ratos libres** *spare time*
el **tiempo libre** *free time*
favorito/a *favorite*
pasar el tiempo *to spend time*

A escuchar

1 **Una estudiante muy activa** Every day, Laura does many things. Number the drawings in the order in which you hear Laura mention them.

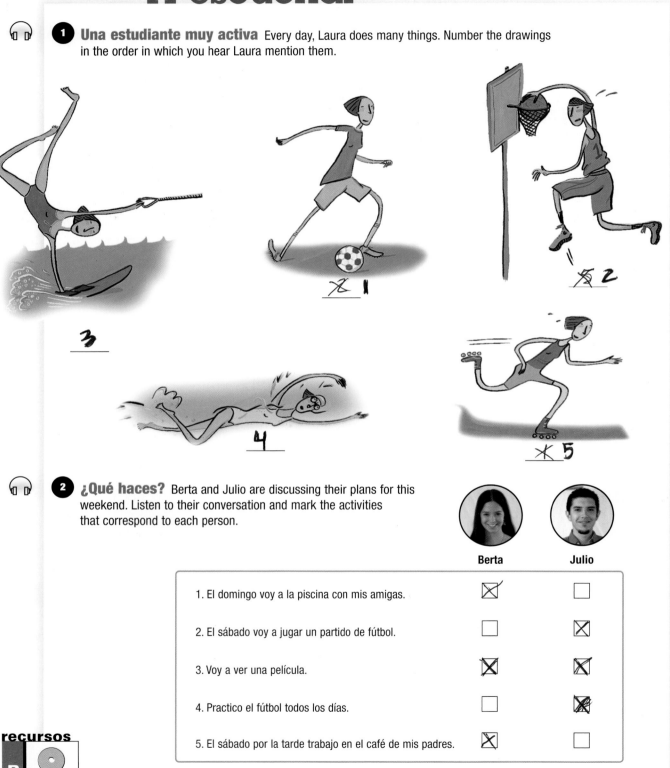

2 **¿Qué haces?** Berta and Julio are discussing their plans for this weekend. Listen to their conversation and mark the activities that correspond to each person.

	Berta	Julio
1. El domingo voy a la piscina con mis amigas.	☒	☐
2. El sábado voy a jugar un partido de fútbol.	☐	☒
3. Voy a ver una película.	☒	☒
4. Practico el fútbol todos los días.	☐	☒
5. El sábado por la tarde trabajo en el café de mis padres.	☒	☐

recursos

R | Textbook CD
Lección 4

A practicar

3 **Tiempo libre** Indicate whether each statement is **cierto** or **falso**.

Gustavo y Simón

Las chicas

José

Don Fernando

Maribel   **Doña Leonor**

1. __C__ Gustavo y Simón pasean por la ciudad en bicicleta.
2. __C__ Las chicas juegan al fútbol.
3. __F__ José hace una excursión a las montañas.
4. __C__ Don Fernando lee el periódico en el parque.
5. __F__ Maribel patina en línea.
6. __C__ Doña Leonor pasea por la ciudad.

4 **Los pasatiempos** Circle the word or phrase that doesn't belong.

1. bucear • ir de excursión • leer una revista • esquiar
2. el baloncesto • el ciclismo • el voleibol • el fútbol
3. la natación • el cine • el café • la iglesia
4. el golf • la aficionada • el jugador • el excursionista
5. el periódico • el pasatiempo • la revista • el correo
6. ver películas • ir al museo • practicar el hockey • leer un periódico

5 **Dos amigos** Complete the conversation with the words given.

LUISA ¿Cómo te gusta _____ los ratos libres, Manuel?

MANUEL Bueno, Luisa, no tengo mucho _____ libre,
pero los fines de _____ me gusta ver películas.
Y tú, Luisa, ¿cuáles son tus _____ favoritos?

centro	pasar	semana
cine	pasatiempos	tiempo
gimnasio	piscina	voleibol

LUISA Voy al _____. Nado en la _____.
Y los sábados juego al _____.

MANUEL ¡Uf! ¿Y qué haces para descansar?

LUISA Pues… para descansar me gusta ver películas.

MANUEL ¡Excelente! Hay una buena en un _____ del _____. ¿Quieres ir?

LUISA Sí, Manuel. Buena idea.

A conversar

6 **¿Y tú?** Interview your partner using these questions.

1. ¿Te gustan los deportes?
2. ¿Qué deportes practicas?
3. ¿Cuál es tu deporte favorito? ¿Por qué te gusta?
4. ¿Te gusta pasear en bicicleta? ¿Dónde paseas y con quién?
5. ¿Escribes muchos mensajes electrónicos? ¿Te gusta recibir mensajes electrónicos?
6. ¿Qué periódicos y revistas lees? ¿Por qué?

7 **En el campus** With a partner, describe what the people in the illustration are doing.

8 **¿Quién soy?** Using **yo** forms, write a description of a famous athlete and read it to the class, mentioning the athlete's initials (**iniciales**). The class will guess who you described.

> **modelo**
>
> **Estudiante:** Soy muy famosa. Vivo en la Florida con mi familia. Practico el tenis. Soy una jugadora profesional. Mi hermana practica el tenis también. Mis iniciales son V. W. ¿Quién soy?
>
> **Clase:** ¿Eres Venus Williams?
>
> **Estudiante:** ¡Sí!

🎧 Pronunciación

Word stress

pe-lí-cu-la   **e-di-fi-cio**   **ver**   **yo**

Every Spanish syllable contains at least one vowel. When two vowels (two weak vowels or one strong and one weak) are joined in the same syllable, they form a **diphthong**. A **monosyllable** is a word formed by a single syllable.

bi-blio-te-ca   **vi-si-tar**   **par-que**   **fút-bol**

The syllable of a Spanish word that is pronounced most emphatically is the "stressed" syllable.

pe-lo-ta   **pis-ci-na**   **ra-tos**   **ha-blan**

Words that end in **n, s,** or a **vowel** are usually stressed on the next-to-last syllable.

na-ta-ción   **pa-pá**   **in-glés**   **Jo-sé**

If words that end in **n, s,** or a **vowel** are stressed on the last syllable, they must carry an accent mark on the stressed syllable.

bai-lar   **es-pa-ñol**   **u-ni-ver-si-dad**   **tra-ba-ja-dor**

Words that do **not** end in **n, s,** or a **vowel** are usually stressed on the last syllable.

béis-bol   **lá-piz**   **ár-bol**   **Gó-mez**

If words that do **not** end in **n, s,** or a **vowel** are stressed on the next-to-last syllable, they must carry an accent mark on the stressed syllable.

Práctica Pronounce each word, stressing the correct syllable. Then give the word stress rule for each word.

1. profesor
2. Puebla
3. ¿Cuántos?
4. Mazatlán
5. examen
6. ¿Cómo?
7. niños
8. Guadalajara
9. programador
10. México
11. están
12. geografía

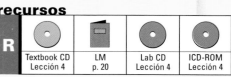

En la unión está la fuerza.[2]

Quien ríe de último, ríe mejor.[1]

Oraciones Read the conversation aloud to practice word stress.

MARINA Hola, Carlos. ¿Qué tal?

CARLOS Bien. Oye, ¿a qué hora es el partido de fútbol?

MARINA Creo que es a las siete.

CARLOS ¿Quieres ir?

MARINA Lo siento, pero no puedo. Tengo que estudiar biología.

Refranes Read these sayings aloud to practice word stress.

1 He who laughs last laughs loudest.
2 In unity, there is strength.

recursos

R	Textbook CD Lección 4	LM p. 20	Lab CD Lección 4	ICD-ROM Lección 4

¡Vamos al parque!

Los estudiantes pasean por la ciudad y hablan de sus pasatiempos.

DON FRANCISCO Tienen una hora libre. Pueden explorar la ciudad, si quieren.

JAVIER Inés, ¿quieres ir a pasear por la ciudad?
INÉS Sí, vamos.

ÁLEX ¿Por qué no vamos al parque, Maite? Podemos hablar y tomar el sol.
MAITE ¡Buena idea! También quiero escribir unas postales.

ÁLEX ¡Maite!
MAITE ¡Dios mío!

JOVEN Mil perdones. Lo siento muchísimo.
MAITE ¡No es nada! Estoy bien.

ÁLEX Ya son las dos y treinta. Debemos regresar al autobús, ¿no?
MAITE Tienes razón.
ÁLEX Oye, Maite, ¿qué vas a hacer esta noche?
MAITE No tengo planes. ¿Por qué?

recursos

| R | Video/VCD-Rom Lección 4 | VM pp.175-176 | ICD-ROM Lección 4 |

Personajes

DON FRANCISCO

JAVIER

INÉS

ÁLEX

MAITE

JOVEN

4

MAITE ¿Eres aficionado a los deportes, Álex?

ÁLEX Sí, me gusta mucho el fútbol. Me gusta también nadar, correr e ir de excursión a las montañas.

MAITE Yo también corro mucho.

5

ÁLEX Oye, Maite, ¿por qué no jugamos al fútbol con él?

MAITE Mmm... No quiero.
Voy a terminar de escribir unas postales.

9

ÁLEX Eh, este... A veces salgo a correr por la noche. ¿Quieres venir a correr conmigo?

MAITE Sí, vamos. ¿A qué hora?

ÁLEX ¿A las seis?

MAITE Perfecto.

10

DON FRANCISCO Esta noche van a correr. ¡Y yo no tengo energía para pasear!

¿Qué piensas?

1 Ordenar Put the following events in order from 1 to 5.

_____ a. Álex y Maite deciden ir al parque.

_____ b. Álex y el joven juegan al fútbol.

_____ c. Maite y Álex vuelven al autobús.

_____ d. Maite decide escribir unas postales.

_____ e. El joven causa un accidente.

2 Pasatiempos Scan **Aventuras** and indicate which pastimes the characters mention. Then indicate whether you participate in each pastime.

ÁLEX

el futbol - No
excursion a las montañas - Si
tambien

MAITE

_____

_____

_____

3 Preguntas Get together with a partner and take turns asking each other these questions.

1. ¿Qué desean hacer Inés y Javier?

_____

2. ¿Cuáles son los deportes favoritos de Álex?

_____

3. ¿Qué desea hacer Maite en el parque?

_____

4. ¿Qué desea hacer Álex en el parque?

_____

5. ¿Qué deciden hacer Álex y Maite esta noche?

_____

6. ¿Cuáles son tus pasatiempos favoritos?

_____

7. ¿Cuáles son los pasatiempos favoritos de tu mejor (*best*) amigo/a?

_____

Exploración
El fútbol: pasión de multitudes

El portero (*goal keeper*) colombiano Óscar Córdoba juega (*plays*) en el equipo Boca Juniors de Buenos Aires. Es considerado uno de los mejores (*best*) porteros del mundo.

El Real Madrid, equipo español, ha ganado (*has won*) la Copa de Europa nueve veces.

El fútbol es el deporte más popular en todo el mundo hispanohablante. El Estadio Azteca de la Ciudad de México tiene una capacidad de 106.000 (ciento seis mil) espectadores. Es el estadio más grande (*the biggest*) de los países hispanohablantes.

Estadísticas del fútbol

Ganadores de la Copa del Mundo:

Argentina (2), Uruguay (2), Brasil (5)

Goleadores célebres:

Cuauhtémoc Blanco (México), Gabriel Batistuta (Argentina), Ronaldo (Brasil)

Equipos célebres:

Barcelona, Real Madrid, Boca Juniors, River Plate

Coméntalo

With a classmate, discuss these questions.

- ¿Te gusta el fútbol? Explica por qué.
- ¿Crees que el fútbol va a ser más (*is going to be more*) popular en los Estados Unidos?
- ¿Se juega (*do they play*) al fútbol en tu comunidad?

recursos

R

vistahigher learning.com

4 GRAMÁTICA

4.1 The present tense of ir

ir (to go)

Singular forms		Plural forms	
yo	voy	nosotros/as	vamos
tú	vas	vosotros/as	vais
Ud./él/ella	va	Uds./ellos/ellas	van

▸ The verb **ir** (*to go*) is irregular in the present tense.

▸ **Ir** is often used with the preposition **a** (*to*). When **a** is followed by the article **el,** they form the contraction **al**. There is no contraction when **a** is followed by **la**, **las**, and **los**.

a + el = al

Voy al cine con María.
I'm going to the movies with María.

Ellos van a las montañas.
They are going to the mountains.

▸ The construction **ir a** + [*infinitive*] expresses actions that are going to happen in the future. It is equivalent to the English *to be going to* + [*infinitive*].

Voy a escribir unas postales.

Álex y Maite van a volver al autobús.

▸ **Vamos a** + [*infinitive*] can also express the idea of *let's (do something)*.

Vamos a pasear.
Let's take a stroll.

¡Vamos a ver!
Let's see!

¡ojo! Use **adónde** instead of **dónde** when asking a question with **ir**.

¿Adónde vas?
Where are you going?

¿Adónde van hoy?
Where are they going today?

¡Manos a la obra!

 Provide the present tense forms of **ir**.

1. Ellos <u>van</u>.
2. Yo _____.
3. Tu novio _____.
4. Adela _____.
5. Mi prima y yo _____.
6. Tú _____.
7. Uds. _____.
8. Nosotros _____.
9. Ud. _____.
10. Nosotras _____.
11. Miguel _____.
12. Ellos _____.

Práctica

1 **Adivina** Roberto has gone to see Doña Imelda, a fortune teller. Using **ira** + [*infinitive*], say what Doña Imelda predicts.

modelo

Tu hermano Gabriel ___va a___ ir a Europa.

1. Tú _____ correr en el Maratón de Boston.
2. Tú y tu familia _____ escalar el monte Everest.
3. Tu hermano Pablo _____ jugar en la Liga Nacional de Fútbol.
4. Tu hermana Tina _____ recibir una carta misteriosa.
5. Tu hermana Rosario _____ patinar en los Juegos Olímpicos.
6. Tus padres _____ tomar el sol en Acapulco.
7. Tú _____ ver las pinturas (*paintings*) de tu amiga en el Museo Nacional de Arte.
8. ¡Y yo _____ ser muy, muy rica!

2 **¿Adónde vas?** You and some friends are visiting Madrid. Work with a partner and ask each other which sites you will visit today. Use the clues provided in the map.

modelo

Estudiante 1: ¿Adónde va Ricardo?
Estudiante 2: Va al Palacio Real.

Conversación

3 **Situaciones** With a partner, say where you and your friends go in the following situations.

1. Cuando deseo descansar…

2. Cuando mi novio/a tiene que estudiar…

3. Si mis amigos necesitan practicar el español…

4. Si deseo hablar con unos amigos…

5. Cuando tengo dinero (*money*)…

6. Cuando mis amigos y yo tenemos hambre…

7. Si tengo tiempo libre…

8. Cuando mis amigos desean esquiar…

9. Si estoy de vacaciones (*on vacation*)…

10. Si quiero leer…

4 **Encuesta** Walk around the class and ask your classmates if they are going to do these activities today. Try to find at least two people for each item and write their names on the worksheet. Report your findings to the class.

Actividades	Nombres
1. Comer en un restaurante	_____
2. Mirar la televisión	_____
3. Leer una revista	_____
4. Escribir un mensaje electrónico	_____
5. Correr	_____
6. Ver una película	_____
7. Pasear en bicicleta	_____
8. Estudiar en la biblioteca	_____

5 **Entrevista** Interview two classmates to find out what they are going to do this weekend.

modelo

Estudiante 1: ¿Adónde vas este (*this*) fin de semana?

Estudiante 2: Voy a Guadalajara con mis amigos.

Estudiante 1: ¿Y qué van a hacer (*to do*) Uds. en Guadalajara?

Estudiante 2: Vamos a visitar unos monumentos y museos.

Identificar

Scan the advertisement above, and identify the instances where the **ir a** + [*infinitive*] construction is used.

Preguntas

1. ¿Quiénes son las personas de la familia?

2. ¿Cómo va a estar la familia?

3. ¿Qué va a hacer (*to do*) el hijo?

4. En tu opinión, ¿por qué el hijo escoge (*does he choose*) el Banco Atlantis?

4.2 Stem-changing verbs: e → ie, o → ue

▶ In stem-changing verbs, the stressed vowel of the stem changes when the verb is conjugated.

INFINITIVE	VERB STEM	STEM CHANGE	CONJUGATED FORM
empezar	empez-	empiez-	empiezo
volver	volv-	vuelv-	vuelvo

▶ In many verbs, such as **empezar** (*to begin*), the stem vowel changes from **e** to **ie**. Note that the **nosotros/as** and **vosotros/as** forms don't have a stem change.

empezar (e:ie)

Singular forms		Plural forms	
yo	empiezo	nosotros/as	empezamos
tú	empiezas	vosotros/as	empezáis
Ud./él/ella	empieza	Uds./ellos/ellas	empiezan

Álex y Maite vuelven al autobús.

Álex empieza a enviar mensajes.

▶ In many other verbs, such as **volver** (*to return*), the stem vowel changes from **o** to **ue**. The **nosotros/as** and **vosotros/as** forms have no stem change.

volver (o:ue)

Singular forms		Plural forms	
yo	vuelvo	nosotros/as	volvemos
tú	vuelves	vosotros/as	volvéis
Ud./él/ella	vuelve	Uds./ellos/ellas	vuelven

▶ To help you identify stem-changing verbs, they will appear as follows throughout the text:

empezar (e:ie)   volver (o:ue)

Práctica

1 **Preferencias** With a partner, take turns asking and answering questions about what these people want to do.

modelo

> Guillermo: estudiar / pasear en bicicleta
> Estudiante 1: ¿Quiere estudiar Guillermo?
> Estudiante 2: No, prefiere pasear en bicicleta.

1. **tú**: trabajar / dormir
   _____

2. **Uds.**: mirar la televisión / ir al cine
   _____

3. **tus amigos**: ir de excursión / descansar
   _____

4. **tú**: comer en la cafetería / ir a un restaurante
   _____

5. **Elisa**: ver una película / leer una revista
   _____

6. **María y su hermana**: tomar el sol / practicar el esquí _____

2 **El día del partido** Complete this game-day conversation between two friends with the appropriate verb forms. Then act it out with a partner.

PABLO	Óscar, voy al centro ahora. ¿_____ [querer] venir?
ÓSCAR	No, yo _____ [preferir] descansar un poco y ver la televisión.
PABLO	¡Qué perezoso (*how lazy*) eres!
ÓSCAR	No, hombre. Es que estoy muy cansado.
PABLO	Todos los días la misma cosa…
ÓSCAR	Vas a ver, vas a ver… Oye, ¿a qué hora _____ [pensar] regresar? El partido de fútbol _____ [empezar] a las dos.
PABLO	A la una. _____ [querer] ver el partido también.
ÓSCAR	¿_____ [pensar] que (*that*) nuestro equipo _____ [poder] ganar?
PABLO	No, _____ [pensar] que vamos a _____ [perder]. Los jugadores del Guadalajara _____ [jugar] muy bien.

Conversación

3 **En la televisión** Read the listing of sports events to be televised this weekend and choose the programs you want to watch. Compare your choices with a classmate and explain why you made them. Then agree on one program you will watch together on each day.

sábado

13:30 NATACIÓN
1   Copa Mundial *(World Cup)* de Natación
15:00 TENIS
8   Abierto *(Open)* Mexicano de Tenis: Alejandro Hernández (México) vs. Jacobo Díaz (España) Semifinales
16:00 FÚTBOL NACIONAL
3   Chivas vs. Monterrey
16:30 FÚTBOL AMERICANO PROFESIONAL
21 los Vaqueros de Dallas vs. los Leones de Detroit
20:00 BALONCESTO PROFESIONAL
16 los Knicks de Nueva York vs. los Toros de Chicago

domingo

13:00 GOLF
40 Audi Senior Classic: Lee Treviño, Jack Nicklaus, Arnold Palmer
14:30 VOLEIBOL
1   Campeonato *(Championship)* Nacional de México
16:00 BALONCESTO
3   Campeonato de Cimeba: los Correcaminos de Tampico vs. los Santos de San Luis Final
17:00 ESQUÍ ALPINO
19 Eslálom
18:30 FÚTBOL INTERNACIONAL
30 Copa América: México vs. Argentina. Ronda final
20:00 PATINAJE ARTÍSTICO
16 Exhibición mundial

4 **Turistas** You and two classmates are spending a long weekend in a new city. Talk about the things you want to do, then fill in the day-planner with the things you plan to do each day.

SÁBADO	DOMINGO
8am	8am
9	9
10	10
11	11
12pm	12pm
1	1
2	
3	
4	
5	
6	
7	
8	8

Common stem-changing verbs

e:ie		o:ue	
cerrar	*to close*	dormir	*to sleep*
comenzar	*to begin*	encontrar	*to find*
empezar	*to begin*	mostrar	*to show*
entender	*to understand*	poder	*to be able to; can*
pensar	*to think*	recordar	*to remember*
perder	*to lose; to miss*	volver	*to return*
preferir	*to prefer*		
querer	*to want; to love*		

▸ **Jugar** (*to play* a sport or a game) is the only Spanish verb that has a **u:ue** stem change. **Jugar** is followed by **a** + [*definite article*] when the name of a sport or game is mentioned.

> Me gusta mucho jugar al fútbol.

> Álex y el joven juegan al fútbol.

▸ **Comenzar** and **empezar** require the preposition **a** when they are followed by an infinitive.

Comienzan a jugar a las siete.
They begin playing at seven.

Ana **empieza a** escribir una postal.
Ana starts to write a postcard.

▸ **Pensar** + [*infinitive*] means *to plan* or *to intend to do something*. **Pensar en** means *to think about someone or something*.

¿Piensan ir al gimnasio?
Are you planning to go to the gym?

¿En qué **piensas?**
What are you thinking about?

¡Manos a la obra!

Provide the correct forms of the verbs.

cerrar (e:ie)	dormir (o:ue)
1. Uds. <u>cierran</u>.	1. Mi abuela no <u>duerme</u>.
2. Tú _____.	2. Yo no_____.
3. Nosotras _____.	3. Tú no _____.
4. Mi hermano _____.	4. Mis hijos no _____.
5. Yo _____.	5. Ud. no _____.
6. Ud. _____.	6. Nosotros no _____.
7. Los chicos _____.	7. Él no _____.
8. Ella _____.	8. Uds. no _____.

4.3 Stem-changing verbs: e → i

▶ In some verbs, such as **pedir** (*to ask for; to request*), the stressed vowel in the stem changes from **e** to **i**, as shown in the diagram.

INFINITIVE	VERB STEM	STEM CHANGE	CONJUGATED FORM
pedir	ped-	pid-	pido

▶ As with other stem-changing verbs you have learned, there is no stem change in the **nosotros/as** or **vosotros/as** forms in the present tense.

pedir (e:i)

Singular forms		Plural forms	
yo	pido	nosotros/as	pedimos
tú	pides	vosotros/as	pedís
Ud./él/ella	pide	Uds./ellos/ellas	piden

▶ To help you identify verbs with the **e:i** stem change, they will appear as follows throughout the text:

pedir (e:i)

▶ The following are the most common **e:i** stem-changing verbs:

conseguir	repetir	seguir
to get; to obtain	*to repeat*	*to follow; to continue; to keep (doing something)*

Le pido un favor a un amigo.
I'm asking a friend for a favor.
Sigue esperando.
He keeps waiting.

Repito la pregunta.
I repeat the question.
Consiguen ver buenas películas.
They get to see good movies.

¡ojo! The **yo** forms of **seguir** and **conseguir** have a spelling change as well as a stem change.

Sigo su plan.
I'm following their plan.

Consigo novelas en la librería.
I get novels at the bookstore.

¡Manos a la obra!

Provide the correct forms of the verbs.

repetir (e:i)	pedir (e:i)	seguir (e:i)
1. Arturo y Eva _repiten_ .	1. Yo _pido_ .	1. Yo _sigo_ .
2. Yo _____ .	2. Él _____.	2. Nosotros _____.
3. Nosotros _____.	3. Tú _____.	3. Tú _____.
4. Julia _____.	4. Ud. _____.	4. Los chicos _____.
5. Sofía y yo _____.	5. Ellas _____.	5. Ud. _____.
6. Tú _____.	6. Nosotros _____.	6. Anita _____.

Práctica

1 En la clase You're teaching Spanish at an elementary school. Fill in the blanks to describe a typical day in your class.

1. Yo entro en la clase y _____ [cerrar] la puerta.
2. La clase _____ [comenzar] a las nueve en punto.
3. Yo _____ [pedir] la tarea del día anterior (*previous*).
4. Los estudiantes _____ [repetir] las palabras del vocabulario.
5. Pablo no _____ [seguir] mis instrucciones.
6. Pedro _____ [perder] su lápiz.
7. Otro estudiante _____ [encontrar] el lápiz de Pedro.
8. La clase termina y yo _____ [volver] a casa muy cansado/a.

2 Combinar Combine words from the columns to create sentences about yourself and people you know.

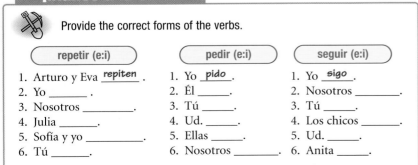

Yo
Mi compañero/a de cuarto
Mi mejor (*best*) amigo/a
Mi familia
Mis amigos/as
Mis amigos y yo
Mis padres
Mi hermano/a
Mi profesor(a) de español

pedir muchos favores
dormir hasta el mediodía
nunca (*never*) pedir perdón
nunca seguir las instrucciones del profesor
siempre seguir las instrucciones del profesor
conseguir libros en Internet
poder hablar dos lenguas extranjeras
repetir el vocabulario
siempre perder sus libros

Conversación

3 **Las películas** Use these questions to interview a classmate.

1. ¿Prefieres las películas románticas, las películas de acción o las películas de horror? ¿Por qué?

2. ¿Dónde consigues información sobre (*about*) una película?

3. ¿Dónde consigues las entradas (*tickets*) para una película?

4. Para decidir qué películas vas a ver, ¿sigues las recomendaciones de los críticos?

5. ¿Qué cines en tu comunidad muestran las mejores (*best*) películas?

6. ¿Vas a ver una película esta semana? ¿A qué hora empieza la película?

4 **El fin de semana** Ask a classmate if he or she does these things on a weekend. Report the results to the class.

Actividad	Sí	No
1. Dormir hasta la una de la tarde	____	____
2. Pedir una pizza por teléfono	____	____
3. Jugar al tenis	____	____
4. Ir a un partido de fútbol/ baloncesto/béisbol	____	____
5. Pasear	____	____
6. Ir a un museo	____	____
7. Escribir mensajes electrónicos	____	____
8. Patinar	____	____
9. Ir al gimnasio	____	____

Español en vivo

Identificar

Scan the movie poster above and identify the stem-changing verbs.

Preguntas

1. ¿Qué palabras indican que *Un mundo azul oscuro* (*Dark Blue World*) es una película dramática?

2. ¿Cuántas personas hay en el póster?

3. ¿Cómo son las personas del póster? ¿Qué relación tienen?

4. ¿Te gustan las películas como ésta (*this one*)?

4.4 Verbs with irregular yo forms

▸ In Spanish, several verbs have irregular **yo** forms in the present tense.

▸ The verbs **hacer** (*to do, to make*), **poner** (*to put, to place*), **salir** (*to leave*), **suponer** (*to suppose*), and **traer** (*to bring*) have **yo** forms that end in **–go**. The other forms are regular.

Verbs with irregular yo forms

	hacer	poner	salir	suponer	traer
yo	hago	pongo	salgo	supongo	traigo
tú	haces	pones	sales	supones	traes
Ud./él/ella	hace	pone	sale	supone	trae
nosotros/as	hacemos	ponemos	salimos	suponemos	traemos
vosotros/as	hacéis	ponéis	salís	suponéis	traéis
Uds./ellos/ellas	hacen	ponen	salen	suponen	traen

A veces salgo a correr por la noche.

Nunca salgo a correr, no hago ejercicio, pero sí tengo energía... ¡para leer el periódico y tomar un café!

▸ **Poner** can mean *to turn on* a household appliance.

Carlos **pone** la radio.
Carlos turns on the radio.

María **pone** la televisión.
María turns on the television.

▸ **Salir de** is used to indicate that someone is leaving a particular place.

Hoy **salgo del** hospital.
Today I leave the hospital.

Sale de la clase a las cuatro.
He leaves class at four.

▸ **Salir para** is used to indicate someone's destination.

Mañana **salgo para** México.
Tomorrow I leave for Mexico.

Hoy **salen para** España.
Today they leave for Spain.

▸ **Salir con** means *to leave with someone or something,* or *to date someone.*

Alberto **sale con** su amigo.
Alberto is leaving with his friend.

Margarita **sale con** Guillermo.
Margarita is going out with Guillermo.

Hoy voy a **salir con** mi hermana.
Today I'm going out with my sister.

Mi primo **sale con** una chica muy bonita.
My cousin is going out with a very pretty girl.

Práctica

1 Completar Complete this conversation with the appropriate verb forms. Then act it out with a partner.

ERNESTO David, ¿qué _hace_ [hacer] hoy?

DAVID Ahora estudio biología, pero esta noche _salgo_ [salir] con Luisa. Vamos al cine. Queremos _ver_ [ver] la nueva (*new*) película de Almodóvar.

ERNESTO ¿Y Diana? ¿Qué _hace_ [hacer] ella?

DAVID _Sale_ [salir] a comer con sus padres.

ERNESTO ¿Qué _hacen_ [hacer] Andrés y Javier?

DAVID Tienen que _hacen_ [hacer] las maletas. _Salen_ [salir] para Monterrey mañana.

ERNESTO Pues, ¿qué _hago_ [hacer] yo?

DAVID _Supongo_ [suponer] que puedes estudiar o _ver_ [ver] la televisión.

ERNESTO No quiero estudiar. Mejor _pongo_ [poner] la televisión.

2 Describir Form complete sentences with the cues provided.

Fernán/poner

Yo/traer

Nosotras/ver

El estudiante/hacer

3 Oraciones Form sentences using the clues given.

modelo
Tú / ? / los libros / debajo de / escritorio
Tú pones los libros debajo del escritorio.

1. Nosotros / ? / mucha / tarea _Nosotros hacemos mucha_
2. ¿Tú / ? / la radio? _¿Tú_
3. Yo / no / ? / el problema _Yo_
4. Marta / ? / una grabadora / clase
5. Los señores Marín / ? / su casa / siete
6. Yo / ? / que (*that*) / tú / ir / cine / ¿no?

Conversación

4 Preguntas Get together with a classmate and ask each other these questions.

1. ¿A qué hora sales de tu residencia o de tu casa por la mañana? ¿A qué hora llegas a la universidad?
2. ¿A qué hora comienza la clase de español?
3. ¿Traes un diccionario a la clase de español? ¿Por qué? ¿Qué más traes?
4. ¿A qué hora salimos de la clase de español?
5. Cuando vuelves a la casa, ¿dónde pones tus libros? ¿Siempre (*always*) pones tus cosas en su lugar?
6. ¿Pones fotos de tu familia en tu casa? ¿De quiénes son las fotos?
7. ¿Cuándo estudias? ¿Haces la tarea cada (*each*) noche o prefieres ver la televisión?
8. ¿Oyes la radio cuando estudias?
9. ¿Qué vas a hacer mañana?
10. ¿Qué haces los fines de semana? ¿Sales con los amigos? ¿Adónde van?

5 Charadas In groups, play a game of charades. Each person should think of a phrase using **hacer, poner, salir, oír, traer,** or **ver** and act out the phrase. The first person to guess correctly acts out the next charade.

6 Situación Ask a classmate if he or she wants to go out. He or she will accept. Then find out what activities your classmate prefers so you can decide where you want to go. Finally, negotiate the place and the time for your date with your classmate.

The verbs ver and oír

▶ The verb **ver** (*to see*) has an irregular **yo** form. The other forms of **ver** are regular.

ver (to see)

Singular forms		Plural forms	
yo	veo	nosotros/as	vemos
tú	ves	vosotros/as	veis
Ud./él/ella	ve	Uds./ellos/ellas	ven

Oye, ¿por qué no jugamos al fútbol?

Maite ve la pelota.

▶ The verb **oír** (*to hear*) has an irregular **yo** form and a spelling change in the **tú, usted, él, ella, ustedes, ellos,** and **ellas** forms. The **nosotros/as** and **vosotros/as** forms have an accent mark.

oír (to hear)

Singular forms		Plural forms	
yo	oigo	nosotros/as	oímos
tú	oyes	vosotros/as	oís
Ud./él/ella	oye	Uds./ellos/ellas	oyen

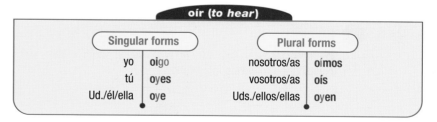

Oigo a unas personas en la otra sala.
I hear some people in the other room.

¿**Oyes** la música latina?
Do you hear the Latin music?

¡Manos a la obra!

Provide the correct forms of the verbs.

1. **salir**   Isabel __sale__.   Nosotros __salimos__.   Yo __salgo__.
2. **ver**   Yo _____.   Uds. _____.   Tú _____.
3. **poner**   Rita y yo _____.   Yo _____.   Los niños _____.
4. **hacer**   Yo _____.   Tú _____.   Ud. _____.
5. **oír**   Él _____.   Nosotros _____.   Yo _____.
6. **traer**   Ellas _____.   Yo _____.   Tú _____.
7. **suponer**   Yo _____.   Mi amigo _____.   Nosotras _____.

Ampliación

1 Escuchar

A First you will hear José talking, then Anabela. Which person does each statement best describe?

⭐ **TIP Listen for general meaning.** You will be surprised at how much you can understand even if you don't know every word.

Descripción	José	Anabela
1. Es muy aficionado/a a los deportes.	☐	☐
2. Usa mucho la computadora.	☐	☐
3. Va mucho al cine.	☐	☐
4. Es una persona muy activa.	☐	☐
5. Le gusta descansar por la tarde.	☐	☐
6. Es una persona estudiosa.	☐	☐
7. Su deporte favorito es el ciclismo.	☐	☐
8. A veces va a ver un partido de béisbol.	☐	☐

B ¿Tienes más en común (*more in common*) con José o con Anabela? Explica tu respuesta.

2 Conversar

You are planning to visit a friend who lives in another state. Call your friend and discuss your plans, including the following information:

- When you are going to arrive
- How long you are planning to stay
- What places you want to visit
- A few activities you can do together.

recursos

Ampliación

Escribir

Write a flyer describing the sports and recreational activities offered at your school.

⭐ **TIP** **Use bilingual dictionaries carefully.** Use a Spanish-English dictionary to look up words you don't know, but consider each entry carefully in order to find the best word for your needs.

Organízalo	List the activities you could include in the flyer. Use an idea map to organize them.
Escríbelo	Using your idea map, write the first draft of your flyer.
Corrígelo	Exchange papers with a classmate and comment on the organization, style, and grammatical correctness of each other's work. Then revise your first draft, keeping your classmate's comments in mind.
Compártelo	Exchange papers with a new partner. Note any words that are new to you, so you can look them up later. Then turn your paper in to your teacher.

4 Un paso más

Prepare a radio broadcast of weekend sports events for a major city in the Spanish-speaking world. Include the following in your broadcast:

- An introduction of yourself and your program
- A list of local sports events
- The location and time of each event
- A brief sign-off.

🖥️ **En Internet**

Investiga estos temas en el sitio vistahigherlearning.com.

- Los deportes más (*most*) populares del mundo hispano
- Los pasatiempos más populares del mundo hispano

Antes de leer

The following article appeared in one of Mexico City's daily newspapers. Scan the headings and the visual elements of the article. Based on what you see, what do you think the reading is about?

Can you guess the meaning of the following cognates that appear in the article?

baladas	misticismo
concierto	naturaleza
exposición	realista
festival	recomendar
isla	romántico/a
majestuosidad	pintor
misterio	serenidad

GUÍA para el fin

CINE

Festival de cine argentino

Para los aficionados al cine este fin de semana comienza El Festival de cine argentino en el Cine Rex. Se muestran las últimas películas de directores como Juan José Campanella, Fito Páez, Gabriela Tagliavini y Aníbal Di Salvo. Recomendamos especialmente la película *El hijo de la novia* del director Juan José Campanella. Esta película fue nominada para el Óscar como mejor película extranjera.

Fechas: 10-14 de marzo
Hora: 8:00 p.m.
Lugar: Cine Rex
Dirección: Calle del Espanto, 152

CONCIERTO

Canta Maribel Puértolas

Si quiere escuchar música, la cantante Maribel Puértolas va a ofrecer un concierto en el Café Los Amigos. Puértolas, de origen puertorriqueño, es una joven cantante. Sus baladas están en el nuevo CD *Verano de amor.* Si quiere pasar una noche muy romántica con su novio o novia, recomendamos este concierto.

Fecha: 15 de marzo
Hora: 7:00 p.m.
Lugar: Café Los Amigos
Dirección: Avenida Bolívar, 345

de semana

EXPOSICIÓN

El pintor Tomás Sánchez

El Museo de Arte Moderno ofrece una exposición del pintor cubano Tomás Sánchez. Las obras de Sánchez son paisajes realistas de la naturaleza de la isla de Cuba. Las pinturas expresan la serenidad y majestuosidad de la selva tropical cubana, en una atmósfera de misterio y misticismo. Tomás Sánchez es tal vez uno de los pintores cubanos contemporáneos más conocidos.

Fechas: 12 de marzo – 8 de abril
Lugar: Museo de Arte Moderno
Dirección: Avenida Juárez, 248

Después de leer

¿Comprendiste?

Based on the article, are these statements **cierto** or **falso**?

Cierto	Falso	
———	———	1. El artículo presenta noticias sobre eventos deportivos.
———	———	2. La película *El hijo de la novia* fue nominada para un Óscar.
———	———	3. Maribel Puértolas es una cantante de baladas.
———	———	4. Las pinturas de Tomás Sánchez se exhiben en el Cine Rex.
———	———	5. Juan José Campanella es un director de cine argentino.
———	———	6. En el Café Los Amigos hay una exposición de arte.

Preguntas

Answer these questions based on the information provided in the reading.

1. ¿De dónde es Maribel Puértolas?
   _____

2. ¿Qué clase de canciones (*songs*) canta ella?
   _____

3. ¿Cómo son las pinturas de Tomás Sánchez?
   _____

4. ¿Dónde está la exposición de Tomás Sánchez?
   _____

5 ¿Qué película está dirigida por Juan José Campanella?
   _____

6 ¿Dónde es el festival de cine?
   _____

Coméntalo

Get together with several classmates. Discuss which of the activities in the article you would each prefer to do on a weekend and why.

últimas	*latest*
fue nominada para	*was nominated for*
extranjera	*foreign*
cantante	*singer*
ofrecer	*to offer*
verano	*summer*
paisajes	*landscapes*
selva	*jungle*

recursos

R | vistahigher learning.com

Actividades

bucear	to scuba dive
escalar montañas (f. pl.)	to climb mountains
escribir una carta	to write a letter
un mensaje electrónico	an e-mail message
una (tarjeta) postal	a postcard
esquiar	to ski
ganar	to win
ir de excursión (a las montañas)	to go for a hike (in the mountains)
leer el correo electrónico	to read e-mail
un periódico	a newspaper
una revista	a magazine
nadar	to swim
pasar el tiempo	to spend time
pasear en bicicleta	to ride a bicycle
pasear por la ciudad/el pueblo	to walk around the city/town
patinar (en línea)	to skate (in-line)
practicar deportes (m. pl.)	to play sports
ser aficionado/a (a)	to be a fan (of)
tomar el sol	to sunbathe
ver películas (f. pl.)	to see movies
visitar un monumento	to visit a monument
la diversión	fun activity; entertainment
el/la excursionista	hiker
el fin de semana	weekend
el pasatiempo	pastime, hobby
los ratos libres	spare time
el tiempo libre	free time

Deportes

el baloncesto	basketball
el béisbol	baseball
el ciclismo	cycling
el equipo	team
el esquí (acuático)	(water) skiing
el fútbol	soccer
el fútbol americano	football
el golf	golf
el hockey	hockey
el/la jugador(a)	player
la natación	swimming
el partido	game
la pelota	ball
el tenis	tennis
el voleibol	volleyball

Verbos

cerrar (e:ie)	to close
comenzar (e:ie)	to begin
conseguir (e:i)	to get; to obtain
dormir (o:ue)	to sleep
empezar (e:ie)	to begin
encontrar (o:ue)	to find
entender (e:ie)	to understand
hacer	to do; to make
ir	to go
jugar (u:ue)	to play
mostrar (o:ue)	to show
oír	to hear
pedir (e:i)	to ask for; to request
pensar (e:ie)	to think
pensar (+ inf.)	to intend; to plan
pensar en	to think about
perder (e:ie)	to lose; to miss
poder (o:ue)	to be able to; can
poner	to put; to place
preferir (e:ie)	to prefer
querer (e:ie)	to want; to love
recordar (o:ue)	to remember
repetir (e:i)	to repeat
salir	to leave
seguir (e:i)	to follow; to continue
suponer	to suppose
traer	to bring
ver	to see
volver (o:ue)	to return

Adjetivos

deportivo/a	sports-related
favorito/a	favorite

Lugares

el café	café
la casa	house
el centro	downtown
el cine	movie theater
el gimnasio	gymnasium
la iglesia	church
el lugar	place
el museo	museum
el parque	park
la piscina	swimming pool
el restaurante	restaurant

Expresiones útiles	See page 85.

recursos

R	Lab CD Lección 4	LM p. 24

AVENTURAS EN LOS PAÍSES HISPANOS

En Acapulco, un saltador (*diver*) salta desde un acantilado (*cliff*) frente al Océano Pacífico. El lugar se llama La Quebrada y miles de turistas lo visitan cada (*each*) día. ¿Te gustaría (*would you like*) visitarlo algún (*some*) día?

MÉXICO

MÉXICO

Área: 1.972.550 km² (761.603 millas²)
Población: 101.851.000
Capital: México, D.F. – 18.372.000
Ciudades importantes: Guadalajara – 4.017.000, Monterrey – 3.514.000, Puebla – 2.025.000, Cancún – 1.325.000, Ciudad Juárez – 1.226.000
Moneda: peso mexicano

SOURCE: Population Division, UN Secretariat

CELEBRACIONES

El 5 de mayo

El 5 de mayo, los mexico-americanos celebran la victoria de México contra Francia en la Batalla de Puebla en 1862. La victoria mexicana simboliza la unidad y la independencia del país y se celebra con fiestas y desfiles (*parades*).

ESTADOS UNIDOS

Ciudad Juárez

Baja California

Golfo de California

Sierra Madre Occidental

Sierra Madre Oriental

Río Bra

Océano Pacífico

Puerto Vallarta

Guadalaj

ARTE

Diego Rivera y Frida Kahlo

Frida Kahlo y Diego Rivera son los pintores mexicanos más famosos. Casados (*married*) en 1929, los dos se interesaron (*became interested*) en las condiciones sociales de la gente indígena y de los campesinos (*farmers*) de su país. Puedes ver algunas de sus obras (*works*) en el Museo de Arte Moderno de la Ciudad de México.

Los mayas

La cultura maya habitó (*inhabited*) la región del sur de México, la península de Yucatán y otros países de Centroamérica. Los mayas crearon (*created*) formidables ciudades con templos religiosos en forma de pirámide, que hoy día son visitados (*are visited*) por millones de turistas.

Grande

Monterrey

Golfo
de México

Península
de Yucatán
Mérida

Cancún

Bahía de
Campeche

Veracruz

Istmo de
Tehuantepec

BELICE

GUATEMALA

de

COMIDA

Las tortillas

La base de la comida mexicana es la tortilla, que está hecha (*is made from*) de maíz (*corn*) y de harina (*wheat flour*).
Los tacos, las enchiladas y las quesadillas están hechos (*are made*) con tortillas y son tan populares en México como en los Estados Unidos. ¿Conoces un restaurante mexicano en tu comunidad?

¿Qué aprendiste?

1 **¿Cierto o falso?** Say whether the following statements are **cierto** or **falso**, based on what you've learned about Mexico.

Cierto	Falso	
_____	_____	1. Guadalajara tiene una población mayor que *(greater than)* la de México, D.F.
_____	_____	2. Frida Kahlo es una pintora.
_____	_____	3. El 5 de mayo es una celebración religiosa.
_____	_____	4. Los mayas inventaron *(invented)* las tortillas.
_____	_____	5. En la Batalla de Puebla, México venció *(defeated)* a Francia.
_____	_____	6. Los mexicanos hacen las tortillas con tomates.
_____	_____	7. Diego Rivera fue *(was)* el esposo de Frida Kahlo.
_____	_____	8. Puebla es la capital de México.
_____	_____	9. La harina es la base de la comida mexicana.
_____	_____	10. La moneda mexicana es el dólar mexicano.

2 **Preguntas** Answer the following questions, based on what you've learned about Mexico.

1. ¿Qué aspecto cultural te interesa más *(interests you most)* de México: el arte, la historia o la comida? Explica tu respuesta.
2. ¿Celebran el 5 de mayo en tu comunidad? ¿Cómo lo celebran?
3. ¿Te gustan los cuadros de Diego Rivera y Frida Kahlo? Explica por qué.
4. ¿Por qué piensas que los mayas son importantes en la historia de México?
5. ¿Qué platos *(dishes)* típicos de México te gustan más? ¿Por qué?
6. ¿Por qué Diego Rivera y Frida Kahlo decidieron pintar *(decided to paint)* la gente indígena y los campesinos?

En Internet

Busca más información sobre estos temas en el sitio vistahigherlearning.com. **Presenta la información a tus compañeros/as de clase.**

- El 5 de mayo
- Frida Kahlo y Diego Rivera
- Los mayas
- La comida mexicana

5 Las vacaciones

Communicative Goals

You will learn how to:
- talk to hotel personnel
- describe a hotel
- talk about how you feel

RECURSOS

These student supplements provide additional practice:
- Textbook Audio CD
- Workbook/Video Manual (WB/VM)
- Lab Manual (LM)
- WB/VM/LM Answer Key
- Lab Audio CDs
- Video CD-ROM
- Interactive CD-ROM

LAS VACACIONES

el pasaporte
passport

la estación del tren
train station

LAS VACACIONES Y LOS VIAJES

el aeropuerto *airport*
la agencia de viajes *travel agency*
el/la agente de viajes *travel agent*
la estación de autobuses *bus station*
          del metro *subway station*
el/la inspector(a) de aduanas *customs officer*
el pasaje (de ida y vuelta) *(round-trip) ticket*
la tienda de campaña *tent*
el/la viajero/a *traveler*

¿QUÉ TIEMPO HACE?

¿Qué tiempo hace? *How's the weather?; what's the weather like?*
Está despejado. *It's clear.*
     (muy) nublado. *It's (very) cloudy.*
Hace buen/mal tiempo. *It's nice/bad weather.*
     (mucho) calor. *It's (very) hot.*
     fresco. *It's cool.*
     (mucho) frío. *It's (very) cold.*
     (mucho) sol. *It's (very) sunny.*
     (mucho) viento. *It's (very) windy.*
Hay (mucha) niebla. *It's (very) foggy.*

llover (o:ue) *to rain*
Llueve. *It's raining.*
nevar (e:ie) *to snow*
Nieva. *It's snowing.*

el botones
bellhop

EN EL HOTEL

el alojamiento *lodging*
la cabaña *cabin*
la cama *bed*
el/la empleado/a *employee*
la habitación *room*
     individual *single room*
     doble *double room*
el hotel *hotel*
el/la huésped *guest*
la pensión *boarding house*
el piso *floor (of a building)*
la planta baja *ground floor*

la llave
key

recursos

R	Textbook CD Lección 5	WB pp. 45-46	LM p. 25	Lab CD Lección 5	ICD-ROM Lección 5

ACTIVIDADES

acampar *to camp*

confirmar una reservación *to confirm a reservation*

estar de vacaciones *to be on vacation*

hacer turismo (m.) *to go sightseeing*

un viaje *to take a trip*

una excursión *to go on a hike, to go on a tour*

ir a la playa *to go to the beach*

ir de pesca *to go fishing*

de vacaciones *to go on vacation*

ir en autobús (m.) *to go by bus*

en auto(móvil) (m.) *to go by car*

en avión (m.) *to go by plane*

en barco (m.) *to go by boat*

en taxi (m.) *to go by taxi*

pasar por la aduana *to go through customs*

pescar *to fish*

ir en motocicleta (f.)
to go by motorcycle

hacer las maletas
to pack (one's suitcases)

sacar fotos (f. pl.)
to take pictures

montar a caballo
to go horseback riding

LAS ESTACIONES Y LOS MESES

el invierno *winter*

la primavera *spring*

el verano *summer*

el otoño *fall, autumn*

el año *year*

la estación *season*

el mes *month*

NÚMEROS ORDINALES

primer, primero/a *first*

segundo/a *second*

tercer, tercero/a *third*

cuarto/a *fourth*

quinto/a *fifth*

sexto/a *sixth*

séptimo/a *seventh*

octavo/a *eighth*

noveno/a *ninth*

décimo *tenth*

OTRAS PALABRAS Y EXPRESIONES

el ascensor *elevator*

el campo *countryside*

el equipaje *luggage*

la llegada *arrival*

el mar *ocean, sea*

la salida *departure; exit*

¿Cuál es la fecha de hoy? *What is today's date?*

Hoy es el primero (dos, tres,...) de marzo. *Today is March first (second, third,...).*

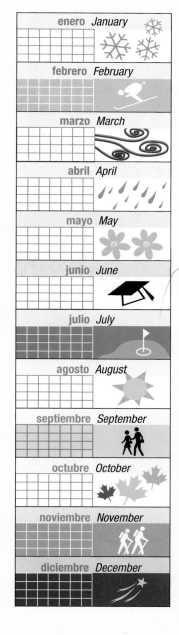

enero *January*

febrero *February*

marzo *March*

abril *April*

mayo *May*

junio *June*

julio *July*

agosto *August*

septiembre *September*

octubre *October*

noviembre *November*

diciembre *December*

A escuchar

🎧 **1** **Escuchar** Indicate who would probably make each statement you hear. Each answer is used twice.

El agente de viajes	La inspectora de aduanas	El empleado del hotel

El agente de viajes

1. _____
2. _____
3. _____
4. _____
5. _____
6. _____

La inspectora de aduanas

1. _____
2. _____
3. _____
4. _____
5. _____
6. _____

El empleado del hotel

1. _____
2. _____
3. _____
4. _____
5. _____
6. _____

🎧 **2** **¿Cierto o falso?** Listen to each sentence and indicate whether it is **cierto** or **falso**. Correct the false statements.

Cierto   **Falso**

_____ _____ 1. _____

_____ _____ 2. _____

_____ _____ 3. _____

_____ _____ 4. _____

_____ _____ 5. _____

_____ _____ 6. _____

_____ _____ 7. _____

_____ _____ 8. _____

recursos

R ◉ Textbook CD
Lección 5

A practicar

3 **Analogías** Complete the analogies.

equipaje	huésped	sacar
inspector	habitación	mar
febrero	llover	viajar
pasaporte		

1. primero → segundo ⊜ enero → _____
2. aeropuerto → viajero ⊜ hotel → _____
3. invierno → nevar ⊜ primavera → _____
4. mes → año ⊜ maleta → _____
5. hotel → botones ⊜ aduana → _____
6. pasaje → avión ⊜ llave → _____
7. acampar → campo ⊜ pescar → _____
8. estudiante → libro ⊜ turista → _____
9. llave → abrir ⊜ pasaje → _____
10. maleta → hacer ⊜ foto → _____

4 **Contestar** Answer these questions with a classmate.

modelo

¿Cuál es el primer mes de la primavera?
Estudiante 1: ¿Cuál es el primer mes de la primavera?
Estudiante 2: Marzo.

1. ¿Cuál es la fecha de hoy?
2. ¿Qué estación es? ¿Te gusta esta (*this*) estación?
3. ¿Cuál es el segundo mes del verano?
4. ¿Cuál es el primer mes del invierno?
5. ¿Cuál es la cuarta estación del año?
6. ¿Prefieres el otoño o la primavera? ¿Por qué?
7. ¿Prefieres el mar o la montaña? ¿Por qué?
8. ¿Te gusta más el campo o la ciudad?
9. Cuando estás de vacaciones, qué clima prefieres: ¿el calor o el frío?
10. ¿En qué mes piensas ir de vacaciones este año? ¿Adónde quieres ir?
11. ¿Cómo vas a ir: en barco, en motocicleta…?
12. ¿Prefieres comprar el pasaje en una agencia de viajes o en Internet?

A conversar

5 **Describir** With a partner, describe what these people are doing.

Enrique y Juan   **Josefina**   **Ricardo**

Don Luis   **Amalia**   **El Sr. y la Sra. Montes**

6 **Mis vacaciones** With a partner, have a conversation in Spanish about how you prepare for vacation and what you like to do on vacation. Use these questions as a guide.

1. During what months or seasons do you prefer to travel?
2. What resources do you use to help you plan your trip (travel agents, books, the Internet, etc.)?
3. Do you spend your vacations with family? With friends?
4. Do you prefer to go to the beach, to the mountains, or to a favorite city or country? What is the weather like there?
5. What activities do you enjoy doing while on vacation?

🎧 Pronunciación

Spanish **b** and **v**

bueno   **v**olei**b**ol   **b**i**b**lioteca   **v**i**v**ir

There is no difference in pronunciation between the Spanish letters **b** and **v**. However, each letter can be pronounced two different ways, depending on which letters appear next to them.

bonito   **v**iajar   tam**b**ién   in**v**estigar

B and **v** are pronounced like the English hard *b* when they appear either as the first letter of a word, at the beginning of a phrase, or after **m** or **n**.

de**b**er   no**v**io   a**b**ril   cer**v**eza

In all other positions, **b** and **v** have a softer pronunciation, which has no equivalent in English. Unlike the hard **b**, which is produced by tightly closing the lips and stopping the flow of air, the soft **b** is produced by keeping the lips slightly open.

bola   **v**ela   Cari**b**e   decli**v**e

In both pronunciations, there is no difference between **b** and **v**. The English *v* sound, produced by friction between the upper teeth and lower lip, does not exist in Spanish. Instead, the soft **b** comes from friction between the two lips.

Verónica y su esposo canta**n b**oleros.

When **b** or **v** begins a word, its pronunciation depends on the previous word. At the beginning of a phrase or after a word that ends in **m** or **n**, it is pronounced as a hard **b**.

Benito es de **B**oquerón pero **v**ive en **V**ictoria.

Words that begin with **b** or **v** are pronounced with a soft **b** if they appear immediately after a word that ends in a vowel or any consonant other than **m** or **n**.

Práctica   Read these words aloud to practice the **b** and the **v**.

1. hablamos	4. van	7. doble	10. cabaña
2. trabajar	5. contabilidad	8. novia	11. llave
3. botones	6. bien	9. béisbol	12. invierno

Oraciones   Read these sentences aloud to practice the **b** and the **v**.

1. Vamos a Guaynabo en autobús.
2. Voy de vacaciones a la Isla Culebra.
3. Tengo una habitación individual en el octavo piso.
4. Víctor y Eva van en avión al Caribe.
5. La planta baja es bonita también.

Refranes   Read these sayings aloud to practice the **b** and the **v**.

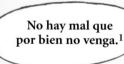

No hay mal que por bien no venga.[1]

Hombre prevenido vale por dos.[2]

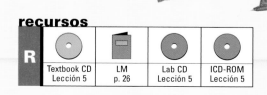

1 Every cloud has a silver lining.
2 An ounce of prevention equals a pound of cure.

recursos

R	Textbook CD Lección 5	LM p. 26	Lab CD Lección 5	ICD-ROM Lección 5

Tenemos una reservación.

Don Francisco y los estudiantes llegan al hotel.

EMPLEADA ¿En qué puedo servirles?

DON FRANCISCO Mire, yo soy Francisco Castillo Moreno y tenemos una reservación a mi nombre.

EMPLEADA Mmm… No veo su nombre aquí. No está.

DON FRANCISCO ¿Está segura, señorita? Quizás la reservación está a nombre de la agencia de viajes, Ecuatur.

EMPLEADA Pues sí, aquí está... dos habitaciones dobles y una individual, de la ciento uno a la ciento tres... todas en las primeras cabañas.

DON FRANCISCO Gracias, señorita. Muy amable.

BOTONES Bueno, la habitación ciento dos… Por favor.

INÉS Oigan, yo estoy aburrida. ¿Quieren hacer algo?

JAVIER ¿Por qué no vamos a explorar la ciudad un poco más?

INÉS ¡Excelente idea! ¡Vamos!

MAITE No, yo no voy. Estoy cansada y quiero descansar un poco porque a las seis voy a correr con Álex.

ÁLEX Y yo quiero escribir un mensaje electrónico antes de ir a correr.

JAVIER Pues nosotros estamos listos, ¿verdad, Inés?

INÉS Sí, vamos.

MAITE Adiós.

INÉS & JAVIER ¡Chau!

recursos

| R | Video/VCD-ROM Lección 5 | VM pp. 177-178 | ICD-ROM Lección 5 |

Personajes

DON FRANCISCO   JAVIER   INÉS   ÁLEX   MAITE   EMPLEADA   BOTONES

4

ÁLEX Hola, chicas. ¿Qué están haciendo?

MAITE Estamos descansando.

5

JAVIER Oigan, no están nada mal las cabañas, ¿verdad?

INÉS Y todo está muy limpio y ordenado.

ÁLEX Sí, es excelente.

MAITE Y las camas son tan cómodas.

9

ÁLEX Bueno, nos vemos a las seis.

MAITE Sí, hasta luego.

ÁLEX Adiós.

10

MAITE ¿Inés y Javier? Juntos otra vez.

Expresiones útiles

Talking to hotel personnel

¿En qué puedo servirles?
How can I help you?

Tenemos una reservación a mi nombre.
We have a reservation in my name.

Mmm… No veo su nombre. No está.
I don't see your name. It's not here.

¿Está seguro/a? Quizás/Tal vez está a nombre de Ecuatur.
Are you sure? Maybe it's in the name of Ecuatur.

Aquí está… dos habitaciones dobles y una individual.
Here it is, two double rooms and one single.

Aquí tienen las llaves.
Here are your keys.

Gracias, señorita. Muy amable.
Thank you, miss. Very kind/nice.

¿Dónde pongo las maletas?
Where do I put the suitcases?

Allí, encima de la cama.
There, on the bed.

Describing a hotel

No están nada mal las cabañas.
The cabins aren't bad at all.

Todo está muy limpio y ordenado.
Everything is very clean and orderly.

Es excelente/estupendo/ fabuloso/fenomenal.
It's excellent/stupendous/ fabulous/great.

Es increíble/magnífico/ maravilloso/perfecto.
It's incredible/magnificent/ marvelous/perfect.

Las camas son tan cómodas.
The beds are so comfortable.

Talking about how you feel

Estoy un poco aburrido/a/cansado/a.
I'm a little bored/tired.

¿Qué piensas?

1 Ordenar Put these events in the correct order.

_____ a. Las chicas descansan en su habitación.

_____ b. Javier e Inés deciden ir a explorar la ciudad.

_____ c. Don Francisco habla con la empleada del hotel.

_____ d. Javier, Maite, Inés y Álex hablan en la habitación de las chicas.

_____ e. El botones pone las maletas en la cama.

2 Completar Complete these sentences using the words below.

descansar	aburrida	el empleado
habitación individual	las camas	habitaciones dobles
las maletas	hacer las maletas	
cansada	la agencia de viajes	

1. La reservación para el hotel está a nombre de _____.

2. Los estudiantes tienen dos _____.

3. Don Francisco tiene una _____.

4. Maite va a _____ porque está _____.

5. El botones lleva _____ a las habitaciones.

6. Las habitaciones son buenas y _____ son cómodas.

3 Minidrama With two or three classmates, prepare a skit with the following scenes:

Scene 1: You call your travel agent and make a hotel reservation for a specific date.

Scene 2: You go to the front desk at the hotel to check in and find out that there are problems with your reservation. You solve the problems and check in.

Scene 3: You find a bellhop to take your bags to your room.

Scene 4: Your bellhop shows you to your room and asks you where to put your bags. You tell the bellhop where to put them and thank him or her.

Exploración
El alojamiento

España tiene unos paradores impresionantes. Generalmente los paradores son castillos o palacios que reflejan la cultura de la región.

Hay muchos tipos de alojamiento para las personas que viajan a los países hispanos. Por ejemplo, hay muchos hoteles elegantes como el Hotel San Juan en San Juan, Puerto Rico. Está cerca de la playa y ofrece hermosas (*beautiful*) habitaciones y jardines (*gardens*) tropicales.

Muchos estudiantes prefieren los albergues juveniles (*youth hostels*) porque son baratos (*inexpensive*). Además, los huéspedes tienen la oportunidad de conocer (*meet*) a personas de todo el mundo (*around the world*).

Estadísticas de hoteles

Cadenas de hoteles más importantes:
- Sol Meliá (España)
- Posadas de México (México)
- N.H. Hoteles (España)

Hoteles más grandes del mundo hispano:
- Moon Palace Hotel (Cancún, México)
- Oasis Cancún Hotel (Cancún, México)
- Sheraton María Isabel Hotel & Towers (México, D.F.)
- Hilton (Caracas, Venezuela)
- Catalonia Bávaro Resort (República Dominicana)
- Caribe Hilton Hotel (San Juan, Puerto Rico)

Coméntalo

With a classmate, discuss these questions.

- Imagina que vas de vacaciones. ¿Prefieres estar en un hotel, un parador o en un albergue juvenil? ¿Por qué?
- ¿Hay un albergue juvenil en tu comunidad? ¿Hay un lugar similar a un parador?

recursos

R

vistahigher learning.com

5.1 Estar with conditions and emotions

▶ **Estar** is used to talk about how you are and to say where nouns are located.

Estoy bien, gracias.
I'm fine, thanks.

Juan **está** en la biblioteca.
Juan is at the library.

▶ **Estar** is used with adjectives to describe the physical condition of nouns.

La puerta **está** cerrada.
The door is closed.

Todo **está** muy limpio.
Everything is very clean.

▶ **Estar** is also used with adjectives to describe how people feel.

Estoy
aburrida.

Estoy
cansada.

Adjectives that describe emotions and conditions

abierto/a	*open*	equivocado/a	*wrong; mistaken*
aburrido/a	*bored; boring*	feliz	*happy*
alegre	*happy, joyful*	limpio/a	*clean*
avergonzado/a	*embarrassed*	nervioso/a	*nervous*
cansado/a	*tired*	ocupado/a	*busy*
cerrado/a	*closed*	ordenado/a	*orderly*
cómodo/a	*comfortable*	preocupado/a (por)	*worried (about)*
contento/a	*happy, content*	seguro/a	*sure; safe*
desordenado/a	*disorderly; messy*	sucio/a	*dirty*
enamorado/a (de)	*in love (with)*	triste	*sad*
enojado/a	*mad, angry*		

¡Manos a la obra!

 Provide the correct forms of **estar.**

1. La biblioteca __está__ cerrada los domingos por la noche.
2. Nosotros _____ muy ocupados todos los lunes.
3. Ellas _____ alegres porque tienen tiempo libre.
4. Javier _____ enamorado de Maribel.
5. Diana _____ enojada con su novio.
6. Yo _____ nerviosa por el examen.
7. La habitación _____ ordenada cuando vienen sus padres.
8. Uds. _____ equivocados.
9. Ana _____ cansada.

Práctica

1 **Un viaje** Tere is going on a trip. Say how she, her family, and her friends are feeling.

Tere

nerviosa	enojado	felices
equivocados	están	estamos
estoy	está	

1. Hoy yo _____ muy contenta porque mañana voy a hacer un viaje a Chicago.
2. También estoy _____ porque voy en avión.
3. Mis padres _____ preocupados porque voy sola (*alone*).
4. Mi amiga Patricia y yo _____ tristes porque ella no puede ir.
5. Es que Patricia _____ ocupada con sus clases.
6. Mi novio César está _____ porque no puede ir.
7. Mis hermanos Juan y Rafael están _____ porque no voy a estar en casa.
8. Todos (*they all*) piensan que voy a tener problemas. Creo que están _____.

2 **¿Dónde están y cómo están?** Indicate where these people are and how they feel.

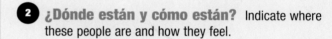

Sebastián

Olivia y Marco

1. _____

3. _____

Mónica

El profesor Olmos

2. _____

4. _____

Conversación

3 **Situaciones** With a partner, talk about how you feel in these situations.

1. Cuando estoy de vacaciones...
2. Cuando hago un examen...
3. Cuando estoy con la familia...
4. Cuando estoy en la clase de español...
5. Cuando llueve...
6. Cuando asisto a un funeral...
7. Cuando mi novio/a sale con otro/a chico/a...

4 **Describir** With a partner, describe the following people and places.

Anabela

Juan y Luisa

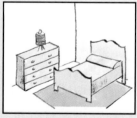

la habitación de Teresa

la habitación de César

5 **Preguntas** Use these questions to interview your partner.

1. ¿Estás ocupado/a este fin de semana? ¿Qué vas a hacer?
2. ¿Estás enamorado/a? ¿De quién?
3. ¿Qué haces cuando estás contento/a?
4. ¿Qué haces cuando estás aburrido/a?
5. ¿Qué haces cuando estás cansado/a?
6. ¿Qué haces cuando estás nervioso/a?

Español en vivo

TÚ: en la ciudad. Estás muy ocupado, cansado y nervioso.

Si crees que el invierno es así para todos, estás equivocado.

OFERTA ESPECIAL $797

CURAÇAO

Donde siempre es verano

El paquete incluye:
- Pasaje de ida y vuelta
- Cómoda estancia de 5 días en habitación doble
- Excursiones en barco a los maravillosos lugares de la isla

Consulte su Agencia de Viajes.

ELLOS: de vacaciones en Curaçao. Están felices y relajados. ¿Estás listo para hacer tus maletas?

Identificar

Scan the above advertisement and identify the adjectives that take the verb **estar**.

Preguntas

1. ¿Cómo están las personas del anuncio?
2. ¿Cuál es el aspecto más atractivo de la oferta (*offer*)?
3. ¿Te identificas (*do you identify*) con la descripción de la vida en la ciudad?

5.2 The present progressive

▶ Both Spanish and English have a present progressive tense, which consists of the present tense of the verb *to be* and the present participle (the *-ing* form of the verb in English).

Los chicos **están jugando.**
The kids are playing.

Los turistas **están viajando.**
The tourists are traveling.

Estoy escribiendo una postal.
I am writing a postcard.

Estás mirando la televisión.
You are watching television.

¿Qué están haciendo?

Estamos descansando.

▶ The present progressive is formed with **estar** and the present participle of the main verb.

ESTAR + PRESENT PARTICIPLE
Están cantando.
They are singing.

Estamos esperando.
We are waiting.

ESTAR + PRESENT PARTICIPLE
Estoy comiendo.
I am eating.

Ella **está trabajando.**
She is working.

▶ The present participle of regular verbs is formed as follows:

INFINITIVE	STEM	ENDING	PRESENT PARTICIPLE
hablar	habl-	-ando	hablando
comer	com-	-iendo	comiendo
escribir	escrib-	-iendo	escribiendo

▶ When the stem of an **–er** or **–ir** verb ends in a vowel, the present participle ends in **–yendo**.

INFINITIVE	STEM	ENDING	PRESENT PARTICIPLE
leer	le-	-yendo	leyendo
oír	o-	-yendo	oyendo
traer	tra-	-yendo	trayendo

Práctica

1 **De vacaciones** Mauricio and his family are vacationing in Mazatlán, Mexico. Complete his description of what everyone is doing right now.

1. Yo _____

4. Mi mamá _____

2. Mi hermana Elena _____

5. Mis hermanos _____

3. Mi papá _____

6. Mi abuela _____

2 **Un amigo preguntón** You are on summer vacation. A nosy friend calls you at all hours to see what you're doing. Look at the clocks and tell him.

modelo

Estoy descansando.

1. _____ 3. _____

2. _____ 4. _____

Conversación

3 **¿Qué están haciendo?** With a partner, say what these celebrities are doing right now, using the cues provided.

 modelo   Tiger Woods está jugando al golf.

Tiger Woods

Carlos Costa

Nomar Garciaparra

Marion Jones

Michelle Kwan

Carlos Santana

Christina Aguilera

4 **Describir** With a partner, describe what's going on in this picture.

Irregular present participles

▶ The verbs **ir, poder,** and **venir** have irregular present participles (**yendo, pudiendo, viniendo**). Several other verbs have irregular present participles.

-*ir* stem changing verbs

e:ie in the present tense		PRESENT PARTICIPLE
preferir	→	prefiriendo
sentir		sintiendo
e:i in the present tense		
conseguir		consiguiendo
pedir	→	pidiendo
seguir		siguiendo
o:ue in the present tense		
dormir	→	durmiendo

Using the present progressive

▶ The present progressive is used less in Spanish than in English. In Spanish, the present progressive emphasizes that an action is *in progress*.

Ella todavía **está escuchando** música.
She is still listening to music.

Javier **está dibujando** ahora mismo.
Javier is drawing right now.

▶ In English, the present progressive is used with actions that occur over time or in the future. In Spanish, the simple present tense is used.

Practican fútbol este verano.
They're playing soccer this summer.

Salgo hoy a las tres.
I'm leaving today at three.

¡Manos a la obra!

 Create complete sentences using the present progressive.

1. Mis amigos / descansar en la playa _Mis amigos están descansando en la playa._
2. Nosotros / practicar deportes _____
3. Carmen / comer en casa _____
4. Nuestro equipo / ganar el partido _____
5. Yo / leer el periódico _____
6. Él / pensar en comprar una bicicleta _____
7. Uds. / explicar la lección _____
8. José y Francisco / dormir _____
9. Marisa / leer el correo electrónico _____
10. Yo / preparar sándwiches _____
11. Carlos / tomar fotos _____
12. ¿Tú / dormir? _____

5.3 Comparing **ser** and **estar**

▸ **Ser** and **estar** both mean *to be,* but are used for different purposes.

Uses of *ser*

Nationality and place of origin	Los Gómez son peruanos.
	Luisa es de Cuzco.
Profession or occupation	Adela es ingeniera.
	Ana y yo somos médicos.
Traits of people and things	Sus padres son amables.
	El hotel es muy grande.
Generalizations	Es necesario trabajar.
Possession	Las postales son de Maite.
What something is made of	Las llaves son de metal.
Date and time	¿Qué hora es? Son las tres.
	¿Qué día es hoy? Hoy es lunes.
	Hoy es el dos de abril.
Where or when events occur	La fiesta es en mi casa.
	El concierto es a las ocho.

Soy Francisco Castillo Moreno. Yo soy de la agencia Ecuatur.

Su nombre no está en mi lista.

Uses of *estar*

Location or spatial relationships	El hotel no está lejos.
	Álex está en el cine.
Health	¿Cómo estás?
	Estoy enfermo.
Physical states and conditions	El conductor está cansado.
	Las puertas están cerradas.
Emotional states	Silvio está aburrido.
	Estoy contenta con el viaje.
Certain weather expressions	Está despejado.
	Está nublado.
On-going actions (progressive)	Estamos buscando el museo.
	Chela está durmiendo.

Práctica

1 Completar Complete this conversation with the correct forms of **ser** and **estar**.

TINA ¡Hola, Ricardo! ¿Cómo _____?

RICARDO Hola, Tina. Bien, gracias. ¡Qué guapa _____ hoy!

TINA Gracias. _____ muy amable. Oye, ¿qué _____ haciendo? ¿_____ ocupado?

RICARDO No, sólo _____ escribiendo un mensaje electrónico a mi amigo Sancho.

TINA ¿De dónde _____ él?

RICARDO Sancho _____ de Ponce, pero ahora él y su familia _____ de vacaciones en Nueva York.

TINA Y… ¿cómo _____ Sancho?

RICARDO _____ moreno y un poco bajo. También _____ muy listo. Quiere _____ ingeniero.

2 En el aeropuerto What do the people in the picture look like? How are they feeling? What are they doing?

Conversación

3 **Adivinar** Using the questions below as a guide, describe a few classmates to your partner. Don't mention their names. Your partner should guess which classmates you are describing. For a challenge, describe a couple of celebrities and your partner will guess their identities.

- ¿Cómo es?
- ¿Cómo está?
- ¿De dónde es?
- ¿Dónde está?
- ¿Qué está haciendo?

4 **Describir** With a partner, describe the people in the drawing. Your descriptions should answer these questions.

1. ¿Quiénes son?
2. ¿Dónde están?
3. ¿Cómo son?
4. ¿Cómo están?
5. ¿Qué están haciendo?
6. ¿Qué estación es?
7. ¿Qué tiempo hace?

Ser and estar with adjectives

▶ With many adjectives, both **ser** and **estar** can be used, but with different connotations. Statements with **ser** describe inherent, permanent qualities. **Estar** is used to describe temporary and changeable conditions.

Juan **es** nervioso.
Juan is nervous.

Juan **está** nervioso hoy.
Juan is nervous today.

Ana siempre **es** feliz.
Ana is always happy.

Ana **está** feliz hoy.
Ana is happy today.

▶ Some adjectives change in meaning depending on whether they are used with **ser** or **estar.**

With *ser*

El chico **es listo**.
*The boy is **smart**.*

La profesora **es mala**.
*The professor is **bad**.*

Jaime **es aburrido**.
*Jaime is **boring**.*

Las peras **son verdes**.
*The pears are **green**.*

El gato **es muy vivo**.
*The cat is very **lively**.*

El puente **es seguro**.
*The bridge is **safe**.*

With *estar*

El chico **está listo**.
*The boy is **ready**.*

La profesora **está mala**.
*The professor is **sick**.*

Jaime **está aburrido**.
*Jaime is **bored**.*

Las peras **están verdes**.
*The pears are **not ripe**.*

El gato **está vivo**.
*The cat is **alive**.*

Él no **está seguro**.
*He's not **sure**.*

¡Manos a la obra!

Form complete sentences with **ser** or **estar**.

1. Alejandra / cansado
   Alejandra está cansada.
2. Ellos / guapo hoy
3. Carmen / alto
4. Yo / la clase de español
5. Película / a las once
6. Hoy / viernes
7. Nosotras / enojado
8. Antonio / médico
9. Romeo y Julieta / enamorado
10. Libros / de Ana
11. Marisa y Juan / estudiando
12. Fiesta / gimnasio

5.4 Direct object nouns and pronouns

▸ A direct object noun receives the action of the verb directly and generally follows the verb. In the example below, the direct object noun answers the question *what is Maite writing?*

SUBJECT	VERB	DIRECT OBJECT NOUN
Maite *Maite*	está escribiendo *is writing*	unas postales. *some postcards.*

¿Dónde pongo las maletas?

Puede ponerlas encima de la cama.

Hay muchos lugares interesantes por aquí. ¿Quieren ir a verlos?

▸ When a direct object noun is a person or a pet, it is preceded by the word **a**. The "personal **a**" has no English equivalent.

Marta busca **a** sus amigos.
Marta looks for her friends.

Escucho **al** profesor.
I listen to the professor.

Direct object pronouns

Singular forms		Plural forms	
me	*me*	nos	*us*
te	*you (fam.)*	os	*you (fam.)*
lo	*you (m., form.);* *him; it (m.)*	los	*you (m., form.);* *them (m.)*
la	*you (f., form.);* *her; it (f.)*	las	*you (f., form.);* *them (f.)*

▸ Direct object pronouns replace direct object nouns. Like English, Spanish sometimes uses a direct object pronoun to avoid repetition.

DIRECT OBJECT	DIRECT OBJECT PRONOUN
Maribel hace las maletas. Felipe compra el sombrero. Vicky tiene la llave.	Maribel las hace. Felipe lo compra. Vicky la tiene.

¡ojo! In Spain and parts of Latin America, **le** and **les** are used when referring to people.

No **le** veo.
I don't see him/her.

No **les** escucha.
He/she doesn't listen to them.

Práctica

1 **Seleccionar** Choose the correct response.

1. ¿El artista quiere dibujarte con tu mamá?
   a. Sí, quiere dibujarlos mañana.
   b. Sí, nos quiere dibujar mañana.
   c. Sí, quiere dibujarte mañana.

2. ¿Quién tiene los pasajes?
   a. Yo lo tengo.
   b. Rita las lleva al aeropuerto.
   c. Mónica los tiene.

3. ¿Vas a llevar a tu hermana a la playa?
   a. No, no voy a llevarlas.
   b. No, no voy a llevarte.
   c. No, no voy a llevarla.

4. ¿Vas a hacer las maletas?
   a. Sí, voy a hacerla.
   b. Sí, voy a hacerlas.
   c. Sí, los voy a hacer.

5. ¿Quién tiene la llave de nuestra habitación?
   a. Yo no la tengo.
   b. Amalia los tiene.
   c. Yo lo tengo.

6. ¿Me puedes llevar al partido de fútbol?
   a. No, no las puedo llevar.
   b. Sí, los puedo llevar.
   c. Sí, te puedo llevar.

2 **¿Qué estás haciendo?** A classmate has called to find out what you are doing to prepare for your trip to Cancún. Answer his or her questions.

modelo

buscar tu cámara

Estudiante 1: ¿Estás buscando tu cámara?
Estudiante 2: No, no estoy buscándola.
Estudiante 1: ¿Cuándo la vas a buscar?
Estudiante 2: Voy a buscarla mañana (el lunes, a las dos, etc.).

1. preparar los documentos de viaje
2. confirmar tus reservaciones
3. buscar tu pasaje
4. buscar tu mochila
5. hacer tus maletas

Conversación

3 Entrevista Use these questions to interview a classmate. Your classmate should respond using direct object pronouns.

1. ¿Quién prepara la comida (*food*) en tu casa?
2. ¿Visitas mucho a tus abuelos?
3. ¿Cuándo ves a tus amigos?
4. ¿Estudias español todos los días?
5. ¿Traes tu libro a clase? ¿Y tu cuaderno?
6. ¿Cuándo vas a hacer la tarea de la clase de español?
7. ¿Ves mucho la televisión? ¿Cuándo vas a ver tu programa favorito?
8. ¿Tienes las llaves de tu casa? ¿De tu carro (*car*)?

4 En un café Get together with a partner and take turns asking each other questions about the drawing.

modelo

Estudiante 1: ¿Quién está leyendo el mapa?
Estudiante 2: El Sr. Torres está leyéndolo.

Ana
Santiago
La Sra. Torres
El Sr. Torres
Mario

Using direct object pronouns

▶ In affirmative sentences, direct object pronouns generally appear before the conjugated verb. In negative sentences, the pronoun is placed between the word **no** and the verb.

Katia tiene las llaves. ▶ **Katia** las **tiene.**
Marcos no practica el tenis. ▶ **Marcos** no lo **practica.**

▶ In the present progressive and in infinitive constructions, such as **ir a** + [*infinitive*], the direct object pronoun can be placed before the conjugated form, or attached to the present participle or infinitive.

Vamos a hacer las maletas. ▶ Las **vamos a hacer.**
Vamos a hacerlas.

Quiero ver el estadio. ▶ Lo **quiero ver.**
Quiero verlo.

▶ When a pronoun is attached to the present participle, an accent mark is added to maintain the proper stress.

Están buscando la llave. ▶ La **están buscando.**
Están buscándola.

¿**Estás mirando** el programa? ▶ ¿Lo **estás mirando?**
¿**Estás mirándolo?**

¡Manos a la obra!

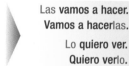

Write new sentences, changing the direct object nouns into pronouns and making any other necessary changes.

1. Juan tiene el pasaporte.
   Juan lo tiene.
2. Confirman la reservación.
   _____
3. Leemos la lección.
   _____
4. Estudio el vocabulario.
   _____
5. Aprendemos las palabras.
   _____
6. Escucho al profesor.
   _____
7. Escribe los párrafos.
   _____
8. Tengo los pasajes.
   _____
9. Quiero las llaves.
   _____
10. Van a ver la película.
    _____
11. Quiero ver los monumentos.
    _____
12. Vamos a tener el examen.
    _____
13. ¿Cuándo vas a hacer la tarea?
    _____
14. Están explorando el pueblo.
    _____
15. Él está comprando los libros.
    _____
16. Estoy leyendo las cartas.
    _____

Ampliación

 1 Escuchar

A Listen to the weather report by Hernán Jiménez and indicate which of these phrases are correct.

 TIP Listen for key words. Listening for key words and phrases will help you identify the subject and main ideas, as well as some of the details.

Santo Domingo
___ 1. hace sol
___ 2. va a hacer frío
___ 3. una mañana de mal tiempo
___ 4. va a estar nublado
___ 5. buena tarde para tomar el sol
___ 6. buena mañana para ir a la playa

San Francisco de Macorís
___ 1. hace frío
___ 2. hace sol
___ 3. va a nevar
___ 4. va a llover
___ 5. hay niebla
___ 6. buen día para excursiones

B ¿Qué tiempo hace en Santo Domingo ahora? ¿Y en San Francisco de Macorís? ¿Qué tiempo hace en tu ciudad?

 2 Conversar

Get together with a classmate you don't know very well and ask each other questions using **ser**, **estar**, and other verbs. Be sure to ask about the following topics.

- Las clases
- La familia
- Los amigos
- Los pasatiempos
- Las vacaciones
- Los parientes
- El tiempo
- Los compañeros de clase

Ampliación

Descripción del sitio (con foto)
A. Playa Grande
1. Playas seguras y limpias
2. Ideal para tomar el sol y descansar
B. El hotel
1. Abierto los 365 días del año
2. Piscina grande

3 Escribir

Write a tourist brochure for a hotel or resort.

 TIP **Make an outline.** Separate topics and subtopics in order to provide a framework for the information you want to present.

Organízalo — Jot down the most attractive aspects of your hotel or resort. Then, organize your ideas into an outline.

Escríbelo — Using the outline you have compiled, write the first draft of your brochure.

Corrígelo — Exchange papers with a classmate and comment on the brochure's completeness, organization, grammatical correctness, and level of interest. Then revise your first draft, keeping your classmate's comments in mind.

Compártelo — Swap brochures with a classmate. After you have read the brochure, name the three aspects of the hotel or resort that appeal to you most or least.

4 Un paso más

Create a real or simulated website to promote a travel package to a resort in a Spanish-speaking country. Include images whenever possible. Your website should consist of the following pages:

- A home page with a general description of the tour and links to your other pages
- A page describing the means of transportation
- A page describing hotels and accommodations
- A page about the locations to be visited
- A page detailing activities available to travelers.

Excursión por Puerto Rico: La Isla del Encanto

excursión de 4 días

excursión de 7 días

Agencia de Viajes El Morro
Tel: 787-234-5678
Fax: 787-876-5432

 En Internet

Investiga estos temas en el sitio vistahigherlearning.com.

- Balnearios (*resorts*) de España
- Balnearios de la América del Sur
- Balnearios de México, Centroamérica y el Caribe

Antes de leer

By scanning for specific information, you can learn a great deal about a text without reading it word for word. For example, you can scan a document to identify its format, to find cognates, or to find specific facts.

Examinar el texto

Scan the reading selection for cognates and write a few of them down.

1. _____
2. _____
3. _____
4. _____
5. _____

Based on the cognates you found, what do you think this document is about?

_____

_____

Preguntas

Read the following questions. Then scan the document again to look for answers to the questions.

1. What is the format of the reading selection?

_____

2. What place is the document about?

_____

3. What are some of the visual cues this document provides? What do they tell you about the content of the document?

_____

_____

4. Who produced the document, and what do you think the document is for?

_____

_____

¡Descubre el Viejo San Juan!

El Morro

El Morro es una fortaleza que defendió la bahía de San Juan entre los años 1500 y 1900. La arquitectura del lugar es extraordinaria. El Morro tiene numerosos túneles secretos, oscuras mazmorras y fantásticas vistas de la bahía. Además, en su interior hay un museo donde se explica la historia de la fortaleza.

La Iglesia de San José

La Iglesia de San José está en el norte de la ciudad, en la famosa plaza del mismo nombre. Esta iglesia es una construcción de 1532. De hecho, es la iglesia más antigua de la isla y un excelente ejemplo de la arquitectura gótica española del siglo XVI.

El Museo Pablo Casals

Pablo Casals es un famoso violonchelista español, que vivió los últimos años de su vida, de 1956 a 1973, en la isla de Puerto Rico. El Museo Pablo Casals es un interesante edificio del siglo XVIII. En su interior hay muchos objetos personales del músico, como su chelo, su piano y una gran cantidad de manuscritos y fotografías.

Hermosos hoteles y cafés

El Viejo San Juan ofrece unos hoteles impresionantes, con habitaciones lujosas y vistas increíbles de la ciudad y del mar. Cerca de los hoteles hay cafés muy agradables, donde los viajeros pueden conversar y escuchar diferentes estilos de música.

Después de leer

¿Comprendiste?

Indicate whether each statement is **cierto** or **falso**.

Cierto	Falso	
_____	_____	1. El Morro es una fortaleza en la bahía de San Juan.
_____	_____	2. El Viejo San Juan no tiene hoteles buenos.
_____	_____	3. El Museo Pablo Casals tiene muchos artículos personales del famoso violonchelista.
_____	_____	4. La Iglesia de San José tiene un museo donde se explica la historia de Puerto Rico.
_____	_____	5. El Museo Pablo Casals es un edificio del siglo XVIII.
_____	_____	6. La Iglesia de San José es de estilo moderno.

Preguntas

1. ¿Dónde pasa Pablo Casals los últimos años de su vida?
   _____

2. Describe la arquitectura de la Iglesia de San José.
   _____

3. ¿Qué podemos hacer en los cafés del Viejo San Juan?
   _____

4. ¿Qué hay en el interior de El Morro?
   _____

5. ¿Dónde está la Iglesia de San José?
   _____

Coméntalo

Imagina que vas de vacaciones al Viejo San Juan. ¿En qué mes del año deseas ir? ¿Por qué? ¿Cómo prefieres viajar, en avión o en barco? ¿Quieres visitar los lugares mencionados aquí? ¿Por qué?

mazmorras	dungeons
se explica	they explain; (something) is explained
además	besides
de hecho	in fact
más antigua	oldest
siglo	century
edificio	building
lujosas	luxurious

recursos

R

vistahigher learning.com

Los viajes y las vacaciones

el aeropuerto	airport
la agencia de viajes	travel agency
el/la agente de viajes	travel agent
la estación de autobuses	bus station
del metro	subway station
del tren	train station
el/la inspector(a) de aduanas	customs inspector
el pasaje (de ida y vuelta)	(round-trip) ticket
el pasaporte	passport
la tienda de campaña	tent
el/la viajero/a	traveler
acampar	to camp
confirmar una reservación	to confirm a reservation
estar de vacaciones	to be on vacation
hacer las maletas	to pack (one's suitcases)
hacer un viaje	to take a trip
una excursión	to go on a hike; to go on a tour
hacer turismo (m.)	to go sightseeing
ir a la playa	to go to the beach
ir de pesca	to go fishing
de vacaciones	to go on vacation
ir en autobús (m.)	to go by bus
en auto(móvil) (m.)	to go by car
en avión (m.)	to go by plane
en barco (m.)	to go by boat
en motocicleta (f.)	to go by motorcycle
en taxi (m.)	to go by taxi
montar a caballo	to ride a horse
pasar por la aduana	to go through customs
pescar	to fish
sacar fotos (f. pl.)	to take pictures

En el hotel

el alojamiento	lodging
el/la botones	bellhop
la cabaña	cabin
la cama	bed
el/la empleado/a	employee
la habitación	room
individual	single room
doble	double room
el hotel	hotel
el/la huésped	guest
la llave	key
la pensión	boarding house
el piso	floor (of a building)
la planta baja	ground floor

Adjetivos

abierto/a	open
aburrido/a	bored; boring
alegre	happy, joyful
amable	nice; friendly
avergonzado/a	embarrassed
cansado/a	tired
cerrado/a	closed
cómodo/a	comfortable
contento/a	happy, content
desordenado/a	disorderly; messy
enamorado/a (de)	in love (with)
enojado/a	mad, angry
equivocado/a	wrong; mistaken
feliz	happy
limpio/a	clean
listo/a	ready; smart
nervioso/a	nervous
ocupado/a	busy
ordenado/a	orderly
preocupado/a (por)	worried (about)
seguro/a	sure; safe
sucio/a	dirty
triste	sad

¿Qué tiempo hace?

¿Qué tiempo hace?	How's the weather?; What's the weather like?
Está despejado.	It's clear.
(muy) nublado.	It's (very) cloudy.
Hace buen/mal tiempo.	It's nice/bad weather.
(mucho) calor.	It's (very) hot.
fresco.	It's cool.
(mucho) frío.	It's (very) cold.
(mucho) sol.	It's (very) sunny.
(mucho) viento.	It's (very) windy.
Hay (mucha) niebla.	It's (very) foggy.
llover (o:ue)	to rain
Llueve.	It's raining.
nevar (e:ie)	to snow
Nieva.	It's snowing.

Palabras y expresiones adicionales

el ascensor	elevator
el campo	countryside
el equipaje	luggage
la llegada	arrival
el mar	ocean, sea
la salida	departure; exit
ahora mismo	right now
todavía	yet; still
¿Cuál es la fecha de hoy?	What is today's date?
Hoy es el primero (dos, tres,...) de marzo.	Today is March first (second, third,...).

Las estaciones y los meses	See page 107.
Ordinal Numbers	See page 107.
Expresiones útiles	See page 113.
Direct object pronouns	See page 122.

recursos

| R | Lab CD Lección 5 | LM p. 30 |

6 ¡De compras!

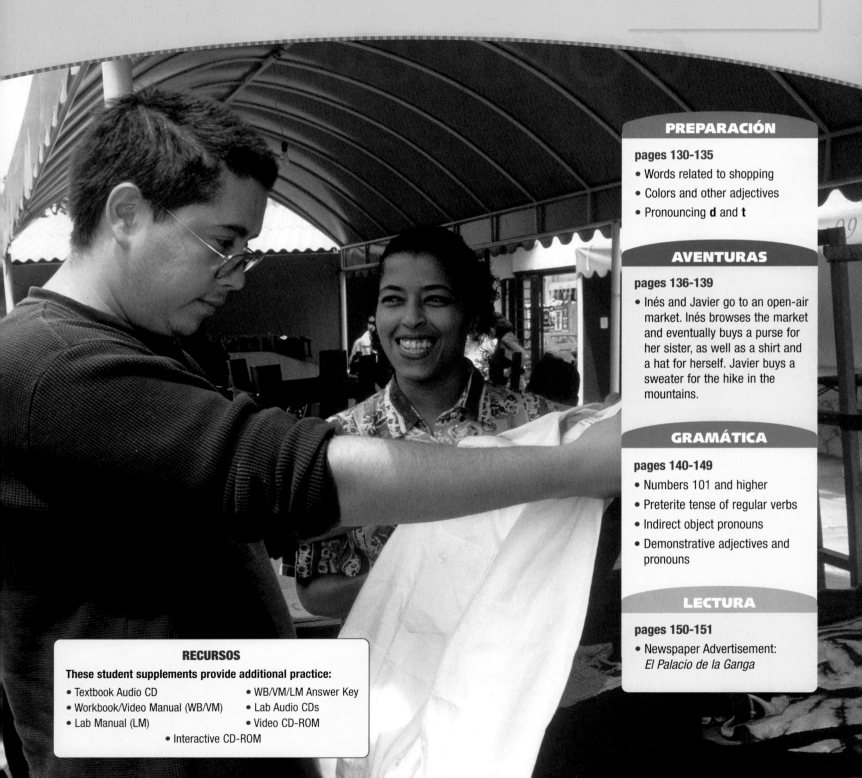

Communicative Goals

You will learn how to:
- discuss how much things cost
- talk about clothing
- talk to salespeople

PREPARACIÓN

pages 130-135
- Words related to shopping
- Colors and other adjectives
- Pronouncing **d** and **t**

AVENTURAS

pages 136-139
- Inés and Javier go to an open-air market. Inés browses the market and eventually buys a purse for her sister, as well as a shirt and a hat for herself. Javier buys a sweater for the hike in the mountains.

GRAMÁTICA

pages 140-149
- Numbers 101 and higher
- Preterite tense of regular verbs
- Indirect object pronouns
- Demonstrative adjectives and pronouns

LECTURA

pages 150-151
- Newspaper Advertisement: *El Palacio de la Ganga*

¡DE COMPRAS!

DE COMPRAS

el almacén *department store*
la caja *cash register*
el centro comercial *shopping mall*
el/la cliente/a *client*
el/la dependiente/a *clerk*
el mercado (al aire libre) *(open-air) market*
la rebaja *sale*
la tienda *shop, store*
el/la vendedor(a) *salesperson*

costar (o:ue) *to cost*
gastar *to spend (money)*
hacer juego (con) *to match*
ir de compras *to go shopping*
llevar *to wear*
regatear *to bargain*
usar *to wear; to use*
vender *to sell*

el precio (fijo)
(fixed, set) price

la tarjeta de crédito
credit card

el dinero
money

recursos

R	Textbook CD Lección 6	WB pp. 53-54	LM p. 31	Lab CD Lección 6	ICD-ROM Lección 6

LA ROPA

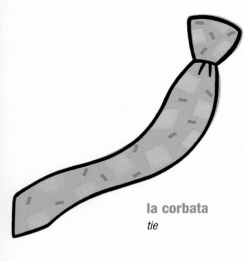

la corbata
tie

las gafas de sol
sunglasses

el abrigo *coat*
los bluejeans *jeans*
la blusa *blouse*
la bolsa *bag; purse*
las botas *boots*
los calcetines *socks*
la camisa *shirt*
la camiseta *t-shirt*
la cartera *wallet*
la chaqueta *jacket*
el cinturón *belt*
la falda *skirt*
los guantes *gloves*
el impermeable *raincoat*

las medias *pantyhose, stockings*
los pantalones *pants*
   cortos *shorts*
el par *pair*
la ropa *clothing, clothes*
   interior *underwear*
las sandalias *sandals*
el sombrero *hat*
el suéter *sweater*
el traje *suit*
   de baño *bathing suit*
el vestido *dress*
los zapatos de tenis *sneakers*

los zapatos
shoes

LOS COLORES

amarillo/a *yellow*

anaranjado/a *orange*

blanco/a *white*

rojo/a *red*

gris *gray*

rosado/a *pink*

negro/a *black*

morado/a *purple*

café *brown*

verde *green*

azul *blue*

ADJETIVOS

barato/a *cheap*
bueno/a *good*
cada *each*
caro/a *expensive*
corto/a *short*
elegante *elegant*
hermoso/a *beautiful*
largo/a *long*
loco/a *crazy*
nuevo/a *new*
otro/a *other; another*
pobre *poor*
rico/a *rich*

A escuchar

1 Escuchar Listen to Juanita and Vicente talk about what they're packing for their vacations. Indicate who is packing each item. If both are packing an item, write both names. If neither is packing an item, write an X.

Vicente

Juanita

Artículo	Nombre(s)	Artículo	Nombre(s)
1. abrigo	_____	7. gafas de sol	_____
2. zapatos de tenis	_____	8. camisetas	_____
3. impermeable	_____	9. traje de baño	_____
4. chaqueta	_____	10. botas	_____
5. sandalias	_____	11. pantalones cortos	_____
6. bluejeans	_____	12. suéter	_____

2 ¿Cierto o falso? Look at the drawing and indicate whether each statement you hear is **cierto** or **falso**.

	Cierto	Falso
1.	_____	_____
2.	_____	_____
3.	_____	_____
4.	_____	_____
5.	_____	_____
6.	_____	_____
7.	_____	_____
8.	_____	_____

recursos

Textbook CD
Lección 6

A practicar

3 **Escoger** Which item in each group does not belong?

1. bolsa • camiseta • blusa
2. medias • calcetines • sombrero
3. chaqueta • falda • abrigo
4. almacén • vendedora • tienda • mercado
5. regatear • gastar • llevar • costar
6. vestido • dinero • caja • tarjeta de crédito

4 **Anita la contraria** Your friend Anita always contradicts you. Indicate how she would respond to each sentence.

modelo El suéter nuevo de Tina es muy hermoso.
No, su suéter es muy feo.

1. Las sandalias de Rufino están sucias. _____

2. El impermeable de don José es muy grande. _____

3. La corbata del Sr. Garza es larga. _____

4. Los trajes de Mauricio son bonitos. _____

5. Los zapatos de tenis de Noelia son nuevos. _____

6. El cinturón de Amalia es caro. _____

5 **Preguntas** Answer these questions with a classmate.

1. ¿De qué color es el suéter?

2. ¿De qué color es la corbata?

3. ¿De qué color es la planta?

4. ¿De qué color es la rosa de Texas?

5. ¿De qué color es la casa donde vive el presidente de EE.UU?

6. ¿De qué color es una cebra?

A conversar

 6 **Marta y el Sr. Vega** With a classmate, answer the questions about the drawing.

Marta   **El señor Vega**

1. ¿Qué lleva Marta?

2. ¿De qué color es su vestido?

3. ¿De qué color son sus zapatos?

4. ¿De qué color son su sombrero y su bolsa?

5. ¿Qué lleva el Sr. Vega?

6. ¿De qué color es su camisa?

7. ¿De qué color son sus pantalones?

8. ¿Hacen juego la chaqueta, la camisa y los pantalones del Sr. Vega?

 7 **Entrevista** Use these questions to interview a classmate. Then report your findings to the class.

1. ¿Adónde vas para (*in order to*) comprar ropa? ¿Por qué?

2. En tu opinión, ¿es importante comprar frecuentemente ropa nueva?

3. ¿Cuánto dinero gastas en ropa cada mes? ¿Cada año?

4. Cuando vas de compras, ¿buscas rebajas?

5. ¿Regateas cuando compras ropa?

6. ¿Prefieres pagar en efectivo (*cash*) o con una tarjeta de crédito?

🎧 Pronunciación

The consonants **d** and **t**

¿Dónde?   ven**d**er   na**d**ar   ver**d**a**d**

Like **b** and **v**, the Spanish **d** can also have a hard sound or a soft sound, depending on which letters appear next to it.

Don   **d**inero   tie**n**da   fal**d**a

At the beginning of a phrase and after **n** or **l**, the letter **d** is pronounced with a hard sound. This sound is similar to the English *d* in *dog*, but a little softer and duller. The tongue should touch the back of the upper teeth, not the roof of the mouth.

me**d**ias   ver**d**e   vesti**d**o   huéspe**d**

In all other positions, **d** has a soft sound. It is similar to the English *th* in *there*, but a little softer.

Don **D**iego no tiene e**l d**iccionario.

When **d** begins a word, its pronunciation depends on the previous word. At the beginning of a phrase or after a word that ends in **n** or **l**, it is pronounced as a hard **d**.

Doña **D**olores e**s d**e la capital.

Words that begin with **d** are pronounced with a soft **d** if they appear immediately after a word that ends in a vowel or any consonant other than **n** or **l**.

traje   pan**t**alones   **t**arje**t**a   **t**ienda

When pronouncing the Spanish **t**, the tongue should touch the back of the upper teeth, not the roof of the mouth. Unlike the English *t*, no air is expelled from the mouth.

Práctica Read these phrases aloud to practice the **d** and the **t**.

1. Hasta pronto.
2. De nada.
3. Mucho gusto.
4. Lo siento.
5. No hay de qué.
6. ¿De dónde es usted?
7. ¡Todos a bordo!
8. No puedo.
9. Es estupendo.
10. No tengo computadora.
11. ¿Cuándo vienen?
12. Son las tres y media.

Una tienda Read these sentences aloud to practice the **d** and the **t**.

1. Don Teodoro tiene una tienda en un almacén en La Habana.

2. Don Teodoro vende muchos trajes, vestidos y zapatos todos los días.

3. Un día un turista, Federico Machado, entra en la tienda para comprar un par de botas.

4. Federico regatea con don Teodoro y compra las botas y también un par de sandalias.

Refranes Read these sayings aloud to practice the **d** and the **t**.

En la variedad está el gusto.[1]

Aunque la mona se vista de seda, mona se queda.[2]

1 *Variety is the spice of life.*
2 *You can't make a silk purse out of a sow's ear.*

recursos

| R | Textbook CD Lección 6 | LM p. 32 | Lab CD Lección 6 | ICD-ROM Lección 6 |

¡Qué ropa más bonita!

Javier e Inés van de compras al mercado.

1

INÉS Javier, ¡qué ropa más bonita! A mí me gusta esa camisa blanca y azul. Debe ser de algodón. ¿Te gusta?

JAVIER Yo prefiero la camisa de la izquierda, la gris con rayas rojas. Hace juego con mis botas marrones.

2

INÉS Está bien, Javier. Mira, necesito comprarle un regalo a mi hermana Graciela. Acaba de empezar un nuevo trabajo…

JAVIER ¿Tal vez una bolsa?

3

VENDEDOR Esas bolsas son típicas de las montañas. ¿Le gustan?

INÉS Sí. Quiero comprarle una a mi hermana.

6

VENDEDOR Buenas tardes, joven. ¿Le puedo servir en algo?

JAVIER Sí. Voy a ir de excursión a las montañas y necesito un buen suéter.

VENDEDOR ¿Qué talla usa Ud.?

JAVIER Uso talla grande.

7

VENDEDOR Éstos son de talla grande.

JAVIER ¿Qué precio tiene ése?

VENDEDOR ¿Le gusta este suéter? Le cuesta ciento cincuenta mil sucres.

JAVIER Quiero comprarlo. Pero, señor, no soy rico. ¿Ciento veinte mil sucres?

8

VENDEDOR Bueno, para usted… sólo ciento treinta mil sucres.

JAVIER Está bien, señor.

Personajes

JAVIER

INÉS

EL VENDEDOR

INÉS Me gusta aquélla. ¿Cuánto cuesta?

VENDEDOR Ésa cuesta ciento sesenta mil sucres. ¡Es de muy buena calidad!

INÉS Uy, demasiado cara. Quizás otro día.

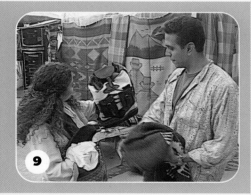

JAVIER Acabo de comprarme un suéter. Y tú, ¿qué compraste?

INÉS Compré esta bolsa para mi hermana.

INÉS También compré una camisa y un sombrero. ¿Qué tal me veo?

JAVIER ¡Guapa, muy guapa!

Expresiones útiles

Talking about clothing
¡Qué ropa más bonita!
What pretty clothes!
Me gusta esta/esa camisa blanca de rayas negras.
I like this/that white shirt with black stripes.
Está de moda.
It's in fashion.
Debe ser de algodón/lana/seda.
It must be cotton/wool/silk.
Es de cuadros/lunares/rayas.
It's plaid/polka-dotted/striped.
Me gusta este/ese suéter.
I like this/that sweater.
Es de muy buena calidad.
It's very good quality.
¿Qué talla lleva/usa Ud.?
What size do you wear?
Llevo/uso talla grande.
I wear a large.
¿Qué número calza Ud.?
What (shoe) size do you wear?
Calzo el treinta y seis.
I wear a size six.

Talking about how much things cost
¿Cuánto cuesta?
How much does it cost?
Sólo cuesta noventa mil sucres.
It only costs ninety thousand sucres.
Demasiado caro/a.
Too expensive.
Es una ganga.
It's a bargain.

Saying what you bought
¿Qué compró Ud./él/ella?
What did you (form.)/he/she buy?
Compré esta bolsa para mi hermana.
I bought this bag for my sister.
¿Qué compraste?
What did you buy?
Acabo de comprarme un sombrero.
I just bought myself a hat.

¿Qué piensas?

1 **¿Cierto o falso?** Indicate whether each sentence is **cierto** or **falso**. Correct the false statements.

Cierto **Falso**

_____ _____ 1. A Inés le gusta la camisa verde y amarilla.

_____

_____ _____ 2. Javier necesita comprarle un regalo a su hermana.

_____

_____ _____ 3. Las bolsas del mercado son típicas de las montañas.

_____

_____ _____ 4. Javier busca un traje de baño en el mercado.

_____

_____ _____ 5. Inés compró un sombrero, un suéter y una bolsa.

_____

_____ _____ 6. Javier regatea con el vendedor.

_____

2 **Contestar** Answer these questions about the **Aventuras** episode.

1. Inés quiere comprarle un regalo a su hermana. ¿Por qué?

_____

2. ¿Cuánto cuesta la bolsa típica de las montañas?

_____

3. ¿Por qué necesita Javier un buen suéter?

_____

4. ¿Cuánto cuesta el suéter que compra Javier?

_____

5. ¿Cuántas cosas compró Inés en el mercado?

_____

6. ¿Qué talla usa Javier?

_____

3 **Conversar** With a classmate, role-play a conversation in which the salesperson greets a customer in an open-air market and offers assistance. The customer is looking for a particular item of clothing. The salesperson and the customer discuss colors, sizes, and negotiate a price.

Exploración
De compras en los países hispanos

Las tiendas pequeñas son muy populares en los países hispanos. El nombre de muchas de estas tiendas se refiere al producto que venden. Por ejemplo, una tienda que vende zapatos es una zapatería y una tienda que vende libros es una librería.

Los mercados al aire libre son muy importantes en el mundo hispano. En ellos se venden muchos productos como ropa, comida (*food*) y libros. En estos mercados tienes que pagar en efectivo (*cash*), pero puedes regatear. El Rastro en Madrid es un mercado muy conocido (*well-known*).

Datos interesantes

- El centro comercial Larcomar en Lima, Perú, está situado sobre un espléndido acantilado (*cliff*).

- En los pueblos pequeños las tiendas generalmente cierran durante la hora del almuerzo (*lunch*).

- El Centro Sambil en Caracas, Venezuela, es el centro comercial más grande de Suramérica. Tiene una terraza, con restaurantes y cafés, que ofrece una vista espectacular de la ciudad.

Muchas ciudades grandes, como la Ciudad de México, Caracas y Madrid, tienen centros comerciales que ofrecen tiendas exclusivas, restaurantes y música en vivo (*live music*).

Coméntalo

Con un(a) compañero/a, contesta las siguientes preguntas.

- ¿Conoces alguna tienda que tiene un nombre similar al producto que vende?
- Piensa en los artículos que te gusta comprar. ¿Dónde prefieres comprarlos?
- ¿Hay un mercado al aire libre o un centro comercial en tu comunidad?

recursos

R

vistahigher
learning.com

6.1 Numbers 101 and higher

▶ Note that Spanish uses a period, rather than a comma, to indicate thousands and millions.

Numbers 101 and higher			
101	ciento uno	1.000	mil
200	doscientos/as	1.100	mil cien
300	trescientos/as	2.000	dos mil
400	cuatrocientos/as	5.000	cinco mil
500	quinientos/as	100.000	cien mil
600	seiscientos/as	200.000	doscientos mil
700	setecientos/as	550.000	quinientos cincuenta mil
800	ochocientos/as	1.000.000	un millón (de)
900	novecientos/as	8.000.000	ocho millones (de)

Ésa cuesta ciento sesenta mil sucres.

Aquí está la reservación... dos habitaciones dobles y una individual, de la ciento uno a la ciento tres.

▶ The numbers **200** through **999** agree in gender with the nouns they modify.

324 tiendas
trescien**tas** veinticuatro tiendas

873 habitaciones
ochocien**tas** setenta y tres habitaciones

500 mujeres
quinien**tas** mujeres

605 clientes
seiscient**os** cinco clientes

990 euros
novecient**os** noventa euros

257 estudiantes
doscient**os** cincuenta y siete estudiantes

▶ **Mil** can mean *a thousand* or *one thousand*. The plural form **miles** is rarely used. The plural form of **un millón** (*a million* or *one million*), is **millones**, which has no accent.

1.000 dólares
mil dólares

1.000 aviones
mil aviones

5.000 bicicletas
cinco mil bicicletas

2.000.000 de pesos
dos millones de pesos

1.000.000 de personas
un millón de personas

1.000.000 de aficionados
un millón de aficionados

Práctica

1 **Completar** Complete these sequences in Spanish.

1. 100, 120, 140, ... 200

_____

_____

2. 5.000, 10.000, 15.000, ... 30.000

_____

_____

3. 50.000, 100.000, 150.000, ... 300.000

_____

_____

4. 100.000.000, 200.000.000, 300.000.000, ... 900.000.000

_____

_____

2 **Resolver** Read the math problems aloud and solve them.

modelo
$$\begin{array}{r} 300 \\ +400 \\ \hline 700 \end{array}$$

Trescientos más cuatrocientos son setecientos.

(+ más − menos = es (singular)/son (plural))

1. $\begin{array}{r} 150 \\ +150 \\ \hline \end{array}$

5. $\begin{array}{r} 3.000 \\ +\ \ 753 \\ \hline \end{array}$

2. $\begin{array}{r} 43.000 \\ -10.000 \\ \hline \end{array}$

6. $\begin{array}{r} 200.000 \\ +350.000 \\ \hline \end{array}$

3. $\begin{array}{r} 20.000 \\ +\ \ \ 555 \\ \hline \end{array}$

7. $\begin{array}{r} 1.000.000 \\ -\ \ 75.000 \\ \hline \end{array}$

4. $\begin{array}{r} 32.000 \\ -30.000 \\ \hline \end{array}$

8. $\begin{array}{r} 800.000 \\ +175.000 \\ \hline \end{array}$

Conversación

3 **¿Cuándo?** With a partner, look at the timeline and say when these events occur.

1914-1918	1939-1945	1968	1969	1997
Primera Guerra Mundial	Segunda Guerra Mundial	Martin Luther King Jr. es asesinado.	Los astronautas llegan a la Luna.	El *Pathfinder* llega al planeta Marte.

1. La Primera Guerra Mundial comienza.

2. El *Pathfinder* llega al planeta Marte.

3. Martin Luther King Jr. es asesinado.

4. La Primera Guerra Mundial termina.

5. La Segunda Guerra Mundial termina.

6. Los astronautas llegan a la Luna (*moon*).

7. La Segunda Guerra Mundial comienza.

4 **¿Cuánto cuesta?** Ask your partner how much each item costs.

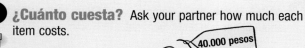
40.000 pesos

Estudiante 1: ¿Cuánto cuestan las gafas de sol?
Estudiante 2: Cuarenta mil pesos.

1.
210.000 pesos

4.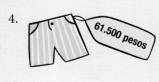
61.500 pesos

2.
160.150 pesos

5.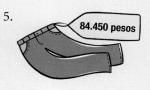
84.450 pesos

3.
48.200 pesos

6.
22.790 pesos

Using numbers

▶ In Spanish, years are not expressed as pairs of 2-digit numbers as they are in English (*1979, nineteen seventy-nine*):

1945	**2005**
mil novecientos cuarenta y cinco	dos mil cinco
1898	**1220**
mil ochocientos noventa y ocho	mil doscientos veinte

Bueno, para usted... sólo ciento treinta mil sucres.

Le cuesta ciento cincuenta mil sucres.

Pero, señor, no soy rico. ¿Ciento veinte mil sucres?

▶ When **millón** or **millones** is used before a noun, place **de** between the two.

1.000.000 **de** hombres = un **millón de** hombres
12.000.000 **de** aviones = doce **millones de** aviones
15.000.000 **de** personas = quince **millones de** personas

¡ojo! Note this difference between Spanish and English:

mil millones
a billion (1.000.000.000)

un billón
a trillion (1.000.000.000.000)

Hay **mil millones** de personas en China.
There are a billion people in China.

Hay un **billón** de planetas en el universo.
There are a trillion planets in the universe.

¡Manos a la obra!

Give the Spanish equivalent of each number.

1. 102 ___ciento dos___
2. 935 _____
3. 5.000.000 _____
4. 2001 _____
5. 1776 _____
6. 345 _____
7. 550.300 _____
8. 235 _____
9. 1999 _____
10. 113 _____
11. 205 _____
12. 2.105 _____
13. 17.123 _____
14. 497 _____

6.2 The preterite tense of regular verbs

▶ The preterite is used to talk about actions or states completed in the past.

Preterite of regular –ar, –er, and –ir verbs		
	comprar	vender	escribir
yo	compré / *I bought*	vendí / *I sold*	escribí / *I wrote*
tú	compraste	vendiste	escribiste
Ud./él/ella	compró	vendió	escribió
nosotros/as	compramos	vendimos	escribimos
vosotros/as	comprasteis	vendisteis	escribisteis
Uds./ellos/ellas	compraron	vendieron	escribieron

▶ The preterite endings for regular **–er** and **–ir** verbs are identical. Also, note that all **yo** and **Ud./él/ella** forms have accents on the last syllable.

¿Qué compraste?

Compré esta bolsa.

▶ Note that the **nosotros/as** forms of regular **–ar** and **–ir** verbs in the preterite are identical to the present tense forms. The context will help you tell the difference.

En invierno **compramos** suéteres.
In the winter we buy sweaters.

Anoche **compramos** unas sandalias.
Last night we bought some sandals.

Escribimos poemas en clase.
We write poems in class.

Ya **escribimos** dos veces al presidente.
We already wrote to the president twice.

▶ **–Ar** and **–er** verbs that have a stem change in the present tense do *not* have a stem change in the preterite.

INFINITIVE	PRESENT	PRETERITE
cerrar (e:ie)	Ana cierra la puerta.	Ana cerró la puerta.
volver (o:ue)	Memo vuelve a las dos.	Memo volvió a las dos.
jugar (u:ue)	Él juega al fútbol.	Él jugó al fútbol.
pensar (e:ie)	Pienso mucho.	Pensé mucho.

Práctica

1 **Preguntas** A pesky friend keeps asking you questions. Respond that you already did or have just done what he/she asks.

modelo

leer la lección
Estudiante 1: ¿Leíste la lección?
Estudiante 2: Sí, ya la leí./Sí, acabo de leerla.

1. lavar (*to wash*) la ropa

2. encontrar tu tarjeta de crédito

3. comprar los suéteres

4. practicar los verbos

5. empezar la composición

6. ver la película *La momia* (*The Mummy*)

2 **¿Qué hicieron?** Combine words from each list to talk about things you and others did.

modelo

Yo leí un buen libro la semana pasada.

¿Quién?	¿Qué?	¿Cuándo?
yo	ver la televisión	anoche
mi compañero/a de cuarto	hablar con un(a) chico/a guapo/a	anteayer
mis amigos y yo	estudiar español	ayer
mis padres	comprar ropa nueva	la semana pasada
mi abuelo/a	leer un buen libro	el año pasado
el/la profesor(a) de español	bailar en el centro comercial	una vez
el presidente de los Estados Unidos	viajar a la Luna (*moon*)	dos veces
mi perro (*dog*)	llegar tarde a clase	
	viajar a Europa	
	escribir una carta	
	llevar ropa muy fea	
	comer siete hamburguesas	

Conversación

3 Encuesta Find out if your partner did the activities listed. Report the results to the class.

modelo

llevar un impermeable ayer
Estudiante 1: ¿Llevaste un impermeable ayer?
Estudiante 2: No, no llevé un impermeable ayer.

Actividades	Respuestas
1. Ver cuatro películas de aventura el año pasado	_____
2. Escribir una telenovela (*soap opera*) el año pasado	_____
3. Viajar a Latinoamérica el verano pasado	_____
4. Salir con una persona famosa la semana pasada	_____
5. Comprar ropa interior ayer	_____
6. Recibir un regalo (*gift*) de un(a) "admirador(a) secreto/a" ayer	_____

4 Nuestras vacaciones You took these photos on a vacation with friends. Use the pictures to tell your partner about the trip.

5 ¿Qué hiciste ayer? Get together with a partner and take turns asking each other what you did yesterday, the day before yesterday, and last week.

Verbs with spelling changes

▶ Verbs that end in **–car**, **–gar**, and **–zar** have a spelling change in the **yo** form of the preterite. All the other forms are regular.

bus**car** → bus**qué**   lle**gar** → lle**gué**   empe**zar** → empe**cé**

▶ **Creer**, **leer**, and **oír** have spelling changes in the preterite.

creer	creí, creíste, creyó, creímos, creísteis, creyeron
leer	leí, leíste, leyó, leímos, leísteis, leyeron
oír	oí, oíste, oyó, oímos, oísteis, oyeron

▶ **Ver** is regular in the preterite, but none of its forms has an accent.

ver → vi, viste, vio, vimos, visteis, vieron

Words commonly used with the preterite			
anoche	*last night*	desde... hasta...	*from... until...*
anteayer	*the day before yesterday*	pasado/a	*(adj.) last; past*
		la semana pasada	*last week*
el año pasado	*last year*	una vez	*once; one time*
ayer	*yesterday*	dos veces	*twice; two times*
de repente	*suddenly*	ya	*already*

Compré una camisa **ayer**.   Miré la televisión **anoche**.
I bought a shirt yesterday.   *I watched TV last night.*

Useful phrases	
¿Qué hiciste?	*What did you (fam.) do?*
¿Qué hizo usted?	*What did you (form., sing.) do?*
¿Qué hicieron ustedes?	*What did you (form., pl.) do?*
¿Qué hizo él/ella?	*What did he/she do?*
¿Qué hicieron ellos/ellas?	*What did they do?*

¡ojo! **Acabar de** + [*infinitive*] is used to say that something has just occurred. Note that **acabar** is in the present tense in this construction:

Acabo de comprar un suéter.   **Acabas de ir** de compras.
I just bought a sweater.   *You just went shopping.*

¡Manos a la obra!

Give the preterite form of each verb.

1. Elena ___celebró___ [celebrar].
2. Ellos _____ [oír].
3. Emilio y yo _____ [comprar].
4. Los niños _____ [comer].
5. Ud. _____ [salir].
6. Yo _____ [llegar].
7. Yo _____ [empezar].
8. Tú _____ [vender].
9. Uds. _____ [escribir].
10. Juan _____ [ver].

6.3 Indirect object pronouns

SUBJECT	INDIRECT OBJECT	VERB	DIRECT OBJECT	INDIRECT OBJECT
Roberto	le	prestó	cien pesos	a Luisa.
Roberto		*loaned*	*100 pesos*	*to Luisa.*

▶ An indirect object is the noun or pronoun that answers the question *to whom* or *for whom* an action is done. In the example above, the indirect object answers this question: **¿A quién le prestó Roberto cien pesos?** *To whom did Roberto loan 100 pesos?*

Indirect object pronouns

Singular forms
me	*(to, for) me*
te	*(to, for) you (fam.)*
le	*(to, for) you (form.)*
	(to, for) him; (to, for) her

Plural forms
nos	*(to, for) us*
os	*(to, for) you (fam.)*
les	*(to, for) you (form.);*
	(to, for) them

¿Le puedo servir en algo?

Sí, necesito comprarme un buen suéter.

▶ The indirect object pronoun and the indirect object noun (to which the pronoun refers) are often used in the same sentence. This is done to emphasize or clarify *to whom* the pronoun refers. The indirect object pronoun is often used without its indirect object noun when the person for whom the action is being done is known.

Iván **le** prestó un lápiz **a Rico**.
Iván loaned a pencil to Rico.

También **le** prestó papel.
He also loaned him paper.

Sabrina **le** compró un café **a Sarah**.
Sabrina bought Sarah a coffee.

También **le** compró un sándwich.
She also bought her a sandwich.

¡ojo! Since **le** and **les** have multiple meanings, **a** + [*noun*] or **a** + [*pronoun*] are often used to clarify to whom the pronouns refer.

Unclear
Ella **les** vendió ropa.
Yo **le** presté una camisa.

Clearer
Ella **les** vendió ropa **a ellos**.
Yo **le** presté una camisa **a Luis**.

Práctica

1 Completar Complete Emilio's description of his family's holiday shopping.

1. Yo _____ compré una cartera a mi padre.
2. Mi tía _____ compró una corbata muy fea.
3. Mis primos _____ compraron a mis padres dos pares de guantes.
4. A mi mamá yo _____ compré un suéter azul.
5. A nosotros mis abuelos _____ compraron muchos regalos.
6. Y yo _____ compré una camiseta bonita a mi novia.

2 Minidiálogos Supply the missing words.

ESPOSO ¿Vas a comprarme una cartera? ¿Un cinturón?
ESPOSA No, _____ ropa interior.

· · ·

PACO ¿Vas a comprarle un regalo a tu novio?
GISELA ¡No _____ nada!

· · ·

NIÑOS Mamá, ¿vas a leernos un cuento (*story*)?
MAMÁ Sí, _____ "Blancanieves" (*Snow White*).

· · ·

PROFESORA Andrés, ¿ _____ la verdad?
ANDRÉS Claro que (*of course*) le digo la verdad, profesora.

· · ·

ALFREDO Ramón, _____ tu bicicleta hoy?
RAMÓN No, no te puedo prestar mi bicicleta. Lo siento, pero es que tienes muchos accidentes.

· · ·

ELISA ¿_____ una tarjeta postal a Maripili?
NACHO No, estoy escribiéndoles una tarjeta postal a Laura y Enrique. ¿Por qué?

Conversación

 Describir With a partner, describe what's happening in these photos based on the cues provided. Use indirect object pronouns.

1. escribir / mensaje electrónico

3. mostrar / fotos

2. pedir / llaves

4. vender / suéter

 Entrevista Use these questions to interview a classmate.

1. ¿Te gusta ir de compras?
2. ¿Qué tiendas, almacenes o centros comerciales prefieres?
3. ¿Le compras mucha ropa a tu novio/a?
4. ¿Les compras regalos a tus amigos cuando hay rebajas?
5. ¿Te prestan tus padres la tarjeta de crédito?
6. ¿Me compraste un regalo el año pasado?
7. Quiero ir de compras. ¿Cuánto dinero me puedes prestar?
8. ¿Siempre (*always*) le dices la verdad al profesor?

5 **¡Somos ricos!** You and your classmates are very rich and want to spend money on your loved ones. In groups of three, discuss what each person is buying for family and friends.

modelo

Estudiante 1: *Quiero comprarle un vestido nuevo a mi mamá y una camiseta a mi novio.*

Estudiante 2: *Y yo voy a darles un carro nuevo a mis padres. A mis compañeras de cuarto les voy a comprar blusas y faldas nuevas.*

Estudiante 3: *Voy a comprarles una casa a mis padres. Pero a mis amigos no les voy a dar nada.*

Estudiante 1: *¡Qué malo eres!*

Using indirect object pronouns

▶ Indirect object pronouns usually precede the conjugated verb. In negative phrases, place the pronoun between **no** and the conjugated verb.

Le compré un abrigo.
I bought him a coat.

No le compré nada.
I didn't buy him anything.

▶ When an infinitive or present participle follows the conjugated verb, the indirect object pronoun may be placed before the conjugated verb, or attached to the infinitive or present participle. When a pronoun is attached to a present participle, an accent mark is added.

Estoy mostrándo**les** las fotos.
Les estoy mostrando las fotos.
I'm showing them the photos.

¿Vas a comprar**le** un regalo?
¿**Le** vas a comprar un regalo?
Are you going to buy a gift for her?

▶ The irregular verbs **dar** (*to give*) and **decir** (*to say; to tell*) often occur with object pronouns.

Dar and decir

	dar	decir
yo	doy	digo
tú	das	dices
Ud./él/ella	da	dice
nosotros/as	damos	decimos
vosotros/as	dais	decís
Uds./ellos/ellas	dan	dicen
Present Participle	dando	diciendo

Mi abuela **me da** muchos regalos.
My grandmother gives me lots of gifts.

Te digo la verdad.
I'm telling you the truth.

Voy a **darle** un beso.
I'm going to give her a kiss.

No **digo** mentiras.
I don't tell lies.

¡Manos a la obra!

 Rewrite the following sentences, attaching the indirect object pronoun to the end of the infinitive or present participle. Add accent marks when necessary.

1. Susana te está escribiendo una carta. <u>Susana está escribiéndote una carta.</u>
2. Le tienes que pedir un lápiz al profesor. _____
3. Mi novia me va a comprar una camisa. _____
4. Mi novio me está preparando unos tacos. _____
5. La mamá le va a leer un libro al niño. _____

6.4 Demonstrative adjectives and pronouns

Demonstrative adjectives

▶ Demonstrative adjectives demonstrate or point out nouns. Demonstrative adjectives precede the nouns they modify and agree with them in gender and number.

este vestido
this dress

esos zapatos
those shoes

aquella tienda
that store (over there)

Demonstrative adjectives

Singular forms		Plural forms		
MASCULINE	FEMININE	MASCULINE	FEMININE	
este	esta	estos	estas	*this; these*
ese	esa	esos	esas	*that; those*
aquel	aquella	aquellos	aquellas	*that; those (over there)*

▶ The demonstrative adjectives **este**, **esta**, **estos**, and **estas** are used to point out nouns that are close to both the speaker and the listener.

Me gusta este vestido.

▶ The demonstrative adjectives **ese**, **esa**, **esos**, and **esas** are used to point out nouns that are not close to the speaker. The objects may, however, be close to the listener.

¡Pero esos zapatos son horrendos!

▶ The demonstrative adjectives **aquel**, **aquella**, **aquellos**, and **aquellas** are used to point out nouns that are far away from both the speaker and the listener.

Aquella tienda es mi favorita.

Práctica

1 **En un almacén** Gabriel and María are at a department store. Complete their conversation.

MARÍA No me gustan _____ (*those*) pantalones. Voy a comprar _____ (*these*).

GABRIEL Yo prefiero _____ (*those over there*).

MARÍA Sí, me gustan a mí también. ¿Qué piensas de _____ (*these*) cinturones?

GABRIEL _____ (*these*) cuestan demasiado (*too much*).

MARÍA También busco un vestido elegante. ¿Te gusta _____ (*this one*)?

GABRIEL No, es muy feo. ¿Necesitas una falda nueva? _____ (*this one*) es bonita.

MARÍA No, no necesito una falda. Vamos, Gabriel. Me gusta _____ (*this*) almacén, pero _____ (*that one over there*) es mejor (*better*).

2 **¿De qué color es?** Use demonstrative adjectives and pronouns to discuss the colors of your classmates' clothing.

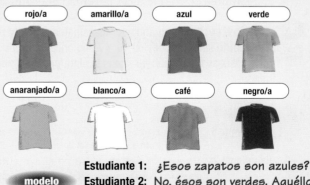

rojo/a   amarillo/a   azul   verde

anaranjado/a   blanco/a   café   negro/a

modelo

Estudiante 1: ¿Esos zapatos son azules?
Estudiante 2: No, ésos son verdes. Aquéllos son azules.
Estudiante 1: Y esa camiseta, ¿es roja?
Estudiante 2: No, ésa es blanca. Aquélla es roja.

Conversación

3 **Nuestros compañeros** Get together with a partner and take turns asking each other questions about the people around you.

¿Cómo se llama… ?	**¿Cómo es/son… ?**
¿Qué clases toma(n)… ?	**¿De dónde es/son… ?**
¿Cuándo… ?	**¿De quién es/son… ?**
¿A qué hora… ?	**¿Cuántos años tiene(n)… ?**

modelo

Estudiante 1: ¿De dónde es ese chico?
Estudiante 2: Es de Nueva York. ¿De dónde es esa chica?
Estudiante 1: Creo que es de Los Ángeles. ¿Qué clases toma aquella chica?
Estudiante 2: Ella toma inglés, español y arte.

4 **En una tienda** You and a classmate are in a small clothing store. Look at the illustration, then have a conversation about what you see around you.

modelo

Estudiante 1: ¿Te gusta esa chaqueta que está debajo de las camisas?
Estudiante 2: No, prefiero aquélla que está al lado de los pantalones. ¿Dónde están los zapatos?
Estudiante 1: Están en el centro de la tienda.

Demonstrative pronouns

▶ Demonstrative pronouns are identical to demonstrative adjectives, except that they carry an accent mark on the stressed vowel. They agree in number and gender with the corresponding noun.

No me gusta **este** suéter. Prefiero **ése**.
I don't like this sweater. I prefer that one.

Ella quiere comprar **esa** bolsa, no **aquélla**.
She wants to buy that purse, not that one over there.

No voy a comprar **estos** zapatos. Quiero **aquéllos**.
I'm not going to buy these shoes. I want those ones over there.

¿Qué precio tienen **esos** pantalones? **Ésos** cuestan quince dólares.
How much do those pants cost? Those cost fifteen dollars.

Demonstrative pronouns				
Singular forms		**Plural forms**		
MASCULINE	FEMININE	MASCULINE	FEMININE	
éste	ésta	éstos	éstas	*this one; these*
ése	ésa	ésos	ésas	*that one; those*
aquél	aquélla	aquéllos	aquéllas	*that one; those (over there)*

▶ There are three neuter forms: **esto**, **eso**, and **aquello**. These forms refer to unidentified or unspecified nouns, situations, and ideas. They do not change in gender or number and never carry an accent mark.

¿Qué es **esto**?	**Eso** es interesante.	**Aquello** es bonito.
What's this?	*That's interesting.*	*That's pretty.*

¡Manos a la obra!

Provide the correct form of the demonstrative adjective and demonstrative pronoun for these nouns.

1. la falda / este
   esta falda; ésta

2. los estudiantes / este

3. los países / aquel

4. la ventana / ese

5. los periodistas / ese

6. las empleadas / ese

7. el chico / aquel

8. las sandalias / este

9. el autobús / ese

10. las chicas / aquel

11. el abrigo / aquel

12. los pantalones / este

13. las medias / ese

14. la bolsa / aquel

Ampliación

1 Escuchar

A Listen to Marisol and Alicia's conversation. Make a list of the clothing items that each person mentions, then note if she actually purchased it.

TIP Listen for linguistic cues. Listening for the verb endings of conjugated verbs will help you identify when an event occurs—in the past, present, or future. Verb endings also give clues as to who is participating in the action.

Marisol	Alicia
1. _____	1. _____
2. _____	2. _____
3. _____	3. _____
4. _____	4. _____

B ¿Crees que la moda (*fashion*) es importante para Alicia? ¿Y para Marisol? ¿Por qué? En tu opinión, ¿es importante estar a la moda (*to be in fashion*)?

2 Conversar

With a classmate, take turns playing the roles of a shopper and a clerk in a clothing store. Use the following guidelines.

- The shopper talks about the clothing he/she is looking for as a gift, mentions for whom the clothes are intended, and says what he/she bought for the same person last year.
- The clerk recommends items, based on the shopper's descriptions.
- The shopper asks how much items cost, and the clerk answers.

recursos

R	Textbook CD Lección 6	WB pp. 55-62	LM pp. 33-36	Lab CD Lección 6	ICD-ROM Lección 6	vistahigher learning.com

Ampliación

❸ Escribir

Write a report for the school newspaper about an interview you conducted with a student concerning his or her shopping habits and clothing preferences.

 TIP Reporting an interview. You may transcribe the interview verbatim, simply summarize it, or summarize it with occasional speaker quotes. Your report will be more interesting if you include a title and introduction, and end with a conclusion.

Organízalo	Use an idea map to organize the interview questions and develop an outline for your report. Then brainstorm a title for your report.
Escríbelo	Using your outline as a guide, write the first draft of your report.
Corrígelo	Exchange papers with a classmate and comment on the report's title, introduction, conclusion, organization, level of interest, and correctness. Then revise your first draft, with your classmate's comments in mind.
Compártelo	Exchange reports in groups of four. Give a superlative title to each report on the basis of its strongest points, for example, "best use of Spanish" or "most interesting questions."

❹ Un paso más

Develop a business plan to open a store in a Spanish–speaking country.

- Decide which products you are going to sell and select an appealing name for your store.
- Choose a location for your store.
- Include a visual presentation of your products.
- Itemize your products' prices and your expected profits.
- Explain why you think your store will be successful.

 En Internet

Investiga estos temas en el sitio vistahigherlearning.com.
- Tiendas y almacenes famosos
- La moneda de los países hispanos

Antes de leer

Skimming involves quickly reading through a document to absorb its general meaning. This strategy allows you to understand the main ideas without having to read word for word. Skim the reading selection to get its general meaning.

Examinar el texto

Look at the format of the reading selection. How is it organized? What does the organization of the document tell you about its content?

Buscar cognados

Scan the reading selection to locate cognates and write a few of them down. Based on the cognates, what is the reading selection about?

1. _____
2. _____
3. _____
4. _____
5. _____
6. The reading selection is about _____ .

Impresiones generales

Now skim the reading selection to understand its general meaning. Jot down your impressions. What new information did you learn about the document by skimming it? Based on all the information you now have, answer these questions.

1. Who produced this document?
2. What is its purpose?
3. Who is its intended audience?

El Palacio de la

¡Donde la rebaja es la reina! ¡Aproveche nuestras ofert

Abierto de lunes a viernes de 10 a 21 horas • sábado de 12 a 20 hor

Suéter de algodón para mujeres/todas las tallas Rebajados de 3.450,00 PESOS A SÓLO 2.760,00 PESOS

Pantalones formales para caballeros/colores gris, negro y azul con el 30% de rebaja, de 5.200,00 PESOS A SÓLO 3.640,00 PESOS

Hermosas **blusas** de seda para damas/tallas mediana y grande Rebajadas de 2.030,00 PESOS al increíble precio de 1.450,00 PESOS

Elegantes **chaquetas** para caballeros/colores café, negro, azul y verde con rebaja del 25%, de 5.370,00 PESOS A SÓLO 4.027,50 PESOS

GANGA

Aceptamos todas las tarjetas de crédito.

Faldas largas para mujeres/colores café, morado, azul y gris
rebajadas de **2.468,00** PESOS A SÓLO **1.974,00** PESOS

Baratos **trajes de baño**
para hombres en amarillo, blanco, azul, verde y morado
Con rebaja del 40%, de **1.384,00** PESOS A SÓLO **830,40** PESOS

Nuevo **modelo de botas**
para mujeres
Números 35 a 38
rebajados de **3.370,00** PESOS A SÓLO **2.596,00** PESOS

Zapatos de tenis
Para hombres
Números 40 a 45
rebajados de **2.976,00** PESOS A SÓLO **2.315,00** PESOS

Después de leer

¿Comprendiste?

Indicate whether each statement is **cierto** or **falso**. Correct the false statements.

Cierto	Falso	
_____	_____	1. Con 4.000 pesos un cliente puede comprar un pantalón formal para hombre.
_____	_____	2. Normalmente las blusas de seda cuestan más de 2.000 pesos.
_____	_____	3. El Palacio de la Ganga abre a las diez de la mañana los domingos.
_____	_____	4. Una elegante chaqueta azul cuesta 4.027,50 pesos.
_____	_____	5. Los trajes de baño para hombre tienen una rebaja del veinticinco por ciento.
_____	_____	6. Hay rebaja de suéteres de algodón para hombres.
_____	_____	7. El Palacio de la Ganga acepta tarjetas de crédito.
_____	_____	8. El Palacio de la Ganga está abierto (*open*) los sábados.

Preguntas

1. ¿Cuánto cuestan los zapatos de tenis?
   _____

2. ¿Hay rebaja de blusas de algodón?
   _____

3. ¿Hay rebaja de ropa para niños en el Palacio de la Ganga? _____

4. ¿Hay rebaja de minifaldas? _____

Coméntalo

Imagina que vas a ir al Palacio de la Ganga. ¿Qué ropa vas a comprar? ¿Hay tiendas similares al Palacio de la Ganga en tu comunidad? ¿Cómo se llaman? ¿Tienen muchas rebajas?

el palacio	*palace*
la reina	*queen*
aproveche	*take advantage of*
abierto	*open*
caballeros	*gentlemen*
damas	*ladies*

recursos

R

vistahigher
learning.com

La ropa

el abrigo	coat
los bluejeans	jeans
la blusa	blouse
la bolsa	purse; bag
las botas	boots
los calcetines	socks
la camisa	shirt
la camiseta	t-shirt
la cartera	wallet
la chaqueta	jacket
el cinturón	belt
la corbata	tie
la falda	skirt
las gafas (de sol)	(sun)glasses
los guantes	gloves
el impermeable	raincoat
las medias	pantyhose, stockings
los pantalones	pants
cortos	shorts
el par	pair
la ropa interior	clothing, clothes underwear
las sandalias	sandals
el sombrero	hat
el suéter	sweater
el traje de baño	suit bathing suit
el vestido	dress
los zapatos de tenis	shoes sneakers

Adjetivos

barato/a	cheap
bueno/a	good
cada	each
caro/a	expensive
corto/a	short
elegante	elegant
hermoso/a	beautiful
largo/a	long
loco/a	crazy
nuevo/a	new
otro/a	other; another
pobre	poor
rico/a	rich

Ir de compras

el almacén	department store
la caja	cash register
el centro comercial	shopping mall
el/la cliente/a	customer
el/la dependiente/a	clerk
el dinero	money
el mercado (al aire libre)	(open-air) market
el precio (fijo)	(fixed; set) price
la rebaja	sale
el regalo	gift
la tarjeta de crédito	credit card
la tienda	shop, store
el/la vendedor(a)	salesperson
costar (o:ue)	to cost
gastar	to spend (money)
hacer juego (con)	to match
ir de compras	to go shopping
llevar	to wear
regatear	to bargain
usar	to wear; to use
vender	to sell

Palabras y expresiones

anoche	last night
anteayer	the day before yesterday
ayer	yesterday
de repente	suddenly
desde	from; since
hasta	until
pasado/a	last; past
el año pasado	last year
la semana pasada	last week
una vez	once; one time
dos veces	twice; two times
ya	already
el beso	kiss
la mentira	lie
la verdad	truth
¿Qué hiciste?	What did you (fam.) do?
¿Qué hizo usted?	What did you (form., sing.) do?
¿Qué hizo él/ella?	What did he/she do?
¿Qué hicieron ustedes?	What did you (form., pl.) do?
¿Qué hicieron ellos/ellas?	What did they do?
acabar de (+ inf.)	to have just done something
dar	to give
decir (que)	to say (that); to tell
prestar	to lend; to loan

Colors	See page 131.
Expresiones útiles	See page 137.
Numbers 101 and higher	See page 140.
Indirect object pronouns	See page 144.
Demonstrative adjectives and pronouns	See pages 146-147.

recursos

R | Lab CD Lección 6 | LM p. 36

AVENTURAS EN LOS PAÍSES HISPANOS

Una mujer baila flamenco en Sevilla. El flamenco, el baile y su música, expresa las pasiones de la gente de España. Tiene raíces *(roots)* judías *(Jewish)*, árabes y africanas. Hoy es popular en todo el mundo. ¿Te gusta la música flamenca?

ESPAÑA

Estadísticas

Área: 504.750 km^2 (kilómetros cuadrados) o 194.884 millas^2, incluyendo las islas Baleares y las islas Canarias

Población: 41.166.000

Capital: Madrid - 5.309.000

Ciudades importantes: Barcelona-4.760.000, Valencia-2.210.000, Sevilla-1.720.000, Zaragoza-827.999

Moneda: – euro

SOURCE: Population Division, UN Secretariat

Madrid: La Plaza Mayor

La Plaza Mayor de Madrid es uno de los lugares turísticos más *(most)* importantes de Madrid. Fue construida *(was built)* en 1617 y está totalmente rodeada *(surrounded)* por edificios *(buildings)* de tres pisos con balcones y pórticos antiguos. En la Plaza Mayor hay muchas cafeterías, donde la gente pasa el tiempo bebiendo café y hablando con amigos.

La Tomatina

En Buñol, un pequeño pueblo de Valencia, la producción de tomates es un recurso *(resource)* muy importante. Cada año en agosto se celebra el festival de La Tomatina. Durante *(during)* todo un día, miles de personas se arrojan *(throw)* tomates unas a otras. Llegan turistas de todo el mundo y se usan varias toneladas *(tons)* de tomates.

Mar Cantábrico

La Coruña

Salamanca

Madrid

PORTUGAL

ESPAÑA

Sevilla

Estrecho de Gibraltar

Ceuta

MARRUECOS

FRANCIA

Sebastián

ANDORRA

Pirineos

Zaragoza

Barcelona

Islas Baleares

Menorca

Mallorca

Valencia

Ibiza

Mar Mediterráneo

a Nevada

a

La Unión Europea

Desde 1992 España participa en la Unión Europea, un grupo de países europeos que trabajan para desarrollar *(to develop)* una política económica y social común en Europa. La moneda de España era *(was)* la peseta, pero desde enero de 2002 tiene la misma moneda de los países de la Unión Europea: el euro.

Artes

Velázquez y el Prado

El Prado, en Madrid, es uno de los museos más famosos del mundo. En el Prado hay miles de pinturas *(paintings)* importantes, incluyendo obras *(works)* de Botticelli, el Greco, y de los españoles Goya y Velázquez. Diego Velázquez pintó *(painted) Las Meninas* en 1656 y es su obra más famosa. Actualmente, *Las Meninas* está en el Museo del Prado.

¿Qué aprendiste?

1 **¿Cierto o falso?** Say whether the following statements are true or false, based on what you've learned about Spain.

	Cierto	Falso
1. La moneda de España es la peseta.	_____	_____
2. El flamenco es un instrumento musical.	_____	_____
3. El flamenco es hoy popular en todo el mundo.	_____	_____
4. En la Plaza Mayor no hay cafeterías.	_____	_____
5. La Plaza mayor fue construida en 1617.	_____	_____
6. En Buñol, los tomates son un recurso importante.	_____	_____
7. Durante La Tomatina, se arrojan pelotas.	_____	_____
8. España participa en la Unión Europea desde 1992.	_____	_____
9. En el Museo del Prado hay miles de pinturas importantes.	_____	_____
10. *Las Meninas* es la obra más famosa de Botticelli.	_____	_____

2 **Preguntas** Answer the following questions, based on what you have learned about Spain.

1. ¿Qué expresa el flamenco?

2. ¿Qué hace la gente en las cafeterías de la Plaza Mayor?

3. ¿Crees que el festival de La Tomatina es triste? ¿Crees que es divertido *(fun)*? ¿Por qué?

4. ¿Desde cuándo el euro es la moneda de España?

5. ¿Por qué crees que el Prado es uno de los museos más importantes del mundo?

En Internet

Busca más información sobre estos temas en el sitio vistahigherlearning.com. Presenta la información a tus compañeros/as de clase.

- La Plaza Mayor
- La Tomatina
- La Unión Europea
- Velázquez y el Prado

7 La vida diaria

Communicative Goals

You will learn how to:
- tell where you went
- talk about daily routines and personal hygiene
- reassure someone

PREPARACIÓN

pages 158-163
- Words related to personal hygiene and daily routines
- Sequencing expressions
- Pronouncing **r** and **rr**

AVENTURAS

pages 164-167
- Javier shows Álex the sweater he bought at the market. They discuss getting up early the next day. Álex agrees to wake Javier after his morning run. Don Francisco reminds them that the bus will leave at 8:30 a.m. tomorrow.

GRAMÁTICA

pages 168-177
- Reflexive verbs
- Indefinite and negative words
- Preterite of **ser** and **ir**
- **Gustar** and verbs like **gustar**

LECTURA

pages 178-179
- Magazine article: *¡Una mañana desastrosa!*

RECURSOS

These student supplements provide additional practice:
- Textbook Audio CD
- Workbook/Video Manual (WB/VM)
- Lab Manual (LM)
- WB/VM/LM Answer Key
- Lab Audio CDs
- Video CD-ROM
- Interactive CD-ROM

LA VIDA DIARIA

LA HIGIENE PERSONAL

cepillarse el pelo *to brush one's hair*
ducharse *to shower*
lavarse la cara *to wash one's face*
las manos *to wash one's hands*
maquillarse *to put on makeup*
peinarse *to comb one's hair*

el baño *bathroom*
el champú *shampoo*
la crema de afeitar *shaving cream*
el maquillaje *makeup*
la rutina diaria *daily routine*
la toalla *towel*

el espejo
mirror

el despertador
alarm clock

el jabón
soap

cepillarse los dientes
to brush one's teeth

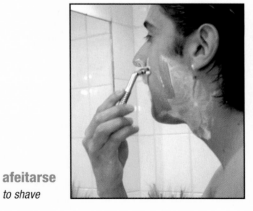

afeitarse
to shave

bañarse
to bathe; to take a bath

recursos

| R | Textbook CD Lección 7 | WB pp. 65-66 | LM p. 37 | Lab CD Lección 7 | ICD-ROM Lección 7 |

POR LA MAÑANA Y POR LA NOCHE

acostarse (o:ue) *to lie down; to go to bed*
despertarse (e:ie) *to wake up*
vestirse (e:i) *to get dressed*

dormirse (o:ue)
to go to sleep; to fall asleep

levantarse
to get up

OTRAS PALABRAS Y EXPRESIONES

Se acuesta. *He/she goes to bed; you (form.) go to bed.*
Se afeita. *He/she shaves; you shave.*
Se cepilla los dientes. *He/she brushes his/her teeth; you brush your teeth.*
Se despierta. *He/she wakes up; you wake up.*
Se peina. *He/she combs his/her hair; you comb your hair.*
Se viste. *He/she gets dressed; you get dressed.*

Se lava las manos.
She washes her hands.

ADVERBIOS Y PREPOSICIONES DE TIEMPO

antes (de) *before*
después *afterwards; then*
después de *after*
durante *during*
entonces *then*
luego *afterwards; then*
más tarde *later*
por la mañana *in the morning*
por la noche *at night*
por la tarde *in the afternoon; in the (early) evening*
por último *finally*

Se ducha.
He takes a shower.

A escuchar

 1 **¿Cierto o falso?** Escucha las frases, mira las fotos e indica si cada frase es **cierta** o **falsa**.

	Cierto	Falso
1.	_____	_____
2.	_____	_____
3.	_____	_____
4.	_____	_____
5.	_____	_____
6.	_____	_____
7.	_____	_____
8.	_____	_____

1.
2.
3.
4.
5.
6.
7.
8.

 2 **Escuchar** Escucha las frases e indica si cada frase es **lógica** o **ilógica**.

	Lógico	Ilógico
1.	_____	_____
2.	_____	_____
3.	_____	_____
4.	_____	_____
5.	_____	_____
6.	_____	_____

recursos

R
Textbook CD
Lección 7

A practicar

3 Ordenar Pon (*put*) esta historia (*story*) en orden.

_____ a. Después de afeitarse, cepillarse los dientes y vestirse, sale para las clases.

_____ b. Por último, se acuesta a las once y media de la noche.

_____ c. Entonces se ducha antes de afeitarse.

_____ d. Por la noche come un poco. Luego estudia antes de acostarse.

_____ e. Asiste a todas sus clases y vuelve a casa por la tarde.

_____ f. Por la mañana, Fabio se despierta a las seis y media.

4 Identificar Con un(a) compañero/a, indica las cosas que cada persona necesita.

modelo

Manuel / vestirse
Estudiante 1: ¿Qué necesita Manuel para (*in order to*) vestirse?
Estudiante 2: Necesita una camiseta y unos pantalones.

Daniel / acostarse   Raúl / despertarse   Mercedes / lavarse la cara

Leonardo / afeitarse   Sofía / lavarse el pelo   Yolanda / maquillarse

A conversar

5 **La rutina diaria** Con un(a) compañero/a, mira las fotos y describe lo que hace cada (*each*) persona.

modelo

Estudiante 1: ¿Qué hace Armando?
Estudiante 2: Se afeita.

Armando

Rocío

Noelia

don Carlos

doña Juana

Marisela

Néstor

6 **Describir** Trabajen en parejas (*pairs*) para describir la rutina diaria de dos o tres de estas personas. Pueden usar las palabras de la lista.

1. mi mejor (*best*) amigo/a
2. nuestro/a profesor(a) de español
3. mi padre/madre
4. mi compañero/a de cuarto
5. Kobe Bryant
6. Shakira
7. Ben Affleck
8. el presidente de los Estados Unidos

primero	durante el día	después
luego	antes	después de
entonces	antes de	por último

🎧 Pronunciación

The consonants r and rr

ropa	**r**utina	**r**ico	**R**amón

In Spanish, **r** has a strong trilled sound at the beginning of a word. No English words have a trill, but English speakers often produce a trill when they imitate the sound of a motor.

gusta**r**	du**r**ante	p**r**imero	c**r**ema

In any other position, **r** has a weak sound similar to the English *tt* in *better* or the English *dd* in *ladder*.
In contrast to English, the tongue touches the roof of the mouth behind the teeth.

piza**rr**a	co**rr**o	ma**rr**ón	abu**rr**ido

The letter **rr**, which only appears between vowels, always has a strong trilled sound.

ca**r**o	ca**rr**o	pe**r**o	pe**rr**o

Between vowels, the difference between the strong trilled **rr** and the weak **r** is very important, as a mispronunciation could lead to confusion between two different words.

Práctica Lee las palabras en voz alta, prestando (*paying*) atención a la pronunciación de la **r** y la **rr**.

1. Perú
2. Rosa
3. borrador
4. madre
5. comprar
6. favor
7. rubio
8. reloj
9. Arequipa
10. tarde
11. cerrar
12. despertador

Oraciones Lee las oraciones en voz alta, prestando atención a la pronunciación de la **r** y la **rr**.

1. Ramón Robles Ruiz es programador. Su esposa Rosaura es artista.
2. A Rosaura Robles le encanta regatear en el mercado.
3. Ramón nunca regatea… le aburre regatear.
4. Rosaura siempre compra cosas baratas.
5. Ramón no es rico, pero prefiere comprar cosas muy caras.
6. ¡El martes Ramón compró un carro nuevo!

Refranes Lee en voz alta los refranes, prestando atención a la **r** y a la **rr**.

Perro que ladra no muerde.[1]

No se ganó Zamora en una hora.[2]

1 The dog's bark is worse than its bite.
2 Rome wasn't built in a day.

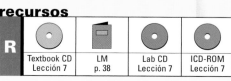

recursos

| R | Textbook CD Lección 7 | LM p. 38 | Lab CD Lección 7 | ICD-ROM Lección 7 |

¡Jamás me levanto temprano!

Álex y Javier hablan de sus rutinas diarias.

JAVIER Hola, Álex. ¿Qué estás haciendo?

ÁLEX Nada… Sólo estoy leyendo mi correo electrónico. ¿Adónde fueron?

JAVIER Inés y yo fuimos a un mercado. Fue muy divertido. Mira, compré este suéter. Me encanta. No fue barato, pero es chévere, ¿no?

ÁLEX Sí, es ideal para las montañas.

JAVIER ¡Qué interesantes son los mercados al aire libre! Me gustaría volver, pero ya es tarde. Oye, Álex, ¿sabes que mañana tenemos que levantarnos temprano?

ÁLEX Ningún problema.

JAVIER ¡Increíble! ¡Álex, el superhombre!

ÁLEX Oye, Javier, ¿por qué no puedes levantarte temprano?

JAVIER Es que por la noche no quiero dormir, sino dibujar y escuchar música. Por eso es difícil despertarme por la mañana.

JAVIER El autobús no sale hasta las ocho y media. ¿Vas a levantarte mañana a las seis también?

ÁLEX No, pero tengo que levantarme a las siete menos cuarto porque voy a correr.

JAVIER Ah, ya… ¿Puedes despertarme después de correr?

ÁLEX Éste es el plan para mañana. Me levanto a las siete menos cuarto y corro por treinta minutos. Vuelvo, me ducho, me visto y a las siete y media te despierto. ¿De acuerdo?

JAVIER ¡Absolutamente ninguna objeción!

recursos

| Video/VCD-ROM Lección 7 | VM pp.181-182 | ICD-ROM Lección 7 |

Personajes

DON FRANCISCO

ÁLEX

JAVIER

4

JAVIER ¿Seguro? Pues yo jamás me levanto temprano. Nunca oigo el despertador cuando estoy en casa y mi mamá se enoja mucho.

ÁLEX Tranquilo, Javier. Yo tengo una solución.

5

ÁLEX Cuando estoy en casa en la Ciudad de México, siempre me despierto a las seis en punto. Me ducho en cinco minutos y luego me cepillo los dientes. Después me afeito, me visto y ¡listo! ¡Me voy!

9

DON FRANCISCO Hola, chicos. Mañana salimos temprano, a las ocho y media… ni un minuto antes ni un minuto después.

ÁLEX No se preocupe, don Francisco. Todo está bajo control.

DON FRANCISCO Bueno, pues, hasta mañana.

10

DON FRANCISCO ¡Ay, los estudiantes! Siempre se acuestan tarde. ¡Qué vida!

¿Qué piensas?

1 **¿Cierto o falso?** Indica si las frases son **ciertas** o **falsas**. Corrige (*correct*) las frases falsas.

Cierto **Falso**

_____ _____ 1. Álex siempre se despierta a las seis cuando está en casa.

_____

_____ _____ 2. Álex está mirando la televisión.

_____

_____ _____ 3. El suéter que Javier acaba de comprar es caro, pero es muy bonito.

_____

_____ _____ 4. A Javier le gusta mucho dibujar y escuchar música por la noche.

_____

_____ _____ 5. Javier cree que los mercados al aire libre son aburridos.

_____

_____ _____ 6. El autobús va a salir hoy a las siete y media en punto.

_____

_____ _____ 7. Álex va a nadar por la mañana.

_____

_____ _____ 8. Javier siempre oye el despertador cuando está en casa.

_____

2 **Los planes de Álex** Ordena correctamente los planes que tiene Álex para mañana. Si hay algo (*something*) que Álex no menciona, escribe una **X.**

_____ a. Voy a lavarme las manos.

_____ b. Voy a vestirme.

_____ c. Voy a correr por media hora.

_____ d. Voy a acostarme temprano.

_____ e. Voy a despertar a mi amigo a las siete y media.

_____ f. Voy a volver a la habitación.

_____ g. Voy a levantarme a las siete menos cuarto.

_____ h. Voy a ducharme.

3 **Conversación** En parejas (*pairs*), preparen una conversación sobre sus rutinas diarias. Pregunten a qué hora hacen las actividades más importantes.

> **modelo**
>
> **Estudiante 1:** ¿Prefieres levantarte temprano o tarde?
> **Estudiante 2:** Prefiero levantarme tarde... muy tarde.
> **Estudiante 1:** ¿A qué hora te levantas durante la semana?
> **Estudiante 2:** A las once. ¿Y tú?

Exploración
La vida diaria

Alejandra Arce de Valera vive en Barcelona, España. Va a la oficina a las ocho de la mañana y trabaja hasta las cinco. Durante la mañana ella y dos o tres colegas (*colleagues*) descansan de quince a treinta minutos. Pero no se quedan en la oficina para descansar; van a un café para relajarse (*relax*), tomar un café (*have a cup of coffee*) y conversar.

Margarita Benítez Morales vive en Caracas, Venezuela. Trabaja en casa cuidando de (*taking care of*) sus hijas. ¡Pero Margarita no se queda (*doesn't stay*) en el sofá mirando la televisión! Durante un día típico, prepara tres comidas (*meals*), arregla la casa (*straightens the house*), va de compras, juega con las niñas y les lee varios cuentos (*stories*).

Luis Romero Reyes tiene diecinueve años y es estudiante de la Universidad Nacional Autónoma de México (UNAM). En un día típico se levanta temprano, asiste a una clase y estudia en la biblioteca. Va a su casa para comer al mediodía, pero después vuelve al campus para asistir a las clases de la tarde.

Observaciones

- Hay mujeres hispanas que prefieren ser amas de casa (*housewives*). Pero cada año hay más mujeres que escogen (*choose*) una carrera profesional.

- La costumbre de la siesta (un descanso de dos o tres horas durante el día) no es hoy tan común como (*as common as*) antes. Cuando España entró en la Unión Europea, por ejemplo, muchas empresas (*businesses*) eliminaron la siesta para tener el mismo horario que los otros países.

- La siesta es más común en los pueblos pequeños que en las ciudades grandes.

Coméntalo

Con un(a) compañero/a, contesta las siguientes preguntas.

- Piensa en la rutina diaria de tu familia y de tus amigos/as. ¿Es similar a la rutina diaria de Margarita Benítez Morales, Alejandra Arce de Valera y Luis Romero Reyes?

- ¿Descansas un poco durante un día típico? ¿Cuándo y dónde descansas?

recursos

R | vistahigher learning.com

7.1 Reflexive verbs

▶ A reflexive verb is used to indicate that the subject does something to or for himself or herself. Reflexive verbs always use reflexive pronouns.

SUBJECT   REFLEXIVE VERB

Carlos   **se afeita** todos los días.

Reflexive verbs

(**lavarse**)

to wash oneself

yo	me lavo	*I wash (myself)*
tú	te lavas	*you wash (yourself)*
Ud.	se lava	*you wash (yourself)*
él/ella	se lava	*he/she washes (himself/herself)*
nosotros/as	nos lavamos	*we wash (ourselves)*
vosotros/as	os laváis	*you wash (yourselves)*
Uds.	se lavan	*you wash (yourselves)*
ellos/ellas	se lavan	*they wash (themselves)*

▶ The pronoun **se** attached to an infinitive identifies it as a reflexive verb, as in **lavarse** (*to wash oneself*) and **levantarse** (*to get up*).

Me ducho, me cepillo los dientes, me visto y ¡listo!

¡Ay, los estudiantes! ¡Siempre se acuestan tarde!

▶ Reflexive pronouns follow the same rules for placement as object pronouns. They are placed before the conjugated verb, or attached to the infinitive or present participle. When a pronoun is attached to the participle, an accent mark is added.

José **se** levanta temprano.   José **se** va a levantar temprano.
José gets up early.   José va a levantar**se** temprano.
   José is going to get up early.

Carlos **se** afeita.   Carlos está afeitándo**se**.
Carlos shaves.   Carlos **se** está afeitando.
   Carlos is shaving.

¡ojo! The definite article, not a possessive article, is usually used when referring to clothing or parts of the body.

La niña se quitó **los** zapatos.   Me cepillé **los** dientes.

Práctica

1 Emparejar Empareja las fotos con las frases que siguen.

1

4

2
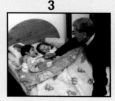

5

3

6

_____ a. Julia se enoja.

_____ b. Juan y Enrique se despiden.

_____ c. Manuela baña a su hija.

_____ d. Estela se pone los calcetines.

_____ e. El abuelo despierta a sus nietas.

_____ f. Ramón se cepilla los dientes.

2 Conversaciones Completa las conversaciones.

MARIO Tú _____ [lavar / lavarse] los platos ayer, ¿no?

TOMÁS Sí, los _____ [lavar / lavarse] después de las clases.

• • •

BEATRIZ ¿Normalmente _____ [duchar / ducharse] antes de ir a clase?

DAVID Sí, _____ [duchar / ducharse] por la mañana después de despertarme.

• • •

MAMÁ ¿Anoche _____ [acostar / acostarse] a los niños a las ocho?

PAPÁ No, no los _____ [acostar / acostarse] a las ocho.

• • •

ANA Yo _____ [sentir / sentirse] nerviosa hoy.

PATRICIA Bueno…tú siempre (*always*) _____ [sentir / sentirse] nerviosa antes de un examen de biología.

Conversación

3 **Preguntas** Usa estas preguntas para entrevistar (*interview*) a un(a) compañero/a.

1. ¿Cuándo te enojas?
2. ¿Cuándo te sientes feliz?
3. ¿Cuándo te preocupas?
4. ¿Te duermes en la clase de español?
5. ¿Te lavas las manos antes de comer?
6. ¿A qué hora te despertaste ayer?
7. ¿A qué hora te levantaste hoy?
8. ¿Te cepillaste los dientes esta mañana?
9. ¿Te duchaste esta mañana?
10. ¿A qué hora te vas a acostar esta noche?

4 **Charadas** Piensa en una frase con un verbo reflexivo y dramatízala en frente de dos o tres compañeros/as. La primera persona que adivina (*guesses*) la frase dramatiza la próxima (*next*) charada.

5 **Entrevista** Prepara un horario con las actividades que hiciste (*you did*) anoche. Después de completar el horario, trabajen en parejas, comparen las actividades y tomen apuntes (*notes*) de lo que hizo el/la compañero/a.

6 pm.	En el Centro Comercial. Me he probado un vestido bien bonito.
7 pm.	En la cafetería con Luis. ¡Siempre se pone tan pesado!
7.30 pm.	Cine con Javier. Muy aburrido. Casi me duermo.
9 pm.	Cena en el restaurante "El cangrejo".
11 pm.	Fiesta en casa de Antonio. Me despido de mis amigos.
2 am.	Me acuesto. No me duermo hasta muy tarde

Common reflexive verbs

Common reflexive verbs			
acordarse (de) (o:ue)	to remember	levantarse	to get up
acostarse (o:ue)	to go to bed	llamarse	to be called/named
afeitarse	to shave	maquillarse	to put on makeup
bañarse	to bathe; to take a bath	peinarse	to comb one's hair
		ponerse	to put on
cepillarse	to brush	ponerse + adj.	to become + adj.
despedirse (de) (e:i)	to say goodbye (to)	preocuparse (por)	to worry (about)
despertarse (e:ie)	to wake up	probarse (o:ue)	to try on
dormirse (o:ue)	to go to sleep	quedarse	to stay, to remain
ducharse	to shower	quitarse	to take off
enojarse (con)	to get angry (with)	sentarse (e:ie)	to sit down
irse	to go away; to leave	sentirse (e:ie)	to feel
		vestirse (e:i)	to get dressed
lavarse	to wash oneself		

▶ Most Spanish verbs can be reflexive. If the verb acts on the subject, use the reflexive form. If it acts on something else, use the non-reflexive form.

Lola **lava** los platos.

Lola **se lava** la cara.

¡ojo! Reflexive verbs and their non-reflexive counterparts sometimes have different meanings.

acordar *to agree*   **acordarse** *to remember*
levantar *to lift*   **levantarse** *to get up*

¡Manos a la obra!

Indica el presente de los verbos reflexivos.

despertarse

1. Ellos _se despiertan_ tarde.
2. Tú _____ tarde.
3. Nosotros _____ tarde.
4. Benito _____ tarde.
5. Yo _____ tarde.
6. Uds. _____ tarde.

ponerse

1. Ella _se pone_ la blusa.
2. Yo _____ la blusa.
3. Ud. _____ la blusa.
4. Nosotras _____ la blusa.
5. Las niñas _____ la blusa.
6. Tú _____ la blusa.

7.2 Indefinite and negative words

▸ Indefinite words, like *someone* or *something*, refer to people and things that are not specific. Negative words, like *no one* or *nothing*, deny the existence of people and things or contradict statements.

Indefinite and negative words

Indefinite words		Negative words	
algo	*something; anything*	nada	*nothing; not anything*
alguien	*someone; anyone*	nadie	*no one; not anyone*
alguno/a(s), algún	*some; any*	ninguno/a,	*no; none; not any*
o… o	*either… or*	ningún	
siempre	*always*	ni… ni	*neither… nor*
también	*also; too*	nunca, jamás	*never*
		tampoco	*neither; not either*

▸ There are two ways to form negative sentences in Spanish. You can place the negative word before the verb, or you can place **no** before the verb and the negative word after the verb.

Nadie está en casa.
No está **nadie** en casa.
Nobody is staying home.

Ellos **no** se enojan **nunca**.
Ellos **nunca** se enojan.
They never get angry.

Ninguno me gusta.
No me gusta **ninguno**.
I don't like any.

Nada me despierta.
No me despierta **nada**.
Nothing wakes me.

Yo siempre
me despierto
a las seis.

Yo jamás me
levanto temprano. Nunca
oigo el despertador.

▸ In Spanish, sentences frequently contain two or more negative words. Once a sentence is negative, all indefinite ideas must be expressed in the negative.

Ella **no** tiene **ninguna** idea.
She doesn't have any idea.

Nunca te pido **nada**.
I never ask you for anything.

Jamás me preocupo por **nada**.
I never worry about anything.

Tampoco me despido de **nadie**.
I don't say goodbye to anyone either.

Práctica

1 La familia de Claudia Completa las frases con **pero** o **sino**.

> **modelo**
>
> Mi abuela es aburrida, ___pero___ amable.

1. No me ducho por la mañana, _____ por la noche.
2. A mí no me gusta nadar, _____ correr.
3. Mi hermana María Luisa es alta, _____ delgada.
4. Mi hermano Emilio no es moreno, _____ rubio.
5. Mis padres no se acuestan temprano, _____ tarde.
6. Mi primo Manuel es inteligente, _____ no es interesante.
7. Mi madre y yo siempre nos despertamos temprano, _____ nunca estamos cansadas.
8. Mi amiga Mariana es pequeña, _____ fuerte.

2 Completar Completa la conversación con palabras negativas.

AURELIO Ana María, ¿encontraste algún regalo para Eliana?

ANA MARÍA _____

AURELIO ¿Viste a algunas amigas en el centro comercial?

ANA MARÍA _____

AURELIO Ana María, ¿quieres ir al teatro o al cine esta noche?

ANA MARÍA _____

AURELIO ¿Quieres salir a comer?

ANA MARÍA _____

AURELIO ¿Hay algo interesante en la televisión esta noche?

ANA MARÍA _____

AURELIO ¿Tienes algún problema?

ANA MARÍA _____

AURELIO ¿Eres siempre tan antipática?

ANA MARÍA _____

Conversación

3 **Quejas** Con un(a) compañero/a, prepara una lista de las quejas (*complaints*) comunes de los estudiantes universitarios.

modelo ¡Nadie me entiende!
¡Jamás puedo levantarme tarde!

Ahora preparen una lista de las quejas que los padres tienen de sus hijos.

modelo ¡Nunca limpian sus habitaciones!
¡No se lavan las manos tampoco!

4 **Anuncios** Mira el anuncio (*ad*). Con un(a) compañero/a, prepara otro anuncio usando expresiones indefinidas o negativas.

¿Buscas algún producto especial?

¡Siempre hay algo para todos en las tiendas García!

Using indefinite words

▶ **Alguien** and **nadie** are often used with the personal **a**. The personal **a** is also used before **alguno/a**, **algunos/as**, and **ninguno/a** when these words refer to people.

—Carlos, ¿ves **a alguien** allí? —¿Oyes **a alguno** de los chicos?
—No, no veo **a nadie**. —No, no oigo **a ninguno**.

¡ojo! Before a masculine, singular noun, **alguno** and **ninguno** are shortened to **algún** and **ningún**.

—¿Tienen Uds. **algún** amigo peruano? —No, no tenemos **ningún** amigo peruano.

▶ Although **pero** and **sino** both mean *but*, they are not interchangeable. **Sino** is used when the first part of a sentence is negative and the second part contradicts it. In this context, **sino** means *but rather* or *on the contrary*. **Pero** is used in all other cases.

No se acuesta temprano, **sino** tarde.
He doesn't get up early, but rather late.

Canto, **pero** nunca en público.
I sing, but never in public.

No queremos irnos, **sino** quedarnos.
We don't want to leave, but rather stay.

Me desperté a las once, **pero** estoy cansada.
I woke up at eleven, but I'm tired.

¡Manos a la obra!

 Cambia las frases para que sean negativas.

1. Siempre se viste bien. _Nunca_ se viste bien. _No_ se viste bien _nunca_.
2. Alguien se ducha. _____ se ducha. _____ se ducha _____.
3. Ellas van también. Ellas _____ van. Ellas _____ van _____.
4. Alguien se pone nervioso. _____ se pone nervioso. _____ se pone nervioso _____.
5. Tú siempre te lavas las manos. Tú _____ te lavas las manos. Tú _____ te lavas las manos _____.
6. Juan también se afeita. Juan _____ se afeita. Juan _____ se afeita _____.
7. Voy a traer algo. _____ voy a traer _____.
8. Mis amigos viven en una residencia o en una casa. Mis amigos _____ viven _____ en una residencia _____ en una casa.
9. La profesora hace algo en su escritorio. La profesora _____ hace _____ en su escritorio.
10. Tú y yo vamos al mercado. _____ tú _____ yo vamos al mercado.
11. Tienen un espejo en su casa. _____ tienen _____ espejo en su casa.
12. Algunos niños se ponen el abrigo. _____ niño se pone el abrigo.

7.3 Preterite of ser and ir

▸ The preterite forms of **ir** (*to go*) and **ser** (*to be*) are irregular, so you will need to memorize them. None of these forms has an accent mark.

Preterite of *ser* and *ir*

	ser	ir
	to be	*to go*
yo	fui	fui
tú	fuiste	fuiste
Ud./él/ella	fue	fue
nosotros/as	fuimos	fuimos
vosotros/as	fuisteis	fuisteis
Uds./ellos/ellas	fueron	fueron

▸ The preterite forms of **ser** and **ir** are identical. The context clarifies which of the two verbs is being used.

Lina **fue** a ver una película.
Lina went to see a film.

La película **fue** muy interesante.
The film was very interesting.

Fui a Barcelona el año pasado.
I went to Barcelona last year.

Fue un viaje maravilloso.
It was a wonderful trip.

¿Adónde fueron Uds.?

Fuimos a un mercado. Fue muy divertido.

¡Manos a la obra!

Completa las siguientes frases usando el pretérito de **ir** y **ser**.

ir

1. Los viajeros ___fueron___ a Perú.
2. Patricia _____ a Cuzco.
3. Tú _____ a Iquitos.
4. Gregorio y yo _____ a Lima.
5. Yo _____ a Trujillo.
6. Uds. _____ a Arequipa.
7. Mi padre _____ a Lima.
8. Nosotras _____ a Cuzco.

ser

1. Ud. ___fue___ muy amable.
2. Yo _____ muy cordial.
3. Ellos _____ muy simpáticos.
4. Nosotros _____ muy impacientes.
5. Ella _____ muy antipática.
6. Tú _____ muy listo.
7. Uds. _____ muy cordiales.
8. La gente _____ muy paciente.

Práctica

1 **Conversación** Andrés y Laura están chismeando (*gossiping*). Completa su conversación con el pretérito de **ser** e **ir**.

ANDRÉS Cristina y Vicente _____ novios, ¿no?

LAURA Sí, pero ahora no salen. Anoche Cristina _____ a comer con Luis y la semana pasada ellos _____ al partido de fútbol.

ANDRÉS ¿Ah, sí? Mercedes y yo _____ al partido y no los vimos.

LAURA ¿_____ tú con Mercedes? Y después del partido, ¿adónde _____ ustedes?

ANDRÉS _____ al café Paraíso y vimos a Vicente con otra chica.

LAURA ¿Él _____ al café Paraíso con otra chica? ¡Qué horror!

2 **Frases** Forma frases con los siguientes elementos. Usa el pretérito.

Sujetos	Verbos	Actividades
yo tú mis amigos nosotros/as Uds. Antonio Banderas Gloria Estefan	(no) ir (no) ser	a un restaurante en autobús a Nueva York estudiante(s) a una discoteca en Buenos Aires por avión a Europa a casa muy tarde a la playa con su novio/a dependiente/a en una tienda

Conversación

3 Preguntas En parejas, túrnense (*take turns*) para hacerse las siguientes preguntas.

1. ¿Adónde fuiste de vacaciones este año?
2. ¿Con quién fuiste de vacaciones?
3. ¿Cómo fueron tus vacaciones?
4. ¿Fuiste de compras esta semana? ¿Qué compraste?
5. ¿Cómo se llama la última (*last*) película que viste?
6. ¿Cuándo fuiste a ver esta película?
7. ¿Cómo fue la película?
8. ¿Adónde fuiste durante el fin de semana? ¿Por qué?

4 El fin de semana pasado En parejas, hablen de lo que hicieron (*you did*) ustedes el fin de semana pasado por la mañana, por la tarde y por la noche. Luego reporten la información a la clase.

	Yo	Mi compañero/a
Por la mañana	_____	_____
	_____	_____
	_____	_____
Por la tarde	_____	_____
	_____	_____
	_____	_____
Por la noche	_____	_____
	_____	_____
	_____	_____

5 Personas famosas En grupos pequeños, cada estudiante debe pensar en una persona famosa del pasado. Luego, los otros miembros del grupo tienen que hacer preguntas usando el pretérito hasta que adivinen (*they guess*) la identidad de la persona. Por ejemplo, pueden hacer preguntas acerca de (*about*) su profesión, su nacionalidad, su personalidad o su apariencia (*appearance*) física.

Fue una experiencia increíble.

Cuando fui a Caldea, me olvidé de todo. Fui para despedirme de todas mis preocupaciones y descubrir los efectos calmantes del agua de las lagunas. Después de bañarme en las aguas termales, se me fueron el cansancio y el estrés. Fueron unas vacaciones extraordinarias.

caldea

SIEMPRE TE ESTAMOS ESPERANDO.

Identificar

Lee el anuncio (*advertisement*) y busca ejemplos del pretérito de los verbos **ser** e **ir**.

Preguntas

1. ¿Cómo se siente el hombre del anuncio?
2. ¿Por qué fue a Caldea? ¿Cómo fue su visita?
3. En tu opinión, ¿se acuerda este hombre de sus responsabilidades diarias mientras (*while*) está en Caldea?
4. En tu opinión, ¿va a volver a Caldea este hombre? ¿Por qué?

Antes de leer

Predicting content from the title will help you increase your reading comprehension in Spanish. We can usually predict the content of a newspaper article in English from its headline, for example.

Examinar el texto

Lee el título de la lectura y haz tres predicciones sobre el contenido. Escribe tus predicciones en una hoja de papel.

Compartir

Comparte tus ideas con un(a) compañero/a de clase.

Cognados

Escribe una lista de cuatro cognados que encuentres en la lectura.

1. _____
2. _____
3. _____
4. _____

¿Qué te dicen los cognados sobre el tema de la lectura?

15 de octubre

¡Una mañana desastrosa!

—Me levanté de la cama a las seis y media

Esta mañana me levanté de la cama a las seis y media y corrí a despertar a mis dos hijas. —Yola▪ Dolores, van a perder el autobús de la escuela, —les grité. Pero ellas no se despertaron. Jamás s▪ despiertan temprano. Siempre se sientan a ver ▪ televisión por la noche y se acuestan muy tard▪

—Corrimos para llegar a la parada del autobús.

Yolanda y Dolores salieron de la casa sin cepillarse los dientes, pero eso no importa. Por lo menos se acordaron de ponerse las botas y el abrigo antes de irse. Corrimos para llegar a la parada del autobús de la escuela, que pasa a las siete de la mañana.

—Nunca llegó el autobú▪

Esperamos media hora, pero nunca llegó el autobús. Regresamos a casa. Llamamo▪ por teléfono a la escuela, pero nadie contestó. Tomamos el automóvil y salimos de casa.

—¡Por fin se despertaron mis hijas!

¡Por fin se despertaron! Medio dormidas y medio enojadas, ellas entraron al baño para lavarse la cara y peinarse. Luego volvieron a su habitación para vestirse. Yo fui a la cocina para prepararles el desayuno. A mis hijas les encanta comer un buen desayuno, pero hoy les di cereales y les preparé dos sándwiches para el almuerzo.

—¡Hoy es sábado!

Llegamos a la escuela antes de las ocho y entonces me di cuenta de que hoy es sábado. ¡Y los sábados no hay clases!

Después de leer

¿Comprendiste?

Selecciona la respuesta *(answer)* correcta.

1. ¿Quién es el/la narrador(a)?
   a. el padre de las chicas   b. Yolanda
   c. Dolores
2. ¿A qué hora se despertó el papá?
   a. a las seis de la mañana   b. a las seis y media
   c. a las siete y media
3. ¿Qué comieron las chicas antes de salir de la casa?
   a. un sándwich   b. cereales
   c. dos sándwiches
4. ¿Cómo fueron las chicas a la escuela?
   a. Corrieron.   b. Fueron en autobús.
   c. Fueron en automóvil.

Preguntas

1. ¿Por qué nunca se despiertan temprano las chicas?
   _____
2. ¿Se bañaron las chicas esta mañana?
   _____
3. ¿A qué hora llega generalmente el autobús?
   _____
4. ¿A qué hora llegó el autobús hoy?
   _____
5. ¿Por qué no contestó nadie cuando llamaron a la escuela?
   _____

Coméntalo

¿Qué crees que le dicen Yolanda y Dolores a su papá después de volver de la escuela? Imagina que eres el papá. ¿Cómo respondes a lo que te dicen las chicas?

grité	*I shouted*
medio dormidas y medio enojadas	*half asleep and half mad*
desayuno	*breakfast*
almuerzo	*lunch*
sin	*without*
di	*I gave*
parada	*stop*
llamamos por teléfono	*we called on the phone*
me di cuenta de que	*I realized that*

recursos

R

vistahigher
learning.com

Los verbos reflexivos

acordarse (de) (o:ue)	to remember
acostarse (o:ue)	to go to bed
afeitarse	to shave
bañarse	to bathe; to take a bath
cepillarse el pelo	to brush one's hair
los dientes	to brush one's teeth
despedirse (de) (e:i)	to say goodbye (to)
despertarse (e:ie)	to wake up
dormirse (o:ue)	to go to sleep, to fall asleep
ducharse	to shower, to take a shower
enojarse (con)	to get angry (with)
irse	to go away; to leave
lavarse la cara	to wash one's face
las manos	to wash one's hands
levantarse	to get up
llamarse	to be called; to be named
maquillarse	to put on makeup
peinarse	to comb one's hair
ponerse	to put on
ponerse + adj.	to become + adj.
preocuparse (por)	to worry (about)
probarse (o:ue)	to try on
quedarse	to be left over; to fit
quitarse	to take off
sentarse (e:ie)	to sit down
sentirse (e:ie)	to feel
vestirse (e:i)	to get dressed

En el baño

el baño	bathroom
el champú	shampoo
la crema de afeitar	shaving cream
el espejo	mirror
el jabón	soap
el maquillaje	makeup
la toalla	towel

Adverbios y preposiciones de tiempo

antes (de)	before
después	afterwards; then
después de	after
durante	during
entonces	then
luego	afterwards; then
más tarde	later
por último	finally

Verbs like *gustar*

aburrir	to bore
encantar	to like very much; to love (inanimate objects)
faltar	to lack; to need
fascinar	to fascinate
gustar	to be pleasing to; to like
importar	to be important to; to matter
interesar	to be interesting to; to interest
me gustaría(n)...	I would like...
molestar	to bother; to annoy
quedar	to be left over; to fit (clothing)

Otras palabras y expresiones

el despertador	alarm clock
por la mañana	in the morning
por la noche	at night
por la tarde	in the afternoon; in the (early) evening
la rutina diaria	daily routine

Expresiones útiles	See page 165.
Indefinite and negative words	See page 170.

recursos

R — Lab CD Lección 7 — LM p. 42

8 ¡A comer!

Communicative Goals

You will learn how to:
- talk about food
- order at a restaurant
- talk about where you are
- discuss familiar people and places

RECURSOS

These student supplements provide additional practice:
- Textbook Audio CD
- Workbook/Video Manual (WB/VM)
- Lab Manual (LM)
- Interactive CD-ROM
- WB/VM/LM Answer Key
- Lab Audio CDs
- Video CD-ROM

OFERTA
MANDARINA ELENDALE
3 k $149

MANZANA
DELICIA
2 k $299

¡A COMER!

el camarero
waiter

EN UN RESTAURANTE

el plato (principal) *(main) dish*

la sección de (no) fumadores *(non) smoking section*

el almuerzo *lunch*

la cena *dinner*

la comida *food; meal*

el desayuno *breakfast*

almorzar (o:ue) *to have lunch*

cenar *to have dinner*

desayunar *to have breakfast*

pedir (e:i) *to order (food)*

probar (o:ue) *to taste; to try*

recomendar (e:ie) *to recommend*

servir (e:i) *to serve*

el menú
menu

MENÚ

Entremeses
Pan tostado con
• Queso frito • Mantequilla y jalea
Tortillas con
• Ajicomino (chile, comino) • Ajiaceite (chile, aceite)

Sopas
• Cebolla • Verduras • Pollo y huevo • Mariscos

Platos Principales
Chilaquil
(tortilla de maíz, queso, hierbas y chile)
Tomatícan
(tomate, papas, maíz, chile, guisantes, zanahorias y verduras)
Tamales
(maíz, azúcar, ajo, cebolla)
Frijoles enchilados
(frijoles negros, carne de cerdo o de res, arroz, chile)

Postres
• Helado de piña • Plátanos caribeños
• Uvate (uvas, azúcar de caña y ron) • Pastel de yogur

Bebidas
• Té helado • Vino tinto
• Vino blanco • Agua mineral • Jugos
• Chilate (maíz, chile y cacao)

los entremeses
hors d'oeuvres

CARNES Y MARISCOS

el atún *tuna*

los camarones *shrimp*

la carne *meat*

la carne de res *beef*

la chuleta de cerdo *pork chop*

la hamburguesa *hamburger*

el jamón *ham*

la langosta *lobster*

el pavo *turkey*

el pescado *fish*

la salchicha *sausage*

el salmón *salmon*

el bistec
steak

LOS SABORES

agrio/a *sour*

delicioso/a *delicious*

dulce *sweet*

picante *hot, spicy*

rico/a *tasty; delicious*

sabroso/a *tasty; delicious*

salado/a *salty*

el pollo (asado)
(roast) chicken

los mariscos
seafood

recursos

R	Textbook CD Lección 8	WB pp. 75-76	LM p. 43	Lab CD Lección 8	ICD-ROM Lección 8

LAS FRUTAS

la banana *banana*
el limón *lemon*
la manzana *apple*
la naranja *orange*
las uvas *grapes*

las frutas
fruit

GRANOS Y VERDURAS

las arvejas *peas*
la cebolla *onion*
los frijoles *beans*
la lechuga *lettuce*
el maíz *corn*
la papa/patata *potato*
el tomate *tomato*
la zanahoria *carrot*

los champiñones
mushrooms

las verduras
vegetables

OTRAS COMIDAS

el aceite *oil*
el ajo *garlic*
el arroz *rice*
el azúcar *sugar*
los cereales *cereal; grain*
la ensalada *salad*
el huevo *egg*
la mantequilla *butter*
la margarina *margarine*
la mayonesa *mayonnaise*
el pan (tostado) *(toasted) bread*
las papas/patatas fritas *French fries*
el queso *cheese*
la sal *salt*
la sopa *soup*
el vinagre *vinegar*

la pimienta
pepper

el sándwich
sandwich

BEBIDAS

la bebida *drink*
la cerveza *beer*
el jugo (de naranja) *(orange) juice*
la leche *milk*
el refresco *soft drink*
el té helado *iced tea*
el vino tinto *red wine*

el agua (f.) (mineral)
(mineral) water

el café
coffee

A escuchar

 1 **¿Lógico o ilógico?** Escucha las frases e indica si son **lógicas** o **ilógicas**.

	Lógico	Ilógico
1.	_____	_____
2.	_____	_____
3.	_____	_____
4.	_____	_____
5.	_____	_____
6.	_____	_____
7.	_____	_____
8.	_____	_____

2 **¿Qué pide Nora?** Escucha la conversación entre Nora y el camarero en un restaurante. Luego indica las comidas y bebidas que Nora pide.

ENTREMESES
___ papas fritas
___ cóctel de frutas con queso
___ sopa de verduras
___ sopa de pollo
___ pan con mantequilla

PLATOS PRINCIPALES
___ sándwich de jamón y queso
___ pollo asado
___ hamburguesa
___ hamburguesa con queso
___ enchiladas de res
___ enchiladas de queso

BEBIDAS
___ agua mineral
___ té helado
___ leche
___ café
___ jugo de naranja

Restaurante Las Fuentes

Avenida Las Lomas, 22

recursos

R
Textbook CD
Lección 8

A practicar

3 **¿Qué es?** Identifica estas comidas. Luego indica si son **carnes, frutas, verduras, bebidas** o **condimentos.**

modelo

Un limón:
es una fruta.

1. _____

2. _____

3. _____

4. _____

5. _____

6. _____

7. _____

8. _____

4 **La comida** Indica la palabra que no está relacionada con su grupo.

1. mariscos • manzana • banana
2. salmón • cereales • camarones
3. frijoles • champiñón • naranja • cebolla
4. mantequilla • salchicha • carne de res • jamón
5. arvejas • lechuga • zanahoria • cerveza
6. refresco • sopa • agua mineral • leche

5 **Completar** Completa las frases con las palabras correctas.

1. El hombre que sirve la comida en un restaurante es el _____.
2. Camarero, ¿puedo ver el _____, por favor?
3. El bistec y el jamón son dos tipos de _____.
4. El té helado, el café y el refresco son ejemplos de _____.
5. El condimento blanco que pongo en mi café es el _____.
6. Las tres comidas principales del día son el _____, el almuerzo y la cena.

A conversar

6 **¿Te gusta(n)?** Mira la lista e indica si te gusta cada comida o bebida.

¿Te gusta(n)?	Me gusta(n)	No me gusta(n)
1. el vino tinto	_____	_____
2. la hamburguesa	_____	_____
3. el queso	_____	_____
4. los camarones	_____	_____
5. el tomate	_____	_____
6. los champiñones	_____	_____
7. los huevos	_____	_____
8. los limones	_____	_____

Ahora compara tus reacciones con las opiniones de un(a) compañero/a.

modelo

la carne de res
Estudiante 1: A mí me gusta mucho la carne de res.
Estudiante 2: A mí no. Prefiero el pollo.

7 **Conversación** En grupos, contesten las preguntas.

1. ¿Desayunas? ¿Qué comes y bebes por la mañana?
2. ¿A qué hora, dónde y con quién almuerzas?
3. ¿Cuáles son las comidas típicas de tu almuerzo?
4. ¿A qué hora, dónde y con quién cenas?
5. ¿Qué comidas prefieres para la cena?
6. ¿Cuáles son las comidas y bebidas más frecuentes en tu dieta?
7. ¿Te gusta cocinar (to cook)? ¿Qué comidas preparas para tus amigos? ¿Y para tu familia?
8. ¿Qué comida les recomiendas a tus amigos? ¿Por qué?
9. ¿Qué comidas te gustaría probar?
10. ¿Eres vegetariano/a? ¿Crees que ser vegetariano/a es una buena idea? ¿Por qué?

🎧 Pronunciación

ll, ñ, c, and z

pollo	llave	ella	cebolla

Most Spanish speakers pronounce the letter **ll** like the *y* in *yes*.

mañana	señor	baño	niña

The letter **ñ** is pronounced much like the *ny* in *canyon*.

café	colombiano	cuando	rico

Before **a**, **o**, or **u**, the Spanish **c** is pronounced like the *c* in *car*.

cereales	delicioso	conducir	conocer

Before **e** or **i**, the Spanish **c** is pronounced like the *s* in *sit*. (In parts of Spain, **c** before **e** or **i** is pronounced like the *th* in *think*.)

zeta	zanahoria	almuerzo	cerveza

The Spanish **z** is pronounced like the *s* in *sit*. (In parts of Spain, **z** before a vowel is pronounced like the *th* in *think*.)

Práctica Lee las palabras en voz alta.

1. mantequilla
2. cuñado
3. aceite
4. manzana
5. español
6. cepillo
7. zapato
8. azúcar
9. quince
10. compañera
11. almorzar
12. calle

Oraciones Lee las oraciones en voz alta.

1. Mi compañero de cuarto se llama Toño Núñez. Su familia es de la Ciudad de Guatemala y de Quetzaltenango.

2. Dice que la comida de su mamá es deliciosa, especialmente su pollo al champiñón y sus tortillas de maíz.

3. Creo que Toño tiene razón porque hoy cené en su casa y quiero volver mañana para cenar allí otra vez.

Refranes Lee los refranes en voz alta.

Panza llena, corazón contento.[2]

Las apariencias engañan.[1]

1 Looks can be deceiving.
2 A full belly makes a happy heart.

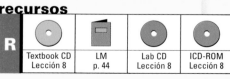

recursos

R	Textbook CD Lección 8	LM p. 44	Lab CD Lección 8	ICD-ROM Lección 8

¿Qué tal la comida?

Don Francisco y los estudiantes van al restaurante El Cráter.

JAVIER ¿Sabes dónde estamos?

INÉS Mmm, no sé. Oiga, don Francisco, ¿sabe Ud. dónde estamos?

DON FRANCISCO Estamos cerca de Cotacachi.

ÁLEX ¿Dónde vamos a almorzar, don Francisco? ¿Conoce un buen restaurante en Cotacachi?

DON FRANCISCO Pues, conozco a doña Rita Perales, la dueña del mejor restaurante de la ciudad, el restaurante El Cráter.

DOÑA RITA Hombre, don Paco, ¿Ud. por aquí?

DON FRANCISCO Sí, doña Rita… y hoy le traigo clientes. Le presento a Maite, Inés, Álex y Javier. Los llevo a las montañas para ir de excursión.

MAITE Voy a tomar un caldo de patas y un lomo a la plancha.

JAVIER Para mí las tortillas de maíz y el ceviche de camarón.

ÁLEX Yo también quisiera las tortillas de maíz y el ceviche de camarón.

INÉS Voy a pedir caldo de patas y lomo a la plancha.

DON FRANCISCO Yo quiero tortillas de maíz y una fuente de fritada, por favor.

DOÑA RITA Y de tomar, les recomiendo el jugo de piña, frutilla y mora. ¿Se lo traigo a todos?

TODOS Sí, perfecto.

CAMARERO ¿Qué plato pidió Ud.?

MAITE Un caldo de patas y lomo a la plancha.

recursos

| R | Video/VCD-ROM Lección 8 | VM pp. 183-184 | ICD-ROM Lección 8 |

Personajes

DON FRANCISCO   JAVIER   INÉS   ÁLEX   MAITE   DOÑA RITA   CAMARERO

DOÑA RITA ¡Bienvenidos al restaurante El Cráter! Están en muy buenas manos… don Francisco es el mejor conductor del país. Y no hay nada más bonito que nuestras montañas. Pero, si van a ir de excursión, deben comer bien. Vengan, chicos, por aquí.

JAVIER ¿Qué nos recomienda Ud.?
DOÑA RITA Bueno, las tortillas de maíz son riquísimas. La especialidad de la casa es el caldo de patas… ¡tienen que probarlo! El lomo a la plancha es un poquito más caro que el caldo, pero es sabrosísimo. También les recomiendo el ceviche de camarón y la fuente de fritada.

DOÑA RITA ¿Qué tal la comida? ¿Rica?
JAVIER Rica, no. ¡Riquísima!
ÁLEX Sí, y nos la sirvieron tan rápidamente.
MAITE Una comida deliciosa, gracias.

DON FRANCISCO Hoy es el cumpleaños de Maite…
DOÑA RITA ¡Ah! Tenemos unos pasteles que están como para chuparse los dedos…

Expresiones útiles

Finding out where you are
¿Sabe Ud./sabes dónde estamos?
Do you know where we are?
Estamos cerca de Cotacachi.
We're near Cotacachi.

Talking about people and places you're familiar with
¿Conoce Ud./conoces un buen restaurante en Cotacachi?
Do you know a good restaurant in Cotacachi?
Sí, conozco varios.
Yes, I know several.
¿Conoce/conoces a doña Rita?
Do you know Doña Rita?
Sí, es la dueña del mejor restaurante de la ciudad.
Yes, she's the owner of the best restaurant in the city.

Ordering food
¿Qué le puedo traer?
What can I bring you?
Voy a tomar/pedir un caldo de patas y un lomo a la plancha.
I am going to have/to order the beef soup and grilled flank steak.
Para mí las tortillas de maíz y el ceviche de camarón, por favor.
Corn tortillas and lemon-marinated shrimp for me, please.
Yo también quisiera…
I would also like…
Y de tomar, el jugo de piña, frutilla y mora.
And to drink, pineapple-strawberry-blackberry juice.
¿Qué plato pidió Ud.?
What did you order?
Yo pedí un caldo de patas.
I ordered the beef soup.

Talking about the food at a restaurant
¿Qué tal la comida?
How is the food?
Muy rica, gracias.
Very tasty, thanks.
¡Riquísima!
Extremely delicious!

¿Qué piensas?

1 **En el restaurante** Escoge la respuesta (*answer*) que completa cada oración.

1. Inés va a pedir

   a. las tortillas de maíz y la fuente de fritada (*mixed grill*).   b. el ceviche y el caldo de patas.
   c. el caldo de patas y el lomo a la plancha.

2. Doña Rita es

   a. la hermana de don Francisco.   b. la dueña del restaurante.
   c. una camarera que trabaja en El Cráter.

3. Don Francisco lleva a los estudiantes a

   a. cenar.   b. desayunar.
   c. almorzar.

4. Doña Rita les recomienda a los viajeros

   a. el caldo de patas y el lomo a la plancha.   b. el bistec, las verduras frescas y el vino tinto.
   c. unos pasteles (*cakes*).

2 **Preguntas** Contesta las preguntas.

1. ¿Dónde comieron don Francisco y los estudiantes? _____

2. Según (*according to*) doña Rita, ¿por qué deben comer bien los viajeros? _____

   _____

3. ¿Cuál es la especialidad del restaurante? _____

4. ¿Qué pidió Maite? _____

5. ¿Qué pidió Álex? _____

6. ¿Qué tomaron todos? _____

7. ¿Cuándo es el cumpleaños (*birthday*) de Maite? _____

8. ¿Qué tal son los pasteles (*cakes*) en El Cráter? _____

3 **Dos situaciones**

1. Prepara con un(a) compañero/a una conversación en
   la que le preguntas si conoce algún buen restaurante
   en su comunidad. Tu compañero/a responde que
   sí conoce un restaurante donde sirven comida deliciosa.
   Lo/la invitas a cenar y él/ella acepta. Determinan la hora
   para verse en el restaurante y se despiden.

2. Trabaja con un(a) compañero/a para representar
   un diálogo entre un(a) cliente/a y un(a) camarero/a
   en un restaurante. El/la camarero/a te pregunta qué te
   puede servir y tú preguntas cuál es la especialidad del
   restaurante. El/la camarero/a te lo dice y te recomienda algunos platos del menú.
   Tú pides entremeses, un plato principal y una bebida. El/la camarero/a te da las
   gracias y luego te sirve la comida.

Exploración
La comida hispana

El asado es la barbacoa (*barbecue*) argentina. Un asado típico consiste en chorizos (*sausages*) y otras carnes a la parrilla (*grilled*). Según los argentinos, el secreto de un buen asado es el corte (*cut*) de la carne y el control del fuego (*fire*).

La paella es el plato típico de España. Tradicionalmente se prepara al aire libre. Los ingredientes principales son: arroz, mariscos, pescado, carne y verduras.

El ceviche es una comida muy popular en el Perú y el Ecuador. En su preparación, se combina el jugo de limón con pescado o mariscos crudos (*raw*).

Observaciones

- Hay cerca de 4.000 variedades de papa.

- La palabra **papa** es de origen quechua (la lengua de los incas).

- En el Perú, hay 35 variedades de maíz, más que en ningún otro país del mundo.

- En Madrid, España, el restaurante más antiguo es la Casa Botín, fundado en el año 1725.

Coméntalo

Con un(a) compañero/a, contesta las siguientes preguntas.

- ¿Te gustaría probar los platos mencionados en esta página?

- Describe los platos tradicionales de tu región o comunidad. ¿Los preparas con frecuencia en tu casa? ¿Son fáciles o difíciles de preparar?

recursos

R
vistahigher
learning.com

8.1 Preterite of stem-changing verbs

▶ As you know, **–ar** and **–er** stem-changing verbs have no stem change in the preterite. **–Ir** stem-changing verbs, however, do have a stem change.

Preterite of –ir stem-changing verbs

	servir (e→i)	morir (to die) (o→u)
yo	serví *I served*	morí *I died*
tú	serviste	moriste
Ud./él/ella	sirvió	murió
nosotros/as	servimos	morimos
vosotros/as	servisteis	moristeis
Uds./ellos/ellas	sirvieron	murieron

▶ Stem-changing **–ir** verbs, in the preterite only, have an **e** to **i** or **o** to **u** stem change in the third-person forms.

INFINITIVE	VERB STEM	STEM CHANGE	PRETERITE
pedir	ped-	pid-	pidió, pidieron
dormir	dor-	dur-	durmió, durmieron

> Perdón, ¿quiénes pidieron las tortillas de maíz?

> ¿Y qué plato pidió usted?

¡Manos a la obra!

Cambia los infinitivos al pretérito.

1. yo [servir, dormir, pedir, preferir, repetir, seguir]
   serví, dormí, pedí, preferí, repetí, seguí

2. Ud. [morir, conseguir, pedir, sentirse, despedirse, vestirse]
   _____

3. tú [conseguir, servir, morir, pedir, dormir, repetir]
   _____

4. ellas [repetir, dormir, seguir, preferir, morir, servir]
   _____

5. nosotros [seguir, preferir, servir, vestirse, despedirse, dormirse]
   _____

6. Uds. [sentirse, vestirse, conseguir, pedir, despedirse, dormirse]
   _____

Práctica

1 **¡Pobre Sr. Suárez!** Completa las frases.

1. Los Sres. Suárez llegaron al restaurante a las ocho y _____ [seguir] al camarero a una mesa.

2. El Sr. Suárez _____ [pedir] una chuleta de cerdo. La Sra. Suárez decidió probar los camarones.

3. Para tomar, los dos _____ [pedir] vino.

4. El camarero _____ [repetir] el pedido (*the order*) para confirmarlo.

5. La comida tardó mucho (*took a long time*) en llegar y los Sres. Suárez casi (*almost*) _____ [dormirse] esperándola.

6. A las nueve les _____ [servir] la comida.

7. Después de comer la chuleta de cerdo, el Sr. Suárez _____ [sentirse] muy mal.

8. De repente, el Sr. Suárez se _____ [morir].

9. ¡Pobre Sr. Suárez! ¿Por qué no _____ [pedir] los camarones?

2 **El camarero loco** Indica lo que los clientes pidieron y lo que el camarero loco les sirvió.

modelo

Claudia / hamburguesa
Claudia pidió una hamburguesa, pero el camarero le sirvió zanahorias.

1. Juan y Rafael / té helado   3. Laura / arroz
_____   _____

2. Nosotros / papas fritas   4. Margarita / salmón
_____   _____

Conversación

3 **Preguntas** Usa estas preguntas para entrevistar a tu compañero/a.

> ¿Te acostaste tarde o temprano anoche?

> Me acosté tarde, a la una de la mañana.

1. ¿Te acostaste tarde o temprano anoche? ¿A qué hora te dormiste? ¿Dormiste bien?

2. ¿A qué hora te despertaste esta mañana? ¿A qué hora te levantaste?

3. ¿Llegaste a tiempo (*on time*) a la clase de español?

4. ¿Cuándo empezaste a estudiar español?

5. ¿Se durmió alguien en alguna de tus clases la semana pasada? ¿En qué clase?

6. ¿Quién preparó anoche la cena en tu casa? ¿Y quién la sirvió?

4 **Una cena romántica** En grupos, describan la cena romántica de Eduardo y Rosa. Usen la foto y las preguntas como guía (*as a guide*).

- ¿Adónde salieron a cenar?
- ¿Qué pidieron?
- ¿Les sirvieron rápidamente (*quickly*) la comida?
- ¿Les gustó la comida?
- ¿Cuánto costó?
- ¿Van a volver otra vez a ese restaurante en el futuro?

Español en vivo

> Buenos días, Mamá y Papá:
> ¿Durmieron bien?
> Me levanté temprano y les preparé el desayuno, como me pidieron. Lo dejé en el horno. Un gran beso, Camilo

007Mundo.com piensa en todo lo que necesitas para estar en Internet. Explora ese mundo ideal.

007mundo.com

Identificar

Lee el anuncio (*advertisement*) e identifica los verbos que cambian de raíz (*stem*) en el pretérito.

Preguntas

1. ¿Quién escribió la nota del anuncio?

2. ¿Qué les preguntó Camilo a sus padres?

3. En tu opinión ¿se sintieron los padres felices o infelices cuando se despertaron?

8.2 Double object pronouns

▸ In previous lessons you learned that direct and indirect object pronouns replace nouns. You'll now learn how to use direct and indirect object pronouns together.

INDIRECT OBJECT PRONOUNS			DIRECT OBJECT PRONOUNS	
me	nos		lo	los
te	os	**+**		
le (se)	les (se)		la	las

▸ When direct and indirect object pronouns are used together, the indirect object pronoun goes before the direct object pronoun.

I.O.	D.O.		DOUBLE OBJECT PRONOUNS
El camarero **me muestra** el menú.			El camarero **me lo muestra.**
The waiter shows me the menu.			*The waiter shows it to me.*
Nos **sirven** los platos.			Nos los **sirven.**
They serve us the dishes.			*They serve them to us.*
Maribel **te pidió** una hamburguesa.			Maribel **te la pidió.**
Maribel ordered a hamburger for you.			*Maribel ordered it for you.*

> Y de tomar, les recomiendo el jugo de piña... ¿Se lo traigo a todos?

> Sí, perfecto.

▸ The indirect object pronouns **le** and **les** always change to **se** when they are used with **lo, los, la,** and **las.**

I.O.	D.O.		DOUBLE OBJECT PRONOUNS
Le **escribí** la carta.			Se la **escribí.**
I wrote him the letter.			*I wrote it to him.*
Les **sirvió** los entremeses.			Se los **sirvió.**
He served them the hors d'oeuvres.			*He served them to them.*
Le **pedimos** un café.			Se lo **pedimos.**
We ordered him a coffee.			*We ordered it for him.*

Práctica

1 **En un restaurante** Imagínate que trabajas de camarero/a en un restaurante. Indica lo que se dicen (*say to each other*) tú y tus clientes.

modelo

Sra. Guzmán

Sra. Guzmán: Una hamburguesa, por favor.
Camarero/a: Enseguida (*right away*) se la traigo.

1. Tus compañeros/as de cuarto

4. Tus padres

2. Tu profesor(a) de español

5. Srta. Salas

3. Sr. Ramos

6. Dr. Cifuentes

2 **¿Quién?** La Sra. Cevallos está hablando sola de los planes para una cena. Cambia los sustantivos subrayados (*underlined nouns*) por pronombres de objeto directo.

modelo ¿Quién va a traerme <u>la carne</u> del supermercado? [Mi esposo]
Mi esposo va a traérmela./Mi esposo me la va a traer.

1. ¿Quién les mandó <u>las invitaciones</u> a los invitados (*guests*)? [Mi hija] _____

2. ¿Quién me puede comprar <u>el pan</u>? [Mi hijo]

   _____

3. ¿Quién puede prestarme <u>los platos</u> que necesito? [Mi mamá] _____

4. Nos falta mantequilla. ¿Quién nos trae <u>la mantequilla</u>? [Mi cuñada] _____

5. ¡Los postres (*desserts*)! ¿Quién está preparándonos <u>los postres</u>? [Silvia y Renata] _____

6. ¿Quién puede pedirle <u>el azúcar</u> a Mónica? [Mi hijo] _____

Conversación

 3 **Contestar** Trabajen en parejas (*pairs*) y formulen preguntas usando las palabras interrogativas **¿Quién?** o **¿Cuándo?**

modelo

nos enseña español
Estudiante 1: ¿Quién nos enseña español?
Estudiante 2: La profesora Castro nos lo enseña.

Preguntas	Respuestas
1. te escribe mensajes electrónicos	_____
2. me vas a prestar tu computadora	_____
3. les vende los libros de texto a los estudiantes	_____
4. le enseñó español al/a la profesor(a)	_____
5. te compró esa camiseta	_____
6. me vas a mostrar tu casa o apartamento	_____

 4 **Preguntas** Contesta estas preguntas con un(a) compañero/a.

1. ¿Me prestas tu coche (*car*)? ¿Ya le prestaste tu coche a otro amigo?
2. ¿Me puedes comprar un coche nuevo?
3. ¿Quién te presta dinero cuando lo necesitas?
4. ¿Les prestas dinero a tus amigos? ¿Por qué?
5. ¿Les prestas tu casa o apartamento a tus amigos? ¿Por qué?
6. ¿Nos compras el almuerzo a mí y a los otros compañeros de clase?
7. ¿Me describes tu casa?
8. ¿Quién te va a preparar la cena esta noche?
9. ¿Quién te va a preparar el desayuno mañana?
10. ¿Vas a leerles el cuento (*story*) de "Blancanieves" (*Snow White*) a tus nietos? ¿Qué otros cuentos les vas a leer?

▶ Because **se** has multiple meanings, Spanish speakers clarify to whom the pronoun refers by adding **a Ud., a él, a ella, a Uds., a ellos,** or **a ellas.**

¿El sombrero? Carlos **se** lo vendió **a ella.**	¿Las verduras? Ellos **se** las compran **a Ud.**
The hat? Carlos sold it to her.	*The vegetables? They buy them for you.*

▶ Double object pronouns are placed before a conjugated verb. With infinitives and present participles, double object pronouns may be placed before the conjugated verb or attached to the end of the infinitive or present participle.

▶ When double object pronouns are attached to an infinitive or a present participle, an accent mark is added to maintain the original stress.

Me lo estoy comiendo.	**Se la** van a traer.
Estoy comiéndo**melo.**	Van a traér**sela.**
I am eating it.	*They are going to bring it to you.*

DOUBLE OBJECT PRONOUNS	DOUBLE OBJECT PRONOUNS
Te lo **voy a mostrar.**	Voy a mostrár**telo.**
Nos las **están sirviendo.**	Están sirviéndo**noslas.**

Qué tal la comida, ¿rica?

Sí, y nos la sirvieron tan rápidamente.

¡Manos a la obra!

 Escribe el pronombre de objeto directo o indirecto que falta en cada frase.

Objeto directo

1. ¿La ensalada? El camarero nos ___la___ sirvió.
2. ¿El salmón? La dueña me _____ recomienda.
3. ¿La comida? Voy a preparárte _____.
4. ¿Las bebidas? Estamos pidiéndose _____.
5. ¿Los refrescos? Te _____ puedo traer ahora.
6. ¿Los platos de arroz? Van a servírnos _____ después.

Objeto indirecto

1. ¿Puedes traerme tu plato? No, no ___te___ lo puedo traer.
2. ¿Quieres mostrarle la carta? Sí, voy a mostrár _____ la ahora.
3. ¿Les serviste la carne? No, no _____ la serví.
4. ¿Vas a leerle el menú? No, no _____ lo voy a leer.
5. ¿Me recomiendas la langosta? Sí, _____ la recomiendo.
6. ¿Cuándo vas a prepararnos la cena? _____ la voy a preparar en una hora.

8.3 Saber and conocer

▶ Spanish has two verbs that mean *to know*, **saber** and **conocer**, but they are used differently. Note that only the **yo** forms of **saber** and **conocer** are irregular in the present tense.

Saber and conocer			
	saber		conocer
yo	sé		cono**zco**
tú	sabes		conoces
Ud./él/ella	sabe		conoce
nosotros/as	sabemos		conocemos
vosotros/as	sabéis		conocéis
Uds./ellos/ellas	saben		conocen

▶ **Saber** means *to know a fact or piece(s) of information* or *to know how to do something.*

No **sé** tu número de teléfono.
I don't know your telephone number.

Mi hermana **sabe** hablar francés.
My sister knows how to speak French.

▶ **Conocer** means *to know or be familiar/acquainted with a person, place, or thing.*

¿**Conoces** la ciudad de Nueva York?
Do you know New York City?

No **conozco** a tu amigo Esteban.
I don't know your friend Esteban.

▶ When the direct object of **conocer** is a person or pet, the personal **a** is used. Compare these sentences.

¿**Conoces a** Rigoberta Menchú?

¿**Conoces** ese restaurante?

¡ojo! These verbs are conjugated like **conocer**.

conducir (*to drive*)	condu**zco**, conduces, conduce, etc.
ofrecer (*to offer*)	ofre**zco**, ofreces, ofrece, etc.
parecer (*to seem*)	pare**zco**, pareces, parece, etc.
traducir (*to translate*)	tradu**zco**, traduces, traduce, etc.

¡Manos a la obra!

Escribe las formas apropiadas de **saber** y **conocer**.

1. José no ___*sabe*___ la hora.
2. Ud. y yo _____ bien Miami.
3. Mis padres _____ hablar japonés.
4. Nadie me _____ bien.
5. ¿_____ tú a la tía de Eduardo?
6. ¿Por qué no _____ tú estos verbos?
7. Mis hermanas no _____ nadar.
8. Yo _____ a qué hora empieza la clase.
9. ¿_____ Ud. las librerías de Madrid?
10. Sara y yo _____ jugar al tenis.

Práctica

1 **Completar** Completa las frases con la forma apropiada de **saber** o **conocer**.

Quetzaltenango

1. —¿_____ Uds. dónde vive Pilar?
   —No, nosotras no lo _____.
2. Mi amiga Carla _____ conducir, pero yo no
   _____.
3. —¿_____ a Mateo, mi hermano mayor?
   —No, no lo _____.
4. —Todavía no _____ a tu novio.
   —Sí, ya lo _____.
5. Tú _____ esquiar, pero Tino y Luis son pequeños y no _____.
6. —Nosotros no _____ Guatemala.
   —Ah, ¿no? Yo _____ bien las ciudades de Escuintla, Quetzaltenango y Antigua.
7. Roberto _____ bien el *Popol Vuh*, el libro sagrado de los mayas; también _____ leer los jeroglíficos de los templos mayas.

2 **Oraciones** Combina las palabras de las tres columnas para hacer oraciones completas.

modelo

No conozco a Cher. Yo conozco a Andy García.

Sujetos	Verbos	Objetos directos
Katie Couric		Cameron Díaz
Cher		Andy García
Ozzy Osbourne		cantar
Tom Hanks		el lago de Maracaibo en Venezuela
Carlos Santana	(no) conocer	hablar dos lenguas extranjeras
Manny Ramírez	(no) saber	hacer reír (*laugh*) a la gente
yo		la fecha de hoy
tú		escribir novelas de terror
tu compañero/a		programar computadoras
tu profesor(a)		muchas personas importantes

Conversación

3 Deportes Pregúntale a un(a) compañero/a qué deportes practica y por qué.

modelo

Estudiante 1: ¿Sabes esquiar?
Estudiante 2: Sí, sé esquiar porque aprendí de niño./ Sí, sé esquiar porque me gusta mucho el invierno.

4 Preguntas Con un(a) compañero/a, contesten las siguientes preguntas.

1. ¿Qué restaurantes buenos conoces? ¿Cenas en los restaurantes frecuentemente (*frequently*)?

2. En tu familia, ¿quién sabe cantar mejor (*best*)? ¿Tu opinión es objetiva?

3. ¿Conoces a algún/alguna artista hispano/a?

4. ¿Sabes usar bien Internet? ¿Te parece fácil o difícil usar la computadora?

5. ¿Sabes escuchar cuando alguien te habla de sus problemas?

6. ¿Conoces a algún/alguna chef famoso/a? ¿Qué tipo de comida prepara?

7. ¿Conoces a algún/alguna escritor(a) famoso/a?

8. ¿Sabes si ofrecen cursos de administración de empresas en tu universidad?

Español en vivo

Él sabe dónde comer lo que más le gusta

Él sabe cómo jugar cuatro horas seguidas

Él sabe dónde está su regalo de cumpleaños

Él sabe dónde divertirse

... y usted sabe dónde puede encontrar un poco de todo. ¿Conoce algún otro lugar como éste?

Oviedo Centro Comercial

Sabe lo que te gusta

Identificar

Lee el anuncio (*advertisement*) y busca ejemplos de los verbos **saber** y **conocer.**

Preguntas

1. Después de leer el anuncio, ¿qué sabes del Centro Comercial Oviedo?

2. ¿Qué puedes hacer en el Centro Comercial Oviedo?

3. ¿A quién está dirigido el anuncio?

4. ¿Conoces un centro comercial como éste? ¿Cómo se llama? ¿En qué ciudad está?

8.4 Comparisons and superlatives

Comparisons of inequality

▶ Comparisons of inequality are formed by placing **más** (*more*) or **menos** (*less*) before adjectives, adverbs, and nouns and **que** (*than*) after them. When the comparison involves a numerical expression, **de** is used before the number.

Tengo más hambre que un elefante.

El lomo a la plancha es un poquito más caro que el caldo.

El té es **más caro que** el jugo.
The tea is more expensive than the juice.

Susana es **menos generosa que** su prima.
Susana is less generous than her cousin.

Tú eres **más alto que** Jorge.
You are taller than Jorge.

Hay **más de cincuenta** naranjas.
There are more than fifty oranges.

▶ With verbs, use this construction to make comparisons of inequality: [*verb*] + **más/menos que**.

Mis hermanos **comen más que** yo.
My brothers eat more than I do.

Antonio **viaja más que** tú.
Antonio travels more than you do.

Arturo **duerme menos que** su padre.
Arturo sleeps less than his father does.

Ana **habla menos que** yo.
Ana talks less than I do.

Comparisons of equality

▶ The constructions **tan** + [*adverb, adjective*] + **como** and **tanto/a(s)** + [*singular noun, plural noun*] + **como** are used to make comparisons of equality.

Este plato es **tan delicioso como** aquél.
This dish is as delicious as that one.

Yo comí **tanta comida como** tú.
I ate as much food as you did.

Tu amigo es **tan simpático como** tú.
Your friend is as nice as you.

Uds. probaron **tantos platos como** ellos.
You tried as many dishes as they did.

▶ Comparisons of equality with verbs are formed by placing **tanto como** after the verb. Note that **tanto** does not change in number or gender.

No **duermo tanto como** mi tía.
I don't sleep as much as my aunt.

Estudiamos **tanto como** ustedes.
We study as much as you do.

Práctica

1 **Tita y Lucila** Escoge (*choose*) la palabra correcta para comparar a dos hermanas muy diferentes. Haz (*make*) las adaptaciones necesarias.

1. Lucila es más alta y más bonita _____ [de, más, menos, que] Tita.

2. Tita es más delgada porque practica deportes _____ [de, más, menos, que] que su hermana.

3. Lucila es más _____ [listo, simpático, bajo] que Tita porque es alegre.

4. A Tita le gusta quedarse en casa. Va a _____ [de, más, menos, que] fiestas que su hermana.

5. Tita es tímida e inteligente. _____ [abrir, oír, estudiar] más que Lucila. Ahora está tomando más _____ [de, más, menos, que] cinco clases.

6. Lucila se preocupa _____ [de, más, menos, que] que Tita por estudiar. ¡Son _____ [como, tan, tanto] diferentes!

2 **Mario y Luis** Completa las oraciones (*sentences*) con las palabras correctas para comparar a Mario y a Luis, los novios de Lucila y Tita.

tantas	tan interesante
tan guapo	amigos extranjeros
diferencia	tantos
como	francés

1. Mario es _____ como Luis.

2. Mario viaja tanto _____ Luis.

3. Luis habla _____ lenguas extranjeras como Mario.

4. Luis habla _____ tan bien como Mario.

5. Mario tiene tantos _____ como Luis.

6. ¡Qué casualidad (*coincidence*)! Mario y Luis también son hermanos, pero no hay tanta _____ entre ellos como entre Lucila y Tita.

Conversación

3 **Comparaciones** En parejas, conversen sobre los siguientes temas u otros.

> **modelo** papas fritas

Estudiante 1: Las papas fritas del restaurante Los Pinos son las mejores del mundo.

Estudiante 2: Pues yo creo que las papas fritas del restaurante López son tan buenas como las papas fritas del restaurante Los Pinos.

Estudiante 1: No, porque son más saladas que las papas fritas del restaurante Los Pinos.

restaurantes en tu comunidad	revistas favoritas
cafés en tu comunidad	libros favoritos
tiendas en tu comunidad	comidas favoritas
periódicos en tu comunidad	los profesores
	los cursos que tomas
	las personas famosas

4 **La familia García** En grupos, túrnense (*take turns*) para hacer comparaciones entre Rafael, Eva, Esteban y Lourdes García.

> 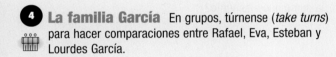 **modelo**

Estudiante 1: Esteban es el más guapo de la familia.

Estudiante 2: Pues yo creo que Rafael es tan guapo como Esteban.

Estudiante 1: Mmm, pero Esteban es mucho más alto.

Superlatives

▸ The following construction is used to form superlatives:

> el/la/los/las + [*noun*] + más/menos + [*adjective*] + de

Es el café más rico del país.
It's the most delicious coffee in the country.

Es el menú menos caro de todos éstos.
It is the least expensive menu of all of these.

▸ The noun in a superlative construction can be omitted if it is clear to whom or what the superlative refers.

¿El restaurante El Cráter?
Es el más elegante de la ciudad.
The El Cráter restaurant? It's the most elegant (one) in the city.

Recomiendo el pollo asado.
Es el más sabroso del menú.
I recommend the roast chicken. It's the most delicious item on the menu.

¡ojo! The absolute superlative, which ends in **–ísimo**, is equivalent to the English *extremely/very* + [*adjective*] or *extremely/very* + [*adverb*]. For example: **muchísimo** (*very much*), **malísimo** (*very bad*), **facilísimo** (*extremely easy*).

Irregular comparisons and superlatives

Irregular comparative and superlative forms					
Adjective		**Comparative form**		**Superlative form**	
bueno/a	good	mejor	better	el/la mejor	(the) best
malo/a	bad	peor	worse	el/la peor	(the) worst
grande	big	mayor	bigger	el/la mayor	(the) biggest
pequeño/a	small	menor	smaller	el/la menor	(the) smallest
joven	young	menor	younger	el/la menor	(the) youngest
viejo/a	old	mayor	older	el/la mayor	(the) oldest

▸ When **grande** and **pequeño/a** refer to age, the irregular comparative and superlative forms, **mayor/menor**, are used. However, when **grande** and **pequeño/a** refer to size, the regular forms, **más grande/más pequeño/a**, are used.

Isabel es **la mayor de** los hermanos.
Isabel is the biggest (eldest) of the siblings.

Tu ensalada es **más grande que** ésa.
Your salad is bigger than that one.

▸ The adverbs **bien** and **mal** have the same irregular comparative forms as **bueno/a** and **malo/a**.

Julio nada **mejor que** los otros chicos.
Julio swims better than the other boys.

Ellas cantan **peor que** las otras chicas.
They sing worse than the other girls.

Ampliación

1 Escuchar

A Escucha a Ramón Acevedo. Toma apuntes (*notes*) de las instrucciones que él da.

> ⭐ **TIP** **Jot down notes as you listen.** Jotting down notes while you listen will help you to focus actively on comprehension rather than on remembering what you have heard.

Ingredientes del relleno:	Poner dentro del pavo:
_____	_____
_____	_____
_____	_____
_____	
_____	
_____	
_____	

- Untarlo con _____.
- Cubrirlo con _____ de aluminio.
- Ponerlo en el horno a _____ grados, por unas _____ horas.

B ¿Es similar el plato que prepara Ramón Acevedo a algún plato que tu familia come habitualmente? ¿En qué es similar? ¿En qué es distinto?

2 Conversar

En parejas, túrnense (*take turns*) para contestar estas preguntas. Luego informen a la clase de los resultados.

- ¿Con quién comiste la semana pasada?
- ¿A qué restaurante fueron?
- ¿Qué pidieron? ¿Les gustó la comida?
- ¿Se la sirvieron rápidamente (*quickly*)?
- ¿Fue mejor o peor que la comida que comes en casa? ¿Fue muy cara?
- ¿Van a volver a ese restaurante en el futuro?

recursos

R	Textbook CD Lección 8	WB pp. 77-84	LM pp. 45-48	Lab CD Lección 8	ICD-ROM Lección 8	vistahigher learning.com

Ampliación

3 Escribir

Escribe una crítica culinaria sobre un restaurante local para el periódico de la universidad.

 TIP **Expressing and supporting opinions.** Use details, facts, examples, and other forms of evidence to convince your readers to take your opinions seriously.

Organízalo	Usa un mapa de ideas para organizar tus comentarios sobre la comida, el servicio, el ambiente (*atmosphere*) y otras informaciones sobre el restaurante.
Escríbelo	Utiliza tus notas para escribir el primer borrador de tu artículo culinario.
Corrígelo	Intercambia (*exchange*) tu composición con un(a) compañero/a. Comenta sobre el título, la organización, los detalles específicos y los errores de gramática o de ortografía.
Compártelo	Revisa el primer borrador según las indicaciones de tu compañero/a. Incorpora nuevas ideas y/o más información para reforzar (*support*) tu opinión. Luego entrégale (*hand it in*) la crítica culinaria a tu profesor(a).

4 Un paso más

Diseña el menú de un nuevo restaurante en la capital de un país hispano.

- Decide en qué país y ciudad vas a abrir el restaurante.
- Investiga cuáles son las comidas típicas y los platos más populares del país.
- Diseña el menú, incluyendo entremeses, platos principales, ensaladas, postres (*desserts*) y bebidas.
- Indica los precios de los platos en la moneda del país.
- Intercambia tu menú con tres o cuatro compañeros y comparen los platos que escogieron.

 En Internet

Investiga estos temas en el sitio vistahigherlearning.com.

- Capitales de los países hispanos
- Comidas del mundo hispano

El Tamalito

Especialidades guatemaltecas

5a calle (Los Próceres)
Zona 4
Tel: (502) 345 89 76
Fax: (502) 243 56 34

Antes de leer

Reading for the main idea is a useful strategy; it involves locating the topic sentences of each paragraph in order to determine the author's purpose for writing a particular piece. The first sentence in each paragraph can provide clues about the content of each paragraph, as well as impressions of how the entire reading selection is organized.

Examinar el texto

En esta sección tenemos dos textos diferentes. ¿Qué estrategias puedes usar para leer la crítica culinaria? ¿Cuáles son las apropiadas para familiarizarte con el menú? Utiliza las estrategias más eficaces para cada texto. ¿Qué tienen en común?

Identificar la idea principal

Lee la primera frase de cada párrafo de la crítica culinaria del restaurante **El Palmito**. Apunta el tema principal de cada párrafo. Luego lee todo el primer párrafo. ¿Crees que el restaurante le gustó a la autora de la crítica culinaria? ¿Por qué? Ahora lee la crítica entera. En tu opinión, ¿cuál es la idea principal de la crítica? ¿Por qué la escribió la autora? Compara tus opiniones con las de un(a) compañero/a.

37E

Restaurantes

Cinco estrellas para El Palmito

Margarita Galán, crítica de restaurantes

El viernes pasado cené en el restaurante **El Palmito,** donde se unen de una manera extraordinaria la comida tradicional de nuestra región y la belleza arquitectónica de nuestra ciudad. Su propietario, Héctor Suárez, es uno de los jefes de cocina más respetados del país.

El exterior del restaurante refleja el estilo colonial de la ciudad. Por dentro, la decoración rústica crea un ambiente cálido. Hay que mencionar también el hermoso patio, lleno de plantas y flores, donde muchas personas se reúnen para tomar un café en un ambiente relajado y cordial.

Uno no se puede quejar del servicio de **El Palmito.** El personal del restaurante es muy amable y atento, desde los cocineros que preparan la comida hasta los meseros que la sirven.

La comida del restaurante es exquisita. Las tortillas, que se sirven con ajiaceite, son deliciosas. La sopa de pollo y huevo es excelente, y los frijoles enchilados, ricos. También recomiendo el tomaticán, cocinado con una gran variedad de verduras muy ricas. De postre, don Héctor me preparó su especialidad, un rico pastel de yogur.

Les recomiendo que visiten **El Palmito** cuando tengan ocasión.

El Palmito
de lunes a sábado 10:00am-11:00pm
domingo 11:00am-10:00pm

Comida ★★★★★
Servicio ★★★★★
Ambiente ★★★★★
Precio ★★★★

MENÚ

Entremeses

Pan tostado con
- Queso frito   • Mantequilla y jalea

Tortillas con
- Ajicomino (chile, comino)   • Ajiaceite (chile, aceite)

Sopas

- Cebolla   • Verduras   • Pollo y huevo   • Mariscos

Platos Principales

Chilaquil
(tortilla de maíz, queso, hierbas y chile)

Tomaticán
(tomate, papas, maíz, chile, arvejas, zanahorias y verduras)

Tamales
(maíz, azúcar, ajo, cebolla)

Frijoles enchilados
(frijoles negros, carne de cerdo o de res, arroz, chile)

Postres

- Helado de piña   • Plátanos caribeños
- Uvate (uvas, azúcar de caña y ron)   • Pastel de yogur

Bebidas

- Té helado   • Vino tinto
- Vino blanco   • Agua mineral   • Jugos
- Chilate (maíz, chile y cacao)

Después de leer

¿Comprendiste?

Selecciona las palabras que mejor completan cada frase.

1. La arquitectura del restaurante es _____ [moderna, colonial, fea].

2. [Los clientes, Los cocineros, Los camareros] _____ sirven la comida.

3. [Los clientes, Los cocineros, Los camareros] _____ preparan la comida.

4. El dueño del restaurante es uno de los _____ [peores, menores, mejores] jefes de cocina del país.

5. La comida en este restaurante, según la autora, es _____ [muy buena, mala, regular].

Preguntas

1. ¿Cómo se llama el dueño del restaurante?
   _____

2. ¿Qué tipo de comida se sirve en El Palmito?
   _____

3. ¿Cómo es el ambiente del restaurante?
   _____

4. ¿Quién escribió este artículo?
   _____

5. ¿Cuántos platos probó la autora del artículo?
   _____

Coméntalo

¿Te interesan las comidas y bebidas que sirven en El Palmito? ¿Cuáles te interesan más? ¿Por qué? ¿Se sirven platos y bebidas similares a éstos en tu región o comunidad?

postres	*desserts*
cálido	*warm*
por dentro	*inside*
hay que	*one must*
jefe de cocina	*head chef*
lleno	*full*
relajado	*relaxed*
ambiente	*atmosphere*
uno no se puede quejar	*one can't complain*
cuando tengan ocasión	*when you have the opportunity*

recursos

R

vistahigher
learning.com

Comidas

el/la camarero/a	waiter
el/la dueño/a	owner
el menú	menu
la sección de (no) fumadores	(non) smoking section
el almuerzo	lunch
la cena	dinner
la comida	food; meal
el desayuno	breakfast
los entremeses	hors d'oeuvres
el plato (principal)	(main) dish
agrio/a	sour
delicioso/a	delicious
dulce	sweet
picante	hot, spicy
rico/a	tasty; delicious
sabroso/a	tasty; delicious
salado/a	salty
almorzar (o:ue)	to have lunch
cenar	to have dinner
desayunar	to have breakfast
pedir (e:i)	to order (food)
probar (o:ue)	to taste; to try
recomendar (e:ie)	to recommend
servir (e:i)	to serve

Verduras

las arvejas	peas
la cebolla	onion
el champiñón	mushroom
la ensalada	salad
los frijoles	beans
la lechuga	lettuce
el maíz	corn
las papas/patatas	potatoes
el tomate	tomato
las verduras	vegetables
la zanahoria	carrot

La carne y el pescado

el atún	tuna
el bistec	steak
los camarones	shrimp
la carne	meat
la carne de res	beef
la chuleta de cerdo	pork chop
la hamburguesa	hamburger
el jamón	ham
la langosta	lobster
los mariscos	seafood
el pavo	turkey
el pescado	fish
el pollo (asado)	(roast) chicken
la salchicha	sausage
el salmón	salmon

Otras comidas

el aceite	oil
el ajo	garlic
el arroz	rice
el azúcar	sugar
los cereales	cereal; grains
el huevo	egg
la mantequilla	butter
la margarina	margarine
la mayonesa	mayonnaise
el pan (tostado)	(toasted) bread
las papas/patatas fritas	fried potatoes; French fries
la pimienta	pepper
el queso	cheese
la sal	salt
el sándwich	sandwich
la sopa	soup
el vinagre	vinegar

Verbos

conocer	to know; to be acquainted with
conducir	to drive
morir (o:ue)	to die
ofrecer	to offer
parecer	to seem; to appear
saber	to know; to know how
servir (e:i)	to serve
traducir	to translate

Expresiones útiles	See page 189.
Comparisons and superlatives	See pages 198-199.

Bebidas

el agua (f.) (mineral)	(mineral) water
la bebida	drink
el café	coffee
la cerveza	beer
el jugo (de fruta)	(fruit) juice
la leche	milk
el refresco	soft drink
el té (helado)	(iced) tea
el vino (blanco/tinto)	(white/red) wine

Las frutas

la banana	banana
las frutas	fruit
el limón	lemon
la manzana	apple
la naranja	orange
las uvas	grapes

recursos

R	Lab CD Lección 8	LM p. 48

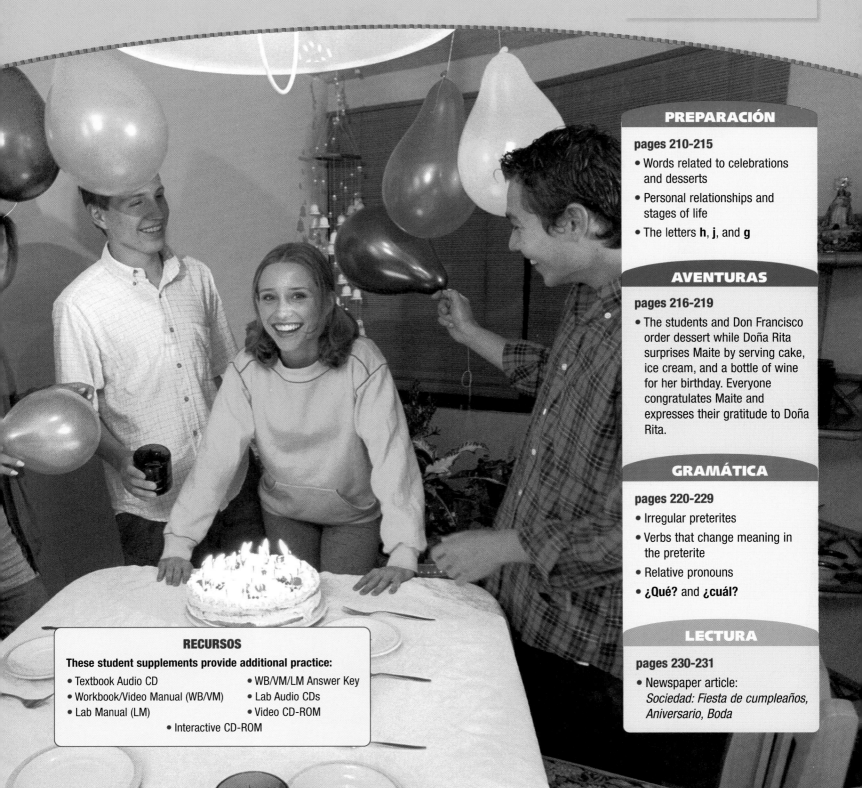

9 Las celebraciones

Communicative Goals

You will learn how to:
- wish somebody a happy birthday
- talk about celebrations and personal relationships
- ask for the bill in a restaurant
- express gratitude

PREPARACIÓN

pages 210-215
- Words related to celebrations and desserts
- Personal relationships and stages of life
- The letters **h**, **j**, and **g**

AVENTURAS

pages 216-219
- The students and Don Francisco order dessert while Doña Rita surprises Maite by serving cake, ice cream, and a bottle of wine for her birthday. Everyone congratulates Maite and expresses their gratitude to Doña Rita.

GRAMÁTICA

pages 220-229
- Irregular preterites
- Verbs that change meaning in the preterite
- Relative pronouns
- **¿Qué?** and **¿cuál?**

LECTURA

pages 230-231
- Newspaper article:
  Sociedad: Fiesta de cumpleaños, Aniversario, Boda

RECURSOS

These student supplements provide additional practice:
- Textbook Audio CD
- Workbook/Video Manual (WB/VM)
- Lab Manual (LM)
- WB/VM/LM Answer Key
- Lab Audio CDs
- Video CD-ROM
- Interactive CD-ROM

LAS CELEBRACIONES

la boda
wedding

LAS FIESTAS

el aniversario (de bodas) *(wedding) anniversary*
el día de fiesta *holiday*
la fiesta *party*
el/la invitado/a *guest*
la Navidad *Christmas*
la quinceañera *young woman's fifteenth birthday celebration*
la sorpresa *surprise*

cambiar (de) *to change*
celebrar *to celebrate*
cumplir años *to have a birthday*
dejar una propina *to leave a tip*
divertirse (e:ie) *to have fun*
invitar *to invite*
pagar la cuenta *to pay the bill*
pasarlo bien/mal *to have a good/bad time*
regalar *to give (a gift)*
reírse (e:i) *to laugh*
relajarse *to relax*
sonreír (e:i) *to smile*
sorprender *to surprise*

el cumpleaños
birthday

brindar
to toast

graduarse (de)
to graduate (from)

POSTRES Y OTRAS COMIDAS

la botella de vino *bottle of wine*
los dulces *sweets*
el helado *ice cream*
el pastel *cake*
   de cumpleaños *birthday cake*
los postres *desserts*

las galletas
cookies

el flan
baked custard

el champán
champagne

recursos

R	Textbook CD Lección 9	WB pp. 89-90	LM p. 49	Lab CD Lección 9	ICD-ROM Lección 9

LAS ETAPAS DE LA VIDA

la etapa *stage*
la juventud *youth*
el nacimiento *birth*
la vida *life*

jubilarse *to retire (from work)*
nacer *to be born*

la niñez
childhood

la adolescencia
adolescence

LAS RELACIONES PERSONALES

la alegría *happiness*
la amistad *friendship*
el amor *love*
el divorcio *divorce*
el estado civil *marital status*
el matrimonio *marriage; married couple*
la pareja *couple; partner*
el/la recién casado/a *newlywed*

casado/a *married*
divorciado/a *divorced*
juntos/as *together*
separado/a *separated*
soltero/a *single*
viudo/a *widowed*

la madurez
maturity; middle-age

casarse (con) *to get married (to)*
comprometerse (con) *to get engaged (to)*
divorciarse (de) *to get divorced (from)*
enamorarse (de) *to fall in love (with)*
llevarse bien/mal (con) *to get along well/badly (with)*
odiar *to hate*
romper (con) *to break up (with)*
salir (con) *to go out (with); to date*
separarse (de) *to separate (from)*
tener una cita *to have a date; to have an appointment*

la vejez
old age

OTRAS PALABRAS

el apellido *last name*
el consejo *advice*
la respuesta *answer*

la muerte
death

A escuchar

1 **¿Lógico o ilógico?** Escucha las oraciones e indica si son **lógicas** o **ilógicas**.

	Lógico	Ilógico
1.	_____	_____
2.	_____	_____
3.	_____	_____
4.	_____	_____
5.	_____	_____
6.	_____	_____
7.	_____	_____
8.	_____	_____

2 **¡Feliz cumpleaños!** Los amigos de Silvia están preparándole una fiesta de cumpleaños. Escucha la conversación y contesta las preguntas.

1. ¿Sabe Silvia que sus amigos le van a dar una fiesta? _____

2. ¿Qué van a comer los amigos en la fiesta? _____

3. ¿A Silvia le gusta el chocolate? _____

4. ¿Dónde compraron el helado? _____

5. ¿Por qué no quieren comer el helado de la cafetería? _____

6. ¿Cuántos años cumple Silvia? _____

7. ¿Con qué brindan los amigos? _____

8. ¿Silvia es mayor o menor que sus amigos? _____

recursos

R | Textbook CD
Lección 9

A practicar

3 **Seleccionar** Selecciona la mejor expresión o palabra.

lo pasaron mal	se llevan bien
dejó una propina	se casaron
sonrió	nació
tenemos una cita	nos divertimos
se jubiló	

1. Nelson y Mildred _____ el septiembre pasado. La boda fue maravillosa.

2. Mi tía le _____ muy grande al camarero.

3. Mi padrastro _____ hace un año.

4. A Alejandra le gustan las galletas. Ella _____ después de comérselas todas.

5. Luis y yo _____ en la fiesta. Bailamos y comimos mucho.

6. ¡Tengo una nueva sobrina! Ella _____ ayer por la mañana.

7. Irene y su esposo _____. Son muy felices.

8. Rocío y Eddie _____ en el cine. La película fue muy mala.

9. Isabel y yo _____ esta noche. Vamos a ir a un restaurante muy elegante.

4 **La fiesta de Susana** Completa las frases con palabras adecuadas.

1. Susana siempre _____ su cumpleaños con su familia y sus amigos.

2. Su mamá invitó a mucha gente; todos los _____ llegaron tarde.

3. Su papá contó chistes (*told jokes*) y todos _____.

4. A Susana le _____ muchos regalos.

5. El hermano de Susana comió muchos trozos (*pieces*) de _____.

6. Su amiga Anabela va a _____ con su novio en dos semanas.

7. Susana está un poco triste porque ayer _____ su novio.

8. Pero Susana _____ el próximo viernes con su amigo Jorge.

5 **Te equivocas** Túrnate (*take turns*) con un(a) compañero/a para decir que sus afirmaciones son falsas. Corrige las afirmaciones falsas usando el opuesto de las expresiones subrayadas.

> **modelo**
> Nuestros amigos lo pasaron mal en la playa.
> **Estudiante 1:** Nuestros amigos lo pasaron mal en la playa.
> **Estudiante 2:** No, te equivocas (*you're wrong*). Ellos lo pasaron bien.

1. El nacimiento es el fin de la vida.

2. A los sesenta y cinco años muchas personas comienzan a trabajar.

3. Francisco y Gloria se divorcian mañana.

4. Pancho se comprometió con Yolanda.

5. Marcela odia a Ramón.

6. La juventud es la etapa de la vida cuando nos jubilamos.

A conversar

6 **Planes para una fiesta** Trabaja con dos compañeros/as para planear una fiesta. Recuerda incluir la siguiente información.

1. ¿Qué tipo de fiesta es?
2. ¿Dónde va a ser? ¿Cuándo va a ser?
3. ¿A quién van a invitar?
4. ¿Qué van a comer? ¿Quién va a llevar o a preparar la comida?
5. ¿Qué van a beber? ¿Quién va a traer las bebidas?
6. ¿Qué van a hacer todos durante la fiesta?
7. Después de la fiesta, ¿qué van a hacer?

7 **Encuesta** Pregunta a dos o tres compañeros/as para saber qué actitudes (*attitudes*) tienen en sus relaciones personales. Comparte los resultados de la encuesta con la clase.

Preguntas	Nombres	Actitudes
1. ¿Te importa la amistad? ¿Por qué?	_____	_____
2. ¿Es mejor tener un(a) buen(a) amigo/a o muchos amigos?	_____	_____
3. ¿Cuáles son las características que buscas en tus amigos?	_____	_____
4. ¿Tienes novio/a? ¿A qué edad (*age*) es posible enamorarse?	_____	_____
5. ¿Debe la pareja hacer todas las cosas juntos?	_____	_____
6. ¿Debe la pareja tener siempre las mismas opiniones? ¿Por qué?	_____	_____

8 **Una fiesta memorable** Cuéntale (*tell*) a un(a) compañero/a cómo fue una fiesta memorable. Incluye los siguientes elementos.

- ¿Qué?
- ¿Por qué?
- ¿Cuándo?
- ¿Dónde?
- ¿Cómo?
- ¿Quién?
- ¿Cuántos?

🎧 Pronunciación

The letters **h**, **j**, and **g**

| **h**elado | **h**ombre | **h**ola | **h**ermosa |

The Spanish **h** is always silent.

| **J**osé | **j**ubilarse | de**j**ar | pare**j**a |

The letter **j** is pronounced much like the English *h* in *his*.

| a**g**encia | **g**eneral | **G**il | **G**isela |

The letter **g** can be pronounced three different ways. Before **e** or **i**, the letter **g** is pronounced much like the English *h*.

Gustavo, **g**racias por llamar el domi**ng**o.

At the beginning of a phrase or after the letter **n**, the Spanish **g** is pronounced like the English *g* in *girl*.

Me **g**radué en a**g**osto.

In any other position, the Spanish **g** has a somewhat softer sound.

| **G**ue**rr**a | conse**gui**r | **gua**ntes | a**gua** |

In the combinations **gue** and **gui**, the **g** has a hard sound and the **u** is silent. In the combination **gua**, the **g** has a hard sound and the **u** is pronounced like the English *w*.

Práctica Lee las palabras en voz alta, prestando atención a la **h**, la **j** y la **g**.

1. hamburguesa
2. jugar
3. oreja
4. guapa
5. geografía
6. magnífico
7. espejo
8. hago
9. seguir
10. gracias
11. hijo
12. galleta
13. Jorge
14. tengo
15. ahora
16. guantes

Oraciones Lee las oraciones en voz alta, prestando atención a la **h**, la **j** y la **g**.

1. Hola. Me llamo Gustavo Hinojosa Lugones y vivo en Santiago de Chile.
2. Tengo una familia grande; somos tres hermanos y tres hermanas.
3. Voy a graduarme en mayo.
4. Para celebrar mi graduación mis padres van a regalarme un viaje a Egipto.
5. ¡Qué generosos son!

Refranes Lee los refranes en voz alta, prestando atención a la **h**, la **j** y la **g**.

El hábito no hace al monje.[2]

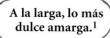

A la larga, lo más dulce amarga.[1]

1 Too much of a good thing.
2 The clothes don't make the man.

recursos

| R | Textbook CD Lección 9 | LM p. 50 | Lab CD Lección 9 | ICD-ROM Lección 9 |

¡Feliz cumpleaños, Maite!

Don Francisco y los estudiantes celebran el cumpleaños de Maite en el restaurante El Cráter.

INÉS A mí me encantan los dulces. Maite, ¿tú qué vas a pedir?

MAITE Ay, no sé. Todo parece tan delicioso. Quizás el pastel de chocolate.

JAVIER Para mí el pastel de chocolate con helado. Me encanta el chocolate. Y tú Álex, ¿qué vas a pedir?

ÁLEX Generalmente prefiero la fruta, pero hoy creo que voy a probar el pastel de chocolate.

DON FRANCISCO Yo siempre tomo un flan y un café.

DOÑA RITA & CAMARERO ¡Feliz cumpleaños, Maite!

INÉS ¿Hoy es tu cumpleaños, Maite?

MAITE Sí, el 22 de junio. Y parece que vamos a celebrarlo.

TODOS MENOS MAITE ¡Felicidades!

ÁLEX Yo también acabo de cumplir los veintitrés años.

MAITE ¿Cuándo?

ÁLEX El cuatro de mayo.

DOÑA RITA Aquí tienen un flan, pastel de chocolate con helado… y una botella de vino para dar alegría.

MAITE ¡Qué sorpresa! ¡No sé qué decir! Muchísimas gracias.

DON FRANCISCO El conductor no puede tomar vino. Doña Rita, gracias por todo. ¿Puede traernos la cuenta?

DOÑA RITA Enseguida, Paco.

recursos

| Video/VCD-ROM Lección 9 | VM pp. 185-186 | ICD-ROM Lección 9 |

Personajes

DON FRANCISCO

JAVIER

INÉS

ÁLEX

MAITE

DOÑA RITA

CAMARERO

MAITE ¡Gracias! Pero, ¿quién le dijo que es mi cumpleaños?

DOÑA RITA Lo supe por don Francisco.

ÁLEX Ayer te lo pregunté, ¡y no quisiste decírmelo! ¿Eh? ¡Qué mala eres!

JAVIER ¿Cuántos años cumples?

MAITE Veintitrés.

INÉS Creo que debemos dejar una buena propina. ¿Qué les parece?

MAITE Sí, vamos a darle una buena propina a la Sra. Perales. Es simpatiquísima.

DON FRANCISCO Gracias una vez más. Siempre lo paso muy bien aquí.

MAITE Muchísimas gracias, Sra. Perales. Por la comida, por la sorpresa y por ser tan amable con nosotros.

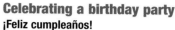

Expresiones útiles

Celebrating a birthday party

¡Feliz cumpleaños!
Happy birthday!

¡Felicidades!
Congratulations! (for an event such as a birthday or anniversary)

¡Felicitaciones!
Congratulations! (for an event such as an engagement or a good grade on a test)

¿Quién le dijo que es mi cumpleaños?
Who told you that it's my birthday?

Lo supe por don Francisco.
I found out from Don Francisco.

¿Cuántos años cumples/cumple Ud.?
How old are you now?

Veintitrés.
Twenty-three.

Asking for the bill

¿Puede traernos la cuenta?
Can you bring us the bill?

La cuenta, por favor.
The bill, please.

Enseguida, señor/señora/señorita.
Right away, sir/ma'am/miss.

Expressing gratitude

¡(Muchas) gracias!
Thank you (very much)!

Muchísimas gracias.
Thank you very, very much.

Gracias por todo.
Thanks for everything.

Gracias una vez más.
Thanks once again.

Leaving a tip

Creo que debemos dejar una buena propina. ¿Qué les parece?
I think we should leave a good tip. What do you guys think?

Sí, vamos a darle una buena propina.
Yes, let's give him/her a good tip.

¿Qué piensas?

1 Completar Completa las frases con la información correcta.

1. De postre, don Francisco siempre pide _____ .
2. A Javier le encanta _____ .
3. Álex cumplió los _____ años _____ .
4. Hoy Álex quiere probar algo diferente. De postre, va a pedir _____ .
5. El conductor no puede _____ .
6. Los estudiantes van a dejar _____ a doña Rita.

2 Seleccionar Selecciona algunas de las opciones de la lista para completar las frases.

pedir	una sorpresa
una botella de vino	comer
la cuenta	veintitrés
la quinceañera	¡Qué sorpresa!
veintidós	el postre

1. Hoy Maite cumple _____ años.
2. Maite no sabe que van a celebrar su cumpleaños porque es _____ .
3. Cuando una pareja celebra su aniversario y quiere tomar algo especial, compra _____ .
4. Después de una cena o un almuerzo, es normal pedir _____ .
5. De postre, Inés y Maite no saben exactamente lo que van a _____ .
6. Álex tiene _____ años.

3 Situación Trabajen en grupos para representar una conversación. Uno/a de Uds. está celebrando su cumpleaños en un restaurante. Un(a) amigo/a le desea feliz cumpleaños y le pregunta cuántos años cumple. Luego, cada uno/a le pide al/a la camarero/a un postre y algo para beber. Después de comer los postres, un(a) amigo/a pide la cuenta y otro/a habla de dejar una propina. Los amigos dicen que quieren pagar la cuenta y la persona que cumple años les da las gracias por todo.

Exploración
Fiestas y celebraciones

En Sevilla, la Semana Santa (*Holy Week*) es especialmente colorida (*colorful*) y emocionante. Las procesiones religiosas son muy famosas y muchos turistas quieren verlas.

Argentina celebra su independencia el 25 de mayo, fecha en que, en 1810, los argentinos establecieron su propio gobierno (*own government*). La celebración es en la Plaza de Mayo de Buenos Aires; hay discursos oficiales y fuegos artificiales (*speeches and fireworks*).

En México, se celebra el Día de los Muertos (*the dead*) el primero y el dos de noviembre. Mucha gente va al cementerio para honrar a sus seres queridos (*loved ones*). Es común ofrecerles flores, incienso y comida a los muertos.

Observaciones

- Los españoles celebran el Año Nuevo comiendo rápidamente doce uvas.

- En las regiones de la América del Sur donde hace calor en diciembre, es común celebrar la Navidad en la playa.

- En el Ecuador se celebra el Carnaval tirando (*throwing*) agua a todos los que pasan.

Coméntalo

Con un(a) compañero/a, contesta las siguientes preguntas.

- ¿Cuál de estas celebraciones te interesa más? ¿Por qué?
- ¿Son similares o diferentes a los días de fiesta en tu comunidad?
- ¿Cuáles son las fiestas más populares en tu comunidad o región? ¿Cómo las celebras?

recursos

R

vistahigher
learning.com

9.1 Irregular preterites

▶ You already know that **ir** and **ser** are irregular in the preterite. Here are some other verbs that are irregular in the preterite.

Preterite of *tener*, *venir*, and *decir*

	tener (e → u)	venir (e → i)	decir (e → i)
yo	**tuv**e	**vin**e	**dij**e
tú	**tuv**iste	**vin**iste	**dij**iste
Ud./él/ella	**tuv**o	**vin**o	**dij**o
nosotros/as	**tuv**imos	**vin**imos	**dij**imos
vosotros/as	**tuv**isteis	**vin**isteis	**dij**isteis
Uds./ellos/ellas	**tuv**ieron	**vin**ieron	**dij**eron

▶ Observe the stem changes in the chart: the **e** in **tener** changes to **u**, and the **e** in **venir** and **decir** changes to **i**. Note also that the **c** in **decir** changes to **j**. None of these verbs have written accents in the **yo** or **Ud./él/ella** forms.

▶ These verbs have similar stem changes.

INFINITIVE	U-STEM	PRETERITE FORMS
poder	pud-	pude, pudiste, pudo, pudimos, pudisteis, pudieron
poner	pus-	puse, pusiste, puso, pusimos, pusisteis, pusieron
saber	sup-	supe, supiste, supo, supimos, supisteis, supieron
estar	estuv-	estuve, estuviste, estuvo, estuvimos, estuvisteis, estuvieron

INFINITIVE	I-STEM	
querer	quis-	quise, quisiste, quiso, quisimos, quisisteis, quisieron
hacer	hic-	hice, hiciste, hizo, hicimos, hicisteis, hicieron

INFINITIVE	J-STEM	
traer	traj-	traje, trajiste, trajo, trajimos, trajisteis, trajeron
conducir	conduj-	conduje, condujiste, condujo, condujimos, condujisteis, condujeron
traducir	traduj-	traduje, tradujiste, tradujo, tradujimos, tradujisteis, tradujeron

¡ojo! Verbs with **j**-stems omit the letter **i** in the **Uds.** form. For example, **tener ➤ tuvieron**, but **decir ➤ dijeron**.

Most verbs that end in **–cir** are **j**-stem verbs in the preterite. For example, **producir ➤ produje, produjiste**, etc.

ORBITEL
$5.000
$10.000
$20.000

¿Dijiste larga distancia?
En tarjetas prepagadas ninguna te da más minutos para hablar

Práctica

1 **Una fiesta sorpresa** Completa estas frases con el pretérito de los verbos indicados.

1. El sábado _____ [haber] una fiesta sorpresa para Elsa en mi casa.

2. Sofía _____ [hacer] un pastel para la fiesta y Miguel _____ [traer] un flan.

3. Los amigos y parientes de Elsa _____ [venir] y _____ [traer] regalos.

4. El hermano de Elsa no _____ [venir] porque _____ [tener] que trabajar.

5. Su tía María Dolores tampoco _____ [poder] venir.

6. Cuando Elsa abrió la puerta, todos gritaron (*shouted*): "¡Feliz cumpleaños!" y su esposo le _____ [dar] un beso.

7. Al final de la fiesta, todos _____ [decir] que se divirtieron mucho.

8. La fiesta le _____ [dar] a Elsa tanta alegría que no _____ [poder] dormir esa noche.

2 **¿Qué hicieron?** Usa los verbos apropiados para describir lo que hicieron estas personas.

dar	hacer	venir	traducir
estar	poner	tener	traer

1. El Sr. López/dinero

3. Nosotros/fiesta

2. Norma/pavo

4. Roberto y Elena/regalo

Conversación

3 Preguntas En parejas, túrnense para contestar estas preguntas.

1. ¿Qué hiciste anoche?
2. ¿Quiénes no estuvieron en clase la semana pasada?
3. ¿Qué trajiste a clase ayer?
4. ¿Qué trajiste a clase hoy?
5. ¿Hiciste la tarea para esta clase?
6. ¿Cuándo hiciste la tarea? ¿Se la diste al/a la profesor(a)?
7. ¿Hubo una fiesta en tu casa o residencia el sábado pasado?
8. ¿Alguien dio una fiesta para tu cumpleaños el año pasado? ¿Quién?
9. ¿Cuándo fue la última (*last*) vez que tus parientes vinieron a visitarte? ¿Te trajeron algo? ¿Qué te trajeron?
10. ¿Les diste a tus padres un regalo para su aniversario de bodas? ¿Qué les regalaste?
11. ¿Le dijiste una mentira a tu novio/a o esposo/a la semana pasada?

4 Encuesta Circula por la clase y formula preguntas hasta que encuentres a alguien que corresponda a alguna descripción de la lista. Luego informa a la clase de los resultados de tu encuesta.

Descripciones	Nombres
1. Tuvo un examen ayer.	_____
2. Trajo dulces a clase.	_____
3. Condujo su carro (*car*) a clase.	_____
4. Estuvo en la biblioteca ayer.	_____
5. Le dio consejos a alguien ayer.	_____
6. No pudo levantarse esta mañana.	_____
7. Tuvo que levantarse temprano ayer.	_____
8. Hizo un viaje a un país hispano el verano pasado.	_____
9. Tuvo una cita anoche.	_____
10. Dijo una mentira ayer.	_____
11. Fue a una fiesta el fin de semana pasado.	_____
12. Tuvo que trabajar el sábado pasado.	_____

The preterite of dar

The preterite of *dar*

yo	di	nosotros/as	dimos
tú	diste	vosotros/as	disteis
Ud./él/ella	dio	Uds./ellos/ellas	dieron

▶ The endings for **dar** are the same as the regular preterite endings for **–er** and **–ir** verbs, but there are no written accent marks.

La camarera me **dio** el menú.
The waitress gave me the menu.

Los invitados le **dieron** un regalo.
The guests gave him a gift.

Le **di** a Juan algunos consejos.
I gave Juan some advice.

Nosotros **dimos** una gran fiesta.
We gave a great party.

▶ The preterite of **hay** (*inf.* **haber**) is **hubo** (*there was/were*).

Hubo una fiesta el sábado pasado.
There was a party last Saturday.

Hubo una sorpresa especial para mi hermana.
There was a special surprise for my sister.

Hubo muchos invitados.
There were a lot of guests.

También **hubo** muchos regalos y champán.
There were also a lot of gifts and champagne.

Hubo una fiesta en el restaurante El Cráter.

Doña Rita les dio una botella de vino a los viajeros.

¡Manos a la obra!

 Escribe en cada espacio en blanco la forma correcta del pretérito de cada verbo.

1. Tú ___quisiste___ [querer].
2. Ud. _____ [decir].
3. Nosotras _____ [hacer].
4. Yo _____ [traer].
5. Ellas _____ [conducir].
6. Ella _____ [estar].
7. Tú _____ [tener].
8. Ella y yo _____ [dar].
9. Yo _____ [traducir].
10. Ayer _____ [haber].
11. Ud. _____ [saber].
12. Ellos _____ [poner].
13. Yo _____ [venir].
14. Tú _____ [poder].
15. Uds. _____ [querer].
16. Nosotras _____ [estar].
17. Tú _____ [decir].
18. Ellos _____ [saber].
19. Él _____ [hacer].
20. Yo _____ [poner].
21. Nosotras _____ [traer].
22. Yo _____ [tener].
23. Tú _____ [dar].
24. Uds. _____ [poder].

9.2 Verbs that change meaning in the preterite

▸ **Conocer, saber, poder,** and **querer** change meanings in the preterite.

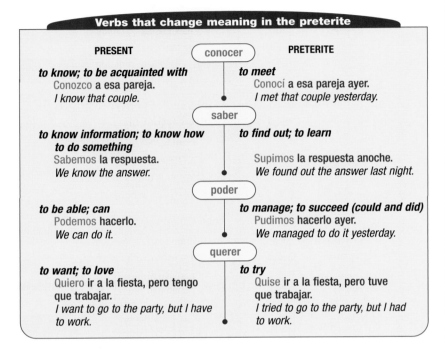

Verbs that change meaning in the preterite

PRESENT	conocer	PRETERITE
to know; to be acquainted with		**to meet**
Conozco a esa pareja.		Conocí a esa pareja ayer.
I know that couple.		I met that couple yesterday.

saber	
to know information; to know how to do something	**to find out; to learn**
Sabemos la respuesta.	Supimos la respuesta anoche.
We know the answer.	We found out the answer last night.

poder	
to be able; can	**to manage; to succeed (could and did)**
Podemos hacerlo.	Pudimos hacerlo ayer.
We can do it.	We managed to do it yesterday.

querer	
to want; to love	**to try**
Quiero ir a la fiesta, pero tengo que trabajar.	Quise ir a la fiesta, pero tuve que trabajar.
I want to go to the party, but I have to work.	I tried to go to the party, but I had to work.

▸ In the preterite, **poder** and **querer** have different meanings, depending on whether they are used in affirmative or negative sentences.

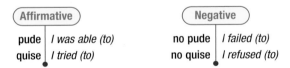

Affirmative	
pude	I was able (to)
quise	I tried (to)

Negative	
no pude	I failed (to)
no quise	I refused (to)

¡Manos a la obra!

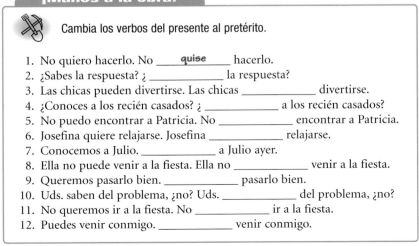

Cambia los verbos del presente al pretérito.

1. No quiero hacerlo. No ____quise____ hacerlo.
2. ¿Sabes la respuesta? ¿ _____ la respuesta?
3. Las chicas pueden divertirse. Las chicas _____ divertirse.
4. ¿Conoces a los recién casados? ¿ _____ a los recién casados?
5. No puedo encontrar a Patricia. No _____ encontrar a Patricia.
6. Josefina quiere relajarse. Josefina _____ relajarse.
7. Conocemos a Julio. _____ a Julio ayer.
8. Ella no puede venir a la fiesta. Ella no _____ venir a la fiesta.
9. Queremos pasarlo bien. _____ pasarlo bien.
10. Uds. saben del problema, ¿no? Uds. _____ del problema, ¿no?
11. No queremos ir a la fiesta. No _____ ir a la fiesta.
12. Puedes venir conmigo. _____ venir conmigo.

Práctica

1 **Oraciones** Forma frases con los siguientes elementos. Usa el pretérito.

modelo

Mis padres / no querer / venir / fiesta
Mis padres no quisieron venir a la fiesta.

1. Anoche / nosotros / saber / que / Carlos y Eva / divorciarse _____

2. Tú / conocer / Nora / clase / historia / ¿no?
_____

3. ¿Poder / Uds. / visitar / la Isla de Pascua?
_____

4. Ayer / yo / saber / que / Paco / querer / romper / Olivia _____

5. El señor Navarro / querer / jubilarse / pero / no poder _____

6. Gustavo y Elena / conocer / mi esposo / quinceañera de Ana _____

7. Yolanda / no poder / dormir / anoche
_____

8. Irma / saber / que / nosotros / comer / galletas
_____

9. Ayer / yo / no poder / llamar / tú
_____

10. Nosotros / querer / pagar la cuenta
_____

2 **Completar** Completa estas frases de una manera lógica.

1. Ayer yo supe…
2. Ayer mi compañero/a de cuarto supo…
3. Esta mañana no pude…
4. El fin de semana pasado mis amigos y yo no pudimos…
5. Conocí a mi mejor amigo/a en…
6. Mis padres no quisieron…
7. Mi mejor amigo/a no pudo…
8. Mi novio/a y yo nos conocimos en…
9. La semana pasada supe…
10. Ayer mis amigos quisieron…
11. Mis abuelos pudieron…

Conversación

3 **Telenovela** En parejas, preparen un diálogo para una escena de una telenovela (*soap opera*). La escena trata de (*is about*) una situación amorosa entre tres personas: Mirta, Daniel y Raúl. Usen el pretérito de **conocer, poder, querer** y **saber** en su diálogo.

Daniel

Mirta

Raúl

PASIÓN
HECHICERÍA

AVENTURA
INQUISICIÓN

LA MUJER DOBLE

4 **El fin de semana** Escribe dos listas: las cosas que hiciste durante el fin de semana pasado y las cosas que quisiste hacer, pero no pudiste. Luego, con un(a) compañero/a, comparen sus listas y expliquen por qué no pudieron hacer esas cosas.

Cosas que hice	Cosas que quise hacer
1. _____	1. _____
2. _____	2. _____
3. _____	3. _____
4. _____	4. _____
5. _____	5. _____
6. _____	6. _____
7. _____	7. _____
8. _____	8. _____
9. _____	9. _____
10. _____	10. _____

Español en vivo

Hubo un día en el que la humanidad quiso ir más allá de sus límites. Pudo conocer un mundo increíble. Supo asegurar su futuro.

Ahora todos lo pueden hacer.

BANCO DAVIVIENDA

Identificar

Lee el anuncio e identifica los verbos en el pretérito.

Preguntas

1. ¿Qué quiso hacer la humanidad? ¿Qué pudo conocer?
2. ¿Cuándo llegó el hombre a la Luna (*to the Moon*)?
3. ¿Qué tipo de compañía es la del anuncio?
4. ¿Es eficaz (*effective*) la conexión entre el viaje a la Luna y los servicios bancarios?

9.3 Relative pronouns

▶ Relative pronouns are used to combine two sentences or clauses that share a common element, such as a noun or pronoun. Study the following diagrams.

Éste es el flan.
This is the flan.

Manuela preparó el flan.
Manuela made the flan.

Éste es el flan que **Manuela preparó.**
This is the flan that Manuela made.

Lourdes **es muy inteligente.**
Lourdes is very intelligent.

Lourdes **estudia español.**
Lourdes studies Spanish.

Lourdes, quien **estudia español, es muy inteligente.**
Lourdes, who studies Spanish, is very intelligent.

La comida que pidieron fue muy sabrosa.

Doña Rita, quien les sirve el vino, es la dueña del restaurante.

▶ Spanish has three commonly used relative pronouns. Note that relative pronouns never carry an accent, unlike interrogative words like **¿qué?** and **¿quién(es)?**.

> **Common relative pronouns**
>
> | | |
> |---|---|
> | que | *that; which; who* |
> | quien(es) | *who; whom; that* |
> | lo que | *that which; what* |

▶ **Que**, the most frequently used relative pronoun, can refer to things or to people. Unlike the English *that*, **que** is never omitted.

¿Dónde está el pastel **que** pedí?
Where is the cake (that) I ordered?

El hombre **que** sirve la comida se llama Diego.
The man who serves the food is named Diego.

Práctica

1 **Una fiesta de aniversario** Amparo está hablando de la fiesta de aniversario de sus abuelos. Completa las oraciones con las expresiones de la lista.

> | | |
> |---|---|
> | que saqué | de quienes te hablé |
> | quien se jubiló | a quien conozco muy bien, se llama Ana |
> | quien es la novia de Ramón | que se graduó |

1. El sábado fui a la fiesta de aniversario de mis abuelos, _____ la semana pasada.
2. Éstas son las fotos _____ durante la fiesta.
3. Éste es Ramón, mi primo. Es el chico _____ de la universidad en junio.
4. Éste es mi abuelo, _____ el año pasado.
5. La mujer en esta foto, _____ .
6. Y ésta es Lucita, _____ .

2 **Una fiesta de cumpleaños** Describe la fiesta sorpresa que van a dar Jaime y Tina, usando los pronombres relativos **que, quien, quienes** y **lo que**.

1. Jaime y Tina son las personas _____ están planeando la fiesta.
2. Manuela, _____ cumple veintiún años mañana, no sabe que ellos están planeando una fiesta.
3. Éstas son las personas _____ van a invitar.
4. Juan y Luz, _____ son los hermanos de Manuela, van a venir.
5. Marco, _____ es el novio de Manuela, va a venir también.
6. _____ Jaime y Tina van a servir de postre es un pastel de chocolate.
7. Después del pastel, _____ está delicioso, todos brindan con champán.

Conversación

3 **Entrevista** En parejas, túrnense para hacerse las siguientes preguntas.

1. ¿Qué es lo que más te gusta de los días de fiesta? ¿Por qué?
2. ¿Qué es lo que menos te gusta de los días de fiesta? ¿Por qué?
3. ¿Quiénes son las personas con quienes celebras tu cumpleaños?
4. ¿Quién es el/la pariente o amigo/a a quien más le gustan los cumpleaños? ¿Por qué le gustan tanto?
5. ¿Dónde compras los regalos que le regalas a tu mejor amigo/a?
6. ¿Tienes hermanos o amigos que están casados? ¿Dónde viven?
7. ¿Quién es la persona que más te importa?
8. ¿Quiénes son las personas con quienes te diviertes más? ¿Por qué lo pasas bien con ellos/ellas?

4 **Definiciones** En parejas, definan las siguientes palabras, usando **que, quien(es)** y **lo que**. Luego compartan sus definiciones con la clase.

> **modelo**
>
> un pastel de cumpleaños
>
> **Estudiante 1:** ¿Qué es un pastel de cumpleaños?
> **Estudiante 2:** Es un postre que comes en tu cumpleaños./Es lo que comes en tu cumpleaños.

1. el helado
2. el champán
3. una propina
4. una boda
5. un invitado
6. la Navidad
7. una recién casada
8. el divorcio
9. la juventud
10. la vejez
11. una viuda
12. una quinceañera

Uses of **que, quien(es),** and **lo que**

▶ **Que** is used like the English *that* after verbs like **creer, decir, pensar,** and **suponer.**

Creo que la fiesta es mañana.	Ana **dice que** no puede venir.
I think (that) the party is tomorrow.	*Ana says (that) she can't come.*
Pienso que hiciste bien.	**Supongo que** va a llover.
I think (that) you did well.	*I suppose (that) it's going to rain.*

▶ **Quien** (singular) and **quienes** (plural) refer only to people and are often used after a preposition or the personal **a.**

Eva, **a quien** vi anoche, cumple veinticinco años hoy.	¿Son ésas las chicas **de quienes** me hablaste la semana pasada?
Eva, whom I saw last night, turns twenty-five today.	*Are those the girls you told me about last week?*

▶ **Quien(es)** is occasionally used instead of **que** in clauses set off by commas.

Lola, **quien** es cubana, es médica.	Su tía, **que** es alemana, ya llegó.
Lola, who is Cuban, is a doctor.	*Her aunt, who is German, already arrived.*
Mi hermana, **quien** vive en Madrid, me llamó por teléfono.	Juan, **que** estuvo muy contento, brindó conmigo.
My sister, who lives in Madrid, called me on the phone.	*Juan, who was very happy, toasted with me.*

▶ **Lo que** refers to an idea, a situation, or a past event and means *what, that which,* or *the thing that.*

Juana tiene todo **lo que** necesitamos.	**Lo que** me molesta es el calor.
Juana has everything we need.	*What bothers me is the heat.*
Lo que quiero es verte.	**Lo que** más te gusta es divertirte.
What I want is to see you.	*What you like most is to have fun.*

¡Manos a la obra!

 Completa las siguientes oraciones con pronombres relativos.

1. La chica ____que____ me invitó a la fiesta se llama Anabel.
2. Ese mercado tiene todo _____ necesitamos.
3. Úrsula, _____ es la dueña del restaurante, es de Uruguay.
4. Enrique dice _____ va a dar una fiesta.
5. Creo _____ la fiesta va a ser muy divertida.
6. Donaldo, a _____ viste en la fiesta, es chileno.
7. A Cecilia no le gusta el regalo _____ le compré.
8. No me gusta hablar con personas a _____ no conozco.
9. Rosana es la chica de _____ te hablé.
10. El chico _____ está a la izquierda es mi primo.
11. Ana, con _____ voy a la fiesta, es muy simpática.
12. _____ me sorprendió fue ver a tantos invitados.

9.4 ¿Qué? and ¿cuál?

▶ As you know, **¿qué?** and **¿cuál?** or **¿cuáles?** mean *what?* or *which?*. However, they are not interchangeable.

▶ **¿Qué?** is used to ask for a definition or explanation.

¿Qué es un flan?
What is flan?

¿Qué estudias?
What do you study?

▶ **¿Cuál(es)?** is used when there is a choice among several possibilities.

¿Cuáles quieres, éstos o ésos?

Which (ones) do you want, these ones or those ones?

¿Cuál es tu apellido, Martínez o Vilanova?

What is your last name, Martínez or Vilanova?

▶ **¿Cuál(es)?** cannot be used before a noun. **¿Qué?** is used instead.

¿Cuál es tu color favorito?
What is your favorite color?

¿Qué colores te gustan?
What colors do you like?

▶ **¿Qué?** used before a noun has the same meaning as **¿cuál?.**

¿Qué regalo te gusta?
What/which gift do you like?

¿Qué dulces quieren Uds.?
What/which sweets do you want?

Interrogative words and phrases

¿a qué hora?	at what time?	¿cuánto/a?	how much?
¿adónde?	(to) where?	¿cuántos/as?	how many?
¿cómo?	how?	¿de dónde?	from where?
¿cuál(es)?	what?; which?	¿dónde?	where?
¿cuándo?	when?	¿qué?	what?; which?
		¿quién(es)?	who?

¡Manos a la obra!

Completa las preguntas con **¿qué?** o **¿cuál(es)?**, según el contexto.

1. ¿ _Cuál_ te gusta más?
2. ¿_____es tu teléfono?
3. ¿_____tipo de pastel pediste?
4. ¿_____es una quinceañera?
5. ¿_____ haces ahora?
6. ¿_____son tus platos favoritos?
7. ¿_____ bebidas te gustan más?
8. ¿_____ es esto?
9. ¿_____ es el mejor?
10. ¿_____ es tu opinión?
11. ¿_____ fiestas celebras tú?
12. ¿_____ vino prefieres?
13. ¿_____ es tu clase favorita?
14. ¿_____ pones en la mesa?
15. ¿_____ restaurante prefieres?
16. ¿_____ clases tomas?
17. ¿_____ quieres comer ahora?
18. ¿_____ es la tarea para mañana?
19. ¿_____ color prefieres?
20. ¿_____ opinas?

Práctica

1 **Minidiálogos** Completa los minidiálogos con las palabras interrogativas correctas.

SORAYA ¿_____ es la fiesta de aniversario de tus padres?
ERNESTO El sábado por la noche.

• • •

MICAELA ¿_____ va a ser la fiesta de cumpleaños?
TIMOTEO En casa de mi primo.

• • •

MARCIA ¿_____ es tu clase favorita?
CARLOS La clase de arte es mi favorita.

• • •

TOMÁS ¿_____ dinero te van a dar tus abuelos para tu graduación de la universidad?
MERCEDES Dicen que van a darme dos mil dólares.

• • •

LIDIA ¿_____ compraste para tu sobrino?
MARTA Una raqueta de tenis.

• • •

BLAS ¿_____ vas después de la boda?
GIL Mi novia y yo vamos al cine. ¿Quieres venir?

2 **Completar** Completa estas preguntas con una palabra interrogativa. A veces se puede usar más de una palabra interrogativa.

1. ¿En _____ país nacieron tus padres?
2. ¿_____ es la fecha de tu cumpleaños?
3. ¿_____ naciste?
4. ¿_____ es tu estado civil?
5. ¿_____ te relajas?
6. ¿_____ son tus programas favoritos de la televisión?
7. ¿_____ es tu mejor amigo?
8. ¿_____ van tus amigos para divertirse?
9. ¿_____ postres te gustan? ¿_____ te gusta más?
10. ¿_____ problemas tuviste el primer día de clase?
11. ¿_____ primos tienes?

Conversación

3 **Una invitación** En parejas, lean esta invitación. Luego, túrnense para hacerse (*ask each other*) preguntas basadas en la información de la invitación.

FERNANDO SANDOVAL VALERA   LORENZO VÁSQUEZ AMARAL

ISABEL ARZIPE DE SANDOVAL   ELENA SOTO DE VÁSQUEZ

TIENEN EL AGRADO DE INVITARLOS
A LA BODA DE SUS HIJOS

MARÍA LUISA Y JOSÉ ANTONIO

LA CEREMONIA RELIGIOSA TENDRÁ LUGAR
EL SÁBADO 10 DE JUNIO A LAS DOS DE LA TARDE
EN EL TEMPLO DE SANTO DOMINGO
(CALLE SANTO DOMINGO, 961).

DESPUÉS DE LA CEREMONIA SÍRVANSE PASAR A LA RECEPCIÓN EN EL SALÓN
DE BAILE DEL HOTEL METRÓPOLI (SOTERO DEL RÍO, 465).

4 **Preguntas** Con un(a) compañero/a, formula preguntas sobre las fotos.

modelo

Estudiante 1: ¿Quién es esta mujer?
Estudiante 2: Es una estudiante.
Estudiante 1: ¿Dónde está?
Estudiante 2: En la biblioteca.
Estudiante 1: ¿Qué está haciendo?
Estudiante 2: Está estudiando.

1.

3.

2.

4.

Español en vivo

¿Con quién quieres compartir tus momentos mágicos?
¿Cuáles son tus prioridades en la vida?
¿Qué te sugiere la palabra "libertad"?
Tú eliges cómo vivir.

BMW

¿Te gusta conducir?

Identificar

Lee el anuncio e identifica las palabras interrogativas.

Preguntas

1. ¿Qué puedes hacer con un coche (*car*) como éste?

2. ¿Te gustaría comprar un coche como éste? ¿Por qué?

3. ¿Te gusta este anuncio? ¿Por qué? ¿Crees que es eficaz (*effective*)?

Ampliación

1 Escuchar

A Escucha la conversación entre Josefina y Rosa. Cuando oigas una de las palabras de la **columna A**, usa el contexto para identificar un sinónimo en la **columna B**.

 TIP **Guess meaning through context.** Listen to the words and phrases around an unfamiliar word to guess its meaning.

A	B
_____ 1. festejar	a. conmemoración religiosa de una muerte
_____ 2. yo lo disfruté (disfrutar)	b. tolera
_____ 3. dicha	c. suerte
_____ 4. bien parecido	d. celebrar
_____ 5. finge (fingir)	e. me divertí
_____ 6. soporta (soportar)	f. horror
	g. crea una ficción
	h. guapo

B ¿Son solteras Rosa y Josefina? ¿Cómo lo sabes?

Margarita Robles de García
y Roberto García Olmos

Piden su presencia en la celebración
del segundo aniversario de bodas
el día 13 de marzo de 2001
con una misa en la Iglesia Virgen del Coromoto
a las 6:30

Seguida por cena y baile
en el restaurante El Campanero,
Calle Principal, Las Mercedes
a las 8:30

2 Conversar

Trabaja con un(a) compañero/a para comparar cómo celebraron Uds. el Día de Acción de Gracias (*Thanksgiving Day*) el año pasado. Incluyan la siguiente información en la conversación.

• ¿Dónde celebraron el día de fiesta? ¿Lo pasaron bien?

• ¿Cuál fue el menú? ¿Quiénes prepararon la comida?

• ¿Trajeron Uds. algo? ¿Qué trajeron?

• ¿Quiénes vinieron a comer? ¿Conocieron a alguien?

recursos

R	Textbook CD Lección 9	WB pp. 91-97	LM pp. 51-54	Lab CD Lección 9	ICD-ROM Lección 9	vistahigher learning.com

Ampliación

③ Escribir

En una composición, compara dos celebraciones a las que tú asististe recientemente.

 TIP **Use Venn diagrams.** Use Venn diagrams to organize your ideas visually before comparing and contrasting people, places, objects, events, or issues. Differences are listed in the outer circles, similarities where the two circles overlap.

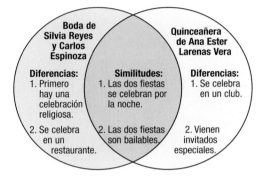

Boda de Silvia Reyes y Carlos Espinoza

Diferencias:
1. Primero hay una celebración religiosa.
2. Se celebra en un restaurante.

Similitudes:
1. Las dos fiestas se celebran por la noche.
2. Las dos fiestas son bailables.

Quinceañera de Ana Ester Larenas Vera

Diferencias:
1. Se celebra en un club.
2. Vienen invitados especiales.

Organízalo Utiliza un diagrama de Venn para anotar las similitudes y las diferencias entre las dos celebraciones.

Escríbelo Utiliza tus notas para escribir el primer borrador de tu composición.

Corrígelo Intercambia tu composición con un(a) compañero/a. Ofrécele algunas sugerencias y si ves errores gramaticales u ortográficos, coméntaselos.

Compártelo Revisa el primer borrador según las indicaciones de tu compañero/a. Incorpora nuevas ideas y/o más información para ampliar la comparación. Luego comparte tu composición con otro/a compañero/a.

④ Un paso más

Imagina que eres un(a) periodista de un país hispano. Escribe un artículo sobre un día de fiesta o una celebración que viste.

- Investiga las fiestas, las celebraciones y los festivales de tu país. Elige la celebración que más te interese.
- Incluye en el artículo el nombre de la celebración, cuándo fue y cómo la celebraron.
- Incluye información sobre la ropa especial que llevaron, la comida, la música y el baile.
- Indica qué hiciste tú durante la celebración.
- Presenta el artículo a la clase. Es importante explicar los detalles y mostrar fotos.

En Internet

Investiga estos temas en el sitio vistahigherlearning.com.
- Festivales nacionales del mundo hispano
- Fiestas religiosas del mundo hispano

Antes de leer

Recognizing root words and word families can help you guess the meaning of words in context, ensuring better comprehension of a reading selection. Using this strategy will enrich your Spanish vocabulary as well. Look through the reading selection and find words related to the following terms.

Give the meanings of both sets of words, based on context and on your knowledge of these words or similar words.

Root word	Related word	Meaning
1. sabroso	_____	_____
2. amar	_____	_____
3. exitoso	_____	_____
4. la diversión	_____	_____
5. el oficial	_____	_____
6. la familia	_____	_____

SOCIEDAD

Fiesta de cumpleaños
Marisa Castillo Solís

Marisa Castillo Solís cumplió 21 años el martes pasado. Para celebrarlo, sus amigos Cristina Montes Vallejo y Tomás Méndez Esquivel le organizaron una fiesta sorpresa en casa de Cristina. Marisa estudia periodismo en la Universidad de Buenos Aires y es una gran amante del cine.

A la fiesta acudió un grupo de amigos de Marisa y su hermano mayor Martín, que viajó desde Mendoza para traerle un regalo muy especial: una colección de las mejores películas argentinas de las últimas décadas. La fiesta fue un gran éxito. Todos los invitados disfrutaron de la comida y se divirtieron bailando al son de diferentes ritmos musicales. De postre, Tomás preparó un delicioso pastel. ¡Felicidades, Marisa!

Aniversario
Lola Navarro de Ibáñez y Bernardo Ibáñez Narváez

Lola Navarro de Ibáñez y Bernardo Ibáñez Narváez celebraron sus cincuenta años de matrimonio en compañía de sus hijos y nietos. La celebración tuvo lugar en el restaurante El Tulipán, donde los invitados saborearon un delicioso banquete. Después de la cena, la Orquesta Armonía animó la fiesta con canciones para todas las edades. Como regalo de aniversario de bodas, los hijos de Lola y Bernardo les organizaron un viaje a Cádiz, ciudad de la costa andaluza española donde se conocieron de niños.

Boda

José Luis Pastor Gómez y Elena Limón Ávila

El pasado 10 de agosto, a las 19 horas, se celebró la boda entre José Luis y Elena en Buenos Aires. La ceremonia fue muy emotiva al ser oficiada por un amigo de la pareja. Tras la breve e íntima ceremonia religiosa, los novios se reunieron con sus invitados en la casa de los padres de José Luis. Allí tuvo lugar el banquete nupcial, que comenzó a las 22:15 de la noche y terminó la mañana siguiente.

Después de leer

¿Comprendiste?

Indica si lo que se dice en cada oración es **cierto** o **falso**. Corrige las oraciones falsas.

Cierto	Falso	
_____	_____	1. Bernardo Ibáñez Narváez y Lola Navarro de Ibáñez tuvieron una fiesta en su casa para celebrar su aniversario de bodas.
_____	_____	2. Martín no pudo asistir a la fiesta de cumpleaños de su hermana.
_____	_____	3. A Marisa le encantan las películas.
_____	_____	4. José Luis Pastor Gómez y Elena Limón Ávila se casaron en una ceremonia religiosa.
_____	_____	5. Después de la boda de José Luis Pastor Gómez y Elena Limón Ávila, los invitados no comieron nada.

Preguntas

1. ¿Qué les regalaron a Bernardo y Lola sus hijos?

_____

2. ¿Cuántos años cumplió Marisa?

_____

3. ¿Dónde tuvo lugar el banquete después de la boda?

_____

4. ¿Qué le regaló Martín a su hermana Marisa?

_____

5. ¿Cuántos años de matrimonio celebran Lola y Bernardo?

_____

Coméntalo

¿Hay una sección de notas sociales en el periódico de tu universidad, comunidad o región? ¿Qué tipo de información encuentras en la sección de notas sociales? ¿La lees normalmente? ¿Por qué?

amante del cine	film lover
acudió	attended
últimas	last few
son	sound
éxito	success
disfrutaron de	enjoyed
saborearon	enjoyed (with respect to food)
animó	livened up
tuvo lugar	took place

recursos

R

vistahigher learning.com

Celebraciones

el aniversario (de bodas)	(wedding) anniversary
la boda	wedding
el cumpleaños	birthday
el día de fiesta	holiday
la fiesta	party
el/la invitado/a	guest
la Navidad	Christmas
la quinceañera	young woman's fifteenth birthday celebration
la sorpresa	surprise
brindar	to toast (drink)
cambiar (de)	to change
celebrar	to celebrate
cumplir años	to have a birthday
dejar una propina	to leave a tip
divertirse (e:ie)	to have fun
graduarse (de)	to graduate (from)
invitar	to invite
pagar la cuenta	to pay the bill
pasarlo bien/mal	to have a good/bad time
regalar	to give (a gift)
reírse (e:i)	to laugh
relajarse	to relax
sonreír (e:i)	to smile
sorprender	to surprise

Postres y otras comidas

la botella de vino	bottle of wine
el champán	champagne
los dulces	sweets; candy
el flan	baked custard
las galletas	cookies
el helado	ice cream
el pastel	cake
el pastel de cumpleaños	birthday cake
los postres	desserts

Relaciones personales

la alegría	happiness
la amistad	friendship
el amor	love
el divorcio	divorce
el estado civil	marital status
el matrimonio	marriage; married couple
la pareja	couple; partner
el/la recién casado/a	newlywed
casado/a	married
divorciado/a	divorced
juntos/as	together
separado/a	separated
soltero/a	single
viudo/a	widowed
casarse (con)	to get married (to)
comprometerse (con)	to get engaged (to)
divorciarse (de)	to get divorced (from)
enamorarse (de)	to fall in love (with)
llevarse bien/mal (con)	to get along well/badly (with)
odiar	to hate
romper (con)	to break up (with)
salir (con)	to go out (with); to date
separarse (de)	to separate (from)
tener una cita	to have a date; to have an appointment

Palabras adicionales

el apellido	last name
el consejo	advice
la respuesta	answer

Las etapas de la vida

la adolescencia	adolescence
la etapa	stage
la juventud	youth
la madurez	maturity; middle-age
la muerte	death
el nacimiento	birth
la niñez	childhood
la vejez	old age
la vida	life
jubilarse	to retire (from work)
nacer	to be born

Expresiones útiles	See page 217.
Relative pronouns	See page 224.
Interrogative words and phrases	See page 226.

recursos

R	Lab CD Lección 9	LM p. 54

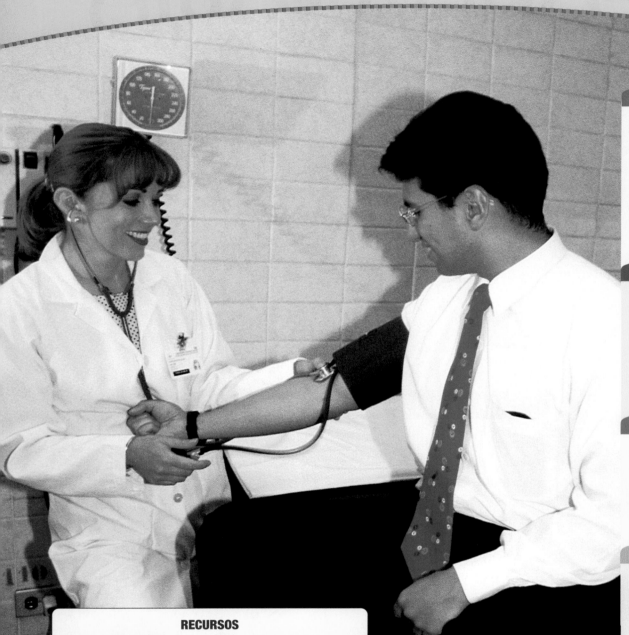

10 En el consultorio

Communicative Goals

You will learn how to:
- discuss medical conditions
- describe your health
- talk about the body

EN EL CONSULTORIO

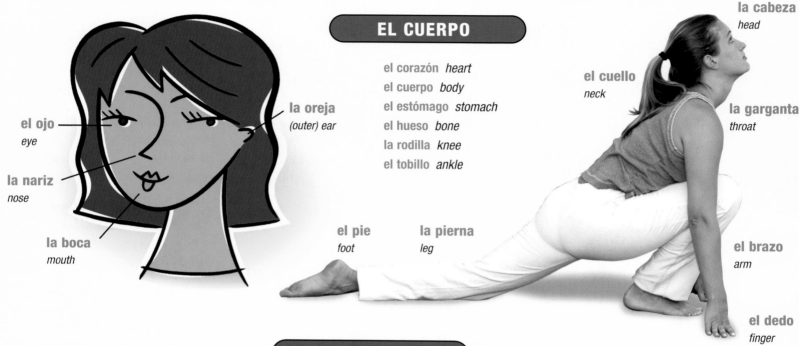

EL CUERPO

el corazón *heart*
el cuerpo *body*
el estómago *stomach*
el hueso *bone*
la rodilla *knee*
el tobillo *ankle*

la cabeza
head

el cuello
neck

la garganta
throat

el ojo
eye

la oreja
(outer) ear

la nariz
nose

la boca
mouth

el pie
foot

la pierna
leg

el brazo
arm

el dedo
finger

LA SALUD

el accidente *accident*
la clínica *clinic*
el consultorio *doctor's office*
el/la doctor(a) *doctor*
el/la enfermero/a *nurse*
el examen médico *physical exam*
el hospital *hospital*
el/la paciente *patient*
la operación *operation*
la radiografía *X-ray*
la sala de emergencia(s) *emergency room*
la salud *health*

el dentista
dentist

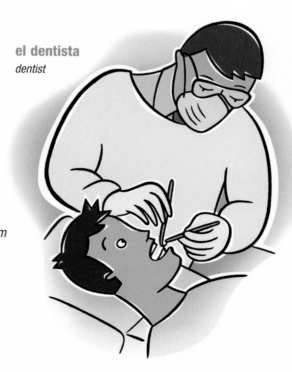

la farmacia
pharmacy

recursos

R	Textbook CD Lección 10	WB pp. 99-100	LM p. 55	Lab CD Lección 10	ICD-ROM Lección 10

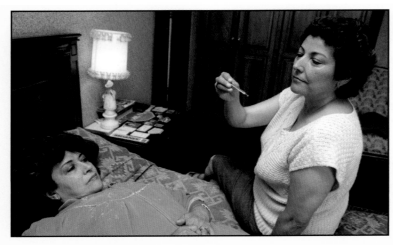

tomar(le) la temperatura (a alguien)
to take (someone's) temperature

VERBOS

caerse *to fall (down)*
enfermarse *to get sick*
lastimarse (el pie) *to injure oneself (one's foot)*
poner una inyección *to give an injection*
recetar *to prescribe*
romperse (la pierna) *to break (one's leg)*
sacar(se) una muela *to have a tooth pulled*
torcerse (el tobillo) *to sprain (one's ankle)*

ENFERMEDADES Y SÍNTOMAS

el dolor (de cabeza) *(head)ache; pain*
la enfermedad *illness; sickness*
la gripe *flu*
la infección *infection*
el resfriado *cold*
el síntoma *symptom*
la tos *cough*

congestionado/a *congested; stuffed-up*
mareado/a *dizzy; nauseated*

doler (o:ue) *to hurt*
estar enfermo/a *to be sick*
ser alérgico/a (a) *to be allergic (to)*
tener fiebre (f.) *to have a fever*
toser *to cough*

estornudar
to sneeze

LOS MEDICAMENTOS

el antibiótico *antibiotic*
el medicamento *medication*
la medicina *medicine*
las pastillas *pills; tablets*
la receta *prescription*

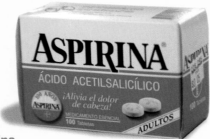

la aspirina
aspirin

ADJETIVOS

embarazada *pregnant*
grave *grave; serious*
médico/a *medical*
saludable *healthy*
sano/a *healthy*

A escuchar

1 **Escuchar** Escucha las frases y selecciona la respuesta más adecuada.

1. _____	a. Tengo dolor de cabeza y fiebre.
2. _____	b. No fui a la clase porque estaba enfermo.
3. _____	c. Me caí ayer jugando al tenis.
4. _____	d. Debes ir a la farmacia.
5. _____	e. Porque tengo gripe.
6. _____	f. Sí, tengo mucha tos por las noches.
7. _____	g. Lo llevaron directamente a la sala de emergencia.
8. _____	h. No sé. Todavía tienen que tomarme la temperatura.

2 **Me duele** Escucha la conversación entre Virginia Cubillos y el doctor Dávila. Luego indica las frases que resumen (*sum up*) la conversación.

_____ 1. Virginia le dice a la enfermera que le duelen las rodillas.

_____ 2. La chica dice que tomó una aspirina anoche.

_____ 3. El médico le pregunta a Virginia si se cayó o tuvo un accidente.

_____ 4. Virginia dice que ayer corrió cinco kilómetros con un amigo.

_____ 5. El Dr. Dávila le receta un antibiótico a Virginia.

_____ 6. El médico le dice a Virginia que puede correr mañana si se toma las pastillas.

_____ 7. El médico le recomienda tomar dos pastillas al día.

_____ 8. El Dr. Dávila le dice a Virginia que no debe correr por siete días.

recursos

R | Textbook CD
Lección 10

A practicar

3 **Actividades** En parejas, identifiquen las partes del cuerpo que Uds. asocian con las siguientes actividades.

modelo

nadar
Estudiante 1: Usamos los brazos para nadar.
Estudiante 2: También usamos las piernas.

1. estudiar biología
2. llevar zapatos
3. toser
4. comer arroz con pollo
5. comprar un perfume
6. ver una película
7. hablar por teléfono
8. correr en el parque
9. tocar el piano
10. escuchar música

4 **Cuestionario** Selecciona las respuestas que mejor reflejen tus experiencias. Suma (*add*) los puntos de cada respuesta y anota el resultado. Después, compara los resultados con el resto de la clase.

¿Tienes buena salud?

27-30 puntos   Salud y hábitos excelentes
23-26 puntos   Salud y hábitos buenos
22 puntos o menos Salud y hábitos problemáticos

1. ¿Con qué frecuencia te enfermas (resfriados, gripe, etc.)?
   • Cuatro veces por año o más. (1 punto)
   • Dos o tres veces por año. (2 puntos)
   • Casi nunca. (3 puntos)

2. ¿Con qué frecuencia tienes dolor de estómago o problemas digestivos?
   • Con mucha frecuencia. (1 punto)
   • A veces. (2 puntos)
   • Casi nunca. (3 puntos)

3. ¿Con qué frecuencia tienes dolor de cabeza?
   • Frecuentemente. (1 punto)
   • A veces. (2 puntos)
   • Casi nunca. (3 puntos)

4. ¿Comes verduras y frutas?
   • No, casi nunca. (1 punto)
   • Sí, a veces. (2 puntos)
   • Sí, todos los días. (3 puntos)

5. ¿Eres alérgico/a a algo?
   • Sí, a muchas cosas. (1 punto)
   • Sí, a algunas cosas. (2 puntos)
   • No. (3 puntos)

6. ¿Haces ejercicios aeróbicos?
   • No, casi nunca hago ejercicios aeróbicos. (1 punto)
   • Sí, a veces. (2 puntos)
   • Sí, con frecuencia. (3 puntos)

7. ¿Con qué frecuencia te haces un examen médico?
   • Nunca o casi nunca. (1 punto)
   • Cada dos años. (2 puntos)
   • Cada año y/o antes de practicar un deporte. (3 puntos)

8. ¿Con qué frecuencia vas al dentista?
   • Nunca voy al dentista. (1 punto)
   • Sólo cuando me duele una muela. (2 puntos)
   • Por lo menos una vez por año. (3 puntos)

9. ¿Qué comes normalmente por la mañana?
   • No como nada. (1 punto)
   • Tomo una bebida dietética. (2 puntos)
   • Como cereales y fruta. (3 puntos)

10. ¿Con qué frecuencia te sientes mareado/a?
    • Frecuentemente. (1 punto)
    • A veces. (2 puntos)
    • Casi nunca. (3 puntos)

A conversar

5 **¿Cuáles son sus síntomas?** En parejas, túrnense para representar los papeles (*roles*) de un(a) médico/a y su paciente.

Estudiante 1: ¿Cuáles son sus síntomas?
Estudiante 2: Me duele la garganta y toso.
Estudiante 1: Creo que Ud. tiene una infección de la garganta. Voy a recetarle un antibiótico.

6 **¿Qué le pasó?** En un grupo de dos o tres, hablen de lo que les pasó y de cómo se sienten estas personas.

Víctor

La Sra. Naranjo

Gabriela

El Sr. Ayala

7 **Un accidente** Cuéntale (*tell*) a la clase cómo fue un accidente o una enfermedad que tuviste. Incluye información que conteste las siguientes preguntas.

- ¿Qué ocurrió?
- ¿Dónde y cuándo ocurrió?
- ¿Cómo ocurrió?
- ¿Quién te ayudó y cómo?

Ortografía

El acento y las sílabas fuertes

In Spanish, written accent marks are used on many words. Here is a review of some of the principles governing word stress and the use of written accents.

· ·

as-pi-ri-na   **gri-pe**   **to-man**   **an-tes**

In Spanish, when a word ends in a vowel, **-n**, or **-s**, the spoken stress usually falls on the next-to-last syllable. Words of this type are very common and do not need a written accent.

· ·

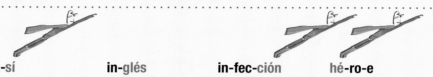

a-sí   **in-glés**   **in-fec-ción**   **hé-ro-e**

When a word ends in a vowel, **-n**, or **-s**, and the spoken stress does *not* fall on the next-to-last syllable, then a written accent is needed.

· ·

hos-pi-tal   **na-riz**   **re-ce-tar**   **to-ser**

When a word ends in any consonant *other* than **-n** or **-s**, the spoken stress usually falls on the last syllable. Words of this type are very common and do not need a written accent.

· ·

lá-piz   **fút-bol**   **hués-ped**   **sué-ter**

When a word ends in any consonant *other* than **-n** or **-s** and the spoken stress does *not* fall on the last syllable, then a written accent is needed.

· ·

far-ma-cia   **bio-lo-gí-a**   **su-cio**   **frí-o**

Diphthongs (two weak vowels or a strong and weak vowel together) are normally pronounced as a single syllable. A written accent is needed when a diphthong is broken into two syllables.

· ·

sol   **pan**   **mar**   **tos**

Spanish words of only one syllable do not usually carry a written accent.

· ·

Práctica Busca las palabras que necesitan acento y escribe su forma correcta.

1. sal-mon
2. ins-pec-tor
3. nu-me-ro
4. fa-cil
5. ju-go
6. a-bri-go
7. ra-pi-do
8. sa-ba-do
9. vez
10. me-nu
11. o-pe-ra-cion
12. im-per-me-a-ble
13. a-de-mas
14. re-ga-te-ar
15. an-ti-pa-ti-co
16. far-ma-cia
17. es-qui
18. pen-sion
19. pa-is
20. per-don

El ahorcado Juega al ahorcado (*hangman*) para adivinar las palabras.

1. __ l __ __ __ __ __ a   Vas allí cuando estás enfermo.

2. __ __ __ __ e __ c __ __ n   Se usa para poner una vacuna (*vaccination*).

3. __ __ __ d __ o __ __ __ __ __ a   Se usa para ver los huesos.

4. __ __ __ __ i __ o   Trabaja en un hospital.

5. a __ __ __ b __ __ __ __ __ __   Es una medicina.

recursos

R   ICD-ROM
    Lección 10

¡Uf! ¡Qué dolor!

Don Francisco y Javier van a la clínica de la doctora Márquez.

1

JAVIER Estoy aburrido…
Tengo ganas de dibujar.
Con permiso.

2

INÉS ¡Javier! ¿Qué te pasó?

JAVIER ¡Ay! ¡Uf! ¡Qué dolor! ¡Creo que me rompí el tobillo!

3

DON FRANCISCO No te preocupes, Javier. Estamos cerca de la clínica donde trabaja la doctora Márquez, mi amiga.

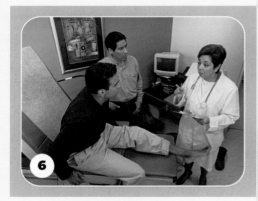

6

DRA. MÁRQUEZ ¿Cuánto tiempo hace que se cayó?

JAVIER Ya se me olvidó… déjeme ver… este… eran más o menos las dos o dos y media cuando me caí… o sea hace más de una hora. ¡Me duele mucho!

DRA. MÁRQUEZ Bueno, vamos a sacarle una radiografía. Queremos ver si se rompió uno de los huesos del pie.

7

DON FRANCISCO Sabes, Javier, cuando era chico yo les tenía mucho miedo a los médicos. Visitaba mucho al doctor porque me enfermaba con mucha frecuencia… Tenía muchas infecciones de la garganta. No me gustaban las inyecciones ni las pastillas. Una vez me rompí la pierna jugando al fútbol…

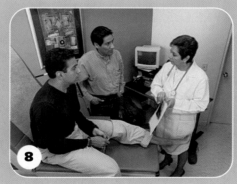

8

JAVIER ¡Doctora! ¿Qué dice? ¿Está roto el tobillo?

DRA. MÁRQUEZ Tranquilo, le tengo buenas noticias, Javier. No está roto el tobillo. Apenas está torcido.

recursos

Video/ VCD-ROM Lección 10	VM pp.187-188	ICD-ROM Lección 10

R

Personajes

DON FRANCISCO

JAVIER

INÉS

DRA. MÁRQUEZ

4

JAVIER ¿Tengo dolor? Sí, mucho. ¿Dónde? En el tobillo. ¿Tengo fiebre? No lo creo. ¿Estoy mareado? Un poco. ¿Soy alérgico a algún medicamento? No. ¿Embarazada? Definitivamente NO.

5

DRA. MÁRQUEZ ¿Cómo se lastimó el pie?

JAVIER Me caí cuando estaba en el autobús.

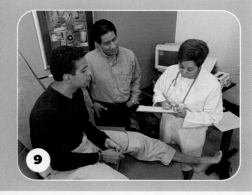

9

JAVIER Pero, ¿voy a poder ir de excursión con mis amigos?

DRA. MÁRQUEZ Creo que sí. Pero debe descansar y no caminar mucho durante un par de días. Le receto unas pastillas para el dolor.

10

DRA. MÁRQUEZ Adiós, Francisco. Adiós, Javier. ¡Cuidado! ¡Buena suerte en las montañas!

Expresiones útiles

Discussing medical conditions

¿Cómo se lastimó el pie?
How did you hurt your foot?

¿Te duele el tobillo?
Does your ankle hurt? (fam.)

¿Le duele el tobillo?
Does your ankle hurt? (form.)

Sí, (me duele) mucho.
Yes, (it hurts) a lot.

¿Es Ud. alérgico/a a algún medicamento?
Are you allergic to any medication?

Sí, soy alérgico/a a la penicilina.
Yes, I'm allergic to penicillin.

¿Está roto el tobillo?
Is the ankle broken?

No está roto. Apenas está torcido.
It's not broken. It's just twisted.

¿Te enfermabas frecuentemente?
Did you used to get sick frequently? (fam.)

Sí, me enfermaba frecuentemente.
Yes, I used to get sick frequently.

Tenía muchas infecciones.
I used to get a lot of infections.

Other expressions

hace + [*period of time*] + que + [*present tense*]:

¿Cuánto tiempo hace que te duele?
How long has it been hurting?

Hace una hora que me duele.
It's been hurting for an hour.

hace + [*period of time*] + que + [*preterite*]:

¿Cuánto tiempo hace que se cayó?
How long ago did you fall?

Me caí hace más de una hora./Hace más de una hora que me caí.
I fell more than an hour ago.

¿Qué piensas?

1 **¿Cierto o falso?** Decide si las siguientes frases sobre Javier son **ciertas** o **falsas.** Corrige las frases falsas.

Cierto   Falso

_____   _____   1. Está aburrido y tiene ganas de hacer algo creativo.

_____

_____   _____   2. Cree que se rompió la rodilla.

_____

_____   _____   3. Se lastimó cuando se cayó en el autobús.

_____

_____   _____   4. Hace menos de una hora que se cayó.

_____

_____   _____   5. Es alérgico a dos medicamentos.

_____

_____   _____   6. No está mareado, pero sí tiene un poco de fiebre.

_____

2 **Ordenar** Pon los siguientes eventos en el orden correcto.

_____   a. La doctora le saca una radiografía.

_____   b. La doctora le receta unas pastillas para el dolor.

_____   c. Javier se lastima el tobillo en el autobús.

_____   d. Don Francisco le habla a Javier de cuando era chico.

_____   e. Javier quiere dibujar un rato (*a while*).

_____   f. Don Francisco lo lleva a una clínica.

3 **En el consultorio** En parejas, preparen una conversación entre un(a) médico/a y su paciente. El/la paciente se cayó en su casa y piensa que se rompió un dedo. El/la médico/a le pregunta al/a la paciente si le duele y cuánto tiempo hace que se cayó. El/la paciente describe su dolor. Finalmente, el/la médico/a le recomienda un tratamiento (*treatment*). Usen las siguientes preguntas y frases en su conversación.

Estoy…	Hace… que me lastimé…	¿Es usted alérgico/a a algún medicamento?
Tengo…	¿Le duele…?	
¿Cómo se lastimó…?	¿Cuánto tiempo hace que le duele…?	Usted debe…
¿Cuánto tiempo hace que se lastimó…?	Hace… que me duele.	

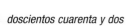

Exploración
La medicina en los países hispanos

En España y en muchos países de Hispanoamérica, hay clínicas y hospitales públicos donde los servicios médicos son gratuitos.

Para las personas que no quieren visitar las instalaciones (*facilities*) públicas, hay clínicas y hospitales privados.

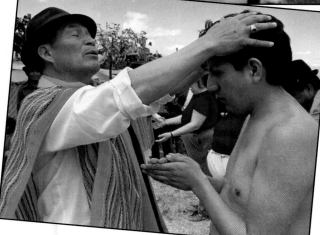

En algunas regiones del mundo hispano, especialmente en las áreas rurales, los curanderos (*healers*) son muy populares. Los curanderos usan plantas y hierbas para tratar (*treat*) las enfermedades.

Médicos célebres

- El médico argentino **René Favaloro** fue el pionero de la operación conocida (*known*) como el *bypass*.

- El **Dr. Manuel Elkin Patarroyo**, de Colombia, descubrió la vacuna (*vaccine*) contra la malaria.

- La **Dra. Antonia Novello**, puertorriqueña, fue la primera mujer y la primera hispana en asumir el puesto de Cirujana-General (*Surgeon General*) de los Estados Unidos.

- El **Dr. Pedro Penzini Fleury** tiene mucha fama en Venezuela por sus artículos de periódico y sus programas de radio sobre medicina y nutrición.

Coméntalo

Con un(a) compañero/a, contesta las siguientes preguntas.

- ¿Debe ofrecer el gobierno servicios médicos gratuitos? ¿Por qué?
- ¿Hay servicios médicos públicos en tu comunidad o región?
- ¿Qué piensas de la medicina alternativa? ¿Por qué?

recursos

R | vistahigher learning.com

10.1 The imperfect tense

▶ In Lesson 6, you learned the preterite tense. Now you will learn the imperfect tense, which describes past activities in a different way.

The imperfect of regular verbs

	cantar	beber	escribir
yo	cantaba	bebía	escribía
tú	cantabas	bebías	escribías
Ud./él/ella	cantaba	bebía	escribía
nosotros/as	cantábamos	bebíamos	escribíamos
vosotros/as	cantabais	bebíais	escribíais
Uds./ellos/ellas	cantaban	bebían	escribían

¡ojo! The imperfect endings of **–er** and **–ir** verbs are the same. The **nosotros** form of **–ar** verbs has an accent on the first **a** of the ending. **–Er** and **–ir** verb forms carry an accent on the first **i** of the ending.

> Cuando era chico yo les tenía mucho miedo a los médicos.

> Tenía que ir mucho a una clínica. ¡No me gustaban nada las inyecciones!

▶ There are no stem changes in the imperfect tense.

Me **duelen** los pies.
My feet hurt.

Me **dolían** los pies.
My feet were hurting.

▶ The imperfect form of **hay** is **había** (*there was/were/used to be*).

Había sólo un médico.
There was only one doctor.

Había dos pacientes allí.
There were two patients there.

¡ojo! **Ir, ser,** and **ver** are the only irregular verbs in the imperfect.

Irregular verbs in the imperfect

	ir	ser	ver
yo	iba	era	veía
tú	ibas	eras	veías
Ud./él/ella	iba	era	veía
nosotros/as	íbamos	éramos	veíamos
vosotros/as	ibais	erais	veíais
Uds./ellos/ellas	iban	eran	veían

Práctica

1 **¡Pobre Miguelito!** Completa las frases con el imperfecto. Luego, pon las oraciones en un orden lógico.

_____ a. Miguelito no _____ [ir] a jugar más. Ahora quería ir a casa a descansar.

_____ b. El doctor dijo que no _____ nada [ser] grave.

_____ c. El niño le dijo a la enfermera que _____ [dolerle] la nariz.

_____ d. Los niños _____ [jugar] en el patio.

_____ e. Su mamá _____ [estar] dibujando cuando Miguelito entró llorando.

_____ f. _____ [ser] las dos de la tarde.

_____ g. Miguelito _____ [tener] mucho dolor. Fueron a la sala de emergencias.

_____ h. El doctor _____ [querer] examinar la nariz del niño.

2 **La salud** Completa las frases con el imperfecto.

doler	mirar	querer	enfermarse
esperar	estar	poder	sentirse
estornudar	toser	tener	caerse

1. Después de correr, a Dora le _____ los pies.

2. Ana _____ el termómetro; con tanta fiebre no _____ leerlo.

3. Él _____ porque la enfermera _____ muy ocupada.

4. Ellos _____ y _____ congestionados porque _____ gripe.

5. Lorenzo _____ dolor de muelas, pero no _____ ir al dentista.

6. Paco y Luis _____ dolor de estómago y _____ unas pastillas para el dolor.

7. Le _____ la cabeza y _____ mareado.

8. Luisa _____ porque es alérgica al polen.

9. Antes de la operación, le _____ todo el cuerpo.

10. De niño, nunca _____ ir al médico.

11. Ella _____ con frecuencia cuando era pequeña.

12. Juan Carlos siempre _____ de la bicicleta.

Conversación

3 Entrevista Trabajen en parejas. Un(a) estudiante entrevista a su compañero/a. Luego compartan los resultados de la entrevista con la clase.

Preguntas	Respuestas
1. ¿Cuántos años tenías en 1988? ¿Y en 1997?	
2. ¿Veías mucha televisión cuando eras niño/a?	
3. Cuando eras niño/a, ¿qué hacía tu familia durante las vacaciones?	
4. Cuando eras estudiante de primaria, ¿te gustaban tus profesores?	
5. Cuando tenías diez años, ¿cuál era tu programa de televisión favorito?	
6. Cuando tenías quince años, ¿cuál era tu grupo musical favorito?	
7. Cuando eras estudiante de secundaria, ¿qué hacías con tus amigos?	
8. Antes de tomar esta clase, ¿sabías hablar español?	

4 Describir En parejas, túrnense para describir lo que hacían durante algunos momentos de sus vidas. Pueden usar las sugerencias de la lista u otras ideas. Luego informen a la clase sobre la vida del/de la compañero/a.

modelo

De niña, mi familia y yo siempre íbamos a Puntarenas. Tomábamos el tren. Salíamos a las 6 de la mañana. Todos los días nadábamos. En Navidad mis papás siempre hacían una gran fiesta. Mi mamá y mis tías preparaban mucha comida. Toda la familia venía.

- Las vacaciones cuando eras niño/a
- Ocasiones especiales
- Qué hacías durante el verano
- Celebraciones con tus amigos
- Celebraciones con tu familia
- Cómo era tu escuela
- Cómo eran tus amigos
- Los viajes que hacías
- A qué jugabas
- Cuando estabas enfermo/a

Uses of the imperfect

▶ The imperfect is used to describe past events in a different way than the preterite. Generally, the imperfect describes actions which are seen by the speaker as incomplete or continuing, while the preterite describes actions which have been completed. The imperfect expresses what was happening at a certain time or how things used to be.

—¿Qué te **pasó**?
What happened to you?

—Me **torcí** el tobillo.
I sprained my ankle.

—¿Dónde **vivías** de niño?
Where did you live as a child?

—**Vivía** en San José.
I lived in San José.

▶ Use the following words and expressions with the imperfect to express habitual or repeated actions: **de niño/a** (*as a child*), **todos los días** (*every day*), **mientras** (*while*).

Uses of the imperfect

Habitual or repeated actions	Íbamos al parque los domingos. *We used to go to the park on Sundays.*
Events or actions that were in progress	Yo leía mientras él estudiaba. *I was reading while he was studying.*
Time-telling	Eran las tres y media. *It was 3:30.*
Age	Los niños tenían seis años. *The children were six years old.*
Physical characteristics	Era alto y guapo. *He was tall and handsome.*
Mental or emotional states	Quería mucho a su familia. *He loved his family very much.*

¡Manos a la obra!

Indica la forma correcta de cada verbo en el imperfecto.

1. Yo [hablar, bailar, descansar, correr, comer, decidir, vivir]
   hablaba, bailaba, descansaba, corría, comía, decidía, vivía

2. Tú [nadar, encontrar, comprender, venir, ir, ser, ver]

3. Ud. [hacer, regatear, asistir, ser, pasear, poder, ir]

4. Nosotras [ser, tomar, ir, poner, seguir, ver, pensar]

5. Ellos [salir, viajar, ir, querer, ser, pedir, empezar]

6. Yo [ver, estornudar, sufrir, ir, dar, ser, toser]

10.2 Constructions with **se**

Impersonal constructions with **se**

▸ As you know, **se** can be used as a reflexive pronoun (**Él se despierta.**). **Se** is also used in other ways.

▸ Non-reflexive verbs can be used with **se** to form impersonal constructions. In impersonal constructions, the person performing the action is not expressed or defined. In English, the passive voice or indefinite subjects (*you, they, one*) are used.

Se habla español en Costa Rica.
Spanish is spoken in Costa Rica.

Se puede leer en la sala de espera.
You can read in the waiting room.

¡ojo! The third person singular verb form is used with singular nouns and the third person plural form is used with plural nouns:

Se vende ropa.   **Se venden camisas.**

▸ You often see the impersonal **se** in signs and advertisements.

SE PROHÍBE NADAR

Se necesitan programadores
GRUPO TECNO
Tel. 778-34-34

ENTRADA

Se entra por la izquierda

Se for unplanned events

▸ **Se** is used to de-emphasize the person who performs the action in question, so as to imply that the accident or event is not his/her direct responsibility. These statements are constructed using the following pattern.

se	+	INDIRECT OBJECT PRONOUN	+	VERB	+	SUBJECT
Se		**me**		**cayó**		**la pluma.**

▸ In this construction, what would normally be the direct object of the sentence becomes the subject and agrees with the verb.

	I.O. PRONOUN	VERB	SUBJECT
Se	me te le nos os les	perdieron cayó dañó rompieron olvidaron	las llaves. la taza. el radio. las botellas. las pastillas.

Práctica

1 **¿Cierto o falso?** Lee estas oraciones sobre la vida en 1901. Indica si lo que dice cada oración es **cierto** o **falso**. Luego corrige las oraciones falsas.

Cierto Falso

_____ _____ 1. Se veía mucha televisión.

_____ _____ 2. Se escribían muchos libros.

_____ _____ 3. Se viajaba mucho en tren.

_____ _____ 4. Se montaba a caballo.

_____ _____ 5. Se mandaba mucho correo electrónico.

_____ _____ 6. Se preparaban muchas comidas en casa.

_____ _____ 7. Se llevaban minifaldas.

_____ _____ 8. Se pasaba mucho tiempo con la familia.

2 **Anuncios** Traduce estos anuncios (*ads*) al español con el **se** impersonal.

ENGINEERS NEEDED

NO TALKING

1. _____   6. _____

EATING AND DRINKING PROHIBITED

TEACHER NEEDED

2. _____   7. _____

PROGRAMMERS SOUGHT

WE SELL BOOKS

3. _____   8. _____

WE SPEAK ENGLISH

DO NOT ENTER

4. _____   9. _____

WE SELL COMPUTERS

SPANISH SPOKEN

5. _____   10. _____

Conversación

3 Preguntas Trabajen en parejas y usen estas preguntas para entrevistarse.

1. ¿Qué comidas se sirven en tu restaurante favorito?
2. ¿Se te olvidó invitar a alguien a tu última fiesta o cena?
3. ¿A qué hora se abre la cafetería de tu universidad?
4. ¿Alguna vez se te quedó algo importante en casa?
5. ¿Alguna vez se te perdió algo importante durante un viaje?
6. ¿Qué se vende en la librería de la universidad?
7. ¿Sabes si en la librería se aceptan cheques?
8. ¿Alguna vez se te rompió un plato o un vaso (*glass*)?
9. ¿Alguna vez se te cayó una botella de vino?

4 Minidiálogos En parejas, preparen los siguientes minidiálogos. Luego preséntenlos a la clase.

1. A Spanish professor asks for a student's workbook. The student explains why he or she doesn't have it.
2. A tourist asks the bellhop where the best food in the city is served, and the bellhop gives several suggestions.
3. A patient tells the doctor that he or she can't walk. The doctor examines the patient and explains what's wrong.
4. A parent asks a child how the plates got broken. The child apologizes profusely and explains what happened.

5 Anuncios En grupos, preparen dos anuncios de televisión para presentar a la clase. Deben usar el imperfecto y dos construcciones con **se.**

> **modelo**
>
> Se me cayeron unos libros en el pie y ¡Ayyyyy! Sentía mucho, pero mucho dolor. Pero ya no, gracias a Superaspirina 500. ¡Tomé dos pastillas y se me fue el dolor! ¡Se puede comprar Superaspirina 500 en todas las farmacias Recetamax!

▶ These verbs are often used with **se** to describe unplanned events.

caer	to fall; to drop	perder (e:ie)	to lose
dañar	to damage; to break down	quedar	to be left behind
olvidar	to forget	romper	to break

¡ojo! **Dejar caer** (*let fall*) is often used to mean *to drop*.

Elena **dejó caer** el libro.
Elena dropped the book.

El médico **dejó caer** la aspirina.
The doctor dropped the aspirin.

¿Cuánto tiempo hace que se cayó?

Ya se me olvidó.

Bueno, vamos a sacarle una radiografía para ver si se le rompió un hueso.

▶ **A** + [*noun*] or **a** + [*prepositional pronoun*] is frequently used to clarify or emphasize who is involved in the action.

Al estudiante se le perdió la tarea.
The student lost his homework.

A mí se me olvidó ir a clase ayer.
I forgot to go to class yesterday.

¡Manos a la obra!

 Completa las frases de la primera columna con **se** impersonal y el tiempo presente. Completa las frases de la segunda columna con **se** para sucesos imprevistos (*unplanned events*) y los verbos en pretérito.

Presente

1. ___Se enseñan___ [enseñar] cinco lenguas en esta universidad.
2. _____ [comer] muy bien en El Cráter.
3. _____ [vender] muchas camisetas allí.
4. _____ [servir] platos exquisitos cada noche.
5. _____ [necesitar] mucho dinero.
6. _____ [buscar] secretaria.

Pretérito

1. ___Se me rompieron___ [*I broke*] las gafas.
2. _____ [*you* (fam.) *dropped*] las pastillas.
3. _____ [*they lost*] la receta.
4. _____ [*you* (form.) *left*] aquí la radiografía.
5. _____ [*we forgot*] pagar la medicina.
6. _____ [*they left*] los cuadernos en casa.

10.3 Adverbs

▶ Adverbs describe how, when, and where actions take place. They modify verbs, adjectives, and even other adverbs. The list below contains some adverbs you have already learned.

bien	nunca	temprano
mal	hoy	ayer
muy	siempre	aquí

▶ Most adverbs end in **–mente**. These are equivalent to the English adverbs which end in *-ly*.

lentamente	*slowly*
verdaderamente	*truly, really*
generalmente	*generally*
simplemente	*simply*

▶ To form adverbs which end in **–mente**, add **–mente** to the feminine form of the adjective. If the adjective does not have a feminine form, just add **–mente** to the standard form.

ADJECTIVE	FEMININE FORM	SUFFIX	ADVERB
lento	lenta	-mente	lentamente
fabuloso	fabulosa	-mente	fabulosamente
enorme		-mente	enormemente
feliz		-mente	felizmente

▶ Adverbs that end in **–mente** generally follow the verb, while adverbs that modify an adjective or another adverb precede the word they modify.

Javier dibuja **maravillosamente**.
Javier draws wonderfully.

Inés está **casi siempre** ocupada.
Inés is almost always busy.

Common adverbs and adverbial expressions

a menudo	*often*	así	*like this; so*	menos	*less*
a tiempo	*on time*	bastante	*enough; quite*	muchas veces	*a lot; many times*
a veces	*sometimes*	casi	*almost*	poco	*little*
además (de)	*furthermore; besides*	con frecuencia	*frequently*	por lo menos	*at least*
apenas	*hardly; scarcely*	de vez en cuando	*from time to time*	pronto	*soon*

¡Manos a la obra!

Transforma los siguientes adjetivos en adverbios.

1. alegre ___alegremente___
2. constante _____
3. gradual _____
4. perfecto _____
5. real _____
6. frecuente _____
7. tranquilo _____
8. regular _____
9. maravilloso _____
10. normal _____
11. básico _____
12. afortunado _____

Práctica

1 **En la clínica** Completa las oraciones con los adverbios adecuados.

1. La cita era a las nueve, pero llegamos _____ [aquí, nunca, tarde].

2. El problema fue que _____ [aquí, ayer, así] se nos rompió el despertador.

3. La recepcionista no se enojó porque sabía que normalmente llegábamos _____ [a veces, a tiempo, poco].

4. El doctor estaba _____ [por lo menos, mal, casi] listo.

5. _____ [así, además, apenas] tuvimos que esperar cinco minutos.

6. El doctor dijo que nuestra hija Irene necesitaba una operación _____ [temprano, menos, inmediatamente].

7. Cuando Irene salió de la operación, le preguntamos _____ [con frecuencia, nerviosamente, muchas veces] al doctor cómo estaba nuestra hija.

8. _____ [por lo menos, afortunadamente, a menudo] el médico nos contestó que Irene estaba bien.

2 **Oraciones** Combina palabras de las tres columnas para formar oraciones completas.

modelo

Mi mejor amigo se enferma frecuentemente.
Britney Spears conduce rápidamente.

Sujetos	Verbos	Adverbios
mi mejor amigo/a	caerse	bien
mi(s) padre(s)	casarse	fabulosamente
el/la profesor(a) de español	conducir	felizmente
yo	divertirse	mal
los jóvenes	enfermarse	frecuentemente
Tiger Woods	estornudar	muchas veces
Britney Spears	ir	poco
Tina Turner	levantarse	rápidamente
todos nosotros	llevarse	pronto
	vestirse	tarde
		temprano
		tranquilamente

Conversación

 3 **Preguntas** Usa estas preguntas para entrevistar a tu compañero/a.

1. ¿Qué sabes hacer muy bien?
2. ¿Vas al doctor de vez en cuando?
3. ¿Qué estudias además de español?
4. ¿Hay compañeros/as de clase a quienes apenas conoces?
5. ¿Te enfermas a menudo?
6. ¿Con qué frecuencia cenas en un restaurante?
7. ¿Generalmente, llegas a tiempo a las clases y citas?
8. ¿Qué haces si te sientes congestionado/a y estornudas muchas veces?

4 **¿Con qué frecuencia?** Circula por la clase y pregúntales a tus compañeros/as con qué frecuencia hacen las actividades que se mencionan en la lista. Comparte la información con la clase.

modelo pasear en bicicleta

Estudiante 1: De vez en cuando, ¿paseas en bicicleta?
Estudiante 2: Sí, paseo en bicicleta con mucha frecuencia./No, casi nunca paseo en bicicleta.

Actividades	con mucha frecuencia	de vez en cuando	casi nunca	nunca
1. Nadar	——	——	——	——
2. Jugar al tenis	——	——	——	——
3. Hacer la tarea	——	——	——	——
4. Salir a bailar	——	——	——	——
5. Mirar la televisión	——	——	——	——
6. Dormir en clase	——	——	——	——
7. Perder las gafas	——	——	——	——
8. Tomar una medicina	——	——	——	——
9. Ir al dentista	——	——	——	——

No Hay Tiempo Para el Dolor de Cabeza

Si tienes prisa, o simplemente si quieres que tu dolor de cabeza se vaya muy pronto, piensa en Bayer. Se asimila mejor y actúa rápidamente. Ya no se puede perder tiempo por un dolor de cabeza.

ASPIRINA

Bayer
Siempre a tu lado.

Identificar

Lee el anuncio e identifica los adverbios.

Preguntas

1. Según el anuncio, ¿cuáles son las ventajas (*advantages*) de este tipo de aspirina? ¿Cuáles son sus cualidades?
2. ¿Te duele a menudo la cabeza? ¿Tomas aspirina cuando te duele la cabeza?
3. ¿Necesitas una receta del médico para comprar aspirina?
4. Cuando estás enfermo/a, ¿prefieres tomar un medicamento o llamar antes al doctor?

Ampliación

1 Escuchar

A Escucha la conversación de la Srta. Méndez y Carlos Peña. Marca las frases donde se mencionan los síntomas de Carlos.

> ⭐ **TIP** **Listen for specific information.** Identify the subject of a conversation and use your background knowledge to predict what kinds of information you might hear. For example, what would you expect to hear in a conversation between a sick person and a doctor's receptionist?

_____ 1. Tiene infección en los ojos.

_____ 2. Se lastimó el dedo.

_____ 3. No puede dormir.

_____ 4. Siente dolor en los huesos.

_____ 5. Está mareado.

_____ 6. Está congestionado.

_____ 7. Le duele el estómago.

_____ 8. Le duele la cabeza.

_____ 9. Es alérgico a la aspirina.

_____ 10. Tiene tos.

_____ 11. Le duele la garganta.

_____ 12. Se rompió la pierna.

_____ 13. Le duele la rodilla.

_____ 14. Tiene frío.

B En tu opinión, ¿qué tiene Carlos? ¿Una gripe? ¿Un resfriado? ¿Una alergia? Explica tu opinión.

2 Conversar

Con un(a) compañero/a, prepara una conversación entre un(a) estudiante hipocondríaco/a y el/la enfermero/a. Presenten la conversación a la clase.

- Decidan qué síntomas tiene el/la estudiante y con qué frecuencia los tiene.

- Decidan qué preguntas le va a hacer el/la enfermero/a. (Por ejemplo: ¿Cuánto tiempo hace que comenzaron los síntomas? ¿Tenía el mismo problema cuando era niño/a? ¿Lo tenía la semana pasada?)

- Decidan qué consejos le va a dar el/la enfermero/a.

recursos

R	Textbook CD Lección 10	WB pp. 101-106	LM pp. 57-59	Lab CD Lección 10	ICD-ROM Lección 10	vistahigher learning.com

Ampliación

③ Escribir

Eres un(a) enfermero/a en la sala de emergencias de un hospital. Tienes que escribir cada día un parte (*report*) médico para tu supervisor(a).

 TIP **Avoid redundancies.** To avoid repetition of verbs and nouns, consult a Spanish language thesaurus. Use direct object pronouns, possessive adjectives, demonstrative adjectives and pronouns, and prepositional pronouns to streamline your writing.

Organízalo	Utiliza un mapa de ideas para organizar tu parte médico. Incluye información sobre los pacientes, sus síntomas y el resultado de los tratamientos.
Escríbelo	Utiliza tus apuntes para escribir el primer borrador de tu parte médico.
Corrígelo	Intercambia tu composición con un(a) compañero/a. Lee su borrador y anota los aspectos mejor escritos (*written*). Ofrécele sugerencias para evitar (*avoid*) redundancias, y si ves algunos errores gramaticales u ortográficos, coméntaselos.
Compártelo	Revisa el primer borrador según las indicaciones de tu compañero/a. Incorpora nuevas ideas y/o más información si es necesario antes de escribir la versión final del parte médico.

Susana se lastimó la rodilla ayer. ~~Susana~~ Ella estaba corriendo por el parque cuando se cayó y se ~~la~~ lastimó la rodilla.

④ Un paso más

Prepara una presentación sobre el sistema de servicios médicos de un país hispano. Tu presentación debe contestar las siguientes preguntas.

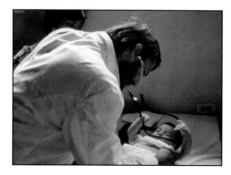

- ¿Qué servicios médicos públicos hay en el país?
- ¿Cuál es el papel (*role*) de las clínicas y los hospitales privados?
- ¿Cómo son los servicios médicos en las ciudades y en las áreas rurales?
- ¿Son populares los tratamientos alternativos?
- ¿Hay personas reconocidas por sus contribuciones a la medicina?

 En Internet

Investiga estos temas en el sitio vistahigherlearning.com.

- Hospitales en el mundo hispano
- Clínicas en el mundo hispano
- Médicos famosos del mundo hispano

Antes de leer

Using what you already know about a particular subject will often help you better understand a reading selection. For example, if you read an article about a recent medical discovery, you might think about what you already know about health in order to understand unfamiliar words or concepts.

At a glance, what does this reading selection appear to be about?

_____

_____

What type of document is this, and how can you tell?

_____

_____

Based on what you know about documents of this type, what types of information do you expect to find in this reading selection?

_____

_____

El consultorio
Dra. Fernanda Jiménez Ocaña

P: Soy una madre española y le escribo para hacerle una consulta sobre mi hijo. Tiene ocho años y hace una semana que ni come ni duerme bien. Además, desde hace cuatro días tose constantemente. Al no tomar la cantidad de alimentos necesarios ni dormir lo suficiente, mi hijo no tiene energía para realizar sus actividades diarias. Estoy un poco preocupada, porque es la primera vez que el niño presenta este tipo de síntomas. Todavía no fuimos al médico porque me interesa conocer primero su punto de vista. Muchísimas gracias por su ayuda.

R: Querida madre española: Gracias por escribir a mi columna. Cuando un niño de la edad de su hijo presenta este tipo de síntomas, puede ser señal de que tiene una pequeña infección en las vías respiratorias, producida por una bacteria o por un virus. Creo que debe llevar pronto a su hijo al consultorio de su médico, para evitar la aparición de una enfermedad crónica como la bronquitis. Si tiene alguna pregunta más o si desea contarme cómo evoluciona su hijo, ya sabe que puede escribirme otra vez.

P: Hola, doctora. Soy un ciclista profesional de Colombia. Hace dos semanas tuve un accidente con mi bicicleta y me lastimé la rodilla. Fui a la sala de emergencias y el médico me hizo una radiografía para ver si tenía un hueso roto. Afortunadamente, los resultados de la radiografía fueron muy buenos y sólo me recetaron unas pastillas y mucho reposo. Le escribo porque, después de este tiempo, sigo sintiendo dolor en la zona de la rodilla. ¿Qué puedo hacer?

R: Querido amigo ciclista: Creo que, en su caso, necesita tener más paciencia. Hay que comprender que algunas veces el cuerpo requiere más tiempo para recuperarse. Creo que tiene que esperar dos semanas más para ver si el dolor va desapareciendo o no. Si sigue las indicaciones de su médico y no nota ningún cambio, debe volver al hospital. En mi opinión, no debe hacer ningún movimiento con la pierna y debe seguir tomándose las pastillas que le recetaron.

P: Le escribo desde Puerto Rico para pedirle su opinión. Durante este mes y el anterior, tengo los síntomas de un resfriado que no desaparece nunca. Toso, estoy congestionado y tengo la garganta y los ojos irritados. Mi novia opina que soy alérgico a algo. ¿Cree que eso es posible?

R: Estimado amigo puertorriqueño: Debe empezar por observar dónde y cuándo aparecen sus síntomas. El otoño y la primavera son las épocas del año en que suele haber más reacciones alérgicas del tipo que usted presenta. Creo que debe ir al médico y esperar los resultados de las pruebas. Si le diagnostican un tipo de alergia, no debe preocuparse. En la actualidad, existen tratamientos excelentes, incluyendo antihistaminas e inyecciones, que calman los efectos de las reacciones alérgicas y lo ayudan a llevar una vida normal.

¡Salud! Dra. Fernanda Jiménez Ocaña

Después de leer

¿Comprendiste?

Indica si cada oración es **cierta** o **falsa**. Corrige las oraciones falsas.

Cierto	Falso	
_____	_____	1. La doctora cree que el chico puertorriqueño puede tener alergias.
_____	_____	2. La madre española no come bien.
_____	_____	3. La doctora piensa que el ciclista debe practicar más el ciclismo.
_____	_____	4. La doctora piensa que el hijo de la española puede tener una infección.
_____	_____	5. La radiografía indica que el ciclista colombiano tiene algunos huesos rotos.
_____	_____	6. Hace dos meses que el puertorriqueño tiene los síntomas de un resfriado.

Preguntas

1. ¿Con qué frecuencia tose el hijo de la madre española?
2. ¿Cuánto tiempo hace que el colombiano se lastimó la rodilla?
3. ¿Qué hizo el médico cuando el ciclista fue a la sala de emergencias?
4. ¿Por qué debe ser paciente el ciclista?
5. ¿Qué debe hacer la madre española?
6. Según (*according to*) la doctora, ¿cuándo ocurren más frecuentemente las reacciones alérgicas?

Coméntalo

¿Hay una columna de consejos médicos en el periódico de tu ciudad? ¿La lees frecuentemente? ¿Por qué sí o por qué no? ¿Es bueno depender de los consejos que aparecen en las revistas y en los periódicos? Imagina que tú escribes esta columna. ¿Qué deben hacer las tres personas que pidieron consejos?

desde hace cuatro días	*since four days ago*
alimentos	*foods*
Querido/a	*Dear*
señal	*sign*
vías	*passages*
Hay que	*It is necessary to*
el anterior	*the previous one*
Estimado/a	*Dear*
suele haber	*there are customarily*
pruebas	*tests*

recursos

R

vistahigher
learning.com

El cuerpo

la boca	mouth
el brazo	arm
la cabeza	head
el corazón	heart
el cuello	neck
el cuerpo	body
el dedo	finger
el estómago	stomach
la garganta	throat
el hueso	bone
la nariz	nose
el ojo	eye
la oreja	(outer) ear
el pie	foot
la pierna	leg
la rodilla	knee
el tobillo	ankle

Verbos

caerse	to fall (down)
dañar	to damage; to break down
doler (o:ue)	to hurt
enfermarse	to get sick
estar enfermo/a	to be sick
estornudar	to sneeze
lastimarse (el pie)	to injure oneself (one's foot)
olvidar	to forget
poner una inyección	to give an injection
prohibir	to prohibit
quedar	to be left behind
recetar	to prescribe
romper	to break
romperse (la pierna)	to break (one's leg)
sacar(se) una muela	to have a tooth pulled
ser alérgico/a (a)	to be allergic (to)
tener fiebre (f.)	to have a fever
tomar(le) la temperatura (a alguien)	to take someone's temperature
torcerse (el tobillo)	to sprain (one's ankle)
toser	to cough

La salud

el accidente	accident
el antibiótico	antibiotic
la aspirina	aspirin
la clínica	clinic
el consultorio	doctor's office
el/la dentista	dentist
el/la doctor(a)	doctor
el dolor (de cabeza)	(head)ache; pain
la enfermedad	illness; sickness
el/la enfermero/a	nurse
el examen médico	physical exam
la farmacia	pharmacy
la gripe	flu
el hospital	hospital
la infección	infection
el medicamento	medication
la medicina	medicine
la operación	operation
el/la paciente	patient
las pastillas	pills; tablets
la radiografía	X-ray
la receta	prescription
el resfriado	cold
la sala de emergencia(s)	emergency room
la salud	health
el síntoma	symptom
la tos	cough

Adjetivos

congestionado/a	congested; stuffed-up
embarazada	pregnant
grave	grave; serious
mareado/a	dizzy; nauseated
médico/a	medical
saludable	healthy
sano/a	healthy

Otras palabras y expresiones

Hace + [time] + **que** + [present]	to have been doing something for a period of time
Hace + [time] + **que** + [preterite]	to have done something in the past (ago)

Expresiones útiles	See page 241.
Adverbs	See page 248.

recursos

R		
	Lab CD Lección 10	LM p. 59

AVENTURAS EN LOS PAÍSES HISPANOS

Un esquiador salta (*jumps*) en el centro de esquí Portillo, uno de los más famosos y antiguos (*old*) de Chile. El esquí y el snowboard se pueden practicar en las montañas nevadas (*snow-capped mountains*) de la Cordillera de los Andes, que se extiende por todo el país. Gente de todo el mundo va a Chile a practicar los deportes de invierno. ¿Te gustaría esquiar en Chile?

SURAMÉRICA II

Argentina

Área: 2.780.400 km^2 (1.074.000 millas^2)

Población: 38.853.000

Capital: Buenos Aires – 12.355.000

Ciudades principales: Córdoba–1.440.000, Rosario–1.352.000, Mendoza–1.007.000

Moneda: peso argentino

SOURCE: Population Division, UN Secretariat

Chile

Área: 756.950 km^2 (292.259 millas^2)

Población: 15.957.000

Capital: Santiago de Chile – 5.971.000

Ciudades principales: Concepción–405.000, Viña del Mar–361.000, Valparaíso–290.000, Temuco–304.000

Moneda: peso chileno

SOURCE: Population Division, UN Secretariat

Uruguay

Área: 176.220 km^2 (68.039 millas^2)

Población: 3.432.000

Capital: Montevideo – 1.346.000

Ciudades principales: Salto, Paysandú, Las Piedras, Rivera

Moneda: peso uruguayo

SOURCE: Population Division, UN Secretariat

Paraguay

Área: 406.750 km^2 (157.046 millas^2)

Población: 6.068.000

Capital: Asunción – 1.427.000

Ciudades principales: Ciudad del Este–355.000, San Lorenzo, Lambaré, Fernando de la Mora

Moneda: guaraní

SOURCE: Population Division, UN Secretariat

Bolivia

Área: 1.098.580 km^2 (412.162 millas^2)

Población: 9.085.000

Capital: La Paz, sede del gobierno (*seat of government*), capital administrativa – 1.620.000; **Sucre,** capital constitucional y judicial–201.000

Ciudades principales: Santa Cruz de la Sierra–1.242.0000, Cochabamba–605.000, Oruro–230.000, Potosí–139.000

Moneda: peso boliviano

SOURCE: Population Division, UN Secretariat

⭐ La Paz

Océano Pacífico

Arica •

Sucre ⭐

Iquique •

Antofagasta •

Salta •

CHILE

ARGENTIN

Córdoba •

Valparaíso • ⭐
Mendoza

Santiago

Concepción •

Bahía Blan

Cordillera de los Andes

Puerto Montt •

Estrecho de
Magallanes •

Punta Arenas •

Tierra
del Fuego

Artes

El tango argentino

El tango es una música y un baile que tienen ritmos y sonidos *(sounds)* de raíces africanas y europeas. Es uno de los símbolos culturales más importantes de la Argentina, y nació en Buenos Aires en la década de 1880. El tango también tiene un lenguaje propio *(own)*: el lunfardo *(Buenos Aires slang)*. En un principio *(in the beginning)*, el tango era un baile provocativo y violento, pero comenzó a ser más romántico desde 1930. Hoy en día es popular en todo el mundo.

Ciudades

La Paz, Bolivia

La Paz es la capital más alta del mundo. Su aeropuerto está a una altitud de 3.600 metros (12.000 pies). La gran altura provoca a veces un malestar *(discomfort)* conocido como *soroche*, que en la lengua nativa aimará significa "mal de montaña" *(mountain sickness)*. La región de La Paz tiene montañas nevadas, desierto y selva *(jungle)* de clima subtropical.

BRASIL

ARAGUAY

⭐ Asunción

osario **URUGUAY**

⭐ ⭐ Montevideo

Buenos Aires

Malvinas

Costumbres

La carne y el mate

La ganadería *(cattle raising)* es una de las actividades económicas principales de Uruguay y Argentina. La carne de res forma parte de la dieta diaria de los dos países. Los platos más comunes son el asado *(barbecue)*, la parrillada *(grilled meat)* y el chivito *(goat)*. El mate es un té verde que se bebe en una taza hecha de calabaza *(gourd)* a través de *(through)* un popote metálico *(metal straw)* llamado bombilla. Es una bebida de origen indígena que se bebe a diario *(every day)* y reemplaza al café.

Naturaleza

Los ríos Paraguay y Paraná

Aunque *(although)* Paraguay no tiene costa *(coast)*, sus dos ríos *(rivers)* principales, el Paraguay y el Paraná, lo comunican con el océano Atlántico. El río Paraguay es el principal afluente *(tributary)* del río Paraná. Divide a Paraguay en dos regiones distintas y le da su nombre.

El río Paraná confluye *(meets)* con el río Iguazú en la frontera *(border)* entre Brasil, Argentina y Paraguay. Allí forman las famosas cataratas *(waterfalls)* del Iguazú, uno de los sitios turísticos más visitados en Suramérica. Situadas *(located)* en el Parque Nacional de Iguazú, estas hermosas y extensas cataratas tienen unos 70 m (230 pies) de altura *(height)*.

¿Qué aprendiste?

1 **¿Cierto o falso?** Decide si lo que dicen las siguientes frases es **cierto** o **falso**.

	Cierto	Falso
1. Rosario es la ciudad de más población de Argentina.	_____	_____
2. Viña del Mar y Concepción son dos de las ciudades principales de Chile.	_____	_____
3. Asunción es la capital de Uruguay.	_____	_____
4. En un principio, el tango era un baile tranquilo.	_____	_____
5. El tango es uno de los símbolos culturales más importantes de Argentina.	_____	_____
6. La Paz es la capital más baja del mundo.	_____	_____
7. La región alrededor de La Paz tiene montañas nevadas, desierto y selva.	_____	_____
8. La carne de res forma parte de la dieta diaria de Argentina y Uruguay.	_____	_____
9. El mate es un té verde.	_____	_____
10. Paraguay tiene costa en el océano Atlántico.	_____	_____
11. El río Paraná es el principal afluente del río Paraguay.	_____	_____
12. Las cataratas del Iguazú están en la frontera entre Brasil, Paraguay y Argentina.	_____	_____

2 **Preguntas** Contesta las siguientes preguntas.

1. ¿Qué país de Suramérica crees que es bueno para practicar los deportes de invierno?
2. ¿Viste gente bailando tango? Si es así, ¿dónde la viste?
3. ¿Comiste asado alguna vez? Si no, ¿crees que te gustaría?
4. ¿Crees que sería fácil correr una maratón en La Paz? ¿Por qué sí o por qué no?
5. ¿Te gustaría visitar La Paz? ¿Por qué?
6. ¿Por qué crees que el Parque Nacional de Iguazú es uno de los sitios turísticos más visitados de Suramérica?

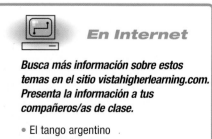

En Internet

Busca más información sobre estos temas en el sitio vistahigherlearning.com. Presenta la información a tus compañeros/as de clase.

- El tango argentino
- La ciudad de La Paz
- La carne y el mate
- Los ríos Paraguay y Paraná

11 El carro y la tecnología

Communicative Goals
You will learn how to:
- answer the telephone
- talk about bus or car problems
- say how far away things are
- express surprise

RECURSOS

These student supplements provide additional practice:
- Textbook Audio CD
- Workbook/Video Manual (WB/VM)
- Lab Manual (LM)
- WB/VM/LM Answer Key
- Lab Audio CDs
- Video CD-ROM
- Interactive CD-ROM

EL CARRO Y LA TECNOLOGÍA

EN LA CALLE

la calle *street*

el camino *route*

el garaje *mechanic's shop*

la gasolina *gasoline*

la gasolinera *gas station*

el kilómetro *kilometer*

el/la mecánico/a *mechanic*

la milla *mile*

la multa *fine*

el policía/la mujer policía *police officer*

la policía *police (force)*

el taller (mecánico) *(mechanic's) garage; repair shop*

el tráfico *traffic*

la velocidad máxima *speed limit*

arrancar *to start*

arreglar *to fix; to arrange*

bajar *to go down*

bajar(se) de *to get off/out of (a vehicle)*

chocar (con) *to run into; to crash*

conducir *to drive*

estacionar *to park*

manejar *to drive*

parar *to stop*

revisar (el aceite) *to check (the oil)*

subir *to go up*

subir(se) a *to get on/into (a vehicle)*

el semáforo
traffic light

LAS PARTES DEL CARRO

el carro *car, automobile*

el coche *car, automobile*

los frenos *brakes*

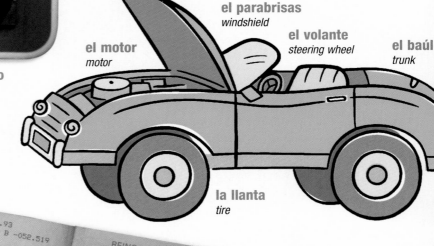

el capó
(car) hood

el parabrisas
windshield

el volante
steering wheel

el baúl
trunk

el motor
motor

la llanta
tire

la licencia de conducir
driver's license

llenar (el tanque)
to fill up (the tank)

recursos

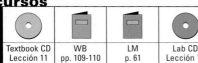

| R | Textbook CD Lección 11 | WB pp. 109-110 | LM p. 61 | Lab CD Lección 11 | ICD-ROM Lección 11 |

el televisor
television set

LA TECNOLOGÍA

la cinta *(audio) tape*
la contestadora *answering machine*
el control remoto *remote control*
el disco compacto *compact disc*
el estéreo *stereo*
el fax *fax (machine)*
el radio *radio (set)*
el teléfono celular *cellular phone*
la televisión por cable *cable television*
el tocadiscos compacto *compact disc player*
el videocasete *videocassette*
la videocasetera *VCR*

apagar *to turn off*
funcionar *to work*
llamar *to call*
poner *to turn on*
prender *to turn on*
sonar (o:ue) *to ring*

la cámara (de vídeo)
(video) camera

la calculadora
calculator

ADJETIVOS

descompuesto/a *not working; out of order*
lento/a *slow*
lleno/a *full*

INTERNET Y LA COMPUTADORA

el archivo *file*
la computadora portátil *laptop*
el disco *disk*
el módem *modem*
la página principal *homepage*
la pantalla *screen*
el programa de computación *software*
la Red *the Web, the Internet*
el sitio Web *website*

guardar *to save*
imprimir *to print*
navegar en Internet *to surf the Internet*

la computadora
the computer

el monitor
monitor

el ratón
mouse

la impresora
printer

el teclado
keyboard

A escuchar

1 **¿Qué necesitas?** Identifica oralmente los dibujos. Luego escucha las frases e indica el objeto que necesitas para cada actividad.

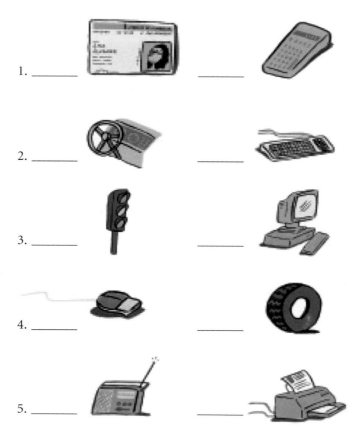

1. _____   _____

2. _____   _____

3. _____   _____

4. _____   _____

5. _____   _____

2 **En una gasolinera** Escucha la conversación entre un joven y el empleado de una gasolinera. Después completa las oraciones.

1. El empleado de la gasolinera llena el tanque, revisa el aceite y
   a. estaciona el carro.   b. limpia el parabrisas.   c. maneja el coche.

2. La próxima semana el joven tiene que
   a. manejar hasta Córdoba.   b. llenar el tanque.   c. revisar las llantas.

3. El joven va a volver mañana porque el empleado
   a. va a llenar el tanque.   b. va a revisar los frenos.   c. va a darle una multa.

4. Para revisar los frenos, el empleado necesita
   a. un par de minutos.   b. un par de días.   c. un par de horas.

5. Hoy el joven va
   a. a Córdoba.   b. a las montañas.   c. a la playa.

6. La gasolina cuesta
   a. 22 pesos.   b. 32 pesos.   c. 24 pesos.

recursos

R   Textbook CD
     Lección 11

A practicar

3 **Oraciones** Escribe oraciones usando los siguientes elementos. Usa el pretérito y añade (*add*) las palabras necesarias.

1. Jaime / decidir / comprar / calculadora / nuevo

_____

2. Yo / apagar / radio / diez / noche

_____

3. teléfono / sonar / pero / yo / no contestar

_____

4. Sara y yo / ir / gasolinera / para / llenar / tanque

_____

5. Sandra / perder / disco compacto

_____

6. Marisa / poner / su / maletas / baúl

_____

4 **Problemas con la computadora** Completa el diálogo con las palabras correctas.

arreglar	descompuesto	el ratón
funciona	la impresora	imprimir
llamar	navegar	la pantalla
prendiste	el disco	el teléfono celular

JUAN CARLOS Mariana, la computadora no _____. No veo nada en _____.

MARIANA Pues, ¿la _____?

JUAN CARLOS Ah sí, tienes razón; no estaba prendida. Mariana, ahora no puedo conectarme a Internet. Parece que el módem está _____. ¿Sabes cómo lo puedo_____?

MARIANA ¡Ay, mi amor! No es eso. Es que estoy hablando por teléfono con Sara. Si quieres, la puedo _____ por _____.

JUAN CARLOS Sí, gracias… Bueno, ahora sí estoy conectado. Voy a _____ un rato y después voy a _____ el trabajo para mi clase de historia… Pero, Mariana, ¿dónde está _____?

MARIANA Lo siento, ésa sí que está descompuesta. Pablo la está arreglando. No sé cómo vas a imprimir tu trabajo ahora.

JUAN CARLOS No te preocupes. Puedo llevar _____ a la universidad e imprimirlo allá.

MARIANA ¡Qué buena idea! ¡Eres tan inteligente, mi amor!

A conversar

5 **Preguntas** Trabajen en grupos para contestar las siguientes preguntas. Después compartan sus respuestas con la clase.

1. ¿Tienes licencia de conducir? ¿Cuánto tiempo hace que la recibiste? ¿Tienes carro?

2. ¿Siempre paras cuando ves la luz amarilla del semáforo? ¿Manejas rápidamente? ¿A veces sobrepasas (*do you exceed*) la velocidad máxima?

3. ¿Tienes una gasolinera favorita? ¿Y un taller mecánico favorito? ¿Por qué te gustan?

4. ¿Cuáles de las siguientes actividades haces tú normalmente: llenar el tanque, limpiar el parabrisas, lavar el coche, revisar el aceite, cambiar el aceite, revisar las llantas, arreglar el carro?

5. ¿Cómo escuchas música: por radio, tocadiscos compacto o por computadora?

6. Para comunicarte con tus amigos, ¿qué utilizas más: el teléfono, el teléfono celular o el correo electrónico? ¿Cuáles son las ventajas (*advantages*) y desventajas de los diferentes medios (*means*) de comunicación?

7. ¿Cómo usas la tecnología para divertirte? ¿Y para comunicarte? ¿Y para trabajar?

6 **En el taller** En parejas, preparen una conversación entre un(a) mecánico/a y un(a) cliente/a cuyo (*whose*) coche se dañó en un accidente. El/la cliente/a le dice al/a la mecánico/a qué ocurrió en el accidente y los dos hablan de las partes dañadas.

7 **Situación** Con un(a) compañero/a de clase, prepara una conversación entre el/la director(a) de ventas (*sales*) de una tienda de computadoras y uno de los clientes siguientes. El/la director(a) de ventas pregunta lo que el/la cliente/a desea hacer con la computadora y le muestra la computadora que éste/a necesita.

- El padre o la madre de un niño de seis años
- Una jubilada (*retired woman*) que quiere aprender Internet
- Una mujer que va a crear una nueva empresa (*business*) en su casa
- Un estudiante que no sabe nada de computadoras
- Un hombre de negocios (*businessman*) que viaja mucho

Ortografía

La acentuación de palabras similares

Although accent marks usually indicate which syllable in a word is stressed, they are also used to distinguish between words that have the same or similar spellings.

. . . .

Él maneja el **coche.**   **Sí, voy** si **quieres.**

Although one-syllable words do not usually carry written accents, some *do* have accent marks to distinguish them from words that have the same spelling but different meanings.

. . . .

Sé cocinar.   **Se baña.**   **¿Tomas** té?   **Te duermes.**

Sé (*I know*) and **té** (*tea*) have accent marks to distinguish them from the pronouns **se** and **te**.

para mí   **mi cámara**   **Tú lees.**   **tu estéreo**

Mí (*me*) and **tú** (*you*) have accent marks to distinguish them from the possessive pronouns **mi** and **tu**.

. . . .

¿Por qué vas?   **Voy porque quiero.**

Several words of more than one syllable also have accent marks to distinguish them from words that have the same or similar spellings.

. . . .

Éste es rápido.   **Este módem es rápido.**

Demonstrative pronouns have accent marks to distinguish them from demonstrative adjectives.

. . . .

¿Cuándo fuiste?   **Fui cuando me llamó.**

¿Dónde trabajas?   **Voy al taller donde trabajo.**

Adverbs have accent marks when they are used to convey a question.

. . . .

Práctica Marca los acentos en las palabras que los necesitan.

ANA Alo, soy Ana. ¿Que tal?
JUAN Hola, pero… ¿por que me llamas tan tarde?
ANA Porque mañana tienes que llevarme a la universidad. Mi auto esta dañado.
JUAN ¿Como se daño?
ANA Se daño el sabado. Un vecino (*neighbor*) choco con el.

Crucigrama Utiliza las siguientes pistas (*clues*) para completar el crucigrama. ¡Ojo con los acentos!

Horizontales
1. Él _____ levanta.
4. No voy _____ no puedo.
7. Tú _____ acuestas.
9. ¿ _____ es el examen?
10. Quiero este vídeo y _____ .

Verticales
2. ¿Cómo _____ Ud.?
3. Eres _____ mi hermano.
5. ¿ _____ tal?
6. Me gusta _____ suéter.
8. Navego _____ la Red.

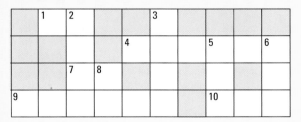

Tecnohombre, ¡mi héroe!

El autobús se daña.

ÁLEX ¿Bueno? … Con él habla… Ah, ¿cómo estás? … Aquí, yo muy bien. Vamos para Ibarra. ¿Sabes lo que pasó? Esta tarde íbamos para Ibarra cuando Javier tuvo un accidente en el autobús. Se cayó y tuvimos que llevarlo a una clínica.

JAVIER Episodio veintiuno: Tecnohombre y los superamigos suyos salvan el mundo una vez más.

INÉS Oh, Tecnohombre, ¡mi héroe!

MAITE ¡Qué cómicos! Un día de éstos, ya van a ver…

ÁLEX Van a ver quién es realmente Tecnohombre. Mis superamigos y yo nos hablamos todos los días por el teléfono Internet, trabajando para salvar el mundo. Pero ahora, con su permiso, quiero escribirle un mensaje electrónico a mi mamá y navegar en la Red un ratito.

INÉS Pues… no sé… creo que es el alternador. A ver… sí… Mire, don Francisco… está quemado el alternador.

DON FRANCISCO Ah, sí. Pero aquí no podemos arreglarlo. Conozco a un mecánico, pero está en Ibarra, a veinte kilómetros de aquí.

ÁLEX ¡Tecnohombre, a sus órdenes!

DON FRANCISCO ¡Eres la salvación, Álex! Llama al Sr. Fonseca al cinco, treinta y dos, cuarenta y siete, noventa y uno. Nos conocemos muy bien. Seguro que nos ayuda.

ÁLEX Buenas tardes. ¿Con el Sr. Fonseca por favor? … Soy Álex Morales, cliente de Ecuatur. Le hablo de parte del señor Francisco Castillo… Es que íbamos para Ibarra y se nos dañó el autobús…. Pensamos que es el… el alternador… Estamos a veinte kilómetros de la ciudad…

recursos

| R | Video/VCD-ROM Lección 11 | VM pp.189-190 | ICD-ROM Lección 11 |

Personajes

DON FRANCISCO

JAVIER

INÉS

ÁLEX

MAITE

SR. FONSECA

DON FRANCISCO Chicos, creo que tenemos un problema con el autobús. ¿Por qué no se bajan?

DON FRANCISCO Mmm, no veo el problema.

INÉS Cuando estaba en la escuela secundaria, trabajé en el taller de mi tío. Me enseñó mucho sobre mecánica. Por suerte, arreglé unos autobuses como éste.

DON FRANCISCO ¡No me digas! Bueno, ¿qué piensas?

SR. FONSECA Creo que va a ser mejor arreglar el autobús allí mismo. Tranquilo, enseguida salgo.

ÁLEX Buenas noticias. El Sr. Fonseca viene enseguida. Piensa que puede arreglar el autobús aquí mismo.

MAITE ¡La Mujer Mecánica y Tecnohombre, mis héroes!

DON FRANCISCO ¡Y los míos también!

Expresiones útiles

Talking on the telephone
¿Aló?/¿Bueno?/¿Diga?
Hello?
¿Quién habla?
Who is speaking?
¿De parte de quién?
Who is calling?
Con él/ella habla.
This is he/she.
Le hablo de parte de Francisco Castillo.
I'm speaking to you on behalf of Francisco Castillo.
¿Puedo dejar un recado?
May I leave a message?
Está bien. Llamo más tarde.
That's fine. I'll call later.

Talking about bus or car problems
¿Qué pasó?
What happened?
Se nos dañó el autobús.
The bus broke down.
Se nos pinchó una llanta.
We got a flat tire.
Está quemado el alternador.
The alternator is burned out.

Saying how far away things are
Está a veinte kilómetros de aquí.
It's twenty kilometers from here.
Estamos a veinte kilómetros de la ciudad.
We're twenty kilometers from the city.

Expressing surprise
¡No me diga! (form.)/¡No me digas! (fam.)
You don't say!

Offering assistance
A sus órdenes.
At your service.

Additional vocabulary
aquí mismo
right here

¿Qué piensas?

1 Seleccionar Selecciona las opciones que completan correctamente las siguientes frases.

1. Álex quiere

   a. llamar a su mamá por el teléfono celular.   b. escribirle a su mamá y navegar en la Red.
   c. hablar por el teléfono celular y navegar en la Red.

2. Se les dañó el autobús. Inés dice que

   a. el alternador está quemado.   b. se les pinchó una llanta.
   c. el taller está quemado.

3. Álex llama al mecánico, el señor

   a. Castillo.   b. Ibarra.
   c. Fonseca.

4. Maite llama a Inés la "Mujer Mecánica" porque antes

   a. trabajaba en el taller de su tío.   b. arreglaba computadoras.
   c. conocía a muchos mecánicos.

5. El grupo está a _____ de la ciudad.

   a. veinte millas   b. veinte grados centígrados
   c. veinte kilómetros

2 ¿Quién? Contesta las preguntas.

1. ¿Quién tiene un teléfono en el autobús? _____

2. ¿Quién conoce a un mecánico en la ciudad? _____

3. ¿Quién diagnostica el problema del autobús? _____

4. ¿Quién llama al mecánico? _____

5. ¿Quién dice que puede arreglar el autobús? _____

6. ¿Quién dice que Inés y Álex son sus héroes? _____

3 Situación Trabaja con un(a) compañero/a para representar los papeles de un(a) mecánico/a y un(a) conductor(a). El/la conductor(a) llama al/a la mecánico/a por teléfono y le explica cuál es el problema del coche. Después le indica dónde está con relación al taller. El/la mecánico/a le dice que puede ir enseguida. Usen estas preguntas y frases en su conversación.

Aló. /¿Bueno?/Diga.	¿Quién habla?
Con él/ella habla.	¿Qué pasó?
Se me dañó el coche.	Estoy a… kilómetros de…

Exploración
El transporte en la ciudad

Observaciones

- En México, D.F., hay unos 80.000 taxis y éstos hacen diariamente más de 780.000 viajes.
- La ciudad de Medellín es la única ciudad en Colombia que tiene metro. Bogotá, la capital, no tiene metro.
- En Caracas, Venezuela, el tiempo de viaje en automóvil se duplica (*doubles*) durante la hora pico (*rush hour*).
- En Argentina hay cuatro nombres para el autobús: ómnibus, colectivo, micro y bondi.

Los taxis son un medio de transporte muy popular en México, D.F., la capital. Muchos de los taxis son de marca Volkswagen y generalmente son de color verde o amarillo brillante.

La chiva es uno de los símbolos folclóricos de Colombia. Las chivas están pintadas de colores vibrantes y viajan de un pueblo a otro. También hay chivas turísticas que viajan dentro de las ciudades. Muchas de las chivas no tienen ventanas de cristal—la cabina está al aire libre.

Madrid, Barcelona, y Bilbao son tres ciudades españolas que tienen metro. Los metros de Madrid (1919) y Barcelona (1924) son muy antiguos. El metro de Bilbao tiene la forma de la letra 'Y' por causa del trayecto del río Nervión.

Coméntalo

Con un(a) compañero/a, contesta las siguientes preguntas.

- ¿Cuál es tu medio de transporte preferido? ¿Por qué? ¿Tienes carro?
- ¿Usas el transporte público? ¿Hay transporte público en tu comunidad?
- ¿Es más importante el transporte público en las ciudades pequeñas o en las grandes?

recursos

R

vistahigher
learning.com

11.1 The preterite and the imperfect

▶ The preterite and the imperfect are not interchangeable. The choice between these two tenses depends on the context and on the point of view of the speaker.

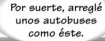

Por suerte, arreglé unos autobuses como éste.

Íbamos para Ibarra y se nos dañó el autobús.

Uses of the preterite

To express actions that are viewed by the speaker as completed	Don Francisco estacionó el autobús. *Don Francisco parked the bus.* Fueron a Valparaíso ayer. *They went to Valparaíso yesterday.*
To express the beginning or end of a past action	La película empezó a las nueve. *The movie began at nine o'clock.* Ayer terminé el proyecto. *Yesterday I finished the project.*
To narrate a series of past actions or events	Don Francisco paró el autobús, abrió la ventanilla y saludó a doña Rita. *Don Francisco stopped the bus, opened the window, and greeted Doña Rita.*

Uses of the imperfect

To describe an on-going past action with no reference to its beginning or end	Maite conducía muy rápido en Madrid. *Maite was driving very fast in Madrid.* Javier esperaba en el garaje. *Javier was waiting in the garage.*
To express habitual past actions and events	Cuando era joven, jugaba al tenis. *When I was young, I used to play tennis.* Álex siempre revisaba su correo electrónico a las tres. *Álex always checked his e-mail messages at three o'clock.*
To describe mental, physical, and emotional states or conditions	La chica quería descansar. Se sentía mal y tenía dolor de cabeza. *The girl wanted to rest. She felt ill and had a headache.* Ellos eran altos y tenían ojos verdes. *They were tall and had green eyes.* Estábamos felices de ver a la familia. *We were happy to see the family.*

Práctica

1 **Un accidente** Completa este artículo de periódico con las formas correctas del pretérito o del imperfecto.

Un trágico accidente

Ayer temprano por la mañana _____ [haber] un trágico accidente en el centro de Lima, cuando un autobús _____ [chocar] con un carro. La mujer que _____ [manejar] el carro _____ [morir] al instante. Los paramédicos llevaron al conductor del autobús al hospital porque _____ [tener] varias fracturas y una conmoción cerebral (*concussion*). Su estado de salud es todavía muy grave. El conductor del autobús _____ [decir] que no _____ [ver] el carro hasta el último (*last*) momento porque _____ [haber] mucha niebla y _____ [estar] lloviendo. Él _____ [intentar] (*to attempt*) dar un viraje brusco (*to swerve*), pero _____ [perder] el control del autobús y no _____ [poder] evitar (*to avoid*) el choque. Según nos informaron, no _____ [lastimarse] ningún pasajero.

2 **Combinar** Combina elementos de las tres columnas para hablar de lo que hicieron y lo que hacían las personas de la primera columna.

Sujetos	Verbos	Adverbios
el mecánico	arreglar	ayer
Dale Earnhardt (hijo)	caerse	bien
la mujer policía	chocar	con frecuencia
Bill Gates	conducir	de vez en cuando
las computadoras	decir	fácilmente
mis amigos y yo	enamorarse	lentamente
Jennifer López	funcionar	por aquí
yo	lastimarse	por fin
	navegar	todos los días
	olvidar	una vez

Conversación

 3 **Frases** En parejas, completen las frases usando el pretérito o el imperfecto. Luego comparen sus respuestas.

modelo De niño/a, yo...

Estudiante 1: De niña, yo vivía con mis abuelos en un apartamento cerca de la escuela.

Estudiante 2: Pues mi mamá, mis hermanos y yo vivíamos en una casita con un jardín.

Estudiante 1: De niña, me lastimé una vez la rodilla. Mientras corría, me caí.

Estudiante 2: En cambio, yo nunca me hice daño en la rodilla, pero me lastimaba constantemente las manos.

1. El verano pasado…
2. Yo manejaba el coche mientras…
3. Anoche mi novio/a…
4. Ayer el/la profesor(a)…
5. La semana pasada un(a) amigo/a…
6. A menudo mi madre…
7. Esta mañana en la cafetería…
8. Navegábamos en la Red cuando…

 4 **Tu primer(a) novio/a** Entrevista a un(a) compañero/a acerca de su primer(a) novio/a. Si quieres, puedes añadir (*to add*) otras preguntas.

1. ¿Quién fue tu primer(a) novio/a?
2. ¿Cuántos años tenías cuando lo/la conociste?
3. ¿Cómo era él/ella?
4. ¿Qué le gustaba hacer? ¿Tenían ustedes los mismos pasatiempos?
5. ¿Por cuánto tiempo salieron Uds.?
6. ¿Adónde iban Uds. cuando salían?
7. ¿Pensaban casarse?
8. ¿Cuándo y por qué rompieron Uds.?

 5 **Un robo misterioso** Anoche alguien robó (*stole*) el examen de la Lección 11 de la oficina de tu profesor(a) y tú tienes que averiguar (*to find out*) quién lo hizo. Pregúntales a varios compañeros dónde estaban, con quién estaban y qué hicieron entre las ocho y las doce de la noche. Luego decide quién robó el examen.

▶ When the preterite and the imperfect appear in the same sentence, the imperfect describes what was happening, and the preterite describes the action that interrupted the on-going activity.

Navegaba en la Red cuando **sonó** el teléfono.

I was surfing the Web when the phone rang.

Maite **leía** el periódico cuando **llegó** Álex.

Maite was reading the newspaper when Álex arrived.

▶ The preterite and the imperfect are often used together in lengthy narratives such as fiction stories and news stories. The imperfect provides the background information, such as the time, the weather, and the location. The preterite indicates the specific events.

Eran las dos de la mañana y el detective ya no **podía** mantenerse despierto. **Se bajó** lentamente del coche, **estiró** las piernas y **levantó** los brazos hacia el cielo oscuro.

It was two in the morning, and the detective could no longer stay awake. He slowly stepped out of the car, stretched his legs, and raised his arms towards the dark sky.

La luna **estaba** llena y no **había** en el cielo ni una sola nube. De repente, el detective **escuchó** un grito espeluznante proveniente del parque.

The moon was full and there wasn't a single cloud in the sky. Suddenly, the detective heard a piercing scream coming from the park.

NASA • La sonda se estrelló antes de orbitar

Mars cayó en Marte

La agencia espacial estadounidense perdió la comunicación con la sonda Mars Climate Orbiter, justo en el momento en que se ponía en órbita alrededor de Marte. La nave se estrelló por un error de navegación importante. Se habían invertido USD 25 millones e iba a ser la primera estación meteorológica interplanetaria. PASE A LA A6

¡Manos a la obra!

 Escribe la forma correcta de los verbos.

Pretérito

1. Tomás y yo __fuimos__ [ir] al parque ayer.
2. _____ [nadar] por la tarde.
3. Después _____ [tomar] el sol.
4. _____ [regresar] a casa a las cinco.
5. Tomás preparó la cena. Yo _____ [leer] el periódico.
6. Mientras Tomás veía una película, yo _____ [dormirse].

Imperfecto

1. __Eran__ [ser] las doce.
2. _____ [haber] mucha gente en la calle.
3. Los novios _____ [estar] en el café.
4. Todos los días ellos _____ [almorzar] juntos.
5. El camarero les _____ [servir] ensaladas.
6. Cuando los novios salieron del café, _____ [llover].

11.2 Por and para

▶ Both **por** and **para** mean *for*, but they are not interchangeable. Study their uses on the charts.

Es para usted. Es un cliente de don Paco.

Álex habla por teléfono.

Uses of *por*

Motion or a general location (around, through, along, by)	La excursión nos llevó **por** el centro. *The tour took us through downtown.*
	Pasamos **por** el parque y **por** el río. *We passed by the park and along the river.*
Duration of an action (for, during, in)	Estuve en Montevideo **por** un mes. *I was in Montevideo for a month.*
	Miguel estudió **por** la noche. *Miguel studied during the night.*
Object of a search (for, in search of)	Vengo **por** ti a las ocho. *I'm coming for you at eight.*
	Maite fue **por** su cámara. *Maite went in search of her camera.*
Means by which something is done (by, by way of, by means of)	Ellos viajan **por** la autopista. *They travel by way of the highway.*
	¿Hablaste con la policía **por** teléfono? *Did you talk to the police by phone?*
Exchange or substitution (for, in exchange for)	Le di dinero **por** la videocasetera. *I gave him money for the VCR.*
	Muchas gracias **por** el vídeo. *Thank you very much for the video.*
Unit of measure (per, by)	José manejaba a 120 kilómetros **por** hora. *José was driving 120 kilometers per hour.*

▶ **Por** is used in several idiomatic expressions.

por aquí	*around here*		**por eso**	*that's why; therefore*
por ejemplo	*for example*		**por fin**	*finally*

¡ojo! When giving an exact time, **de** is used instead of **por** before **la mañana, la tarde,** and **la noche.**

Llegué a las diez **de la noche.**
I arrived at ten p.m.

Me gusta estudiar **por la noche.**
I like to study at night.

Práctica

1 Un viaje a Buenos Aires Completa este párrafo con las preposiciones **por** o **para**.

El mes pasado, mi esposo y yo hicimos un viaje a Buenos Aires y sólo pagamos dos mil dólares _____ los pasajes. Estuvimos en Buenos Aires _____ una semana y exploramos toda la ciudad. Durante el día caminamos _____ la plaza San Martín, el microcentro y el barrio de La Boca, donde viven muchos artistas. _____ la noche fuimos a una tanguería, que es un tipo de teatro, _____ mirar a la gente bailar tango. Dos días después decidimos hacer una excursión _____ las Pampas _____ ver el paisaje (*countryside*) y un rodeo con gauchos. _____ eso, alquilamos (*we rented*) un carro y pasamos unos días muy agradables. El último (*last*) día que estuvimos en Buenos Aires fuimos a Galerías Pacíficas _____ comprar recuerdos (*souvenirs*) _____ nuestros hijos y nietos. Compramos tantos regalos que, al regresar, tuvimos que pagar impuestos (*duties*) cuando pasamos _____ la aduana.

2 ¿Qué pasa aquí? Usa **por** o **para** y el tiempo presente para describir estos dibujos.

1. _____

4. _____

2. _____

5. _____

3. _____

6. _____

Conversación

3 **Completar** Usa **por** o **para** y completa estas frases de una manera (*manner*) lógica. Luego, compara tus respuestas con las de un(a) compañero/a.

1. El año pasado compré un regalo…
2. Ayer fui al taller…
3. Necesito hacer la tarea…
4. En casa, hablo con mis amigos…
5. Los miércoles tengo clases…
6. A veces voy a la biblioteca…
7. Necesito… dólares…
8. Esta noche tengo que estudiar…
9. Mi padre/madre trabaja…
10. Mi mejor amigo/a estudia…

4 **Encuesta** Camina por la clase haciendo preguntas hasta que encuentres a alguien que corresponda a cada descripción. Luego presenta los resultados a la clase.

Descripciones	Nombres
1. En casa, tiene televisión por cable.	
2. Anoche durmió por ocho horas.	
3. Viajó por Europa.	
4. Hoy pasó por la gasolinera.	
5. Se preocupa por sus amigos.	
6. Habla por teléfono celular.	
7. Quiere estudiar para médico/a.	
8. Las clases son fáciles para él/ella.	
9. Escucha música por la noche.	
10. Va a la biblioteca para estudiar.	

5 **Una subasta** Trabajen en grupos para dramatizar una subasta (*auction*). Cada estudiante debe traer un objeto o una foto del objeto para vender a la clase. Luego, un(a) estudiante es el/la vendedor(a) y los otros son los postores (*bidders*).

modelo

Vendedor(a): ¿Quién me ofrece $200,00 por la cámara de vídeo? Es una ganga a este precio. Yo pagué $400,00 por ella.

Postor(a) 1: Te doy $175,00.

Uses of *para*

Destination *(toward, in the direction of)*	Salimos para Mérida el sábado. *We are leaving for Mérida on Saturday.* Voy para el banco. *I'm going to the bank.*
Deadline or a specific time in the future *(by, for)*	Él va a arreglar el carro para el viernes. *He will fix the car by Friday.*
Purpose or goal + [*infinitive*] *(in order to)*	Juan estudia para (ser) mecánico. *Juan is studying to be a mechanic.*
Purpose + [*noun*] *(for, used for)*	Es una llanta para el carro. *It's a tire for the car.* Un módem sirve para navegar en la Red. *A modem is used to surf the Web.*
The recipient of something *(for)*	Compré una calculadora para mi hijo. *I bought a calculator for my son.*
Comparisons or opinions *(for, considering)*	Para ser joven, es demasiado serio. *For a young person, he is too serious.* Para mí, esta lección no es difícil. *For me, this lesson isn't difficult.*
Employment *(for)*	Sara trabaja para Telecom. *Sara works for Telecom.*

▶ Often, either **por** or **para** can be used in a sentence. The meaning of the sentence changes, depending on which one is used.

Caminé **por** el parque.
I walked through the park.

Caminé **para** el parque.
I walked to (toward) the park.

Trabajó **por** su padre.
He worked for (in place of) his father.

Trabajó **para** su padre.
He worked for his father('s business).

Se exhibió **por** todo el pueblo.
It was shown throughout (around) the whole town.

Se exhibió **para** todo el pueblo.
It was shown for the whole town.

¡Manos a la obra!

 Completa las frases con **por** o **para**.

1. Dormimos ___*por*___ la mañana.
2. Necesitas un módem _____ navegar en la Red.
3. Entraron _____ la puerta.
4. Es un pasaje _____ Buenos Aires.
5. _____ arrancar el carro, necesito la llave.
6. Arreglé el televisor _____ ti.
7. Estuvieron nerviosos _____ el examen.
8. ¿Hay una gasolinera _____ aquí?
9. Esta computadora es _____ Ud.
10. Juan está enfermo. Tengo que trabajar _____ él.
11. Estuvimos en Cancún _____ dos meses.
12. _____ mí, el español es difícil.
13. Tengo que estudiar la lección _____ el lunes.
14. Voy a ir _____ ese camino.
15. Compré dulces _____ mi novia.
16. Lo compró _____ un buen precio.

11.3 Stressed possessive adjectives and pronouns

▸ Spanish has two types of possessive adjectives: the unstressed (short) forms you learned in Lesson 3 and the stressed (long) forms. The stressed possessive adjectives are used for emphasis or to express the English phrases *(of) mine, (of) yours, (of) his,* and so on.

Stressed possessive adjectives

Singular forms		Plural forms		
MASCULINE	**FEMININE**	**MASCULINE**	**FEMININE**	
mío	mía	míos	mías	*my; (of) mine*
tuyo	tuya	tuyos	tuyas	*your; (of) yours (fam.)*
suyo	suya	suyos	suyas	*your; (of) yours (form.); his; (of) his; her; (of) hers; its*
nuestro	nuestra	nuestros	nuestras	*our; (of) ours*
vuestro	vuestra	vuestros	vuestras	*your; (of) yours (fam.)*
suyo	suya	suyos	suyas	*your; (of) yours (form.); their; (of) theirs*

▸ Stressed possessive adjectives must agree in gender and number with the nouns they modify.

mi **impresora**	la **impresor**a **mía**
my printer	*my printer*
nuestros televisores	los televisores **nuestros**
our television sets	*our television sets*

▸ Stressed possessive adjectives are placed after the nouns they modify. Unstressed possessive adjectives are placed before the noun.

Son **mis** llaves.   Son las llaves **mías**.
They are my keys.   *They are my keys.*

▸ A definite article, an indefinite article, or a demonstrative adjective usually precedes a noun modified by a stressed possessive adjective.

Alberto tenía
unos discos **tuyos.**   *Alberto had some disks of yours.*
los discos **tuyos.**   *Alberto had your disks.*
estos discos **tuyos.**   *Alberto had these disks of yours.*

▸ **Suyo, suya, suyos,** and **suyas** have more than one meaning. You can avoid confusion by using the construction: [*article*] + [*noun*] + **de** + [*subject pronoun* or *noun*].

el teclado **suyo**
el teclado **de él/ella**   *his/her keyboard*
el teclado **de Ud./Uds.**   *your keyboard*
el teclado **de ellos/ellas**   *their keyboard*
el teclado **de Ramón**   *Ramón's keyboard*

▸ **El** and **la** are usually omitted when a stressed possessive adjective follows the verb **ser**.

¿**Es suya** esta cámara?   No, no **es mía**.

Práctica

1 **Frases** Forma frases en el presente con las siguientes palabras.

1. yo / necesitar / usar / impresora / de Miguel / porque / mío / no / funcionar

2. pero / él / no poder / ayudarme / porque / suyo / tampoco / funcionar

3. Me gustaría / pedirle / a Juana / su ratón, / pero / suyo / estar / descompuesto

4. yo / no poder / usar / teclado / de Conchita / porque / suyo / estar descompuesto / también

5. y si / yo / pedirte / computadora, / estar / seguro / que / ir / decirme / que / no poder / usar / tuyo

2 **¿Es suyo?** Un policía ha capturado al hombre que robó (*robbed*) en tu casa. Ahora el policía quiere saber qué cosas son tuyas. Túrnate con un(a) compañero/a para hacer el papel del policía y usa las pistas (*clues*) para contestar las preguntas.

 modelo

No / pequeño
Policía: Esta computadora, ¿es suya?
Estudiante: No, no es mía. La mía es más pequeña.

1. Sí

4. No / viejo

2. Sí

5. Sí

3. No / nuevo

6. No / caro

Conversación

3 **¿Son tuyas estas cintas?** Trabajen en grupos. Cada estudiante trae tres objetos. Pongan (*put*) todos los objetos juntos. Luego, un(a) estudiante escoge uno o dos objetos y le pregunta a otro/a si esos objetos son suyos. Usen los adjetivos posesivos en sus preguntas.

modelo

Estudiante 1: José Luis, ¿son tuyas estas cintas?
Estudiante 2: Sí, son mías. / No, no son mías. Son las cintas de Felipe.

4 **Anuncios** Lee este anuncio (*ad*) con un(a) compañero/a. Luego, preparen su propio (*own*) anuncio usando los adjetivos o los pronombres posesivos. Después, conviértanlo en un anuncio de televisión (*commercial*) y preséntenlo a la clase.

Esta computadora y esta impresora pueden ser suyas por sólo

$1799

Características de la computadora
- Procesador: Intel Pentium III a 3000 Mhz
- 640Mb de memoria
- Disco duro de 100 Gb
- Sistema operativo: Linux

Características de la impresora
- Velocidad: 20 páginas por minuto en blanco y negro
- Resolución de 1200 x 1200

El precio incluye un año de servicio de Internet gratis. Para más información, llame al 362-1990 o visite nuestro sitio Web www.fiera.com.

Possessive pronouns

▶ Possessive pronouns are used to replace [*noun*] + [*possessive adjective*]. In Spanish, the possessive pronouns have the same forms as the stressed possessive adjectives, and they are preceded by a definite article.

la **calculadora** nuestra → la nuestra
el **fax** tuyo → el tuyo
los **archivos** suyos → los suyos

> Episodio veintiuno: Tecnohombre y los superamigos suyos salvan el mundo una vez más.

> La Mujer Mecánica y Tecnohombre, ¡mis héroes!

> ¡Y los míos también!

▶ Possessive pronouns agree in number and gender with the nouns they replace.

—Aquí está **mi coche.** ¿Dónde está **el tuyo**?
Here's my car. Where is yours?

—**El mío** está en el taller de mi hermano Armando.
Mine is at my brother Armando's garage.

—¿Tienes **las cintas** de Carlos?
Do you have Carlos' tapes?

—No, pero tengo **las nuestras**.
No, but I have ours.

¡Manos a la obra!

Indica las formas tónicas *(stressed)* de estos adjetivos posesivos y los pronombres posesivos correspondientes.

	adjetivos	pronombres
1. su videocasetera	la videocasetera suya	la suya
2. mi televisor		
3. nuestros discos		
4. tus cintas		
5. su módem		
6. mis vídeos		
7. nuestra impresora		
8. tu estéreo		
9. nuestro carro		
10. mi computadora		

Ampliación

1 Escuchar

A Mientras escuchas a Ricardo Moreno, selecciona el género al que corresponde su discurso. Luego, identifica de qué habla y su propósito (*purpose*).

 TIP **Recognize the genre of spoken discourse.** Identifying the genre (for example: political speech, radio interview, news broadcast) of what you hear can help you figure out what kinds of things you are likely to hear. It will also help you identify the speaker's motives and intentions.

1. ¿Qué tipo de discurso es?
   a. las noticias por radio o televisión   b. un anuncio comercial
   c. una reseña (*review*) de una película
2. ¿De qué habla?
   a. de su vida   b. de un producto o servicio
   c. de algo que oyó o vio
3. ¿Cuál es el propósito?
   a. relacionarse con alguien   b. informar
   c. vender

B ¿Qué te indicó el género de este discurso?

2 Conversar

Con un(a) compañero/a, prepara una conversación sobre la primera vez que manejaste un carro o el día en que fuiste al Departamento de Tráfico para conseguir tu licencia de conducir.

modelo

Estudiante 1: Conseguí la licencia de conducir cuando tenía dieciséis años. Hacía sol y mi mamá me acompañó al Departamento de Tráfico. ¿Tú también conseguiste la tuya a los dieciséis años?

Estudiante 2: No, todavía no tengo la mía. En mi estado no podemos conseguir una licencia de conducir hasta los dieciocho años. ¿Cómo fue la primera vez que manejaste?

Estudiante 1: Estaba despejado y hacía sol. Eran las tres y media de la tarde, después de clases. Tenía un poco de miedo, pero quería hacerlo. Después de conducir, me sentí muy bien.

recursos

R	Textbook CD Lección 11	WB pp. 113-118	LM pp. 63-65	Lab CD Lección 11	ICD-ROM Lección 11	vistahigher learning.com

Ampliación

3 Escribir

Escribe una historia acerca de una experiencia tuya con una máquina electrónica o con el carro.

 TIP **Master the simple past tenses.** To write about events that occurred in the past, you will need to know when to use the preterite and the imperfect. The box on this page contains a summary of their uses.

Preterite	
● Actions viewed as completed	
● Beginning or end of past actions	
● Series of past actions	
Imperfect	
● On-going past actions	
● Habitual past actions	
● Mental, physical, and emotional states in the past	

Organízalo	Prepara una lista de todos los detalles que quieres narrar (*narrate*).
Escríbelo	Utiliza tu lista para escribir el primer borrador de tu historia.
Corrígelo	Intercambia tu historia con un(a) compañero/a. Lee su borrador y reflexiona sobre las partes mejor escritas. Ofrécele sugerencias sobre los detalles, la lógica de la secuencia de eventos y el uso del pretérito y del imperfecto.
Compártelo	Revisa el primer borrador según las indicaciones de tu compañero/a. Incorpora nuevas ideas para enriquecer la narración de los eventos. Escribe la versión final de tu historia y compártela con la clase.

4 Un paso más

Busca información sobre los cibercafés en los países hispanos e inventa un cibercafé nuevo. Crea un anuncio de revista (*magazine advertisement*) para promocionarlo. El anuncio debe incluir los siguientes elementos:

- Una descripción del lugar donde está ubicado (*located*) el cibercafé
- Una descripción de la tecnología y de los servicios que se ofrecen a los clientes
- Fotos o dibujos
- Por qué este cibercafé es mejor que otros
- Los precios.

 En Internet

Investiga estos temas en el sitio vistahigherlearning.com.

- Cibercafés en el mundo hispano
- Internet en el mundo hispano
- La tecnología en el mundo hispano

Antes de leer

One way languages grow is by borrowing words from each other. English words that relate to technology are often borrowed by Spanish and other languages throughout the world. Sometimes the words are modified slightly to fit the sounds of the languages that borrow them. When reading in Spanish, you can often increase your understanding by looking for words borrowed from English or other languages you know.

Examinar el texto

Mira brevemente la selección. ¿De qué trata? ¿Cómo lo sabes?

Buscar

Esta lectura contiene varias palabras tomadas del inglés. Trabaja con un(a) compañero/a para encontrarlas.

Inteligencia y memoria: la inteligencia artificial
Alfonso Santamaría

Una de las principales características de la película de ciencia ficción *2001: una odisea del espacio* es la gran inteligencia de su protagonista no humano, la computadora HAL-9000. Para muchas personas, la genial película de Stanley Kubrick es una reflexión sobre la evolución de la inteligencia, desde que el hombre utilizó por primera vez un hueso como herramienta hasta la llegada de la inteligencia artificial (I.A.).

Ahora que vivimos en el siglo XXI, en un mundo en el que Internet y el fax son ya comunes, podemos preguntarnos: ¿consiguieron los científicos especialistas en I.A. crear una computadora como HAL? La respuesta es no. Hoy en día no existe una computadora con las capacidades intelectuales de HAL porque todavía no existen *inteligencias artificiales generales* que demuestren lo que llamamos "sentido común". Sin embargo, la I.A. está progresando mucho en el desarrollo de las *inteligencias especializadas*. El ejemplo más famoso es Deep Blue, la computadora de IBM especializada en jugar al ajedrez.

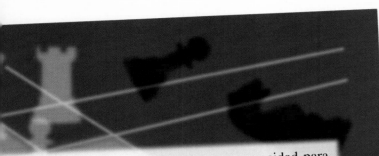

La idea de crear una máquina con capacidad para jugar al ajedrez se originó en 1950. En esa década, el científico Claude Shannon desarrolló una teoría que se convirtió en realidad en 1967, cuando apareció el primer programa que le permitió a una computadora competir, aunque sin éxito, en un campeonato de ajedrez. Más de veinte años después, un grupo de expertos en I.A. fue al centro de investigación Thomas J. Watson de Nueva York para desarrollar Deep Blue, la computadora que en 1997 derrotó al campeón mundial de ajedrez Garry Kasparov. Esta extraordinaria computadora pudo ganar al maestro ruso de ajedrez porque estaba diseñada para procesar 200 millones de jugadas por segundo. Además, Deep Blue guardaba en su memoria una recopilación de los movimientos de ajedrez más brillantes de toda la historia, entre ellos los que Kasparov efectuó en sus competiciones anteriores.

Para muchas personas la victoria de Deep Blue sobre Kasparov simbolizó la victoria de la inteligencia artificial sobre la del ser humano. Debemos reconocer los grandes avances científicos en el área de las computadoras y las ventajas que pueden traernos en un futuro, pero también sus limitaciones. Las computadoras generan nuevos modelos con conocimientos muy definidos, pero todavía no tienen sentido común: una computadora como Deep Blue puede ganar una partida de ajedrez, pero no puede explicar la diferencia entre una reina y un peón. Tampoco puede crear algo nuevo y original a partir de lo establecido, como hicieron Mozart o Picasso.

Las inteligencias artificiales especializadas son una realidad. ¿Pero una inteligencia como la de HAL-9000? Pura ciencia ficción.

Después de leer

¿Comprendiste?

Indica si las frases son **ciertas** o **falsas**. Corrige las falsas.

Cierto	Falso	
_____	_____	1. La computadora HAL-9000 era muy inteligente.
_____	_____	2. Deep Blue es un buen ejemplo de la inteligencia artificial general.
	_____	3. El maestro de ajedrez Garry Kasparov le ganó a Deep Blue en 1997.
_____	_____	4. Las computadoras no tienen la creatividad de Mozart y Picasso.
_____		5. Hoy hay computadoras como HAL-9000.

Preguntas

1. ¿Qué tipo de inteligencia se relaciona con HAL-9000?

_____

2. ¿Qué tipo de inteligencia tienen las computadoras como Deep Blue?

_____

3. ¿Cuándo se originó la idea de crear una máquina para jugar al ajedrez?

_____

4. ¿Qué compañía inventó Deep Blue?

_____

5. ¿Por qué Deep Blue le pudo ganar a Garry Kasparov?

_____

Coméntalo

¿Son las computadoras más inteligentes que los seres humanos? ¿Para qué cosas son mejores las computadoras, y para qué cosas son mejores los seres humanos? ¿Por qué? En el futuro, ¿van a tener las computadoras la inteligencia de los seres humanos? ¿Cuándo?

herramienta	*tool*
sentido común	*common sense*
desarrollo	*development*
ajedrez	*chess*
éxito	*success*
campeonato	*championship*
jugadas	*moves*
derrotó	*defeated*
la del ser humano	*that of the human being*
ventajas	*advantages*
conocimientos	*knowledge*
partida	*match*
reina	*queen*
peón	*pawn*

recursos

R

vistahigher learning.com

El carro

el baúl	trunk
la calle	street
el camino	route
el capó	hood
el carro	car
el coche	car
los frenos	brakes
el taller (mecánico)	(mechanic's) repair shop
el garaje	mechanic's shop
la gasolina	gasoline
la gasolinera	gas station
el kilómetro	kilometer
la licencia de conducir	driver's license
la llanta	tire
el/la mecánico/a	mechanic
la milla	mile
el motor	motor
la multa	fine
el parabrisas	windshield
el policía/la mujer policía	police officer
la policía	police (force)
el semáforo	traffic light
el tráfico	traffic
la velocidad máxima	speed limit
el volante	steering wheel
arrancar	to start
arreglar	to fix; to arrange
bajar	to go down
bajar(se) de	to get off of/out of (a vehicle)
chocar (con)	to run into; to crash
conducir	to drive
estacionar	to park
llenar (el tanque)	to fill (the tank)
manejar	to drive
parar	to stop
revisar (el aceite)	to check (the oil)
subir	to go up
subir(se) a	to get on/into (a vehicle)

La tecnología

la calculadora	calculator
la cámara (de vídeo)	(video) camera
la cinta	(audio)tape
la contestadora	answering machine
el control remoto	remote control
el disco compacto	compact disc
el estéreo	stereo
el fax	fax (machine)
el radio	radio (set)
el teléfono (celular)	(cellular) telephone
la televisión por cable	cable television
el televisor	television set
el tocadiscos compacto	compact disc player
el videocasete	videocassette
la videocasetera	VCR
apagar	to turn off
funcionar	to work
llamar	to call
poner	to turn on
prender	to turn on
sonar (o:ue)	to ring
descompuesto/a	not working; out of order
lento/a	slow
lleno/a	full

Internet y la computadora

el archivo	file
la computadora portátil	portable computer; laptop
el disco	(computer) disk
la impresora	printer
Internet	Internet
el módem	modem
el monitor	(computer) monitor
la página principal	home page
la pantalla	screen
el programa de computación	software
el ratón	mouse
la Red	the Web
el sitio Web	website
el teclado	keyboard
guardar	to save
imprimir	to print
navegar (en la Red)	to surf (the Internet)

Otras palabras y expresiones

para	for; in order to
por	for; by; by means of; through; along; during; in; because of; due to; in exchange for; for the sake of; on behalf of
por aquí	around here
por ejemplo	for example
por eso	that's why; therefore
por fin	finally

Expresiones útiles	See page 267.
Stressed possessive adjectives and pronouns	See pages 274–275.

recursos

R	Lab CD Lección 11	LM p. 65

12 Hogar, dulce hogar

HOGAR, DULCE HOGAR

LA CASA Y SUS CUARTOS

la escalera
stairs; stairway

la alcoba *bedroom*
el altillo *attic*
el balcón *balcony*
la cocina *kitchen*
el comedor *dining room*
la entrada *entrance*
el garaje *garage*
la oficina *office*
el pasillo *hallway*
el patio *patio*
la sala *living room*
el sótano *basement, cellar*

el jardín
garden; yard

LA MESA

la copa *wine glass; goblet*
la cuchara *spoon*
el cuchillo *knife*
el plato *plate*
la servilleta *napkin*
la taza *cup*
el tenedor *fork*
el vaso *glass*

LOS ELECTRODOMÉSTICOS

la estufa *stove*
el horno (de microondas) *(microwave) oven*
la lavadora *washing machine*
el lavaplatos *dishwasher*
el refrigerador *refrigerator*
la secadora *clothes dryer*

los electrodomésticos
electrical appliances

recursos

Textbook CD Lección 12	WB pp. 119-120	LM p. 67	Lab CD Lección 12	ICD-ROM Lección 12

LOS QUEHACERES DOMÉSTICOS

arreglar *to neaten; to straighten up*
cocinar *to cook*
ensuciar *to get (something) dirty*
hacer los quehaceres domésticos *to do household chores*
lavar (el suelo, los platos) *to wash (the floor, the dishes)*
limpiar la casa *to clean the house*
pasar la aspiradora *to vacuum*
poner la mesa *to set the table*
quitar la mesa *to clear the table*
sacar la basura *to take out the trash*
sacudir los muebles *to dust the furniture*

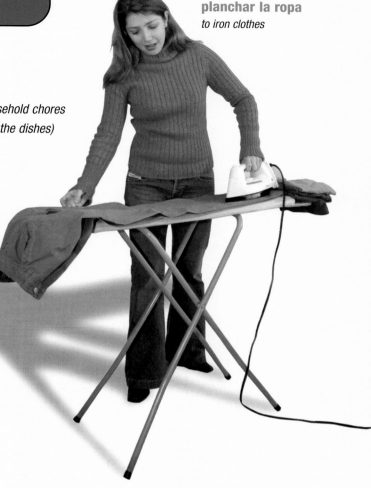

planchar la ropa
to iron clothes

barrer el suelo
to sweep the floor

hacer la cama
to make the bed

LOS MUEBLES

la alfombra *rug*
la almohada *pillow*
el armario *closet*
la cómoda *chest with drawers*
las cortinas *curtains*
el cuadro *painting*
el estante *bookcase; bookshelves*
la lámpara *lamp*
la luz *light*
la manta *blanket*
la mesita *side/end table*
la mesita de noche *night stand*
la pared *wall*
la pintura *painting; picture*
el sillón *armchair*
el sofá *sofa; couch*

los muebles
furniture

OTRAS PALABRAS

las afueras *suburbs; outskirts*
la agencia de bienes raíces *real estate agency*
el alquiler *rent (payment)*
el ama (m., f.) de casa *housekeeper; caretaker*
el barrio *neighborhood*
el edificio de apartamentos *apartment building*
el hogar *home*
el/la vecino/a *neighbor*
la vivienda *housing*

alquilar *to rent*
mudarse *to move (residences)*

A escuchar

 1 **Escoger** Escucha las preguntas e indica la respuesta correcta.

1. _____ Al pasillo.

   _____ Al balcón.

2. _____ En el lavaplatos.

   _____ En la mesita de noche.

3. _____ Al barrio.

   _____ A las afueras.

4. _____ En la secadora.

   _____ En la basura.

5. _____ El balcón.

   _____ Las escaleras.

6. _____ En las paredes.

   _____ En la estufa.

7. _____ El horno.

   _____ La aspiradora.

8. _____ En la alfombra.

   _____ En la alcoba.

 2 **Escuchar** Escucha la conversación y completa las frases.

1. Pedro va a limpiar _____ primero.

2. Paula va a comenzar por _____.

3. Pedro le recuerda (*reminds*) a Paula que debe _____ en la alcoba de huéspedes.

4. Pedro va a _____ en el sótano.

5. Pedro también va a limpiar _____.

6. Ellos están limpiando la casa porque _____.

A practicar

3 **Definiciones** En parejas, identifiquen lo que se describe en cada descripción. Luego inventen sus propias descripciones de algunas palabras de **Preparación**.

modelo

Si vives en un apartamento, lo tienes que pagar cada mes.
Estudiante 1: Si vives en un **apartamento, lo tienes que pagar cada mes.**
Estudiante 2: El **alquiler.**

1. Es donde pones la cabeza cuando duermes.

2. Es el quehacer doméstico que haces después de comer.

3. Cubren (*they cover*) las ventanas y decoran la sala a la vez (*at the same time*).

4. Algunos ejemplos son la cómoda, la mesita y los sillones.

5. Son las personas que viven en tu barrio.

4 **Emparejar** Identifica los dibujos. Luego indica la letra del dibujo que corresponde a cada descripción.

_____ 1. Lo usas para tomar agua.

_____ 2. Lo necesitas para comer un bistec.

_____ 3. Necesitas este objeto para la sopa.

_____ 4. La necesitas para tomar café.

_____ 5. La necesitas para tomar vino.

_____ 6. Necesitas este objeto para limpiarte la boca después de comer.

a._____ b._____ c._____

d._____ e._____ f._____

5 **Los quehaceres domésticos** Trabajen en grupos para indicar quién hace los siguientes quehaceres domésticos en sus casas. Luego contesten las preguntas.

pasar la aspiradora	sacar la basura	cocinar
sacudir los muebles	hacer las camas	lavar la ropa
barrer el suelo	lavar los platos	planchar la ropa

• ¿Quién hace más quehaceres, tú o tus compañeros/as?

• ¿Cúales son los quehaceres que más te molesta hacer?

• ¿Piensas que debes hacer más quehaceres? ¿Por qué?

A conversar

6 Dos habitaciones En parejas, describan las habitaciones que ven en las fotos. Identifiquen y describan seis muebles o adornos (*accessories*) de cada foto y luego indiquen los quehaceres domésticos que se pueden hacer en cada habitación.

7 Mi apartamento Dibuja el plano de un apartamento amueblado (*furnished*) y escribe los nombres de las habitaciones y los muebles. En parejas, un(a) compañero/a describe su apartamento mientras el/la otro/a lo dibuja. Cuando terminen, miren el dibujo. ¿Es similar al dibujo original? Hablen de los cambios que se necesitan para mejorarlo. Repitan la actividad, intercambiando los papeles (*roles*).

8 Un(a) corredor(a) de bienes raíces Trabajen en grupos para representar a un(a) corredor(a) de bienes raíces (*real estate agent*) y a sus clientes. El/la corredor(a) tiene varias casas para vender; debe mostrarlas, hablar de los muebles y del barrio que más les convienen (*suit*) a los siguientes clientes.

- Una pareja que está esperando su segundo hijo
- Una pareja de jubilados (*retirees*) que quiere tranquilidad
- Un grupo de estudiantes universitarios que quiere vivir fuera del campus (*off-campus*)
- Una familia con cinco niños

Ortografía

Las mayúsculas y las minúsculas

Here are some of the rules that govern the use of capital letters (**mayúsculas**) and lowercase letters (**minúsculas**) in Spanish.

Los estudiantes llegaron al aeropuerto a las dos. Luego fueron al hotel.

In both Spanish and English, the first letter of every sentence is capitalized.

Rubén Blades   **Panamá**   **Colón**   **los Andes**

The first letter of all proper nouns (names of people, countries, cities, geographical features, etc.) is capitalized.

Cien años de soledad   ***Don Quijote de la Mancha***   ***El País***   ***Muy Interesante***

The first letter of the first word in titles of books, films, and works of art is generally capitalized, as well as the first letter of any proper names. In newspaper and magazine titles, as well as other short titles, the initial letter of each word is often capitalized.

la señora Ramos   **don Francisco**   **el presidente**   **Sra. Vives**

Titles associated with people are *not* capitalized unless they appear as the first word in a sentence. Note, however, that the first letter of an abbreviated title is capitalized.

Último   **Álex**   **MENÚ**   **PERDÓN**

Accent marks should be retained on capital letters. In practice, however, this rule is often ignored.

lunes   **viernes**   **marzo**   **primavera**

The first letter of days, months, and seasons is *not* capitalized.

español   **estadounidense**   **japonés**   **panameños**

The first letter of nationalities and languages is *not* capitalized.

Práctica Corrige las mayúsculas y minúsculas incorrectas.

1. soy lourdes romero. Soy Colombiana.
2. éste Es mi Hermano álex.
3. somos De panamá.
4. ¿es ud. La sra. benavides?
5. ud. Llegó el Lunes, ¿no?

Oraciones Lee el diálogo de las serpientes. Ordena las letras para saber de qué palabras se trata. Después escribe las letras indicadas para descubrir por qué llora Pepito.

Profesor Herrera, ¿es cierto que somos venenosas?

Sí, Pepito. ¿Por qué lloras?

m n a a P á   y a U r u g u

s t e m r a   r o ñ e s a

i g s l é n

¡ ___orque ___e acabo de morder la ___ en ___u ___!

venenosas *venomous*
morder *to bite*

1 Respuestas: Panamá, martes, inglés, Uruguay, señora. ¡Porque me acabo de morder la lengua!

recursos R ICD-ROM Lección 12

¡Les va a encantar la casa!

Don Francisco y los estudiantes llegan a Ibarra.

SRA. VIVES ¡Hola, bienvenidos!

DON FRANCISCO Sra. Vives, le presento a los chicos. Chicos, ésta es la Sra. Vives, el ama de casa.

SRA. VIVES Encantada. Síganme, que quiero mostrarles la casa. ¡Les va a encantar!

SRA. VIVES Esta alcoba es para los chicos. Tienen dos camas, una mesita de noche, una cómoda… En el armario hay más mantas y almohadas por si las necesitan.

SRA. VIVES Ésta es la sala. El sofá y los sillones son muy cómodos. Pero, por favor, ¡no los ensucien!

SRA. VIVES Allí están la cocina y el comedor. Al fondo del pasillo hay un baño.

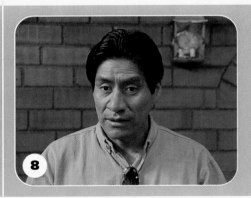

DON FRANCISCO Chicos, a ver… ¡atención! La Sra. Vives les va a preparar las comidas. Pero quiero que Uds. la ayuden con los quehaceres domésticos. Quiero que arreglen sus alcobas, que hagan las camas, que pongan la mesa… ¿entendido?

JAVIER No se preocupe… La vamos a ayudar en todo lo posible.

ÁLEX Sí, cuente con nosotros.

recursos

| R | Video/VCD-ROM Lección 12 | VM pp.191-192 | ICD-ROM Lección 12 |

Personajes

DON FRANCISCO **JAVIER** **INÉS** **ÁLEX** **MAITE** **SRA. VIVES**

SRA. VIVES Javier, no ponga las maletas en la cama. Póngalas en el piso, por favor.

SRA. VIVES Tomen Uds. esta alcoba, chicas.

INÉS Insistimos en que nos deje ayudarla a preparar la comida.
SRA. VIVES No, chicos, no es para tanto, pero gracias por la oferta. Descansen un rato que seguramente están cansados.
ÁLEX Gracias. A mí me gustaría pasear por la ciudad.

INÉS Perdone, don Francisco, ¿a qué hora viene el guía mañana?
DON FRANCISCO ¿Martín? Viene temprano, a las siete de la mañana. Les aconsejo que se acuesten temprano esta noche. ¡Nada de televisión ni de conversaciones largas!
ESTUDIANTES ¡Ay, don Francisco!

Expresiones útiles

Welcoming people
¡Bienvenido(s)/a(s)!
Welcome!

Showing people around the house
Síganme, que quiero mostrarles la casa.
Follow me, I want to show you the house.
Allí están la cocina y el comedor.
The kitchen and dining room are over there.
Al fondo del pasillo hay un baño.
At the end of the hall there is a bathroom.

Telling people what to do
Quiero que la ayude(n) con los quehaceres domésticos.
I want you to help her with the household chores.
Quiero que arregle(n) su(s) alcoba(s).
I want you to straighten your room(s).
Quiero que haga(n) las camas.
I want you to make the beds.
Quiero que ponga(n) la mesa.
I want you to set the table.
Cuente con nosotros.
You can count on us.
Insistimos en que nos deje ayudarla a preparar la comida.
We insist that you let us help you make the food.
Le(s) aconsejo que se acueste(n) temprano.
I advise you to go to bed early.

Other expressions
No es para tanto.
It's not a big deal.
Gracias por la oferta.
Thanks for the offer.

¿Qué piensas?

1 **¿Cierto o falso?** Indica si las siguientes frases son **ciertas** o **falsas**. Corrige las frases falsas.

Cierto   Falso

_____   _____   1. La alcoba de los chicos tiene dos camas,
dos mesitas de noche y una cómoda.
_____

_____   _____   2. La señora Vives no quiere que Javier ponga
las maletas en la cama.
_____

_____   _____   3. El sofá y los sillones están en la sala.
_____

_____   _____   4. Los estudiantes tienen que sacudir
los muebles y sacar la basura.
_____

_____   _____   5. Los estudiantes van a preparar las comidas.
_____

2 **En la casa de Ibarra** Contesta las preguntas.

1. ¿Quién les muestra la casa a los estudiantes?
_____

2. Si Álex y Javier necesitan mantas y almohadas, ¿dónde deben buscarlas?
_____

3. ¿Quién les dice a los estudiantes que deben ayudar a la Sra. Vives?
_____

4. ¿Quién dice que los estudiantes pueden ayudar a preparar la comida?
_____

5. ¿A qué hora va a llegar el guía mañana?
_____

3 **Mi casa** Dibuja el plano (*floor plan*) de una casa o un apartamento donde te gustaría vivir.
Después, en parejas, comenten las actividades que se pueden realizar (*can be carried out*)
en las distintas habitaciones. Pueden usar estas frases en su conversación.

Quiero mostrarte…	**Allí yo (preparo la comida).**
Al fondo hay…	**Ésta es (la cocina).**
Aquí es donde **yo (pongo la basura).**	

Exploración
La vivienda en el mundo hispano

Muchas casas antiguas en España y América Latina están construidas alrededor de un patio central. Desde el patio, se pueden ver las puertas de todas las habitaciones.

En el lago de Maracaibo, en Venezuela, hay casas que se llaman palafitos, suspendidas sobre el agua. Los palafitos son reminiscentes de la ciudad italiana de Venecia, de donde viene el nombre "Venezuela", que significa "pequeña Venecia".

Las casas colgantes (*hanging*) de Cuenca, España, son muy famosas. Estas casas están situadas en un acantilado (*cliff*) y forman parte del paisaje único (*unique landscape*) de la ciudad.

Observaciones

- Los aztecas de México tenían sistemas de drenaje (*sewer systems*) en sus viviendas.
- La Gran Francia en Granada, Nicaragua, es una antigua casa colonial convertida en hotel.
- La Casa de las Gárgolas (*gargoyles*), en Santo Domingo, tiene seis gárgolas en su fachada (*façade*). Se dice que vienen de la Catedral de Santo Domingo.

Coméntalo

Con un(a) compañero/a, contesta las siguientes preguntas.

- ¿Cuál de las viviendas mencionadas en esta página te interesa más? ¿Por qué?
- En tu comunidad, ¿dónde vive la mayoría de la gente: en casas o en apartamentos?
- Describe tu casa o apartamento ideal.

recursos

R vistahigher learning.com

12.1 Formal (Ud. and Uds.) commands

▸ Command forms are used to give orders or advice. Use formal commands with people you address as **Ud.** or **Uds.**

Hable con ellos, don Francisco.
Talk to them, Don Francisco.

Coma frutas y verduras.
Eat fruits and vegetables.

Laven los platos ahora mismo.
Wash the dishes right now.

Beban menos té y café.
Drink less tea and coffee.

▸ The **Ud.** and **Uds.** commands are formed by dropping the final **–o** of the **yo** form of the present tense. For **–ar** verbs, add **–e** or **–en**. For **–er** and **–ir** verbs, add **–a** or **–an**.

Formal commands (*Ud.* and *Uds.*)

Infinitive	Present tense *yo* form	*Ud.* command	*Uds.* command
barrer	barro	barra	barran
decir	digo	diga	digan
limpiar	limpio	limpie	limpien
sacudir	sacudo	sacuda	sacudan
salir	salgo	salga	salgan
servir	sirvo	sirva	sirvan
venir	vengo	venga	vengan
volver	vuelvo	vuelva	vuelvan

No se preocupe... La vamos a ayudar en todo lo posible.

Sí, cuente con nosotros.

▸ Verbs with irregular **yo** forms have the same irregularity in their formal commands. These verbs include **conducir, conocer, decir, hacer, ofrecer, oír, poner, salir, tener, traducir, traer, venir,** and **ver**.

Oiga, don Francisco…
Listen, Don Francisco…

¡Salga inmediatamente!
Leave immediately!

Ponga la mesa, por favor.
Set the table, please.

Hagan la cama antes de salir.
Make the bed before leaving.

▸ Stem-changing verbs maintain their stem changes in **Ud.** and **Uds.** commands.

e:ie
No **pierda** la llave.
Cierren la puerta.

o:ue
Vuelva temprano, joven.
Duerman bien, chicos.

e:i
Sirva la sopa, por favor.
Repitan las frases.

Práctica

1 **Consejos para la Sra. González** La Sra. González quiere mudarse. Ayúdala a organizarse, indicando el mandato (*command*) formal de cada verbo.

1. _____ [leer] los anuncios (*ads*) del periódico y _____ [guardarlos].

2. _____ [ir] personalmente y _____ [ver] las casas Ud. misma.

3. Decida qué casa quiere y _____ [llamar] al agente. _____ [pedirle] un contrato de alquiler.

4. _____ [alquilar] un camión (*truck*) para el día de la mudanza (*moving day*) y _____ [preguntarles] la hora exacta de llegada.

5. _____ [decirles] a todos en casa que tienen que ayudar. No _____ [decirles] que Ud. va a hacerlo todo.

6. _____ [tomar] tiempo para hacer las maletas tranquilamente. No _____ [hacerles] las maletas a los niños más grandes.

7. El día de la mudanza no _____ [estar] nerviosa.

8. No _____ [preocuparse]. _____ [saber] que todo va a salir bien.

2 **¿Qué dicen?** Mira los dibujos y escribe un mandato lógico para cada uno.

1. _____

4. _____

2. _____

5. _____

3. _____

6. _____

Conversación

 Problemas y soluciones Trabajen en parejas para hablar de los siguientes problemas. Usen mandatos y túrnense para ofrecer soluciones.

> **modelo**
> Me torcí el tobillo jugando al tenis.
> Es la tercera vez.
> **Estudiante 1:** Me torcí el tobillo jugando
> al tenis. Es la tercera vez.
> **Estudiante 2:** No juegue más al tenis. /
> Vaya a ver a un médico.

1. Me enfermé después de volver de las vacaciones.
2. Mi compañero/a de cuarto y yo siempre llegamos tarde a la clase.
3. Nuestra casa es demasiado pequeña para nuestra familia.
4. Se me cayó la botella de vino que traía para la cena.
5. Se me perdió el libro de español en la biblioteca.
6. Se nos quedaron los pasajes en casa. El avión sale en una hora.
7. ¡Se me olvidó estudiar para el examen!

 Un programa de consejos En parejas, túrnense para representar los papeles de una persona que da consejos en la radio y los radioyentes (*radio listeners*) que la llaman con los siguientes problemas.

- problemas sentimentales o familiares
- problemas académicos
- problemas con los amigos
- problemas financieros
- problemas médicos
- problemas con la casa o el apartamento
- problemas con el coche

5 **Un anuncio de televisión** En grupos, presenten un anuncio de televisión (*TV commercial*) a la clase. Debe tratar de (*be about*) un detergente, un electrodoméstico o una agencia de bienes raíces. Usen mandatos, los pronombres relativos (**que, quien(es)** o **lo que**) y el **se** impersonal.

> **modelo**
> Compre el lavaplatos Corona. Tiene todo lo que Ud. desea. Es el lavaplatos que mejor funciona. Venga a verlo ahora mismo... No pierda ni un minuto más. Se aceptan tarjetas de crédito.

Irregular commands

▶ Verbs ending in **-car, -gar,** and **-zar** have a spelling change in the command forms.

sacar	c	qu	saque, saquen
jugar	g	gu	juegue, jueguen
almorzar	z	c	almuerce, almuercen

▶ The following verbs have irregular formal commands.

INFINITIVE	Ud. COMMAND	Uds. COMMAND
dar	dé	den
estar	esté	estén
ir	vaya	vayan
saber	sepa	sepan
ser	sea	sean

▶ To make a command negative, place **no** before the verb.

No ponga las maletas en la cama.
Don't put the suitcases on the bed.

No ensucien los sillones.
Don't dirty the armchairs.

▶ In affirmative commands, reflexive and object pronouns are attached to the end of the verb. Note that when a pronoun is attached to a verb that has two or more syllables, an accent mark is added.

Siéntense, por favor.
Dígamelo.

Acuéstense ahora.
Pónganlas en el suelo, por favor.

▶ In negative commands, the pronouns precede the verb.

No se preocupe.
No me lo dé.

No los ensucien.
No nos las traigan.

▶ **Ud.** and **Uds.** can be used after command forms for a more formal, polite tone.

Muéstrele Ud. la foto a su amigo.
Show the photo to your friend.

Tomen Uds. esta alcoba.
Take this bedroom.

¡Manos a la obra!

 Indica los mandatos (*commands*) afirmativos y negativos.

	Afirmativo	Negativo
1. escucharlo (Ud.)	Escúchelo	No lo escuche
2. decírmelo (Uds.)	_____	_____
3. salir (Ud.)	_____	_____
4. servírnoslo (Uds.)	_____	_____
5. barrerla (Ud.)	_____	_____
6. hacerlo (Ud.)	_____	_____
7. ir (Uds.)	_____	_____
8. sentarse (Uds.)	_____	_____

12.2 The present subjunctive

▶ The subjunctive mood expresses the speaker's attitudes toward events, actions, or states that the speaker views as uncertain or hypothetical.

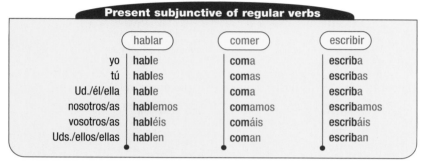

Present subjunctive of regular verbs

	hablar	comer	escribir
yo	hable	coma	escriba
tú	hables	comas	escribas
Ud./él/ella	hable	coma	escriba
nosotros/as	hablemos	comamos	escribamos
vosotros/as	habléis	comáis	escribáis
Uds./ellos/ellas	hablen	coman	escriban

▶ To form the present subjunctive of regular verbs, drop the **–o** ending from the **yo** form of the present indicative, and replace it with the subjunctive endings.

INFINITIVE	PRESENT INDICATIVE	PRESENT SUBJUNCTIVE
hablar	hablo	hable
comer	como	coma
escribir	escribo	escriba

▶ Verbs with irregular **yo** forms in the present indicative tense have the same irregularity in the present subjunctive.

INFINITIVE	PRESENT INDICATIVE	PRESENT SUBJUNCTIVE
conducir	conduzco	conduzca
conocer	conozco	conozca
decir	digo	diga
hacer	hago	haga
ofrecer	ofrezco	ofrezca
oír	oigo	oiga
parecer	parezco	parezca
poner	pongo	ponga
tener	tengo	tenga
traducir	traduzco	traduzca
traer	traigo	traiga
venir	vengo	venga
ver	veo	vea

▶ To maintain the **-c, -g,** and **-z** sounds, verbs ending in **-car, -gar,** and **-zar** have a spelling change in all forms of the present subjunctive.

sacar	saque, saques, saque, saquemos, saquéis, saquen
jugar	juegue, juegues, juegue, juguemos, juguéis, jueguen
almorzar	almuerce, almuerces, almuerce, almorcemos, almorcéis, almuercen

Práctica

1 **Emparejar** Completa las oraciones conjugando los verbos indicados. Luego empareja las oraciones del primer grupo con las del segundo grupo.

1. Es mejor que _____ [nosotros, cenar] en casa.
2. Es importante que _____ [yo, tomar] algo para el dolor de cabeza.
3. Señora, es urgente que le _____ [yo, sacar] la muela. Parece que tiene una infección.
4. Es malo que Ana les _____ [dar] tantos dulces a los niños.
5. Es necesario que _____ [Uds., llegar] a la una de la tarde.
6. Es importante que _____ [nosotros, acostarse] temprano.

. . .

a. Es importante que _____ [ellos, comer] más verduras.
b. No, es mejor que _____ [nosotros, salir] a comer.
c. Y yo creo que es urgente que _____ [tú, llamar] al médico.
d. En mi opinión, no es necesario que _____ [nosotros, dormir] tanto.
e. ¿Ah, sí? ¿Es necesario que me _____ [yo, tomar] un antibiótico también?
f. Para llegar a tiempo, es necesario que _____ [nosotros, almorzar] temprano.

2 **Oraciones** Combina los elementos de las tres columnas para formar frases.

Expresiones	Sujetos	Actividades
Es bueno que	yo	hacer la cama
Es mejor que	mi hermano	levantarse
Es malo que	los padres	sacar la basura
Es importante que	Oprah Winfrey	gritar
Es necesario que	mis amigos	lavar los platos
Es urgente que	Calista Flockhart	cocinar
	mi profesor(a)	barrer el suelo
		despertarse
		ensuciar
		comer

Conversación

 3 **Minidiálogos** En parejas, completen los minidiálogos de una manera lógica usando el subjuntivo.

modelo

> **Miguelito:** Mamá, no quiero arreglar mi cuarto.
> **Sra. Casas:** Es necesario que lo arregles. Y es importante que sacudas los muebles también.

MIGUELITO Mamá, no quiero estudiar. Quiero salir a jugar con mis amigos.

SRA. CASAS _____.

. . .

MIGUELITO Mamá, es que no me gustan las verduras. Prefiero comer pasteles.

SRA. CASAS _____.

. . .

MIGUELITO ¿Tengo que poner la mesa, mamá?
SRA. CASAS _____.

. . .

MIGUELITO No me siento bien, mamá. Me duele todo el cuerpo y tengo fiebre.

SRA. CASAS _____.

4 **Entrevista** En parejas, usen estas preguntas para entrevistarse. Expliquen sus respuestas.

1. ¿Es importante que los niños ayuden con los quehaceres domésticos?

2. ¿Es urgente que los norteamericanos aprendan otras lenguas?

3. Si un(a) norteamericano/a quiere aprender francés, ¿es mejor que lo aprenda en Francia?

4. En tu universidad, ¿es necesario que los estudiantes vivan en residencias estudiantiles?

5. ¿Es bueno que todos los estudiantes practiquen algún deporte?

6. ¿Es importante que todos los estudiantes asistan a las clases?

▶ **-Ar** and **-er** stem-changing verbs have the same stem changes in the present subjunctive and in the present indicative tenses.

entender (e:ie)	entienda, entiendas, entienda, entendamos, entendáis, entiendan
pensar (e:ie)	piense, pienses, piense, pensemos, penséis, piensen
mostrar (o:ue)	muestre, muestres, muestre, mostremos, mostréis, muestren
volver (o:ue)	vuelva, vuelvas, vuelva, volvamos, volváis, vuelvan

▶ **–Ir** stem-changing verbs maintain the stem changes of the present indicative in the present subjunctive. In addition, the **nosotros/as** and **vosotros/as** forms also undergo a stem change, from unstressed **e** to **i**, and unstressed **o** to **u**.

dormir (o:ue)	duerma, duermas, duerma, durmamos, durmáis, duerman
pedir (e:i)	pida, pidas, pida, pidamos, pidáis, pidan
sentir (e:ie)	sienta, sientas, sienta, sintamos, sintáis, sientan

▶ These five verbs are irregular in the present subjunctive.

	dar	estar	ir	saber	ser
yo	dé	esté	vaya	sepa	sea
tú	des	estés	vayas	sepas	seas
Ud./él/ella	dé	esté	vaya	sepa	sea
nosotros/as	demos	estemos	vayamos	sepamos	seamos
vosotros/as	deis	estéis	vayáis	sepáis	seáis
Uds./ellos/ellas	den	estén	vayan	sepan	sean

¡ojo! The subjunctive form of **hay** is **haya**.

General uses of the subjunctive

▶ As you will soon learn, the subjunctive is mainly used to express: 1) will and influence, 2) emotion, 3) doubt, disbelief, and denial, and 4) indefiniteness and non-existence.

▶ The subjunctive is usually used in complex sentences that consist of a main clause and a subordinate clause. The main clause contains a verb or expression that triggers the use of the subjunctive. The word **que** connects the subordinate clause to the main clause.

▶ Some expressions are always followed by clauses in the subjunctive. These include:

Es bueno (malo, mejor) que...
It's good (bad, better) that...

Es importante (necesario, urgente) que...
It's important (necessary, urgent) that...

Es mejor que vayas con él.
It's better that you go with him.

Es urgente que sepa la verdad.
It's urgent that she know the truth.

12.3 Subjunctive with verbs of will and influence

▶ The subjunctive is used with verbs and expressions of will and influence.

Quiero que tengas **dientes más blancos.**

▶ Verbs of will and influence are often used when someone wants to affect the actions of other people.

Enrique **quiere** que **salgamos** a cenar.
Enrique wants us to go out for dinner.

Paola **prefiere** que **cenemos** en casa.
Paola prefers that we have dinner at home.

Ana **insiste** en que la **llamemos.**
Ana insists that we call her.

Mi madre nos **ruega** que **vayamos** a verla.
My mother begs us to come see her.

▶ Here are some verbs of will and influence.

Verbs of will and influence

aconsejar	to advise	pedir (e:i)	to ask (for)
desear	to wish; to desire	preferir (e:ie)	to prefer
importar	to be important; to matter	prohibir	to prohibit
		querer (e:ie)	to want
insistir (en)	to insist (on)	recomendar (e:ie)	to recommend
mandar	to order	rogar (o:ue)	to beg; to plead
necesitar	to need	sugerir (e:ie)	to suggest

▶ Some impersonal expressions convey will or influence, such as **es necesario que, es importante que, es mejor que,** and **es urgente que.**

Es importante que duermas bien.
It's important that you sleep well.

Es urgente que él lo **haga** hoy.
It's urgent that he do it today.

▶ When the main clause contains an expression of will or influence and the subordinate clause has a different subject, the subjunctive is required.

Main clause	Connector	Subordinate clause
VERB OF WILL	▼	SUBJUNCTIVE
Mi mamá prefiere	**que**	**yo** saque la basura.

Práctica

1 **Entre amigas** Completa el diálogo con las palabras indicadas.

ponga	sea	saber	haga
prohíbe	quiere	comas	diga
cocina	sé	ser	vaya

IRENE Tengo problemas con Vilma. ¿Qué me recomiendas que le _____?

JULIA Necesito _____ más para aconsejarte.

IRENE Me _____ que traiga dulces a la casa.

JULIA Tiene razón. Es mejor que tú no _____ dulces.

IRENE Quiero que _____ más flexible. Pero insiste en que yo _____ todo en la casa.

JULIA Yo _____ que Vilma _____ y hace los quehaceres todos los días.

IRENE Sí, pero siempre me pide que _____ los cubiertos en la mesa y que _____ al sótano por las servilletas.

JULIA ¡Vilma sólo _____ que ayudes en la casa!

2 **Unos consejos** Lee lo que dice cada persona. Luego da consejos lógicos usando verbos como **aconsejar, recomendar** y **prohibir**. Tus consejos deben ser diferentes de lo que la persona quiere hacer.

modelo

El presidente: Quiero comprar la Casa Blanca.
Le aconsejo que compre otra casa.

1. **Tu mamá:** Pienso poner la secadora en la entrada de la casa.

2. **Martha Stewart:** Voy a ir a la gasolinera para comprar unas elegantes copas de cristal.

3. **Tu amigo:** Voy a ponerme mi traje de baño en la clase.

4. **Tu primo:** Voy a comprar tazas y platos en el taller El Coche Feliz.

5. **Tu profesora:** No voy a poner servilletas para los cuarenta invitados.

6. **Enrique Iglesias:** Pienso poner todos mis muebles nuevos en el altillo.

7. **Shakira:** Hay una fiesta en mi casa esta noche, pero no quiero arreglar la casa.

8. **Tu papá:** Hoy no tengo ganas de hacer las camas.

Conversación

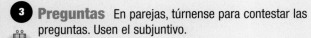

3 **Preguntas** En parejas, túrnense para contestar las preguntas. Usen el subjuntivo.

1. ¿Te dan consejos tus amigos? ¿Qué te aconsejan? ¿Aceptas sus consejos? ¿Por qué?

2. ¿Qué te sugieren tus profesores antes de terminar los cursos que tomas?

3. ¿Insisten tus amigos en que salgas mucho con ellos?

4. ¿Qué quieres que te regalen tu familia y tus amigos/as para tu cumpleaños?

5. ¿Qué le recomiendas tú a un(a) amigo/a que no quiere salir los sábados con su novio/a?

6. ¿Qué les aconsejas a los nuevos estudiantes de tu universidad?

4 **Recomendaciones** En parejas, preparen una lista de seis personas famosas. Un(a) estudiante da el nombre de una persona famosa y el/la otro/a le da un consejo.

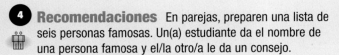

Estudiante 1: Judge Judy.
Estudiante 2: Le recomiendo que sea más simpática con la gente.
Estudiante 1: Leonardo DiCaprio.
Estudiante 2: Le aconsejo que haga más películas.

5 **El apartamento de Luisa** En parejas, miren la ilustración y denle consejos a Luisa sobre cómo arreglar su apartamento. Usen expresiones impersonales y verbos como **aconsejar, sugerir** y **recomendar**.

modelo

Es mejor que arregles el apartamento más a menudo. Te aconsejo que no dejes para mañana lo que puedas hacer hoy.

> *Quiero que arreglen sus alcobas, que hagan las camas, que pongan la mesa...*

> *...y les aconsejo que se acuesten temprano esta noche.*

▶ Indirect object pronouns are often used with verbs of permission, suggestion or request, such as **aconsejar, mandar, pedir, recomendar, rogar** and **sugerir**.

Te aconsejo que estudies.
I advise you to study.

Le sugiero que vaya a casa.
I suggest that he go home.

Les recomiendo que barran el suelo.
I recommend that you sweep the floor.

Le ruego que no venga.
I beg you not to come.

▶ All the forms of **prohibir** in the present tense carry a written accent, except for the **nosotros** form.

Ella les **prohíbe** que miren la televisión.
She prohibits them from watching television.

Nos **prohíben** que nademos en la piscina.
They prohibit us from swimming in the pool.

▶ The infinitive is used with expressions of will and influence if there is no change of subject.

No quiero **sacudir** los muebles.
I don't want to dust the furniture.

Paco prefiere **descansar**.
Paco prefers to rest.

Es importante **sacar** la basura.
It's important to take out the trash.

No es necesario **quitar** la mesa.
It's not necessary to clear the table.

¡Manos a la obra!

 Completa cada oración con la forma correcta del verbo indicado.

1. Te sugiero que ___vayas___ [ir] con ella al supermercado.
2. Él necesita que yo le _____ [prestar] dinero.
3. No queremos que tú _____ [hacer] nada especial para nosotros.
4. Mis papás quieren que yo _____ [limpiar] mi cuarto.
5. Nos piden que la _____ [ayudar] a preparar la comida.
6. Quieren que tú _____ [sacar] la basura todos los días.
7. Quiero _____ [descansar] esta noche.
8. Es importante que Uds. _____ [limpiar] la casa.
9. Su tía les manda que _____ [poner] la mesa.
10. Te aconsejo que no _____ [salir] con él.
11. Mi tío insiste en que mi prima _____ [hacer] la cama.
12. Prefiero _____ [ir] al cine.
13. Es necesario _____ [estudiar].
14. Recomiendo que ustedes _____ [pasar] la aspiradora.

Ampliación

1 Escuchar

A Mira los anuncios en esta página y escucha la conversación entre el Sr. Núñez, Adriana y Felipe. Luego indica si cada descripción se refiere a la casa ideal de Adriana y Felipe, a la casa del anuncio o al apartamento del anuncio.

 TIP Use visual cues. Visual cues, like illustrations and headings, provide useful clues about what you will hear. For example, what sort of visuals might appear in a real estate ad?

18G

Bienes raíces

 Se vende.
4 alcobas, 3 baños, cocina moderna, jardín con árboles frutales.
B/. 225.000

 Se alquila.
2 alcobas, 1 baño.
Balcón. Urbanización Las Brisas. 525

Descripciones	La casa ideal	La casa del anuncio	El apartamento del anuncio
1. Es barato.	☐	☐	☐
2. Tiene cuatro alcobas.	☐	☐	☐
3. Tiene una oficina.	☐	☐	☐
4. Tiene un balcón.	☐	☐	☐
5. Tiene una cocina moderna.	☐	☐	☐
6. Tiene un jardín muy grande.	☐	☐	☐
7. Tiene un patio.	☐	☐	☐

B Usa la información de los dibujos y la conversación para entender lo que dice Adriana al final. ¿Qué significa "todo a su debido tiempo"?

2 Conversar

Con un(a) compañero/a, preparen una conversación entre el Dr. Freud y un(a) paciente que lo consulta sobre un problema personal (la familia, el/la novio/a, etc.). Luego presenten la conversación a la clase.

modelo

Estudiante 1: Buenos días, Dr. Freud, me llamo Alicia. Mi mamá no quiere que yo vaya a ver a mis amigas. No le importa que me aburra. Me prohíbe conducir por la noche.

recursos

R	Textbook CD Lección 12	WB pp. 121-126	LM pp. 69-71	Lab CD Lección 12	ICD-ROM Lección 12	vistahigher learning.com

Ampliación

③ Escribir

Eres el/la administrador(a) de un edificio de apartamentos. Prepara un contrato de arrendamiento (*lease*) para los nuevos inquilinos (*tenants*).

 TIP **Use linking words.** To make your writing more sophisticated, use linking words to connect simple sentences or ideas. Some common linking words are: **y, o, cuando, mientras, pero, porque, pues, que, quien(es),** and **sino**.

Organízalo	Utiliza un mapa de ideas para organizar la información sobre las fechas del contrato, el precio del alquiler y otros aspectos importantes.
Escríbelo	Escribe el primer borrador de tu contrato de arrendamiento.
Corrígelo	Intercambia el contrato con un(a) compañero/a. Anota los aspectos mejor escritos (*written*), especialmente el uso de las palabras de enlace (*linking words*). Ofrécele sugerencias, y si ves algunos errores, coméntaselos.
Compártelo	Revisa el primer borrador según las indicaciones de tu compañero/a. Incorpora nuevas ideas y/o más información si es necesario, antes de escribir la versión final.

> Here are some technical terms that might help you in writing your contract:
> **arrendatario** (tenant);
> **arrendador** (landlord);
> **propietario** (owner);
> **estipulaciones** (stipulations);
> **parte** (party);
> **de anticipación, de antelación** (in advance).

④ Un paso más

Imagina que quieres construir una casa de vacaciones en un país hispano. Prepara para la clase una presentación sobre la casa. Toma en cuenta las siguientes preguntas.

- ¿Dónde quieres construir la casa? ¿Prefieres que esté en la selva (*jungle*), en una isla, en una montaña o en un lugar con vistas al mar?

- ¿Cómo va a ser la casa? ¿Quieres que sea grande? ¿Cuántos pisos y cuántos cuartos va a tener?

- ¿Qué efectos visuales puedes usar para hacer más interesante la presentación? ¿Tienes mapas, fotos o planos (*blueprints*) de la casa?

- ¿Qué muebles quieres poner en cada cuarto?

 En Internet

Investiga estos temas en el sitio vistahigherlearning.com.
- Lugares turísticos del mundo hispano
- Agencias de bienes raíces en el mundo hispano
- Mueblerías (*furniture stores*) en el mundo hispano

Antes de leer

Did you know that a text written in Spanish is often longer than the same text written in English? Because the Spanish language often uses more words to express ideas, you may encounter a few long sentences when reading in Spanish. Of course, the length of sentences varies with genre and with authors' individual styles. To help you understand long sentences, identify the main parts of the sentence before trying to read it in its entirety. First, locate the main verb of the sentence, along with its subject, ignoring any words or phrases set off by commas. Then re-read the sentence, adding details like direct and indirect objects, transitional words, and prepositional phrases. Practice this strategy on a few sentences from this reading selection.

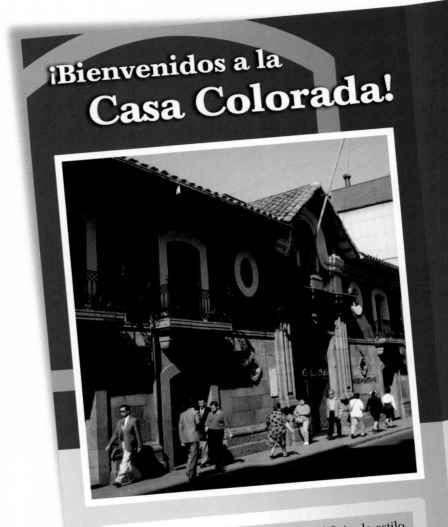

¡Bienvenidos a la Casa Colorada!

La Casa Colorada es un atractivo edificio de estilo colonial, construido en 1769. Está situado en el centro de Santiago de Chile, en la calle Merced. En sus orígenes fue la vivienda de Mateo de Toro y Zambrano, un aristócrata chileno conocido por sus actividades en el ejército, los negocios y la administración de la ciudad. En la actualidad, la Casa Colorada no está habitada por nadie.

El edificio se convirtió en un espacio público en el siglo XX y en su interior están el Museo de Santiago, la Oficina de Turismo y la Fundación de Vicente Huidobro, donde se encuentra abundante información sobre la vida y la obra de este escritor chileno. El Museo de Santiago ofrece una exhibición permanente sobre la historia de la ciudad, desde la época precolombina hasta nuestros días.

La Casa Colorada es una obra del arquitecto portugués Joseph de la Vega. Los materiales fundamentales que se utilizaron en su construcción fueron el adobe, la madera y la cal. Desde el primer momento, esta casa se convirtió en el centro de atención de la sociedad santiaguina por la elegancia de su diseño. Además, una característica que la diferenciaba de otras viviendas del mismo estilo arquitectónico es que su fachada estaba recubierta de piedra hasta el primer piso. El edificio empezó a llamarse Casa Colorada en 1888, año en que pintaron su fachada de color rojo.

La composición exterior del edificio es simétrica. En el centro de la fachada hay una gran puerta que sirve de acceso principal a la vivienda; a los lados se ven unos arcos que forman puertas adicionales en el primer piso y ventanas con balcones de hierro forjado en el segundo. Otra característica interesante del exterior de la casa es la elevación triangular del tejado sobre la puerta principal.

Después de leer

¿Comprendiste?

Completa las frases con las palabras adecuadas.

1. En el siglo XVIII, Mateo de Toro y Zambrano, un aristócrata de _____ , vivió en la Casa Colorada.
2. Ahora _____ vive en la Casa Colorada.
3. El exterior de la casa es de color _____ .
4. La _____ principal está en el centro de la fachada.
5. Los materiales que se utilizaron en su construcción fueron
_____ .
6. En el Museo de Santiago hay una exhibición sobre la _____ de la ciudad.

Preguntas

1. ¿Cómo se llamaba el arquitecto de la Casa Colorada?
_____
2. ¿Cuándo se construyó la Casa Colorada?
_____
3. ¿Cuándo se convirtió en lugar público?
_____
4. ¿Por qué este edificio se llama la Casa Colorada?
_____
5. ¿Por qué la Casa Colorada se diferenciaba de otras viviendas del mismo estilo arquitectónico?
_____
6. ¿Dónde están el Museo de Santiago, la Oficina de Turismo y la Fundación de Vicente Huidobro?
_____

Coméntalo

¿Te gustaría visitar la Casa Colorada? ¿Por qué? ¿Te gustaría vivir en una casa similar a ésta? Explica tu respuesta. ¿Hay edificios históricos en tu ciudad o comunidad? Descríbelos.

ejército	*army*
negocios	*business*
En la actualidad	*At the present time*
siglo	*century*
obra	*work*
madera	*wood*
cal	*lime*
santiaguina	*of Santiago*
diseño	*design*
fachada	*façade*
recubierta de piedra	*covered with stone*
hierro forjado	*wrought iron*
tejado	*roof*

recursos

R

vistahigher
learning.com

La vivienda

las afueras	suburbs; outskirts
la agencia de bienes raíces	real estate agency
el alquiler	rent (payment)
el ama (m., f.) de casa	housekeeper; caretaker
el barrio	neighborhood
el edificio de apartamentos	apartment building
el hogar	home
el/la vecino/a	neighbor
la vivienda	housing
alquilar	to rent
mudarse	to move (residences)

Cuartos y otros lugares

la alcoba	bedroom
el altillo	attic
el balcón	balcony
la cocina	kitchen
el comedor	dining room
la entrada	entrance
la escalera	stairs; stairway
el garaje	garage
el jardín	garden; yard
la oficina	office
el pasillo	hallway
el patio	patio
la sala	living room
el sótano	basement; cellar

Muebles y otras cosas

la alfombra	rug
la almohada	pillow
el armario	closet
la cómoda	chest of drawers
las cortinas	curtains
el cuadro	painting
el estante	bookcase; bookshelves
la lámpara	lamp
la luz	light
la manta	blanket
la mesita	side/end table
la mesita de noche	night stand
los muebles	furniture
la pared	wall
la pintura	painting; picture
el sillón	armchair
el sofá	couch; sofa

Electrodomésticos

la estufa	stove
el electrodoméstico	electric appliance
el horno (de microondas)	(microwave) oven
la lavadora	washing machine
el lavaplatos	dishwasher
el refrigerador	refrigerator
la secadora	clothes dryer

La mesa

la copa	wineglass; goblet
la cuchara	spoon
el cuchillo	knife
el plato	plate
la servilleta	napkin
la taza	cup
el tenedor	fork
el vaso	glass

Quehaceres domésticos

arreglar	to neaten; to straighten up
barrer el suelo	to sweep the floor
cocinar	to cook
ensuciar	to get (something) dirty
hacer la cama	to make the bed
hacer los quehaceres domésticos	to do household chores
lavar (el suelo, los platos)	to wash (the floor, the dishes)
limpiar la casa	to clean the house
pasar la aspiradora	to vacuum
planchar la ropa	to iron clothes
poner la mesa	to set the table
quitar la mesa	to clear the table
sacar la basura	to take out the trash
sacudir los muebles	to dust the furniture

Expresiones útiles	See page 289.
Verbs and expressions of will and influence	See page 296.

recursos

R	Lab CD Lección 12	LM p. 71

AVENTURAS EN LOS PAÍSES HISPANOS

La ropa tradicional de los guatemaltecos se llama *huipil* y muestra el amor de la cultura maya por la naturaleza *(nature)*. Tiene colores vivos y los diseños *(designs)* indican el origen, la edad y el sexo de la persona que lo lleva.

AMÉRICA CENTRAL I

Guatemala

Área: 108.890 km^2 (42.042 millas^2)

Población: 12.627.000

Capital: Ciudad de Guatemala – 3.741.000

Ciudades principales:
Quetzaltenango –104.000, Escuintla–70.000, Mazatenango–44.000, Puerto Barrios–40.000

Moneda: quetzal

SOURCE: Population Division, UN Secretariat

Honduras

Área: 112.492 km^2 (43.870 millas^2)

Población: 7.044.000

Capital: Tegucigalpa – 1.083.000

Ciudades principales: San Pedro Sula–500.000, El Progreso–82.000

Moneda: lempira

SOURCE: Population Division, UN Secretariat

El Salvador

Área: 21.040 km^2 (8.124 millas^2)

Población: 6.759.000

Capital: San Salvador – 1.496.000

Ciudades principales: Apopa–402.000, Santa Ana–168.000, San Miguel–187.000

Moneda: colón

SOURCE: Population Division, UN Secretariat

Map labels

Sierra de Lacandón

Lago Petén Itza

BELICE

MÉXICO

Río Usumacinta

Río de la Pasión

Golfo de Honduras

Lago de Izabal

Puerto Barrios

La Ceiba

GUATEMALA

San Pedro Su...

Río Motagua

Sierra Espíritu Santo

El Progreso

Sierra Madre

Sierra Grita

Sierra Ri...

Lago de Atitlán

Ciudad de
Guatemala

Lago de Yojoa

Lago de Guija

Tegucigalpa

Quetzaltenango

Mazatenango

Antigua Guatemala

Río Lempa

Escuintla

Río de la Paz

Santa Ana

San Salvador

La Libertad

San Miguel

Río Cho...

Río Lempa

La Unión

EL SALVADOR

Océano Pacífico

La Antigua Guatemala

La Antigua Guatemala era la capital del país, hasta que un
terremoto *(earthquake)* la destruyó *(destroyed)* en 1773. Tiene
una arquitectura colonial hermosa y es un importante
centro turístico de Guatemala. La Antigua Guatemala es
también muy famosa en el mundo por su celebración anual
de la Semana Santa *(Holy Week)*.

Mar Caribe

Islas de la Bahía

HONDURAS

rra de Payas

Río Patuca

Montañas de Colón

Río Coco

Laguna de Caratasca

NICARAGUA

COSTA RICA

Lugares

Copán

Copán está en Honduras, en el límite *(border)* con Guatemala. Miles de turistas van a las ruinas mayas de Copán durante todo el año. Los mayas fueron una antigua *(ancient)* civilización indígena que vivió en el sur de México, Guatemala, Honduras y El Salvador por más de 2.000 años. Era una civilización muy avanzada. Construyeron *(built)* pirámides, templos y observatorios. También descubrieron *(discovered)* y usaron el cero antes que los europeos e hicieron un calendario complejo y preciso. Una de las actividades más importantes de Copán era la astronomía. Allí se hacían congresos *(conventions)* de astrónomos.

Naturaleza

El Parque Nacional Montecristo

El Parque Nacional Montecristo está en el norte de El Salvador, en el límite con Honduras y Guatemala. Este bosque *(forest)* tiene árboles *(trees)* muy altos que forman una bóveda *(vault)* natural. La luz del sol no puede pasar a través de *(through)* ella. El bosque tiene un 100% de humedad. Allí hay muchas especies interesantes de plantas y animales, como orquídeas, hongos *(fungi)*, pumas, quetzales y tucanes.

¿Qué aprendiste?

1 **¿Cierto o falso?** Indica si las siguientes frases son **ciertas** o **falsas**.

	Cierto	Falso
1. La ropa tradicional de los guatemaltecos se llama Quetzaltenango.	_____	_____
2. Los diseños del *huipil* indican el origen de la persona que lo lleva.	_____	_____
3. Tegucigalpa es la capital de Honduras.	_____	_____
4. La lempira es la moneda de Guatemala.	_____	_____
5. Los mayas descubrieron el cero antes que los europeos.	_____	_____
6. En Copán se hacían congresos de geografía.	_____	_____
7. La Antigua Guatemala es la capital de Guatemala.	_____	_____
8. La Antigua Guatemala es muy famosa por su celebración de la Semana Santa.	_____	_____
9. El Parque Nacional Montecristo está en El Salvador, en el límite con Honduras y Guatemala.	_____	_____
10. El bosque del Parque Nacional Montecristo tiene un 50% de humedad.	_____	_____

2 **Preguntas** Contesta las siguientes preguntas.

1. ¿Qué muestra el *huipil*? ¿Qué indican sus diseños?
2. ¿Crees que los países de esta lección son muy poblados *(populated)* o poco poblados?
3. ¿Crees que la civilización maya era avanzada? ¿Por qué?
4. ¿Por qué crees que la Antigua Guatemala es un importante centro turístico?
5. ¿Por qué la luz del sol no puede pasar a través de los árboles del Parque Nacional Montecristo?

En Internet

Busca más información sobre estos temas en el sitio vistahigherlearning.com. Presenta la información a tus compañeros/as de clase.

- Copán
- La Antigua Guatemala
- El Parque Nacional Montecristo

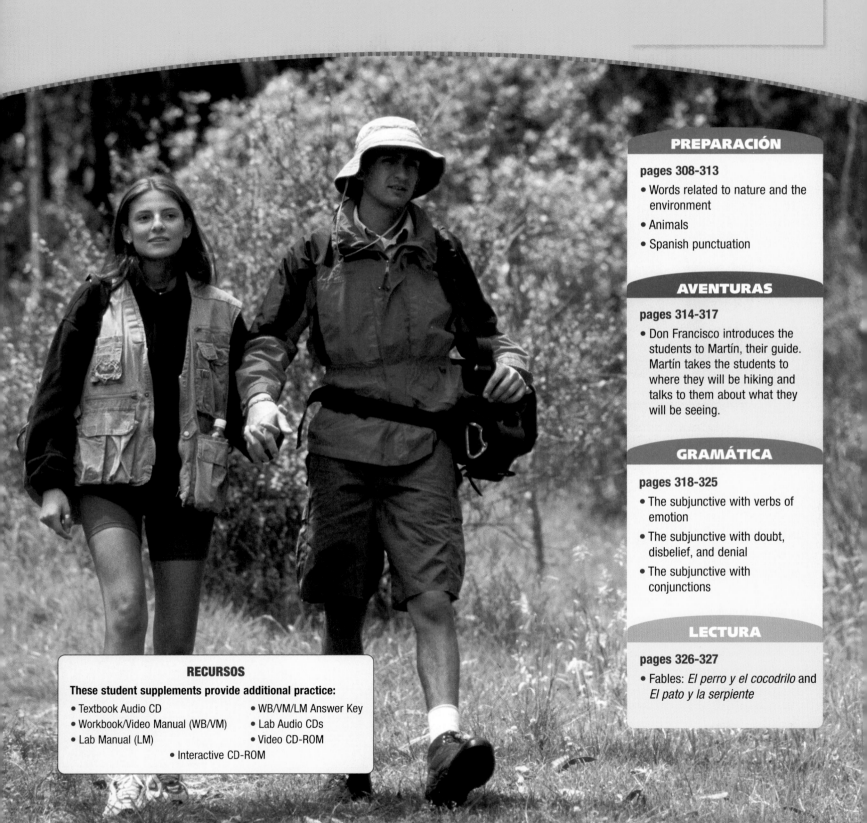

13 La naturaleza

Communicative Goals

You will learn how to:
- talk about the natural world
- discuss environmental conditions
- express wishes, desires, and doubts

RECURSOS

These student supplements provide additional practice:
- Textbook Audio CD
- Workbook/Video Manual (WB/VM)
- Lab Manual (LM)
- WB/VM/LM Answer Key
- Lab Audio CDs
- Video CD-ROM
- Interactive CD-ROM

LA NATURALEZA

el volcán
volcano

LA NATURALEZA

el árbol *tree*
el bosque (tropical) *(tropical; rain) forest*
el cielo *sky*
el cráter *crater*
el desierto *desert*
la estrella *star*
la hierba *grass*
el lago *lake*
la luna *moon*
el mundo *world*
la naturaleza *nature*
la nube *cloud*
el océano *ocean*
el paisaje *landscape*
la piedra *rock; stone*
la planta *plant*
la región *region; area*
el río *river*
la selva *jungle*
el sendero *trail*
el sol *sun*
la tierra *land; soil*
el valle *valley*

la flor
flower

EL MEDIO AMBIENTE

la conservación *conservation*
la contaminación (del aire; del agua) *(air; water) pollution*
la ecología *ecology*
el ecoturismo *ecotourism*
la energía (solar) *(solar) energy*
la extinción *extinction*
el gobierno *government*
la ley *law*
la lluvia (ácida) *(acid) rain*
el medio ambiente *environment*
el peligro *danger*
la población *population*
el reciclaje *recycling*
el recurso natural *natural resource*
la solución *solution*

la energía nuclear
nuclear energy

la deforestación
deforestation

recursos

R	Textbook CD Lección 13	WB pp. 131–132	LM p. 73	Lab CD Lección 13	ICD-ROM Lección 13

el gato
cat

el animal *animal*

el pez *fish*

la vaca *cow*

el perro
dog

VERBOS

conservar *to conserve*

contaminar *to pollute*

controlar *to control*

cuidar *to take care of*

dejar de + (inf.) *to stop (doing something)*

desarrollar *to develop*

descubrir *to discover*

destruir *to destroy*

estar afectado/a (por) *to be affected (by)*

evitar *to avoid*

mejorar *to improve*

proteger *to protect*

reciclar *to recycle*

recoger *to pick up*

reducir *to reduce*

resolver (o:ue) *to resolve; to solve*

respirar *to breathe*

el pájaro
bird

la botella de vidrio
glass bottle

OTRAS PALABRAS Y EXPRESIONES

el envase de plástico *plastic container*

puro/a *pure*

la lata de aluminio
aluminum can

estar contaminado/a
to be polluted

A escuchar

 1 **Escuchar** Mientras escuchas las frases, anota los sustantivos (*nouns*) que se refieren a **las plantas**, **los animales**, **la tierra** y **el cielo**.

Plantas	Animales	Tierra	Cielo
_____	_____	_____	_____
_____	_____	_____	_____
_____	_____	_____	_____

 2 **Seleccionar** Escucha las descripciones e indica qué foto corresponde a cada descripción.

a. _____

c. _____

b. _____

d. _____

recursos

Textbook CD
Lección 13

A practicar

3 **La naturaleza** ¿Qué palabra no está relacionada con cada grupo?

1. sol • desierto • luna • estrella
2. océano • lluvia • sendero • río
3. naturaleza • paisaje • ecoturismo • gato
4. piedra • pájaro • pez • perro
5. volcán • vaca • cráter • piedra
6. recurso natural • lluvia ácida • contaminación • deforestación
7. nube • aire • cielo • lago
8. solución • selva • bosque • desierto
9. lluvia • nube • peligro • cielo
10. valle • árbol • hierba • flor

4 **Completar** Completa las frases.

1. Si vemos basura en las calles, la debemos _____.
2. Los científicos trabajan para _____ nuevas soluciones.
3. Es necesario que todos trabajemos juntos para _____ los problemas del medio ambiente.
4. Debemos _____ el medio ambiente porque está en peligro.
5. Muchas leyes nuevas _____ el número de árboles que se pueden cortar (*cut down*).
6. Las primeras civilizaciones _____ cerca de los ríos, los lagos y los océanos.
7. Todas las personas del mundo _____ por la contaminación.
8. Los turistas deben tener cuidado de no _____ las regiones que visitan.
9. Podemos conservar los recursos si _____ el aluminio, el vidrio y el plástico.
10. La lluvia ácida, la contaminación y la deforestación _____ el medio ambiente.

contaminar	destruyen	reciclamosre
controlan	están afectadas	recoger
cuidan	mejoramos	resolver
descubrir	proteger	se desarrollaron

5 **Definir** Trabaja con un(a) compañero/a para definir o describir cada palabra.

¿Qué es el cielo?

El cielo está sobre la tierra y tiene nubes.

1. la población
2. un valle
3. la lluvia
4. la naturaleza
5. un desierto
6. la extinción
7. la ecología
8. un sendero

A conversar

6 **Entrevista** Pregúntale a un(a) compañero/a qué importancia tienen para él/ella los siguientes problemas. Luego, comparte los resultados con la clase.

modelo
la deforestación
Estudiante 1: ¿Qué importancia tiene la deforestación?
Estudiante 2: Pienso que el problema de la deforestación es importantísimo.

importantísimo *****	
muy importante ****	
importante ***	
poco importante **	
no es importante *	

Problemas	Importancia
1. la lluvia ácida	_____
2. la contaminación del agua	_____
3. la contaminación del aire	_____
4. la reducción de los recursos naturales	_____
5. la población de las ciudades	_____
6. los animales en peligro de extinción	_____

7 **Preguntas** Mira otra vez la lista de problemas de la práctica anterior (*previous*). Luego, con un(a) compañero/a, contesta las siguientes preguntas.

1. ¿Qué problema consideras tú el más grave? ¿Por qué?
2. ¿Cuál de esos problemas es el menos importante?
3. ¿Es necesario resolver el problema menos importante? ¿Por qué?
4. ¿Está en peligro el medio ambiente de tu ciudad o región? ¿Qué problemas hay?
5. ¿Qué se puede hacer para resolver esos problemas?

8 **Situaciones** Trabajen en grupos pequeños para representar una de las siguientes situaciones.

• Un(a) representante de una agencia ambiental (*environmental*) habla con el/la presidente/a de una compañía industrial que está contaminando un río o el aire.
• Un(a) guía de ecoturismo habla con un grupo sobre cómo disfrutar del (*to enjoy*) medio ambiente y conservarlo.
• Un(a) representante de la universidad habla con un grupo de nuevos estudiantes sobre la campaña (*campaign*) ambiental de la universidad y trata de reclutar (*tries to recruit*) miembros para un club que trabaja para la protección del medio ambiente.

Ortografía

Los signos de puntuación

In Spanish, as in English, punctuation marks are important because they help you express your ideas in a clear, organized way.

No podía ver las llaves. Las buscó por los estantes, las mesas, las sillas, el suelo; minutos después, decidió mirar por la ventana. Allí estaban…

The **punto y coma (;)**, the **tres puntos (…)**, and the **punto (.)** are used in very similar ways in Spanish and English.

Argentina, Brasil, Paraguay y Uruguay son miembros de Mercosur.

In Spanish, the **coma (,)** is not used before **y** or **o** in a series.

13,5%	29,2°	3.000.000	$2.999,99

In numbers, Spanish uses a **coma** where English uses a decimal point and a **punto** where English uses a comma.

¿Cómo te llamas?　　**¿Dónde está?**　　**¡Ven aquí!**　　**¡Hola!**

Questions in Spanish are preceded and followed by **signos de interrogación (¿ ?)**, and exclamations are preceded and followed by **signos de exclamación (¡ !)**.

Práctica Lee el párrafo e indica los signos de puntuación necesarios.

Ayer recibí la invitación de boda de Marta mi amiga colombiana inmediatamente empecé a pensar en un posible regalo fui al almacén donde Marta y su novio tenían una lista de regalos había de todo copas cafeteras tostadoras finalmente decidí regalarles un perro ya sé que es un regalo extraño pero espero que les guste a los dos

¿Palabras de amor? El siguiente diálogo tiene diferentes significados (*meanings*), dependiendo de los signos de puntuación que utilizas y el lugar donde los pones. Intenta encontrar los diferentes significados.

JULIÁN　me quieres

MARISOL　no puedo vivir sin ti

JULIÁN　me quieres dejar

MARISOL　no me parece mala idea

JULIÁN　no eres feliz conmigo

MARISOL　no soy feliz

¡Qué paisaje más hermoso!

Martín y los estudiantes visitan el sendero en las montañas.

DON FRANCISCO Chicos, les presento a Martín Dávalos, el guía de la excursión. Martín, nuestros pasajeros: Maite, Javier, Inés y Álex.

MARTÍN Mucho gusto. Voy a llevarlos al área donde vamos a ir de excursión mañana. ¿Qué les parece?

ESTUDIANTES ¡Sí! ¡Vamos!

MAITE ¡Qué paisaje más hermoso!

INÉS No creo que haya lugares más bonitos en el mundo.

JAVIER Entiendo que mañana vamos a cruzar un río. ¿Está contaminado?

MARTÍN En las montañas el río no parece estar afectado por la contaminación. Cerca de las ciudades, sin embargo, el río tiene bastante contaminación.

ÁLEX ¡Qué aire tan puro se respira aquí! No es como en la Ciudad de México..... Tenemos un problema gravísimo de contaminación.

MARTÍN A menos que resuelvan ese problema, los habitantes van a sufrir muchas enfermedades en el futuro.

INÉS Creo que todos debemos hacer algo para proteger el medio ambiente.

MAITE Yo creo que todos los países deben establecer leyes que controlen el uso de automóviles.

recursos

| R | Video/VCD-ROM Lección 13 | VM pp.193-194 | ICD-ROM Lección 13 |

Personajes

DON FRANCISCO

JAVIER

INÉS

ÁLEX

MAITE

MARTÍN

4

MARTÍN Esperamos que Uds. se diviertan mucho, pero es necesario que cuiden la naturaleza.

JAVIER Se pueden tomar fotos, ¿verdad?

MARTÍN Sí, con tal de que no toques las flores o las plantas.

5

ÁLEX ¿Hay problemas de contaminación en esta región?

MARTÍN La contaminación es un problema en todo el mundo. Pero aquí tenemos un programa de reciclaje. Si ves por el sendero botellas, papeles o latas, recógelos.

9

JAVIER Pero Maite, ¿tú vas a dejar de usar tu carro en Madrid?

MAITE Pues, voy a tener que usar el Metro… Pero tú sabes que mi coche es tan pequeñito… casi no contamina nada.

10

INÉS ¡Ven, Javier!

JAVIER ¡¡Ya voy!!

Expresiones útiles

Talking about the environment

No creo que haya lugares más bonitos en el mundo.
I don't think there are any prettier places in the world.

¿Hay problemas de contaminación en esta región?
Are there problems with pollution in this region/area?

Es un problema en todo el mundo.
It's a problem throughout the world.

El río no parece estar afectado por la contaminación.
The river does not seem to be affected by pollution.

El río tiene bastante contaminación.
The river is quite polluted.

Es necesario que cuiden la naturaleza.
It's necessary that you take care of nature.

Puedes tomar fotos, con tal de que no toques las plantas.
You can take pictures, provided that you don't touch the plants.

Tenemos un problema gravísimo de contaminación.
We have an extremely serious problem with pollution.

A menos que resuelvan el problema, los habitantes van a sufrir muchas enfermedades.
Unless they solve the problem, the inhabitants are going to suffer a lot of illnesses.

Si ves botellas, papeles o latas, recógelos.
If you see bottles, papers, or cans, pick them up.

¿Qué piensas?

1 **Seleccionar** Selecciona la opción más lógica para cada frase.

1. Martín va a llevar a los estudiantes al lugar donde van a
   a. contaminar el río.   b. bailar.
   c. ir de excursión.

2. El río está más afectado por la contaminación
   a. cerca de los bosques.   b. en las ciudades.
   c. en las montañas.

3. Martín quiere que los estudiantes
   a. recojan la basura de los senderos.   b. descubran nuevos senderos.
   c. no usen sus autos.

4. La contaminación del aire puede producir
   a. problemas de estómago.   b. enfermedades respiratorias.
   c. enfermedades mentales.

2 **Preguntas** Responde a las siguientes preguntas.

1. Según Martín, ¿qué es necesario que hagan los estudiantes? ¿Qué no pueden hacer?
   _____

2. ¿Qué problemas del medio ambiente mencionan Martín y los estudiantes?
   _____

3. ¿Qué cree Maite que deben hacer los países?
   _____

4. ¿Qué cosas se pueden reciclar en el programa que menciona Martín?
   _____

5. Si Maite no puede usar su carro en Madrid, ¿qué medio de transporte va a usar?
   _____

3 **Situación** Eres el/la guía de un grupo de turistas que quiere hacer una excursión a las montañas. Conversa con ellos/as (tus compañeros/as) sobre las cosas que van a ver y sobre lo que deben y no deben hacer durante la excursión.

Exploración
Atracciones naturales del mundo hispano

Nicaragua tiene más de 25 volcanes, como el Cerro Negro, en la zona pacífica del país. Algunos de ellos son activos y de vez en cuando entran en erupción (*erupt*).

Observaciones

- Hay más de 1.640 especies de pájaros en el Ecuador.

- El árbol de Tule en Oaxaca, México, tiene más de 2.000 años de edad y un diámetro de 10 metros —el más grande del mundo.

- La Bahía Piñas es el lugar de pesca más famoso de Panamá.

- En Puerto Rico, hay 16 especies nativas de coquí, ranas arbóreas (*tree frogs*).

- El volcán Momotombo de Nicaragua aparece frecuentemente en los versos del gran poeta nicaragüense Rubén Darío.

Muchas personas consideran que Guatemala es el país de la eterna primavera, por sus bellezas naturales. Para conservar los recursos naturales, en Guatemala se estableció un sistema de biotopos —parques nacionales y reservas naturales. Los biotopos sirven para preservar la flora y la fauna únicas del país.

En la Quebrada de los Cuervos, en Uruguay, se puede hacer turismo de aventura y, al mismo tiempo, estar en contacto con la naturaleza. Desde 1986, forma parte de la primera área natural protegida (*protected*) de Uruguay.

Coméntalo

Con un(a) compañero/a, contesta las siguientes preguntas.

- ¿Quieres visitar algunos de los lugares mencionados en esta página? ¿Por qué?
- ¿Cuáles son los lugares naturales más bonitos que conoces? ¿Cómo son?
- ¿Hay parques nacionales cerca de tu comunidad? ¿Qué se puede hacer allí?

recursos

R

vistahigher
learning.com

13.1 The subjunctive with verbs of emotion

Main clause	Connector	Subordinate clause
Marta espera	que	yo vaya al lago este fin de semana.

▶ When the main clause of a sentence expresses an emotion or feeling, the subjunctive is required in the subordinate clause.

Nos alegramos de que te **gusten** las flores.
We are happy that you like the flowers.

Siento que tú no **vengas** mañana.
I'm sorry that you're not coming tomorrow.

Temo que Ana no **pueda** ir mañana con nosotros.
I'm afraid that Ana won't be able to go with us tomorrow.

Le **sorprende** que Juan **sea** tan joven.
It surprises him that Juan is so young.

Esperamos que Uds. se diviertan mucho en la excursión.

Es triste que tengamos un problema grave de contaminación en la Ciudad de México.

Common verbs and expressions of emotion

alegrarse (de)	to be happy	tener miedo (de)	to be afraid (of)
esperar	to hope; to wish	es extraño	it's strange
gustar	to be pleasing; to like	es una lástima	it's a shame
		es ridículo	it's ridiculous
molestar	to bother	es terrible	it's terrible
sentir (e:ie)	to be sorry; to regret	es triste	it's sad
sorprender	to surprise	ojalá (que)	I hope (that);
temer	to be afraid; to fear		I wish (that)

Me molesta que la gente no **recicle** el plástico.
It bothers me that people don't recycle plastic.

Me gusta que **respiremos** aire limpio.
I like that we breathe clean air.

Es una lástima que no controlemos la deforestación.
It's a shame we don't control deforestation.

Espera que las leyes **cuiden** las selvas.
He hopes that the laws protect the jungles.

Práctica

1 **Olga y Sara** Completa el diálogo con palabras de la lista.

alegro	lleguen	puedan
encuentren	molesta	tengo miedo de
estén	ojalá	vayan
		visitar

OLGA Me alegro de que Adriana y Raquel _____ a Colombia.

SARA Sí. Es una lástima que _____ tarde. Ojalá que la universidad las ayude a buscar casa. _____ que no consigan dónde vivir.

OLGA Me _____ que seas tan pesimista. Yo espero que _____ gente simpática.

SARA Sí, ojalá. Van a estudiar la deforestación en las costas. Es triste que en tantos países los recursos naturales _____ en peligro.

OLGA Me _____ de que no se queden en la capital por la contaminación, pero _____ tengan tiempo de viajar por el país.

SARA Sí, espero que _____ ir al Museo del Oro. Sé que también esperan _____ la Catedral de Sal de Zipaquirá.

2 **Frases** Combina elementos de las tres columnas para formar frases.

modelo **Es triste que algunas personas no cuiden la naturaleza.**

Expresiones	Sujetos	Actividades
Me alegro de que	yo	desarrollar programas de reciclaje
Espero que	tú	proteger el medio ambiente
Es extraño que	el gobierno	
Me gusta que	el/la profesor(a)	destruir los bosques
Tengo miedo de que	la universidad	contaminar el aire
	las fábricas	poner en peligro la naturaleza
Es triste que	algunas personas	
Ojalá que	los centros comerciales	cuidar la naturaleza
	mis amigos y yo	

Conversación

3 **Diálogo** Usa los siguientes elementos para crear una conversación entre Juan y la madre de su novia. Añade palabras si es necesario. Luego, con un(a) compañero/a, preséntala a la clase.

1. Juan, / esperar / (tú) escribirle / Raquel. / Ser / tu / novia. / Ojalá / no / sentirse / sola
2. molestarme / (Ud.) decirme / lo que / tener / hacer. / Ahora / mismo / estarle / escribiendo
3. alegrarme / oírte / decir / eso. / Ser / terrible / estar / lejos / cuando / nadie / recordarte
4. señora, / ¡yo / tener / miedo / (ella) no recordarme / mí! / Ser / triste / estar / sin / novia
5. ser / ridículo / (tú) sentirte / así. / Tú / saber / ella / querer / casarse / contigo
6. ridículo / o / no, / sorprenderme / todos preocuparse / ella / y / (nadie) acordarse / mí

4 **Comentar** En parejas, conversen sobre su ciudad, sus clases o algún otro tema, usando expresiones como **me alegro de que, temo que** y **es extraño que.** Luego reaccionen a los comentarios de su compañero/a.

modelo

Estudiante 1: Me alegro de que vayan a limpiar el río.
Estudiante 2: Yo también. Me preocupa que el agua del río esté tan contaminada.
Estudiante 1: Espero que mis profesores de español y matemáticas den menos tarea.
Estudiante 2: Pues yo temo que todos mis profesores piensen dar más tarea.

5 **Problemas** Prepara una lista de problemas ecológicos que te preocupen. Luego, describe cada problema a varios compañeros. Escribe las soluciones que te ofrecen. Después, comparte la información con la clase.

Problemas	Soluciones
_____	_____
_____	_____
_____	_____
_____	_____
_____	_____
_____	_____
_____	_____
_____	_____

Using the subjunctive

▶ The infinitive is used after an expression of emotion when there is no change of subject.

Temo **llegar** tarde.
I'm afraid I'll arrive late.

Temo que mi novio **llegue** tarde.
I'm afraid my boyfriend will arrive late.

Me molesta **ver** el bosque tropical en peligro.
It bothers me to see the rain forest in danger.

Me alegro de que el gobierno **se preocupe** por el medio ambiente.
I'm happy that the government worries about the environment.

▶ The expression **ojalá (que)** is always followed by the subjunctive. The use of **que** is optional.

Ojalá (que) se conserven nuestros recursos naturales.
I hope (that) our natural resources will be conserved.

Ojalá (que) recojan la basura muy pronto.
I hope (that) they collect the garbage soon.

Esperamos
que nuestros hijos vean el cielo azul y que naden en aguas limpias...
Tenemos que enseñarles a conservar y reciclar.

¡Manos a la obra!

Completa las oraciones con las formas correctas de los verbos.

1. Ojalá que ellos ___descubran___ [descubrir] nuevas formas de energía.
2. Espero que Ana nos _____ [ayudar] a recoger la basura en la carretera.
3. Es una lástima que la gente no _____ [reciclar] más.
4. Esperamos _____ [proteger] el aire de nuestra comunidad.
5. Me alegro de que mis amigos _____ [querer] conservar la naturaleza.
6. A mis padres les gusta que nosotros _____ [participar] en programas de conservación.
7. Es ridículo _____ [contaminar] el medio ambiente.
8. Espero que tú _____ [venir] a la reunión (*meeting*) del Club de Ecología.
9. Siento que nuestras ciudades _____ [estar] afectadas por la contaminación.
10. Ojalá que yo _____ [poder] hacer algo para reducir la contaminación.

13.2 The subjunctive with doubt, disbelief, and denial

▶ The subjunctive is used with expressions of doubt, disbelief, and denial.

Main clause	Connector	Subordinate clause
Dudan	que	su hijo les diga la verdad.

▶ The subjunctive is used in a subordinate clause when there is a change of subject and the main clause implies negation or uncertainty.

¡No creo que haya lugares más bonitos en el mundo!

Dudo que el río esté contaminado aquí en las montañas.

Expressions of doubt, disbelief, or denial

dudar	to doubt	no es seguro	it's not certain
negar (e:ie)	to deny	no es verdad	it's not true
no creer	not to believe	es imposible	it's impossible
no estar seguro/a (de)	not to be sure	es improbable	it's improbable
no es cierto	it's not true; it's not certain	(no) es posible	it's (not) possible
		(no) es probable	it's (not) probable

El gobierno **niega** que el agua **esté** contaminada.
The government denies that the water is polluted.

Dudo que el gobierno **resuelva** el problema.
I doubt that the government will solve the problem.

▶ In English, the expression *it is probable/possible* indicates a fairly high degree of certainty. In Spanish, however, **es probable/posible** implies uncertainty and therefore triggers the subjunctive in the subordinate clause.

Es posible que **haya** menos bosques y selvas en el futuro.
It's possible that there will be fewer forests and jungles in the future.

Es muy probable que **contaminemos** el medio ambiente.
It's very probable that we pollute the environment.

Práctica

1 **Dudas** Carolina siempre miente. Expresa tus dudas sobre lo que Carolina está diciendo ahora.

> **modelo**
> El próximo año mi familia y yo vamos a ir de vacaciones por diez meses. [dudar]
> **¡Ja! Dudo que vayan de vacaciones por diez meses.**

1. Estoy escribiendo una novela en español. [no creer]

2. Mi tía es la directora del Sierra Club. [no ser verdad]

3. Dos profesores míos juegan para los Osos (*Bears*) de Chicago. [ser imposible]

4. Mi mejor amiga conoce al chef Emeril. [no ser cierto]

5. Mi padre es dueño del Centro Rockefeller. [no ser posible]

6. Yo ya tengo un doctorado en lenguas. [ser improbable]

2 **Conversación** Completa el diálogo. Luego dramatízalo con un(a) compañero/a.

RAÚL Uds. dudan que yo _____ [estudio/estudie]. No niego que a veces me _____ [divierto/divierta], pero no cabe duda de que _____ [tomo/tome] mis estudios en serio. Creo que no _____ [tienen/tengan] razón.

PAPÁ Es posible que tu mamá y yo no _____ [tenemos/tengamos] razón. Es cierto que a veces _____ [dudamos/dudemos] de ti. Pero no hay duda de que te _____ [pasas/pases] toda la noche en Internet y oyendo música. No es seguro que _____ [estás/estés] estudiando.

RAÚL Es verdad que _____ [uso/use] mucho Internet, pero ¿no es posible que _____ [es/sea] para buscar información para mis clases? ¡No hay duda de que Internet _____ [es/sea] el mejor recurso del mundo! Es obvio que Uds. _____ [piensan/piensen] que no hago nada, pero no es cierto.

PAPÁ No dudo que esta conversación nos _____ [va/vaya] a ayudar. Pero tal vez _____ [puedes/puedas] estudiar sin música.

Conversación

3 Hablando con un(a) burócrata En parejas, miren
la foto y preparen un diálogo interesante sobre el medio
ambiente entre un(a) activista y un(a) burócrata del gobierno
(*government bureaucrat*). Luego presenten la conversación a
la clase.

modelo

Activista: *Queremos reducir la contaminación del aire.*
Pero dudo que el gobierno nos ayude.

Burócrata: *Es obvio que el gobierno está haciendo*
muchas cosas para reducir la contaminación
del aire.

4 Adivinar Escribe cinco oraciones sobre tu vida presente
y futura. Cuatro deben ser falsas y sólo una debe ser cierta.
Preséntalas al grupo. El grupo adivina (*guesses*) cuál es la
oración cierta y expresa sus dudas sobre las falsas.

modelo

Estudiante 1: *Quiero irme un año a trabajar en la selva.*
Estudiante 2: *Dudo que te guste vivir en la selva.*
Estudiante 3: *En cinco años voy a ser presidente de*
los Estados Unidos.
Estudiante 2: *No creo que vayas a ser presidente de*
los Estados Unidos en cinco años. ¡Tal
vez en treinta! Algún día pienso enseñar
arte a los niños.
Estudiante 1: *No dudo que vas a ser profesor. Te*
gustan mucho los niños.

5 Debate Con un compañero/a, debate algunas de las
posibles soluciones a los problemas del medio ambiente.

modelo

Estudiante 1: *Para proteger el medio ambiente, creo*
que necesitamos una ley para controlar
el número de coches en cada familia.
Estudiante 2: *Dudo que sea posible controlar el*
número de coches. A muchas personas
*les gusta tener su propio (*own*) coche.*

▶ **Quizás** and **tal vez** imply an uncertain possibility and are usually
followed by the subjunctive.

Quizás haga sol mañana.
Perhaps it will be sunny tomorrow.

Tal vez veamos la luna esta noche.
Perhaps we will see the moon tonight.

▶ The indicative is used in a subordinate clause when the main clause
expresses certainty.

Expressions of certainty			
no dudar	*not to doubt*	estar seguro/a (de)	*to be sure of*
no cabe duda de	*there is no doubt*	es cierto	*it's true; it's certain*
no hay duda de	*there is no doubt*	es seguro	*it's certain*
no negar (e:ie)	*not to deny*	es verdad	*it's true*
		es obvio	*it's obvious*

No negamos que **hay** demasiados
carros en las carreteras.
We don't deny that there are too
many cars on the highways.

No hay duda de que el Amazonas **es**
uno de los ríos más largos del mundo.
There is no doubt that the Amazon is
one of the longest rivers in the world.

Es verdad que Colombia **es** un
país bonito.
It's true that Colombia is a
beautiful country.

Es cierto que los tigres **están** en peligro
de extinción.
It's certain that tigers are in danger
of extinction.

▶ The verb **creer** expresses belief or certainty, so it is followed by the
indicative. **No creer** implies doubt and is followed by the subjunctive.

No creo que **haya** vida en el
planeta Marte.
I don't believe that there is life
on planet Mars.

Creo que **debemos** usar exclusivamente
la energía solar.
I believe we should exclusively use
solar energy.

¡Manos a la obra!

Completa estas frases con la forma correcta del verbo.

1. Dudo que ellos __trabajen__ [trabajar].
2. Es cierto que él _____ [comer] mucho.
3. Es imposible que ellos _____ [salir].
4. Es probable que Uds. _____ [ganar].
5. No creo que ella _____ [volver].
6. Es posible que nosotros _____ [ir].
7. Dudamos que tú _____ [reciclar].
8. Creo que ellos _____ [jugar] al fútbol.
9. No niego que Uds. _____ [estudiar].
10. Es probable que ellos _____ [dormir].
11. Es posible que Marta _____ [llamar].
12. Tal vez Juan no nos _____ [oír].

13.3 The subjunctive with conjunctions

Conjunctions followed by the subjunctive

Se pueden tomar fotos, ¿verdad?

Sí, con tal de que no toques ni las flores ni las plantas.

A menos que resuelvan el problema, los habitantes van a sufrir muchas enfermedades.

▶ Conjunctions are words or phrases that connect other words and clauses in sentences. Certain conjunctions commonly introduce adverbial clauses, which describe *how, why, when,* and *where* an action takes place. The conjunctions listed below always require the subjunctive.

Conjunctions that require the subjunctive			
a menos que	*unless*	en caso (de) que	*in case (that)*
antes (de) que	*before*	para que	*so that*
con tal (de) que	*provided that*	sin que	*without*

Voy a dejar un recado **en caso de que** Gustavo me **llame**.
I'm going to leave a message in case Gustavo calls me.

Voy al supermercado **para que tengas** algo de comer.
I'm going to the supermarket so that you'll have something to eat.

Algunos animales van a morir **a menos que haya** leyes para protegerlos.
Some animals are going to die unless there are laws to protect them.

Voy a tomar esa clase **con tal de que** tú la **tomes** también.
I'm going to take that class provided that you take it too.

¡ojo! The infinitive is used after the prepositions **antes de, para,** and **sin** when there is no change of subject. Compare these sentences.

Te llamamos el viernes **antes de salir** de la casa.
We will call you on Friday before leaving the house.

Te llamamos mañana **antes de que salgas.**
We will call you tomorrow before you leave.

Tus padres trabajan muchísimo **para vivir** bien.
Your parents work very hard in order to live well.

Tus padres trabajan mucho **para que tú puedas** vivir bien.
Your parents work a lot so that you are able to live well.

Práctica

1 Una excursión La Sra. Montero habla de una excursión que quiere hacer con su familia. Completa las oraciones con la forma correcta de cada verbo.

1. Voy a llevar a mis hijos al parque para que _____ [aprender] sobre la naturaleza.

2. Vamos a pasar todo el día allí con tal de que todos nosotros _____ [tener] tiempo.

3. Vamos a alquilar bicicletas en cuanto _____ [llegar] al parque.

4. En bicicleta, podemos explorar el parque sin _____ [caminar] demasiado.

5. Vamos a bajar al cráter a menos que se _____ [prohibir].

6. Siempre llevamos al perro cuando _____ [ir] al parque.

7. En caso de que _____ [llover], vamos a regresar temprano a la casa.

8. Queremos almorzar a la orilla (*shore*) del río cuando _____ [tener] hambre.

9. Mis hijos van a ver muchas cosas interesantes antes de _____ [salir] del parque.

10. Una vez estuvimos en el parque hasta que uno de mis hijos _____ [dormirse].

2 Oraciones Completa las siguientes oraciones.

1. No podemos controlar la contaminación del aire a menos que…

2. Voy a reciclar los productos de papel en cuanto…

3. Protegemos los animales en peligro de extinción para que…

4. Mis amigos y yo vamos a recoger la basura de la universidad después de que…

5. Todos podemos conservar energía cuando…

6. No podemos desarrollar nuevas fuentes (*sources*) de energía sin…

7. Debemos comprar coches eléctricos tan pronto como…

8. Hay que eliminar la contaminación del agua para…

9. No podemos proteger la naturaleza sin que…

Conversación

3 Preguntas En parejas, contesten las siguientes preguntas. Luego, compartan la información con la clase.

1. ¿Qué haces cada noche antes de acostarte?
2. ¿Qué haces en la clase cada día después de que llega el/la profesor(a)?
3. ¿Qué hacen tus padres para que puedas asistir a la universidad?
4. ¿Qué puedes hacer para mejorar tu español?
5. ¿Qué quieres hacer mañana a menos que haga mal tiempo?
6. ¿Qué haces en tus clases sin que los profesores lo sepan?
7. ¿Qué quieres hacer hoy tan pronto como salgas de clase?

4 El fin de semana En parejas, hablen de lo que van a hacer este fin de semana, usando las palabras indicadas.

antes de	después de que	para	tan pronto como
antes de que	en caso de que	para que	
con tal de que	en cuanto	sin	
cuando	hasta que	sin que	

modelo

Estudiante 1: El sábado mis amigos y yo vamos al lago. Después de que volvamos, voy a estudiar para mi examen de química.

Estudiante 2: Todos los sábados llevo a mi primo al parque para que juegue con sus amigos. Pero el sábado que viene, con tal de que no llueva, lo voy a llevar a las montañas.

5 Tic-Tac-Toe Formen dos equipos. Una persona comienza una frase y otra persona de su equipo la termina, usando palabras de la gráfica. El primer equipo que forme tres oraciones seguidas (in a row) gana el tic-tac-toe. Tienen que usar correctamente la conjunción o la preposición y el verbo.

modelo

Estudiante 1: Dudo que podamos eliminar la deforestación...

Estudiante 2: ...sin que nos ayude el gobierno.

cuando	con tal de que	para que
antes de que	para	sin que
hasta que	en caso de que	antes de

Conjunctions with subjunctive or indicative

Cuando veo basura, la recojo.

Voy a formar un club de ecología tan pronto como empiecen las clases.

Conjunctions used with subjunctive or indicative

cuando	when	hasta que	until
después (de) que	after	tan pronto como	as soon as
en cuanto	as soon as		

▸ With the conjunctions above, use the subjunctive in the subordinate clause if the main clause expresses a future action or command.

Vamos a resolver el problema **cuando desarrollemos** nuevas tecnologías.
We are going to solve the problem when we develop new technologies.

Después de que Uds. **tomen** sus refrescos, reciclen las botellas.
After you drink your soft drinks, recycle the bottles.

▸ If the verb in the main clause expresses an action that habitually happens, or that happened in the past, the indicative is used.

Contaminan los ríos **cuando construyen** nuevos edificios.
They pollute the rivers when they build new buildings.

Contaminaron el río **cuando construyeron** ese edificio.
They polluted the river when they built that building.

Siempre vamos de excursión **tan pronto como llega** Rafael.
We always go hiking as soon as Rafael arrives.

Salimos **tan pronto como llegó** Rafael.
We left as soon as Rafael arrived.

¡Manos a la obra!

 Completa las oraciones con las formas correctas de los verbos.

1. Voy a estudiar ecología cuando __vuelva__ [volver] a la universidad.
2. No podemos evitar la lluvia ácida a menos que todos _____ [trabajar] juntos.
3. No podemos conducir sin _____ [contaminar] el aire.
4. Siempre recogemos mucha basura cuando _____ [ir] al parque.
5. Elisa habló con el presidente del club de ecología después de que _____ [terminar] la reunión.
6. Vamos de excursión para _____ [observar] los animales y las plantas.
7. La contaminación va a ser un problema muy serio hasta que _____ [cambiar] nuestros sistemas de producción y transporte.
8. El gobierno debe crear más parques nacionales antes de que los bosques y ríos _____ [estar] completamente contaminados.
9. La gente quiere reciclar, con tal de que no _____ [ser] difícil.

Ampliación

1 Escuchar

A Escucha el discurso de Soledad Morales, una activista preocupada por el medio ambiente. Antes de escuchar, marca las palabras y frases que tú crees que ella va a usar en su discurso. Después marca las palabras y frases que escuchaste.

> ⭐ **TIP** **Use your background knowledge / Guess meaning from context.** Your background knowledge helps you anticipate the content of discourse that you hear in Spanish. If you hear words or expressions you do not understand, you can often guess their meanings based on the surrounding words.

	Antes de escuchar	Después de escuchar
1. el futuro	☐	☐
2. el cine	☐	☐
3. los recursos naturales	☐	☐
4. el aire	☐	☐
5. los ríos	☐	☐
6. la contaminación	☐	☐
7. las diversiones	☐	☐
8. la conservación de la naturaleza	☐	☐

¡Protejamos la Tierra!

B En tu opinión, ¿qué recomendaciones va a dar la señora Morales en la siguiente parte de su discurso?

2 Conversar

Conversa con un(a) compañero/a sobre el estado del medio ambiente en tu comunidad o región. Las siguientes expresiones pueden ser útiles.

Dudo que…	Es cierto que…
No estoy seguro/a de que…	No dudo que…
No es verdad que…	No hay duda de que…
No podemos resolver el problema a menos que…	Es posible resolver el problema con tal de que…
Es probable que…	Tal vez…
Ojalá…	Es una lástima que…
Quizás…	No es cierto que…

recursos

Textbook CD Lección 13	WB pp. 133-138	LM pp. 75-77	Lab CD Lección 13	ICD-ROM Lección 13	vistahigher learning.com

R

Ampliación

- Are you going to comment on one topic or several?
- Are you intending to register a complaint or to inform others?
- Are you hoping to persuade others to adopt your point of view or to take specific action?

3 Escribir

Escribe una carta a un periódico sobre una situación importante que afecta el medio ambiente en tu comunidad.

TIP **Consider your audience and purpose.** Once you have defined both your audience and your purpose, you will be able to decide which genre, vocabulary, and grammatical structures will best serve your needs.

Organízalo	Decide cuál es el propósito de tu carta y planéala.
Escríbelo	Utiliza tus apuntes para escribir el primer borrador de tu carta.
Corrígelo	Intercambia tu carta con un(a) compañero/a. Léela y anota los mejores aspectos. Ofrécele sugerencias para mejorarla. Si ves algunos errores, coméntaselos.
Compártelo	Revisa el primer borrador según las indicaciones de tu compañero/a. Si es necesario, incorpora nuevas ideas y/o más información.

4 Un paso más

Escribe una carta al/a la presidente/a de un país hispano para hablarle de tus dudas, deseos y preocupaciones sobre el futuro de una de las atracciones naturales del país.

Las tortugas marinas están en grave peligro de extinción.

- Investiga algunas de las atracciones naturales del mundo hispano.
- Escoge una y piensa en lo que se puede hacer para protegerla.
- Explica lo que temes de los problemas ambientales, lo que esperas y tus dudas sobre el futuro.
- Formula recomendaciones para proteger este lugar en el futuro.

 En Internet

Investiga estos temas en el sitio vistahigherlearning.com.

- Atracciones naturales de España
- Atracciones naturales de América del Sur
- Atracciones de México, América Central y el Caribe

Antes de leer

When you are faced with an unfamiliar text, it is important to determine the writer's purpose (which is often related to the genre or type of writing). Identifying the purpose of a text will help you anticipate the content of a reading selection. For example, if you are reading an advice column in a newspaper, you know to expect questions about people's problems and suggestions from the columnist. The reading selection for this lesson consists of two fables: "El perro y el cocodrilo" by Félix María Samaniego, and "El pato y la serpiente" by Tomás de Iriarte. In general, what do the writers of fables attempt to accomplish? What kinds of characters do you expect to read about in fables?

_____

_____

_____

_____

Sobre los autores

Félix María Samaniego (1745-1801), nacido en España, escribió las *Fábulas morales*, que ilustran de manera humorística el carácter humano. Los protagonistas de muchas de sus fábulas son animales que hablan.

Tomás de Iriarte (1750-91), nacido en las Islas Canarias, tuvo gran éxito (*success*) con su libro *Fábulas literarias*. Su tendencia a representar la lógica a través de símbolos de la naturaleza fue de gran influencia para muchos autores de su época.

El perro y el cocodrilo

Bebiendo un perro en el Nilo,
al mismo tiempo corría.
"Bebe quieto", le decía
un taimado cocodrilo.

Díjole el perro prudente:
"Dañoso es beber y andar;
pero ¿es sano el aguardar
a que me claves el diente? "

¡Oh qué docto perro viejo!
Yo venero su sentir
en esto de no seguir
del enemigo el consejo.

Nilo	Nile
quieto	in peace
taimado	sly
Díjole	Said to him
Dañoso	Harmful
andar	to walk
¿es sano... diente?	is it good for me to wait for you to sink your teeth into me?
docto	learned; wise
venero	revere
sentir	wisdom

El pato y la serpiente

A orillas de un estanque,
diciendo estaba un pato:
"¿A qué animal dio el cielo
los dones que me ha dado?

"Soy de agua, tierra y aire:
cuando de andar me canso,
si se me antoja, vuelo;
si se me antoja, nado".

Una serpiente astuta
que le estaba escuchando,
le llamó con un silbo,
y le dijo "¡Seo guapo!

"No hay que echar tantas plantas;
pues ni anda como el gamo,
ni vuela como el sacre,
ni nada como el barbo;

"y así tenga sabido
que lo importante y raro
no es entender de todo,
sino ser diestro en algo".

Después de leer

¿Comprendiste?

Escoge la mejor opción para completar cada oración.

1. El cocodrilo _____ perro.
   a. está preocupado por el   b. quiere comerse al
   c. tiene miedo del
2. El perro _____ cocodrilo.
   a. tiene miedo del   b. es amigo del
   c. quiere quedarse con el
3. El pato cree que es un animal
   a. muy famoso.   b. muy hermoso.
   c. de muchos talentos.
4. La serpiente cree que el pato es
   a. muy inteligente.   b. muy tonto.
   c. muy feo.

Preguntas

1. ¿Qué representa el cocodrilo?
   _____

2. ¿Qué representa el pato?
   _____

3. ¿Cuál es la moraleja (*moral*) de "El perro y el cocodrilo"?
   _____

4. ¿Cuál es la moraleja de "El pato y la serpiente"?
   _____

Coméntalo

¿Estás de acuerdo (*do you agree*) con las moralejas de estas fábulas? ¿Por qué? ¿Cuál de estas fábulas te gusta más? ¿Por qué? ¿Conoces otras fábulas? ¿Cuál es su propósito (*purpose*)?

pato	duck	Seo	Señor
orillas	bank	No hay que... plantas	There's no reason to boast
estanque	pond	gamo	deer
cielo	heaven	sacre	falcon
los dones... dado	the gifts that it has given me	barbo	barbel (a type of fish)
me canso	I get tired	lo... raro	the important and rare thing
si se me antoja, vuelo	If I feel like it, I fly	diestro	skillful
silbo	hiss		

recursos

R

vistahigher
learning.com

La naturaleza

el árbol	tree
el bosque (tropical)	(tropical; rain) forest
el cielo	sky
el cráter	crater
el desierto	desert
la estrella	star
la flor	flower
la hierba	grass
el lago	lake
la luna	moon
el mundo	world
la naturaleza	nature
la nube	cloud
el océano	ocean
el paisaje	landscape
la piedra	stone; rock
la planta	plant
la región	region; area
el río	river
la selva	jungle
el sendero	trail
el sol	sun
la tierra	land; soil
el valle	valley
el volcán	volcano

Conjunctions

a menos que	unless
antes (de) que	before
con tal (de) que	provided (that)
después (de) que	after
en caso (de) que	in case
en cuanto	as soon as
hasta que	until
para que	so that
sin que	without
tan pronto como	as soon as

El medio ambiente

la conservación	conservation
la contaminación (del aire; del agua)	(air; water) pollution
la deforestación	deforestation
la ecología	ecology
el ecoturismo	ecotourism
la energía (nuclear; solar)	(nuclear; solar) energy
la extinción	extinction
el gobierno	government
la ley	law
la lluvia (ácida)	(acid) rain
el medio ambiente	environment
el peligro	danger
la población	population
el reciclaje	recycling
el recurso natural	natural resource
la solución	solution
conservar	to conserve
contaminar	to pollute
controlar	to control
cuidar	to take care of
dejar de + (inf.)	to stop (doing something)
desarrollar	to develop
descubrir	to discover
destruir	to destroy
estar afectado/a (por)	to be affected by
estar contaminado/a	to be polluted
evitar	to avoid
mejorar	to improve
proteger	to protect
reciclar	to recycle
recoger	to pick up
reducir	to reduce
resolver (o:ue)	to resolve; to solve
respirar	to breathe
la botella de vidrio	glass botle
el envase de plástico	plastic container
la lata de aluminio	aluminum can
puro/a	pure

Expressions of emotion

alegrarse (de)	to be happy
esperar	to hope; to wish
sentir (e:ie)	to be sorry; to regret
temer	to fear
es extraño	it's strange
es una lástima	it's a shame
es ridículo	it's ridiculous
es terrible	it's terrible
es triste	it's sad
ojalá (que)	I hope (that); I wish (that)

Doubts and certainty

(no) creer	(not) to believe
(no) dudar	(not) to doubt
(no) estar seguro/a (de)	(not) to be sure (of)
(no) negar (e:ie)	(not) to deny
es imposible	it's impossible
es improbable	it's improbable
es obvio	it's obvious
no cabe duda (de) que...	there is no doubt that...
no hay duda (de) que...	there is no doubt that...
(no) es posible	it's (not) possible
(no) es probable	it's (not) probable
(no) es cierto	it's (not) true
(no) es verdad	it's (not) true
(no) es seguro	it's (not) certain

Animales

el animal	animal
el gato	cat
el pájaro	bird
el perro	dog
el pez	fish
la vaca	cow

Expresiones útiles	See page 315.

recursos

R	Lab CD Lección 13	LM p. 77

14 En la ciudad

Communicative Goals

You will learn how to:
- give advice
- talk about errands
- ask for directions

PREPARACIÓN

pages 330-335
- City life
- In the bank and post office
- Abbreviations

AVENTURAS

pages 336-339
- In preparation for the hike, Álex and Maite decide to go food shopping. On their way downtown, they ask a young man for directions.

GRAMÁTICA

pages 340-347
- The subjunctive in adjective clauses
- Familiar (**tú**) commands
- **Nosotros/as** commands

LECTURA

pages 348-349
- Novel: excerpt from *La muerte de Artemio Cruz*

RECURSOS

These student supplements provide additional practice:
- Textbook Audio CD
- Workbook/Video Manual (WB/VM)
- Lab Manual (LM)
- WB/VM/LM Answer Key
- Lab Audio CDs
- Video CD-ROM
- Interactive CD-ROM

EN LA CIUDAD

EN LA CIUDAD

la pescadería
fish market

el banco *bank*

la carnicería *butcher shop*

el correo *post office; mail*

la heladería *ice cream shop*

la joyería *jewelry store*

la lavandería *laundromat*

la panadería *bakery*

la pastelería *pastry shop*

el salón de belleza *beauty salon*

el supermercado *supermarket*

la zapatería *shoe store*

hacer cola *to stand in line*

hacer diligencias *to run errands*

la frutería
fruit store

la peluquería
hairdresser

el cartero
mail carrier

EN EL CORREO

el paquete *package*

los sellos *stamps*

el sobre *envelope*

echar (una carta) al buzón *to put (a letter) in the mailbox; to mail (a letter)*

enviar *to send*

mandar *to send*

las estampillas
stamps

recursos

	R	Textbook CD Lección 14	WB pp. 139-140	LM p. 79	Lab CD Lección 14	ICD-ROM Lección 14

EN EL BANCO

el cheque de viajero *traveler's cheque*

la cuenta corriente *checking account*

la cuenta de ahorros *savings account*

ahorrar *to save (money)*

cobrar *to cash (a check); to charge (for a product or service)*

depositar *to deposit*

llenar (un formulario) *to fill out (a form)*

pagar al contado *to pay in cash*

pagar a plazos *to pay in installments*

pedir prestado *to borrow*

pedir un préstamo *to apply for a loan*

ser gratis *to be free of charge*

el cheque
check

Este cheque tiene papel de seguridad con marca de agua, verifíquela antes de aceptarlo.

SERIE KY 5296221
Diamante 787
Valparaíso

0-744679-00-5
JUAN FLORES GARCÍA

$ 2387.00

044-0365
011

8 de noviembre de 2002

Páguese a la orden de María Eugenia Castano

la suma de dos mil trescientos ochenta y siete con 00/100   o, al portador

pesos m/l

BANCO ATLANTIS

Juan Flores García
Firma autorizada

:54892332.A 0440900657008- 01

firmar
to sign

el cajero automático
automatic teller machine, ATM

el letrero
sign

OTRAS PALABRAS Y EXPRESIONES

la cuadra *(city) block*

la dirección *address*

la esquina *corner*

cruzar *to cross*

doblar *to turn*

estar perdido/a *to be lost*

quedar *to be located*

(al) este *(to the) east*

(al) oeste *(to the) west*

(al) norte *(to the) north*

(al) sur *(to the) south*

derecho *straight (ahead)*

enfrente de *opposite; facing*

hacia *toward*

dar direcciones
to give directions

A escuchar

1 **¿Lógico o ilógico?** Escucha las frases e indica si cada frase es **lógica** o **ilógica.**

	Lógico	Ilógico
1.	_____	_____
2.	_____	_____
3.	_____	_____
4.	_____	_____
5.	_____	_____
6.	_____	_____
7.	_____	_____
8.	_____	_____

2 **¿Adónde fue?** Óscar está hablándote de las diligencias que hizo ayer. Indica adónde fue.

1. _____

4. _____

2. _____

5. _____

3. _____

6. _____

A practicar

3 **Emparejar** Empareja los lugares con la actividad que se pueda hacer en cada lugar.

Lugares	Actividades
1. carnicería _____	a. comprar galletas
2. pastelería _____	b. comprar manzanas
3. frutería _____	c. comprar un collar (*necklace*)
4. joyería _____	d. cortarse (*to cut*) el pelo
5. lavandería _____	e. lavar la ropa
6. pescadería _____	f. comprar pescado
7. salón de belleza _____	g. comprar pollo
8. zapatería _____	h. comprar unas sandalias

4 **Completar** Llena los espacios en blanco con las palabras más adecuadas.

1. El banco me regaló un reloj. Lo conseguí _____ .
2. Me gusta _____ dinero, pero no me molesta gastarlo.
3. Tengo que _____ el cheque en el dorso (*on the back*) para cobrarlo.
4. Para pagar con un cheque, necesito tener dinero en mi _____ .
5. Mi madre va a un _____ para obtener dinero.
6. Julio lleva su cheque al banco y lo _____ para tener dinero.
7. Ana lleva su cheque al banco y lo _____ en su cuenta de ahorros.
8. Anoche en el restaurante, Marco _____ en vez de usar una tarjeta de crédito.
9. Cuando viajas, es buena idea llevar cheques _____ .
10. Para pedir un préstamo, Miguel y Susana tuvieron que _____ cuatro formularios.

cobra	**firmar**
de viajero	**gratis**
deposita	**llenar**
cuenta corriente	**ahorrar**
cajero automático	**pagó al contado**

5 **Conversación** Completa el diálogo entre Juanita y el cartero con las palabras más adecuadas.

CARTERO Buenas tardes, ¿es Ud. la Srta. Ramírez? Le traigo un _____ .

JUANITA Sí, soy yo. ¿Quién lo envía?

CARTERO La Sra. Ramírez. Y también tiene Ud. dos _____ .

JUANITA Ay, pero ¡ninguna es de mi novio! ¿No llegó nada de Manuel Fuentes?

CARTERO Sí, pero él echó la carta al _____ sin poner un _____ en el sobre.

JUANITA Entonces, ¿qué recomienda Ud. que haga?

CARTERO Sugiero que vaya al _____ . Si Ud. paga el costo del sello, se le puede dar la carta.

A conversar

6 **Situaciones** En parejas, representen los papeles (*roles*) de un(a) empleado/a del banco y de uno/a de los/las siguientes clientes/as.

- un(a) estudiante universitario/a que quiere abrir una cuenta corriente.

- una pareja de recién casados que quiere pedir un préstamo para comprar una casa.

- una persona que quiere información de los servicios que ofrece el banco.

- un(a) estudiante que va a ir a estudiar al extranjero (*abroad*).

7 **El Hatillo** Trabajen en parejas para representar los papeles (*roles*) de un(a) turista que está perdido/a en El Hatillo, Venezuela, y de un(a) residente de la ciudad que quiere ayudarlo/a.

El Hatillo

Plaza Bolívar
Plaza Sucre
Banco
Casa de la Cultura
Farmacia
Iglesia
Terminal
Escuela
E Estacionamiento (*parking lot*)
Joyería
Zapatería
Café Primavera

 modelo

Plaza Sucre, Café Primavera
Estudiante 1: *Perdón, ¿por dónde queda la Plaza Sucre?*
Estudiante 2: *Del Café Primavera, camine derecho por la calle Sucre hasta cruzar la calle Comercio. Doble a la izquierda y camine una cuadra. Allí está la plaza.*

1. Plaza Bolívar, farmacia
2. Casa de la Cultura, Plaza Sucre
3. banco, terminal
4. estacionamiento (este), escuela

5. Plaza Sucre, estacionamiento (oeste)
6. joyería, banco
7. farmacia, joyería
8. zapatería, iglesia

8 **Direcciones** En grupos, escriban un minidrama en el que unos/as turistas están preguntando cómo llegar a diferentes sitios de la comunidad en la que viven Uds. Luego preséntenlo a la clase.

Ortografía

Las abreviaturas

In Spanish, as in English, abbreviations are often used in order to save space and time while writing. Here are some of the most commonly used abbreviations in Spanish.

usted → Ud.   **ustedes** → Uds.

As you have already learned, the subject pronouns **usted** and **ustedes** are often abbreviated.

don → D.   **doña** → Dña.   **doctor(a)** → Dr(a).

señor → Sr.   **señora** → Sra.   **señorita** → Srta.

These titles are frequently abbreviated.

centímetro → cm   **metro** → m   **kilómetro** → km

litro → l   **gramo** → g; gr   **kilogramo** → kg

The abbreviations for these units of measurement are often used, but without periods.

por ejemplo → p. ej.   **página(s)** → pág(s).

These abbreviations are often seen in books.

derecha → dcha.   **izquierda** → izq. (izqda.)

código postal → C.P.   **número** → n.º

These abbreviations are often used in mailing addresses.

Sra. Emilia F. Bazán
Cía. Romero, S.A.
3336
Calle Lozano, n.º 37
Caracas, Venezuela

Banco → Bco.   **Compañía** → Cía.

cuenta corriente → c/c.   **Sociedad Anónima (*Inc.*)** → S.A.

These abbreviations are frequently used in the business world.

Práctica Escribe otra vez la siguiente información usando las abreviaturas adecuadas.

1. doña María   5. Banco de Santander
2. señora Pérez   6. doctor Medina
3. Compañía Mexicana de Inversiones 7. Código Postal 03697
4. usted   8. cuenta corriente número 20-453

Emparejar En la tabla hay 9 abreviaturas. Empareja los cuadros necesarios para formarlas.

S.	c.	C.	c	co.	U
B	c/	Sr	A.	D	dc
ta.	P.	ña.	ha.	m	d.

Estamos perdidos.

Maite y Álex hacen diligencias en el centro.

1

MARTÍN & DON FRANCISCO Buenas tardes.

JAVIER Hola. ¿Qué tal? Estamos conversando sobre la excursión de mañana.

2

DON FRANCISCO ¿Y ya tienen todo lo que necesitan? A todos los excursionistas yo siempre les recomiendo llevar zapatos cómodos, una mochila, gafas oscuras y un suéter por si hace frío.

JAVIER Todo listo, don Francisco.

3

MARTÍN Les aconsejo que traigan algo de comer.

ÁLEX Mmm… no pensamos en eso.

MAITE ¡Deja de preocuparte tanto, Álex! Podemos comprar algo en el supermercado ahora mismo. ¿Vamos?

6

JOVEN ¡Hola! ¿Puedo ayudarte en algo?

MAITE Sí, estamos perdidos. ¿Hay un banco por aquí con cajero automático?

JOVEN Mmm… no hay ningún banco en esta calle que tenga cajero automático.

7

JOVEN Pero conozco uno en la calle Pedro Moncayo que sí tiene cajero automático. Cruzas esta calle y luego doblas a la izquierda. Sigues todo derecho y antes de que lleguen a la Joyería Crespo van a ver un letrero grande del Banco del Pacífico.

8

MAITE También buscamos un supermercado.

JOVEN Pues, allí mismo enfrente del banco hay un supermercado pequeño. Fácil, ¿no?

MAITE Creo que sí. Muchas gracias por su ayuda.

recursos

| R | Video/VCD-ROM Lección 14 | VM pp.195-196 | ICD-ROM Lección 14 |

onajes

JAVIER

INÉS

ÁLEX

MAITE

MARTÍN
JOVEN

DON NCISCO

ÁLEX ¡Excelente idea! En cuanto termine mi café te acompaño.

MAITE Necesito pasar por el banco y por el correo para mandar unas cartas.

ÁLEX Está bien.

ÁLEX ¿Necesitan algo del centro?

INÉS ¡Sí! Cuando vayan al correo, ¿pueden echar estas postales al buzón? Además necesito unas estampillas.

ÁLEX Por supuesto.

MAITE Ten, guapa, tus sellos.

INÉS Gracias, Maite. ¿Qué tal les fue en el centro?

MAITE ¡Superbien! Fuimos al banco y al correo. Luego en el supermercado compramos comida para la excursión. Y antes de regresar, paramos en una heladería.

MAITE ¡Ah! Y otra cosa. Cuando llegamos al centro conocimos a un joven muy simpático que nos dio direcciones. Era muy amable... ¡y muy guapo!

Expresiones útiles

Giving advice

Les recomiendo/hay que llevar zapatos cómodos.
I recommend that you/it's necessary to wear comfortable shoes.

Les aconsejo que traigan algo de comer.
I advise you to bring something to eat.

Trae gafas oscuras.
Bring sunglasses. (fam., sing.)

Talking about errands

Necesito pasar por el banco.
I need to go by the bank.

Te acompaño.
I'll go with you.

Getting directions

¿Hay un banco por aquí?
Is there a bank around here?

Dobla a la izquierda/derecha.
Turn to the left/right. (fam., sing.)

Sigue todo derecho.
Go straight ahead.(fam., sing.)

Van a ver un letrero grande.
You're going to see a big sign.

¿Por dónde queda... ?
Where is…?

Está a dos cuadras de aquí.
It's two blocks from here.

Allí mismo enfrente del banco hay un supermercado.
Right in front of the bank there is a supermarket.

¿Qué piensas?

1 **¿Cierto o falso?** Decide si las siguientes frases son **ciertas** o **falsas**. Corrige las frases falsas.

Cierto	Falso	
_____	_____	1. Don Francisco insiste en que los excursionistas lleven una cámara.
		_____
_____	_____	2. Inés escribió unas postales y ahora necesita mandarlas por correo.
		_____
_____	_____	3. El joven dice que el Banco del Atlántico tiene un cajero automático.
		_____
_____	_____	4. Enfrente del banco hay una heladería.
		_____

2 **Ordenar** Pon los eventos en el orden correcto.

_____ a. Álex y Maite comen un helado.

_____ b. Maite y Álex van al supermercado y compran comida.

_____ c. Álex termina su café.

_____ d. Inés les da unas postales a Maite y a Álex para echar al buzón.

_____ e. Un joven ayuda a Álex y a Maite a encontrar el banco porque están perdidos.

_____ f. Maite y Álex van al banco y al correo.

3 **Conversación** Un(a) compañero/a y tú son vecinos/as. Uno/a de Uds. acaba de mudarse y necesita ayuda porque no conoce la ciudad. Preparen una breve conversación en la que hagan planes para ir a los siguientes lugares usando las palabras indicadas.

primero	*first*	**¿Qué te parece?**	*What do you think?*
luego	*then*	**¡Cómo no!**	*Why not!*
¿Sabes dónde queda… ?	*Do you know where… is?*		

• un banco

• una lavandería

• un supermercado

• una heladería

• una panadería

Exploración
En el centro

La Puerta del Sol en Madrid, España, está en el "kilómetro cero" de la ciudad. Se dice que allí comienzan todas las calles principales. Cerca hay muchos bares, restaurantes, tiendas y otros negocios.

En muchos países hispanos, la plaza mayor es el centro social de la ciudad. Es donde la gente va para reunirse con sus amigos, para tomar un café o para ir de compras. Normalmente, está localizada en el centro de la ciudad.

Muchas personas dicen que Buenos Aires, Argentina, es "la ciudad que nunca duerme". La ciudad tiene discotecas, bares, restaurantes y otras atracciones que están abiertas toda la noche...o por lo menos (*at least*) hasta la madrugada (*early morning*), siete días a la semana.

Observaciones

- En México, se usa el término **zócalo** en lugar de **plaza mayor**.

- En la Plaza de Armas de Lima, Perú, se hace el cambio de guardia (*changing of the guard*) todos los días, como un tributo público a la bandera (*flag*) peruana.

- El Parque San Antonio de Medellín, Colombia, tiene cuatro grandes esculturas del famoso artista Fernando Botero.

- La zona viva es el corazón comercial de Tegucigalpa, Honduras, donde se encuentran las tiendas y los restaurantes más importantes.

Coméntalo

Con un(a) compañero/a, contesta las siguientes preguntas.

- ¿Te gustaría visitar algunos de los lugares mencionados en esta página? ¿Cuáles?
- ¿Prefieres las ciudades grandes, medianas (*medium-sized*) o pequeñas? ¿Por qué?
- Describe el centro de una ciudad que conoces. ¿Qué se puede hacer allí?

recursos

R

vistahigher
learning.com

14.1 The subjunctive in adjective clauses

▸ Adjective clauses modify nouns or pronouns. The subjunctive can be used in adjective clauses to indicate that the existence of someone or something is uncertain or indefinite.

¿Hay un banco por aquí que tenga cajero automático?

No hay ningún banco en esta calle que tenga cajero automático.

▸ The subjunctive is used in an adjective clause that refers to a person, place, thing, or idea that either does not exist or whose existence is uncertain or indefinite.

Adjective clauses

Indicative	Subjunctive
Necesito el libro **que** tiene **información sobre Venezuela.**	**Necesito** un libro **que** tenga **información sobre Venezuela.**
I need the book that has information about Venezuela.	*I need a book that has information about Venezuela.*
Quiero vivir en esta casa **que** tiene **jardín.**	**Quiero vivir en** una casa **que** tenga **jardín.**
I want to live in this house that has a garden.	*I want to live in a house that has a garden.*
En mi barrio, hay una heladería **que** vende **helado de mango.**	**En mi barrio, no hay** ninguna heladería **que** venda **helado de mango.**
In my neighborhood, there's an ice cream shop that sells mango ice cream.	*In my neighborhood, there is no ice cream shop that sells mango ice cream.*

▸ When the adjective clause refers to a person, place, thing, or idea that is certain or definite, the indicative is used.

Quiero ir **al restaurante** que **está** en frente de la biblioteca.
I want to go to the restaurant that's in front of the library.

Busco **al profesor** que **enseña** japonés.
I'm looking for the professor who teaches Japanese.

Conozco a **alguien** que **va** a esa peluquería.
I know someone who goes to that beauty salon.

Tengo **un amigo** que **vive** cerca de mi casa.
I have a friend who lives near my house.

Práctica

1 **Minidiálogos** Completa los minidiálogos con la forma correcta de los verbos indicados.

MARCIA Buscamos un hotel que _____ [tener] piscina.

MARTÍN Hay tres o cuatro hoteles por aquí que _____ [tener] piscina.

• • •

EDUARDO ¿Hay algún buzón por aquí donde yo _____ [poder] echar una carta?

SUSANA Hay un buzón en la esquina donde _____ [poder] echar una carta.

• • •

ANA Queremos encontrar un restaurante que _____ [servir] comida venezolana.

BENITO Creo que el restaurante en esta cuadra _____ [servir] comida venezolana.

• • •

VICENTE Necesitas al empleado que _____ [entender] este nuevo programa de computación.

MARISOL No hay nadie que _____ [entender] este programa.

2 **Anuncios clasificados** En parejas, lean estos anuncios y luego describan el tipo de persona u objeto que se busca.

CLASIFICADOS

VENDEDOR(A) Se necesita persona dinámica y responsable con buena presencia. Experiencia mínima de un año. Horario de trabajo flexible. Llamar a Joyería Aurora de 10 a 13h y de 16 a 18h. Tel: 263-7553.

PELUQUERÍA UNISEX Se busca persona con experiencia en peluquería y maquillaje para trabajar tiempo completo. Llamar de 9 a 13h. Tel: 261-3548.

COMPARTIR APARTAMENTO Se necesita compañera para compartir apartamento de 2 alcobas en el Chaco. Alquiler 300.000 bolívares por mes. No fumar. Llamar al 951-3642 entre 19 y 22h.

CLASES DE INGLÉS Profesor de Inglaterra con diez años de experiencia ofrece clases para grupos o instrucción privada para individuos. Llamar al 933-4110 de 16:30 a 18:30.

SE BUSCA CONDOMINIO Se busca condominio en Sabana Grande con 3 alcobas, 2 baños, sala, comedor y aire acondicionado. Tel: 977-2018.

EJECUTIVO DE CUENTAS Se requiere joven profesional con al menos dos años de experiencia en el sector financiero. Se ofrecen beneficios excelentes. Enviar currículum vitae al Banco Unión, Avda. Urdaneta 263, Caracas.

Conversación

3 **Completar** Completa estas frases de una manera lógica. Luego, compara tus respuestas con las de un(a) compañero/a.

1. Tengo un(a) amigo/a que…
2. Algún día espero tener un apartamento o una casa que…
3. Quiero visitar un país que…
4. No tengo ningún profesor que…
5. Me gustaría conocer a alguien que…
6. Mi compañero/a de cuarto busca una lavandería que…
7. Un(a) consejero/a (*advisor*) debe ser una persona que…
8. Mi novio/a desea un perro que…
9. En esta clase no hay nadie que…
10. Mis padres buscan un carro que…

4 **Encuesta** Circula por la clase y pregúntales a tus compañeros/as si conocen a alguien que corresponda a cada descripción de la lista. Si dicen que conocen a una persona así, pregúntales quién es y anota sus respuestas. Luego informa a la clase de los resultados de tu encuesta.

Actividades	Nombres	Respuestas
1. Dar direcciones buenas	_____	_____
2. Hablar japonés	_____	_____
3. Comprender el subjuntivo	_____	_____
4. Necesitar un préstamo	_____	_____
5. Pedir prestado un carro	_____	_____
6. Odiar ir de compras	_____	_____
7. Ser venezolano/a	_____	_____
8. No saber nadar	_____	_____
9. Manejar una motocicleta	_____	_____
10. Trabajar en una zapatería	_____	_____
11. No tener tarjeta de crédito	_____	_____
12. Graduarse este año	_____	_____

▶ The personal **a** is not used with direct objects that are hypothetical people. However, **alguien** and **nadie** are always preceded by the personal **a** when they function as direct objects.

Necesitamos **un empleado** que **sepa** usar computadoras.
We need an employee who knows how to use computers.

Necesitamos **al empleado** que **sabe** usar computadoras.
We need the employee who knows how to use computers.

Buscamos **a alguien** que **pueda** cocinar.
We're looking for someone who can cook.

No conocemos **a nadie** que **pueda** cocinar.
We don't know anyone who can cook.

▶ The subjunctive is commonly used in questions when the speaker is uncertain. However, if the person who responds to the question knows the information, the indicative is used.

—¿Hay un parque que **esté** cerca de nuestro hotel?
Is there a park that's close to our hotel?

—Sí, hay un parque que **está** muy cerca del hotel.
Yes, there's a park that's very close to the hotel.

¡Qué fácil encontrarlo todo con cosmoguía.com! La ciudad a tu alcance.

Buscar –
✓ restaurante que sirva paella (Mamá)
✓ librería que venda libros de texto (Juan, historia)
✓ tutor que enseñe inglés (niños)

¡Manos a la obra!

Escoge entre el subjuntivo o el indicativo para completar cada oración.

1. Necesito una persona que ___pueda___ [puede/pueda] cantar bien.
2. Buscamos a alguien que _____ [tiene/tenga] paciencia.
3. ¿Hay restaurantes aquí que _____ [sirven/sirvan] comida japonesa?
4. Tengo una amiga que _____ [saca/saque] fotografías muy bonitas.
5. Hay una carnicería que _____ [está/esté] cerca de aquí.
6. No vemos ningún apartamento que nos _____ [interesa/interese].
7. Conozco a un estudiante que _____ [come/coma] hamburguesas todos los días.
8. ¿Hay alguien que _____ [dice/diga] la verdad?

14.2 Familiar (tú) commands

▸ Familiar (**tú**) commands are used when you want to give advice to or instruct someone you address with **tú**.

Trae algo de comer.

No te preocupes, el supermercado está cerca.

Negative *tú* commands

Infinitive	Present subjunctive	Negative *tú* command
cuidar	tú cuides	no cuides (tú)
tocar	tú toques	no toques (tú)
temer	tú temas	no temas (tú)
volver	tú vuelvas	no vuelvas (tú)
insistir	tú insistas	no insistas (tú)
pedir	tú pidas	no pidas (tú)

▸ Negative **tú** commands have the same form as the **tú** form of the present subjunctive. The pronoun **tú** is used only for emphasis.

Julia, **no cruces** la calle.
Julia, don't cross the street.

Carlos, **no eches** eso al buzón.
Carlos, don't put that in the mailbox.

▸ The negative familiar commands keep the same stem changes as the indicative.

Affirmative *tú* commands

Infinitive	Present indicative	Affirmative *tú* command
cuidar	él/ella/Ud. cuida	cuida (tú)
tocar	él/ella/Ud. toca	toca (tú)
temer	él/ella/Ud. teme	teme (tú)
volver	él/ella/Ud. vuelve	vuelve (tú)
insistir	él/ella/Ud. insiste	insiste (tú)
pedir	él/ella/Ud. pide	pide (tú)

▸ Affirmative **tú** commands usually have the same form as the third person singular of the present indicative.

Paga al contado.
Pay in cash.

Pide un préstamo.
Ask for a loan.

Práctica

1 Unas diligencias La Sra. Pujol quiere que su esposo haga unas diligencias en el centro. Completa las frases con las formas correctas.

1. Enrique, _____ [ir] al banco, por favor.
2. Cuando llegues al banco, _____ [depositar] este cheque en nuestra cuenta corriente.
3. No lo _____ [depositar] en la cuenta de ahorros y, por favor, no _____ [pedir] un préstamo.
4. Luego _____ [pasar] por la zapatería y _____ [recoger] mis zapatos.
5. No _____ [pagar] al contado, sino con un cheque.
6. Luego _____ [comprar] un pastel en la pastelería. Por favor, no _____ [comprar] un pastel de chocolate. Mi tío Felipe viene a cenar y es alérgico al chocolate.

2 Quehaceres Pedro y Marina no pueden ponerse de acuerdo (*agree*) cuando le dan órdenes a su hijo Miguel. Lee los quehaceres que Pedro le da a Miguel. Después, usa la información entre paréntesis para formar las órdenes que le da Marina. Sigue el modelo.

 modelo
Recoge la basura. (poner la mesa)
No la recojas, Miguel. Pon la mesa.

1. Barre el suelo. (pasar la aspiradora)
2. Plancha la ropa. (hacer las camas)
3. Saca la basura. (quitar la mesa)
4. Ve a la joyería. (ir a la frutería)
5. Dale los libros a Katia. (dárselos a Juan)
6. Prepara la cena. (limpiar el carro)
7. Echa las cartas al buzón. (dárselas al cartero)
8. Corta el césped. (bañar al gato)

3 Oraciones La Sra. Morales está dándoles órdenes a su esposo y a sus hijos. Forma los mandatos que ella les da.

modelo
Pilar / sacar / basura
Pilar, saca la basura.

1. Gloria / poner / sello / el sobre
2. Manolo / ir / banco / cobrar / este / cheques
3. Lidia / no poner / televisión
4. Esteban / hacer / camas
5. Gloria / barrer / suelo / no lavar / platos
6. Manolo / firmar / este / formularios

Conversación

4 **Estoy perdido/a** Con un(a) compañero/a, prepara una breve conversación entre un(a) estudiante nuevo/a en la universidad y otro estudiante que le da direcciones.

modelo

Estudiante 1: Quiero ir al Edificio de Ciencias, pero estoy perdido. ¿Me puedes ayudar?

Estudiante 2: Sí. Sigue derecho hasta que llegues al Edificio de Negocios. Dobla a la izquierda y sigue hasta llegar al Edificio de Artes. Dobla a la derecha y el Edificio de Ciencias es el primer edificio a la izquierda.

5 **Diálogo** En parejas, preparen un diálogo entre Ramón y Luisa Aguilera. Ellos están hablando sobre lo que tienen que hacer para llegar a tiempo a una fiesta. Usen mandatos afirmativos y negativos. Luego presenten el diálogo a la clase.

modelo

Luisa: ¡Sal del cuarto de baño ya!

Ramón: ¡No me des órdenes!

Luisa: Pero tengo que maquillarme.

Ramón: Y yo tengo que ducharme. Oye, ¿qué hora es?

Luisa: Son las siete menos veinte.

Ramón: ¡Ay! ¡Tráeme una toalla!

6 **Órdenes** Circula por la clase e intercambia órdenes con tus compañeros/as. Debes seguir las órdenes que ellos te dan o reaccionar apropiadamente.

modelo

Estudiante 1: Dame todo tu dinero.

Estudiante 2: No, no quiero dártelo. Muéstrame tu cuaderno.

Estudiante 1: Aquí está.

Estudiante 3: Ve a la pizarra y escribe tu nombre.

Estudiante 4: No quiero. Hazlo tú.

Irregular tú commands

▸ There are eight irregular affirmative **tú** commands.

decir	di	salir	sal
hacer	haz	ser	sé
ir	ve	tener	ten
poner	pon	venir	ven

¡Ten cuidado con el perro!
Be careful with the dog!

Pon la estampilla en el sobre.
Put the stamp on the envelope.

¡Sal de aquí ahora mismo!
Leave here at once!

Haz los ejercicios.
Do the exercises.

▸ **Ir** and **ver** have the same **tú** command. Context will determine the meaning.

Ve al supermercado con José.
Go to the supermarket with José.

Ve al banco esta tarde.
Go to the bank this afternoon.

Ve ese programa… es muy interesante.
See that program… it's very interesting.

Ve esa película con tu hermano.
See that movie with your brother.

▸ The placement of reflexive and object pronouns in **tú** commands follows the same rules as in formal commands. When a pronoun is attached to a command of more than two syllables, a written accent is used.

Informal	Formal
¡Alégra**te!**	¡Alégren**se!**
Be happy!	*Be happy!*
No **te** sientas triste.	No **se** sientan tristes.
Don't feel sad.	*Don't feel sad.*
Di**me.**	Díga**me.**
Tell me.	*Tell me.*
No **me lo** digas.	No **me lo** diga.
Don't tell me (it).	*Don't tell me (it).*

¡Manos a la obra!

Indica los mandatos (*commands*) familiares de estos verbos.

	Mandato afirmativo	Mandato negativo
1. cambiar	_Cambia_ el aceite.	No _cambies_ el aceite.
2. correr	_____ más rápido.	No _____ más rápido.
3. salir	_____ ahora.	No _____ ahora.
4. tocar	_____ las flores.	No _____ las flores.
5. venir	_____ aquí.	No _____ aquí.
6. levantarse	_____ temprano.	No _____ temprano.
7. volver	_____ pronto.	No _____ pronto.
8. hacerlo	_____ ya.	No _____ ahora.

14.3 Nosotros/as commands

▶ **Nosotros/as** commands, which correspond to the English equivalent of *let's* + [*verb*], are used to give orders or suggestions that include yourself and other people.

Crucemos la calle.
Let's cross the street.

No crucemos la calle.
Let's not cross the street.

▶ Both affirmative and negative **nosotros/as** commands are generally formed by using the first person plural form of the present subjunctive.

▶ The affirmative *let's* + [*verb*] may also be expressed with **vamos a** + [*infinitive*]. Remember, however, that **vamos a** + [*infinitive*] can also mean *we are going to (do something)*. Context and tone will determine which meaning is being expressed.

Vamos a cruzar la calle.
Let's cross the street.

Vamos a trabajar mucho.
We're going to work a lot.

¿Quieres ir al supermercado?

¡Excelente idea! ¡Vamos!

▶ To express *let's go*, the present indicative form of **ir** is used. For the negative command, the present subjunctive (**vayamos**) is used.

(Affirmative)

Vamos a la pescadería.
Let's go to the fish market.

Vamos a tomar un café.
Let's go have a coffee.

(Negative)

No vayamos a la pescadería.
Let's not go to the fish market.

No vayamos a tomar un café.
Let's not go have a coffee.

¡Hagamos un viaje!
¡Compremos un caballo!
¡Pidamos un préstamo!
BANCOSUR. LLÁMANOS.

Práctica

1 **Conversación** Completa esta conversación con los mandatos de **nosotros/as.** Luego, represéntala con un(a) compañero/a.

MARÍA Sergio, ¿quieres hacer diligencias ahora o por la tarde?

SERGIO No _____ [dejarlas] para más tarde. _____ [hacerlas] ahora.

MARÍA Necesito comprar sellos.

SERGIO Yo también. _____ [ir] al correo.

MARÍA Pues, antes de ir al correo, necesito sacar dinero de mi cuenta corriente.

SERGIO Bueno, _____ [buscar] un cajero automático.

MARÍA ¿Tienes hambre?

SERGIO Sí. _____ [cruzar] la calle y _____ [comer] algo en ese café.

MARÍA Buena idea.

SERGIO ¿Nos sentamos aquí?

MARÍA No, no _____ [sentarse] aquí; _____ [sentarse] enfrente de la ventana.

SERGIO ¿Qué pedimos?

MARÍA _____ [pedir] café y pan dulce.

2 **Hagámoslo** Responde a cada oración según las indicaciones.

> **modelo**
> Vamos a vender el carro. (Sí)
> **Sí, vendámoslo.**

1. Vamos a levantarnos a las seis. (Sí)

2. Vamos a enviar los paquetes. (No)

3. Vamos al supermercado. (No)

4. Vamos a mandar esta tarjeta postal a nuestros amigos. (No)

5. Vamos a limpiar la habitación. (Sí)

6. Vamos a mirar la televisión. (No)

7. Vamos a bailar. (Sí)

8. Vamos a arreglar la sala. (No)

9. Vamos a comprar estampillas. (Sí)

Conversación

3 Decisiones Tú y un(a) compañero/a están en Tegucigalpa, Honduras. Túrnense para hacerse estas preguntas. Contesten las preguntas con un mandato afirmativo o negativo de **nosotros/as.**

1. ¿Nos quedamos en un hotel o en una pensión?
2. ¿Cruzamos la calle aquí o caminamos una cuadra más?
3. ¿Vamos a casa o comemos en un restaurante?
4. ¿Vamos al cine en taxi o en autobús?
5. ¿Salimos para el cine a las seis o a las seis y media?
6. ¿Hacemos cola o buscamos otra película?
7. ¿Volvemos al hotel después de la película o tomamos algo en un café?
8. ¿Pagamos la cuenta al contado o con tarjeta de crédito?

4 Turistas Tú y dos o tres amigos/as están en Caracas por dos días. Lean esta página de una guía turística sobre la ciudad y decidan qué van a hacer hoy por la mañana, por la tarde y por la noche.

> **modelo**

Estudiante 1: Visitemos el Museo de Arte Contemporáneo Sofía Imber esta mañana. Quiero ver las esculturas (*sculptures*) de Jesús Rafael Soto.

Estudiante 2: Sí. Después vamos a la Casa Natal de Simón Bolívar. ¡Qué interesante!

Estudiante 3: Está bien. Esta noche salgamos a un restaurante, pero no vayamos al Restaurante El Coyuco. Es muy caro.

Guía de Caracas

MUSEOS
- **Museo de Arte Colonial** Avenida Panteón
- **Museo de Arte Contemporáneo Sofía Imber** Parque Central Esculturas de Jesús Rafael Soto y pinturas de Miró, Chagall y Picasso.
- **Galería de Arte Nacional** Parque Central. Colección de más de 4.000 obras de arte venezolano.

SITIOS DE INTERÉS
- **Plaza Bolívar**
- **Jardín Botánico** Avenida Interna UCV. De 8:00 a 5:00.
- **Parque del Este** Avenida Francisco de Miranda. Parque más grande de la ciudad con serpentarium.
- **Casa Natal de Simón Bolívar** Esquinas San Jacinto y Traposos. Casa colonial donde nació Simón Bolívar.

RESTAURANTES
- **El Barquero** Avenida Luis Roche
- **Restaurante El Coyuco** Avenida Urdaneta
- **Restaurante Sorrento** Avenida Francisco Solano
- **Café Tonino** Avenida Andrés Bello

Nosotros commands and object pronouns

▶ Object pronouns are attached to affirmative **nosotros/as** commands. A written accent is added to maintain the original stress.

Firmemos el cheque.
Let's sign the check.

Firmémoslo.
Let's sign it.

Escribamos a Ana y Raúl.
Let's write to Ana and Raúl.

Escribámosles.
Let's write to them.

▶ Object pronouns are placed in front of negative **nosotros/as** commands.

No **les paguemos** el préstamo.
Let's not pay them the loan.

No **se lo digamos** a ellos.
Let's not tell them.

No **lo compremos.**
Let's not buy it.

No **se la presentemos.**
Let's not introduce her.

▶ When **nos** or **se** is attached to an affirmative **nosotros/as** command, the final **–s** is dropped.

Démoselo a ella.
Let's give it to her.

Mandémoselo a ellos.
Let's send it to them.

Sentémonos allí.
Let's sit down there.

Levantémonos temprano.
Let's get up early.

▶ The **nosotros/as** command form of **irse** (*to go away*) is **vámonos**. Its negative form is **no nos vayamos.**

¡Vámonos de vacaciones!
Let's go away on vacation!

No nos vayamos de aquí.
Let's not go away from here.

> **¡Manos a la obra!**

Indica los mandatos afirmativos y negativos de la primera persona del plural (**nosotros/as**) de los siguientes verbos.

	afirmativo	negativo
1. estudiar	estudiemos	no estudiemos
2. cenar		
3. leer		
4. decidir		
5. perder		
6. seguir		
7. practicar		
8. conocer		
9. decir		
10. cerrar		
11. levantarse		
12. irse		
13. dormir		
14. escribirle		
15. comprarlo		
16. pedírselo		

Ampliación

① Escuchar

A Lee estas frases y luego escucha la conversación entre Alberto y Eduardo. Indica si cada verbo se refiere a algo en el pasado, en el presente o en el futuro.

 TIP **Listen for specific information/linguistic cues.** You can often get the facts you need by listening for specific pieces of information. By listening for verb endings, you can figure out whether the verbs describe past, present, or future actions. Verb endings also indicate who is performing the action.

Acciones

1. Demetrio / comprar en Macro _____
2. Alberto / comprar en Macro _____
3. Alberto / estudiar psicología _____
4. carro / tener frenos malos _____
5. Eduardo / comprar un anillo para Rebeca _____
6. Eduardo / estudiar _____

B ¿Crees que Alberto y Eduardo viven en una ciudad grande o en un pueblo? ¿Cómo lo sabes?

② Conversar

Tú y un(a) compañero/a viven juntos/as en un apartamento y tienen problemas económicos. Describan los problemas y sugieran algunas soluciones.

modelo

Estudiante 1: No sé qué hacer. Casi no tengo el dinero para el alquiler.

Estudiante 2: Debes ahorrar más dinero—y yo también. No comamos en restaurantes. Comamos en casa.

Estudiante 1: Tal vez necesitemos mudarnos. Necesitamos un apartamento que sea más barato.

Estudiante 2: ¡Uy! No quiero mudarme. Pídele un préstamo a tu papá, mejor.

Estudiante 1: No lo puedo hacer cada mes. Pero tienes razón, podemos ahorrar dinero comiendo en casa.

Estudiante 2: Y no usemos más los cajeros automáticos. Paguemos todo de la cuenta corriente para saber mejor adónde va el dinero.

recursos

R	Textbook CD Lección 14	WB pp. 141-146	LM pp. 81-83	ICD-ROM Lección 14	vistahigher learning.com

Ampliación

③ Escribir

Escribe una carta a un(a) amigo/a en la cual le explicas claramente cómo llegar a tu casa desde el aeropuerto. Incluye también un mapa detallado para que no se confunda.

 TIP List key words. When you give directions, you use prepositions that describe location, such as **enfrente de, al lado de**, and **detrás de**. Making a list of these expressions will help you write your directions more efficiently.

Organízalo	Planea la mejor ruta para llegar a tu casa. Apunta las expresiones útiles para dar direcciones, como los nombres de las calles y de los monumentos.
Escríbelo	Dibuja un mapa y utilízalo para escribir el primer borrador de tu carta.
Corrígelo	Intercambia tu carta con un(a) compañero/a. Anota los aspectos mejor escritos. Ofrécele sugerencias. ¿Hay suficientes detalles? ¿Está claro el mapa? Si ves algunos errores, coméntaselos.
Compártelo	Revisa el primer borrador de la carta y el mapa según las indicaciones de tu compañero/a. Incorpora nuevas ideas y/o más información si es necesario antes de escribir la versión final.

④ Un paso más

Imagina que eres miembro de un grupo que está diseñando y promocionando una comunidad modelo en un país hispano. Diseña el folleto (*brochure*) publicitario para la comunidad.

- Escoge el lugar ideal para el proyecto. Considera el acceso a las ciudades grandes, los eventos culturales y las atracciones naturales.
- Incluye un mapa del país elegido que indique dónde está localizada la comunidad modelo.
- Crea un mapa de la zona que muestre las atracciones principales del centro de la comunidad.
- Explica las características de la comunidad.

 En Internet

Investiga estos temas en el sitio vistahigherlearning.com.

- Ciudades en España
- Ciudades en México, el Caribe y Centroamérica
- Ciudades en América del Sur

Antes de leer

You can understand a narrative more completely if you identify the point of view of the narrator. You can do this by simply asking yourself from whose perspective the story is being told. Some stories are narrated in the first person. That is, the narrator is a character in the story, and everything you read is filtered through that person's thoughts, emotions, and opinions. Other stories have an omniscient narrator who is not one of the story's characters, but reports the thoughts and actions of all the characters. This reading selection consists of an excerpt from the novel *La muerte de Artemio Cruz*, by Carlos Fuentes. Is this selection narrated in the first person or by an omniscient narrator? How can you tell?

_____

_____

Sobre el autor

Carlos Fuentes (1928-) es un renombrado escritor mexicano que ha ganado varios premios (*has won several prizes*) internacionales. Sus escritos demuestran una profunda preocupación por las cuestiones sociales y políticas.

La muerte de Artemio Cruz

(fragmento)
Carlos Fuentes

En la Ciudad de México, un hombre de negocios va en limusina al edificio donde trabaja.

Él vio pasar el domo naranja y las columnas blancas, gordas, del Palacio de Bellas Artes (...), la portada ocre, veneciana del Correo y las esculturas frondosas, las ubres plenas y las cornucopias vaciadas del Banco de México:

acarició la banda de seda del sombrero de fieltro marrón (...): los mosaicos azules de Sanborn's y la piedra labrada y negruzca del convento de San Francisco. El automóvil se detuvo en la esquina de Isabel la Católica y el chófer le abrió la puerta y se quitó la gorra y él, en cambio, se colocó el fieltro, peinándose con los dedos (...).

(…) y esa corte de vendedores (…) y mujeres enrebozadas y niños con el labio superior embarrado de moco lo rodearon hasta que pasó las puertas giratorias y se ajustó la corbata frente al vidrio del vestíbulo y atrás, en el segundo vidrio, el que daba a la calle de Madero, un hombre idéntico a él (…) se arreglaba el nudo de la corbata también, con los mismos dedos manchados de nicotina, el mismo traje cruzado, pero sin color, rodeado de los mendigos y dejaba caer la mano al mismo tiempo que él y luego le daba la espalda y caminaba al centro de la calle, mientras él buscaba el ascensor, desorientado por un instante.

Después de leer

¿Comprendiste?

Indica si las oraciones son **ciertas** o **falsas**. Corrige las oraciones falsas.

Cierto	Falso	
_____	_____	1. El hombre de negocios condujo su carro al centro.
_____	_____	2. El hombre de negocios tiene un sombrero que es de seda.
_____	_____	3. Mientras va al trabajo, el hombre ve el Palacio de Bellas Artes.
_____	_____	4. Mientras entraba en el edificio, lo rodeó un grupo de mendigos.
_____	_____	5. El hombre buscaba las escaleras.

Preguntas

1. ¿Es rico o pobre el hombre de negocios? ¿Cómo lo sabes?

_____

2. Cuando entra en el edificio donde trabaja, el hombre ve un grupo de mendigos. ¿Es indiferente a su sufrimiento?

_____

3. El hombre ve su propio reflejo en el vidrio, caminando hacia los pobres, y se siente desorientado. ¿Por qué?

_____

4. En tu opinión, ¿representa el reflejo otro aspecto de su personalidad?

_____

Coméntalo

¿Hay lugares mencionados en la lectura que tengan un valor (*value*) simbólico? ¿Qué simbolizan las personas que se mencionan? En tu opinión, ¿hay un comentario social en esta lectura? ¿Cuál es?

portada ocre	*ochre-colored façade*	**enrebozadas**	*wrapped up in shawls*
esculturas… plenas	*luxuriant sculptures, full udders*	**embarrado de moco**	*covered with snot*
acarició	*gently touched*	**rodearon**	*surrounded*
fieltro marrón	*brown felt*	**giratorias**	*revolving*
piedra labrada	*carved stone*	**atrás**	*behind*
se detuvo	*stopped*	**daba a**	*faced*
gorra	*cap*	**manchados**	*stained*
se colocó	*put on*	**mendigos**	*beggars*

En la ciudad

el banco	bank
la carnicería	butcher shop
el correo	post office
la frutería	fruit store
la heladería	ice cream shop
la joyería	jewelry store
la lavandería	laundromat
la panadería	bakery
la pastelería	pastry shop
la peluquería	hairdresser
la pescadería	fish market
el salón de belleza	beauty salon
el supermercado	supermarket
la zapatería	shoe store
hacer cola	to stand in line
hacer diligencias	to run errands

En el banco

el cajero automático	automatic teller machine, ATM
el cheque	check
el cheque de viajero	traveler's cheque
la cuenta corriente	checking account
la cuenta de ahorros	savings account
ahorrar	to save (money)
cobrar	to cash (a check), to charge (for a product or service)
depositar	to deposit
firmar	to sign
llenar (un formulario)	to fill out (a form)
pagar a plazos	to pay in installments
pagar al contado	to pay in cash
pedir prestado	to borrow
pedir un préstamo	to apply for a loan
ser gratis	to be free of charge

Direcciones

la cuadra	(city) block
la dirección	address
la esquina	corner
el letrero	sign
cruzar	to cross
dar direcciones	to give directions
doblar	to turn
estar perdido/a	to be lost
quedar	to be located
(al) este	(to the) east
(al) oeste	(to the) west
(al) norte	(to the) north
(al) sur	(to the) south
derecho	straight (ahead)
enfrente de	opposite; facing
hacia	toward

Expresiones útiles	See page 337.

En el correo

el cartero	mail carrier
el correo	mail
las estampillas	stamps
el paquete	package
los sellos	stamps
el sobre	envelope
echar (una carta) al buzón	to put (a letter) in the mailbox; to mail (a letter)
enviar	to send
mandar	to send

recursos

| R | Lab CD Lección 14 | LM p. 83 |

AVENTURAS EN LOS PAÍSES HISPANOS

El Canal de Panamá conecta los océanos Pacífico y Atlántico. Se construyó en 1903 y se terminó diez años después. La construcción costó 639 millones de dólares. Actualmente lo usan 38 barcos por día y por él pasan más de 12.000 barcos por año. Es la fuente *(source)* principal de ingresos *(income)* de Panamá. Cada barco paga aproximadamente $40.000 dólares de peaje *(toll)*.

AMÉRICA CENTRAL II

Nicaragua

Área: 129.494 km^2 (49.998 millas^2)

Población: 5.631.000

Capital: Managua – 1.133.000

Ciudades principales: León–164.000, Masaya–126.000, Granada–93.000

Moneda: córdoba oro

SOURCE: Population Division, UN Secretariat

Costa Rica

Área: 51.100 km^2 (19.730 millas^2)

Población: 4.370.000

Capital: San José – 1.055.000

Ciudades principales: Alajuela–174.000, Cartago–121.000, Puntarenas–103.000, Heredia–74.000

Moneda: colón costarricense

SOURCE: Population Division, UN Secretariat

Panamá

Área: 78.200 km^2 (30,193 millas^2)

Población: 3.026.000

Capital: Ciudad de Panamá – 1.276.000

Ciudades importantes: Colón–139.000, David–126.000

Moneda: balboa

SOURCE: Population Division, UN Secretariat

Costa Rica: nación progresista

Costa Rica es uno de los países más progresistas del mundo.
Da servicios médicos gratis a todos sus ciudadanos (*citizens*) y también a
los turistas. En 1870, Costa Rica abolió (*abolish*) la pena de muerte (*death
penalty*). En 1948, disolvió el ejército (*army*) e hizo obligatoria y gratis la
educación para todos los costarricenses.

Río Coco

Cordillera
Isabella

Nicaragua

Río Tuma

Sierra Madre

Cordillera
de Yolaina

● León

Lago de Managua

⭐ Managua

Masaya ●

Granada ● Lago de Nicaragua

Isla Zapatera

Isla Ometepe

Río San Juan

Océano Pacífico

La mola

La mola es un tejido de los cunas, una tribu indígena que vive en las
islas San Blas de Panamá. Las molas se hacen con piezas de tela
(*material*) de muchos colores. Las molas tradicionales tienen dibujos
(*patterns*) geométricos. Antes se usaban como ropa y hoy también se
usan para decorar casas.

Cordillera de
Guanacaste

Puntarenas

San José ⭐

Río Reventazó

Lim

Costa Rica

Cartago ●

Cordil.
Talama

Ernesto Cardenal

El nicaragüense Ernesto Cardenal es poeta, escultor y sacerdote *(priest)* católico. Es uno de los escritores más famosos de América Latina. Ha escrito más de treinta y cinco libros. Estudió en México y Estados Unidos. Cree en el poder *(power)* de la poesía para mejorar la sociedad y el mundo. Siempre ha trabajado para establecer la igualdad *(equality)* y la justicia en su país.

Óscar Arias

Óscar Arias, político costarricense, fue presidente de su país desde 1986 hasta 1990. Estudió en Costa Rica, Estados Unidos e Inglaterra. Fue profesor de Ciencias Políticas en la Universidad de Costa Rica. Cuando fue presidente, hizo un plan para establecer la paz *(peace)* en Centroamérica. Logró *(achieved)* un acuerdo *(agreement)* de paz con los presidentes de El Salvador, Nicaragua, Honduras y Guatemala. Por sus esfuerzos *(efforts)*, ganó el Premio Nobel de la Paz en 1987.

Mar Caribe

ocas del Toro

Canal de Panamá

Islas San Blas

Cordillera de San Blas

Colón

Río Chepo

Serranía de Tabasará

Ciudad de Panamá

Panamá

avid

Isla del Rey

Isla de Coiba

Golfo de Panamá

Colombia

¿Qué aprendiste?

1 **¿Cierto o falso?** Indica si las siguientes frases son **ciertas** o **falsas**.

	Cierto	Falso
1. El Canal de Panamá conecta los océanos Pacífico y Atlántico.	_____	_____
2. Por el Canal de Panamá pasan más de 12.000 barcos por día.	_____	_____
3. La población de Nicaragua es mayor que la de Panamá.	_____	_____
4. San José es la capital de Panamá.	_____	_____
5. En Costa Rica, la educación es gratis y obligatoria para todos los turistas.	_____	_____
6. Costa Rica disolvió el ejército en 1948.	_____	_____
7. La mola es una tribu indígena que vive en Panamá.	_____	_____
8. Las molas se usan hoy para decorar casas.	_____	_____
9. Ernesto Cardenal es uno de los escritores más famosos de América Latina.	_____	_____
10. Ernesto Cardenal estudió en Inglaterra.	_____	_____
11. Óscar Arias fue presidente de Panamá.	_____	_____
12. Óscar Arias ganó el Premio Nobel de la Paz en 1987.	_____	_____

2 **Preguntas** Contesta las siguientes preguntas con frases completas.

1. ¿Crees que el Canal de Panamá es importante? ¿Por qué?
2. ¿Por qué crees que Costa Rica es uno de los países más progresistas del mundo?
3. ¿Qué puedes hacer con una mola hecha por los cunas?
4. ¿Cuántos libros escribió Ernesto Cardenal? ¿Qué profesiones tiene, además de ser escritor?
5. ¿Por qué ganó Óscar Arias el Premio Nobel de la Paz?

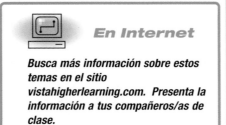

En Internet

Busca más información sobre estos temas en el sitio vistahigherlearning.com. Presenta la información a tus compañeros/as de clase.

- Costa Rica
- La mola
- Ernesto Cardenal
- Óscar Arias

15 El bienestar

Communicative Goals

You will learn how to:

- talk about an outing
- discuss nutrition
- describe an action or event in the immediate past
- describe an event that occurred before another past event

PREPARACIÓN

pages 356-361

- Words related to being healthy
- The gym and nutrition
- The letters **b** and **v**

AVENTURAS

pages 362-365

- The students and Martín go on their long-awaited hike. Don Francisco greets them when they return at the end of the day, and listens to their reactions to what they saw and experienced.

GRAMÁTICA

pages 366-373

- Past participles used as adjectives
- The present perfect
- The past perfect

LECTURA

pages 374-375

- Novel: excerpt from *Indicios pánicos*

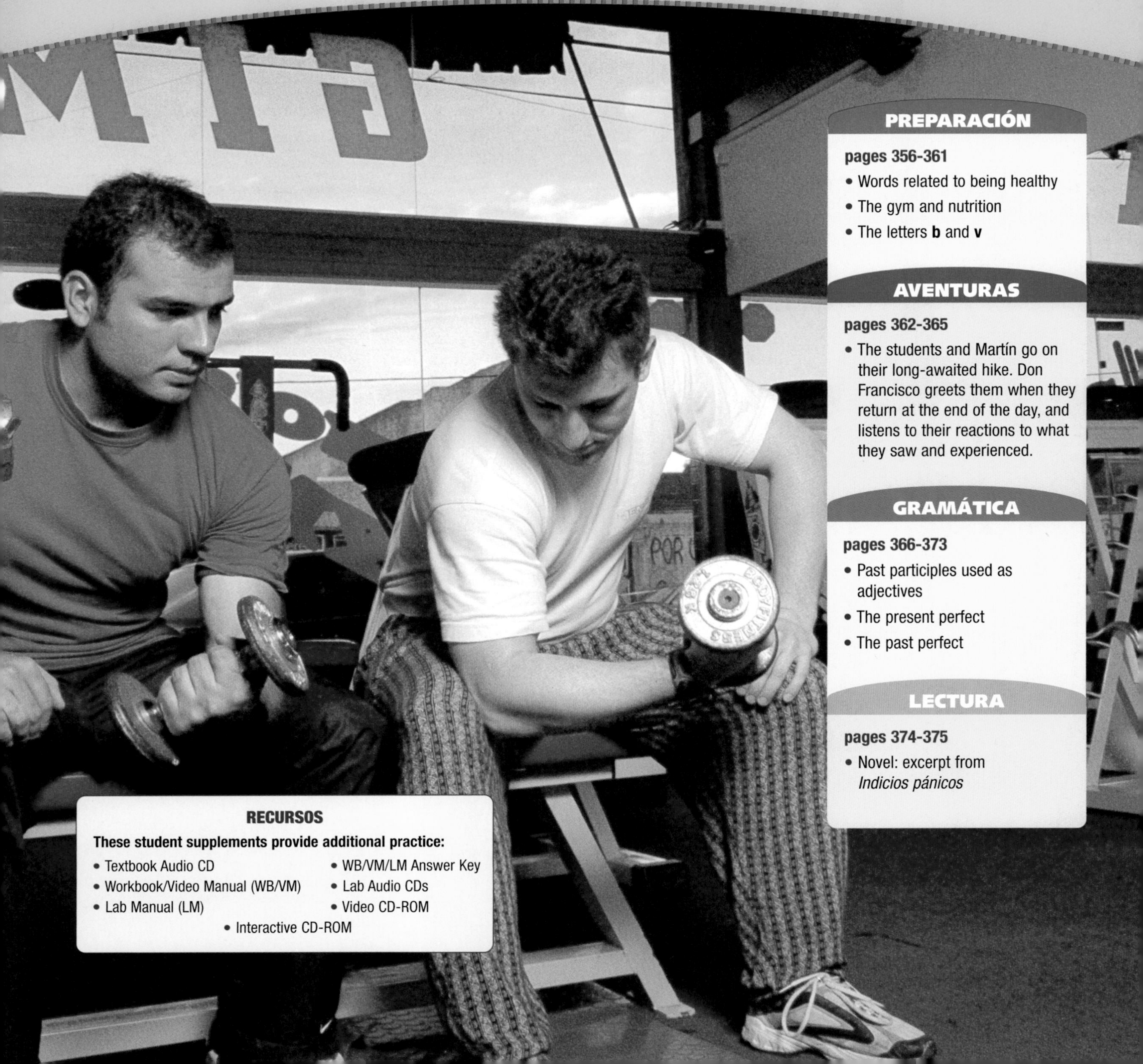

RECURSOS

These student supplements provide additional practice:

- Textbook Audio CD
- Workbook/Video Manual (WB/VM)
- Lab Manual (LM)
- WB/VM/LM Answer Key
- Lab Audio CDs
- Video CD-ROM
- Interactive CD-ROM

EL BIENESTAR

EL BIENESTAR

el bienestar *well-being*

aliviar el estrés/la tensión *to relieve stress/tension*
disfrutar (de) *to enjoy; to reap the benefits (of)*
llevar una vida sana *to lead a healthy lifestyle*
(no) fumar *(not) to smoke*

el masaje
massage

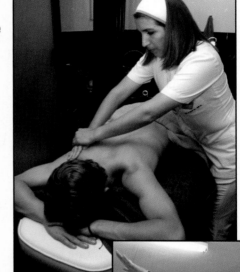

EN EL GIMNASIO

el/la monitor(a) *trainer*
el músculo *muscle*

calentarse (e:ie) *to warm-up*
entrenarse *to practice; to train*
estar en buena forma *to be in good shape*
hacer ejercicio *to exercise*
hacer ejercicios aeróbicos *to do aerobics*
hacer gimnasia *to work out*
mantenerse en forma *to stay in shape*
sudar *to sweat*

levantar pesas
to lift weights

hacer ejercicios de estiramiento
to do stretching exercises

la clase de ejercicios aeróbicos
aerobics class

recursos

R	Textbook CD Lección 15	WB pp. 149-150	LM p. 85	Lab CD Lección 15	ICD-ROM Lección 15

LA NUTRICIÓN

la caloría *calorie*

el colesterol *cholesterol*

la grasa *fat*

la merienda *(afternoon) snack*

los minerales *minerals*

la nutrición *nutrition*

la proteína *protein*

adelgazar *to lose weight; to slim down*

aumentar de peso *to gain weight*

comer una dieta equilibrada *to eat a balanced diet*

consumir alcohol *to consume alcohol*

engordar *to gain weight*

estar a dieta *to be on a diet*

descafeinado/a *decaffeinated*

merendar (e:ie)
to have a (afternoon) snack

las vitaminas
vitamins

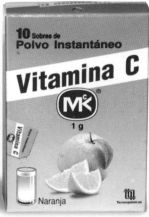

la bebida alcohólica
alcoholic beverage

ADJETIVOS

activo/a *active*

débil *weak*

flexible *flexible*

sedentario/a *sedentary*

tranquilo/a *calm; quiet*

fuerte
strong

OTRAS PALABRAS Y EXPRESIONES

la droga *drug*

el/la drogadicto/a *drug addict*

el/la teleadicto/a *couch potato*

apurarse *to hurry; to rush*

darse prisa *to hurry; to rush*

sufrir muchas presiones *to be under a lot of pressure*

tratar de + (*inf.*) *to try (to do something)*

en exceso *in excess; too much*

sin *without*

A escuchar

1 **¿Lógico o ilógico?** Escucha las frases e indica si cada frase es **lógica** o **ilógica**.

	Lógico	Ilógico
1.	_____	_____
2.	_____	_____
3.	_____	_____
4.	_____	_____
5.	_____	_____
6.	_____	_____
7.	_____	_____
8.	_____	_____

2 **¿Cómo se mantiene en buena forma?** Maribel habla de lo que hace para mantenerse en forma. Indica las cosas que hace.

_____ 1. Hacer ejercicios de estiramiento

_____ 2. Hacer ejercicios aeróbicos

_____ 3. Levantar pesas

_____ 4. Comer una dieta equilibrada

_____ 5. Practicar tenis

_____ 6. Tomar sólo bebidas descafeinadas

_____ 7. Correr

_____ 8. Pasear en bicicleta

_____ 9. Ir al gimnasio

_____ 10. Nadar

A practicar

3 **Identificar** Identifica el opuesto (*opposite*) de cada palabra, usando las palabras indicadas.

1. activo
2. adelgazar
3. débil
4. rígido

5. no tener prisa
6. estar sano
7. engordar
8. nervioso

sin	flexible
sudar	sedentario
tranquilo	en exceso
aumentar de peso	apurarse
fuerte	sufrir muchas presiones
estar enfermo	mantenerse en forma

4 **Combinar** Combina las palabras de las dos columnas para formar diez frases lógicas.

_____ 1. David levanta pesas…

_____ 2. Estás en buena forma…

_____ 3. Felipe se lastimó…

_____ 4. Mi hermano…

_____ 5. Sara hace ejercicios de…

_____ 6. Mis primos están a dieta…

_____ 7. Para llevar una vida sana…

_____ 8. Ellos sufren muchas…

a. aumentó de peso.

b. estiramiento.

c. presiones.

d. porque quieren adelgazar.

e. porque haces ejercicio.

f. un músculo de la pierna.

g. no se debe fumar.

h. y corre mucho.

5 **Describir** Describe lo que ocurre en los dibujos.

1.

3.

2.

4.

15 AVENTURAS

¡Qué buena excursión!

Martín y los estudiantes van de excursión.

1

MARTÍN Buenos días, don Francisco.
DON FRANCISCO ¡Hola, Martín!
MARTÍN Ya veo que han traído lo que necesitan. ¡Todos han venido muy bien equipados!

2

MARTÍN Muy bien. ¡Atención, chicos! Primero hagamos algunos ejercicios de estiramiento…

3

MARTÍN Es bueno que se hayan mantenido en buena forma. Entonces, jóvenes, ¿ya están listos?
JAVIER ¡Sí, listísimos! No puedo creer que finalmente haya llegado el gran día.

6

DON FRANCISCO ¡Hola! ¡Qué alegría verlos! ¿Cómo les fue en la excursión?
JAVIER Increíble, don Efe. Nunca había visto un paisaje tan espectacular. Es un lugar estupendo. Saqué mil fotos y tengo montones de escenas para dibujar.

7

MAITE Nunca había hecho una excursión. ¡Me encantó! Cuando vuelva a España, voy a tener mucho que contarle a mi familia.

8

INÉS Ha sido la mejor excursión de mi vida. Amigos, Martín, don Efe, mil gracias.

recursos

R | Video/VCD-ROM Lección 15 | VM pp.197-198 | ICD-ROM Lección 15

Personajes

DON FRANCISCO

JAVIER

INÉS

ÁLEX

MAITE

MARTÍN

Expresiones útiles

Getting ready to start a hike

Ya veo que han traído lo que necesitan.
I see that you have brought what you need.

¡Todos han venido muy bien equipados!
Everyone has come very well-equipped!

¿(Están) listos?
(Are you) ready?

¡En marcha, pues!
Let's get going, then!

Talking about a hike

¿Cómo les fue en la excursión?
How did the hike go?

Nunca había visto un paisaje tan espectacular.
I had never seen such spectacular scenery.

Nunca había hecho una excursión.
¡Me encantó!
I had never gone on a hike before. I loved it!

Ha sido la mejor excursión de mi vida.
It's been the best hike of my life.

Courtesy expressions

Gracias por todo.
Thanks for everything.

Ha sido un placer.
It's been a pleasure.

¡Cuídense!
Take care!

MARTÍN ¡Fabuloso! ¡En marcha, pues!
DON FRANCISCO ¡Adiós! ¡Cuídense!

Martín y los estudiantes pasan ocho horas caminando en las montañas. Hablan, sacan fotos y disfrutan del paisaje. Se divierten muchísimo.

ÁLEX Sí, gracias, Martín. Gracias por todo.
MARTÍN No hay de qué. Ha sido un placer.

DON FRANCISCO Chicos, pues es hora de volver. Creo que la Sra. Vives nos ha preparado una cena muy especial.

¿Qué piensas?

1 Seleccionar Selecciona la opción que mejor completa cada frase.

1. Antes de salir, Martín les recomienda a los estudiantes que hagan

    a. ejercicios de estiramiento.   b. ejercicios aeróbicos.
    c. gimnasia.

2. Los excursionistas hablaron, _____ en las montañas.

    a. levantaron pesas y se divirtieron   b. caminaron y dibujaron
    c. sacaron fotos y disfrutaron del paisaje

3. Inés dice que ha sido la mejor excursión

    a. del viaje.   b. del año.
    c. de su vida.

4. Cuando Maite vuelva a España, va a

    a. tener montones de escenas para dibujar.   b. tener mucho que contarle a su familia.
    c. tener muchas fotos que enseñarle a su familia.

5. La señora Vives les ha preparado

    a. una cena especial.   b. un día en las montañas muy especial.
    c. una excursión espectacular.

2 Completar Completa las frases.

1. A Javier le duelen los músculos después de caminar tanto.
   Hoy lo que necesita es _____

2. Don Francisco a veces sufre presiones y estrés en su trabajo.
   Debe hacer ejercicio para _____

3. A Inés le encanta salir con amigos o leer un buen libro.
   Ella nunca va a ser una _____

4. Álex trata de comer una dieta equilibrada. Por ejemplo, trata
   de llevar una dieta sin mucha _____

5. A Maite no le duelen los músculos. Cuatro veces por semana
   hace gimnasia para _____

grasa	vitamina
teleadicta	aliviar el estrés
un masaje	mantenerse en forma

3 Minidrama Usando el episodio de **Aventuras** como fuente (*source*) de ideas, trabaja con dos
o tres amigos/as para preparar un minidrama en tres partes, en el que hacen una excursión por la
montaña. El minidrama debe incluir los siguientes elementos.

• Una breve conversación antes de comenzar la excursión.

• Una conversación durante la excursión, mencionando algunas de las cosas que ven y hacen.

• Después de la excursión, una conversación en la que comentan las cosas que ocurrieron.

Exploración
El bienestar en el mundo hispano

España es conocida por su dieta mediterránea, caracterizada por el arroz, los productos lácteos, las frutas y las verduras frescas. El uso del aceite de oliva y el consumo de pescado reducen el colesterol y las proteínas animales en la dieta.

La yerba mate, una bebida similar al té, es popular en Argentina, Uruguay y Paraguay. Se dice que controla el estrés y la obesidad, y que estimula el sistema inmunológico. Tradicionalmente, se toma en una calabaza (*gourd*) con una bombilla filtrante (*tea-filtering straw*).

Observaciones

• Según leyendas indígenas, la yerba mate tiene orígenes divinos.

• El vino tinto, consumido con moderación en las comidas de países como Chile, Argentina y España, combate las enfermedades cardiovasculares.

• Chile tiene mucha actividad geotérmica y una gran cantidad de centros termales para reducir el estrés y mantenerse en forma.

De origen vasco, el deporte jai alai se diseminó por España antes de llegar a México y a la Florida. Parecido a la pelota de frontón (*handball*), tiene fama de ser el deporte más rápido del mundo. También era uno de los más peligrosos, antes de la introducción de los cascos (*helmets*),en 1968.

Coméntalo

Con un(a) compañero/a, contesta las siguientes preguntas.

• ¿Te interesa seguir alguna de las estrategias mencionadas aquí? ¿Cuál y por qué?

• ¿Prefieres lograr *(achieve)* tu bienestar con una dieta, con ejercicios, con métodos alternativos o con un poco de todo?

recursos

R

vistahigher learning.com

15.1 Past participles used as adjectives

Forming past participles

▶ The past participles of English verbs often end in **–ed** (*to turn* ➔ *turned*), but many are also irregular (*to buy* ➔ *bought; to drive* ➔ *driven*).

▶ In Spanish, regular **–ar** verbs form the past participle with **–ado**. Regular **–er** and **–ir** verbs form the past participle with **–ido**.

INFINITIVE		STEM		PAST PARTICIPLE
bailar	▶	bail-	▶	bailado
comer		com-		comido
vivir		viv-		vivido

▶ You already know several past participles used as adjectives: **aburrido, interesado, nublado, perdido,** etc.

Sólo tomo café descafeinado.

Estoy cansada.

▶ Note that all irregular past participles, except for those of **decir (dicho)** and **hacer (hecho)**, end in **–to.**

Irregular past participles

abrir	▶	abierto		morir	▶	muerto
decir		dicho		poner		puesto
describir		descrito		resolver		resuelto
descubrir		descubierto		romper		roto
escribir		escrito		ver		visto
hacer		hecho		volver		vuelto

¡ojo! The past participles of **–er** and **–ir** verbs whose stems end in **–a, –e,** or **–o** carry a written accent mark on the **i** of the **–ido** ending.

caer	▶	caído		oír	▶	oído		sonreír	▶	sonreído
creer		creído		reír		reído		traer		traído
leer		leído								

Práctica

1 **Completar** Completa estas frases con la forma adecuada del participio pasado.

1. El hombre _____ [describir] en ese panfleto es un monitor del gimnasio.
2. Serena Williams es una atleta muy _____ [conocer].
3. ¿Está _____ [descubrir] ya todo el petróleo del mundo?
4. Los libros _____ [usar] son más baratos que los nuevos.
5. Los documentos están _____ [firmar].
6. Creo que el gimnasio está _____ [abrir] veinticuatro horas al día.

2 **Describir** Completa las frases con las palabras indicadas.

no está hecha	están abiertas
están firmados	está muerto
está cerrada	está rota
están aburridos	están descritos

1. Los estudiantes
   _____.

4. Los cheques
   _____.

2. La ventana
   _____.

5. La cama
   _____.

3. La puerta
   _____.

6. El Sr. Vargas
   _____.

Conversación

3 **Preguntas** En parejas, túrnense para hacerse estas preguntas.

1. ¿Qué haces cuando no estás preparado/a para una clase?
2. ¿Qué haces cuando estás perdido/a en una ciudad?
3. ¿Está ordenado tu cuarto?
4. ¿Dejas la luz prendida en tu cuarto?
5. ¿Prefieres comprar libros usados o nuevos? ¿Por qué?
6. ¿Tienes mucho dinero ahorrado?
7. ¿Necesitas pedirles dinero prestado a tus padres?
8. ¿Quiénes están aburridos en la clase?
9. ¿Hay alguien que esté dormido en la clase?
10. ¿Cuándo está abierto el gimnasio de la universidad?

4 **Encuesta** Circula por la clase y pregunta a tus compañeros hasta que encuentres a las personas que correspondan a cada descripción. Anota sus respuestas, luego informa a la clase de los resultados.

Descripciones	Nombres	Otra información
1. Tiene algo roto en casa. (¿Qué es?)		
2. Lleva algo hecho en Europa o en un país hispano. (¿Qué es?)		
3. Tiene su libro abierto. (¿Qué libro?)		
4. Toma café descafeinado. (¿Cuándo?)		
5. Está interesado/a en trabajar en un banco. (¿Por qué?)		
6. Hace ejercicios aeróbicos todos los días. (¿Dónde y por qué?)		
7. Tiene un pariente o un(a) amigo/a muy conocido/a. (¿Quién?)		
8. Es teleadicto/a. (¿Cuáles son sus programas favoritos?)		

Past participles used as adjectives

La ventana está rota.   **La puerta está abierta.**

▶ Past participles can be used as adjectives. They are often used with the verb **estar** to describe a condition or state that results from an action. When used as adjectives, past participles must agree in gender and number with the nouns they modify.

En la entrada, hay algunos letreros **escritos** en español.
In the entrance, there are some signs written in Spanish.

Tenemos la mesa **puesta** y la cena **hecha**.
We have the table set and dinner made.

El gimnasio **está cerrado**.
The gym is closed.

El cheque ya **está firmado**.
The check is already signed.

Revista Capital

Consejos financieros escritos por gente que sabe.

Inclusive si su negocio va mal, su compañía no está acabada. ¡Tenemos la solución y montones de ideas listas para poner en práctica!

¡Manos a la obra!

 Indica la forma correcta del participio pasado de estos verbos.

1. hablar   _hablado_
2. beber _____
3. decidir _____
4. romper _____
5. escribir _____
6. cantar _____
7. oír _____
8. traer _____
9. correr _____
10. leer _____

11. ver _____
12. hacer _____
13. morir _____
14. reír _____
15. mirar _____
16. abrir _____
17. decir _____
18. volver _____
19. poner _____
20. descubrir _____

15.2 The present perfect

▸ The present perfect indicative tense (**el pretérito perfecto de indicativo**) is used to talk about what someone *has done*. It is formed with the present tense of **haber** and a past participle.

Ya veo que han traído todo lo que necesitan.

Todos han venido muy bien equipados.

Present indicative of *haber*

Singular forms		Plural forms	
yo	he	nosotros/as	hemos
tú	has	vosotros/as	habéis
Ud./él/ella	ha	Uds./ellos/ellas	han

Tú no **has cerrado** la puerta.	¿**Ha asistido** Juan a la clase?
You haven't closed the door.	*Has Juan attended class?*
Yo ya **he leído** esos libros.	**Hemos presentado** el proyecto.
I've already read those books.	*We have presented the project.*

▸ The past participle agrees with the noun when it functions as an adjective, but not when it is part of the present perfect tense.

Clara **ha abierto** las ventanas.	Las ventanas están **abiertas**.
Clara has opened the windows.	*The windows are open.*
Yo **he cerrado** la puerta.	La puerta está **cerrada**.
I've closed the door.	*The door is closed.*

▸ The present perfect is generally used just as in English: to talk about what *has occurred*. It usually refers to the recent past.

He trabajado cuarenta horas.	¿Cuál es el último libro que **has leído**?
I have worked forty hours.	*What is the last book that you have read?*

¡ojo! To say that someone has *just done something*, **acabar de** + [*infinitive*] is used.

Juan **acaba de llegar**.	Ellos **acaban de salir**.
Juan has just arrived.	*They have just left.*
Acabo de terminar mi tarea.	**Acabamos de cenar.**
I have just finished my homework.	*We have just eaten dinner.*

Práctica

1 **Completar** Estas oraciones describen el estilo de vida (*lifestyle*) de unos estudiantes. Complétalas con el pretérito perfecto de indicativo de los verbos indicados.

adelgazar	aumentar
comer	sufrir
hacer	llevar

1. Luisa _____ muchas presiones este año.
2. Juan y Raúl _____ de peso porque no hacen ejercicio.
3. Pero María Luisa _____ porque trabaja demasiado y siempre se olvida de comer.
4. Hasta ahora, yo _____ una vida muy sana.
5. Pero tú y yo no _____ gimnasia este semestre.
6. Tampoco _____ una dieta equilibrada recientemente.

2 **Estilos de vida** Marisela ha cambiado su estilo de vida porque quiere llevar una vida sana. Explica lo que ha hecho según el modelo. Luego explica lo que tú has hecho al respecto (*in that regard*).

modelo

Encontrar un buen gimnasio
Marisela ha encontrado un buen gimnasio. Yo no he encontrado un gimnasio, pero sé que debo buscar uno.

1. Tratar de estar en forma
2. Estar a dieta los últimos dos meses
3. Dejar de tomar refrescos
4. Hacerse una prueba de colesterol
5. Entrenar cinco días a la semana este año
6. Cambiar de una vida sedentaria a una vida activa
7. Tomar vitaminas por la noche y por la mañana
8. Hacer ejercicio para relajarse
9. Consumir mucha proteína este mes
10. Dejar de fumar
11. Levantar pesas tres días a la semana
12. Aliviar el estrés

Conversación

3 **¿Qué han hecho estas personas?** En parejas, describan lo que han hecho y lo que no han hecho las personas en cada dibujo. Usen la imaginación.

Jorge y Raúl

Natalia y Diego

Luisa

Ricardo

Jacobo

Carmen

4 **Describir** En parejas, identifiquen a una persona que lleva una vida muy sana. Puede ser una persona que conocen o un personaje que aparece en una película o programa de televisión. Entre los dos, escriban una descripción de lo que la persona ha hecho para llevar una vida sana.

modelo

Sammy Sosa ha llevado una vida muy sana. Ha hecho todo lo posible para mantenerse en forma. Para jugar muy bien al béisbol, él ha ....

Using the present perfect

▸ **Haber** and the past participle cannot be separated.

Siempre **hemos vivido** en Bolivia.
We have always lived in Bolivia.

Ud. nunca **ha venido** a mi oficina.
You have never come to my office.

▸ The word **no** and any object or reflexive pronouns are placed immediately before **haber**.

Yo **no he cobrado** el cheque.
I have not cashed the check.

¿Por qué **no lo has cobrado**?
Why haven't you cashed it?

Susana ya **lo ha hecho**.
Susana has already done it.

Ellos **no lo han arreglado**.
They haven't fixed it.

▸ *To have* can be a main verb or an auxiliary verb. As a main verb, it corresponds to **tener**, while as an auxiliary, it corresponds to **haber**.

Tengo muchos amigos.
I have a lot of friends.

No **he** visto el programa.
I have not seen the program.

Tengo un problema.
I have a problem.

He resuelto mi problema.
I have resolved my problem.

▸ The present perfect of **hay** is **ha habido**.

Ha habido muchos problemas con el nuevo profesor.
There have been a lot of problems with the new professor.

Ha habido un accidente en la calle Central.
There has been an accident on Central Street.

¡Manos a la obra!

 Indica el pretérito perfecto de indicativo de los siguientes verbos.

1. yo *he disfrutado, he comido, he vivido* [disfrutar, comer, vivir]
2. tú _____ [traer, adelgazar, compartir]
3. Ud. _____ [venir, estar, correr]
4. ella _____ [leer, resolver, poner]
5. ellos _____ [decir, romper, hacer]
6. nosotros _____ [mantenerse, dormirse]
7. yo _____ [estar, escribir, ver]
8. él _____ [vivir, correr, morir]

15.3 The past perfect

▸ The past perfect indicative (**el pretérito pluscuamperfecto de indicativo**) is used to talk about what someone *had done* or what *had occurred* before another past action or state. The past perfect uses the imperfect of **haber** plus the past participle.

Nunca había visto un paisaje tan espectacular.

Nunca había hecho una excursión.

Past perfect indicative		
	cerrar	**perder**	**asistir**
yo	había **cerrado**	había **perdido**	había **asistido**
tú	habías **cerrado**	habías **perdido**	habías **asistido**
Ud./él/ella	había **cerrado**	había **perdido**	había **asistido**
nosotros/as	habíamos **cerrado**	habíamos **perdido**	habíamos **asistido**
vosotros/as	habíais **cerrado**	habíais **perdido**	habíais **asistido**
Uds./ellos/ellas	habían **cerrado**	habían **perdido**	habían **asistido**

Antes de 2003, **había vivido** aquí.
Before 2003, I had lived here.

Cuando llegamos, Luis ya **había salido**.
When we arrived, Luis had left already.

▸ The past perfect is often used with the word **ya** (*already*). Note that **ya** cannot be placed between **haber** and the past participle.

Ella ya **había empezado** cuando llamaron.

She had begun already when they called.

Cuando llegué a casa, Raúl **ya se había acostado**.

When I arrived home, Raúl had already gone to bed.

¡Manos a la obra!

Indica el pretérito pluscuamperfecto de indicativo de cada verbo.

1. Nosotros ya <u>habíamos cenado</u> [cenar] cuando nos llamaron.
2. Antes de tomar esta clase, yo no _____ [estudiar] nunca el español.
3. Antes de ir a México, ellos nunca _____ [ir] a otro país.
4. Eduardo nunca _____ [entrenarse] antes de este año.
5. Tú siempre _____ [llevar] una vida sana antes del año pasado.
6. Antes de conocerte, yo ya te _____ [ver] muchas veces.

Práctica

1 Completar Completa los minidiálogos con las formas correctas del pretérito pluscuamperfecto de indicativo.

SARA Antes de cumplir los 15 años, ¿_____ [estudiar] tú otra lengua?

JOSÉ Sí, _____ [tomar] clases de inglés y de italiano.

• • •

DOLORES Antes del 2000, ¿_____ [viajar] tú y tu familia a Europa?

TOMÁS Sí, _____ [visitar] Europa tres veces.

• • •

ANTONIO Antes de este año, ¿_____ [correr] Ud. en un maratón?

SRA. VERA No, nunca lo _____ [hacer].

• • •

SOFÍA Antes de su enfermedad, ¿_____ [sufrir] muchas presiones tu tío?

IRENE Sí… y mi tío nunca _____ [mantenerse] en buena forma.

2 Quehaceres Indica lo que ya había hecho cada miembro de la familia antes de la llegada de la madre, la Sra. Ferrer.

Teresa Carmen el Sr. Ferrer Tomás su suegra Armando

3 Tu vida Indica si ya habías hecho las siguientes cosas antes de cumplir los dieciséis años.

1. Hacer un viaje en avión
2. Escalar una montaña
3. Escribir un poema
4. Leer una novela
5. Enamorarse
6. Tomar una clase de educación física
7. Montar a caballo
8. Ir de pesca
9. Manejar un carro
10. Navegar en Internet

Conversación

 Oraciones En parejas, conversen sobre los siguientes temas, usando el pretérito pluscuamperfecto de indicativo.

1. Cuando yo llamé a mi mejor amigo/a la semana pasada, él/ella ya…

2. Antes de este año, mis amigos y yo nunca…

3. Hasta el año pasado, yo siempre…

4. Antes de cumplir los veinte años, mi mejor amigo/a…

5. Antes de cumplir los treinta años, mis padres ya…

6. Hasta que cumplí los dieciocho años, yo no…

7. Antes de este semestre, el/la profesor(a) de español no…

8. Antes de tomar esta clase, yo nunca…

 Lo dudo Escribe cinco oraciones, algunas ciertas y otras falsas, sobre cosas que habías hecho antes de venir a la universidad. Luego, en grupos, túrnense para leer sus oraciones. Cada miembro del grupo debe decir "es cierto" o "lo dudo" después de cada una. Escribe la reacción de cada compañero/a. ¿Quién obtuvo más respuestas ciertas?

> **modelo**
>
> **Estudiante 1:** Cuando tenía 10 años, ya había manejado el carro de mi papá.
>
> **Estudiante 2:** Lo dudo.
>
> **Estudiante 3:** Es cierto.

 Entrevista En parejas, preparen una conversación en la que un(a) periodista de televisión está entrevistando (*interviewing*) a un(a) actor/actriz famoso/a que está haciendo un vídeo de ejercicios aeróbicos. El/la periodista le hace preguntas para descubrir la siguiente información:

- Si siempre se había mantenido en forma antes de hacer este vídeo

- Si había seguido una dieta especial antes de hacer este vídeo

- Qué le recomienda a la gente que quiere mantenerse en forma

- Qué le recomienda a la gente que quiere adelgazar

- Qué va a hacer cuando termine este vídeo

Español en vivo

¡Acabo de descubrir una nueva vida!

Antes, siempre había preferido mirar la TV en mis ratos libres. ¡Era un teleadicto! Jamás había practicado ningún deporte y había aumentado de peso recientemente.

Ahora, he empezado a comer una dieta más sana y voy al gimnasio. Disfruto de una vida sana y…. ¡Estoy realmente feliz!

Manténgase en forma. Su cuerpo y su mente se lo agradecen.

Gimnasio Olímpico

Identificar

Identifica los ejemplos del pretérito pluscuamperfecto del indicativo en el anuncio.

Preguntas

1. ¿Cómo era la vida del hombre cuando llevaba una vida sedentaria? ¿Cómo es ahora?

2. ¿Te identificas con algunos de los hábitos, presentes o pasados, de este hombre? ¿Con cuáles?

3. ¿Qué les recomienda el hombre del anuncio a los lectores? ¿Crees que les da un buen consejo?

Ampliación

1 Escuchar

A Escucha lo que dice Ofelia Cortez de Bauer. Anota algunos de los cognados que escuchas y también la idea general del discurso.

 TIP **Listen for the gist/cognates.** By listening for the gist, you can get the general idea of what you're hearing. Listening for cognates will help you to fill in the details.

Cognados	Idea general
_____	_____
_____	_____
_____	_____

Ahora indica si las siguientes frases son **ciertas** o **falsas**.

Cierto   Falso

_____   _____   1. La señora Bauer habla de la importancia de estar en buena forma.

_____   _____   2. Según la Sra. Bauer, es importante que todos sigan el mismo programa.

_____   _____   3. La Sra. Bauer participa en actividades individuales y de grupo.

_____   _____   4. Según la Sra. Bauer, el objetivo más importante de cada persona debe ser adelgazar.

B ¿Sigues los consejos de la señora Bauer? Explica tu respuesta. ¿Qué piensas de los consejos que ella da? ¿Hay otra información que ella debía haber incluido?

2 Conversar

Con un(a) compañero/a, preparen una conversación entre el/la enfermero/a de la clínica de la universidad y un(a) estudiante que no se siente bien. Incluyan la siguiente información en su conversación. Luego preséntenla a la clase.

- ¿De dónde viene el problema?
- ¿Tiene buenos hábitos el/la estudiante?
- ¿Qué ha hecho el/la estudiante en los últimos meses? ¿Cómo se ha sentido?
- ¿Qué recomendaciones tiene el/la enfermero/a para el/la estudiante?
- ¿Qué va a hacer el/la estudiante para llevar una vida más sana?

recursos

R	Textbook CD Lección 15	WB pp. 151-156	LM pp. 87-89	Lab CD Lección 15	ICD-ROM Lección 15	vistahigher learning.com

Ampliación

3 Escribir

Desarrolla un plan personal para mejorar tu bienestar físico y emocional. Considera la nutrición, el ejercicio y el estrés.

 TIP Organize your information logically. To make your writing and message clearer to your readers, organize information chronologically or in order of importance.

Organízalo	Escribe tus objetivos. Anota lo que has hecho hasta ahora, lo que no has hecho, y lo que todavía tienes que hacer para conseguir tus objetivos.
Escríbelo	Organiza tus apuntes y escribe el primer borrador de tu plan personal.
Corrígelo	Intercambia tu plan personal con un(a) compañero/a. Ofrécele sugerencias para mejorar la organización. ¿Incluye toda la información pertinente? ¿Es lógica la organización? Si ves algunos errores, coméntaselos.
Compártelo	Prepara la versión final, tomando en cuenta los comentarios de tu compañero/a. Luego júntate con otro/a compañero/a y comparen lo que han escrito. ¿Cómo son similares sus planes? ¿Cómo son diferentes?

4 Un paso más

Imagina que estás a cargo de (*in charge of*) promocionar una excursión de aventuras con actividades deportivas en algún país hispano. Crea un folleto (*brochure*) atractivo para vender la idea de la excursión; compara tu folleto con los de tus compañeros/as.

- Escoge el país y los lugares que van a visitar.
- Describe las actividades deportivas y de aventura que van a hacer en cada lugar.
- Explica los aspectos de la excursión que son importantes para la salud.
- Incluye el costo del viaje.

 En Internet

Investiga estos temas en el sitio vistahigherlearning.com.

- Actividades deportivas en el mundo hispano
- Turismo alternativo en el mundo hispano

Antes de leer

For dramatic effect and to achieve a smoother writing style, authors often do not explicitly supply the reader with all the details of a story. Clues in the text can help you infer those things the writer chooses not to state in a direct manner. You simply "read between the lines" to fill in the missing information and draw conclusions about the story.

Sobre la autora

Cristina Peri Rossi (1941 -) Nació en Uruguay, pero ahora vive en España. En sus cuentos, novelas y poemas explora las pasiones, el aislamiento (*isolation*) y las incertidumbres (*uncertainties*) que sentimos como seres humanos (*human beings*).

14 (De Indicios pánicos)

Cristina Peri Rossi

Ella me ha entregado la felicidad dentro de una caja bien cerrada, y me la ha dado, diciéndome:

—Ten cuidado, no vayas a perderla, no seas distraída, me ha costado un gran esfuerzo conseguirla: los mercados estaban cerrados, en las tiendas ya no había y los pocos vendedores ambulantes que existían se han jubilado, porque tenían los pies cansados. Ésta es la única que pude hallar en la plaza, pero es de las legítimas. Tiene un poco menos brillo que aquella que consumíamos mientras éramos jóvenes y está un poco arrugada, pero si caminas bien, no notarás la diferencia. Si la apoyas en alguna parte, por favor, recógela antes de irte, y si decides tomar un ómnibus, apriétala bien entre las manos: la ciudad está llena de ladrones y fácilmente te la podrían arrebatar.

Después de todas estas recomendaciones soltó la caja y me la puso entre las manos. Mientras caminaba, noté que no pesaba mucho pero que era un poco incómoda de usar: mientras la sostenía no podía tocar otra cosa, ni me animaba a dejarla depositada, para hacer las compras. De manera que no podía entretenerme, y menos aún, detenerme a explorar, como era mi costumbre. A la mitad de la tarde tuve frío. Quería abrirla, para saber si era de las legítimas, pero ella me dijo que se podía evaporar. Cuando desprendí el papel, noté que en la etiqueta venía una leyenda:

"Consérvese sin usar."

Desde ese momento tengo la felicidad guardada en una caja. Los domingos de mañana la llevo a pasear, por la plaza, para que los demás me envidien y lamenten su situación; de noche la guardo en el fondo del ropero. Pero se aproxima el verano y tengo un temor: ¿cómo la defenderé de las polillas?

Después de leer

¿Comprendiste?

1. La persona que narra el cuento, ¿es hombre o es mujer?
2. El regalo, la felicidad, ¿fue fácil o difícil de conseguir?
3. ¿La felicidad se compró en la calle o en una tienda?
4. Según la persona que la dio, ¿esta felicidad es de mejor o de peor calidad que la que tenía de joven?
5. Según ella, ¿hay mucho o poco riesgo de perder la felicidad?
6. ¿Cuál es el problema con la felicidad?
7. Al final, ¿qué hace la narradora con la felicidad?

Preguntas

1. ¿Qué debe hacer la narradora para cuidar la felicidad?
2. ¿Qué límites le impone la felicidad a la narradora?
3. ¿Cómo quiere la narradora que su felicidad afecte a otras personas?
4. ¿Por qué tiene miedo de las polillas la narradora?

Coméntalo

Para ti, ¿qué significa este cuento? ¿Qué dice de la felicidad? ¿Qué dice de la sociedad y las relaciones humanas? ¿Te parecen importantes la edad y el sexo de la persona que narra? ¿Y de la persona que le dio la felicidad? ¿Qué relación tienen las dos personas? En el cuento, ¿cuáles son las ventajas (*advantages*) y desventajas de tener la felicidad? ¿Te parece un buen regalo? ¿Qué recomendaciones tienes para la narradora del cuento?

me… caja	*handed me happiness in a box*
esfuerzo	*effort*
la única que	*the only one*
pude hallar	*I could find*
brillo	*shine*
arrugada	*wrinkled*
no notarás	*you won't notice*
Si… parte	*If you set it down somewhere*
apriétala	*hold*
ladrones	*thieves*
arrebatar	*to snatch*
soltó	*let go of*
pesaba	*weighed*
desprendí	*I took off*
etiqueta	*label*
leyenda	*inscription*
envidien	*envy*
en… ropero	*in the back of the closet*
defenderé	*will I defend*
polillas	*moths*

recursos

R

vistahigher
learning.com

El bienestar

el bienestar	well-being
la clase de ejercicios aeróbicos	aerobics class
la droga	drug
el/la drogadicto/a	drug addict
el masaje	massage
el/la monitor(a)	trainer
el músculo	muscle
el/la teleadicto/a	couch potato; television addict
adelgazar	to lose weight; to slim down
aliviar el estrés/ la tensión	to relieve stress/ tension
apurarse	to hurry; to rush
aumentar de peso	to gain weight
calentarse (e:ie)	to warm up
darse prisa	to hurry up; to rush
disfrutar (de)	to enjoy; to reap the benefits (of)
engordar	to gain weight
entrenarse	to practice; to train
estar a dieta	to be on a diet
estar en buena forma	to be in good shape
(no) fumar	(not) to smoke
hacer ejercicio	to exercise
hacer ejercicios aeróbicos	to do aerobics
hacer ejercicios de estiramiento	to do stretching exercises
hacer gimnasia	to work out
levantar pesas	to lift weights
llevar una vida sana	to lead a healthy lifestyle
mantenerse en forma	to stay in shape
sudar	to sweat
sufrir muchas presiones	to be under a lot of pressure
tratar de + (inf.)	to try (to do something)
activo/a	active
débil	weak
flexible	flexible
fuerte	strong
sedentario/a	sedentary
tranquilo/a	calm; quiet

La nutrición

la bebida alcohólica	alcoholic beverage
la caloría	calorie
el colesterol	cholesterol
la grasa	fat
la merienda	(afternoon) snack
los minerales	minerals
la nutrición	nutrition
la proteína	protein
las vitaminas	vitamins
comer una dieta equilibrada	to eat a balanced diet
consumir alcohol	to consume alcohol
merendar (e:ie)	to have a(n) (afternoon) snack
descafeinado/a	decaffeinated

Palabras adicionales

en exceso	in excess; too much
sin	without

Expresiones útiles	See page 363.
Irregular past participles	See page 366.

recursos

| R | Lab CD Lección 89 | LM p. 89 |

16 El mundo del trabajo

EL MUNDO DEL TRABAJO

el científico
scientist

LAS OCUPACIONES

el/la abogado/a *lawyer*

la actriz *actress*

el/la arquitecto/a *architect*

el/la arqueólogo/a *archeologist*

el bailarín *dancer*

la bailarina *dancer*

el/la cantante *singer*

el/la carpintero/a *carpenter*

el/la consejero/a *counselor; advisor*

el/la contador(a) *accountant*

el/la corredor(a) de bolsa *stockbroker*

el/la diseñador(a) *designer*

el/la electricista *electrician*

el/la escritor(a) *writer*

el/la escultor(a) *sculptor*

el/la gerente *manager*

el hombre/la mujer de negocios *businessperson*

el/la jefe/a *boss*

el/la maestro/a *elementary school teacher*

el/la pintor(a) *painter*

el/la poeta *poet*

el/la político/a *politician*

el/la reportero/a *reporter*

el/la secretario/a *secretary*

el/la técnico/a *technician*

el cocinero
cook; chef

la peluquera
hairdresser

el actor
actor

el bombero
firefighter

el psicólogo
psychologist

recursos

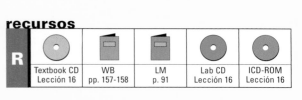

R				
Textbook CD Lección 16	WB pp. 157-158	LM p. 91	Lab CD Lección 16	ICD-ROM Lección 16

Se busca diseñador gráfico.

Ofrecemos excelentes beneficios.
Para mayor información,
diríjase a nuestra oficina principal,
Calle Castilla, no. 44.

el anuncio
advertisement

LAS ENTREVISTAS

el/la aspirante *candidate; applicant*
los beneficios *benefits*
el/la entrevistador(a) *interviewer*
el puesto *position; job*
el salario *salary*
la solicitud (de trabajo) *(job) application*
el sueldo *salary*

contratar *to hire*
entrevistar *to interview*
ganar *to earn*
obtener *to obtain; to get*
solicitar *to apply (for a job)*

el currículum
résumé

DATOS PERSONALES
Nombre y apellidos: **Carmelo Roca**
Fecha de nacimiento: **14 de diciembre de 1978**
Lugar de nacimiento: **Salamanca**
D.N.I.: **7885270-R**
Dirección: **Calle Ferrara 17, 5**
37500 Salamanca
Teléfono: **923 270 118**
Correo electrónico: **rocac@teleline.com**

FORMACIÓN ACADÉMICA
• 2001-2002 Máster en Administración y Dirección de Empresas, Universidad Autónoma de Madrid
• 1996-2001 Licenciado en Administración y Dirección de Empresas por la Universidad de Salamanca

CURSOS Y SEMINARIOS
• 2001 "Gestión y Creación de Empresas", Universidad de Córdoba

EXPERIENCIA PROFESIONAL
• 1999-2000 Contrato de un año en la empresa RAMA, S.L., realizando tareas administrativas
• 1998-1999 Contrato de trabajo haciendo prácticas en Banco Sol

IDIOMAS
• INGLÉS Nivel alto. Título de la Escuela Oficial de Idiomas
• ITALIANO Nivel Medio

INFORMÁTICA/COMPUTACIÓN
• Conocimientos de usuario de Mac / Windows
• MS Office

EL MUNDO DEL TRABAJO

el ascenso *promotion*
el aumento de sueldo *raise*
la carrera *career*
la compañía *company; firm*
el empleo *job; employment*
la empresa *company; firm*
la especialización *field of study*
los negocios *business; commerce*
la ocupación *occupation*
el oficio *trade*
la profesión *profession*
el teletrabajo *tele-commuting*
el trabajo *job; work*
la videoconferencia *videoconference*

dejar *to quit; to leave behind*
despedir (e:i) *to fire*
invertir (e:ie) *to invest*
renunciar (a) *to resign (from)*
tener éxito *to be successful*

comercial *commercial; business-related*

la reunión
meeting

la entrevista
interview

A escuchar

1 **¿Lógico o ilógico?** Escucha las frases e indica si cada frase es **lógica** o **ilógica**.

	Lógico	Ilógico
1.	_____	_____
2.	_____	_____
3.	_____	_____
4.	_____	_____
5.	_____	_____
6.	_____	_____
7.	_____	_____
8.	_____	_____

2 **Escuchar** Escucha la descripción que hace Alejandro Dávila de su profesión y luego completa las frases con las palabras adecuadas.

1. Alejandro Dávila es un

   a. poeta.   b. hombre de negocios.   c. escultor.

2. El Sr. Dávila trabaja como _____ en una compañía multinacional.

   a. secretario   b. técnico   c. gerente

3. Al Sr. Dávila le interesaba _____ en la cual pudiera trabajar en otros países.

   a. una carrera   b. un ascenso   c. un aumento de sueldo

4. En sus negocios con empresas extranjeras, el Sr. Dávila prefiere

   a. usar las videoconferencias.   b. conocer a la gente personalmente.
   c. mandar correos electrónicos.

recursos

R   Textbook CD
Lección 16

A practicar

3 **Ocupaciones** ¿Quién realiza las siguientes actividades? Escoge entre las ocupaciones indicadas.

1. Arregla las computadoras. _____
2. Enseña a los niños. _____
3. Diseña ropa. _____
4. Canta para el público. _____
5. Arregla los electrodomésticos. _____
6. Desarrolla teorías de biología, química, física, etc. _____
7. Construye (*builds*) sillas, mesas, casas y otras cosas de madera (*wood*). _____
8. Ayuda a la gente a invertir su dinero. _____
9. Trabaja con números y arregla las cuentas de diferentes negocios. _____
10. Combate los fuegos (*fires*) que destruyen los edificios y los bosques. _____

la carpintera	**la técnica**
el bombero	**el diseñador**
la contadora	**la electricista**
la cantante	**el maestro**
el corredor de bolsa	**el científico**

4 **Asociaciones** ¿Qué profesiones asocias con las siguientes palabras? Escoge de la lista.

1. pelo _____
2. novelas _____
3. emociones _____
4. teatro _____
5. periódico _____
6. pinturas _____
7. elecciones _____
8. baile _____
9. leyes _____
10. consejos _____

escritor	**psicóloga**
actriz	**abogado**
pintor	**reportero**
arqueólogo	**política**
peluquera	**bailarín**
consejero	**electricista**

5 **Completar** Completa las frases.

1. Quiero conseguir un puesto con
   a. oficios.   b. beneficios.   c. ocupación.
2. Luisa tiene la oportunidad de _____ la empresa donde trabaja.
   a. despedir   b. entrevistar   c. invertir en
3. Mi vecino dejó su _____ porque no le gustaba su jefe.
   a. puesto   b. anuncio   c. ascenso
4. Raúl va a _____ su empleo antes de empezar su propia empresa.
   a. solicitar   b. tener éxito   c. renunciar a
5. Mi madre _____ su carrera como escultora.
   a. tuvo éxito en   b. invirtió   c. entrevistó
6. ¿Cuándo obtuviste _____ más reciente?
   a. la reunión   b. la videoconferencia   c. el aumento de sueldo
7. Jorge llegó tarde a la _____ esta mañana.
   a. reunión   b. especialización   c. carrera

A conversar

6 **Conversación** Contesta las preguntas con un(a) compañero/a.

1. ¿Te gusta tu especialización?
2. ¿Lees los anuncios de empleos en el periódico con regularidad?
3. ¿Cómo te preparas para una entrevista?
4. ¿Obtienes siempre los puestos que quieres?
5. ¿Qué características tiene un(a) jefe/a bueno/a?
6. ¿Te gustaría más un teletrabajo o un trabajo en una oficina? ¿Por qué?
7. ¿Quieres tener tu propia empresa?
8. ¿Cuál es tu carrera ideal? ¿Por qué?

7 **Entrevista** Trabaja con un(a) compañero/a para representar los papeles de un(a) aspirante a un puesto de trabajo y el de un(a) entrevistador(a).

El/la entrevistador(a) debe describir…
- el empleo
- las responsabilidades
- el salario
- los beneficios.

El/la aspirante debe…
- presentar su experiencia
- preguntar los detalles del puesto.

Entonces…
- el/la entrevistador(a) debe decidir si va a contratar al/a la aspirante
- el/la aspirante debe decidir si va a aceptar el puesto.

8 **Una feria de trabajo** La clase va a organizar una feria (*fair*) de trabajo. Unos estudiantes son los representantes de las compañías y otros son los/las aspirantes que están buscando nuevos puestos de trabajo.

Representantes	**Aspirantes**
• Preparan carteles con el nombre de su compañía. • Escriben los puestos de trabajo que ofrecen. • Contestan las preguntas de los aspirantes y describen los puestos disponibles. • Consiguen los nombres y referencias de los aspirantes.	• Circulan por la feria de trabajo. • Hablan con tres representantes y formulan preguntas sobre los puestos que tienen. • Muestran sus referencias y sus currícula. • Escogen su puesto favorito.

Ortografía

Las letras **y**, **ll** y **h**

The letters **ll** and **y** were not pronounced alike in Old Spanish. Nowadays, however, **ll** and **y** have the same or similar pronunciations in many parts of the Spanish-speaking world. This similarity results in frequent misspellings. The letter **h**, as you already know, is silent in Spanish, and it is often difficult to know whether words should be written with or without it. Here are some of the word groups that are spelled with each letter.

talla	**se**llo	**bot**ella	**amari**llo

The letter **ll** is used in these endings: **–allo/a**, **–ello/a**, **–illo/a**.

llave	**lle**ga	**llo**rar	**llu**via

The letter **ll** is used at the beginning of words in these combinations: **lla-**, **lle-**, **llo-**, **llu-**.

ca**y**endo	le**y**eron	o**y**e	inclu**y**e

The letter **y** is used in some forms of the verbs **caer**, **leer**, and **oír**, and of verbs ending in **–uir**.

hiperactivo	**hosp**ital	**hipo**pótamo	**hum**or

The letter **h** is used at the beginning of words in these combinations: **hiper-**, **hosp-**, **hidr-**, **hipo-**, **hum-**.

hiato	**hie**rba	**hue**so	**hui**r

The letter **h** is also used in words that begin with these combinations: **hia-**, **hie-**, **hue-**, **hui-**.

Práctica Llena los espacios con **h**, **ll** o **y**. Después escribe una frase con cada una de las palabras.

1. cuchi____o
2. ____ielo
3. cue____o
4. estampi____a
5. estre____a
6. ____uésped
7. destru____ó
8. pla____a

Adivinanza Aquí tienes una adivinanza (*riddle*). Intenta descubrir de qué se trata.

Una cajita chiquita, blanca como la nieve: todos la saben abrir, nadie la sabe cerrar.[1]

Pista: Es una comida.

1 El huevo

recursos

R | ICD-ROM Lección 16

Memorias del viaje

Los viajeros recuerdan sus experiencias.

1

INÉS

La excursión a las montañas fue lo que más me gustó del viaje. ¡El paisaje era tan hermoso! Me encantó que mis amigos pudieran disfrutar de la belleza de mi país. Además, fue una oportunidad para que Javier y yo pudiéramos conocernos. Sé que muy pronto será un artista famoso. Nos llevamos muy bien durante el viaje y creo que seremos buenos amigos.

3

JAVIER

Para mí, el paisaje de las montañas fue lo mejor del viaje. Tomé varias fotos e hice muchos dibujos cuando estábamos allí. El próximo verano volveré para pintar más cuadros de lo que vi durante este viaje. Ahora soy un pintor desconocido… pero, cuando la gente vea esos cuadros, seré famoso. Estoy casi seguro de ello. Cuando vuelva, me gustaría que Inés, Maite y Álex vinieran conmigo. El viaje no sería tan divertido sin ellos.

Personajes

JAVIER

INÉS

ÁLEX

MAITE

(2)

ÁLEX

Hola, Mario:

Anoche volvimos a Quito. No quería que el viaje se acabara. Nos lo pasamos muy bien, incluso cuando se nos dañó el autobús cerca de Ibarra. Además, conocí a gente interesante, como Maite, que estudia para ser periodista. Es una chica guapa y muy inteligente. Durante el viaje, salimos juntos en varias ocasiones y creo que volveremos a vernos otra vez. Nunca se sabe, es posible que nos casemos un día de estos.

Tu amigo, Álex

(4)

MAITE

El viaje fue estupendo y me divertí muchísimo. Me sorprendió que mis amigos me organizaran una fiesta de cumpleaños en el restaurante El Cráter. Además, conocí a un chico encantador que se llama Álex. Me dijo que estaba pensando en empezar un negocio en Internet. En un primer momento, dudé que llegáramos a ser buenos amigos. Pero ahora me gustaría conocerlo mejor. ¿Quién sabe? Quizás nos convirtamos en algo más que amigos…

Talking about future plans

Sé que muy pronto será un artista famoso.
I know that soon he will be a famous artist.
Creo que seremos buenos amigos.
I think we'll be good friends.
El próximo verano volveré para pintar más cuadros de lo que vi durante este viaje.
Next summer I'll return to paint more paintings of what I saw during this trip.
Cuando la gente vea esos cuadros, seré famoso.
When people see those paintings, I'll be famous.
Nunca se sabe, es posible que nos casemos un día de estos.
You never know, it's possible that we'll get married one of these days.

Reminiscing

Además, fue una oportunidad para que Javier y yo pudiéramos conocernos.
Besides, it was an opportunity for Javier and me to get to know each other.
Me sorprendió que mis amigos me organizaran una fiesta de cumpleaños en el restaurante El Cráter.
It surprised me that my friends organized a birthday party for me in the El Cráter restaurant.
Dudé que llegáramos a ser buenos amigos.
I doubted that we would become good friends.
No quería que el viaje se acabara.
I didn't want the trip to end.

Expressing hopes and wishes

Pero ahora me gustaría conocerlo mejor.
But now I would like to get to know him better.
Cuando vuelva, me gustaría que Inés, Maite y Álex vinieran conmigo.
When I return, I would like Inés, Maite, and Álex to come with me.

¿Qué piensas?

1 **Seleccionar** Selecciona la respuesta más lógica para cada frase.

1. Inés cree que Javier será

   a. un bombero.   b. un artista famoso.
   c. un científico.

2. Maite estaba sorprendida de que sus amigos le hubieran organizado

   a. una fiesta de cumpleaños.   b. una excursión.
   c. una cena con Álex.

3. Javier volverá el próximo verano para

   a. correr.   b. viajar.
   c. pintar.

4. Álex no quería que el viaje se acabara porque

   a. se le dañó la computadora.   b. lo pasó muy bien.
   c. le gustó la comida de doña Rita.

2 **Preguntas** Responde a las siguientes preguntas.

1. ¿Se habían conocido Inés y Javier antes del viaje? ¿Cómo lo sabes?
   _____

2. ¿Qué piensa Maite de Álex?
   _____

3. ¿Qué le gustó más del viaje a Javier?
   _____

4. ¿Qué opina Álex sobre su futuro con Maite?
   _____

3 **La reunión** En 20 años Maite, Álex, Inés y Javier se vuelven a reunir. En grupos, escriban un diálogo explicando qué ha pasado en sus vidas personales y profesionales después del viaje. Luego, representen el diálogo delante de la clase.

Exploración
Las mujeres en el mundo del trabajo

La indígena guatemalteca Rigoberta Menchú Tum recibió el Premio Nobel de la Paz en 1992. Es conocida por su trabajo en la defensa de los derechos de los pueblos indígenas. En 1983, publicó *Yo, Rigoberta Menchú*, un libro sobre su lucha (*fight*).

Observaciones

- **Gabriela Mistral** fue una poeta y diplomática chilena. En 1945 tuvo el honor de ser la primera escritora latinoamericana en recibir el Premio Nobel de Literatura.

- En 1996, el 49% de los estudiantes que se matricularon (*registered*) en los colegios técnicos públicos de Costa Rica eran mujeres.

- En 1999, **Mireya Moscoso** fue la primera mujer elegida (*elected*) presidenta de Panamá.

La diseñadora venezolana Carolina Herrera es considerada una de las figuras más importantes en el campo de la moda. Tiene mucho éxito en los Estados Unidos y en Latinoamérica. Su ropa es muy popular entre las mujeres profesionales por su estilo clásico y funcional.

La primera mujer que gobernó un país de América Central fue Violeta Barrios de Chamorro. Fue presidenta de Nicaragua desde 1990 hasta 1997. Después, escribió sus memorias en un libro llamado *Sueños del corazón*.

Coméntalo

Con un(a) compañero/a, contesta las siguientes preguntas.

- ¿Por qué son importantes estas mujeres en el mundo en general?
- En parejas, escojan una mujer profesional que admiran. ¿Qué cualidades admiran en esta persona?

recursos

R

vistahigher learning.com

16.1 The future tense

▶ You have already learned how to use **ir a** + [*infinitive*] to express the near future. You will now learn the future tense. Compare these different ways of expressing the future in Spanish.

(Present indicative)

Voy al cine mañana.
I'm going to the movies tomorrow.

(ir a + infinitive)

Voy a ir al cine.
I'm going to go to the movies.

(Present subjunctive)

Ojalá **vaya al cine** mañana.
I hope I will go to the movies tomorrow.

(Future)

Iré al cine.
I will go to the movies.

Future tense of regular verbs

	estudiar	aprender	recibir
yo	estudiaré	aprenderé	recibiré
tú	estudiarás	aprenderás	recibirás
Ud./él/ella	estudiará	aprenderá	recibirá
nosotros/as	estudiaremos	aprenderemos	recibiremos
vosotros/as	estudiaréis	aprenderéis	recibiréis
Uds./ellos/ellas	estudiarán	aprenderán	recibirán

¡ojo! All the forms of the future tense have written accents, except the **nosotros/as** form.

▶ In Spanish, the future tense consists of one word, whereas in English it is made up of *will* or *shall* and a main verb.

¿Cuándo **recibirás** el ascenso?
When will you receive the promotion?

Mañana **aprenderemos** más.
Tomorrow we will learn more.

▶ The future endings are the same for all verbs. For regular verbs, add the endings to the infinitive. For irregular verbs, add the endings to the irregular stem.

Irregular verbs in the future

INFINITIVE	STEM	FUTURE FORMS
decir	dir-	diré
hacer	har-	haré
poder	podr-	podré
poner	pondr-	pondré
querer	querr-	querré
saber	sabr-	sabré
salir	saldr-	saldré
tener	tendr-	tendré
venir	vendr-	vendré

Práctica

1 **Planes** Celia está hablando de sus planes. Repite lo que dice con el tiempo futuro.

modelo
Voy a consultar un diccionario en la biblioteca.
Consultaré un diccionario en la biblioteca.

1. Julián me va a decir dónde puedo buscar trabajo.
2. Voy a buscar un puesto que ofrezca ascensos.
3. Voy a leer los anuncios clasificados todos los días.
4. Voy a obtener un puesto en mi especialización.
5. Mis amigos van a intentar obtener un teletrabajo.

2 **En el futuro** Mario habla de sus planes para el futuro y de los planes de algunos amigos y parientes suyos. Combina los siguientes elementos para formar frases completas.

1. Yo / estudiar / para / exámenes finales / mañana
2. Yo / tener / entrevista de trabajo / en una semana
3. La próxima semana / mis tíos / poner / anuncio para buscar un empleado
4. Pronto / mi hermana / dejar / puesto de cocinera
5. Mis padres / tener mucho éxito / como políticos
6. Mis amigos y yo / tener / puestos interesantes

3 **Preguntas** En parejas, túrnense para hablar del puesto que prefieren y por qué, basándose en los anuncios. Usen las preguntas como guía y formulen también sus propias preguntas.

SE BUSCA DIRECTOR
de mercadeo para empresa privada. Mínimo de 5 años de experiencia en turismo y conexiones con INTUR (Instituto Nicaragüense de Turismo) y ANTUR (Asociación Nicaragüense de Turismo Receptivo). Debe hablar inglés, español y alemán. Salario anual: 306,000 córdobas. Horario flexible. Buenos beneficios. Envíe currículum por fax al 492-38-67.

MUEBLERÍA MANAGUA
busca carpintero/a. Experiencia e fabricación de muebles finos. Horario lunes a viernes de 7:30 a 11:30 y de 1:30 a 5:30. Sueldo semanal: 462 córdobas (y beneficios) Comenzará inmediatamente. Solicite en persona: Calle El Lago, Managua.

1. ¿Cuál será tu trabajo?
2. ¿Qué harás?
3. ¿Cuánto te pagarán?
4. ¿Te ofrecerán beneficios?
5. ¿Qué horario tendrás?
6. ¿Crees que te gustará?
7. ¿Cuándo comenzarás a trab
8. ¿Qué crees que aprenderás?

Conversación

4 **Conversar** Tú y tu compañero/a viajarán a la República Dominicana por siete días. En parejas, conversen sobre sus itinerarios. Digan dónde, cómo, con quién o cuándo harán las actividades escogidas, usando el anuncio como guía. Pueden usar sus propias ideas también.

▸ **modelo**

Estudiante 1: ¿Qué haremos el martes?
Estudiante 2: Visitaremos el Jardín Botánico.
Estudiante 1: Pues, tú visitarás el Jardín Botánico y yo caminaré por el Mercado Modelo.

¡Bienvenido a la República Dominicana!

Se divertirá desde el momento en que llegue al Aeropuerto Internacional de las Américas.

- Visite la ciudad colonial de **Santo Domingo** con su interesante arquitectura.
- Vaya al **Jardín Botánico** y disfrute de nuestra abundante naturaleza.

- En el **Mercado Modelo**, no va a poder resistir la tentación de comprar artesanías.
- No deje de escalar la montaña del **Pico Duarte** (se recomiendan 3 días).
- ¿Le gusta bucear? **Cabarete** tiene todo el equipo que Ud. necesita.
- ¿Desea nadar? **Punta Cana** le ofrece hermosas playas.

---

5 **Una empresa privada** En grupos pequeños, desarrollen planes para formar una empresa privada. Usen las preguntas como guía. Después presenten su plan a la clase.

1. ¿Cómo se llamará y qué tipo de empresa será?
2. ¿Cuántos empleados tendrá y cuáles serán sus oficios?
3. ¿Qué tipo de beneficios se ofrecerán?
4. ¿Quién será el/la gerente y quién será el/la jefe/a?
5. ¿Permitirá su empresa el teletrabajo? ¿Por qué?
6. ¿Qué se hará para que los empleados no dejen el trabajo?
7. ¿Dónde pondrá anuncios para buscar empleados?
8. ¿Qué harán los gerentes para que la empresa tenga éxito?

6 **Predicciones** Con dos o tres compañeros/as, especula sobre lo que ocurrirá en los siguientes años: 2010, 2030 y 2050. Usen su imaginación. Luego compartan sus predicciones con la clase.

¡ojo! The future of **hay** (*inf.* **haber**) is **habrá** (*there will be*).

La próxima semana **habrá** dos reuniones.
Next week there will be two meetings.

Habrá muchos gerentes en la conferencia.
There will be many managers at the conference.

▸ Although *will* can refer to future time, it also refers to someone's willingness to do something. In this case, Spanish uses **querer** + [*infinitive*].

¿**Quieres llamarme**, por favor?
Will you please call me?

¿**Quieren Uds. escucharnos**, por favor?
Will you please listen to us?

▸ English sentences involving expressions such as *I wonder, I bet, must be, may, might,* and *probably* are often conveyed in Spanish using the future of probability, a use of the future that expresses conjecture about present conditions, events, or actions.

—¿Dónde **estarán** mis llaves?
I wonder where my keys are?

—**Estarán** en la cocina.
They're probably in the kitchen.

—¿Qué hora **será**?
What time can it be? (I wonder what time it is?)

—**Serán** las once o las doce.
It must be (it's probably) eleven or twelve.

▸ The future may be used in sentences in which the present subjunctive follows a conjunction of time such as **cuando, después (de) que, en cuanto, hasta que,** and **tan pronto como.**

Cuando llegues a la oficina, **hablaremos**.
When you arrive at the office, we will talk.

Saldremos tan pronto como termine su trabajo.
We will leave as soon as you finish your work.

Después de que obtengas el ascenso, te **invitaré** a cenar.
After you get the promotion, I'll take you out to dinner.

Hasta que contrate otro empleado, el jefe **tendrá** que hacer el trabajo.
Until he hires another employee, the boss will have to do the work.

¡Manos a la obra!

 Conjuga los verbos indicados en futuro.

1. yo [dejar, correr, invertir] _____ *dejaré, correré, invertiré*
2. tú [renunciar, beber, vivir] _____
3. Lola [hacer, poner, venir] _____
4. nosotros [tener, decir, querer] _____
5. Uds. [ir, ser, estar] _____
6. Ud. [solicitar, comer, repetir] _____
7. yo [saber, salir, poder] _____
8. tú [encontrar, jugar, servir] _____

16.2 The conditional tense

▶ The conditional tense expresses what you would do or what would happen under certain circumstances. In Lesson 7, you learned the polite expression **me gustaría…** (*I would like…*), which uses a conditional form of **gustar**.

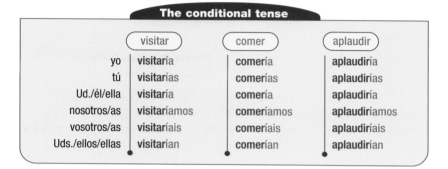

The conditional tense		
	visitar	comer	aplaudir
yo	visitaría	comería	aplaudiría
tú	visitarías	comerías	aplaudirías
Ud./él/ella	visitaría	comería	aplaudiría
nosotros/as	visitaríamos	comeríamos	aplaudiríamos
vosotros/as	visitaríais	comeríais	aplaudiríais
Uds./ellos/ellas	visitarían	comerían	aplaudirían

▶ The conditional endings are the same for all verbs and all forms carry a written accent. For regular verbs, add the endings to the infinitive. For irregular verbs, add the endings to the irregular stem.

INFINITIVE	STEM	CONDITIONAL
decir	dir-	diría
haber	habr-	habría
hacer	har-	haría
poder	podr-	podría
poner	pondr-	pondría
querer	querr-	querría
saber	sabr-	sabría
salir	saldr-	saldría
tener	tendr-	tendría
venir	vendr-	vendría

¡ojo! The conditional form of **hay** is **habría** (*there would be*).

▶ In English, the conditional is made up of *would* and a main verb, but in Spanish, it consists of one word.

Este aspirante **sería** perfecto para el puesto.
This candidate would be perfect for the job.

Querría un puesto con un buen salario.
I would like a job with a good salary.

¿**Vivirían** Uds. en otro país por un trabajo?
Would you live in another country for a job?

Ganarían más en otra compañía.
They would earn more in another company.

Práctica

1 **Un viaje** A la empresa Informática al Día le gustaría tener una conferencia en Puerto Rico. En las siguientes oraciones, los empleados nos cuentan sus planes de viaje. Complétalas con el condicional del verbo indicado.

1. Me _____ [gustar] venir unos días antes de la conferencia para viajar.

2. Ana _____ [salir] primero a la playa para descansar.

3. Yo _____ [decir] que fuéramos a San Juan porque es una ciudad muy divertida.

4. Nosotras _____ [preferir] tener las reuniones por la mañana. Por la tarde _____ [poder] visitar la ciudad.

5. Y nosotros _____ [ver] la zona comercial de la ciudad. Y tú, Luisa, ¿qué _____ [hacer]?

6. El jefe _____ [tener] interés en hacer una videoconferencia. En el fin de semana él _____ [visitar] los museos.

2 **Preguntas** Forma preguntas con las palabras que se dan en cada ocasión. Inventa luego las respuestas para estas preguntas. Usa el condicional.

> **modelo**
>
> Hacer (Uds.) / videoconferencia / con / empresa en Chile
> —¿Harían Uds. una videoconferencia con una empresa en Chile?
> —Sí, haríamos una videoconferencia con una empresa en Chile.

1. contratar (tú) / un miembro de tu familia / para / puesto nuevo

2. invertir (ellos) / dinero / en / compañía nueva

3. solicitar (ella) / trabajo / de abogado

4. renunciar (tú) / puesto / por otro trabajo con mejores beneficios

5. tener (nosotros) / dinero / para empezar / empresa privada

3 **Sugerencias** Beatriz busca trabajo. Dile ocho cosas que tú harías si fueras (*if you were*) ella. Usa el condicional. Luego compara tus sugerencias con las de un(a) compañero/a.

Conversación

4 **En tu lugar…** Lee las situaciones. Responde con lo que harías en esta situación usando la frase **Yo en tu lugar…** (*If I were you…*). Después, compara tus ideas con las de un(a) compañero/a.

> **modelo**
>
> Me encanta mi puesto, pero mi jefe es muy pesado. ¡Nunca me deja hablar!
>
> **Estudiante 1:** Me encanta mi puesto, pero mi jefe es muy pesado. ¡Nunca me deja hablar!
> **Estudiante 2:** Pues, yo en tu lugar hablaría con mi jefe sobre este problema.

1. El año pasado escogí la contabilidad como mi especialización, pero ahora he descubierto que no me gusta trabajar con números todo el día. Si cambio, mis padres quizás se enojen.

2. Me ofrecen un puesto interesantísimo, con un buen sueldo y excelentes beneficios, pero tiene un horario horrible. No volveré a ver a mis amigos jamás.

3. Mi peluquero es maravilloso, pero se va de viaje por dos meses a San Juan. Los otros peluqueros que trabajan en su salón no me gustan. Y tengo que hacer varias presentaciones públicas para mi empresa durante esos dos meses.

5 **¿Qué harías?** Quieres saber qué harían tus compañeros por un millón de dólares. Escribe ocho preguntas en el tiempo condicional. Circula por la clase y pregúntales a tus compañeros. Anota las respuestas e informa a la clase de los resultados de la encuesta.

> **modelo**
>
> **Estudiante 1:** ¿Trabajarías como cantante en Las Vegas?
> **Estudiante 2:** Sí, lo haría. Sería un puesto muy interesante.

Actividades	Nombre de compañero/a
_____	_____
_____	_____
_____	_____
_____	_____
_____	_____
_____	_____

Uses of the conditional

▶ The conditional is commonly used to make polite requests.

¿Podrías llamar al gerente, por favor?
Would you call the manager, please?

¿Sería tan amable de venir ahora?
Would you be so kind as to come now?

▶ In both Spanish and English, the conditional expresses the future in relation to a past action or state of being. The future indicates what *will happen*, whereas the conditional indicates what *would happen*. The future tense is often used if the main verb is in the present tense. The conditional is often used if the main verb is in one of the past tenses.

Creo que mañana **hará** sol.
I think it will be sunny tomorrow.

Creía que hoy **haría** sol.
I thought it would be sunny today.

▶ The English *would* can also mean *used to*, in the sense of past habitual action. To express past habitual actions, Spanish uses the imperfect.

Íbamos al parque los sábados.
We would go to the park on Saturdays.

De adolescentes, **comíamos** mucho.
As teenagers, we used to eat a lot.

▶ English sentences involving expressions such as *I wondered if, probably,* and *must have been* are often conveyed in Spanish using the conditional of probability, a use of the conditional that expresses conjecture or probability about *past* conditions, events, or actions.

Serían las nueve cuando el jefe me llamó.
It must have been 9 o'clock when the boss called.

Sonó el teléfono. **¿Llamaría** Tina para cancelar la cita?
The phone rang. Could it be Tina calling to cancel the appointment?

Sin ti, no sé qué haría.

Sólo tú sabes ordenar mi vida.

Computadoras de Bolsillo Vargas   MM-3000

¡Manos a la obra!

Indica la forma apropiada del condicional de los siguientes verbos.

1. yo [escuchar, leer, escribir] ___ *escucharía, leería, escribiría*
2. tú [invertir, comprender, compartir] _____
3. Marcos [poner, venir, querer] _____
4. nosotras [ser, saber, ir] _____
5. Uds. [presentar, deber, despedir] _____
6. ella [salir, poder, hacer] _____
7. yo [tener, tocar, acostarse] _____
8. tú [decir, ver, renunciar] _____

16.3 The past subjunctive

▸ The past subjunctive (**el imperfecto del subjuntivo**) is also called the imperfect subjunctive. Like the present subjunctive, it is used mainly in multiple-clause sentences that express will, influence, emotion, commands, indefiniteness, and non-existence.

The past subjunctive

	estudiar	aprender	recibir
yo	estudiara	aprendiera	recibiera
tú	estudiaras	aprendieras	recibieras
Ud./él/ella	estudiara	aprendiera	recibiera
nosotros/as	estudiáramos	aprendiéramos	recibiéramos
vosotros/as	estudiarais	aprendierais	recibierais
Uds./ellos/ellas	estudiaran	aprendieran	recibieran

¡ojo! The past subjunctive endings are the same for all verbs. Also, note that the **nosotros/as** forms always have a written accent.

▸ For *all* verbs, the past subjunctive is formed with the **Uds./ellos/ellas** form of the preterite. By dropping the **–ron** ending, you establish the stem for all the past subjunctive forms. You then add the past subjunctive endings.

INFINITIVE	PRETERITE FORM	STEM	PAST SUBJUNCTIVE
hablar	ellos hablaron	habla-	hablara, hablaras, habláramos
beber	ellos bebieron	bebie-	bebiera, bebieras, bebiéramos
escribir	ellos escribieron	escribie-	escribiera, escribieras, escribiéramos

▸ Verbs with irregular preterites use the same stems and endings in the past subjunctive.

INFINITIVE	PRETERITE FORM	STEM	PAST SUBJUNCTIVE
dar	dieron	die-	diera, dieras, diéramos
decir	dijeron	dije-	dijera, dijeras, dijéramos
estar	estuvieron	estuvie-	estuviera, estuvieras, estuviéramos
hacer	hicieron	hicie-	hiciera, hicieras, hiciéramos
ir/ser	fueron	fue-	fuera, fueras, fuéramos
poder	pudieron	pudie-	pudiera, pudieras, pudiéramos
poner	pusieron	pusie-	pusiera, pusieras, pusiéramos
querer	quisieron	quisie-	quisiera, quisieras, quisiéramos
saber	supieron	supie-	supiera, supieras, supiéramos
tener	tuvieron	tuvie-	tuviera, tuvieras, tuviéramos
venir	vinieron	vinie-	viniera, vinieras, viniéramos

Práctica

1 Conversaciones Completa los minidiálogos con el imperfecto del subjuntivo.

PACO ¿Qué le dijo el consejero a Andrés? Quisiera saberlo.

JULIA Le aconsejó que _____ [dejar] los estudios de arte y que _____ [estudiar] una carrera que _____ [pagar] mejor.

PACO Siempre el dinero. ¿No se enojó Andrés de que le _____ [aconsejar] eso?

JULIA Sí, y le dijo que no creía que ninguna carrera le _____ [ir] a gustar más.

• • •

EVA Qué lástima que ellos no te _____ [ofrecer] el puesto de gerente.

LUIS Querían a alguien que _____ [tener] más experiencia.

EVA Pero, ¿cómo? ¿No te molestó que te _____ [decir] eso?

LUIS No, porque les gustó mucho mi currículum. Me pidieron que _____ [volver] en un año y _____ [solicitar] el puesto otra vez.

• • •

CARLA Cuánto me alegro de que tus hijas _____ [venir] ayer a visitarte. ¿Cuándo se van?

ANA Bueno, yo esperaba que se _____ [quedar] dos semanas, pero no pueden. Ojalá _____ [poder]. Hace muchísimo tiempo que no las veo.

2 Transformar Cambia las frases al pasado según el modelo.

modelo

Temo que Juanita no consiga el trabajo.
Temía que Juanita no consiguiera el trabajo.

1. Esperamos que Miguel no renuncie.
2. No hay nadie que responda al anuncio.
3. Me sorprende que ellos no inviertan su dinero.
4. Te piden que no llegues tarde a la oficina.
5. Juan quiere que Marta tome el puesto de contadora.
6. Siento mucho que no tengas éxito en el trabajo nuevo.
7. Quiero que te entrevistes con esta compañía.

Conversación

3 Preguntas Con un(a) compañero/a, completa las siguientes oraciones.

1. Cuando eras niño/a, ¿qué querías que hicieran tus padres?
2. Cuando eras niño/a, ¿esperaban tus padres que trabajaras en una profesión específica?
3. ¿Dudaban tus profesores que tú pudieras llegar a ser lo que querías?
4. ¿Insistían tus padres en que fueras a la universidad? ¿Insistían en otras cosas?
5. ¿Qué te aconsejaron tus amigos que hicieras para tener éxito?
6. ¿Cuál esperabas que fuera tu profesión?

4 Minidiálogos Trabajen en parejas. Uno/a de Uds. ha comprado una casa; el/la otro/a es el/la gerente de la empresa responsable de las reformas (*improvements*) de la casa. El/la cliente/a llama al/a la gerente para quejarse (*to complain*) de que algunos trabajadores todavía no han hecho algunas reformas. Usen las siguientes palabras y el modelo como guía.

modelo el/la técnico/a / conectar / módem

Estudiante 1: Le pedí al técnico que conectara el módem, pero todavía no ha venido.
Estudiante 2: No se preocupe. Yo también le pedí al técnico que fuera a su casa.

1. el/la electricista / conectar / electricidad
2. el/la carpintero/a / construir / balcón
3. el/la diseñador(a) / escoger / muebles
4. el/la pintor(a) / pintar / paredes

5 Situación Claudia dejó su puesto por la forma en que le hablaba el gerente, por el aumento que les dieron a otros empleados (¡pero no a ella!) y por el horario que no le permitía seguir con sus clases. Con un(a) compañero/a, prepara una conversación entre Claudia y el gerente.

modelo

Estudiante 1: No estoy contenta. No me dieron un aumento de sueldo.
Estudiante 2: ¿Quería usted que le diéramos un aumento? ¡No lo sabía!

Past subjunctive of stem-changing verbs

▶ **–Ir** stem-changing verbs and other verbs with spelling changes follow a similar process to form the past subjunctive.

INFINITIVE	PRETERITE FORM	STEM	PAST SUBJUNCTIVE
conducir	condujeron	conduje-	condujera, condujeras, condujéramos
creer	creyeron	creye-	creyera, creyeras, creyéramos
destruir	destruyeron	destruye-	destruyera, destruyeras, destruyéramos
dormir	durmieron	durmie-	durmiera, durmieras, durmiéramos
oír	oyeron	oye-	oyera, oyeras, oyéramos
preferir	prefirieron	prefirie-	prefiriera, prefirieras, prefiriéramos
repetir	repitieron	repitie-	repitiera, repitieras, repitiéramos

No pensé que pudiera terminar la excursión.

Martín mostró mucho interés en que aprendiéramos sobre el medio ambiente.

▶ The past subjunctive is used in the same way as the present subjunctive, except that it generally describes actions or conditions that have already happened. The verb in the main clause is usually in the preterite or the imperfect.

Me pidieron que no **llegara** tarde.
They asked me not to arrive late.

Salió antes de que yo **pudiera** llamar.
He left before I could call.

¡ojo! **Quisiera** is often used to make polite requests.

Quisiera hablar con Marco.
I would like to speak to Marco.

¿**Quisiera** Ud. algo más?
Would you like anything else?

¡Manos a la obra!

 Completa las siguientes frases con el imperfecto de subjuntivo.

1. Quería que tú ___vinieras___ [venir] más temprano.
2. Esperábamos que Uds. _____ [hablar] mucho más en la reunión.
3. No creían que yo _____ [poder] hacerlo.
4. Se opuso a que nosotros _____ [invertir] el dinero ayer.
5. Sentí mucho que Ud. no _____ [estar] con nosotros anoche.
6. No era necesario que ellas _____ [hacer] todo.
7. Me pareció increíble que tú _____ [saber] dónde encontrarlo.
8. No había nadie que _____ [creer] tu historia.
9. Mis padres insistieron en que yo _____ [ir] a la universidad.
10. Queríamos salir antes de que Uds. _____ [llegar].

Ampliación

1 Escuchar

A Escucha la entrevista de la Sra. Sánchez y Rafael Ventura Romero. Antes de escucharla, prepara una lista de la información que esperas oír, según tu conocimiento previo (*prior knowledge*) del tema.

⭐ **TIP** **Use background knowledge/Listen for specific information.** Knowing the subject of what you're going to hear will help you use your background knowledge to anticipate words and phrases you're likely to hear, and to determine important information you should listen for.

Llena el formulario con la información necesaria. Si no oyes un dato (*piece of information*) que necesitas, escribe *Buscar en el currículum*. ¿Oíste toda la información de tu lista?

Puesto solicitado _____

Nombre y apellidos del solicitante _____

Dirección _____ **Tel.** _____

Educación _____

Experiencia profesional: Puesto _____

Empresa _____

¿Cuánto tiempo? _____

Referencias:

Nombre _____

Dirección _____ **Tel.** _____

Nombre _____

Dirección _____ **Tel.** _____

B ¿Cómo sabes si los resultados de la entrevista han sido positivos para Rafael Ventura?

_____

2 Conversar

Con un(a) compañero/a, conversen sobre sus planes para el futuro. Incluyan la siguiente información en su conversación.

- ¿Qué profesión u oficio seguirás en el futuro?
- ¿Por qué te interesa esta carrera?
- ¿Qué se necesita hacer para tener éxito?
- ¿Te mudarías de país por un puesto excelente?

recursos

Textbook CD Lección 16	WB pp. 159-164	LM pp. 93-95	Lab CD Lección 16	ICD-ROM Lección 16	vistahigher learning.com

Ampliación

3 Escribir

Escribe una composición sobre tus planes para el futuro. Formula planes para tu vida personal, profesional y financiera. Termina tu composición con una lista de metas.

 TIP Use note cards. Note cards (**fichas**) can help you organize your information. Label the top of each card with a general subject, such as **lugar** or **empleo**. Number the cards so you can easily flip through them to find information.

Organízalo	Utiliza fichas para apuntar cada plan o meta para el futuro. Asigna un año a cada meta.
Escríbelo	Organiza tus fichas y escribe el primer borrador de tu composición.
Corrígelo	Intercambia tu composición con un(a) compañero/a. Léela y anota sus mejores aspectos. ¿Habla de las metas específicas para su futuro? Ofrécele sugerencias para mejorar la organización. Si ves algunos errores, coméntaselos.
Compártelo	Revisa el primer borrador de tu composición según las indicaciones de tu compañero/a. Incorpora nuevas ideas y/o más información si es necesario, antes de escribir la versión final.

4 Un paso más

Imagina que en el futuro trabajarás para una empresa multinacional que tiene sus oficinas más importantes en algún país hispano. Crea una cronología con texto y fotos de tu futura carrera profesional y compártela con la clase.

- Escoge el país y busca información sobre las industrias y las compañías que operen allá.
- Describe la empresa y sus productos.
- Incluye fotos relacionadas con la empresa y con sus productos.
- Describe tu carrera, desde el comienzo hasta tu jubilación.
- Incluye los puestos que vas a tener en la empresa, y también fotos relacionadas con tu carrera.

 En Internet

Investiga estos temas en el sitio vistahigherlearning.com.

- Empresas en el mundo hispano
- Industrias en el mundo hispano
- Compañías multinacionales en el mundo hispano

Antes de leer

Summarizing a text in your own words can help you understand it better. Before summarizing a text, you may find it helpful to skim it and jot down a few notes about its general meaning. You can then read the text again, writing down important details or noting special characteristics that occur in the text. Your notes will help you summarize what you have read.

The reading selection for this lesson consists of a brief story by Augusto Monterroso. What special characteristics in this text could help you summarize it? Skim the short story and jot down your ideas.

_____

_____

_____

_____

Sobre el autor

Augusto Monterroso (1921-) escritor guatemalteco. Monterroso tiene un estilo conciso, sencillo (*simple*) y accesible. Su trabajo incluye la parodia, el humor negro, la fábula y el ensayo.

Imaginación y Destino
Augusto Monterroso

En la calurosa tarde de verano un hombre descansa acostado, viendo al cielo, bajo un árbol; una manzana cae sobre su cabeza; tiene imaginación, se va a su casa y escribe la Oda a Eva.

En la calurosa tarde de verano un hombre descansa acostado, viendo al cielo, bajo un árbol; una manzana cae sobre su cabeza; tiene imaginación, se va a su casa y establece la Ley de la Gravitación Universal.

En la calurosa tarde de verano un hombre descansa acostado, viendo al cielo, bajo un árbol; una manzana cae sobre su cabeza; tiene imaginación, observa que el árbol no es un manzano sino una encina y descubre, oculto entre las ramas, al muchacho travieso del pueblo que se entretiene arrojando manzanas a los señores que descansan bajo los árboles, viendo al cielo, en las calurosas tardes del verano.

El primero era, o se convierte entonces para siempre en el poeta sir James Calisher; el segundo era, o se convierte entonces para siempre en el físico sir Isaac Newton[1]; el tercero pudo ser o convertirse entonces para siempre en el novelista sir Arthur Conan Doyle[2]; pero se convierte, o era ya irremediablemente desde niño, en el Jefe de Policía de San Blas, S.B.[3]

[1] Sir Isaac Newton (1642 – 1727), matemático y físico británico. Es considerado uno de los científicos más importantes de la historia. Formuló la Ley de la Gravitación Universal.

[2] Sir Arthur Conan Doyle (1859 – 1930), escritor británico. Sus más famosos protagonistas son Sherlock Holmes y su ayudante, el doctor Watson.

[3] S.B. Abreviatura para San Blas, una isla en Panamá. Una de las novelas de Monterroso tiene lugar en San Blas.

Después de leer

¿Comprendiste?

1. ¿Qué estación del año es y qué tiempo hace?

2. ¿Qué hace el primer hombre después de descansar?

3. ¿Qué hace el segundo hombre después de descansar?

4. ¿Qué encuentra el tercer hombre en el árbol?

5. ¿Cuáles son las profesiones de estos tres hombres al final del cuento?

Preguntas

1. ¿Por qué lleva el cuento el título "Imaginación y Destino"?

2. ¿Por qué utiliza el autor tanta repetición?

3. La misma cosa les ocurre a los tres hombres, pero tienen reacciones distintas. ¿Por qué?

4. El autor escribe "o era ya irremediablemente desde niño". ¿Qué significa esta frase en relación con el resto del cuento?

5. Imagina que hay una cuarta persona en la historia. Escribe un párrafo en el estilo del autor sobre qué le pasa a esta persona "cuando una manzana cae sobre su cabeza…"

Coméntalo

En el cuento, los tres personajes tienen la misma experiencia con distintos resultados. ¿Has tenido una experiencia así? Un ejemplo es la graduación: un grupo de personas se gradúa el mismo día, pero ¿qué pasa después? ¿Crees que podemos controlar nuestros destinos? ¿Afectarán tus experiencias actuales tu futuro? ¿Cómo sabes qué profesión quieres ejercer (carry out) en el futuro?

acostado	lying down
viendo	looking up
Ley	law
encina	oak tree
oculto	hidden
ramas	branches
travieso	mischievous
se entretiene	entertains himself
arrojando	throwing

recursos

R

vistahigher
learning.com

Las ocupaciones

el/la abogado/a	lawyer
el actor	actor
la actriz	actress
el/la arqueólogo/a	archeologist
el/la arquitecto/a	architect
el bailarín	dancer
la bailarina	dancer
el/la bombero/a	firefighter
el/la cantante	singer
el/la carpintero/a	carpenter
el/la científico/a	scientist
el/la cocinero/a	cook; chef
el/la consejero/a	counselor; advisor
el/la contador(a)	accountant
el/la corredor(a) de bolsa	stockbroker
el/la diseñador(a)	designer
el/la electricista	electrician
el/la escritor(a)	writer
el/la escultor(a)	sculptor
el/la gerente	manager
el hombre/la mujer de negocios	businessperson
el/la jefe/a	boss
el/la maestro/a	elementary school teacher
el/la peluquero/a	hair dresser
el/la pintor(a)	painter
el/la poeta	poet
el/la político/a	politician
el/la psicólogo/a	psychologist
el/la reportero/a	reporter
el/la secretario/a	secretary
el/la técnico/a	technician

Las entrevistas

el anuncio	advertisement
el/la aspirante	candidate; applicant
los beneficios	benefits
el currículum	résumé
la entrevista	interview
el/la entrevistador(a)	interviewer
el puesto	position; job
el salario	salary
la solicitud (de trabajo)	(job) application
el sueldo	salary
contratar	to hire
entrevistar	to interview
ganar	to earn
obtener	to obtain; to get
solicitar	to apply (for a job)

Palabras adicionales

dentro de (diez años)	within (ten years)
en el futuro	in the future
el porvenir	the future
próximo/a	next

Expresiones útiles	See page 385.

El mundo del trabajo

el ascenso	promotion
el aumento de sueldo	raise
la carrera	career
la compañía	company; firm
el empleo	job; employment
la empresa	company; firm
la especialización	field of study
los negocios	business; commerce
la ocupación	occupation
el oficio	trade
la profesión	profession
la reunión	meeting
el teletrabajo	tele-commuting
el trabajo	job; work
la videoconferencia	videoconference
dejar	to quit; to leave behind
despedir (e:i)	to fire
invertir (e:ie)	to invest
renunciar (a)	to resign (from)
tener éxito	to be successful
comercial	commercial; business-related

recursos

R	Lab CD Lección 16	LM p. 95

AVENTURAS EN LOS PAÍSES HISPANOS

El mar Caribe, de aguas cálidas (*warm*) y transparentes, está al este de América Central y rodea (*surrounds*) a las Islas Antillas. Cuba, Puerto Rico y República Dominicana son tres de estas islas. El Caribe goza de (*enjoys*) un clima tropical todo el año. Las plantas y animales del Caribe son muy variados y exóticos. Personas de todo el mundo viajan al Caribe para disfrutar del clima, la naturaleza y las hermosas playas. ¿Te gustaría ir al Caribe algún día?

EL CARIBE

Puerto Rico

Área: 8.959 km^2 (3.459 millas^2)
Población: 4.057.000
Capital: San Juan – 1.451.000
Ciudades principales: Caguas–244.000, Mayagüez–134.000, Ponce–230.000
Moneda: dólar estadounidense

SOURCE: Population Division, UN Secretariat

Cuba

Área: 110.860 km^2 (42.083 millas^2)
Población: 11.338.000
Capital: La Habana – 2.297.000
Ciudades principales: Santiago de Cuba–449.000, Camagüey–313.000, Holguín–270.000, Guantánamo–207.000
Moneda: peso cubano

SOURCE: Population Division, UN Secretariat

República Dominicana

Área: 48.730 km^2 (18.815 millas^2)
Población: 8.899.000
Capital: Santo Domingo – 2.826.000
Ciudades importantes: Santiago de los Caballeros–879.000, La Vega–330.000
Moneda: peso dominicano

SOURCE: Population Division, UN Secretariat

Lugares

La Habana Vieja

La Habana Vieja es la parte antigua *(old)* de la capital de Cuba. Fue declarada Patrimonio Cultural de la Humanidad por la UNESCO en 1982. Tiene muchos edificios coloniales, como el Palacio de los Capitanes generales, que ahora es un museo. También hay calles estrechas *(narrow)* y casas antiguas con balcones.

Estrecho de la Florida

ISLAS BAHAMAS

★ La Habana

Cordillera de los Órganos

Isla de la Juventud

CUBA

Mar de las Antillas

Camagüey •

Holguín •

Sierra Maestra

Santiago de Cuba •

Guantánar

Deportes

El béisbol

El béisbol es un deporte muy popular en el Caribe. Los primeros países hispanos en tener una liga de béisbol fueron Cuba y México, en el siglo XIX. Actualmente es el deporte nacional de la República Dominicana. Sammy Sosa, Pedro Martínez y Manny Ramírez son tres de los muchos beisbolistas dominicanos que alcanzaron *(achieve)* el éxito y la fama en este deporte.

JAMAICA

Océano
Atlántico

Música

La salsa y el merengue

La música salsa nació en Nueva York entre los inmigrantes de Puerto Rico y Cuba. Esta música es muy rítmica y está hecha para bailar. Tiene ese nombre porque es la "salsa" *(sauce)* de las fiestas. Tres de los músicos de salsa más populares son Tito Puente, Willie Colón y Héctor Lavoe.

El merengue, una música tradicional de la República Dominicana, tiene sus raíces *(roots)* en el campo. Tradicionalmente, las canciones hablaban de los problemas sociales de los campesinos *(country people)*. El merengue también está hecho para bailar. Gracias a Juan Luis Guerra, un cantante internacional dominicano, el merengue se conoce en todo el mundo.

Monumentos

El Morro

El Morro es un fuerte *(fort)* que está en la bahía *(bay)* de San Juan, Puerto Rico. Fue construido en el siglo *(century)* XVI por los españoles para defenderse de los piratas. Actualmente, El Morro es un museo que atrae *(attracts)* a miles de turistas. También es el sitio más fotografiado de Puerto Rico. La arquitectura del fuerte es impresionante. Tiene túneles misteriosos, mazmorras *(dungeons)* y vistas *(views)* fabulosas de la bahía.

Puerto Plata

Santiago

Río Yuna

HAITÍ

LA REPÚBLICA DOMINICANA

Arecibo

San
Juan

Fajardo

Sierra de Neiba

San Pedro
de Macorís

Isla
Culebra

Sierra de Baoruco

Santo
Domingo

Mayagüez

Ponce

Isla de Vieques

PUERTO RICO

Mar Caribe

¿Qué aprendiste?

1 **¿Cierto o falso?** Indica si las siguientes frases son **ciertas** o **falsas**.

	Cierto	Falso
1. El mar Caribe está al Norte de América Central.	_____	_____
2. El área de Cuba es mayor que el área de Puerto Rico.	_____	_____
3. San Juan es la ciudad de Puerto Rico de mayor población.	_____	_____
4. El Morro fue construido por los piratas en el siglo XVI.	_____	_____
5. El Morro es actualmente un museo.	_____	_____
6. La Habana Vieja es Patrimonio Cultural de la Humanidad.	_____	_____
7. La Habana Vieja es la parte nueva de la capital de Cuba.	_____	_____
8. Los primeros países hispanos en tener una liga de béisbol fueron Chile y Uruguay.	_____	_____
9. El béisbol es el deporte nacional de la República Dominicana.	_____	_____
10. La salsa nació en Nueva York.	_____	_____
11. El merengue tiene sus raíces en la ciudad.	_____	_____
12. Juan Luis Guerra es un cantante de merengue.	_____	_____

2 **Preguntas** Contesta las siguientes preguntas con frases completas.

1. ¿Dónde está el mar Caribe? ¿Cómo son sus aguas?
2. ¿Cómo es la arquitectura del fuerte El Morro?
3. ¿Por qué crees que la Habana Vieja fue declarada Patrimonio Cultural de la Humanidad?
4. ¿En qué países del Caribe es popular el béisbol?
5. ¿En qué país nació la música salsa? ¿En qué país nació el merengue?

En Internet

Busca más información sobre estos temas en el sitio vistahigherlearning.com. Presenta la información a tus compañeros/as de clase.

- El Morro
- La Habana Vieja
- El béisbol
- La salsa y el merengue

Glossary of Grammatical Terms

ADJECTIVE A word that modifies or describes a noun or pronoun.

muchos libros	un hombre **rico**
many books	*a **rich** man*
las mujeres **altas**	
*the **tall** women*	

Demonstrative adjective An adjective that points out a specific noun.

esta fiesta	**ese** chico
***this** party*	***that** boy*
aquellas flores	
***those** flowers*	

Possessive adjective An adjective that indicates ownership or possession.

mi mejor vestido	Éste es **mi** hermano.
***my** best dress*	*This is **my** brother*

Stressed possessive adjective A possessive adjective that emphasizes the owner or possessor.

Es un libro **mío**.
*It's **my book**./It's a book **of mine**.*

Es amiga **tuya**; yo no la conozco.
*She's a friend **of yours**; I don't know her.*

ADVERB A word that modifies or describes a verb, adjective, or another adverb.

Pancho escribe **rápidamente**.
*Pancho writes **quickly**.*

Este cuadro es **muy** bonito.
*This picture is **very** pretty.*

ARTICLE A word that points out either a specific (definite) noun or a non-specific (indefinite) noun.

Definite article An article that points out a specific noun.

el libro	**la** maleta
***the** book*	***the** suitcase*
los diccionarios	**las** palabras
***the** dictionaries*	***the** words*

Indefinite article An article that points out a noun in a general, non-specific way.

un lápiz	**una** computadora
***a** pencil*	***a** computer*
unos pájaros	**unas** escuelas
***some** birds*	***some** schools*

CLAUSE A group of words that contains both a conjugated verb and a subject, either expressed or implied.

Main (or Independent) clause A clause that can stand alone as a complete sentence.

Pienso ir a cenar pronto.
I plan to go to dinner soon.

Subordinate (or Dependent) clause A clause that does not express a complete thought and therefore cannot stand alone as a sentence.

Trabajo en la cafetería **porque necesito dinero para la escuela**.
*I work in the cafeteria **because I need money for school**.*

COMPARATIVE A word or construction used with an adjective or adverb to express a comparison between two people, places, or things.

Este programa es **más interesante que** el otro.
*This program is **more interesting than** the other one.*

Tomás no es **tan alto como** Alberto.
*Tomás is not **as tall as** Alberto.*

CONJUGATION A set of the forms of a verb for a specific tense or mood or the process by which these verb forms are presented.

Preterite conjugation of **cantar**

cant**é**	cant**amos**
cant**aste**	cant**asteis**
cant**ó**	cant**aron**

CONJUNCTION A word or phrase used to connect words, clauses, or phrases.

Susana es de Cuba **y** Pedro es de España.
*Susana is from Cuba **and** Pedro is from Spain.*

No quiero estudiar, **pero** tengo que hacerlo.
*I don't want to study, **but** I have to do it.*

CONTRACTION The joining of two words into one. The only contractions in Spanish are **al** and **del**.

Mi hermano fue **al** concierto ayer.
*My brother went **to the** concert yesterday.*

Saqué dinero **del** banco.
*I took money **from the** bank.*

DIRECT OBJECT A noun or pronoun that directly receives the action of the verb.

Tomás lee **el libro**.	**La** pagó ayer.
*Tomás reads **the book**.*	*She paid **it** yesterday.*

GENDER The grammatical categorizing of certain kinds of words, such as nouns and pronouns, as masculine, feminine, or neuter.

Masculine
articles **el**, un**o**
pronouns **él**, **lo**, mí**o**, ést**e**, és**e**, aquell**o**
adjective simpátic**o**

Feminine
articles **la**, un**a**
pronouns **ella**, **la**, mí**a**, ést**a**, és**a**, aquéll**a**
adjective simpátic**a**

IMPERSONAL EXPRESSION A third-person expression with no expressed or specific subject.

Es muy importante.	**Llueve** mucho.
*It's **very important**.*	*It's **raining** hard.*

Aquí **se habla** español.
*Spanish **is spoken** here.*

INDIRECT OBJECT A noun or pronoun that receives the action of the verb indirectly; the object, often a living being, to or for whom an action is performed.

Eduardo **le** dio un libro **a Linda**.
*Eduardo gave a book **to Linda**.*

La profesora **me** dio una C en el examen.
*The professor gave **me** a C on the test.*

INFINITIVE The basic form of a verb. Infinitives in Spanish end in **-ar**, **-er**, or **-ir**.

hablar	correr	abrir
to speak	*to run*	*to open*

INTERROGATIVE An adjective or pronoun used to ask a question.

¿Quién habla?	**¿Cuántos** compraste?
Who is speaking?	**How many** did you buy?

¿Qué piensas hacer hoy?
What do you plan to do today?

INVERSION Changing the word order of a sentence, often to form a question.

Statement: Elena pagó la cuenta del restaurante.

Inversion: ¿Pagó Elena la cuenta del restaurante?

MOOD A grammatical distinction of verbs that indicates whether the verb is intended to make a statement or command, or to express a doubt, emotion, or condition contrary to fact.

Imperative mood Verb forms used to make commands.

Di la verdad.	**Caminen Uds. conmigo.**
Tell the truth.	*Walk with me.*

¡Comamos ahora!
Let's eat now!

Indicative mood Verb forms used to state facts, actions, and states considered to be real.

Sé que **tienes** el dinero.
***I know** that **you have** the money.*

Subjunctive mood Verb forms used principally in subordinate (or dependent) clauses to express wishes, desires, emotions, doubts, and certain conditions, such as contrary-to-fact situations.

Prefieren que **hables** en español.
*They prefer that **you speak** in Spanish.*

Dudo que Luis **tenga** el dinero necesario.
*I doubt that Luis **has** the necessary money.*

NOUN A word that identifies people, animals, places, things, and ideas.

hombre	gato
man	*cat*
México	casa
Mexico	*house*
libertad	
freedom	

NUMBER A grammatical term that refers to singular or plural. Nouns in Spanish and English have number. Other parts of a sentence, such as adjectives, articles, and verbs, can also have number.

Singular	Plural
una cosa	**unas** cosas
a thing	*some things*
el profesor	**los** profesores
the professor	*the professors*

NUMBERS Words that represent amounts.

Cardinal numbers Words that show specific amounts.

cinco minutos
five minutes

el año **dos mil dos**
the year 2002

Ordinal numbers Words that indicate the order of a noun in a series.

el **cuarto** jugador	la **décima** hora
*the **fourth** player*	*the **tenth** hour*

PAST PARTICIPLE A past form of the verb used in compound tenses. The past participle may also be used as an adjective, but it must then agree in number and gender with the word it modifies.

Han **buscado** por todas partes.
*They have **searched** everywhere.*

Yo no había **estudiado** para el examen.
*I hadn't **studied** for the exam.*

Hay una **ventana rota** en la sala.
*There is a **broken window** in the living room.*

PERSON The form of the verb or pronoun that indicates the speaker, the one spoken to, or the one spoken about. In Spanish, as in English, there are three persons: first, second, and third.

Person	Singular		Plural	
1st	**yo**	*I*	**nosotros/as**	*we*
2nd	**tú, Ud.**	*you*	**vosotros/as, Uds.**	*you*
3rd	**él, ella**	*he/she*	**ellos, ellas**	*they*

PREPOSITION A word that describes the relationship, most often in time or space, between two other words.

Anita es **de** California.
*Anita is **from** California.*

La chaqueta está **en** el carro.
*The jacket is **in** the car.*

¿Quieres hablar **con** ella?
*Do you want to talk **to** her?*

PRESENT PARTICIPLE In English, a verb form that ends in *-ing*. In Spanish, the present participle ends in **–ndo**, and is often used with **estar** to form a progressive tense.

Mi hermana está **hablando** por teléfono ahora mismo.
*My sister is **talking** on the phone right now.*

PRONOUN A word that takes the place of a noun or nouns.

Demonstrative pronoun A pronoun that takes the place of a specific noun.

Quiero **ésta**.
*I want **this one**.*

¿Vas a comprar **ése**?
*Are you going to buy **that one**?*

Juan prefirió **aquéllos**.
*Juan preferred **those** (over there).*

Object pronoun A pronoun that functions as a direct or indirect object of the verb.

Te digo la verdad.
*I'm telling **you** the truth.*

Me lo trajo Juan.
*Juan brought **it** to **me**.*

Reflexive pronoun A pronoun that indicates that the action of a verb is performed by the subject on itself. These pronouns are often expressed in English with *-self: myself, yourself,* etc.

Yo **me bañé** antes de salir.
*I **bathed** (**myself**) before going out.*

Elena **se acostó** a las once y media.
*Elena **went to bed** at eleven-thirty.*

Relative pronoun A pronoun that connects a subordinate clause to a main clause.

El chico **que** nos escribió viene a visitarnos mañana.
*The boy **who** wrote us is coming to visit us tomorrow.*

Ya sé **lo que** tenemos que hacer.
*I already know **what** we have to do.*

Subject pronoun A pronoun that replaces the name or title of a person or thing and acts as the subject of a verb.

Tú debes estudiar más.
***You** should study more.*

Él llegó primero.
***He** arrived first.*

SUBJECT A noun or pronoun that performs the action of a verb and is often implied by the verb.

María va al supermercado.
***María** goes to the supermarket.*

(**Ellos**) Trabajan mucho.
***They** work hard.*

Esos **libros** son muy caros.
*Those **books** are very expensive.*

SUPERLATIVE A word or construction used with an adjective or adverb to express the highest or lowest degree of a specific quality among three or more people, places, or things.

Entre todas mis clases, ésta es la **más interesante**.
*Among all my classes, this is the **most interesting**.*

Raúl es el **menos simpático** de los chicos.
*Raúl is the **least pleasant** of the boys.*

TENSE A set of verb forms that indicates the time of an action or state: past, present, or future.

Compound tense A two-word tense made up of an auxiliary verb and a present or past participle. In Spanish, there are two auxiliary verbs: **estar** and **haber**.

En este momento, **estoy estudiando**.
*At this time, **I am studying**.*

El paquete no **ha llegado** todavía.
*The package **has not arrived** yet.*

Simple tense A tense expressed by a single verb form.

María **estaba** mal anoche.
*María **was** ill last night.*

Juana **hablará** con su mamá mañana.
*Juana **will** speak with her mom tomorrow.*

VERB A word that expresses actions or states-of-being.

Auxiliary verb A verb used with a present or past participle to form a compound tense. **Haber** is the most commonly used auxiliary verb in Spanish.

Los chicos **han** visto los elefantes.
*The children **have** seen the elephants.*

Espero que **hayas** comido.
*I hope you **have** eaten.*

Reflexive verb A verb that describes an action performed by the subject on itself and is always used with a reflexive pronoun.

Me compré un carro nuevo.
I bought myself *a new car.*

Pedro y Adela **se levantan** muy temprano.
*Pedro and Adela **get (themselves) up** very early.*

Spelling change verb A verb that undergoes a predictable change in spelling in order to reflect its actual pronunciation in the various conjugations.

practicar	c → qu	practico	practi**qué**
dirigir	g → j	diri**jo**	dirigí
almorzar	z → c	almor**zó**	almor**cé**

Stem-changing verb A verb whose stem vowel undergoes one or more predictable changes in the various conjugations.

entender (i:ie)	enti**e**ndo
pedir (e:i)	p**i**den
dormir (o:ue, u)	d**ue**rmo, d**u**rmieron

Verb conjugation tables

The verb lists

The list of verbs below and the model-verb tables that start on page 410 show you how to conjugate every verb taught in **Aventuras**. Each verb in the list is followed by a model verb conjugated according to the same pattern. The number in parentheses indicates where in the tables you can find the conjugated forms of the model verb. If you want to find out how to conjugate **divertirse**, for example, look up number 33, **sentir**, the model for verbs that follow the **i:ie** stem-change pattern.

How to use the verb tables

In the tables you will find the infinitive, past and present participles, and all the simple forms of each model verb. The formation of the compound tenses of any verb can be inferred from the table of compound tenses, pages 410–417, either by combining the past participle of the verb with a conjugated form of **haber** or combining the present participle with a conjugated form of **estar**.

---

abrazar (z:c) like cruzar (37)
abrir like vivir (3) *except* past participle is abierto
aburrir(se) like vivir (3)
acabar de like hablar (1)
acampar like hablar (1)
acompañar like hablar (1)
aconsejar like hablar (1)
acordarse (o:ue) like contar (24)
acostarse (o:ue) like contar (24)
adelgazar (z:c) like cruzar (37)
afeitarse like hablar (1)
ahorrar like hablar (1)
alegrarse like hablar (1)
aliviar like hablar (1)
almorzar (o:ue) like contar (24) *except* (z:c)
alquilar like hablar (1)
anunciar like hablar (1)
apagar (g:gu) like llegar (41)
aplaudir like vivir (3)
apreciar like hablar (1)
aprender like comer (2)
apurarse like hablar (1)
arrancar (c:qu) like tocar (43)
arreglar like hablar (1)
asistir like vivir (3)
aumentar like hablar (1)
ayudar(se) like hablar (1)

bailar like hablar (1)
bajar(se) like hablar (1)
bañarse like hablar (1)
barrer like comer (2)
beber like comer (2)
besar(se) like hablar (1)
brindar like hablar (1)
bucear like hablar (1)
buscar (c:qu) like tocar (43)
caber (4)
caer(se) (5)
calentarse (e:ie) like pensar (30)
calzar (z:c) like cruzar (37)
cambiar like hablar (1)
caminar like hablar (1)
cantar like hablar (1)
casarse like hablar (1)
celebrar like hablar (1)
cenar like hablar (1)
cepillarse like hablar (1)
cerrar (e:ie) like pensar (30)
chocar (c:qu) like tocar (43)
cobrar like hablar (1)
cocinar like hablar (1)
comenzar (e:ie) (z:c) like empezar (26)
comer (2)
compartir like vivir (3)
comprar like hablar (1)
comprender like comer (2)

comprometerse like comer (2)
comunicarse (c:qu) like tocar (43)
conducir (c:zc) (6)
confirmar like hablar (1)
conocer (c:zc) (35)
conseguir (e:i) like seguir (32)
conservar like hablar (1)
consumir like vivir (3)
contaminar like hablar (1)
contar (o:ue) (24)
controlar like hablar (1)
correr like comer (2)
costar (o:ue) like contar (24)
creer (y) (36)
cruzar (z:c) (37)
cubrir like vivir (3) *except* past participle is cubierto
cuidar like hablar (1)
cumplir like vivir (3)
dañar like hablar (1)
dar(se) (7)
deber like comer (2)
decidir like vivir (3)
decir (e:i) (8)
declarar like hablar (1)
dejar like hablar (1)
depositar like hablar (1)
desarrollar like hablar (1)
desayunar like hablar (1)
descansar like hablar (1)
describir like vivir (3) *except* past

participle is descrito
descubrir like vivir (3) *except* past participle is descubierto
desear like hablar (1)
despedirse (e:i) like pedir (29)
despertarse (e:ie) like pensar (30)
destruir (y) (38)
dibujar like hablar (1)
disfrutar like hablar (1)
divertirse (e:ie) like sentir (33)
divorciarse like hablar (1)
doblar like hablar (1)
doler (o:ue) like volver (34) *except* past participle is regular
dormir(se) (o:ue) (25)
ducharse like hablar (1)
dudar like hablar (1)
durar like hablar (1)
echar like hablar (1)
elegir (e:i) like pedir (29) *except* (g:j)
emitir like vivir (3)
empezar (e:ie) (z:c) (26)
enamorarse like hablar (1)
encantar like hablar (1)
encontrar(se) (o:ue) like contar (24)
enfermarse like hablar (1)
enojarse like hablar (1)
enseñar like hablar (1)
ensuciar like hablar (1)

entender (e:ie) (27)

entrenarse like hablar (1)

entrevistar like hablar (1)

enviar (envío) (39)

escalar like hablar (1)

escribir like vivir (3) *except* past participle is escrito

escuchar like hablar (1)

esculpir like vivir (3)

esperar like hablar (1)

esquiar (esquío) like enviar (39)

establecer (c:zc) like conocer (35)

estacionar like hablar (1)

estar (9)

estornudar like hablar (1)

estudiar like hablar (1)

evitar like hablar (1)

explicar (c:qu) like tocar (43)

explorar like hablar (1)

faltar like hablar (1)

fascinar like hablar (1)

firmar like hablar (1)

fumar like hablar (1)

funcionar like hablar (1)

ganar like hablar (1)

gastar like hablar (1)

graduarse (gradúo) (40)

guardar like hablar (1)

gustar like hablar (1)

haber (hay) (10)

hablar (1)

hacer (11)

importar like hablar (1)

imprimir like vivir (3)

informar like hablar (1)

insistir like vivir (3)

interesar like hablar (1)

invertir (e:ie) like sentir (33)

invitar like hablar (1)

ir(se) (12)

jubilarse like hablar (1)

jugar (u:ue) (g:gu) (28)

lastimarse like hablar (1)

lavar(se) like hablar (1)

leer (y) like creer (36)

levantar(se) like hablar (1)

limpiar like hablar (1)

llamar(se) like hablar (1)

llegar (g:gu) (41)

llenar like hablar (1)

llevar(se) like hablar (1)

llover (o:ue) like volver (34) *except* past participle is regular

luchar like hablar (1)

mandar like hablar (1)

manejar like hablar (1)

mantener(se) (e:ie) like tener (20)

maquillarse like hablar (1)

mejorar like hablar (1)

merendar (e:ie) like pensar (30)

mirar like hablar (1)

molestar like hablar (1)

montar like hablar (1)

morir (o:ue) like dormir (25) *except* past participle is muerto

mostrar (o:ue) like contar (24)

mudarse like hablar (1)

nacer (c:zc) like conocer (35)

nadar like hablar (1)

navegar (g:gu) like llegar (41)

necesitar like hablar (1)

negar (e:ie) like pensar (30) *except* (g:gu)

nevar (e:ie) like pensar (30)

obedecer (c:zc) like conocer (35)

obtener (e:ie) like tener (20)

ocurrir like vivir (3)

odiar like hablar (1)

ofrecer (c:zc) like conocer (35)

oír (13)

olvidar like hablar (1)

pagar (g:gu) like llegar (41)

parar like hablar (1)

parecer (c:zc) like conocer (35)

pasar like hablar (1)

pasear like hablar (1)

patinar like hablar (1)

pedir (e:i) (29)

peinarse like hablar (1)

pensar (e:ie) (30)

perder (e:ie) like entender (27)

pescar (c:qu) like tocar (43)

pintar like hablar (1)

planchar like hablar (1)

poder (o:ue) (14)

poner(se) (15)

practicar (c:qu) like tocar (43)

preferir (e:ie) like sentir (33)

preguntar like hablar (1)

preocuparse like hablar (1)

preparar like hablar (1)

presentar like hablar (1)

prestar like hablar (1)

probar(se) (o:ue) like contar (24)

prohibir like vivir (3)

proteger (g:j) (42)

publicar (c:qu) like tocar (43)

quedar(se) like hablar (1)

querer (e:ie) (16)

quitar(se) like hablar (1)

recetar like hablar (1)

recibir like vivir (3)

reciclar like hablar (1)

recoger (g:j) like proteger (42)

recomendar (e:ie) like pensar (30)

recordar (o:ue) like contar (24)

reducir (c:zc) like conducir (6)

regalar like hablar (1)

regatear like hablar (1)

regresar like hablar (1)

reir(se) (e:i) (31)

relajarse like hablar (1)

renunciar like hablar (1)

repetir (e:i) like pedir (29)

resolver (o:ue) like volver (34)

respirar like hablar (1)

revisar like hablar (1)

rogar (o:ue) like contar (24) *except* (g:gu)

romper(se) like comer (2) *except* past participle is roto

saber (17)

sacar (c:qu) like tocar (43)

sacudir like vivir (3)

salir (18)

saludar(se) like hablar (1)

seguir (e:i) (32)

sentarse (e:ie) like pensar (30)

sentir(se) (e:ie) (33)

separarse like hablar (1)

ser (19)

servir (e:i) like pedir (29)

solicitar like hablar (1)

sonar (o:ue) like contar (24)

sonreír (e:i) like reír(se) (31)

sorprender like comer (2)

subir like vivir (3)

sudar like hablar (1)

sufrir like vivir (3)

sugerir (e:ie) like sentir (33)

suponer like poner (15)

temer like comer (2)

tener (e:ie) (20)

terminar like hablar (1)

tocar (c:qu) (43)

tomar like hablar (1)

torcerse (o:ue) like volver (34) *except* (c:z) and past participle is regular

toser like comer (2)

trabajar like hablar (1)

traducir (c:zc) like conducir (6)

traer (21)

transmitir like vivir (3)

tratar like hablar (1)

usar like hablar (1)

vender like comer (2)

venir (e:ie) (22)

ver (23)

vestirse (e:i) like pedir (29)

viajar like hablar (1)

visitar like hablar (1)

vivir (3)

volver (o:ue) (34)

votar like hablar (1)

Regular verbs: simple tenses

Infinitive	INDICATIVE					SUBJUNCTIVE		IMPERATIVE
	Present	**Imperfect**	**Preterite**	**Future**	**Conditional**	**Present**	**Past**	
1 hablar	hablo	hablaba	hablé	hablaré	hablaría	hable	hablara	
	hablas	hablabas	hablaste	hablarás	hablarías	hables	hablaras	habla tú (no hables)
	habla	hablaba	habló	hablará	hablaría	hable	hablara	hable Ud.
Participles:	hablamos	hablábamos	hablamos	hablaremos	hablaríamos	hablemos	habláramos	hablemos
hablando	habláis	hablabais	hablasteis	hablaréis	hablaríais	habléis	hablarais	hablad (no habléis)
hablado	hablan	hablaban	hablaron	hablarán	hablarían	hablen	hablaran	hablen Uds.
2 comer	como	comía	comí	comeré	comería	coma	comiera	
	comes	comías	comiste	comerás	comerías	comas	comieras	come tú (no comas)
	come	comía	comió	comerá	comería	coma	comiera	coma Ud.
Participles:	comemos	comíamos	comimos	comeremos	comeríamos	comamos	comiéramos	comamos
comiendo	coméis	comíais	comisteis	comeréis	comeríais	comáis	comierais	comed (no comáis)
comido	comen	comían	comieron	comerán	comerían	coman	comieran	coman Uds.
3 vivir	vivo	vivía	viví	viviré	viviría	viva	viviera	
	vives	vivías	viviste	vivirás	vivirías	vivas	vivieras	vive tú (no vivas)
	vive	vivía	vivió	vivirá	viviría	viva	viviera	viva Ud.
Participles:	vivimos	vivíamos	vivimos	viviremos	viviríamos	vivamos	viviéramos	vivamos
viviendo	vivís	vivíais	vivisteis	viviréis	viviríais	viváis	vivierais	vivid (no viváis)
vivido	viven	vivían	vivieron	vivirán	vivirían	vivan	vivieran	vivan Uds.

All verbs: compound tenses

PERFECT TENSES

INDICATIVE				SUBJUNCTIVE	
Present Perfect	**Past Perfect**	**Future Perfect**	**Conditional Perfect**	**Present Perfect**	**Past Perfect**
he	había	habré	habría	haya	hubiera
has	habías	habrás	habrías	hayas	hubieras
ha	había	habrá	habría	haya	hubiera
hemos hablado	habíamos hablado	habremos hablado	habríamos hablado	hayamos hablado	hubiéramos hablado
habéis comido	habíais comido	habréis comido	habríais comido	hayáis comido	hubierais comido
han vivido	habían vivido	habrán vivido	habrían vivido	hayan vivido	hubieran vivido

PROGRESSIVE TENSES

	INDICATIVE				SUBJUNCTIVE	
Present Progressive	Past Progressive	Future Progressive	Conditional Progressive		Present Progressive	Past Progressive
estoy	estaba	estaré	estaría		esté	estuviera
estás	estabas	estarás	estarías		estés	estuvieras
está hablando	estaba hablando	estará hablando	estaría hablando		esté hablando	estuviera
estamos comiendo	estábamos comiendo	estaremos comiendo	estaríamos comiendo		estemos comiendo	estuviéramos
estáis viviendo	estabais viviendo	estaréis viviendo	estaríais viviendo		estéis viviendo	estuvierais
estan	estaban	estarán	estarían		estén	estuvieran

Irregular verbs

Infinitive	INDICATIVE					SUBJUNCTIVE		IMPERATIVE
	Present	Imperfect	Preterite	Future	Conditional	Present	Past	
4 caber	**quepo**	cabía	**cupe**	**cabré**	**cabría**	**quepa**	**cupiera**	
	cabes	cabías	**cupiste**	**cabrás**	**cabrías**	**quepas**	**cupieras**	cabe tú (no **quepas**)
	cabe	cabía	**cupo**	**cabrá**	**cabría**	**quepa**	**cupiera**	**quepa** Ud.
Participles:	cabemos	cabíamos	**cupimos**	**cabremos**	**cabríamos**	**quepamos**	**cupiéramos**	**quepamos**
cabiendo	cabéis	cabíais	**cupisteis**	**cabréis**	**cabríais**	**quepáis**	**cupierais**	cabed (no **quepáis**)
cabido	caben	cabían	**cupieron**	**cabrán**	**cabrían**	**quepan**	**cupieran**	**quepan** Uds.
5 caer(se)	**caigo**	caía	**caí**	caeré	caería	**caiga**	**cayera**	
	caes	caías	**caíste**	caerás	caerías	**caigas**	**cayeras**	cae tú (no **caigas**)
	cae	caía	**cayó**	caerá	caería	**caiga**	**cayera**	**caiga** Ud. (no **caiga**)
Participles:	caemos	caíamos	**caímos**	caeremos	caeríamos	**caigamos**	**cayéramos**	**caigamos**
cayendo	caéis	caíais	**caísteis**	caeréis	caeríais	**caigáis**	**cayerais**	caed (no **caigáis**)
caído	caen	caían	**cayeron**	caerán	caerían	**caigan**	**cayeran**	**caigan** Uds.
6 conducir	**conduzco**	conducía	**conduje**	conduciré	conduciría	**conduzca**	**condujera**	
(c:zc)	conduces	conducías	**condujiste**	conducirás	conducirías	**conduzcas**	**condujeras**	conduce tú (no **conduzcas**)
	conduce	conducía	**condujo**	conducirá	conduciría	**conduzca**	**condujera**	**conduzca** Ud. (no **conduzca**)
Participles:	conducimos	conducíamos	**condujimos**	conduciremos	conduciríamos	**conduzcamos**	**condujéramos**	**conduzcamos**
conduciendo	conducís	conducíais	**condujisteis**	conduciréis	conduciríais	**conduzcáis**	**condujerais**	conducid (no **conduzcáis**)
conducido	conducen	conducían	**condujeron**	conducirán	conducirían	**conduzcan**	**condujeran**	**conduzcan** Uds.

		Infinitive	INDICATIVE Present	Imperfect	Preterite	Future	Conditional	SUBJUNCTIVE Present	Past	IMPERATIVE
7		dar	doy	daba	di	daré	daría	dé	diera	
			das	dabas	diste	darás	darías	des	dieras	da tú (no des)
			da	daba	dio	dará	daría	dé	diera	dé Ud.
		Participles:	damos	dábamos	dimos	daremos	daríamos	demos	diéramos	demos
		dando	dais	dabais	disteis	daréis	daríais	deis	dierais	dad (no deis)
		dado	dan	daban	dieron	darán	darían	den	dieran	den Uds.
8		decir (e:i)	digo	decía	dije	diré	diría	diga	dijera	
			dices	decías	dijiste	dirás	dirías	digas	dijeras	di tú (no digas)
			dice	decía	dijo	dirá	diría	diga	dijera	diga Ud.
		Participles:	decimos	decíamos	dijimos	diremos	diríamos	digamos	dijéramos	digamos
		diciendo	decís	decíais	dijisteis	diréis	diríais	digáis	dijerais	decid (no digáis)
		dicho	dicen	decían	dijeron	dirán	dirían	digan	dijeran	digan Uds.
9		estar	estoy	estaba	estuve	estaré	estaría	esté	estuviera	
			estás	estabas	estuviste	estarás	estarías	estés	estuvieras	está tú (no estés)
			está	estaba	estuvo	estará	estaría	esté	estuviera	esté Ud.
		Participles:	estamos	estábamos	estuvimos	estaremos	estaríamos	estemos	estuviéramos	estemos
		estando	estáis	estabais	estuvisteis	estaréis	estaríais	estéis	estuvierais	estad (no estéis)
		estado	están	estaban	estuvieron	estarán	estarían	estén	estuvieran	estén Uds.
10		haber	he	había	hube	habré	habría	haya	hubiera	
			has	habías	hubiste	habrás	habrías	hayas	hubieras	
			ha	había	hubo	habrá	habría	haya	hubiera	
		Participles:	hemos	habíamos	hubimos	habremos	habríamos	hayamos	hubiéramos	
		habiendo	habéis	habíais	hubisteis	habréis	habríais	hayáis	hubierais	
		habido	han	habían	hubieron	habrán	habrían	hayan	hubieran	
11		hacer	hago	hacía	hice	haré	haría	haga	hiciera	
			haces	hacías	hiciste	harás	harías	hagas	hicieras	haz tú (no hagas)
			hace	hacía	hizo	hará	haría	haga	hiciera	haga Ud.
		Participles:	hacemos	hacíamos	hicimos	haremos	haríamos	hagamos	hiciéramos	hagamos
		haciendo	hacéis	hacíais	hicisteis	haréis	haríais	hagáis	hicierais	haced (no hagáis)
		hecho	hacen	hacían	hicieron	harán	harían	hagan	hicieran	hagan Uds.
12		ir	voy	iba	fui	iré	iría	vaya	fuera	
			vas	ibas	fuiste	irás	irías	vayas	fueras	ve tú (no vayas)
			va	iba	fue	irá	iría	vaya	fuera	vaya Ud.
		Participles:	vamos	íbamos	fuimos	iremos	iríamos	vayamos	fuéramos	vamos
		yendo	vais	ibais	fuisteis	iréis	iríais	vayáis	fuerais	id (no vayáis)
		ido	van	iban	fueron	irán	irían	vayan	fueran	vayan Uds.
13		oír (y)	oigo	oía	oí	oiré	oiría	oiga	oyera	
			oyes	oías	oíste	oirás	oirías	oigas	oyeras	oye tú (no oigas)
			oye	oía	oyó	oirá	oiría	oiga	oyera	oiga Ud.
		Participles:	oímos	oíamos	oímos	oiremos	oiríamos	oigamos	oyéramos	oigamos
		oyendo	oís	oíais	oísteis	oiréis	oiríais	oigáis	oyerais	oíd (no oigáis)
		oído	oyen	oían	oyeron	oirán	oirían	oigan	oyeran	oigan Uds.

14 — poder (o:ue) · Participles: pudiendo, podido

	INDICATIVE					SUBJUNCTIVE		IMPERATIVE
Infinitive	Present	Imperfect	Preterite	Future	Conditional	Present	Past	
poder (o:ue)	**puedo**	podía	**pude**	**podré**	**podría**	**pueda**	**pudiera**	
	puedes	podías	**pudiste**	**podrás**	**podrías**	**puedas**	**pudieras**	**puede** tú (no **puedas**)
Participles:	**puede**	podía	**pudo**	**podrá**	**podría**	**pueda**	**pudiera**	**pueda** Ud.
pudiendo	podemos	podíamos	**pudimos**	**podremos**	**podríamos**	podamos	**pudiéramos**	podamos
podido	podéis	podíais	**pudisteis**	**podréis**	**podríais**	podáis	**pudierais**	poded (no **podáis**)
	pueden	podían	**pudieron**	**podrán**	**podrían**	**puedan**	**pudieran**	**puedan** Uds.

15 — poner · Participles: poniendo, puesto

	INDICATIVE					SUBJUNCTIVE		IMPERATIVE
Infinitive	Present	Imperfect	Preterite	Future	Conditional	Present	Past	
poner	**pongo**	ponía	**puse**	**pondré**	**pondría**	**ponga**	**pusiera**	
	pones	ponías	**pusiste**	**pondrás**	**pondrías**	**pongas**	**pusieras**	**pon** tú (no **pongas**)
Participles:	pone	ponía	**puso**	**pondrá**	**pondría**	**ponga**	**pusiera**	**ponga** Ud.
poniendo	ponemos	poníamos	**pusimos**	**pondremos**	**pondríamos**	**pongamos**	**pusiéramos**	**pongamos**
puesto	ponéis	poníais	**pusisteis**	**pondréis**	**pondríais**	**pongáis**	**pusierais**	poned (no **pongáis**)
	ponen	ponían	**pusieron**	**pondrán**	**pondrían**	**pongan**	**pusieran**	**pongan** Uds.

16 — querer (e:ie) · Participles: queriendo, querido

	INDICATIVE					SUBJUNCTIVE		IMPERATIVE
Infinitive	Present	Imperfect	Preterite	Future	Conditional	Present	Past	
querer (e:ie)	**quiero**	quería	**quise**	**querré**	**querría**	**quiera**	**quisiera**	
	quieres	querías	**quisiste**	**querrás**	**querrías**	**quieras**	**quisieras**	**quiere** tú (no **quieras**)
Participles:	**quiere**	quería	**quiso**	**querrá**	**querría**	**quiera**	**quisiera**	**quiera** Ud.
queriendo	queremos	queríamos	**quisimos**	**querremos**	**querríamos**	queramos	**quisiéramos**	**queramos**
querido	queréis	queríais	**quisisteis**	**querréis**	**querríais**	queráis	**quisierais**	quered (no **queráis**)
	quieren	querían	**quisieron**	**querrán**	**querrían**	**quieran**	**quisieran**	**quieran** Uds.

17 — saber · Participles: sabiendo, sabido

	INDICATIVE					SUBJUNCTIVE		IMPERATIVE
Infinitive	Present	Imperfect	Preterite	Future	Conditional	Present	Past	
saber	**sé**	sabía	**supe**	**sabré**	**sabría**	**sepa**	**supiera**	
	sabes	sabías	**supiste**	**sabrás**	**sabrías**	**sepas**	**supieras**	sabe tú (no **sepas**)
Participles:	sabe	sabía	**supo**	**sabrá**	**sabría**	**sepa**	**supiera**	**sepa** Ud.
sabiendo	sabemos	sabíamos	**supimos**	**sabremos**	**sabríamos**	**sepamos**	**supiéramos**	**sepamos**
sabido	sabéis	sabíais	**supisteis**	**sabréis**	**sabríais**	**sepáis**	**supierais**	sabed (no **sepáis**)
	saben	sabían	**supieron**	**sabrán**	**sabrían**	**sepan**	**supieran**	**sepan** Uds.

18 — salir · Participles: saliendo, salido

	INDICATIVE					SUBJUNCTIVE		IMPERATIVE
Infinitive	Present	Imperfect	Preterite	Future	Conditional	Present	Past	
salir	**salgo**	salía	salí	**saldré**	**saldría**	**salga**	saliera	
	sales	salías	saliste	**saldrás**	**saldrías**	**salgas**	salieras	**sal** tú (no **salgas**)
Participles:	sale	salía	salió	**saldrá**	**saldría**	**salga**	saliera	**salga** Ud.
saliendo	salimos	salíamos	salimos	**saldremos**	**saldríamos**	**salgamos**	saliéramos	**salgamos**
salido	salís	salíais	salisteis	**saldréis**	**saldríais**	**salgáis**	salierais	salid (no **salgáis**)
	salen	salían	salieron	**saldrán**	**saldrían**	**salgan**	salieran	**salgan** Uds.

19 — ser · Participles: siendo, sido

	INDICATIVE					SUBJUNCTIVE		IMPERATIVE
Infinitive	Present	Imperfect	Preterite	Future	Conditional	Present	Past	
ser	**soy**	**era**	**fui**	seré	sería	sea	**fuera**	
	eres	**eras**	**fuiste**	serás	serías	seas	**fueras**	**sé** tú (no **seas**)
Participles:	**es**	**era**	**fue**	será	sería	sea	**fuera**	sea Ud.
siendo	**somos**	**éramos**	**fuimos**	seremos	seríamos	**seamos**	**fuéramos**	**seamos**
sido	**sois**	**erais**	**fuisteis**	seréis	seríais	**seáis**	**fuerais**	sed (no **seáis**)
	son	**eran**	**fueron**	serán	serían	sean	**fueran**	sean Uds.

20 — tener (e:ie) · Participles: teniendo, tenido

	INDICATIVE					SUBJUNCTIVE		IMPERATIVE
Infinitive	Present	Imperfect	Preterite	Future	Conditional	Present	Past	
tener (e:ie)	**tengo**	**tenía**	**tuve**	**tendré**	**tendría**	**tenga**	**tuviera**	
	tienes	**tenías**	**tuviste**	**tendrás**	**tendrías**	**tengas**	**tuvieras**	**ten** tú (no **tengas**)
Participles:	**tiene**	**tenía**	**tuvo**	**tendrá**	**tendría**	**tenga**	**tuviera**	**tenga** Ud.
teniendo	tenemos	**teníamos**	**tuvimos**	**tendremos**	**tendríamos**	**tengamos**	**tuviéramos**	**tengamos**
tenido	tenéis	**teníais**	**tuvisteis**	**tendréis**	**tendríais**	**tengáis**	**tuvierais**	tened (no **tengáis**)
	tienen	**tenían**	**tuvieron**	**tendrán**	**tendrían**	**tengan**	**tuvieran**	**tengan** Uds.

21 — traer

	INDICATIVE					SUBJUNCTIVE		IMPERATIVE
Infinitive	Present	Imperfect	Preterite	Future	Conditional	Present	Past	
traer	**traigo**	traía	**traje**	traeré	traería	**traiga**	**trajera**	
	traes	traías	**trajiste**	traerás	traerías	**traigas**	**trajeras**	trae tú (no **traigas**)
Participles:	trae	traía	**trajo**	traerá	traería	**traiga**	**trajera**	**traiga** Ud.
trayendo	traemos	traíamos	**trajimos**	traeremos	traeríamos	**traigamos**	**trajéramos**	**traigamos**
traído	traéis	traíais	**trajisteis**	traeréis	traeríais	**traigáis**	**trajerais**	traed (no **traigáis**)
	traen	traían	**trajeron**	traerán	traerían	**traigan**	**trajeran**	**traigan** Uds.

22 — venir (e:ie)

	INDICATIVE					SUBJUNCTIVE		IMPERATIVE
Infinitive	Present	Imperfect	Preterite	Future	Conditional	Present	Past	
venir (e:ie)	**vengo**	venía	**vine**	**vendré**	**vendría**	**venga**	**viniera**	
	vienes	venías	**viniste**	**vendrás**	**vendrías**	**vengas**	**vinieras**	**ven** tú (no **vengas**)
Participles:	**viene**	venía	**vino**	**vendrá**	**vendría**	**venga**	**viniera**	**venga** Ud.
viniendo	venimos	veníamos	**vinimos**	**vendremos**	**vendríamos**	**vengamos**	**viniéramos**	**vengamos**
venido	venís	veníais	**vinisteis**	**vendréis**	**vendríais**	**vengáis**	**vinierais**	venid (no **vengáis**)
	vienen	venían	**vinieron**	**vendrán**	**vendrían**	**vengan**	**vinieran**	**vengan** Uds.

23 — ver

	INDICATIVE					SUBJUNCTIVE		IMPERATIVE
Infinitive	Present	Imperfect	Preterite	Future	Conditional	Present	Past	
ver	**veo**	**veía**	vi	veré	vería	**vea**	**viera**	
	ves	**veías**	viste	verás	verías	**veas**	**vieras**	**ve** tú (no **veas**)
Participles:	ve	**veía**	vio	verá	vería	**vea**	**viera**	**vea** Ud.
viendo	vemos	**veíamos**	vimos	veremos	veríamos	**veamos**	**viéramos**	**veamos**
visto	veis	**veíais**	visteis	veréis	veríais	**veáis**	**vierais**	ved (no **veáis**)
	ven	**veían**	vieron	verán	verían	**vean**	**vieran**	**vean** Uds.

Stem changing verbs

24 — contar (o:ue)

	INDICATIVE					SUBJUNCTIVE		IMPERATIVE
Infinitive	Present	Imperfect	Preterite	Future	Conditional	Present	Past	
contar (o:ue)	**cuento**	contaba	conté	contaré	contaría	**cuente**	contara	
	cuentas	contabas	contaste	contarás	contarías	**cuentes**	contaras	**cuenta** tú (no **cuentes**)
Participles:	**cuenta**	contaba	contó	contará	contaría	**cuente**	contara	**cuente** Ud.
contando	contamos	contábamos	contamos	contaremos	contaríamos	contemos	contáramos	contemos
contado	contáis	contabais	contasteis	contaréis	contaríais	contéis	contarais	contad (no **contéis**)
	cuentan	contaban	contaron	contarán	contarían	**cuenten**	contaran	**cuenten** Uds.

25 — dormir (o:ue)

	INDICATIVE					SUBJUNCTIVE		IMPERATIVE
Infinitive	Present	Imperfect	Preterite	Future	Conditional	Present	Past	
dormir (o:ue)	**duermo**	dormía	dormí	dormiré	dormiría	**duerma**	**durmiera**	
	duermes	dormías	dormiste	dormirás	dormirías	**duermas**	**durmieras**	**duerme** tú (no **duermas**)
Participles:	**duerme**	dormía	**durmió**	dormirá	dormiría	**duerma**	**durmiera**	**duerma** Ud.
durmiendo	dormimos	dormíamos	dormimos	dormiremos	dormiríamos	**durmamos**	**durmiéramos**	**durmamos**
dormido	dormís	dormíais	dormisteis	dormiréis	dormiríais	**durmáis**	**durmierais**	dormid (no **durmáis**)
	duermen	dormían	**durmieron**	dormirán	dormirían	**duerman**	**durmieran**	**duerman** Uds.

26 — empezar (e:ie) (c)

	INDICATIVE					SUBJUNCTIVE		IMPERATIVE
Infinitive	Present	Imperfect	Preterite	Future	Conditional	Present	Past	
empezar (e:ie) (c)	**empiezo**	empezaba	**empecé**	empezaré	empezaría	**empiece**	empezara	
	empiezas	empezabas	empezaste	empezarás	empezarías	**empieces**	empezaras	**empieza** tú (no **empieces**)
Participles:	**empieza**	empezaba	empezó	empezará	empezaría	**empiece**	empezara	**empiece** Ud.
empezando	empezamos	empezábamos	empezamos	empezaremos	empezaríamos	**empecemos**	empezáramos	**empecemos**
empezado	empezáis	empezabais	empezasteis	empezaréis	empezaríais	**empecéis**	empezarais	empezad (no **empecéis**)
	empiezan	empezaban	empezaron	empezarán	empezarían	**empiecen**	empezaran	**empiecen** Uds.

27 · entender (e:ie) — Participles: entendiendo, entendido

	INDICATIVE					SUBJUNCTIVE		IMPERATIVE
	Present	Imperfect	Preterite	Future	Conditional	Present	Past	
	entiendo	entendía	entendí	entenderé	entendería	entienda	entendiera	
	entiendes	entendías	entendiste	entenderás	entenderías	entiendas	entendieras	entiende tú (no entiendas)
	entiende	entendía	entendió	entenderá	entendería	entienda	entendiera	entienda Ud.
	entendemos	entendíamos	entendimos	entenderemos	entenderíamos	entendamos	entendiéramos	entendamos
	entendéis	entendíais	entendisteis	entenderéis	entenderíais	entendáis	entendierais	entended (no entendáis)
	entienden	entendían	entendieron	entenderán	entenderían	entiendan	entendieran	entiendan Uds.

28 · jugar (u:ue) (gu) — Participles: jugando, jugado

	INDICATIVE					SUBJUNCTIVE		IMPERATIVE
	Present	Imperfect	Preterite	Future	Conditional	Present	Past	
	juego	jugaba	jugué	jugaré	jugaría	juegue	jugara	
	juegas	jugabas	jugaste	jugarás	jugarías	juegues	jugaras	juega tú (no juegues)
	juega	jugaba	jugó	jugará	jugaría	juegue	jugara	juegue Ud.
	jugamos	jugábamos	jugamos	jugaremos	jugaríamos	juguemos	jugáramos	juguemos
	jugáis	jugabais	jugasteis	jugaréis	jugaríais	juguéis	jugarais	jugad (no juguéis)
	juegan	jugaban	jugaron	jugarán	jugarían	jueguen	jugaran	jueguen Uds.

29 · pedir (e:i) — Participles: pidiendo, pedido

	INDICATIVE					SUBJUNCTIVE		IMPERATIVE
	Present	Imperfect	Preterite	Future	Conditional	Present	Past	
	pido	pedía	pedí	pediré	pediría	pida	pidiera	
	pides	pedías	pediste	pedirás	pedirías	pidas	pidieras	pide tú (no pidas)
	pide	pedía	pidió	pedirá	pediría	pida	pidiera	pida Ud.
	pedimos	pedíamos	pedimos	pediremos	pediríamos	pidamos	pidiéramos	pidamos
	pedís	pedíais	pedisteis	pediréis	pediríais	pidáis	pidierais	pedid (no pidáis)
	piden	pedían	pidieron	pedirán	pedirían	pidan	pidieran	pidan Uds.

30 · pensar (e:ie) — Participles: pensando, pensado

	INDICATIVE					SUBJUNCTIVE		IMPERATIVE
	Present	Imperfect	Preterite	Future	Conditional	Present	Past	
	pienso	pensaba	pensé	pensaré	pensaría	piense	pensara	
	piensas	pensabas	pensaste	pensarás	pensarías	pienses	pensaras	piensa tú (no pienses)
	piensa	pensaba	pensó	pensará	pensaría	piense	pensara	piense Ud.
	pensamos	pensábamos	pensamos	pensaremos	pensaríamos	pensemos	pensáramos	pensemos
	pensáis	pensabais	pensasteis	pensaréis	pensaríais	penséis	pensarais	pensad (no penséis)
	piensan	pensaban	pensaron	pensarán	pensarían	piensen	pensaran	piensen Uds.

31 · reír(se) (e:i) — Participles: riendo, reído

	INDICATIVE					SUBJUNCTIVE		IMPERATIVE
	Present	Imperfect	Preterite	Future	Conditional	Present	Past	
	río	reía	reí	reiré	reiría	ría	riera	
	ríes	reías	reíste	reirás	reirías	rías	rieras	ríe tú (no rías)
	ríe	reía	rió	reirá	reiría	ría	riera	ría Ud.
	reímos	reíamos	reímos	reiremos	reiríamos	riamos	riéramos	riamos
	reís	reíais	reísteis	reiréis	reiríais	riáis	rierais	reíd (no riáis)
	ríen	reían	rieron	reirán	reirían	rían	rieran	rían Uds.

32 · seguir (e:i) (gu) — Participles: siguiendo, seguido

	INDICATIVE					SUBJUNCTIVE		IMPERATIVE
	Present	Imperfect	Preterite	Future	Conditional	Present	Past	
	sigo	seguía	seguí	seguiré	seguiría	siga	siguiera	
	sigues	seguías	seguiste	seguirás	seguirías	sigas	siguieras	sigue tú (no sigas)
	sigue	seguía	siguió	seguirá	seguiría	siga	siguiera	siga Ud.
	seguimos	seguíamos	seguimos	seguiremos	seguiríamos	sigamos	siguiéramos	sigamos
	seguís	seguíais	seguisteis	seguiréis	seguiríais	sigáis	siguierais	seguid (no sigáis)
	siguen	seguían	siguieron	seguirán	seguirían	sigan	siguieran	sigan Uds.

33 · sentir (e:ie) — Participles: sintiendo, sentido

	INDICATIVE					SUBJUNCTIVE		IMPERATIVE
	Present	Imperfect	Preterite	Future	Conditional	Present	Past	
	siento	sentía	sentí	sentiré	sentiría	sienta	sintiera	
	sientes	sentías	sentiste	sentirás	sentirías	sientas	sintieras	siente tú (no sientas)
	siente	sentía	sintió	sentirá	sentiría	sienta	sintiera	sienta Ud.
	sentimos	sentíamos	sentimos	sentiremos	sentiríamos	sintamos	sintiéramos	sintamos
	sentís	sentíais	sentisteis	sentiréis	sentiríais	sintáis	sintierais	sentid (no sintáis)
	sienten	sentían	sintieron	sentirán	sentirían	sientan	sintieran	sientan Uds.

		INDICATIVE					SUBJUNCTIVE		IMPERATIVE
Infinitive	Present	Imperfect	Preterite	Future	Conditional		Present	Past	
34 volver (o:ue)	**vuelvo**	volvía	volví	volveré	volvería		**vuelva**	volviera	
	vuelves	volvías	volviste	volverás	volverías		**vuelvas**	volvieras	**vuelve** tú (no **vuelvas**)
	vuelve	volvía	volvió	volverá	volvería		**vuelva**	volviera	**vuelva** Ud.
Participles:	volvemos	volvíamos	volvimos	volveremos	volveríamos		volvamos	volviéramos	volvamos
volviendo	volvéis	volvíais	volvisteis	volveréis	volveríais		volváis	volvierais	volved (no **volváis**)
vuelto	**vuelven**	volvían	volvieron	volverán	volverían		**vuelvan**	volvieran	**vuelvan** Uds.

Verbs with spelling changes only

		INDICATIVE					SUBJUNCTIVE		IMPERATIVE
Infinitive	Present	Imperfect	Preterite	Future	Conditional		Present	Past	
35 conocer	**conozco**	conocía	conocí	conoceré	conocería		**conozca**	conociera	
(c:zc)	conoces	conocías	conociste	conocerás	conocerías		**conozcas**	conocieras	conoce tú (no **conozcas**)
	conoce	conocía	conoció	conocerá	conocería		**conozca**	conociera	**conozca** Ud.
Participles:	conocemos	conocíamos	conocimos	conoceremos	conoceríamos		**conozcamos**	conociéramos	**conozcamos**
conociendo	conocéis	conocíais	conocisteis	conoceréis	conoceríais		**conozcáis**	conocierais	conoced (no **conozcáis**)
conocido	conocen	conocían	conocieron	conocerán	conocerían		**conozcan**	conocieran	**conozcan** Uds.
36 creer (y)	creo	creía	**creí**	creeré	creería		crea	**creyera**	
	crees	creías	**creíste**	creerás	creerías		creas	**creyeras**	cree tú (no creas)
	cree	creía	**creyó**	creerá	creería		crea	**creyera**	crea Ud.
Participles:	creemos	creíamos	**creímos**	creeremos	creeríamos		creamos	**creyéramos**	creamos
creyendo	creéis	creíais	**creísteis**	creeréis	creeríais		creáis	**creyerais**	creed (no creáis)
creído	creen	creían	**creyeron**	creerán	creerían		crean	**creyeran**	crean Uds.
37 cruzar (c)	cruzo	cruzaba	**crucé**	cruzaré	cruzaría		**cruce**	cruzara	
	cruzas	cruzabas	cruzaste	cruzarás	cruzarías		**cruces**	cruzaras	cruza tú (no **cruces**)
	cruza	cruzaba	cruzó	cruzará	cruzaría		**cruce**	cruzara	**cruce** Ud.
Participles:	cruzamos	cruzábamos	cruzamos	cruzaremos	cruzaríamos		**crucemos**	cruzáramos	**crucemos**
cruzando	cruzáis	cruzabais	cruzasteis	cruzaréis	cruzaríais		**crucéis**	cruzarais	cruzad (no **crucéis**)
cruzado	cruzan	cruzaban	cruzaron	cruzarán	cruzarían		**crucen**	cruzaran	**crucen** Uds.
38 destruir (y)	**destruyo**	destruía	destruí	destruiré	destruiría		**destruya**	**destruyera**	
	destruyes	destruías	destruiste	destruirás	destruirías		**destruyas**	**destruyeras**	**destruye** tú (no **destruyas**)
	destruye	destruía	**destruyó**	destruirá	destruiría		**destruya**	**destruyera**	**destruya** Ud.
Participles:	destruimos	destruíamos	destruimos	destruiremos	destruiríamos		**destruyamos**	**destruyéramos**	**destruyamos**
destruyendo	destruís	destruíais	destruisteis	destruiréis	destruiríais		**destruyáis**	**destruyerais**	destruid (no **destruyáis**)
destruido	**destruyen**	destruían	**destruyeron**	destruirán	destruirían		**destruyan**	**destruyeran**	**destruyan** Uds.
39 enviar	**envío**	enviaba	envié	enviaré	enviaría		**envíe**	enviara	
(envío)	**envías**	enviabas	enviaste	enviarás	enviarías		**envíes**	enviaras	**envía** tú (no **envíes**)
	envía	enviaba	envió	enviará	enviaría		**envíe**	enviara	**envíe** Ud.
Participles:	enviamos	enviábamos	enviamos	enviaremos	enviaríamos		**enviemos**	enviáramos	enviemos
enviando	enviáis	enviabais	enviasteis	enviaréis	enviaríais		**enviéis**	enviarais	enviad (no **enviéis**)
enviado	**envían**	enviaban	enviaron	enviarán	enviarían		**envíen**	enviaran	**envíen** Uds.

Infinitive	INDICATIVE					SUBJUNCTIVE		IMPERATIVE
	Present	Imperfect	Preterite	Future	Conditional	Present	Past	
40 graduarse (gradúo) **Participles:** graduando graduado	**gradúo** **gradúas** **gradúa** **graduamos** **graduáis** **gradúan**	graduaba graduabas graduaba graduábamos graduabais graduaban	gradué graduaste graduó graduamos graduasteis graduaron	graduaré graduarás graduará graduaremos graduaréis graduarán	graduaría graduarías graduaría graduaríamos graduaríais graduarían	**gradúe** **gradúes** **gradúe** **graduemos** **graduéis** **gradúen**	graduara graduaras graduara graduáramos graduarais graduaran	**gradúa** tú (no **gradúes**) **gradúe** Ud. graduemos graduad (no **graduéis**) **gradúen** Uds.
41 llegar (gu) **Participles:** llegando llegado	llego llegas llega llegamos llegáis llegan	llegaba llegabas llegaba llegábamos llegabais llegaban	**llegué** llegaste llegó llegamos llegasteis llegaron	llegaré llegarás llegará llegaremos llegaréis llegarán	llegaría llegarías llegaría llegaríamos llegaríais llegarían	**llegue** **llegues** **llegue** **lleguemos** **lleguéis** **lleguen**	llegara llegaras llegara llegáramos llegarais llegaran	llega tú (no **llegues**) **llegue** Ud. **lleguemos** llegad (no **lleguéis**) **lleguen** Uds.
42 proteger (j) **Participles:** protegiendo protegido	**protejo** proteges protege protegemos protegéis protegen	protegía protegías protegía protegíamos protegíais protegían	protegí protegiste protegió protegimos protegisteis protegieron	protegeré protegerás protegerá protegeremos protegeréis protegerán	protegería protegerías protegería protegeríamos protegeríais protegerían	**proteja** **protejas** **proteja** **protejamos** **protejáis** **protejan**	protegiera protegieras protegiera protegiéramos protegierais protegieran	protege tú (no **protejas**) **proteja** Ud. **protejamos** proteged (no **protejáis**) **protejan** Uds.
43 tocar (qu) **Participles:** tocando tocado	toco tocas toca tocamos tocáis tocan	tocaba tocabas tocaba tocábamos tocabais tocaban	**toqué** tocaste tocó tocamos tocasteis tocaron	tocaré tocarás tocará tocaremos tocaréis tocarán	tocaría tocarías tocaría tocaríamos tocaríais tocarían	**toque** **toques** **toque** **toquemos** **toquéis** **toquen**	tocara tocaras tocara tocáramos tocarais tocaran	toca tú (no **toques**) **toque** Ud. **toquemos** tocad (no **toquéis**) **toquen** Uds.

Guide to Vocabulary

Note on alphabetization

Formerly, **ch**, **ll**, and **ñ** were considered separate letters in the Spanish alphabet, **ch** appearing after **c**, **ll** after **l**, and **ñ** after **n**. In current practice, for purposes of alphabetization, **ch** and **ll** are not treated as separate letters, but **ñ** still follows **n**. Therefore, in this glossary you will find that **año**, for example, appears after **anuncio**.

Abbreviations used in this glossary

adj.	adjective	*interj.*	interjection	*poss.*	possessive
adv.	adverb	*i.o.*	indirect object	*prep.*	preposition
conj.	conjunction	*m.*	masculine	*pron.*	pronoun
d.o.	direct object	*n.*	noun	*ref.*	reflexive
f.	feminine	*obj.*	object	*sing.*	singular
fam.	familiar	*p.p.*	past participle	*sub.*	subject
form.	formal	*pl.*	plural	*v.*	verb

Spanish-English

A

a *prep.* at; to 1
  ¿A qué hora...? At what time . . . ? 1
  a bordo aboard 1
  a dieta on a diet 15
  a la derecha to the right 2
  a la izquierda to the left 2
  a la plancha grilled 8
  a la(s) + *time* at + *time* 1
  a menos que unless 13
  a menudo often 10
  a nombre de in the name of 5
  a plazos in installments 14
  A sus órdenes. At your service. 11
  a tiempo on time 10
  a veces sometimes 10
  a ver let's see 2
¡Abajo! *adv.* Down! 15
abeja *f.* bee
abierto/a *p.p.* open 5
abogado/a *m., f.* lawyer 16
abrazar(se) *v.* to hug; to embrace (each other) 11
abrazo *m.* hug
abrigo *m.* coat 6
abril *m.* April 5
abrir *v.* to open 3
abuelo/a *m., f.* grandfather; grandmother 3
abuelos *pl.* grandparents 3
aburrido/a *adj.* bored; boring 5
aburrir *v.* to bore 7
aburrirse *v.* to get bored
acabar de (+ inf.) *v.* to have just (*done something*) 6
acampar *v.* to camp
accidente *m.* accident 10
acción *f.* action

aceite *m.* oil 8
ácido/a *adj.* acid 13
acompañar *v.* to go with; to accompany 14
aconsejar *v.* to advise 12
acontecimiento *m.* event
acordarse (de) (o:ue) *v.* to remember 7
acostarse (o:ue) *v.* to go to bed 7
activo/a *adj.* active 15
actor *m.* actor 16
actriz *f.* actor 16
actualidades *f., pl.* news; current events
acuático/a *adj.* aquatic 4
adelgazar *v.* to lose weight; to slim down 15
además (de) *adv.* furthermore; besides; in addition (to) 10
adicional *adj.* additional
adiós *m.* good-bye 1
adjetivo *m.* adjective
administración de empresas *f.* business administration 2
adolescencia *f.* adolescence 9
¿adónde? *adv.* where? (desti-nation) 2
aduana *f.* customs 5
aeróbico/a *adj.,* aerobic 15
aeropuerto *m.* airport 5
afectado/a *adj.* affected 13
afeitarse *v.* to shave 7
aficionado/a *adj.* fan 4
afirmativo/a *adj.* affirmative
afueras *f., pl.* suburbs; outskirts 12
agencia de viajes *f.* travel agency 5
agente de viajes *m., f.* travel agent 5
agosto *m.* August 5
agradable *adj.* pleasant 5
agua *f.* water 8
  agua mineral mineral water 8
ahora *adv.* now 2
  ahora mismo right now 5
ahorrar *v.* to save money 14

ahorros *m., pl.* savings 14
aire *m.* air 6
ajo *m.* garlic
al (*contraction of* **a** + **el**) 2
  al aire libre open-air 6
  al contado in cash 14
  al este to the east 14
  al fondo (de) at the end (of) 12
  al lado de beside 2
  al norte to the north 14
  al oeste to the west 14
  al sur to the south 14
alcoba *f.* bedroom 12
alcohol *m.* alcohol 15
alcohólico/a *adj.* alcoholic 15
alegrarse (de) *v.* to be happy 13
alegre *adj.* happy; joyful 5
alegría *f.* joy 9
alemán, alemana *adj.* German 3
alérgico/a *adj.* allergic 10
alfombra *f.* carpet; rug 12
algo *pron.* something; any-thing 7
algodón *m.* cotton 6
alguien *pron.* someone; somebody; anyone 7
algún, alguno/a(s) *adj.* any; some 7
aliviar *v.* to ease; alleviate 15
  aliviar el estrés/la tensión to reduce stress/tension 15
allí *adv.* there 5
  allí mismo right there 14
almacén *m.* department store 6
almohada *f.* pillow 12
almorzar (o:ue) *v.* to have lunch 8
almuerzo *m.* lunch 8
aló *interj.* hello (*on the telephone*) 11
alojamiento *m.* lodging 5
alquilar *v.* to rent 12
alquiler *m.* rent 12
alternador *m.* alternator 11

altillo *m.* attic 12
alto/a *adj.* tall 3
aluminio *m.* aluminum 13
amable *adj.* nice; friendly 5
ama de casa *f.* housekeeper; caretaker; housewife 12
amarillo/a *adj.* yellow 6
amigo/a *m., f.* friend 3
amistad *f.* friendship 9
amor *m.* love 9
anaranjado/a *adj.* orange 6
animal *m.* animal 13
aniversario (de bodas) *m.* (wedding) anniversary 9
anoche *adv.* last night 6
anteayer *adv.* the day before yesterday 6
antes *adv.* before 7
  antes (de) que *conj.* before 13
  antes de *prep.* before 7
antibiótico *m.* antibiotic 10
antipático/a *adj.* unpleasant 3
anunciar *v.* to announce; to advertise
anuncio *m.* advertisement 16
año *m.* year 2, 5
  el año pasado *last* year 6
apagar *v.* to turn off 11
aparato *m.* appliance 12
apartamento *m.* apartment 12
apellido *m.* last name 9
apenas *adv.* hardly; scarcely; just 10
aplaudir *v.* to applaud
apreciar *v.* to appreciate
aprender *v.* to learn 3
apurarse *v.* to hurry; to rush 15
aquel, aquella *adj.* that; those (over there) 6
aquél, aquélla *pron.* that; those (over there) 6
aquello *neuter, pron.* that; that thing; that fact 6
aquellos/as *pl. adj.* that; those (over there) 6
aquéllos/as *pl. pron.* those (ones) (over there) 6
aquí *adv.* here 1
  Aquí está... Here it is . . . 5
    Aquí estamos en... Here we are in . . . 2
    aquí mismo right here 11
árbol *m.* tree 13
archivo *m.* file 11
armario *m.* closet 12
arqueólogo/a *m., f.* archaeologist 16
arquitecto/a *m., f.* architect 16
arrancar *v.* to start (*a car*) 11
arreglar *v.* to fix; to arrange 11
arriba *adv.* up 15
arroz *m.* rice 8
arte *m.* art 2
artes *f., pl.* arts
artesanía *f.* craftsmanship; crafts 17

artículo *m.* article
artista *m., f.* artist 3
artístico/a *adj.* artistic
arveja *m.* pea 8
asado/a *adj.* roasted 8
ascenso *m.* promotion 16
ascensor *m.* elevator 5
así *adj.* thus; so (*in such a way*) 10
  así así so so 1
asistir (a) *v.* to attend 3
aspiradora *f.* vacuum cleaner 12
aspirante *m., f.* candidate; applicant 16
aspirina *f.* aspirin 10
atún *m.* tuna
aumentar *v.* **de peso** to gain weight 15
aumento *m.* increase 16
  aumento de sueldo pay raise 16
aunque *conj.* although
autobús *m.* bus 1
automático/a *adj.* automatic 14
auto(móvil) *m.* auto(mobile) 5
autopista *f.* highway
ave *f.* bird
avenida *f.* avenue
aventura *f.* adventure
avergonzado/a *adj.* embarrassed 5
avión *m.* airplane 5
¡Ay! *interj.* Oh! 10
  ¡Ay, qué dolor! Oh, what pain! 10
ayer *adv.* yesterday 6
ayudar (a) *v.* to help 12
ayudarse *v.* to help each other 11
azúcar *m.* sugar 8
azul *adj. m., f.* blue 6

B

bailar *v.* to dance 2
bailarín/bailarina *m., f.* dancer
baile *m.* dance
bajar(se) *v.* to go down; to get off (of) 11
bajo/a *adj.* short (*in height*) 3
  bajo control under control 7
balcón *m.* balcony
ballet *m.* ballet
baloncesto *m.* basketball 4
banana *f.* banana 8
banco *m.* bank 14
banda *f.* band
bandera *f.* flag
bañarse *v.* to bathe; to take a bath 7
baño *m.* bathroom 7
barato/a *adj.* cheap 6
barco *m.* ship 5
barrer *v.* to sweep 12
  barrer el suelo to sweep the floor 12
barrio *m.* neighborhood 12

bastante *adv.* enough; rather 10; pretty
basura *f.* trash 12
baúl *m.* trunk 11
beber *v.* to drink 3
bebida *f.* drink 8
béisbol *m.* baseball 4
bellas artes *f., pl.* fine arts
belleza *f.* beauty 14
beneficio *m.* benefit 16
besar(se) *v.* to kiss (each other) 11
beso *m.* kiss 9
biblioteca *f.* library 2
bicicleta *f.* bicycle 4
bien *adj.* good; well 1
bienestar *m.* well-being 15
bienvenido/a *adj.* welcome 12
billete *m.* paper money 8
billón *m.* trillion 5
biología *f.* biology 2
bistec *m.* steak 8
bizcocho *m.* biscuit
blanco/a *adj.* white 6
bluejeans *m., pl.* jeans 6
blusa *f.* blouse 6
boca *f.* mouth 10
boda *f.* wedding 9
boleto *m.* ticket
bolsa *f.* purse, bag 6
bombero/a *m., f.* firefighter 16
bonito/a *adj.* pretty 3
borrador *m.* eraser 2
bosque *m.* forest 13
  bosque tropical tropical forest; rainforest 13
bota *f.* boot 6
botella *f.* bottle 9
  botella de vino bottle of wine 9
botones *m., sing.* bellhop 5
brazo *m.* arm 10
brindar *v.* to toast (*drink*) 9
bucear *v.* to (scuba) dive 4
bueno *adv.* well 2
bueno/a, buen *adj.* good 3, 6
  Buen viaje. Have a good trip. 1
  buena forma good shape (*physical*) 15
  Buena idea. Good idea. 4
  Buenas noches. Good evening; Good night. 1
  Buenas tardes. Good afternoon. 1
  buenísimo extremely good 8
  ¿Bueno? Hello. (*on telephone*) 11
  Buenos días. Good morning. 1
bulevar *m.* boulevard
buscar *v.* to look for 2
buzón *m.* mailbox 14

C

caballo *m.* horse 5
cabaña *f.* cabin 5

cabe: no cabe duda (de) que…
    there's no doubt that … 13
cabeza *f.* head 10
cada *adj. m., f.* each 6
caerse *v.* to fall (down) 10
café *m.* café 4; *adj. m., f.* brown 6;
    coffee 8
cafetera *f.* coffee maker
cafetería *f.* cafeteria 2
caído/a *p.p.* fallen 14
caja *f.* cash register 6
cajero/a *m., f.* cashier 14
    cajero automático automatic teller
    machine (ATM) 14
calcetín *m.* sock 6
calculadora *f.* calculator 11
caldo *m.* soup 8
    caldo de patas beef soup 8
calentarse *v.* to warm up 15
calidad *f.* quality 6
calle *f.* street 11
calor *m.* heat 4
caloría *f.* calorie 15
calzar *v.* to take size … shoes 6
cama *f.* bed 5
cámara *f.* camera 11
    cámara de video *f.* videocamera 11
camarero/a *m., f.* waiter 8
camarón *m.* shrimp 8
cambiar *m.* **(de)** *v.* to change 9
cambio *m.* **de moneda** currency
    exchange 8
caminar *v.* to walk 2
camino *m.* road 11
camión *m* truck; bus
camisa *f.* shirt 6
camiseta *f.* t-shirt 6
campo *m.* countryside 5
canadiense *adj.* Canadian 3
canal *m.* channel (TV)
canción *f.* song
candidato/a *m., f.* candidate
cansado/a *adj.* tired 5
cantante *m., f.* singer
cantar *v.* to sing 2
capital *f.* capital (city) 1
capó *m.* hood 11
cara *f.* face 7
caramelo *m.* caramel
carne *f.* meat 8
    carne de res *f.* beef 8
carnicería *f.* butcher shop 14
caro/a *adj.* expensive 6
carpintero/a *m., f.* carpenter 16
carrera *f.* career 16
carretera *f.* highway
carro *m.* car; automobile 11
carta *f.* letter 4; (playing) card 5
cartel *m.* poster
cartera *f.* wallet 6
cartero *m.* mail carrier 14
casa *f.* house; home 4
casado/a *adj.* married 9
casarse (con) *v.* to get married (to) 9
casi *adv.* almost 10

catorce *adj., pron.* fourteen 1
cebolla *f.* onion 8
celebrar *v.* to celebrate 9
celular *adj.* cellular 11
cena *f.* dinner 8
cenar *v.* to have dinner 8
centro *m.* downtown 4
    centro comercial shopping
    mall 6
cepillarse los dientes/el pelo
    v. to brush one's teeth/one's
    hair 7
cerámica *f.* pottery
cerca de *prep.* near 2
cerdo *m.* pork 8
cereales *m., pl.* cereal; grains 8
cero *m.* zero 1
cerrado/a *p.p.* closed 5
cerrar (e:ie) *v.* to close 4
cerveza *f.* beer 8
césped *m.* grass
ceviche *m.* marinated fish dish 8
    ceviche de camarón
    marinated shrimp 8
chaleco *m.* vest 6
champán *m.* champagne
champiñón *m.* mushroom 8
champú *m.* shampoo 7
chaqueta *f.* jacket 6
chau *fam., interj.* bye 1
cheque *m.* (bank) check 14
    cheque de viajero traveler's check
    14
chévere *adj., fam.* terrific
chico/a *m., f.* boy girl 1
chino/a *adj.* Chinese
chocar (con) *v.* to run into 11
chocolate *m.* chocolate
choque *m.* collision 18
chuleta *f.* chop (food) 8
    chuleta de cerdo pork
    chop 8
ciclismo *m.* cycling 4
cielo *m.* sky 13
cien(to) *adj., pron.* one hundred 5
ciencia *f.* science
    ciencia ficción science
    fiction
científico/a *m., f.* scientist 16
cierto *m.* certain; true 13
cifra *f.* figure
cinco *adj., pron.* five 1
cincuenta *adj., pron.* fifty 2
cine *m.* movie theater 4
cinta *f.* (audio)tape 11
cinturón *m.* belt 6
circulación *f.* traffic
cita *f.* date; appointment 9
ciudad *f.* city 4
ciudadano/a *adj.* citizen
claro que sí *fam.* of course 16
clase *f.* class 2
    clase de ejercicios aeróbicos
    f. aerobics class 15
clásico/a *adj.* classical

cliente/a *m., f.* customer 6
clínica *f.* clinic 10
cobrar *v.* to cash a check 14
coche *m.* car; automobile 11
cocina *f.* kitchen; stove
cocinar *v.* to cook 12
cocinero/a *m., f.* cook, chef 16
cola *f.* line 14
colesterol *m.* cholesterol 15
color *m.* color 6
comedia *f.* comedy; play
comedor *m.* dining room 12
comenzar (e:ie) *v.* to begin 4
comer *v.* to eat 3
comercial *adj.* commercial;
    business-related 16
comida *f.* food; meal 8
como *prep.* like as 8
¿cómo? what; how 1
    ¿Cómo es...? What's... like? 3
    ¿Cómo está Ud.? *form.*
    How are you? 1
    ¿Cómo estás? *fam.* How are
    you? 1
    ¿Cómo les fue...? *pl.* How did
    . . . go for you? 15
    ¿Cómo se llama (Ud.)?
    (form.) What's your name? 1
    ¿Cómo te llamas (tú)? *(fam.)*
    What's your name? 1
cómoda *f.* chest of drawers 12
cómodo/a *adj.* comfortable 5
compañero/a de clase *m., f.*
    classmate 2
compañero/a de cuarto *m., f.*
    roommate 2
compañía *f.* company; firm 16
compartir *v.* to share 3
completamente *adv.* completely 16
compositor(a) *m., f.* composer
comprar *v.* to buy 2
compras *f., pl.* purchases 5
    ir de compras go shopping
comprender *v.* to understand 3
comprobar *v.* to check
comprometerse (con) *v.* to get
    engaged (to) 9
computación *f.* computer science 2
computadora *f.* computer 1
computadora portátil *f.* portable
    computer; laptop 11
comunicación *f.* communication
comunicarse (con) *v.* to
    communicate (with)
comunidad *f.* community 1
con *prep.* with 2
    Con él/ella habla. This is
    he/she. *(on telephone)* 11
    con frecuencia *adv.* frequently 10
    Con permiso. Pardon me.,
    Excuse me. 1
    con tal (de) que provided
    (that) 13
concierto *m.* concert
concordar *v.* to agree 8

concurso *m.* contest; game show
conducir *v.* to drive **8, 11**
conductor(a) *m., f.* chauffeur; driver **1**
confirmar *v.* to confirm **5**
confirmar *v.* **la reservación** *f.* to confirm the reservation **5**
congelador *m.* freezer
congestionado/a *adj.* congested; stuffed up **10**
conmigo *pron.* with me **4**
conocer *v.* to know; to be acquainted with **8**
conocido/a *adj.* known **2**
conseguir (e:i) *v.* to get; to obtain **4**
consejero/a *m., f.* counselor; advisor **16**
consejo *m.* advice **9**
conservación *f.* conservation **13**
conservar *v.* to conserve **13**
construir *v.* build
consultorio *m.* doctor's office **10**
consumir *v.* consume **15**
contabilidad *f.* accounting **2**
contador(a) *m., f.* accountant **16**
contaminación *f.* pollution; contamination **4**
contaminación del aire/del agua air/water pollution **13**
contaminado/a *adj.* polluted **13**
contaminar *v.* to pollute **13**
contar (con) *v.* to count (on) **12**
contento/a *adj.* happy; content **5**
contestadora *f.* answering machine **11**
contestar *v.* to answer **2**
contigo *pron.* with you **8**
contratar *v.* to hire **16**
control *m.* control **7**
control remoto remote control
controlar *v.* to control **13**
conversación *f.* conversation **2**
conversar *v.* to talk **2**
copa *f.* wineglass; goblet **12**
corazón *m.* heart **10**
corbata *f.* tie **6**
corredor(a) *m., f.* **de bolsa** stockbroker **16**
correo *m.* post office; mail **14**
correo electrónico e-mail **4**
correr *v.* to run; to jog **3**
cortesía *f.* courtesy
cortinas *f., pl.* curtains **12**
corto/a *adj.* short (*in length*) **6**
cosa *f.* thing **1**
costar (o:ue) *f.* to cost **6**
cráter *m.* crater **13**
creer (en) *v.* to believe (in) **3**
creído/a *p.p.* believed **3**
crema de afeitar *f.* shaving cream **7**
crimen *m.* crime; murder **18**
cruzar *v.* to cross **14**
cuaderno *m.* notebook **1**

cuadra *f.* city block **14**
¿cuál(es)? which?; which ones?; what? **2**
¿Cuál es la fecha (de hoy)? What is the date (today)? **4**
cuadro *m.* picture
cuadros *m., pl.* plaid **6**
cuando *conj.* when **7**
¿cuándo? *adv.* when? **2**
¿cuánto/a(s)? *adv.* how much?, how many? **1**
¿Cuánto cuesta...? How much does . . . cost? **6**
¿Cuántos años tienes? How old are you? **3**
cuarenta *adj., pron.* forty **2**
cuarto *m.* room **7**
cuarto/a *adj.* fourth **5**
menos cuarto quarter to (time)
y cuarto quarter after (time)
cuarto de baño *m.* bathroom **7**
cuatro *adj., pron.* four **1**
cuatrocientos/as *adj., pron.,* four hundred **5**
cubiertos *m., pl.* silverware
cubierto/a *p.p.* covered **14**
cubrir *v.* to cover **14**
cuchara *f.* tablespoon **12**
cuchillo *m.* knife **12**
cuello *m.* neck **10**
cuenta *f.* bill **9**; account **14**
cuenta corriente *f.* checking account **14**
cuenta de ahorros *f.* savings account **14**
cuento *m.* story
cuerpo *m.* body **10**
cuidado *m.* care **3**
cuidar *v.* to take care of **13**
cultura *f.* culture
cumpleaños *m., sing.* birthday **9**
cumplir años *v.* to have a birthday **9**
cuñado/a *m., f.* brother-in-law; sister-in-law **3**
currículum *m.* résumé; curriculum vitae **16**
curso *m.* course **2**

D

danza *f.* dance
dañar *v.* to damage; to breakdown **11**
dar *v.* to give **6**
dar direcciones to give directions **14**
dar un consejo to give advice **6**
darse con *v.* to bump into; to run into
de *prep.* of; from **1**
¿De dónde eres (tú)? *fam.* Where are you from? **1**
¿De dónde es (Ud.)? *form.* Where are you from? **1**

¿De parte de quién? Who is calling? (*on telephone*) **11**
¿de quién? whose (*sing.*) **1**
¿de quiénes? whose (*pl.*) **1**
de algodón (made of) cotton **6**
de aluminio (made of) aluminum **13**
de compras shopping **5**
de cuadros plaid **6**
de excursión hiking **4**
de hecho in fact **5**
de ida y vuelta roundtrip **5**
de la mañana in the morning; A.M. **1**
de la noche in the evening; at night; P.M. **1**
de la tarde in the afternoon; in the early evening; P.M. **1**
de lana (made of) wool **6**
de lunares polka-dotted **6**
de mi vida of my life **15**
de moda in fashion **6**
De nada. You're welcome. **1**
de ninguna manera no way **16**
de niño/a as a child **10**
de parte de on behalf of **11**
de plástico (made of) plastic **13**
de rayas striped **6**
de repente suddenly **6**
de seda (made of) silk **6**
de vaqueros western (genre) **17**
de vez en cuando from time to time **10**
de vidrio (made of) glass **13**
debajo de *prep.* below; under **2**
deber (+ infin.) *v.* to have to (*do something*), should (*do something*) **3**
deber *m.* responsibility; obligation
debido a due to; the fact that **3**
débil *adj.* weak **15**
decidido/a *adj.* decided **14**
decidir *v.* to decide **3**
décimo/a *adj.* tenth **5**
decir *v.* **(que)** to say (that); to tell (that) **6**
declarar *v.* to declare; to say
dedo *m.* finger **10**
deforestación *f.* deforestation **13**
dejar *v.* to let **12**; to quit; to leave behind **16**
dejar de (+ inf.) to stop (*doing something*) **13**
dejar una propina to leave a tip **9**
del (contraction of de + el) of the; from the **1**
delante de *prep.* in front of **2**
delgado/a *adj.* thin; slender **3**
delicioso/a *adj.* delicious **8**
demás *pron.* the rest **5**
demasiado *adv.* too much **6**
dentista *m., f.* dentist **10**
dentro de *adv.* within **16**

dependiente/a *m., f.* clerk **6**
deporte *m.* sport **4**
deportista *m.* sports person **1**
deportivo/a *adj.* sports-loving **4**
depositar *v.* to deposit **14**
derecha *f.* right **2**
derecho/a *adj.* straight **14**
derechos *m., pl.* rights
desarrollar *v.* to develop **13**
desastre natural *m.* natural disaster
desayunar *v.* to have breakfast **8**
desayuno *m.* breakfast **8**
descafeinado/a *adj.* decaffeinated **15**
descansar *v.* to rest **2**
descompuesto/a *adj.* not working; out-of-order **11**
describir *v.* to describe **3**
descrito/a *p.p.* described **14**
descubierto/a *p.p.* discovered **14**
descubrir *v.* to discover **13**
desde *prep.* from; since **6**
desear *v.* to wish; to desire **2**
desempleo *m.* unemployment
desierto *m.* desert **13**
desigualdad *f.* inequality
desordenado/a *adj.* disorderly **5**
despacio *adj.* slowly **8**
despedida *f.* farewell; good-bye
despedir (e:i) *v.* fire **16**
despedirse (de) (e:i) *v.* to say good-bye (to) **7**
despejado/a *adj.* clear (*weather*) **4**
despertador *m.* alarm clock **7**
despertarse (e:ie) *v.* to wake up **7**
después *adv.* afterwards; then **7**
  después de after **7**
  después (de) que *conj.* after **14**
destruir *v.* to destroy **13**
detrás de *prep.* behind **2**
día *m.* day **1**
  día de fiesta holiday **9**
diario *m.* diary **1**; newspaper
  diario/a *adj.* daily **7**
dibujar *v.* to draw **2**
dibujo *m.* drawing **17**
  dibujos animados *m., pl.* cartoons **17**
diccionario *m.* dictionary **1**
dicho/a *p.p.* said **14**
diciembre *m.* December **5**
dictadura *f.* dictatorship
diecinueve *adj., pron.* nineteen **1**
dieciocho *adj., pron.* eighteen **1**
dieciséis *adj., pron.* sixteen **1**
diecisiete *adj., pron.* seventeen **1**
diente *m.* tooth **7**
dieta *f.* diet **15**
  dieta equilibrada balanced diet **15**
diez *adj., pron.* ten **1**
difícil *adj.* hard; difficult **3**
Diga. Hello. (*on telephone*) **11**
diligencia *f.* errand **14**
dinero *m.* money **6**
dirección *f.* address **14**

direcciones *f., pl.* directions **14**
director(a) *m., f.* director; (*musical*) conductor
disco *m.* (computer) disk **11**
disco compacto compact disc (CD) **11**
discriminación *f.* discrimination
discurso *m.* speech
diseñador(a) *m., f.* designer **16**
diseño *m.* design
disfrutar (de) *v.* to enjoy; to reap the benefits (of) **15**
diversión *f.* fun activity **4**
divertido/a *adj.* fun **7**
divertirse (e:ie) *v.* to have fun **9**
divorciado/a *adj.* divorced **9**
divorciarse (de) *v.* to get divorced (from) **9**
divorcio *m.* divorce **9**
doblar *v.* to turn **14**
doce *adj., pron.* twelve **1**
doble *adj.* double
doctor(a) *m., f.* doctor
documental *m.* documentary
documentos de viaje *m., pl.* travel documents
doler (o:ue) *v.* to hurt **10**
dolor *m.* ache; pain **10**
dolor de cabeza *m.* headache **10**
doméstico/a *adj.* domestic
domingo *m.* Sunday **2**
don/doña title of respect used with a person's first name **1**
donde *prep.* where
  ¿Dónde está...? Where is . . . ? **2**
  ¿dónde? where? **2**
dormir (o:ue) *v.* to sleep **4**
dormirse (o:ue) *v.* to go to sleep; to fall asleep **7**
dos *adj., pron.* two **1**
  dos veces twice; two times **6**
doscientos/as *adj., pron.* two hundred **5**
drama *m.* drama; play
dramático/a *adj.* dramatic
dramaturgo/a *m., f.* playwright
droga *f.* drug **15**
drogadicto/a *adj.* drug addict **15**
ducha *f.* shower
ducharse *v.* to shower; to take a shower **7**
duda *f.* doubt **13**
dudar *v.* to doubt **13**
dueño/a *m., f.* owner; landlord **8**
dulces *m., pl.* sweets; candy **9**
durante *prep.* during **7**
durar *v.* to last

E

e *conj.* (*used instead of* **y** *before words beginning with* **i** *and* **hi**) and **4**
echar *v.* to throw **14**
  echar una carta al buzón

to throw a letter in the mailbox **14**
ecología *f.* ecology **13**
economía *f.* economics
ecoturismo *m.* ecotourism **13**
Ecuador *m.* Ecuador **1**
ecuatoriano/a *adj.* Ecuadorian **3**
edad *f.* age **8**
edificio *m.* building **12**
efectivo *m.* cash **14**
ejercicio *m.* exercise **15**
  ejercicios aeróbicos aerobic exercises **15**
  ejercicios de estiramiento stretching exercises **15**
ejército *m.* army **18**
el *m., sing.* the **1**
él *sub. pron.* he **1**; *adj. pron.* him **1**
elección *f.* election
electricista *m., f.* electrician **16**
elegante *adj. m., f.* elegant **6**
elegir *v.* to elect
ella *sub. pron.* she **1**; *obj. pron.* her **1**
ellos/as *sub. pron.* they **1**; them **1**
embarazada *adj.* pregnant **10**
emergencia *f.* emergency **10**
emitir *v.* to broadcast
emocionante *adj.* exciting
empezar (e:ie) *v.* to begin **4**
empleado/a *m., f.* employee **5**
empleo *m.* job; employment **16**
empresa *f.* company; firm **16**
en *prep.* in; on **2**
  en casa at home **7**
  en caso (de) que in case (that) **13**
  en cuanto as soon as **14**
  en efectivo in cash
  en exceso in excess; too much **15**
  en línea in-line **4**
  ¡En marcha! Forward march! **15**
  en mi nombre in my name **5**
  en punto on the dot; exactly; sharp (*time*) **1**
  en qué in what; how **2**
  ¿En qué puedo servirles? How may I help you? **5**
enamorado/a *adj.* **(de)** in love with **5**
enamorarse (de) *v.* to fall in love (with) **9**
encantado/a *adj.* delighted; pleased to meet you **1**
encantar *v.* to like very much; to love (*inanimate things*) **7**
encima de *prep.* on top of **2**
encontrar (o:ue) *v.* to find **4**
encontrar(se) *v.* to meet (each other); to find (each other) **11**
encuesta *f.* poll; survey
energía *f.* energy **13**
enero *m.* January **5**
enfermarse *v.* to get sick **10**
enfermedad *f.* illness **10**
enfermero/a *m., f.* nurse **10**

enfermo/a *adj.* sick 10
enfrente de *adv.* opposite; facing 14
engordar *v.* to gain weight
enojado/a *adj.* mad; angry 5
enojarse (con) *v.* to get angry (with) 7
ensalada *f.* salad 8
enseguida *adv.* right away 9
enseñar *v.* to teach 2
ensuciar *v.* to dirty; to get dirty 12
entender (e:ie) *v.* to understand 4
entonces *adv.* then 7
entrada *f.* entrance 12; ticket
entre *prep.* between; among 2
entremeses *m., pl.* hors
   d'oeuvres; appetizers 8
entrenarse *v.* to practice; to train 15
entrevista *f.* interview 16
entrevistador(a) *m., f.* interviewer 16
entrevistar *v.* to interview 16
envase *m.* container 13
enviar *v.* to send; to mail 14
equilibrado/a *adj.* balanced 15
equipado/a *adj.* equipped 15
equipaje *m.* luggage 5
equipo *m.* team 4
equivocado/a *adj.* mistaken; wrong 5
eres *fam.* you are 1
es he/she/it is 1
   Es (una) lástima que... It's a
      shame that . . . 13
   Es bueno que... It's good
      that . . . 12
   Es de... He/She is from . . . 1
   Es extraño que... It's strange
      that . . . 13
   Es importante que... It's
      important that . . . 12
   Es imposible que... It's
      impossible that . . . 13
   Es improbable que... It's
      improbable that . . . 13
   Es la una. It's one o'clock. 1
   Es malo que... It's bad
      that . . . 12
   Es mejor que... It's better
      that . . . 12
   Es necesario que... It's
      necessary that . . . 12
   Es obvio que... It's
      obvious that . . . 13
   Es ridículo que... It's
      ridiculous that . . . 13
   Es seguro que... It's sure
      that . . . 13
   Es terrible que... It's terrible
      that . . . 13
   Es triste que... It's sad that . . . 13
   Es urgente que... It's urgent
      that . . . 12
   Es verdad que... It's true
      that . . . 13
esa(s) *f., adj.* that; those 6
ésa(s) *f., pron.* those (ones) 6
escalar *v.* to climb 4
   escalar montañas to climb

mountains 4
escalera *f.* stairs; stairway 12
escoger *v.* choose 8
escribir *v.* to write 3
   **escribir un mensaje
      electrónico** to write an
      e-mail message 4
   escribir una (tarjeta) postal
      to write a postcard 4
   escribir una carta to write a
      letter 4
escrito/a *p.p.* written 14
escritor(a) *m., f.* writer
escritorio *m.* desk 2
escuchar *v.* to listen to 2
   escuchar la radio to listen to
      the radio 2
   escuchar música to listen to
      music 2
escuela *f.* school 1
esculpir *v.* to sculpt
escultor(a) *m., f.* sculptor
escultura *f.* sculpture
ese *m., sing., adj.* that 6
ése *m., sing., pron.* that (one) 6
eso *neuter, pron.* that;
   that thing 6
esos *m., pl., adj.* those 6
ésos *m., pl., pron.* those (ones) 6
España *f.* Spain 1
español *m.* Spanish (*language*) 2
español(a) *m., f., adj.* Spanish 3
espárragos *m., pl.* asparagus
especialización *f.* major field of study
   or interest; specialization 16
espectacular *adj.* spectacular 15
espectáculo *m.* show
espejo *m.* mirror 7
esperar *v.* to wait for; to hope 2; to
   wish 13
esposo/a *m., f.* husband/wife; spouse
   3
esquí (acuático) *m.* (water)
   skiing 4
esquiar *v.* to ski 4
esquina *m.* corner 14
está he, she, it is, you are 1
   Está (muy) despejado. It's
      (very) clear. (*weather*) 5
   Está (muy) nublado. It's
      (very) cloudy. (*weather*) 5
   Está bien. That's fine. It's okay. 11
esta(s) *f., adj.* this; these 4
   esta noche tonight 4
ésta(s) *f., pron.* this (one); these
   (ones) 6
   Ésta es... *f.* This is . . .
      (*introducing someone*) 1
establecer *v.* to establish 16
estación *f.* station; season 5
   estación de autobuses
      bus station 5
   estación del metro subway
      station 5
   estación de tren train station 5

estacionar *v.* to park 11
estadio *m.* stadium 2
estado civil *m.* marital status 9
Estados Unidos *m.* (EE.UU.;
   E.U.) United States 1
estadounidense *adj.* from the United
   States 3
estampado/a *adj.* print 6
estampilla *f.* stamp 14
estante *m.* bookcase; bookshelf 12
estar *v.* to be 2
   **estar a (veinte kilómetros)
      de aquí.** to be (20 kilometers)
      from here 11
   estar a dieta to be on a diet
      15
   estar aburrido/a to be
      bored 5
   estar afectado/a por to be
      affected by 13
   estar bajo control to be under
      control 7
   estar cansado/a to be tired 5
   estar contaminado/a to be
      polluted 13
   estar de acuerdo to agree 16
   estar de moda to be in
      fashion 6
   estar de vacaciones to be on
      vacation 5
   estar en buena forma to be in
      good shape 15
   estar enfermo/a to be sick 10
   estar listo/a to be ready 15
   estar perdido/a to be lost 14
   estar roto/a to be broken 10
   estar seguro/a to be sure 5
   estar torcido/a to be twisted;
      to be sprained 10
   (no) está nada mal it's not at
      all bad 5
estatua *f.* statue
este *m.* east 14; umm
este *m., sing., adj.* this 6
éste *m., sing., pron.* this (one) 6
   Éste es... *m.* This is . . .
      (*introducing someone*) 1
estéreo *m.* stereo 11
estilo *m.* style 5
estiramiento *m.* stretching 15
esto *neuter pron.* this; this thing 6
estómago *m.* stomach 10
estornudar *v.* to sneeze 10
estos *m., pl., adj.* these 6
éstos *m., pl., pron.* these (ones) 6
estrella *f.* star 13
   estrella de cine *m., f.* movie
      star 17
estrés *m.* stress 15
estudiante *m., f.* student 1
estudiantil *adj. m., f.* student 2
estudiar *v.* to study 2
estufa *f.* stove 12
estupendo/a *adj.* stupendous 5

etapa *f.* stage; step **9**
evitar *v.* to avoid **13**
examen *m.* test; exam **2**
　examen médico phisical exam **10**
excelente *adj. m., f.* excellent **5**
exceso *m.* excess; too much **15**
excursión *f.* hike; tour; excursion **4**
excursionista *m., f.* hiker **4**
éxito *m.* success **16**
experiencia *f.* experience
explicar *v.* to explain **2**
explorar *v.* to explore **4**
　explorar un pueblo to explore a town **4**
　explorar una ciudad to explore a city **4**
expresión *f.* expression
extinción *f.* extinction **13**
extranjero/a *adj.* foreign **17**
extraño/a *adj.* strange **13**

F

fabuloso/a *adj* fabulous **5**
fácil *adj. m., f.* easy **3**
falda *f.* skirt **6**
faltar *v.* to lack; to need **7**
familia *f.* family **3**
famoso/a *adj.* famous **16**
farmacia *f.* pharmacy **10**
fascinar *v.* to fascinate **7**
favorito/a *adj.* favorite **4**
fax *m.* fax (machine) **11**
febrero *m.* February **5**
fecha *f.* date **5**
feliz *adj.* happy **5**
　¡Felicidades! Congratulations! (*for an event such as a birthday or anniversary*) **9**
　¡Felicitaciones! Congratulations! (*for an event such as an engagement or a good grade on a test*) **9**
　¡Feliz cumpleaños! Happy birthday! **9**
fenomenal *adj.* phenomenal; great **5**
feo/a *adj.* ugly **3**
festival *m.* festival
fiebre *f.* fever **10**
fiesta *f.* party **9**
fijo/a *adj.* set, fixed **6**
fin *m.* end **4**
　fin de semana weekend **4**
finalmente *adv.* finally **15**
firmar *v.* to sign (*a document*) **14**
física *f.* physics **2**
flan (de caramelo) *m.* baked (caramel) custard **9**
flexible *adj.* flexible **15**
flor *f.* flower **13**
folklórico/a *adj.* folk; folkloric
folleto *m.* brochure **5**

fondo *m.* end **12**
forma *f.* shape **15**
formulario *m.* form **14**
foto(grafía) *f.* photograph **1**
francés, francesa *m., f.* French **3**
frecuentemente *adv.* frequently **10**
frenos *m., pl.* brakes **11**
fresco/a *adj.* cool **4**
frijoles *m., pl.* beans **8**
frío/a *adj.* cold **4**
fritada *f.* fried dish (pork, fish, etc.) **8**
frito/a *adj.* fried **8**
fruta *f.* fruit **8**
frutería *f.* fruit store **14**
frutilla *f.* strawberry **8**
fuente de fritada *f.* platter of fried food
fuera *adv.* outside **8**
fuerte *adj. m., f.* strong **15**
fumar *v.* to smoke **15**
funcionar *v.* to work; to function **11**
fútbol *m.* soccer **4**
　fútbol americano football **4**
futuro/a *adj.* future **16**
　en el futuro in the future **16**

G

gafas (de sol) *f., pl.* (sun)glasses **6**
gafas (oscuras) *f., pl.* (sun)glasses
galleta *f.* cookie **9**
ganar *v.* to win **4**; to earn (money) **16**
ganga *f.* bargain **6**
garaje *m.* garage
garganta *f.* throat **10**
gasolina *f.* gasoline **11**
gasolinera *f.* gas station **11**
gastar *v.* to spend (*money*) **6**
gato/a *m., f.* cat **13**
gente *f.* people **3**
geografía *f.* geography **2**
gerente *m., f.* manager **16**
gimnasio *m.* gymnasium **4**
gobierno *m.* government **13**
golf *m.* golf **4**
gordo/a *adj.* fat **3**
grabadora *f.* tape recorder **1**
gracias *f., pl.* thank you; thanks **1**
　Gracias por todo. Thanks for everything. **9**
　Gracias una vez más. Thanks again. **9**
graduarse (en) *v.* to graduate (from) **9**
gran, grande *adj.* big **3**
grasa *f.* fat **15**
gratis *adj. m., f.* free of charge **14**
grave *adj.* grave; serious **10**
gravísimo/a *adj.* extremely serious **13**
grillo *m.* cricket **4**
gripe *f.* flu **10**
gris *adj. m., f.* gray **6**
gritar *v.* to scream **7**

guantes *m., pl.* gloves **6**
guapo/a *adj.* handsome; good-looking **3**
guardar *v.* to save (on a computer) **11**
guerra *f.* war
guía *m., f.* guide **12**
gustar *v.* to be pleasing to; to like **2, 7**
　Me gustaría... I would like **7**
gusto *m.* pleasure **1**
　El gusto es mío. The pleasure is mine. **1**
　Gusto de (+ *inf.*)... It's a pleasure to . . .
　Mucho gusto. Pleased to meet you. **1**

H

haber (*aux.*) *v.* to have (*done something*) **15**
　ha sido un placer it's been a pleasure **15**
habitación *f.* room **5**
　habitación doble double room **5**
　habitación individual single room **5**
hablar *v.* to talk; to speak **2**
hacer *v.* to do; to make; **4**
　Hace buen tiempo. The weather is good.; It's good weather. **5**
　Hace calor. It's hot. (*weather*) **5**
　Hace fresco. It's cool. (*weather*) **5**
　Hace frío. It's cold. (*weather*) **5**
　Hace mal tiempo. The weather is bad.; It's bad weather. **5**
　Hace (mucho) viento. It's (very) windy. (*weather*) **5**
　Hace sol. It's sunny. (*weather*) **5**
　hacer cola to stand in line **14**
　hacer diligencias to do errands; to run errands **14**
　hacer ejercicio to exercise **15**
　hacer ejercicios aeróbicos to do aerobics **15**
　hacer ejercicios de estiramiento to do stretching exercises **15**
　hacer el papel to play a role
　hacer gimnasia to work out **15**
　hacer juego (con) to match **6**
　hacer la cama to make the bed **12**
　hacer las maletas to pack the suitcases **5**
　hacer quehaceres domésticos to do household chores **12**
　hacer turismo to go sightseeing **5**
　hacer un viaje to go on a trip **5**
　hacer una excursión to go on a hike; to go on a tour **5**
hacha *f.* ax **1**

hacia *prep.* toward **14**
hambre *f.* hunger **3**
hamburguesa *f.* hamburger **8**
hasta *prep.* until; toward **1**
   Hasta la vista. See you later. **1**
   Hasta luego. See you later. **1**
   Hasta mañana. See you
     tomorrow. **1**
   hasta que until **14**
   Hasta pronto. See you soon. **1**
hay there is; there are **1**
   Hay (mucha) contaminación.
     It's (very) smoggy. **13**
   Hay (mucha) niebla. It's (very)
     foggy. **5**
   Hay que It is necessary that **14**
   No hay duda que… There's no
     doubt that . . . **13**
   No hay de qué. You're
     welcome. **1**
hecho/a *p.p.* done **14**
heladería *f.* ice cream shop **14**
helado/a *adj.* iced **8**
helado *m.* ice cream **9**
hermanastro/a *m., f.*
   stepbrother/stepsister **3**
hermano/a *m., f.* brother/sister **3**
hermano/a mayor/menor *m., f.*
   older/younger brother/sister **3**
hermanos *m., pl.* brothers and sisters
   3
hermoso/a *adj.* beautiful **6**
hierba *f.* grass **13**
hijastro/a *m., f.* stepson/stepdaughter
   3
hijo/a *m., f.* son/daughter **3**
   hijo/a único/a only child **3**
   hijos *m., pl.* children **3**
historia *f.* history **2**; story
hockey *m.* hockey **4**
hola *interj.* hello; hi **1**
hombre *m.* man **1**
   hombre de negocios
     businessman **16**
hora *f.* hour **1**
horario *m.* schedule **2**
horno *m.* oven **12**
   horno de microondas
     microwave oven **12**
horror *m.* horror **12**
hospital *m.* hospital **10**
hotel *m.* hotel **5**
hoy *adv.* today **2**
   hoy día nowadays **5**
   Hoy es... Today is . . . **2, 5**
huelga *f.* strike (labor)
hueso *m.* bone **10**
huésped *m., f.* guest **5**
huevo *m.* egg **8**
humanidades *f., pl.* humanities
huracán *m.* hurricane

I

ida *f.* one way (*travel*) **5**
idea *f.* idea **4**
iglesia *f.* church **4**
igualdad *f.* equality **18**
igualmente *adv.* likewise **1**
impermeable *m.* raincoat **6**
importante *adj. m., f.* important **3**
importar *v.* to be important to;
   to matter **7**
imposible *adj. m., f.* impossible **13**
impresora *f.* printer **11**
imprimir *v.* to print **11**
improbable *adj. m., f.* improbable **13**
impuesto *m.* tax
incendio *m.* fire
increíble *adj. m., f.* incredible **5**
individual *adj.* private (*room*) **5**
infección *f.* infection **10**
informar *v.* to inform
informe *m.* report; paper (*written
   work*)
ingeniero/a *m., f.* engineer **3**
inglés *m.* English (*language*) **2**
inglés, inglesa *adj.* English **3**
insistir (en) *v.* to insist (on) **12**
inspector(a) de aduanas *m.* customs
   inspector **5**
inteligente *adj. m., f.* intelligent **3**
intercambiar *v.* exchange
interesante *adj. m., f.* interesting **3**
interesar *v.* to be interesting to;
   to interest **7**
internacional *adj. m., f.* international
   18
Internet *m.* Internet **11**
inundación *f.* flood
invertir (i:ie) *v.* to invest **16**
invierno *m.* winter **5**
invitado/a *m., f.* guest (*at a function*)
   9
invitar *v.* to invite **9**
inyección *f.* injection **10**
ir *v.* to go **4**
   ir a (+ inf.) to be going to do
     something **4**
   ir a la playa to go to the beach **5**
   ir de compras to go shopping **6**
   ir de excursión (a las montañas)
     to go for a hike (in the
     mountains) **4**
   ir de pesca to go fishing **5**
   ir de vacaciones to go on
     vacation **5**
   ir en autobús to go by bus **5**
   ir en auto(móvil) to go by
     auto(mobile); to go by car **5**
   ir en barco to go by ship **5**
   ir en metro to go by subway **5**
   ir en motocicleta to go by
     motorcycle **5**
   ir en taxi to go by taxi **5**
   ir en tren to go by train **5**

   ir en avión to go by plane **5**
irse *v.* to go away; to leave **7**
italiano/a *adj.* Italian **3**
izquierdo/a *adj.* left **2**
   a la izquierda de to the left
     of **2**

J

jabón *m.* soap **7**
jamás *adv.* never; not ever **7**
jamón *m.* ham **8**
japonés, japonesa *adj.*
   Japanese **3**
jardín *m.* garden; yard **12**
jefe, jefa *m., f.* boss **16**
joven *adj. m., f.* young **3**
joven *m., f.* youth; young
   person **1**
joyería *f.* jewelry store **14**
jubilarse *v.* to retire (*from work*) **9**
juego *m.* game **5**
jueves *m., sing.* Thursday **2**
jugador(a) *m., f.* player **4**
jugar (u:ue) *v.* to play **4**
   jugar a las cartas to play cards **5**
jugo *m.* juice **8**
   jugo de fruta fruit juice **8**
julio *m.* July **5**
jungla *f.* jungle
junio *m.* June **5**
juntos/as *adj.* together **9**
juventud *f.* youth **9**

K

kilómetro *m.* kilometer **11**

L

la *f., sing., d.o. pron.* her, it,
   form. you **5**
la *f., sing.* the **1**
laboratorio *m.* laboratory **2**
lago *m.* lake **5**
lámpara *f.* lamp **12**
lana *f.* wool **6**
langosta *f.* lobster
lápiz *m.* pencil **1**
largo/a *m.* long (*in length*) **6**
las *f., pl.* the **1**
las *f., pl., d.o.pron.* them; *form.* you **5**
lástima *f.* shame **13**
lastimarse *v.* to injure oneself **10**
   lastimarse el pie to injure one's
     foot **10**
lata *f.* (*tin*) can **13**
lavabo *m.* sink
lavadora *f.* washing machine **12**
lavandería *f.* laundromat **14**
lavaplatos *m., sing.* dishwasher **12**
lavar *v.* to wash **12**

lavarse *v.* to wash oneself **7**
  lavarse la cara to wash one's face **7**
  lavarse las manos to wash one's hands **7**
le *sing., i.o. pron.* to/for him, her, *form.* you **6**
  Le presento a… *form.* I would like to introduce . . . to you. **1**
lección *f.* lesson **1**
leche *f.* milk **8**
lechuga *f.* lettuce **8**
leer *v.* to read **3**
  leer el correo electrónico to read e-mail **4**
  leer el periódico to read the newspaper **4**
  leer la revista to read the magazine **4**
leído/a *p.p.* read **14**
lejos de *prep.* far from **2**
lengua *f.* language **2**
  lenguas extranjeras *f., pl.* foreign languages **2**
lentes de contacto *m., pl.* contact lenses
  lentes de sol sunglasses
lento/a *adj.* slow **11**
les *pl., i.o. pron.* to/for them, *form.* you **5**
letrero *m.* sign **14**
levantar *v.* to lift **15**
  levantar pesas to lift weights **15**
levantarse *v.* to get up **7**
ley *f.* law **13**
libertad *f.* liberty; freedom
libre *adj. m., f.* free **4**
librería *f.* bookstore **2**
libro *m.* book **2**
licencia de conducir *f.* driver's license **11**
limón *m.* lemon **8**
limpiar *v.* to clean **12**
  limpiar la casa to clean the house **12**
limpio/a *adj.* clean **5**
línea *f.* line **4**
listo/a *adj.* smart **5**; ready **15**
literatura *f.* literature
llamar *v.* to call **7**
  llamar por teléfono to call on the phone **11**
  llamarse to be called; to be named **7**
llanta *f.* tire **11**
llave *f.* key **5**
llegada *f.* arrival **5**
llegar *v.* to arrive **2**
llenar *v.* to fill
  llenar el tanque to fill the tank **11**
  llenar un formulario to fill out a form **14**
lleno/a *adj.* full **11**

llevar *v.* to carry; to take **2**; *v.* to wear **6**
  llevar una vida sana to lead a healthy lifestyle **15**
  llevarse bien/mal con to get along well/badly with **9**
llover (o:ue) *v.* to rain **5**
  Llueve. It's raining. **5**
lluvia *f.* rain **13**
  lluvia ácida acid rain **13**
lo *m., sing. d.o. pronoun.* him, it, *form.* you **5**
  lo mejor the best (thing)
  lo pasamos de película we had a great time **18**
  lo peor the worst (thing)
  lo que what; that which **12**
  lo siento I'm sorry **1**
loco/a *adj.* crazy **6**
locutor(a) *m., f.* TV or radio announcer **18**
lomo a la plancha *m.* grilled flank steak **8**
los *m., pl., do. pron.* them, *form.* you **5**
  los *m., pl.* the **1**
luchar (contra), (por) *v.* to fight struggle (against), (for)
luego *adv.* afterwards, then **7**; *adv.* later **1**
lugar *m.* place **4**
luna *f.* moon **13**
lunar *m.* polka dot **6** ; mole
lunes *m., sing.* Monday **2**
luz *f.* light; electricity **12**

M

madrastra *f.* stepmother **3**
madre *f.* mother **3**
madurez *f.* maturity; middle age **9**
maestro/a *m., f.* teacher (*elementary school*) **16**
magnífico/a *adj.* magnificent **6**
maíz *m.* corn **5**
mal, malo/a *adj.* bad **3**
maleta *f.* suitcase **3**
mamá *f.* mom **1**
mañana *f.* morning, A.M. **1**; tomorrow **1**
mandar *v.* to order **12**; to send; to mail **14**
manejar *v.* to drive **11**
manera *f.* way **16**
mano *f.* hand **1**
  ¡Manos arriba! Hands up! **15**
manta *f.* blanket **12**
mantener *v.* to maintain **15**
  mantenerse en forma to stay in shape **15**
mantequilla *f.* butter **8**
manzana *f.* apple **8**
mapa *m.* map **1**
maquillaje *m.* make-up **7**

maquillarse *v.* to put on makeup **7**
mar *m.* sea; ocean **5**
maravilloso/a *adj.* marvelous **5**
mareado/a *adj.* dizzy; nauseated **10**
margarina *f.* margarine
mariscos *m., pl.* shellfish **8**
marrón *adj. m., f.* brown
martes *m., sing.* Tuesday **2**
marzo *m.* March **5**
más *pron.* more **2**
  más de (+ *number*) more than (+ *number*) **8**
  más tarde later **7**
  más… que more . . . than **8**
masaje *m.* massage **15**
matemáticas *f., pl.* mathematics **2**
materia *f.* course
matrimonio *m.* marriage **9**
máximo/a *m., f.* maximum **11**
mayo *m.* May **5**
mayonesa *f.* mayonnaise **8**
mayor *adj.* older **3**
  el/la mayor *adj.* oldest **8**
me *pron.* me **5**
  Me duele mucho. It hurts me a lot. **10**
  Me gusta… I like . . . **2**
  No me gustan nada. I don't like . . . at all. **2**
  Me gustaría(n)… I would like . . . **7**
  Me llamo… My name is . . . **1**
  Me muero por… I'm dying to (for) . . . **1**
mecánico/a *m., f.* mechanic **11**
mediano/a *adj.* medium **6**
medianoche *f.* midnight **1**
medias *f., pl.* pantyhose, stockings **6**
medicamento *m.* medication **10**
medicina *f.* medicine **10**
médico/a *m., f.* doctor **3**; *adj.* medical **10**
medio/a *m. adj.* half **3**
  medio ambiente environment **13**
  medio/a hermano/a half-brother/half-sister **3**
  medios de comunicación *m., pl.* means of communication; media
  y media thirty minutes past the hour (*time*) **1**
mediodía *m.* noon **1**
mejor *adj.* better; best **8**
  el/la mejor *m., f.* the best **8**
mejorar *v.* to improve **13**
melocotón *m.* peach
menor *adj.* younger **3**
  el/la menor *m., f.* youngest **8**
menos *adv.* less **10**
  menos cuarto… menos quince… quarter to . . . (*time*) **1**
  menos de (+ *number*) less than (+ *number*) **8**
  menos… que less . . . than **8**

mensaje electrónico *m.* e-mail message **4**
mentira *f.* lie **9**
menú *m.* menu **8**
mercado *m.* market **6**
  mercado al aire libre open-air market **6**
merendar *v.* to snack in the afternoon; to have an afternoon snack **15**
merienda *f.* afternoon snack **15**
mes *m.* month **5**
mesa *f.* table **2**
mesita *f.* end table **12**
  mesita de noche night stand **12**
metro *m.* subway **5**
mexicano/a *adj.* Mexican **3**
México *m.* Mexico **1**
mí *pron. obj. of prep.* me **8**
mi(s) *poss. adj.* my **3**
microonda *f.* microwave **12**
  horno de microondas microwave oven **12**
miedo *m.* fear **3**
mientras *adv.* while **10**
miércoles *m., sing.* Wednesday **2**
mil *adj., pron.* one thousand **4**
  mil millones billion **5**
  Mil perdones. I'm extremely sorry. (*lit.* A thousand pardons.) **4**
milla *f.* mile **11**
millón *adj., pron.* million **5**
millones (de) *adj., pron.* millions (of) **5**
mineral *m.* mineral **15**
minuto *m.* minute **1**
mío/a(s) *poss.* my; (of) mine **11**
mirar *v.* to watch **2**
  mirar (la) televisión to watch television **2**
mismo/a *adj.* same **3**
mochila *f.* backpack **2**
moda *f.* fashion **6**
módem *m.* modem **11**
moderno/a *adj.* modern
molestar *v.* to bother; to annoy **7**
monitor *m.* (computer) monitor **11**
monitor(a) *m., f.* trainer **15**
montaña *f.* mountain **4**
montar *v.* **a caballo** to ride a horse **5**
monumento *m.* monument **4**
mora *f.* blackberry **8**
morado/a *adj.* purple **6**
moreno/a *adj.* brunet(te) **3**
morir (o:ue) *v.* to die **8**
mostrar (o:ue) *v.* to show **4**
moto(cicleta) *f.* motorcycle **5**
motor *m.* motor **11**
muchacho/a *m., f.* boy; girl **3**
mucho/a *adj., adv.* many; a lot of; much **2, 3**
  muchas veces many times **10**

Muchísimas gracias. Thank you very much. **9**
Mucho gusto. Pleased to meet you. **1**
  (Muchas) gracias. Thank you (very much). Thanks (a lot). **1**
muchísimo *adj., adv.* very much **2**
mudarse *v.* to move (from one house to another) **12**
muebles *m., pl.* furniture **12**
muela *f.* tooth **10**
muerte *f.* death **9**
muerto/a *p.p.* died **14**
mujer *f.* woman **1**
  mujer de negocios business woman **16**
  mujer policía female police officer **11**
multa *f.* fine
mundial *adj.* worldwide **5**
mundo *m.* world **11**
municipal *m. f., adj.* municipal **4**
músculo *m.* muscle **15**
museo *m.* museum **4**
música *f.* music **2**
musical *adj. m., f.* musical
músico/a *m., f.* musician
muy *adv.* very **1**
  Muy amable. That's very kind of you. **5**
Muy bien, gracias. Very well, thank you. **1**

N

nacer *v.* to be born **9**
nacimiento *m.* birth **9**
nacional *adj. m., f.* national
nacionalidad *f.* nationality **1**
nada *pron., adv.* nothing **1**; not anything **7**
  nada mal not bad at all **5**
nadar *v.* to swim **4**
nadie *pron.* no one, nobody, not anyone **7**
naranja *m.* orange **8**
nariz *f.* nose **10**
natación *f.* swimming **4**
natural *adj. m., f.* natural **13**
naturaleza *f.* nature **13**
navegar (en) *v.* to surf (*the Web*) **11**
Navidad *f.* Christmas **9**
necesario/a *adj.* necessary **12**
necesitar *v.* to need **2**
negar (e:ie) *v.* to deny **13**
negativo/a *m.* negative **7**
negocios *m., pl.* business; commerce **16**
negro/a *adj.* black **6**
nervioso/a *adj.* nervous **5**
nevar (e:ie) *v.* to snow **5**
  Nieva. It's snowing. **5**
ni...ni *conj.* neither... nor **7**

niebla *f.* fog **4**
nieto/a *m., f.* grandson/granddaughter **3**
nieve *f.* snow **8**
ningún, ninguno/a(s) *adj.* no; none; not; any **7**
  ningún problema no problem **7**
niñez *f.* childhood **9**
niño/a *m., f.* child **3**
no *adv.* no; not **1**
  No cabe duda (de) que... There is no doubt that . . . **13**
  No es así. That's not the way it is **16**
  No es para tanto. It's no big deal. **12**
  No es seguro que... It's not sure that . . . **13**
  No es verdad que... It's not true that . . . **13**
  No está nada mal. It's not bad at all. **5**
  no estar de acuerdo to disagree **16**
  No estoy seguro. I'm not sure. **1**
  no hay there is not; there are not **1**
  No hay de qué. You're welcome. **1**
  No hay duda (de) que... There is no doubt that . . . **13**
  ¡No me diga(s)! You don't say! **11**
  No me gustan nada. I don't like them at all. **2**
  no muy bien not very well **1**
  ¿no? right? **1**
  no quiero I don't want to **4**
  no sé I don't know **1**
  No se preocupe. Don't worry. **7**
  no tener razón to be wrong **3**
noche *f.* night **1**
nombre *m.* name **5**
norte *m.* north **14**
norteamericano/a *adj.* (North) American **3**
nos *pron.* us **5**
  Nos vemos. See you. **1**
nosotros/as *sub. pron.* we **1**; *ob. pron.* us **8**
noticias *f., pl.* news **18**
noticiero *m.* newscast **18**
novecientos/as *adj.* nine hundred **5**
noveno/a *adj.* ninth **5**
noventa *adj., pron.* ninety **2**
noviembre *m.* November **5**
novio/a *m., f.* boyfriend/girlfriend **3**
nube *f.* cloud **13**
nublado/a *adj.* cloudy **4**
  Está (muy) nublado. It's very cloudy. **4**
nuclear *adj. m., f.* nuclear **13**
nuera *f.* daughter-in-law **3**
nuestro/a(s) *poss. adj.* our **3**

nueve *adj., pron.* nine 1
nuevo/a *adj.* new 6
número *m.* number 1
   número (shoe) size 6
nunca *adj.* never; not ever 7
nutrición *f.* nutrition 15

O

o *conj.* or 7
o... o; *conj.* either . . . or 7
obedecer (c:zc) *v.* to obey
obra *f.* work (*of art, literature, music, etc.*)
   obra maestra masterpiece
obtener *v.* to obtain; to get 16
obvio/a *adj.* obvious 13
océano *m.* ocean; sea 13
ochenta eighty 2
ocho *m.* eight 1
ochocientos/as *adj.* eight hundred 5
octavo/a *adj.* eighth 5
octubre *m.* October 5
ocupación *f.* occupation 16
ocupado/a *adj.* busy 5
ocurrir *v.* to occur; to happen
odiar *v.* to hate 9
oeste *m.* west 14
oferta *f.* offer 12
oficina *f.* office 12
oficio *m.* trade 16
ofrecer (c:zc) *v.* to offer 8
oído *m.* sense of hearing; inner ear 10
oído *p.p.* heard 14
oír *v.* to hear 4
   oigan *form., pl.* listen (*in conversation*) 5
   oye *fam., sing.* listen (*in conversation*) 1
ojalá (que) *interj.* I hope (that); I wish (that) 13
ojo *m.* eye 10
olvidar *v.* to forget 10
once *adj., pron.* eleven 1
ópera *f.* opera
operación *f.* operation 10
ordenado/a *adj.* orderly; well organized 5
ordinal *adj.* ordinal (*number*)
oreja *f.* (outer) ear 10
orquesta *f.* orchestra
ortográfico/a *adj.* spellling
os *fam., pl. pron.* you
otoño *m.* autumn 5
otro/a *adj.* other; another 6
   otra vez again 15

P

paciente *m., f.* patient 10
padrastro *m.* stepfather 3
padre *m.* father 3

padres *m., pl.* parents 3
pagar *v.* to pay 9
   pagar a plazos to pay in installments 14
   pagar al contado to pay in cash 14
   pagar en efectivo to pay in cash 14
   pagar la cuenta to pay the bill 9
página *f.* page 11
   página principal home page 11
país *m.* country 1
paisaje *m.* landscape; countryside 13
pájaro *m.* bird 13
palabra *f.* word 1
pan *m.* bread 8
   pan tostado toasted bread; toast 8
panadería *f.* bakery 14
pantalla *f.* screen 11
pantalones *m., pl.* pants 6
   pantalones cortos shorts 6
papa *f.* potato 8
papas fritas *f., pl.* fried potatoes; french fries 8
papá *m.* dad 3
   papás *m., pl.* parents 3
papel *m.* paper 2; role
paquete *m.* package 14
par *m.* pair 6
para *prep.* for; in order to 11
   para que so that 13
parabrisas *m., sing.* windshield 11
parar *v.* to stop 11
parecer *v.* to seem; to appear 8
pared *f.* wall 12
pareja *f.* (married) couple; partner 9
parientes *m., pl.* relatives 3
parque *m.* park 4
párrafo *m.* paragraph 5
parte: de parte de on behalf of 11
partido *m.* game; match (*sports*) 4
pasado/a *adj.* last; past 6
pasado *p.p.* passed 15
pasaje *m.* ticket 5
   pasaje de ida y vuelta *m.* roundtrip ticket 5
pasajero/a *m., f.* passenger 1
pasaporte *m.* passport 5
pasar *v.* to go by 5; to pass 12;
   pasar la aspiradora to vacuum 12
   pasar por el banco to go by the bank 14
   pasar por la aduana to go through customs 5
   pasar tiempo to spend time 4
   pasarlo bien/mal to have a good/bad time 9
pasatiempo *m.* pastime 4
pasear *v.* to take a walk; to stroll 4

pasear en bicicleta to ride a bicycle 4
pasear por la ciudad/el pueblo to walk around the city/town 4
pasillo *m.* hallway 12
pastel *m.* cake; pie 9
   pastel de chocolate chocolate cake 9
   pastel de cumpleaños birthday cake 9
pastelería *f.* pastry shop 14
pastilla *f.* pill; tablet 10
patata *f.* potato; 8
   patatas fritas *f., pl.* fried potatoes; french fries 8
patinar (en línea) *v.* to skate (in-line) 4
patio *m.* patio; yard
pavo *m.* turkey 8
paz *f.* peace
pedir (e:i) *v.* to ask for; to request 4; to order (*food*) 8
   pedir prestado to borrow 14
   pedir un préstamo to apply for a loan 14
peinarse *v.* to comb one's hair 7
película *f.* movie 4
peligro *m.* danger 13
peligroso/a *adj.* dangerous
pelirrojo/a *adj.* red-headed 3
pelo *m.* hair 7
pelota *f.* ball 4
peluquería *f.* beauty salon 14
peluquero/a *m., f.* hairdresser 16
penicilina *f.* penicillin 10
pensar (e:ie) *v.* to think 4
   pensar (+ inf.) to intend to; to plan to (*do something*) 4
   pensar en to think about 4
pensión *f.* boardinghouse 5
peor *adj.* worse; worst 8
   (el/la) peor the worst 8
pequeño/a *adj.* small 3
pera *f.* pear
perder (e:ie) *v.* to lose 4
perdido/a *adj.* lost 14
Perdón. Pardon me.; Excuse me. 1
perezoso/a *adj.* lazy
perfecto/a *adj.* perfect 5
periódico *m.* newspaper 4
periodismo *m.* journalism 2
periodista *m., f.* journalist 3
permiso *m.* permission 1
pero *conf.* but 2
perro *m.* dog 13
persona *f.* person 3
personaje *m.* character
   personaje principal main character
pesas *f., pl.* weights 15
pesca *f.* fishing 5
pescadería *f.* fish market 14
pescado *m.* fish (*cooked*) 8

pescador(a) *m., f.* fisherman/
fisherwoman 5
pescar *v.* to fish 5
peso *m.* weight 15
pez *m.* fish (*live*) 13
pie *m.* foot 10
piedra *f.* stone 13
pierna *f.* leg 10
pimienta *f.* black pepper 8
piña *f.* pineapple 8
pintar *v.* to paint 16
pintor(a) *m., f.* painter 16
pintura *f.* painting 12
piscina *f.* swimming pool 4
piso *m.* floor (*of a building*) 5
pizarra *f.* blackboard 2
placer *m.* pleasure 15
   Ha sido un placer. It's been a
   pleasure. 15
planchar la ropa *v.* to iron clothes 12
planes *m., pl.* plans 4
planta *f.* plant 13
   planta baja ground floor 5
plástico *m.* plastic 13
plato *m.* dish (*in a meal*) 8; *m.* plate
   12
   plato principal main dish 8
playa *f.* beach 5
plazos *m., pl.* periods; time 14
pluma *f.* pen 2
población *f.* population 13
pobre *adj. m., f.* poor 6
pobreza *f.* poverty 3
poco/a *adj.* little; few 5
poder (o:ue) *v.* to be able to;
   can 4
poema *m.* poem
poesía *f.* poetry
poeta *m., f.* poet
policía *f.* police (force) 11; *m.* (male)
   police officer 11
política *f.* politics
político/a *m., f.* politician 16
pollo *m.* chicken 8
   pollo asado roast chicken 8
ponchar *v.* to deflate; to get a flat
   (*tire*) 11
poner *v.* to put; to place 4; to turn on
   (*electrical appliances*) 11
   poner la mesa to set the
      table 12
   poner una inyección to give
      an injection 10
ponerse (+ adj.) to become
   (+ *adj.*) 7; to put on clothing 7
por *prep.* due to; in exchange for; for
   the sake of 11; for; by; in; through
   11
   por aquí around here 11
   por avión by plane 5
   por ejemplo for example 11
   por eso that's why;
      therefore 11
   Por favor. Please. 1

por fin finally 11
por la mañana in the
   morning 7
por la noche at night 7
por la tarde in the afternoon 7
por lo menos at least 10
¿por qué? why? 2
por supuesto of course 16
por teléfono by phone; on the
   phone 7
por último finally 7
porque *conj.* because 2
portátil *adj.* portable 11
porvenir *m.* future 16
posesivo/a *adj.* possessive 3
posible *adj.* possible 13
postal *f.* postcard 4
postre *m.* dessert 9
practicar *v.* to practice 2
   practicar deportes to play sports 4
precio (fijo) *m.* (fixed; set)
   price 6
preferir (e:ie) *v.* to prefer 4
pregunta *f.* question 2
preguntar *v.* to ask (*a question*) 2
premio *m.* prize; award
prender *v.* to turn on 11
prensa *f.* press
preocupado/a *adj.* worried 5
preocuparse (por) *v.* to worry (about)
   7
preparar *v.* to prepare 2
preposición *f.* preposition
presentación *f.* introduction
presentar *v.* to introduce 1; to put on
   (*a performance*)
presiones *f., pl.* pressures 15
prestado/a *adj.* borrowed 14
préstamo *m.* loan 14
prestar *v.* to lend 6
primavera *f.* spring 5
primer, primero/a *adj.* first 5
primo/a *m., f.* cousin 3
principal *adj. m., f.* main 8
prisa *f.* haste 3
probable *adj. m., f.* probable 13
probar (o:ue) *v.* to taste; to try 8
probarse (o:ue) *v.* to try on 7
problema *m.* problem 1
profesión *f.* profession 16
profesor(a) *m., f.* teacher;
   professor 1
programa *m.* 1
   programa de computación
      software 11
   programa de entrevistas
      talk show
programador(a) *m., f.* programmer 3
prohibir *v.* to prohibit; to
   forbid 10
pronombre *m.* pronoun 8
pronto *adj.* soon 10
propina *f.* tip 9
propio/a *adj.* own 16
proteger *v.* to protect 13

proteína *f.* protein 15
próximo/a *adj.* next 16
prueba *f.* test; quiz 2
psicología *f.* psychology 2
psicólogo/a *m., f.* psychologist 16
publicar *v.* to publish
público *m.* audience
pueblo *m.* town 4
puerta *f.* door 2
Puerto Rico *m.* Puerto Rico 1
puertorriqueño/a *adj.* Puerto Rican 3
pues *conj.* well 2
puesto *m.* position; job 16
puesto/a *p.p.* put 14
puro/a *adj.* pure 13

Q

que *pron.* that; who 12
   ¡Qué...! How . . . ! 3
   ¡Qué dolor! What pain! 10
   ¡Qué gusto + inf.! What a
      pleasure to . . . ! 18
   ¡Qué ropa más bonita!
      What pretty clothes! 6
   ¡Qué sorpresa! What a
      surprise! 9
   ¿qué? what? 1
   ¿Qué día es hoy? What day is
      it? 2
   ¿Qué hay de nuevo? What's
      new?; What's happening? 1
   ¿Qué hora es? What time
      is it? 1
   ¿Qué les parece? What do
      you (*pl.*) think? 9
   ¿Qué pasa? What's going on?
      1
   ¿Qué pasó? What happened?;
      What's wrong? 11
   ¿Qué precio tiene? What is
      the price? 6
   ¿Qué tal? How are you?;
      How is it going? 1; How is/are
      . . . ? 2
   ¿Qué talla lleva/usa? What
      size do you take? 6
   ¿Qué tiempo hace? What's
      the weather like? 5
quedar *v.* to be left over; to fit
   (*clothing*) 7; to be left behind 10;
   to be located 14
quedarse *v.* to stay; to remain 7
quehaceres domésticos *m., pl.*
   household chores 12
quemado/a *adj.* burned (out) 11
querer (e:ie) *v.* to want; to love 4
queso *m.* cheese 8
quien *pron.* who; whom 12
   ¿Quién es...? Who is . . . ? 1
   ¿Quién habla? Who is
      speaking? (*telephone*) 11
   ¿quién(es)? who?; whom? 1
química *f.* chemistry 2

quince *adj., pron.* fifteen **1**
  menos quince quarter to (time) **1**
  y quince quarter after (time) **1**
quinceañera *f.* young woman's fifteenth birthday celebration **9**
quinientos/as *adj.* five hundred **5**
quinto/a *adj.* fifth **5**
quisiera *v.* I would like **8**
quitar la mesa *v.* to clear the table **12**
quitarse *v.* to take off **7**
quizás *adv.* perhaps **5**

R

racismo *m.* racism
radio *f.* radio (*medium*) **2**
radio *m.* radio (set) **2, 11**
radiografía *f.* X-ray **10**
rápido/a *adj.* fast **8**
ratón *m.* mouse **11**
ratos libres *m., pl.* spare time **4**
raya *f.* stripe **6**
razón *f.* reason **3**
rebaja *f.* sale **6**
recado *m.* (telephone) message **11**
receta *f.* prescription **10**
recetar *v.* to prescribe **10**
recibir *v.* to receive **3**
reciclaje *m.* recycling **13**
reciclar *v.* to recycle **13**
recién casado/a *m., f.* newly-wed **9**
recoger *v.* to pick up
recomendar (e:ie) *v.* to recommend **8**
recordar (o:ue) *v.* to remember **4**
recorrer *v.* to tour an area
recurso *m.* resource **13**
  recurso natural natural resource **13**
red *f.* network; Internet
reducir *v.* to reduce **13**
refresco *m.* soft drink **8**
refrigerador *m.* refrigerator **12**
regalar *v.* to give (*as a gift*) **9**
regalo *m.* gift; present **6**
regatear *v.* to bargain **6**
región *f.* region; area **13**
regresar *v.* to return **2**
regular *adj. m., f.* so so.; OK **1**
reído *p.p.* laughed **14**
reírse (e:i) *v.* to laugh **9**
relaciones *f., pl.* relationships
relajarse *v.* to relax **9**
reloj *m.* clock; watch **2**
renunciar (a) *v.* to resign (from) **16**
repetir (e:i) *v.* to repeat **4**
reportaje *m.* report
reportero/a *m., f.* reporter; journalist **16**
representante *m., f.* representative
resfriado *m.* cold (*illness*) **10**

residencia estudiantil *f.* dormitory **2**
resolver (o:ue) *v.* to resolve; to solve **13**
respirar *v.* to breathe **13**
respuesta *f.* answer **9**
restaurante *m.* restaurant **4**
resuelto/a *p.p.* resolved **14**
reunión *f.* meeting **16**
revisar *v.* to check **11**
  revisar el aceite to check the oil **11**
revista *f.* magazine **4**
rico/a *adj.* rich **6;** *adj.* tasty; delicious **8**
ridículo *adj.* ridiculous **13**
río *m.* river **13**
riquísimo/a *adj.* extremely delicious **8**
rodilla *f.* knee **10**
rogar (o:ue) *v.* to beg; to plead **12**
rojo/a *adj.* red **6**
romántico/a *adj.* romantic
romper (con) *v.* to break up (with) **9**
romper(se) *v.* to break **10**
  romperse la pierna to break one's leg **10**
ropa *f.* clothing; clothes **6**
  ropa interior underwear **6**
rosado/a *adj.* pink **6**
roto/a *adj.* broken **10**
rubio/a *adj.* blond(e) **3**
ruso/a *adj.* Russian
rutina *f.* routine **7**
  rutina diaria daily routine **7**

S

sábado *m.* Saturday **2**
saber *v.* to know; to know how to **8**
sabrosísimo/a *adj.* extremely delicious **8**
sabroso/a *adj.* tasty; delicious **8**
sacar *v.* to take out **10**
  sacar fotos to take photographs **5**
  sacar la basura to take out the trash **12**
  sacar(se) una muela to extract a tooth; to pull a tooth **10**
sacudir *v.* to dust **12**
  sacudir los muebles dust the furniture **12**
sal *f.* salt **8**
sala *f.* living room; room **12**
  sala de emergencia emergency room **10**
salario *m.* salary **16**
salchicha *f.* sausage **8**
salida *f.* departure; exit **5**
salir *v.* to leave; to go out **4**
  salir con to go out with; to date

  (*someone*) **4, 9**
  salir de to leave from **4**
  salir para to leave for (*a place*) **4**
salmón *m.* salmon **8**
salón de belleza *m.* beauty salon **14**
salud *f.* health **10**
saludable *adj.* healthy **10**
saludar(se) *v.* to greet (each other) **11**
saludo *m.* greeting **1**
  saludos a... greetings to . . . **1**
sandalia *f.* sandal **6**
sándwich *m.* sandwich **8**
sano/a *adj.* healthy **10**
se *ref.pron.* himself, herself, itself, *form.* yourself, themselves, yourselves **7**
se *impersonal* one **10**
  Se nos dañó... The . . . broke down on us. **11**
  Se hizo... He/she/it became . . . **5**
  Se nos pinchó una llanta. We had a flat tire. **11**
secadora *f.* clothes dryer **12**
sección de (no) fumar *f.* (no) smoking section **8**
secretario/a *m., f.* secretary **16**
secuencia *f.* sequence
sed *f.* thirst **3**
seda *f.* silk **6**
sedentario/a *adj.* sedentary; related to sitting **15**
seguir (e:i) *v.* to follow; to continue **4**
según *prep.* according to
segundo/a *adj.* second **5**
seguro/a *adj.* sure **5**
seis *adj., pron.* six **1**
seiscientos/as *adj., pron.* six hundred **5**
sello *m.* stamp **14**
selva *f.* jungle **13**
semáforo *m.* traffic signal **11**
semana *f.* week **2**
  fin *m.* **de semana** weekend **4**
semestre *m.* semester **2**
sendero *m.* trail; trailhead **13**
sentarse (e:ie) *v.* to sit down **7**
sentir(se) (e:ie) *v.* to be sorry; to feel **7;** to regret **13**
señor (Sr.) *m.* Mr.; sir **1**
señora (Sra.) *f.* Mrs.; ma'am **1**
señorita (Srta.) *f.* Miss **1**
separado/a *adj.* separated **9**
separarse (de) *v.* to separate (from)
septiembre *m.* September **5**
séptimo/a *adj., pron.* seventh **5**
ser *v.* to be **1**
  ser aficionado/a (a) to be a fan (of) **4**
  ser alérgico/a (a) to be allergic (to) **10**
  ser gratis to be free of charge **14**
serio/a *adj.* serious

servilleta *f.* napkin 12
servir (e:i) *v.* to serve 8; to help 5
sesenta *adj., pron.* sixty 2
setecientos/as *adj., pron.* seven hundred 5
setenta *adj., pron.* seventy 2
sexismo *m.* sexism
sexto/a *adj., pron.* sixth 5
sí *adv.* yes 1
si *conj.* if 4
SIDA *m.* AIDS
sido *p.p.* been 15
siempre *adv.* always 7
siete *adj., pron.* seven 1
silla *f.* seat 2
sillón *m.* armchair 12
similar *adj. m., f.* similar
simpático/a *adj.* nice; likeable 3
sin *prep.* without 13, 15
   sin duda without a doubt
   sin embargo *adv.* however
   sin que *conj.* without 13
sino *conj.* but 7
síntoma *m.* symptom 10
sitio *m.* **Web;** Web site 11
situado/a *p.p.* located 14
sobre *m.* envelope 14; *prep.* on; over 2
sobrino/a *m., f.* nephew; niece 3
sociología *f.* sociology 2
sofá *m.* couch; sofa 12
sol *m.* sun 4
solar *adj. m., f.* solar 14
solicitar *v.* to apply (*for a job*) 16
solicitud (de trabajo) *f.* (job) application 16
sólo *adv.* only 3
soltero/a *adj.* single; unmarried 9
solución *f.* solution 13
sombrero *m.* hat 6
Son las... It's . . . o'clock. 1
sonar (o:ue) *v.* to ring 11
sonreído *p.p.* smiled 14
sonreír (e:i) *v.* to smile 9
sopa *f.* soup 8
sorprender *v.* to surprise 9
sorpresa *f.* surprise 9
sótano *m.* basement; cellar
soy I am 1
   Soy yo. That's me. 1
   soy de... I'm from . . . 1
su(s) *poss. adj.* his; her; its; *form.* your; their; 3
subir(se) *v.* to go up; to get on/in (*a vehicle*) 11
sucio/a *adj.* dirty 5
sucre *m.* Ecuadorian currency 6
sudar *v.* to sweat 15
suegro/a *m., f.* father-in-law; mother-in-law 3
sueldo *m.* salary 16
suelo *m.* floor 12
sueño *n.* sleep 3
suerte *f.* luck 3
suéter *m.* sweater 6

sufrir *v.* to suffer 10
   sufrir muchas presiones to be under a lot of pressure 15
   sufrir una enfermedad to suffer (from) an illness 10
sugerir (e:ie) *v.* to suggest 12
supermercado *m.* supermarket 14
suponer *v.* to suppose 4
sur *m.* south 14
sustantivo *m.* noun
suyo/a(s) *poss.* (of) his/her; (of) hers; (of) its; (of) *form.* your, (of) yours, (of) their 11

T

tal vez *adv.* maybe 5
talentoso/a *adj.* talented
talla *f.* size 6
   talla grande large 6
taller *m.* **mecánico** mechanic's repairshop 11
también *adv.* also; too 2
tampoco *adv.* neither; not either 7
tan *adv.* so 5, 8
   tan pronto como as soon as 14
   tan... como as . . . as 8
tanque *m.* tank 11
tanto *adv.* so much 12
   tanto... como as much . . . as 8
   tantos/as... como as many . . . as 8
tarde *adv.* late 7
tarde *f.* afternoon; evening; P.M. 1
tarea *f.* homework 2
tarjeta *f.* (post) card 4
   tarjeta de crédito credit card 6
   tarjeta postal postcard 4
taxi *m.* taxi(cab) 5
taza *f.* cup 12
te *fam. pron.* you 6
   Te presento a... I would like to introduce you to . . . 1
   ¿Te gustaría? Would you like to? 7
   ¿Te gusta(n)... ? Do you like . . . ? 2
té *m.* tea 8
   té helado iced tea 8
teatro *m.* theater
teclado *m.* keyboard 11
técnico/a *m., f.* technician 16
tejido *m.* weaving
teleadicto/a *m., f.* couch potato 15
teléfono (celular) *m.* (cell) telephone 11
telenovela *f.* soap opera
teletrabajo *m.* telecommuting 16
televisión *f.* television 11
   televisión por cable cable television 11

televisor *m.* television set 11
temer *v.* to fear 13
temperatura *f.* temperature 10
temprano *adv.* early 7
tenedor *m.* fork 12
tener *v.* to have 3
   tener... años to be . . . years old 3
   Tengo... años. I'm . . . years old. 3
   tener calor to be hot 3
   tener cuidado to be careful 3
   tener dolor de to have a pain in
   tener éxito to be successful 16
   tener fiebre to have a fever 10
   tener frío to be cold 3
   tener ganas de (+ inf.) to feel like (*doing something*) 3
   tener hambre *f.* to be hungry 3
   tener miedo de to be afraid of; to be scared of 3
   tener miedo (de) que to be afraid that 13
   tener planes to have plans 4
   tener prisa to be in a hurry 3
   tener que (+ inf.) *v.* to have to (*do something*) 3
   tener razón to be right 3
   tener sed to be thirsty 3
   tener sueño to be sleepy 3
   tener suerte to be lucky 3
   tener tiempo to have time 4
   tener una cita to have a date, an appointment 9
tenis *m.* tennis 4
tensión *f.* tension
tercero/a *adj., pron.* third 5
terminar *v.* to end; to finish 2
   terminar de (+inf.) to finish (*doing something*) 4
terremoto *m.* earthquake
terrible *adj. m., f.* terrible 13
ti *prep., obj. of prep., fam.* you 8
tiempo *m.* time; weather 4
   tiempo libre free time 4
tienda *f.* shop; store 6
   tienda de campaña tent 5
tierra *f.* land; soil 13
tinto/a *adj.* red (wine) 8
tío/a *m., f.* uncle; aunt 3
tíos *m.* aunts and uncles 3
título *m.* title
tiza *f.* chalk 2
toalla *f.* towel 7
tobillo *m.* ankle 10
tocadiscos compacto *m.* compact-disc player 11
tocar *v.* to play (*a musical instrument*); to touch 13
todavía *adv.* yet; still 5
todo *m.* everything 5
   todo el mundo the whole world; all over the world 13

Todo está bajo control.
Everything is under control. 7
(todo) derecho straight
ahead 14
¡Todos a bordo! All aboard! 1
todo/a *adj.* whole; all 4
todos *m., pl.* all of us 1; *m., pl.*
everybody; everyone 13
todos los días every day 10
tomar *v.* to take; to drink 2
tomar clases to take
classes 2
tomar el sol to sunbathe 4
tomar en cuenta take into
account 8
tomar fotos to take photos
tomar la temperatura to take
someone's temperature 10
tomate *m.* tomato 8
tonto/a *adj.* silly; foolish 3
torcerse (el tobillo) *v.* to sprain (one's
ankle) 10
torcido/a *adj.* twisted;
sprained 10
tormenta *f.* storm
tornado *m.* tornado
tortilla *f.* kind of flat bread 8
tortillas de maíz flat bread
made of corn flour 8
tos *f., sing.* cough 10
toser *v.* to cough 10
tostado/a *adj.* toasted 8
tostadora *f.* toaster
trabajador(a) *adj.* hardworking 3
trabajar *v.* to work 2
trabajo *m.* job; work; written work 16
traducir *v.* to translate 8
traer *v.* to bring 4
tráfico *m.* traffic 11
tragedia *f.* tragedy
traído/a *p.p.* brought 14
traje *m.* suit 6
traje de baño bathing suit 6
tranquilo/a *adj.* calm; quiet 15
¡Tranquilo! Stay calm! 7
transmitir to broadcast 18
tratar de (+ inf.) *v.* to try to (*do
something*) 15
Trato hecho. It's a deal.
trece *adj., pron.* thirteen 1
treinta *adj., pron.* thirty 1
y treinta thirty minutes past the
hour (time) 1
tren *m.* train 5
tres *adj., pron.* three 1
trescientos/as *adj., pron.* three
hundred 5
trimestre *m.* trimester; quarter 2
triste *adj.* sad 5
tú *fam. sub. pron.* you 1
Tú eres... You are . . . 1
tu(s) *fam. poss. adj.* your 3
turismo *m.* tourism 5
turista *m., f.* tourist 1

turístico/a *adj.* touristic
tuyo/a(s) *fam. poss. pron.* your; (of)
yours 11

Ud. *form., sing.* you 1
Uds. *form., pl.* you 1
último/a *adj.* last 15
un, uno/a *art.* a; one 1
una vez más one more time 9
una vez once; one time 6
único/a *adj.* only 3
universidad *f.* university;
college 2
unos/as *pron.* some 1
urgente *adj.* urgent 12
usar *v.* to wear; to use 6
usted *form., sing.* you 1
ustedes *form., pl.* you 1
útil *adj.* useful 1
uva *f.* grape 8

vaca *f.* cow 13
vacaciones *f., pl.* vacation 5
valle *m.* valley 13
vamos let's go 4
vaquero *m.* cowboy
de vaqueros *m., pl.* western
varios/as *adj. m. f., pl.* various 8
vaso *m.* glass 12
veces *f., pl.* times 6
vecino/a *m., f.* neighbor 12
veinte *adj., pron.* twenty 1
veinticinco *adj., pron.* twenty-five 1
veinticuatro *adj., pron.* twenty-four 1
veintidós *adj., pron.* twenty-two 1
veintinueve *adj., pron.* twenty-nine 1
veintiocho *adj., pron.* twenty-eight 1
veintiséis *adj., pron.* twenty-six 1
veintisiete *adj., pron.* twenty-seven 1
veintitrés *adj., pron.* twenty-three 1
veintiún, veintiuno/a *adj., pron.*
twenty-one 1
vejez *f.* old age 9
velocidad *f.* speed 11
velocidad máxima speed limit 11
vendedor(a) *m., f.* salesperson 6
vender *v.* to sell 6
venir *v.* to come 3
ventana *f.* window 2
ver *v.* to see 4
ver películas to see movies 4
a ver let's see 2
verano *m.* summer 5
verbo *m.* verb
verdad *f.* truth 9
¿verdad? right? 1
verde *adj., m. f.* green 6
verduras *pl., f.* vegetables 8

vestido *m.* dress 6
vestirse (e:i) *v.* to get dressed 7
vez *f.* time 6
viajar *v.* to travel 2
viaje *m.* trip 5
viajero/a *m., f.* traveler 5
vida *f.* life 9
video(casete) *m.* video
(cassette) 11
videocasetera *f.* VCR 11
videoconferencia *f.* video conference
16
vidrio *m.* glass 13
viejo/a *adj.* old 3
viento *m.* wind 4
viernes *m., sing.* Friday 5
vinagre *m.* vinegar
vino *m.* wine 8
vino blanco white wine 8
vino tinto red wine 8
violencia *f.* violence
visitar *v.* to visit 4
visitar monumentos to visit
monuments 4
visto/a *p.p.* seen 14
vitamina *f.* vitamin 14
viudo/a *adj.* widowed 9
vivienda *f.* housing 12
vivir *v.* to live 3
vivo/a *adj.* bright; lively; living 4
volante *m.* steering wheel 11
volcán *m.* volcano 13
vóleibol *m.* volleyball 4
volver (o:ue) *v.* to return 4
volver a ver(te, lo, la) *v.* to see (you)
again
vos *pron.* you 1
vosotros/as *form., pl.* you
votar *v.* to vote 18
vuelta *f.* return trip 5
vuelto/a *p.p.* returned 14
vuestro/a(s) *poss. adj.* your 3

walkman *m.* Walkman

y *conj.* and 1
y cuarto quarter after (time) 1
y media half-past (time) 1
y quince quarter after (time) 1
y treinta thirty (minutes past
the hour) 1
¿Y tú? *fam.* And you? 1
¿Y Ud.? *form.* And you? 1
ya *adv.* already 6
yerno *m.* son-in-law 3
yo *sub. pron.* I 1
Yo soy... I'm . . . 1
yogur *m.* yogurt

Z

zanahoria *f.* carrot **8**
zapatería *f.* shoe store **14**
zapatos (de tenis) *m., pl.* (tennis)
shoes **6**

English-Spanish

A

A.M. **mañana** *f.* 1
able: be able to **poder (o:ue)** *v.* 4
aboard **a bordo** 1
accident **accidente** *m.* 10
accompany **acompañar** *v.* 14
account **cuenta** *f.* 14
accountant **contador(a)** *m., f.* 16
accounting **contabilidad** *f.* 2
ache **dolor** *m.* 10
acid **ácido/a** *adj.* 13
   acid rain **lluvia ácida** 13
acquainted: be acquainted with
   conocer *v.* 8
action **acción** *f.*
active **activo/a** *adj.* 15
actor **actor** *m.*, **actriz** *f.* 16
addict (*drug*) **drogadicto/a**
   adj. 15
additional **adicional** *adj.*
address **dirección** *f.* 14
adjective **adjetivo** *m.*
adolescence **adolescencia** *f.* 9
adventure **aventura** *f.*
advertise **anunciar** *v.*
advertisement **anuncio** *m.* 16
advice **consejo** *m.* 9
   give advice **dar** *v.* **un consejo** 9
advise **aconsejar** *v.* 12
advisor **consejero/a** *m., f.* 16
aerobic **aeróbico/a** *adj.* 15
   aerobic exercises **ejercicios**
      aeróbicos 15
   aerobics class **clase de**
      ejercicios aeróbicos 15
affected **afectado/a** *adj.* 13
   be affected by **estar** *v.*
      afectado/a por 13
affirmative **afirmativo/a** *adj.*
afraid: be afraid (of) **tener miedo (de)**
   3
   be afraid that **tener** *v.* **miedo**
      (de) que 13
after **después de** *prep.* 7 **después (de)**
   que *conj.* 14
afternoon **tarde** *f.* 1
afterward **después** *adv.* 7; **luego** *adv.* 7
again **otra vez** *adv.* 15
age **edad** *f.* 8
agree **concordar** *v.* agree; **estar** *v.* **de**
   acuerdo 16
agreement **acuerdo** *m.* 16
AIDS **SIDA** *m.*
air **aire** *m.* 6
   air pollution **contaminación del**
      aire 13
airplane **avión** *m.* 5
airport **aeropuerto** *m.* 5
alarm clock **despertador** *m.* 7
alcohol **alcohol** *m.* 15

alcoholic **alcohólico/a** *adj.* 15
all **todo/a** *adj.* 4
   All aboard! **¡Todos a bordo!** 1
   all of us **todos** 1
   all over the world **en todo el**
      mundo 13
allergic **alérgico/a** *adj.* 10
   be allergic (to) **ser alérgico/a**
      (a) 10
alleviate **aliviar** *v.* 15
almost **casi** *adv.* 10
alone **solo/a** *adj.*
along **por** *prep.* 11
already **ya** *adv.* 6
also **también** *adv.* 2
alternator **alternador** *m.* 11
although **aunque** *conj.*
aluminum **aluminio** *m.* 13
   (made of) aluminum **de**
      aluminio 13
always **siempre** *adv.* 7
American (*North*) **norteamericano/a**
   adj. 3
among **entre** *prep.* 2
amusement **diversión** *f.* 4
and **y** 1, **e** (*before words beginning*
   with **i** *or* **hi**) 4
   And you? **¿Y tú?** *fam.* 1;
   ¿Y Ud.? *form.* 1
angry **enojado/a** *adj.* 5
   get angry (with) **enojarse** *v.*
      (con) 7
animal **animal** *m.* 13
ankle **tobillo** *m.* 10
anniversary **aniversario** *m.* 9
   (wedding) anniversary
      aniversario (de bodas) 9
announce **anunciar** *v.*
announcer (*TV/radio*) **locutor(a)** *m.,*
   f.
annoy **molestar** *v.* 7
another **otro/a** *adj.* 6
answer **contestar** *v.* 2; **respuesta** *f.* 9
answering machine **contestadora** *f.*
   11
antibiotic **antibiótico** *m.* 10
any **algún, alguno/a(s)** *adj.* 7
anyone **alguien** *pron.* 7
anything **algo** *pron.* 7
apartment **apartamento** *m.* 12
apartment building **edificio de**
   apartamentos 12
appear **parecer** *v.* 8
appetizers **entremeses** *m., pl.* 8
applaud **aplaudir** *v.*
apple **manzana** *f.* 8
appliance (electric) **electrodoméstico**
   m. 12
applicant **aspirante** *m., f.* 16
application **solicitud** *f.* 16
   job application **solicitud de**
      trabajo 16
apply (*for a job*) **solicitar** *v.* 16
   apply for a loan **pedir** *v.*
      préstamo 14

appointment **cita** *f.* 9
   have an appointment **tener** *v.*
      una cita 9
appreciate **apreciar** *v.*
April **abril** *m.* 5
aquatic **acuático/a** *adj.* 4
archaeologist **arqueólogo/a**
   m., f. 16
architect **arquitecto/a** *m., f.* 16
area **región** *f.* 13
arm **brazo** *m.* 10
armchair **sillón** *m.* 12
army **ejército** *m.*
around here **por aquí** 11
arrange **arreglar** *v.* 5
arrival **llegada** *f.* 5
arrive **llegar** *v.* 2
art **arte** *m.* 2
   fine arts **bellas artes** *f., pl.*
article **artículo** *m.*
artist **artista** *m., f.* 3
artistic **artístico/a** *adj.*
arts **artes** *f., pl.* 17
as **como** *conj.* 8
   as . . . as **tan... como** 8
   as a child **de niño/a** 10
   as many . . . as **tantos/as...**
      como 8
   as much . . . as **tanto...**
      como 8
   as soon as **en cuanto** *conj.* 14;
      tan pronto como *conj.* 14
ask (*a question*) **preguntar** *v.* 2
   ask for **pedir (e:i)** *v.* 4
asparagus **espárragos** *m., pl.*
aspirin **aspirina** *f.* 10
at **a** *prep.* 1
   at + *time* **a la(s)** + *time* 1
   at home **en casa** 7
   at least **por lo menos** 10
   at night **por la noche** 7
   at the end (of) **al fondo (de)** 12
   At what time . . . ? **¿A qué**
      hora...? 1
   At your service. **A sus**
      órdenes. 11
attend **asistir (a)** *v.* 3
attic **altillo** *m.* 12
attract **atraer** *v.* 4
audience **público** *m.*
August **agosto** *m.* 5
aunt **tía** *f.* 3
   aunts and uncles **tíos** *m., pl.* 3
automatic **automático/a** *adj.* 14
   automatic teller machine (ATM)
      cajero automático 14
automobile **automóvil** *m.* 5; **carro** *m.*;
   coche *m.* 11
autumn **otoño** *m.* 5
avenue **avenida** *f.*
avoid **evitar** *v.* 13
award **premio** *m.*

B

backpack **mochila** *f.* 2
bad **mal, malo/a** *adj.* 3
   It's bad that . . . **Es malo
     que. . .** 12
   It's not at all bad. **No está
     nada mal.** 5
bag **bolsa** *f.* 6
bakery **panadería** *f.* 14
balanced **equilibrado/a** *adj.* 15
   balanced diet **dieta
     equilibrada** 15
balcony **balcón** *m.*
ball **pelota** *f.* 4
ballet **ballet** *m.*
banana **banana** *f.* 8
band **banda** *f.*
bank **banco** *m.* 14
bargain **ganga** *f.* 6; **regatear** *v.* 6
baseball (*game*) **béisbol** *m.* 4
basement **sótano** *m.*
basketball (*game*) **baloncesto** *m.* 4
bath **baño** *m.*
   take a bath **bañarse** *v.* 7
bathe **bañarse** *v.* 7
bathing suit **traje** *m.* **de baño** 6
bathroom **baño** *m.* 7; **cuarto de baño**
   m.
be **ser** *v.* 1; **estar** *v.* 2
be . . . years old **tener. . . años** 3
beach **playa** *f.* 5
beans **frijoles** *m., pl.* 8
beautiful **hermoso/a** *adj.* 6
beauty **belleza** *f.* 14
   beauty salon **peluquería** *f.* 14;
     salón *m.* **de belleza** 14
because **porque** *conj.* 2
   because of **por** *prep.* 11
become (+ *adj.*) **ponerse (+ *adj.*)** 7;
   convertirse *v.* 6
bed **cama** *f.* 5
   go to bed **acostarse (o:ue)** *v.* 7
bedroom **alcoba** *f.* **cuarto** *m.*
   recámara *f.*
beef **carne** *f.* **de res** 8
   beef soup **caldo** *m.* **de patas** 8
been **sido** *p.p.* 15
beer **cerveza** *f.* 8
before **antes** *adv.* 7; **antes de** *prep.* 7;
   antes (de) que *conj.* 13
beg **rogar (o:ue)** *v.* 12
begin **comenzar (e:ie)** *v.* 4; **empezar
   (e:ie)** *v.* 4
behalf: on behalf of **de parte
   de** 11
behind **detrás de** *prep.* 2
believe (in) **creer** *v.* **(en)** 3
bellhop **botones** *m., sing.* 5
beloved **enamorado/a** *adj.* 5
below **debajo de** *prep.* 2
belt **cinturón** *m.* 6
benefit **beneficio** *m.* 16
beside **al lado de** *prep.* 2
besides **además (de)** *adv.* 10

best **mejor** *adj.* 8
   the best **el/la mejor** *m., f.* 8 **lo
     mejor** *neuter*
better **mejor** *adj.* 8
   It's better that . . . **Es mejor
     que. . .** 12
between **entre** *prep.* 2
bicycle **bicicleta** *f.* 4
big **gran, grande** *adj.* 3
bill **cuenta** *f.* 9
billion: billion **mil millones** *adj., pron.*
   5
biology **biología** *f* . 2
bird **ave** *f.* **pájaro** *m.*
birth **nacimiento** *m.* 9
birthday **cumpleaños** *m., sing.* 9
   birthday cake **pastel de
     cumpleaños** 9
   have a birthday **cumplir** *v.*
     años 9
biscuit **bizcocho** *m.*
black **negro/a** *adj.* 6
blackberry **mora** *f.* 8
blackboard **pizarra** *f.* 2
blanket **manta** *f.* 12
block (city) **cuadra** *f.* 14
blond(e) **rubio/a** *adj.* 3
blouse **blusa** *f.* 6
blue **azul** *adj. m., f.* 6
boarding house **pensión** *f.* 5
boat **barco** *m.* 5
body **cuerpo** *m.* 10
bone **hueso** *m.* 10
book **libro** *m.* 2
bookcase **estante** *m.* 12
bookstore **librería** *f.* 2
boot **bota** *f.* 6
bore **aburrir** *v.* 7
bored **aburrido/a** *adj.* 5
   be bored **estar** *v.* **aburrido/a** 5
   get bored **aburrirse** *v.*
boring **aburrido/a** *adj.* 5
born: be born **nacer** *v.* 9
borrow **pedir prestado** 14
borrowed **prestado/a** *adj.* 14
boss **jefe** *m.*, **jefa** *f.* 16
bottle **botella** *f.* 9
   bottle of wine **botella de
     vino** 9
bother **molestar** *v.* 7
bottom **fondo** *m.* 12
boulevard **bulevar** *m.*
boy **chico** *m.* 1; **muchacho** *m.* 3
boyfriend **novio** *m.* 3
brakes **frenos** *m., pl.* 11
bread **pan** *m.* 8
break **romperse** *v.* 10
   break a leg **romper(se) la
     pierna** 10
   break down: The . . . broke down
     on us. **Se nos dañó
     el/la. . .** 11
   break up (with) **romper** *v.* **(con)** 9
breakfast **desayuno** *m.* 8
   have breakfast **desayunar** *v.* 8

breathe **respirar** *v.* 13
bring **traer** *v.* 4
broadcast **transmitir** *v.;*
   emitir *v.*
brochure **folleto** *m.*
broken **roto/a** *adj.* 10
   be broken **estar roto/a** 10
brother **hermano** *m.* 3
   brother-in-law **cuñado** *m., f.* 3
   brothers and sisters **hermanos**
     m., pl. 3
brought **traído** *p.p.* 14
brown **café** *adj.* 6; **marrón** *adj.*
brunet(te) **moreno/a** *adj.* 3
brush **cepillar** *v.* 7
   brush one's hair **cepillarse el
     pelo** 7
   brush one's teeth **cepillarse los
     dientes** 7
build **construir** *v.* 4
building **edificio** *m.* 12
bullfight **corrida** *f.* **de toros** 4
bump into (*meet accidentally*) **darse
   con**
burned (out) **quemado/a** *adj.* 11
bus **autobús** *m.* 1
   bus station **estación** *f.* **de
     autobuses** 5
business **negocios** *m., pl.* 16
   business administration
     administración *f.* **de empresas** 2
   business-related **comercial** *adj.* 16
businessman **hombre** *m.* **de negocios**
   16
businesswoman **mujer** *f.* **de negocios**
   16
busy **ocupado/a** *adj.* 5
but **pero** *conj.* 2; **sino** *conj.*
   (*in negative sentences*) 7
butcher shop **carnicería** *f.* 14
butter **mantequilla** *f.*
buy **comprar** *v.* 2
by **por** *conj.* 11
   by phone **por teléfono** 7
   by plane **en avión** 5
bye **chau** *interj. fam.*

C

cabin **cabaña** *f.* 5
cable television **televisión** *f.*
   por cable *m.* 11
café **café** *m.* 4
cafeteria **cafetería** *f.* 2
cake **pastel** *m.* 9
calculator **calculadora** *f.* 11
call **llamar** *v.* 7
   call on the phone **llamar por
     teléfono** 11
   be called **llamarse** *v.* 7
calm **tranquilo/a** *adj.* 15
   Stay calm! **¡Tranquilo!** 7
calorie **caloría** *f.* 15
camera **cámara** *f.* 11

camp **acampar** v.

can **lata** f. 13

can **poder (o:ue)** v. 4

Canadian **canadiense** adj. 3

candidate **aspirante** m. f. 16;
    candidate **candidato/a** m., f.

candy **dulces** m., pl. 9

capital (city) **capital** f. 1

car **coche** m. 11; **carro** m. 11;
    auto(móvil) m. 5

caramel **caramelo** m.

card **tarjeta** f. 4; (playing)
    carta f. 5

care **cuidado** m. 3
    take care of **cuidar** v. 13

career **carrera** f. 16

careful: be careful **tener** v.
    cuidado 3

carpenter **carpintero/a** m., f. 16

carpet **alfombra** f. 12

carrot **zanahoria** f. 8

carry **llevar** v. 2

cartoons **dibujos** m., pl. **animados**

case: in case (that) **en caso (de) que**
    13

cash (a check) **cobrar** v. 14;
    efectivo m. 14
    cash register **caja** f. 6
    pay in cash **pagar** v. **al contado**
    pagar en efectivo

cashier **cajero/a** m., f. 14

cat **gato/a** m., f. 13

celebrate **celebrar** v. 9

cellar **sótano** m.

cellular **celular** adj. 11
    cellular telephone **teléfono** m.
        celular 11

cereal **cereales** m., pl. 8

certain **cierto** m.; **seguro** m. 13

chair **silla** f. 2

chalk **tiza** f. 2

champagne **champán** m. 9

change **cambiar** v. **(de)** 9

channel (TV) **canal** m.

character (fictional) **personaje**
    m.
    main character **personaje**
        principal

chauffeur **conductor(a)** m., f. 1

chat **conversar** v. 2

cheap **barato/a** adj. 6

check **comprobar** v.; **revisar** v. 11;
    (bank) **cheque** m. 14
    check the oil **revisar el**
        aceite 11

checking account **cuenta** f.
    corriente 14

cheese **queso** m. 8

chef **cocinero/a** m., f. 16

chemistry **química** f. 2

chest of drawers **cómoda** f. 12

chicken **pollo** m. 8

child **niño/a** m., f. 3

childhood **niñez** f. 9

children **hijos** m., pl. 3

Chinese **chino/a** adj.

chocolate **chocolate** m.
    chocolate cake **pastel** m. **de**
        chocolate 9

cholesterol **colesterol** m. 15

choose **escoger** v. 8

chop (food) **chuleta** f. 8

Christmas **Navidad** f. 9

church **iglesia** f. 4

citizen **ciudadano/a** m., f.

city **ciudad** f. 4

class **clase** f. 2
    take classes **tomar** v. **clases** 2

classical **clásico/a** adj.

classmate **compañero/a** m., f. **de**
    clase 2

clean **limpio/a** adj. 5;
    limpiar v. 12
    clean the house v. **limpiar la**
        casa 12

clear (weather) **despejado/a**
    adj. 5
    clear the table **quitar** v. **la**
        mesa 12
    It's (very) clear. (weather)
        Está (muy) despejado. 5

clerk **dependiente/a** m., f. 6

climb **escalar** v. 4
    climb mountains **escalar**
        montañas 4

clinic **clínica** f. 10

clock **reloj** m. 2

close **cerrar (e:ie)** v. 4

closed **cerrado/a** adj. 5

closet **armario** m. 12

clothes **ropa** f. 6
    clothes dryer **secadora** f. 12

clothing **ropa** f. 6

cloud **nube** f. 13

cloudy **nublado/a** adj. 5
    It's (very) cloudy. **Está (muy)**
        nublado. 5

coat **abrigo** m. 6

coffee **café** m. 8
    coffee maker **cafetera** f.

cold **frío** m. 4; (disease); **resfriado** m.
    10
    be (feel) cold **tener frío** 3
    It's cold. (weather) **Hace frío.** 4

college **universidad** f. 2

collision **choque** m.

color **color** m. 6

comb one's hair **peinarse** v. 7

come **venir** v. 3

comedy **comedia** f.

comfortable **cómodo/a** adj. 5

commerce **negocios** m., pl. 16

commercial **comercial** adj. 16

communicate (with) **comunicarse** v.
    (con)

communication **comunicación** f.
    means of communication
        medios m., pl. **de comunicación**

community **comunidad** f .1

compact disc (CD) **disco** m.
    compacto 11
    compact disc player **tocadiscos** m.
    sing. **compacto** 11

company **compañía** f. 16; **empresa** f.
    16

comparison **comparación** f.

completely **completamente**
    adv. 16

composer **compositor(a)**
    m., f.

computer **computadora** f. 1
    computer disc **disco** m. 11
    computer monitor **monitor**
        m. 11
    computer programmer
        programador(a) m., f. 3
    computer science **computación**
        f. 2

concert **concierto** m.

conductor (musical) **director(a)** m., f.

confirm **confirmar** v. 5
    confirm the reservation **confirmar**
    la reservación 5

congested **congestionado/a**
    adj. 10

Congratulations! (for an event such as
    a birthday or anniversary)
        ¡Felicidades! 9; (for an
        event such as an engagement
        or a good grade on a test)
        f., pl. **¡Felicitaciones!** 9

conservation **conservación** f. 13

conserve **conservar** v. 13

consume **consumir** v. 15

contact lenses **lentes** m. pl. **de**
    contacto

container **envase** m. 13

contamination **contaminación**
    f. 13

content **contento/a** adj. 5

contest **concurso** m.

continue **seguir (e:i)** v. 4

control **control** m. 7; **controlar** v. 13
    be under control **estar bajo**
        control 7

conversation **conversación** f. 2

converse **conversar** v. 2

cook **cocinar** v. 12; **cocinero/a** m., f.
    16

cookie **galleta** f. 9

cool **fresco/a** adj. 5
    It's cool. (weather) **Hace**
        fresco. 5

corn **maíz** m. 5

corner **esquina** m. 14

cost **costar (o:ue)** v. 6

cotton **algodón** m. 6
    (made of) cotton **de algodón** 6

couch **sofá** m. 12

couch potato **teleadicto/a**
    m., f. 15

cough **tos** f. 10; **toser** v. 10

counselor **consejero/a** m., f. 16

count (on) **contar** *v.* **(con)** 12
country (*nation*) **país** *m.* 1
countryside **campo** *m.* 5; **paisaje** *m.* 5
couple (married) **pareja** *f.* 9
course **curso** *m.* 2; **materia** *f.*
courtesy **cortesía** *f.*
cousin **primo/a** *m., f.* 3
cover **cubrir** *v.* 14
covered **cubierto** *p.p.* 14
cow **vaca** *f.* 13
cowboy **vaquero** *m.*
crafts **artesanía** *f.*
craftsmanship **artesanía** *f.*
crater **cráter** *m.* 13
crazy **loco/a** *adj.* 6
create **crear** *v.*
credit **crédito** *m.* 6
    credit card **tarjeta** *f.* **de crédito** 6
crime **crimen** *m.*
cross **cruzar** *v.* 14
culture **cultura** *f.*
cup **taza** *f.* 12
currency exchange **cambio** *m.* **de moneda** 8
current events **actualidades** *f., pl.*
curriculum vitae **currículum** *m.* 16
curtains **cortinas** *f., pl.* 12
custard (*baked*) **flan** *m.* 9
custom **costumbre** *f.* 1
customer **cliente** *m., f.* 6
customs **aduana** *f.* 5
    customs inspector **inspector(a)** *m., f.* **de aduanas** 5
cycling **ciclismo** *m.* 4

D

dad **papá** *m.* 3
daily **diario/a** *adj.* 7
    daily routine **rutina** *f.* **diaria** 7
damage **dañar** *v.* 11
dance **bailar** *v.* 2; **danza** *f.* **baile** *m.*
dancer **bailarín/bailarina** *m., f.* 16
danger **peligro** *m.* 13
dangerous **peligroso/a** *adj.*
date (*appointment*) **cita** *f.* 9; (*calendar*) **fecha** *f.* 5; (*someone*) **salir** *v.* **con (alguien)** 9
    date: have a date **tener** *v.* **una cita** 9
daughter **hija** *f.* 3
    daughter-in-law **nuera** *f.* 3
day **día** *m.* 1
    day before yesterday **anteayer** *adv.* 6
deal **trato** *m.*
    It's a deal. **Trato hecho.**
    It's no big deal. **No es para tanto.** 12
death **muerte** *f.* 9

decaffeinated **descafeinado/a** *adj.* 15
December **diciembre** *m.* 5
decide **decidir** *v.* 3
decided **decidido/a** *adj.* 14
declare **declarar** *v.* 18
deforestation **deforestación** *f.* 13
delicious **delicioso/a** *adj.* 8; **rico/a** *adj.* 8; **sabroso/a** *adj.* 8
delighted **encantado/a** *adj.* 1
dentist **dentista** *m., f.* 10
deny **negar (e: ie)** *v.* 13
department store **almacén** *m.* 6
departure **salida** *f.* 5
deposit **depositar** *v.* 14
describe **describir** *v.* 3
described **descrito/a** *p.p.* 14
desert **desierto** *m.* 13
design **diseño** *m.* 3
designer **diseñador(a)** *m., f.* 16
desire **desear** *v.* 2
desk **escritorio** *m.*2
dessert **postre** *m.* 9
destroy **destruir** *v.* 13
develop **desarrollar** *v.* 13
diary **diario** *m.* 1
dictatorship **dictadura** *f.*
dictionary **diccionario** *m.* 1
die **morir (o:ue)** *v.* 8
died **muerto/a** *p.p.* 14
diet **dieta** *f.* 15
    balanced diet **dieta equilibrada** 15
    be on a diet **estar** *v.* **a dieta** 15
difficult **difícil** *adj. m., f.* 3
dining room **comedor** *m.* 12
dinner **cena** *f.* 8
    have dinner **cenar** *v.* 8
directions **direcciones** *f., pl.* 14
    give directions **dar direcciones** 14
director **director(a)** *m., f.*
dirty **ensuciar** *v.* 12; **sucio/a** *adj.* 5
    get dirty **ensuciar** *v.* 12
disagree **no estar de acuerdo** 16
disaster **desastre** *m.*
discover **descubrir** *v.* 13
discovered **descubierto** *p.p.* 14
discrimination **discriminación** *f.*
dish **plato** *m.* 8
    main dish **plato principal** 8
dishwasher **lavaplatos** *m., sing.* 12
disk **disco** *m.* 11
disorderly **desordenado/a** *adj.* 5
dive **bucear** *v.* 4
divorce **divorcio** *m.* 9
divorced **divorciado/a** *adj.* 9
    get divorced (from) **divorciarse** *v.* **(de)** 9
dizzy **mareado/a** *adj.* 10
do **hacer** *v.* 4
    do aerobics **hacer ejercicios aeróbicos** 15
    do errands **hacer diligencias** 14

do household chores **hacer quehaceres domésticos** 12
do stretching exercises **hacer ejercicios de estiramiento** 15
doctor **doctor(a)** *m., f.* **médico/a** *m., f.*
documentary (*film*) **documental** *m.*
dog **perro/a** *m., f.* 13
domestic **doméstico/a** *adj.*
    domestic appliance **electrodoméstico** *m.* 12
done **hecho/a** *p.p.* 14
door **puerta** *f.* 2
dormitory **residencia** *f.* **estudiantil** 2
double **doble** *adj.* 5
    double room **habitación** *f.* **doble** 5
doubt **duda** *f.* 13; **dudar** *v.* 13
    There is no doubt that . . . **No cabe duda (de) que...** 13; **No hay duda (de) que...** 13
Down with . . . ! **¡Abajo el/ la...!** 15
downtown **centro** *m.* 4
drama **drama** *m.*
dramatic **dramático/a** *adj.*
draw **dibujar** *v.*
drawing **dibujo** *m.* 17
dress **vestido** *m.* 6
    get dressed **vestirse (e:i)** *v.* 7
drink **beber** *v.* 3; **bebida** *f.* 8; **tomar** *v.* 2
    Do you want something to drink? **¿Quieres algo de tomar?** 8
drive **conducir** *v.* 8; **manejar** *v.* 11
driver **conductor(a)** *m., f.* 1
drug *f.* **droga** 15
    drug addict **drogadicto/a** *adj.* 15
due to **por** *prep.* 11
    due to the fact that **debido a** 3
during **durante** *prep.* 7; **por** *prep.* 11
dust **sacudir** *v.* 12
    dust the furniture **sacudir los muebles** 12
dying: I'm dying to (for) . . . **me muero por...** 1

E

each **cada** *adj. m., f.* 6
eagle **águila** *f.* 1
ear (outer) **oreja** *f.* 10
early **temprano** *adv.* 7
earn **ganar** *v.* 16
earthquake **terremoto** *m.*
ease **aliviar** *v.* 15
east **este** *m.* 14
    to the east **al este** 14
easy **fácil** *adj.* 3
eat **comer** *v.* 3

ecology **ecología** *f.* 13
economics **economía** *f.*
ecotourism **ecoturismo** *m.* 13
Ecuador **Ecuador** *m.* 1
Ecuadorian **ecuatoriano/a** *adj.* 3
effective **eficaz** *adj. m., f.* 8
egg **huevo** *m.* 8
eight *adj., pron.* **ocho** 1
eight hundred *adj., pron.*
    ochocientos/as 5
eighteen *adj., pron.* **dieciocho** 1
eighth *adj., pron.* **octavo/a** 5
eighty *adj., pron.* **ochenta** 2
either . . . or **o... o** *conj.* 7
elect **elegir** *v.*
election **elecciones** *f., pl.*
electrician **electricista** *m., f.* 16
electricity **luz** *f.* 12
elegant **elegante** *adj. m., f.* 6
elevator **ascensor** *m.* 5
eleven *adj., pron.* **once** 1
e-mail **correo** *m.* **electrónico** 4
    e-mail message **mensaje** *m.*
        electrónico 4
    read e-mail **leer** *v.* **el correo**
        electrónico 4
embarrassed **avergonzado/a**
    adj. 5
embrace (each other) **abrazar(se)** *v.*
    11
emergency **emergencia** *f.* 10
    emergency room **sala** *f.* **de**
        emergencia 10
employee **empleado/a** *m., f.* 5
employment **empleo** *m.* 16
end **fin** *m.* 4; **terminar** *v.* 2
    end table **mesita** *f.* 12
energy **energía** *f.* 13
engaged: get engaged (to)
    comprometerse *v.* **(con)** 9
engineer **ingeniero/a** *m., f.* 3
English (*language*) **inglés** *m.* 2;
    inglés, inglesa *adj.* 3
enjoy **disfrutar** *v.* **(de)** 15
enough **bastante** *adj.* 10
entertainment **diversión** *f.* 4
entrance **entrada** *f.* 12
envelope **sobre** *m.* 14
environment **medio ambiente**
    m. 13
equality **igualdad** *f.*
equipped **equipado/a** *adj.* 15
eraser **borrador** *m.* 2
errand *f.* **diligencia** 14
establish **establecer** *v.* 16
evening **tarde** *f.* 1
event **acontecimiento** *m.*
every day **todos los días** 10
everybody **todos** *m., pl.* 13
everything **todo** *m.* 5
    Everything is under control.
        Todo está bajo control. 7
exactly **en punto** *adv.* 1
exam **examen** *m.* 2

excellent **excelente** *adj.* 5
excess **exceso** *m.* 15
    in excess **en exceso** 15
exchange **intercambiar** *v.* 8
    in exchange for **por** 11
exciting **emocionante** *adj. m., f.*
excursion **excursión** *f.* 4
excuse **disculpar** *v.* 8
Excuse me. (*May I?*) **Con permiso.** 1;
    (*I beg your pardon.*) **Perdón.** 1
exercise **ejercicio** *m.* 15
    hacer *v.* **ejercicio** 15
exit **salida** *f.* 5
expensive **caro/a** *adj.* 6
experience **experiencia** *f.*
explain **explicar** *v.* 2
explore **explorar** *v.* 4
    explore a city/town **explorar**
        una ciudad/pueblo 4
expression **expresión** *f.*
extinction **extinción** *f.* 13
eye **ojo** *m.* 10

F

fabulous **fabuloso/a** *adj* 5
face **cara** *f.* 7
facing **enfrente de** *prep.* 14
fact: in fact **de hecho** 5
fall (down) **caerse** *v.* 10
    fall asleep **dormirse (o:ue)** *v.* 7
    fall in love (with) **enamorarse**
        v. **(de)** 9
fall (season) **otoño** *m.* 5
fallen **caído** *p.p.* 14
family **familia** *f.* 3
famous **famoso/a** *adj.* 16
fan **aficionado/a** *adj.* 4
    be a fan of **ser aficionado/a**
        a 4
far from **lejos de** *prep.* 2
farewell **despedida** *f.*
fascinate **fascinar** *v.* 7
fashion **moda** *f.* 6
    be in fashion **estar** *v.* **de moda** 6
fast **rápido/a** *adj.* 8
fat **gordo/a** *adj.* 3; **grasa** *f.* 15
father **padre** *m.* 3
father-in-law **suegro** *m.* 3
favorite **favorito/a** *adj.* 4
fax (machine) **fax** *m.* 11
fear **miedo** *m.* 3; fear **temer** *v.* 13
February **febrero** *m.* 5
feel *v.* **sentir(se) (e:ie)** 7
    feel like (*doing something*) **tener**
        ganas de (+ inf.) 3
festival **festival** *m.*
fever **fiebre** *f.* 10
    have a fever **tener** *v.* **fiebre** 10
few **pocos/as** *adj. pl.* 5
field: major field of study
    especialización *f.* 16
fifteen **quince** *adj., pron.* 1

fifth **quinto/a** *adj., pron.* 5
fifty **cincuenta** *adj., pron.* 2
fight **luchar** *v.* **(por)**
figure (*number*) **cifra** *f.*
file **archivo** *m.* 11
fill **llenar** *v.* 11
    fill out a form **llenar un**
        formulario 14
    fill the tank **llenar el**
        tanque 11
finally **finalmente** *adv.* 15; **por último**
    7; **por fin** 11
find **encontrar (o:ue)** *v.* 4
    find (each other) **encontrar(se)** *v.*
    11
fine arts **bellas artes** *f., pl.*
fine **multa** *f.*
    That's fine. **Está bien.** 11
finger **dedo** *m.* 10
finish **terminar** *v.*
    finish (*doing something*)
        terminar *v.* **de (+inf.)** 4
fire **incendio** *m.*; **despedir (e:i)** *v.* 16
firefighter **bombero/a** *m., f.* 16
firm **compañía** *f.* 16; **empresa**
    f. 16
first **primer, primero/a** *adj.* 5
fish (*food*) **pescado** *m.* 8; **pescar** *v.* 5;
    (*live*) **pez** *m.* 13
    fish market **pescadería** *f.* 14
fisherman **pescador** *m.* 5
fisherwoman **pescadora** *f.* 5
fishing **pesca** *f.* 5
fit (*clothing*) **quedar** *v.* 7
five **cinco** *adj., pron.* 1
five hundred **quinientos/as** *adj.,*
    pron. 5
fix (*put in working order*) **arreglar** *v.*
    11
fixed **fijo/a** *adj.* 6
flag **bandera** *f.*
flank steak **lomo** *m.* 8
flat tire: We had a flat tire. **Se nos**
    pinchó una llanta. 11
flexible **flexible** *adj.* 15
flood **inundación** *f.*
floor (*story in a building*) **piso** *m.* 5;
    suelo *m.* 12
    ground floor **planta** *f.* **baja** 5
    top floor **planta** *f.* **alta** 5
flower **flor** *f.* 13
flu **gripe** *f.* 10
fog **niebla** *f.* 4
foggy: It's (very) foggy. **Hay (mucha)**
    niebla. 5
folk **folklórico/a** *adj.*
follow **seguir (e:i)** *v.* 4
food **comida** *f.* 8
foolish **tonto/a** *adj.* 3
foot **pie** *m.* 10
football **fútbol** *m.* **americano** 4
for **para** *prep.* 11; **por** *prep.* 11
    for example **por ejemplo** 11
    for me **para mí** 8

forbid **prohibir** *v.* 10
foreign **extranjero/a** *adj.*
   foreign languages **lenguas**
    f,. pl. **extranjeras** 2
forest **bosque** *m.* 13
forget **olvidar** *v.* 10
fork **tenedor** *m.* 12
form **formulario** *m.* 14
forty **cuarenta** *m.* 2
forward **en marcha** *adv.* 15
four **cuatro** *adj., pron.* 1
four hundred **cuatrocientos/as** *adj.,*
   pron. 5
fourteen **catorce** *adj., pron.* 1
fourth **cuarto/a** *adj., pron.* 5
free **libre** *adj. m., f.* 4
   be free (of charge) **ser gratis** 14
   free time **tiempo** *m.* **libre** 4; **ratos**
    m., pl. **libres** 4
freedom **libertad** *f.*
freezer **congelador** *m.*
French **francés, francesa** *m., f.* 3
   french fries **papas** *f., pl* **fritas** 8
    patatas *f., pl* **fritas** 8
frequently **frecuentemente** *adv.* 10;
   con frecuencia 10
Friday **viernes** *m., sing.* 2
fried **frito/a** *adj.* 8
   fried potatoes **papas** *f., pl.*
    fritas 8; **patatas** *f., pl.*
    fritas 8
friend **amigo/a** *m., f.* 3
friendly **amable** *adj. m., f.* 5
friendship **amistad** *f.* 9
from **de** *prep.* 1; **desde** *prep.* 6
   from the United States
    estadounidense *adj.* 3
   from time to time **de vez en**
    cuando 10
   He/She/It is from . . . **Es de...** 1
fruit **fruta** *f.* 8
   fruit juice **jugo** *m.* **de fruta** 8
   fruit store **frutería** *f.* 14
full **lleno/a** *adj.* 11
fun **divertido/a** *adj.* 7
   fun activity **diversión** *f.* 4
   have fun **divertirse (e:ie)** *v.* 9
function **funcionar** *v.* 11
furniture **muebles** *m., pl.* 12
furthermore **además (de)** *adv.* 10
future **futuro** *adj.* 16; **porvenir** *m.* 16

G

gain weight **aumentar** *v.* **de peso**;
   engordar *v.*
game **juego** *m.* 5; *(match)*
   partido *m.* 4
   game show **concurso** *m.*
garage **garaje** *m.*
garden **jardín** *m.* 12
garlic **ajo** *m.*
gas station **gasolinera** *f.* 11
gasoline **gasolina** *f.* 11
geography **geografía** *f.* 2

German **alemán, alemana** *adj.* 3
get **conseguir (e:i)** *v.* 4; **obtener** *v.* 16
   get along well/badly with
    llevarse bien/mal con 9
   get bored **aburrirse** *v.*
   get off (a vehicle) **bajar** *v.* **(de)**
    11
   get on/in (a vehicle) **subir(se)** *v.* **a**
    11
   get up **levantarse** *v.* 7
gift **regalo** *m.* 6
girl **chica** *f.* 1; **muchacha** *f.* 3
girlfriend **novia** *f.* 3
give **dar** *v.* 9; *(as a gift)* **regalar** 9
glass *(drinking)* **vaso** *m.* 12; **vidrio** *m.*
   13
   (made of) glass **de vidrio** 13
glasses **gafas** *f., pl.* 6
   sunglasses **gafas oscuras/de sol**
gloves **guantes** *m., pl.* 6
go **ir** *v.* 4
   go away **irse** 7
   go by bus **ir en autobús** 5
   go by car **ir en auto(móvil)** 5
   go by motorcycle **ir en**
    motocicleta 5
   go by plane **ir en avión** 5
   go by ship **ir en barco** 5
   go by subway **ir en metro** 5
   go by taxi **ir en taxi** 5
   go by the bank **pasar por el banco**
    14
   go by train **ir en tren** 5
   go by **pasar** *v.* **por** 5
   go down; **bajar(se)** *v.* 11
   go fishing **ir de pesca** 5
   go for a hike (in the mountains) **ir**
    de excursión (a las montañas)
    4
   go out **salir** *v.* 9
   go out with **salir con** 4, 9
   go through customs **pasar por la**
    aduana 5
   go up **subir** *v.* 11
   go with **acompañar** *v.* 14
   Let's go. **Vamos.** 4
goblet **copa** *f.* 12
going to: be going to *(do something)* **ir**
   a (+ *inf.***)** 4
golf **golf** *m.* 4
good **buen, bueno/a** *adj.* 1, 3
   Good afternoon. **Buenas**
    tardes. 1
   Good evening. **Buenas**
    noches. 1
   Good morning. **Buenos días.** 1
   Good night. **Buenas noches.** 1
   I'm good, thanks. **Bien,**
    gracias. 1
   It's good that . . . **Es bueno**
    que... 12
good-bye **adiós** *m.* 1
   say good-bye (to) **despedirse** *v.*
    (de) (e:i) 7
good-looking **guapo/a** *adj.* 3

government **gobierno** *m.* 13
graduate (from) **graduarse** *v.*
   (en) 9
grains **cereales** *m., pl.* 8
granddaughter **nieta** *f.* 3
grandfather **abuelo** *m.* 3
grandmother **abuela** *f.* 3
grandparents **abuelos** *m., pl.* 3
grandson **nieto** *m.* 3
grape **uva** *f.* 8
grass **césped** *m.*; **hierba** *f.* 13
grave **grave** *adj.* 10
gray **gris** *adj. m., f.* 6
great **fenomenal** *adj. m., f.* 5
green **verde** *adj. m., f.* 6
greet (each other) **saludar(se)**
   v. 11
greeting **saludo** *m.* 1
   Greetings to . . . **Saludos a...** 1
grilled *(food)* **a la plancha** 8
   grilled flank steak **lomo a la**
    plancha 8
ground floor **planta** *f.* **baja** 5
guest (at a house/hotel) **huésped** *m., f.*
   5 *(invited to a function)*
    invitado/a *m., f.* 9
guide **guía** *m., f.* 12
gym **gimnasio** *m.* 4
gymnasium **gimnasio** *m.* 4

H

hair **pelo** *m.* 7
hairdresser **peluquero/a** *m., f.* 16
half **medio/a** *adj.* 3
   half-brother **medio hermano** 3;
    half-sister **media hermana** 3
   half-past . . . *(time)* **...y**
    media 1
hallway **pasillo** *m.* 12
ham **jamón** *m.* 8
hamburger **hamburguesa** *f.* 8
hand **mano** *f.* 1
Hands up! **¡Manos arriba!** 15
handsome **guapo** *adj.* 3
happen **ocurrir** *v.*
Happy birthday! **¡Feliz cumpleaños!**
   9
happy **alegre** *adj.* 5; **contento/a** *adj.* 5;
   feliz *adj.* 5
   be happy **alegrarse** *v.* **(de)** 13
hard **difícil** *adj. m., f.* 3
hard-working **trabajador(a)**
   adj. 3
hardly **apenas** *adv.* 10
haste **prisa** *f.* 3
hat **sombrero** *m.* 6
hate **odiar** *v.* 9
have **tener** *v.* 3
   have to *(do something)* **tener**
    que (+ *inf.***)** 3; **deber**
    (+ *inf.***)** 3
head **cabeza** *f.* 10
headache **dolor de cabeza** *m.* 10
health **salud** *f.* 10

healthful **saludable** *adj. m., f.* 10
healthy **sano/a** *adj.* 10
   lead a healthy life **llevar** *v.* **una vida sana** 15
hear **oír** *v.* 4
heard **oído** *p.p.* 14
hearing: sense of hearing **oído** *m.*
heart **corazón** *m.* 10
heat **calor** *m.* 4
Hello. **Hola.** *interj.* 1; (*on the telephone*) **Aló.** 11; **¿Bueno?** 11; **Diga.** 11
help (to) **ayudar** *v.* **(a)** 12; **servir (e:i)** *v.* 5
   help each other **ayudarse** *v.* 11
her **su(s)** *poss. adj.* 3; hers **suyo/a(s)** *poss. pron.* 11
here **aquí** *adv.* 1
   Here it is. **Aquí está.** 5
   Here we are in . . . **Aquí estamos en…** 2
Hi. **Hola.** *interj.* 1
highway **autopista** *f.*; **carretera** *f.*
hike **excursión** *f.* 4
   go on a hike **hacer una excursión; ir de excursión** 5
hiker **excursionista** *m., f.* 4
hiking **de excursión** 4
hire **contratar** *v.* 16
his **su(s)** *poss. adj.* 3; **suyo/a(s)** *poss. pron.* 11
history **historia** *f.* 2
hobby **pasatiempo** *m.* 4
hockey **hockey** *m.* 4
holiday **día** *m.* **de fiesta** 9
home **casa** *f.* 4
   home page **página** *f.* **principal** 11
homework **tarea** *f.* 2
hood **capó** *m.* 11
hope **esperar** *v.* 2
   I hope (that) **Ojalá** *interj.* 13
horror **horror** *m.* 17
hors d'oeuvres **entremeses** *m., pl.* 8
horse **caballo** *m.* 5
hospital **hospital** *m.* 10
hot: be hot (*weather*) **hacer calor** 5; (*feel*) **tener calor** 3
hotel **hotel** *m.* 5
hour **hora** *f.* 1
house **casa** *f.* 4
household chores **quehaceres** *m., pl.* **domésticos** 12
housewife **ama** *f.* **de casa** 12
housing **vivienda** *f.* 12
How . . . ! **¡Qué…!** 3
   how **¿cómo?** *adv.* 1
   How are you? **¿Qué tal?** 1
   How are you? **¿Cómo estás?** *fam.* 1
   How are you? **¿Cómo está usted?** *form.* 1
   How did it go for you . . .? **¿Cómo le/les fue…?** 15

How is it going? **¿Qué tal?** 1
How is/are . . . ? **¿Qué tal...?** 2
How much/many? **¿Cuánto/a(s) ?** 1
How may I help you? **¿En qué puedo servirles?** 5
How much does it cost? **¿Cuánto cuesta…?** 6
How old are you? **¿Cuántos años tienes?** *fam.* 3
however **sin embargo** *adv.*
hug (each other) **abrazar(se)** *v.* 11
humanities **humanidades** *f., pl.*
hunger **hambre** *f.* 3
hundred **ciento** *m.* 2
hungry: be hungry **tener** *v.* **hambre** 3
hurricane **huracán** *m.*
hurry **apurarse** *v.* 15
   be in a hurry **tener** *v.* **prisa** 3
hurt **doler (o:ue)** *v.* 10
   It hurts me a lot . . . **Me duele mucho…** 10
husband **esposo** *m.* 3

I am . . . **Yo soy...** 1
I hope (that) **Ojalá (que)** *interj.* 13
I wish (that) **Ojalá (que)** *interj.* 13
ice cream **helado** *m.* 9
   ice cream shop **heladería** *f.* 14
iced **helado/a** *adj.* 9
   iced tea **té helado** 8
idea **idea** *f.* 4
if **si** *conj.* 4
illness **enfermedad** *f.* 10
important **importante** *adj.* 3
   be important to **importar** *v.* 7
impossible **imposible** *adj.* 13
improbable **improbable** *adj.* 13
improve **mejorar** *v.* 13
in **en** *prep.* 2
   in the afternoon **de la tarde** 1; **por la tarde** 7
   in the evening **de la noche** 1; **por la noche** 7
   in the morning **de la mañana** 1; **por la mañana** 7
   in love with **enamorado/a de** 5
in front of **delante de** *prep.* 2
increase **aumento** *m.* 16
incredible **increíble** *adj.* 5
inequality **desigualdad** *f.*
infection **infección** *f.* 10
inform **informar** *v.*
injection **inyección** *f.* 10
   give an injection **poner** *v.* **una inyección** 10
injure (oneself) **lastimarse** *v.* 10
   injure (one's foot) **lastimarse (el pie)** 10
inner ear **oído** *m.* 10

insist (on) **insistir** *v.* **(en)** 12
installments: pay in installments **pagar** *v.* **a plazos** 14
intelligent **inteligente** *adj.* 3
intend to **pensar** *v.* **(+ inf.)** 4
interest **interesar** *v.* 7
interesting **interesante** *adj.* 3
   be interesting to **interesar** *v.* 7
international **internacional** *adj. m., f.*
Internet **red** *f.*; **Internet** *m.* 11
interview **entrevista** *f.* 16; interview **entrevistar** *v.* 16
interviewer **entrevistador(a)** *m., f.* 16
introduction **presentación** *f.*
invest **invertir (i:ie)** *v.* 16
invite **invitar** *v.* 9
iron (clothes) **planchar** *v.* **la ropa** 12
Italian **italiano/a** *adj.* 3
its **su(s)** *poss. adj.* 3 , **suyo/a(s)** *poss. pron.* 11

jacket **chaqueta** *f.* 6
January **enero** *m.* 5
Japanese **japonés, japonesa** *adj.* 3
jeans **bluejeans** *m., pl.* 6
jewelry store **joyería** *f.* 14
job **empleo** *m.* 16; **puesto** *m.* 16; **trabajo** *m.* 16
   job application **solicitud** *f.* **de trabajo** 16
jog **correr** *v.* 3
journalism **periodismo** *m.* 2
journalist **periodista** *m., f.* 3; **reportero/a** *m., f.* 16
joy **alegría** *f.* 9
   give joy **dar** *v.* **alegría** 9
joyful **alegre** *adj.* 5
juice **jugo** *m.* 8
July **julio** *m.* 5
June **junio** *m.* 5
jungle **selva** *f.* 13, **jungla** *f.*
just **apenas** *adv.* 10
   have just (*done something*) **acabar de (+ inf.)** 6

key **llave** *f.* 5
keyboard **teclado** *m.* 11
kilometer **kilómetro** *m.* 11
kind: That's very kind of you. **Muy amable.** *adj.* 5
kiss (each other) **besar(se)** *v.* 11; **beso** *m.* 9
kitchen **cocina** *f.* 12
knee **rodilla** *f.* 10
knife **cuchillo** *m.* 12
know **saber** *v.* 8; **conocer** *v.* 8

L

laboratory **laboratorio** *m.* 2
lack **faltar** *v.* 7
lake **lago** *m.* 5
lamp **lámpara** *f.* 12
land **tierra** *f.* 13
landlord **dueño/a** *m., f.* 8
landscape **paisaje** *m.* 13
language **lengua** *f.* 2
laptop (computer) **computadora** *f.* **portátil** 11
large (*clothing size*) **talla** *f.* **grande** *adj.* 6
last **durar** *v.*; **pasado/a** *adj.* 6; **último/a** *adj.* 15
   last name **apellido** *m.* 9
   last night **anoche** *adv.* 6
late **tarde** *adv.* 7
later **más tarde** *adv.* 7
   See you later. **Hasta la vista.** 1; **Hasta luego.** 1
laugh **reírse (e:i)** *v.* 9
laughed **reído** *p.p.* 14
laundromat **lavandería** *f.* 14
law **ley** *f.* 13
lawyer **abogado/a** *m., f.* 16
lazy **perezoso/a** *adj.*
learn **aprender** *v.* 3
leave **salir** *v.* 4; **irse** *v.* 7
   leave a tip **dejar una propina** 9
   leave for (*a place*) **salir para** 4
   leave from **salir de** 4
   leave behind **dejar** *v.* 16
left **izquierdo/a** *adj.* 2
   be left over **quedar** *v.* 7
   to the left (of) **a la izquierda (de)** 2
leg **pierna** *f.* 10
lemon **limón** *m.* 8
lend **prestar** *v.* 6
less **menos** *adv.* 10
   less . . . than **menos... que** 8
   less than (+ *number*) **menos de (+ *number*)** 8
lesson **lección** *f.* 1
let **dejar** *v.* 12
   let's see **a ver** 2
letter **carta** *f.* 4
lettuce **lechuga** *f.* 8
liberty **libertad** *f.*
library **biblioteca** *f.* 2
license (*driver's*) **licencia** *f.* **de conducir** 11
lie **mentira** *f.* 9
life **vida** *f.* 9
   in my life **en mi vida** 15
lifestyle: lead a healthy lifestyle **llevar una vida sana** 15
lift **levantar** *v.* 15
   lift weights **levantar pesas** 15
light **luz** *f.* 12
like **como** *prep.* 8; **gustar** *v.* 2
   I like . . . **me gusta(n)...** 2
I like . . . very much *v.* **Me encanta...** 2
Do you like . . . ? **¿Te gusta(n)...?** 2
likeable **simpático/a** *adj.* 3
likewise **igualmente** *adv.* 1
line **línea** *f.* 4; **cola** (*queue*) *f.* 14
listen to **escuchar** *v.* 2
   Listen! (*command*) **¡Oye!** *fam.*, *sing.*1; **¡Oigan!** *form.*, *pl.* 5
   listen to music **escuchar música** 2
   listen to the radio **escuchar la radio** 2
literature **literatura** *f.*
little (*quantity*) **poco/a** *adj.* 5
live **vivir** *v.* 3
living room **sala** *f.* 12
loan **préstamo** *m.*; **prestar** *v.* 6, 14
lobster **langosta** *f.*
located **situado/a** *adj.*
   be located **quedar** *v.* 14
lodging **alojamiento** *m.* 5
long **largo/a** *adj.* 6
look for **buscar** *v.* 2
lose **perder (e:ie)** *v.* 4
   lose weight **adelgazar** *v.* 15
lost **perdido/a** *adj.* 14
   be lost **estar perdido/a** 14
lot of, a **mucho/a** *adj.* 2
love (*another person*) **querer (e:ie)** *v.* 4; (*things*) **encantar** *v.* 7 ; **amor** *m.* 9
   in love **enamorado/a** *adj.* 5
luck **suerte** *f.* 3
lucky: be lucky **tener suerte** *adj.* 3
luggage **equipaje** *m.* 5
lunch **almuerzo** *m.* 8
   have lunch **almorzar (o:ue)** *v.* 8

M

ma'am **señora (Sra.)** *f.* 1
mad **enojado/a** *adj.* 5
magazine **revista** *f.* 4
magnificent **magnífico/a** *adj.* 6
mail **correo** *m.* 14; **enviar** *v.*, **mandar** *v.* 14
   mail carrier **cartero/a** *m.* 14
mailbox **buzón** *m.* 14
main **principal** *adj. m., f.* 8
maintain **mantener** *v.* 15
make **hacer** *v.* 4
   make the bed **hacer la cama** 12
make-up **maquillaje** *m.* 7
man **hombre** *m.* 1
manager **gerente** *m., f.* 16
many **mucho/a** *adj.* 2, 3
   many times **muchas veces** 10
map **mapa** *m.* 1
March **marzo** *m.* 5
margarine **margarina** *f.* 8
marinated fish **ceviche** *m.* 8
   marinated shrimp **ceviche de camarón** 8
marital status **estado** *m.* **civil** 9
market **mercado** *m.* 6
marriage **matrimonio** *m.* 9
married **casado/a** *adj.* 9
   get married (to) **casarse** *v.* **(con)** 9
marvelous **maravilloso/a** *adj.* 5
marvelously **maravillosamente** *adv.* 18
massage **masaje** *m.* 15
masterpiece **obra** *f.* **maestra**
match (*sports*) **partido** *m.* 4
   match **hacer** *v.* **juego (con)** 6
mathematics **matemáticas** *f., pl.* 2
matter **importar** *v.* 7
maturity **madurez** *f.* 9
maximum **máximo/a** *m.* 11
May **mayo** *m.* 5
maybe **tal vez** *adv.* 5; **quizás** *adv.* 5
mayonnaise **mayonesa** *f.* 8
meal **comida** *f.* 8
means of communication **medios** *m., pl.* **de comunicación**
meat **carne** *f.* 8
mechanic **mecánico/a** *m., f.* 11
   mechanic's repair shop **taller** *m.* **mecánico** 11
media **medios** *m., pl.* **de comunicación**
medical **médico/a** *adj.* 10
medication **medicamento** *m.* 10
medicine **medicina** *f.* 10
medium **mediano/a** *adj.* 6
meet (each other) **encontrar(se)** *v.* 11
meeting **reunión** *f.* 16
menu **menú** *m.* 8
message (*telephone*) **recado** *m.* 11
Mexican **mexicano/a** *adj.* 3
Mexico **México** *m.* 1
microwave **microonda** *f.* 12
   microwave oven **horno** *m.* **de microondas** 12
middle age **madurez** *f.* 9
midnight **medianoche** *f.* 1
mile **milla** *f.* 11
milk **leche** *f.* 8
million **millón** *m.* 5
   million of **millón de** 5
mine **mío/a(s)** *poss. pron.* 11
mineral **mineral** *m.* 15
   mineral water **agua** *f.* **mineral** 8
minute **minuto** *m.* 1
mirror **espejo** *m.* 7
Miss **señorita (Srta.)** *f.* 1
mistaken **equivocado/a** *adj.* 5
modem **módem** *m.* 11
modern **moderno/a** *adj.*
mom **mamá** *f.* 1
Monday **lunes** *m., sing.* 2
money **dinero** *m.* 6

monitor **monitor** *m.* 11
month **mes** *m.* 5
monument **monumento** *m.* 4
moon **luna** *f.* 13
more **más**
    more . . . than **más… que** 8
    more than (+ *number*) **más de**
      (+ *number*) 8
morning **mañana** *f.* 1
mother **madre** *f.* 3
mother-in-law **suegra** *f.* 3
motor **motor** *m.* 11
motorcycle **moto(cicleta)** *f.* 5
mountain **montaña** *f.* 4
mouse **ratón** *m.* 11
mouth **boca** *f.* 10
move (*to another house/city/country*)
    mudarse *v.* 12
movie **película** *f.* 4
    movie star **estrella** *f.* **de**
      cine
    movie theater **cine** *m.* 4
Mr. **señor (Sr.)** *m.* 1
Mrs. **señora (Sra.)** *f.* 1
much **mucho/a** *adj.* 2, 3
municipal **municipal** *adj., m., f.* 4
murder **crimen** *m.*
muscle **músculo** *m.* 15
museum **museo** *m.* 4
mushroom **champiñón** *m.* 8
music **música** *f.* 2
musical **musical** *adj.*
musician **músico/a** *m., f.*
must: It must be . . . **Debe ser…** 6
my **mi(s)** *poss. adj.* 3; **mío/a(s)**
    poss. pron. 11

N

name **nombre** *m.* 5
    in the name of **a nombre de** 5
    last name **apellido** *m.* 9
    My name is . . . **Me llamo…** 1
    be named **llamarse** *v.* 7
napkin **servilleta** *f.* 12
national **nacional** *adj., m., f.*
nationality **nacionalidad** *f.* 1
natural **natural** *adj., m., f.* 13
    natural disaster **desastre** *m.*
      natural
    natural resource **recurso** *m.*
      natural 13
nature **naturaleza** *f.* 13
nauseated **mareado/a** *adj.* 10
near **cerca de** *prep.* 2
necessary **necesario/a** *adj.* 12
    It is necessary that . . . **Hay**
      que… 14
neck **cuello** *m.* 10
need **faltar** *v.* 7; **necesitar** *v.* 2
negative **negativo/a** *adj.*
neighbor **vecino/a** *m., f.* 12
neighborhood **barrio** *m.* 12

neither . . . nor **ni… ni** *conj.* 7; neither
    tampoco *adv.* 7
nephew **sobrino** *m.* 3
nervous **nervioso/a** *adj.* 5
network **red** *f.*
never **nunca** *adv.* 7; **jamás** *adv.* 7
new **nuevo/a** *adj.* 6
newlywed **recién casado/a**
    m., f. 9
news **noticias** *f., pl.*; **actualidades**
    f., pl.
newscast **noticiero** *m.*
newspaper **periódico** *m.* 4; **diario**
    m.
next **próximo/a** *adj.* 16
nice **simpático/a** *adj.* 3; **amable** *adj.,*
    m., f. 5
niece **sobrina** *f.* 3
night **noche** *f.* 1
    night stand **mesita** *f.* **de**
      noche 12
nine **nueve** *adj., pron.* 1
nine hundred **novecientos/as** *adj.,*
    pron. 5
nineteen **diecinueve** *adj., pron.* 1
ninety **noventa** *adj., pron.* 2
ninth **noveno/a** *adj., pron.* 5
no no 1; **ningún, ninguno/a(s)** *adj.* 7
    no one **nadie** *pron.* 7
    No problem. **Ningún**
      problema. 7
    no way **de ninguna**
      manera 16
none **ningún, ninguno/a(s)**
    adj. 7
noon **mediodía** *m.* 1
nor **ni** *conj.* 7
north **norte** *m.* 14
    to the north **al norte** 14
nose **nariz** *f.* 10
not no 1
    not any **ningún, ninguno/a(s)**
      adj. 7
    not anyone **nadie** *pron.* 7
    not anything **nada** *pron.* 7
    not bad at all **nada mal** 5
    not either **tampoco** *adv.* 7
    not ever **nunca** *adv.* 7; **jamás**
      adv. 7
    not very well **no muy bien** 1
    not working **descompuesto/a**
      adj. 11
notebook **cuaderno** *m.* 1
nothing **nada** *pron.* 1
noun **sustantivo** *m.*
November **noviembre** *m.* 5
now **ahora** *adv.* 2
nowadays **hoy día** *adv.* 5
nuclear **nuclear** *adj., m., f.* 13
number **número** *m.* 1
nurse **enfermero/a** *m., f.* 10
nutrition **nutrición** *f.* 15

O

o'clock: It's . . . o'clock **Son**
    las… 1
    It's one o'clock. **Es la una.** 1
obey **obedecer (c:zc)** *v.*
obligation **deber** *m.*
obtain **conseguir (e:i)** *v.* 4; **obtener** *v.*
    16
obvious **obvio/a** *adj.* 13
occupation **ocupación** *f.* 16
occur **ocurrir** *v.*
ocean **mar** *m.*; **océano** *m.* 13
October **octubre** *m.* 5
of **de** *prep.* 1
    of course **claro que sí** 16; **por**
      supuesto 16
offer **oferta** *f.* 12; **ofrecer (c:cz)** *v.* 8
office (*medical*) **consultorio** *m.* 10;
    oficina *f.* 12
often **a menudo** *adv.* 10
Oh! **¡Ay!** 10
oil **aceite** *m.* 8
okay **regular** *adj.* 1
    It's okay. **Está bien.** 11
old **viejo/a** *adj.* 3; old age **vejez** *f.* 9
older **mayor** *adj., m., f.* 3
    older brother, sister **hermano/a**
      mayor *m., f.* 3
oldest **el/la mayor** 8
on **en** *prep.* 2: **sobre** *prep.* 2
    on behalf of **por** *prep.* 11
    on the dot **en punto** *adv.* 1
    on time **a tiempo** *adv.* 10
    on top of **encima de** *prep.* 2
once **una vez** 6
one **un, uno/a** *adj., pron.* 1
    one hundred **cien(to)** 5
    one million **un millón** 5
    one more time **una vez más** 9
    one thousand **mil** 4
    one time **una vez** 6
    one way (*travel*) **ida** *f.* 5
onion **cebolla** *f.* 8
only **sólo** *adv.* 3; **único/a** *adj.* 3
    only child **hijo/a único/a**
      m., f. 3
open **abierto/a** *adj.* 5; **abrir** *v.* 3
open-air **al aire libre** 6
opera **ópera** *f.*
operation **operación** *f.* 10
opposite **en frente de** *prep.* 14
or **o** *conj.* 7
orange **anaranjado/a** *adj.* 6; **naranja** *f.*
    8
orchestra **orquesta** *f.*
order **mandar** 12; (*food*) **pedir (e:i)** *v.*
    8
    in order to **para** *prep.* 11
orderly **ordenado/a** *adj.* 5
ordinal (*numbers*) **ordinal** *adj.*
other **otro/a** *adj.* 6

our **nuestro/a(s)** *poss. adj.* 3; *poss. pron.* 11
out of order **descompuesto/a** *adj.* 11
outside **fuera** *adv.* 8
outskirts **afueras** *f., pl.* 12
oven **horno** *m.* 12
over **sobre** *prep.* 2
own **propio/a** *adj.* 16
owner **dueño/a** *m., f.* 8

P

P.M. **tarde** *f.* 1
pack the suitcases **hacer** *v.* **las maletas** 5
package **paquete** *m.* 14
page **página** *f.* 11
pain **dolor** *m.* 10
    have a pain in the (knee) **tener** *v.* **dolor de (rodilla)**
paint **pintar** *v.* 17
painter **pintor(a)** *m., f.* 16
painting **pintura** *f.*
pair **par** *m.* 6
pants **pantalones** *m., pl.* 6
pantyhose **medias** *f., pl.* 6
paper **papel** *m.* 2; (*report*) **informe** *m.*
    paper money **billete** *m.* 8
paragraph **párrafo** *m.* 5
Pardon me. (*May I?*) **con permiso** 1; (*Excuse me.*) Pardon me. **Perdón.** 1
parents **padres** *m., pl.* 3; **papás** *m., pl.* 3
park **estacionar** *v.* 11; **parque** *m.* 4
partner (*one of a married couple*) **pareja** *f.* 9
party **fiesta** *f.* 9
pass **pasar** *v.* 12
passed **pasado/a** *p.p.* 15
passenger **pasajero/a** *m., f.* 1
passport **pasaporte** *m.* 5
past **pasado/a** *adj.* 6
pastime **pasatiempo** *m.* 4
pastry shop **pastelería** *f.* 14
patient **paciente** *m., f.* 10
patio **patio** *m.*
pay in cash **pagar** *v.* **al contado; pagar en efectivo** 14
pay in installments **pagar** *v.* **a plazos** 14
pay the bill **pagar** *v.* **la cuenta** 9
pea **arveja** *m.* 8
peace **paz** *f.*
peach **melocotón** *m.*
pear **pera** *f.*
pen **pluma** *f.* 2
pencil **lápiz** *m.* 1
penicillin **penicilina** *f.* 10
people **gente** *f.* 3
pepper (*black*) **pimienta** *f.* 8

perfect **perfecto/a** *adj.* 5
perhaps **quizás** *adv.* 5; **tal vez** *adv.* 5
periods **plazos** *m., pl.* 14
permission **permiso** *m.* 1
person **persona** *f.* 3
pharmacy **farmacia** *f.* 10
phenomenal **fenomenal** *adj.* 5
photograph **foto(grafía)** *f.* 1
physical (*medical examination*) **examen** *m.* **médico** 10
physician **doctor** *m.* 3
physics **física** *f., sing.* 2
pick up **recoger** *v.* 13
picture **cuadro** *m.* 12
pie **pastel** *m.* 9
pill (*tablet*) **pastilla** *f.* 10
pillow **almohada** *f.* 12
pineapple **piña** *f.* 8
pink **rosado/a** *adj.* 6
place **lugar** *m.* 4; **poner** *v.* 4
plaid **de cuadros** *adj.* 6
plan (*to do something*) **pensar** *v.* (**+ inf.**) 4
plane **avión** *m.* 5
plans **planes** *m., pl.* 4
    have plans **tener** *v.* **planes** 4
plant **planta** *f.* 13
plastic **plástico** *m.* 13
    (made of) plastic **de plástico** 13
plate **plato** *m.* 12
    platter of fried food **fuente** *f.* **de fritada** 8
play **drama** *m.*; **comedia** *f.*; **jugar (u:ue)** *v.* 4; (*a musical instrument*) **tocar** *v.*; (*a role*) **hacer** *v.* **el papel**; (*cards*) **jugar** *v.* **a (las cartas)** 5; (*sports*) **practicar** *v.* **deportes** 4
player **jugador(a)** *m., f.* 4
playwright **dramaturgo/a** *m., f.*
plead **rogar (o:ue)** *v.* 12
pleasant **agradable** *adj.* 5
Please. **Por favor.** 1
Pleased to meet you. **Mucho gusto.** 1; **Encantado/a.** *adj.* 1
pleasing: be pleasing to **gustar** *v.* 7
pleasure **gusto** *m.* 1; **placer** *m.* 15
    It's a pleasure to . . . **Gusto de (+ inf.)**
    It's been a pleasure. **Ha sido un placer.** 15
    The pleasure is mine. **El gusto es mío.** 1
poem **poema** *m.*
poet **poeta** *m., f.*
poetry **poesía** *f.*
police (*force*) **policía** *f.* 11
    police officer **policía** *m.*, **mujer** *f.* **policía** 11
political **político/a** *adj.*

politician **político/a** *m., f.* 16
politics **política** *f.*
polka-dotted **de lunares** *adj.* 6
poll **encuesta** *f.*
pollute **contaminar** *v.* 13
polluted **contaminado/a** *adj. m., f.* 13
    be polluted **estar contaminado/a** 13
pollution **contaminación** *f.* 4
pool **piscina** *f.* 4
poor **pobre** *adj.* 6
population **población** *f.* 13
pork **cerdo** *m.* 8
    pork chop **chuleta** *f.* **de cerdo** 8
portable **portátil** *adj.* 11
    portable computer **computadora** *f.* **portátil** 11
position **puesto** *m.* 16
possessive **posesivo/a** *adj.* 3
possible **posible** *adj.* 13
post office **correo** *m.* 14
postcard **postal** *f.* 4; **tarjeta** *f.* **postal** 4
poster **cartel** *m.*
potato **papa** *f.* 8; **patata** *f.* 8
pottery **cerámica** *f.*
practice **entrenarse** *v.* 15; **practicar** *v.* 2
prefer **preferir (e:ie)** *v.* 4
pregnant **embarazada** *adj. f.* 10
prepare **preparar** *v.* 2
preposition **preposición** *f.*
prescribe (*medicine*) **recetar** *v.* 10
prescription **receta** *f.* 10
present **regalo** *m.* 6; **presentar** *v.*
press **prensa** *f.*
pressure: be under a lot of pressure **sufrir** *v.* **muchas presiones** 15
pretty **bonito/a** *adj.* 3; **bastante** *adv.* 13
price **precio** *m.* 6
    fixed price **precio** *m.* **fijo** 6
print **estampado/a** *adj.* 6; **imprimir** *v.* 11
printer **impresora** *f.* 11
private (*room*) **individual** *adj.* 5
prize **premio** *m.*
probable **probable** *adj.* 13
problem **problema** *m.* 1
profession **profesión** *f.* 3
professor **profesor(a)** *m., f.* 1
program **programa** *m.* 1
programmer **programador(a)** *m., f.* 3
prohibit **prohibir** *v.* 10
promotion (*career*) **ascenso** *m.* 16
pronoun **pronombre** *m.*
protect **proteger** *v.* 13
protein **proteína** *f.* 15
provided that **con tal (de) que** *conj.* 13

psychologist **psicólogo/a**
  m., f. 16
psychology **psicología** *f.* 2
publish **publicar** *v.*
Puerto Rican **puertorriqueño/a** *adj.* 3
Puerto Rico **Puerto Rico** *m.* 1
pull a tooth **sacar** *v.* **una muela** 10
purchases **compras** *f., pl.* 5
pure **puro/a** *adj.* 13
purple **morado/a** *adj.* 6
purse **bolsa** *f.* 6
put **poner** *v.* 4; **puesto/a** *p.p.* 14
  put a letter in the mailbox **echar** *v.*
    una carta al buzón 14
  put on (*a performance*)
    presentar *v.*
  put on (*clothing*) **ponerse** *v.* 7
  put on makeup **maquillarse**
    v. 7

Q

quality **calidad** *f.* 6
quarter **trimestre** *m.* 2
  quarter after (*time*) **y cuarto** 1;
    y quince 1
  quarter to (*time*) **menos cuarto**
    1; **menos quince** 1
question **pregunta** *f.* 2
quickly **rápido** *adv.* 8
quiet **tranquilo/a** *adj.* 15
quit **dejar** *v.* 16
quiz **prueba** *f.* 2

R

racism **racismo** *m.*
radio (*medium*) **radio** *f.* 2; radio
  (*receiver*) **radio** *m.* 2, 11
rain **llover (o:ue)** *v.* 5; **lluvia** *f.* 13
  It's raining. **Llueve.** 5
raincoat **impermeable** *m.* 6
rainforest **bosque** *m.* **tropical** 13
raise (*salary*) **aumento** *v.* **de**
  sueldo 16
read **leer** *v.* 3; **leído/a** *p.p.* 14
ready **listo/a** *adj.* 15
reap the benefits (of) **disfrutar** *v.* **(de)**
  15
reason **razón** *f.* 3
receive **recibir** *v.* 3
recommend **recomendar (e:ie)**
  v. 8
recycle **reciclar** *v.* 13
recycling **reciclaje** *m.* 13
red **rojo/a** *adj.* 6
red-headed **pelirrojo/a** *adj.* 3
reduce **reducir** *v.* 13
  reduce stress/tension **aliviar el**
    estrés/la tensión 15
refrigerator **refrigerador** *m.* 12
region **región** *f.* 13
regret **sentir (e:ie)** *v.* 13
related to sitting **sedentario/a** *adj.* 15

relationships **relaciones** *f., pl.*
relatives **parientes** *m., pl.* 3
relax **relajarse** *v.* 9
remain **quedarse** *v.* 7
remember **acordarse (o:ue)** *v.* **(de)** 7;
  recordar (o:ue) *v.* 4
remote control **control** *m.* **remoto**
rent **alquilar** *v.* 12; **alquiler** *m.* 12
repeat **repetir (e:i)** *v.* 4
report **informe** *m.* 18; **reportaje** *m.*
reporter **reportero/a** *m., f.* 16
representative **representante** *m., f.*
request **pedir (e:i)** *v.* 4
reservation **reservación** *f.* 5
resign (from) **renunciar (a)** *v.* 16
resolve **resolver (o:ue)** *v.* 13
resolved **resuelto/a** *p.p.* 14
resource **recurso** *m.* 13
responsibility **deber** *v.*
rest **descansar** *v.* 2
  the rest **lo/los/las demás**
    pron. 5
restaurant **restaurante** *m.* 4
résumé **currículum** *m.* 16
retire (from work) **jubilarse** *v.* 9
return **regresar** *v.* 2; **volver (o:ue)** *v.* 4
  return trip **vuelta** *f.* 5
returned **vuelto/a** *p.p.* 14
rice **arroz** *m.* 8
rich **rico/a** *adj.* 6
ride **pasear** *v.* 4
  ride a bicycle **pasear en**
    bicicleta 4
  ride a horse **montar a**
    caballo 5
ridiculous **ridículo/a** *adj.* 13
right **derecha** *f.* 2;
  right here **aquí mismo** 11
  right now **ahora mismo** 5
  right there **allí mismo** 14
  right away **enseguida** *adv.* 9
  be right **tener** *v.* **razón** 3
  to the right (of) **a la derecha**
    (de) 2
  right? (*question tag*) **¿no?** 1;
    ¿verdad? 1
rights **derechos** *m., pl.*
ring (*a doorbell*) **sonar (o:ue)**
  v. 11
river **río** *m.* 13
road **camino** *m.* 11
roast chicken **pollo** *m.* **asado** 8
roasted **asado/a** *adj.* 8
role **papel** *m.*
rollerblade **patinar** *v.* **en línea** 4
romantic **romántico/a** *adj.*
room **habitación** *f.* 5; **cuarto**
  m. 7; (*large, living*) **sala** *f.* 12
roommate **compañero/a**
  m., f. **de cuarto** 2
roundtrip **de ida y vuelta** 5
  roundtrip ticket **pasaje** *m.* **de**
    ida y vuelta 5
routine **rutina** *f.* 7
rug **alfombra** *f.* 12

run **correr** *v.* 3
  run errands **hacer**
    diligencias 14
  run into (*have an accident*)
    chocar *v.* **(con)** 11; (*meet*
    accidentally) **darse con** *v.*
rush **apurarse** *v.* 15
Russian **ruso/a** *adj.*

S

sad **triste** *adj.* 5
said **dicho/a** *p.p.* 14
sake: for the sake of **por** *prep.* 11
salad **ensalada** *f.* 8
salary **salario** *m.* 16; **sueldo**
  m. 16
sale **rebaja** *f.* 6
salesperson **vendedor(a)** *m., f.* 6
salmon **salmón** *m.* 8
salt **sal** *f.* 8
same **mismo/a** *adj.* 3
sandal **sandalia** *f.* 6
sandwich **sándwich** *m.* 8
Saturday **sábado** *m.* 2
sausage **salchicha** *f.* 8
save (*on a computer*) **guardar**
  v. 11; save (*money*) **ahorrar**
  v. 14
savings **ahorros** *m., pl.* 14
  savings account **cuenta** *f.* **de**
    ahorros 14
say (that) **decir (que)** *v.* 9; **declarar** *v.*
scarcely **apenas** *adv.* 10
scared: be scared (of) **tener** *v.* **miedo**
  (de) 3
schedule **horario** *m.* 2
school **escuela** *f.* 1
science **ciencia** *f.*
  science fiction **ciencia ficción**
    f.
scientist **científico/a** *m., f.* 16
scream **gritar** *v.* 7
screen **pantalla** *f.* 11
scuba dive **bucear** *v.* 4
sculpt **esculpir** *v.*
sculptor **escultor(a)** *m., f.*
sculpture **escultura** *f.*
sea **mar** *m.* 5; **océano** *m.* 5
season **estación** *f.* 5
seat **silla** *f.* 2
second **segundo/a** *adj.* 5
secretary **secretario/a** *m., f.* 16
sedentary **sedentario/a** *adj.* 15
see **ver** *v.* 4
  see (you) again **volver** *v.* **a**
    ver(te, lo, la)
  see movies **ver películas** 4
  See you. **Nos vemos.** 1
  See you later. **Hasta la vista.** 1;
    Hasta luego. 1
  See you soon. **Hasta pronto.** 1
  See you tomorrow. **Hasta**
    mañana. 1

seem **parecer** *v.* 8
seen **visto/a** *p.p.* 14
sell **vender** *v.* 6
semester **semestre** *m.* 2
send **enviar** *v.*; **mandar** *v.* 14
separate (from) **separarse** *v.*
   (de) 9
separated **separado/a** *adj.*
September **septiembre** *m.* 5
sequence **secuencia** *f.*
serious **grave** *adj.* 10
serve **servir (e:i)** *v.* 8
set (*fixed*) **fijo** *adj.* 6
   set the table **poner** *v.* **la mesa** 12
seven **siete** *adj., pron.* 1
seven hundred **setecientos/as** *adj.,*
   pron. 5
seventeen **diecisiete** *adj., pron.* 1
seventh **séptimo/a** *adj., pron.* 5
seventy **setenta** *adj., pron.* 2
sexism **sexismo** *m.*
shame **lástima** *f.* 13
   It's a shame that . . . **Es (una)**
     lástima que... 13
shampoo **champú** *m.* 7
shape **forma** *f.* 15
   be in good shape **estar en**
     buena forma 15
share **compartir** *v.* 3
sharp (*time*) **en punto** 1
shave **afeitarse** *v.* 7
shaving cream **crema** *f.* **de afeitar** 7
shellfish **mariscos** *m., pl.* 8
ship **barco** *m.* 5
shirt **camisa** *f.* 6
shoe **zapato** *m.* 6
   shoe size **número** *m.* **de zapato** 6
   shoe store **zapatería** *f.* 14
   tennis shoes **zapatos** *m., pl.* **de**
     tenis 6
shop **tienda** *f.* 6
shopping, to go **ir** *v.* **de compras** 6
   shopping mall **centro** *m.*
     comercial 6
short (*in height*) **bajo/a** *adj.* 3; (*in*
   length) **corto/a** *adj.* 6
short story **cuento** *m.*
shorts **pantalones cortos** *m., pl.* 6
should (*do something*) **deber** *v.*
   (+ inf.) 3
show **espectáculo** *m.*; **mostrar (o:ue)**
   v. 4
shower **ducha** *f.*; **ducharse** *v.* 7;
   bañarse *v.* 7
shrimp **camarón** *m.* 8
sick **enfermo/a** *adj.* 10
   be sick **estar enfermo/a** 10
   get sick **enfermarse** *v.* 10
sightseeing: go sightseeing **hacer** *v.*
   turismo 5
sign **firmar** *v.* 14; **letrero** *m.* 14
silk **seda** *f.* 6; (made of) **de**
   seda 6
silly **tonto/a** *adj.* 3
silverware **cubierto** *m.* 12

similar **similar** *adj. m., f.*
since **desde** *prep.* 6
sing **cantar** *v.* 2
singer **cantante** *m., f.*
single **soltero/a** *adj.* 9
   single room **habitación** *f.*
     individual 5
sink **lavabo** *m.*
sir **señor (Sr.)** *m.* 1
sister **hermana** *f.* 3
sister-in-law **cuñada** *f.* 3
sit down **sentarse (e:ie)** *v.* 7
six **seis** *adj., pron.* 1
six hundred **seiscientos/as** *adj.,*
   pron. 5
sixteen **dieciséis** *adj., pron.* 1
sixth **sexto/a** *adj., pron.* 5
sixty **sesenta** *adj., pron.* 2
size **talla** *f.* 6
   shoe size **número** *m.* **de zapato** 6
skate (in-line) **patinar** *v.*
   (en línea) 4
ski **esquiar** *v.* 4
skiing **esquí** *m.* 4
   water-skiing **esquí acuático** 4
skirt **falda** *f.* 6
sky **cielo** *m.* 13
sleep **dormir (o:ue)** *v.* 4; **sueño** *m.* 3
   go to sleep **dormirse**
     (o:ue) *v.* 7
sleepy: be sleepy **tener** *v.* **sueño** 3
slender **delgado/a** *adj.* 3
slim down **adelgazar** *v.* 15
slow **lento/a** *adj.* 11
slowly **despacio** *adv.* 8
small **pequeño/a** *adj.* 3
smart **listo/a** *adj.* 5
smile **sonreír (e:i)** *v.* 9
smiled **sonreído** *p.p.* 14
smoggy: It's (very) smoggy. **Hay**
   (mucha) contaminación. 4
smoke **fumar** *v.* 8, 15
smoking section **sección** *f.* **de fumar**
   8
   (non) smoking section **sección**
     de (no) fumar 8
snack (in the afternoon) **merendar** *v.*
   15; (afternoon snack)
     merienda *f.* 15
   have a snack **merendar** *v.* 15
sneeze **estornudar** *v.* 10
snow **nevar (e:ie)** *v.* 5; **nieve** *f.* 8
snowing: It's snowing. **Nieva.** 5
so (in such a way) **así** *adj.* 10; **tan**
   adv. 8
   so much **tanto** *adv.* 12
   so so **así así** 1, **regular** 1
   so that **para que** *conj.* 13
soap **jabón** *m.* 7
   soap opera **telenovela** *f.*
soccer **fútbol** *m.* 4
sociology **sociología** *f.* 2
sock **calcetín** *m.* 6
sofa **sofá** *m.* 12
soft drink **refresco** *m.* 8

software **programa** *m.* **de**
   computación 11
soil **tierra** *f.* 13
solar (*energy*) **solar** *adj., m., f.* 13
solution **solución** *f.* 13
solve **resolver (o:ue)** *v.* 13
some **algún, alguno/a(s)** *adj.* 7;
   unos/as *pron.* 1
somebody **alguien** *pron.* 7
someone **alguien** *pron.* 7
something **algo** *pron.* 7
sometimes **a veces** *adv.* 10
son **hijo** *m.* 3
song **canción** *f.*
son-in-law **yerno** *m.* 3
soon **pronto** *adj.* 10
   See you soon. **Hasta pronto.** 1
sorry: be sorry **sentir (e:ie)** *v.* 13
   I'm sorry. **Lo siento.** 1
   I'm extremely sorry. **Mil**
     perdones. 4
soup **caldo** *m.* 8; **sopa** *f.* 8
south **sur** *m.* 14
   to the south **al sur** 14
Spain **España** *f.* 1
Spanish (*language*) **español** *m.* 2;
   español(a) *adj.; m., f.* 3
spare time **ratos** *m., pl.* **libres** 4
speak **hablar** *v.* 2
specialization **especialización**
   f. 16
spectacular **espectacular** *adj.* 15
speech **discurso** *m.*
speed **velocidad** *f.* 11
   speed limit **velocidad**
     máxima 11
spelling **ortográfico/a** *adj.*
spend (*money*) **gastar** *v.* 6
   spend time **pasar** *v.* **tiempo** 4
spoon (*table or large*) **cuchara**
   f. 12
sport **deporte** *m.* 4
   sports-loving **deportivo/a**
     adj. 4
   sports-related **deportivo/a**
     adj. 4
spouse **esposo/a** *m., f.* 3
sprain (an ankle) **torcerse** *v.*
   (el tobillo) 10
sprained **torcido/a** *adj.* 10
   be sprained **estar** *v.* **torcido/a** 10
spring **primavera** *f.* 5
stadium **estadio** *m.* 2
stage **etapa** *f.* 9
stairs **escalera** *f.* 12
stairway **escalera** *f.* 12
stamp **estampilla** *f.* 14; **sello**
   m. 14
stand in line **hacer** *v.* **cola** 14
star **estrella** *f.* 13
start (*a vehicle*) **arrancar** *v.* 11
state **estado** *m.* 2
station **estación** *f.* 5
statue **estatua** *f.*
status: marital status **estado** *m.*
   civil 9

stay **quedarse** *v.* 7
   Stay calm! **¡Tranquilo!** *adj.* 7
   stay in shape **mantenerse** *v.* **en forma** 15
steak **bistec** *m.* 8
steering wheel **volante** *m.* 11
step **etapa** *f.* 9
stepbrother **hermanastro** *m.* 3
stepdaughter **hijastra** *f.* 3
stepfather **padrastro** *m.* 3
stepmother **madrastra** *f.* 3
stepsister **hermanastra** *f.* 3
stepson **hijastro** *m.* 3
stereo **estéreo** *m.* 11
still **todavía** *adv.* 5
stock broker **corredor(a)** *m., f.* **de bolsa** 16
stockings **medias** *f., pl.* 6
stomach **estómago** *m.* 10
stone **piedra** *f.* 13
stop **parar** *v.* 11
   stop (*doing something*) **dejar** *v.* **de (+ inf.)** 13
store **tienda** *f.* 6
storm **tormenta** *f.*
story **cuento** *m.;* **historia** *f.*
stove **estufa** *f.*
straight **derecho** *adj.* 14
   straight ahead **(todo) derecho** 14
strange **extraño/a** *adj.* 13
   It's strange that . . . **Es extraño que...** 13
strawberry **frutilla** *f.;* **fresa** *f.* 8
street **calle** *f.* 11
stress **estrés** *m.* 15
stretching **estiramiento** *m.* 15
   stretching exercises **ejercicios** *m., pl.* **de estiramiento** 15
strike (*labor*) **huelga** *f.*
stripe **raya** *f.* 6
   striped **de rayas** *adj.* 6
stroll **pasear** *v.* 4
strong **fuerte** *adj.* 15
struggle (for) **luchar** *v.* **(por)**
student **estudiante** *m., f.* 1; **estudiantil** *adj.* 2
study **estudiar** *v.* 2
stuffed up (*sinuses*) **congestionado/a** *adj.* 10
stupendous **estupendo/a** *adj.* 5
style **estilo** *m.* 5
suburbs **afueras** *f., pl.* 12
subway **metro** *m.* 5
   subway station **estación** *f.* **del metro** 5
success **éxito** *m.* 16
successful: be successful **tener** *v.* **éxito** 16
such as **tales como** 4
suddenly **de repente** *adv.* 6
suffer **sufrir** *v.* 10
   suffer from an illness **sufrir una enfermedad**
sufficient **bastante** *adj.* 10

sugar **azúcar** *m.* 8
suggest **sugerir (e:ie)** *v.* 12
suit **traje** *m.* 6
suitcase **maleta** *f.* 3
summer **verano** *m.* 5
sun **sol** *m.* 4
sunbathe **tomar** *v.* **el sol** 4
Sunday **domingo** *m.* 2
sunglasses **gafas** *f., pl.* **oscuras/de sol; lentes** *m., pl.* **de sol**
sunny: It's (very) sunny. **Hace (mucho) sol.** 5
supermarket **supermercado** *m.* 14
suppose **suponer** *v.* 4
sure **seguro/a** *adj.* 5
   be sure **estar** *v.* **seguro/a** 5
surf (*Internet*) **navegar** *v.* **(en)** 11
surprise **sorprender** *v.* 9; **sorpresa** *f.* 9
survey **encuesta** *f.*
sweat **sudar** *v.* 15
sweater **suéter** *m.* 6
sweep (the floor) **barrer** *v.* **(el suelo)** 12
sweets **dulces** *m., pl.* 9
swim **nadar** *v.* 4
swimming **natación** *f.* 4
   swimming pool **piscina** *f.* 4
symptom **síntoma** *m.* 10

T

table **mesa** *f.* 2
tablespoon **cuchara** *f.* 12
tablet (*pill*) **pastilla** *f.* 10
take **llevar** *v.* 2; **tomar** *v.* 2, 8
   take care of **cuidar** *v.* **de** 13
   take (someone's) temperature **tomar** *v.* **la temperatura (a alguien)** 10
   take (*wear*) a shoe size **calzar** *v.* 6
   take a bath **bañarse** *v.* 7
   take a shower **ducharse** *v.* 7
   take into account **tomar** *v.* **en cuenta** 8
   take off **quitarse** *v.* 7
   take out (the trash) **sacar** *v.* **(la basura)** 10
   take photos **tomar/sacar** *v.* **fotos**
talented **talentoso/a** *adj.*
talk **hablar** *v.* 2; **conversar** *v.* 2
   talk show **programa** *m.* **de entrevistas**
tall **alto/a** *adj.* 3
tank **tanque** *m.* 11
tape (audio) **cinta** *f.* 11
   tape recorder **grabadora** *f.* 1
taste **probar (o:ue)** *v.* 8
tasty **rico/a** *adj.* 8; **sabroso/a** *adj.* 8
tax **impuesto** *m.*
taxi(cab) **taxi** *m.* 5
tea **té** *m.* 8
teach **enseñar** *v.* 2
teacher **profesor(a)** *m., f.* 1;

(*elementary school*) **maestro/a** *m., f.* 16
team **equipo** *m.* 4
technician **técnico/a** *m., f.* 16
telecommuting **teletrabajo** *m.* 16
teleconference **videoconferencia** *f.* 16
telephone **teléfono** *m.* 11
   cellular telephone **teléfono celular** 11
television **televisión** *f.* 11
   television set **televisor** *m.* 11
tell (that) **decir** *v.* **(que)** 9
temperature **temperatura** *f.* 10
ten **diez** *adj., pron.* 1
tennis **tenis** *m.* 4
   tennis shoes **zapatos** *m., pl.* **de tenis** 6
tension **tensión** *f.* 15
tent **tienda** *f.* **de campaña** 5
tenth **décimo/a** *adj., pron.* 5
terrible **terrible** *adj. m., f.* 13
terrific **chévere** *adj.* 1
test **prueba** *f.* 2; **examen** *m.* 2
Thank you. **Gracias.** *f., pl.* 1
   Thank you (very much). **(Muchas) gracias.** 1
   Thank you very much. **Muchísimas gracias.** 9
   Thanks (a lot). **(Muchas) gracias.** 1
   Thanks again. **Gracias una vez más.** 9
   Thanks for everything. **Gracias por todo.** 9
that **que** *conj.* 12
   that (one) **ése, ésa, eso** *pron.* 6; **ese, esa,** *adj.* 6
   that (*over there*) **aquél, aquélla, aquello** *pron.* 6; **aquel, aquella** *adj.* 6
   that which **lo que** *conj.* 12
   that's why **por eso** 11
theater **teatro** *m.*
their **su(s)** *poss., adj.* 3; **suyo/a(s)** *poss., pron.* 11
then **después** (*afterward*) *adv.* 7; **entonces** (*as a result*) *adv.* 7; **luego** (*next*) *adv.* 1; **pues** *adv.* 15
there **allí** *adv.* 5
   There is/are . . . **Hay...** 1;
   There is/are not . . . **No hay...** 1
therefore **por eso** *adv.* 11
thin **delgado/a** *adj.* 3
thing **cosa** *f.* 1
think **pensar (e:ie)** *v.* 4; (*believe*) **creer** *v.* 3
   think about **pensar en** 4
third **tercero/a** *adj., pron.* 5
thirst **sed** *f.* 3
thirsty: be thirsty **tener** *v.* **sed** 3
thirteen **trece** *adj., pron.* 1
thirty **treinta** *adj., pron.* 1; thirty (*minutes past the hour*) **y treinta; y media** 1

this **este, esta** *adj.*; **éste, ésta, esto**
pron. 6
This is . . . (*introduction*)
Éste/a es... 1
This is he/she. (*on telephone*)
Con él/ella habla. 11
thousand **mil** *m.* 5
three **tres** *adj., pron.* 1
three hundred **trescientos/as** *adj.,*
pron. 5
throat **garganta** *f.* 10
through **por** *prep.* 11
throw **echar** *v.* 14
Thursday **jueves** *m., sing.* 2
thus (*in such a way*) **así** *adj.* 10
ticket **boleto** *m;.* **entrada** *f.;* **pasaje** *m.*
5
tie **corbata** *f.* 6
time **vez** *f.* 6; time **tiempo** *m.* 4
buy on time **comprar** *v.* **a plazos**
m., pl.
have a good/bad time **pasarlo** *v.*
bien/mal 9
We had a great time. **Lo**
pasamos de película.
times **veces** *f., pl.* 4
many times **muchas veces** 10
tip **propina** *f.* 9
tire **llanta** *f.* 11
tired **cansado/a** *adj.* 5
be tired **estar** *v.* **cansado/a** 5
title **título** *m.*
to **a** *prep.* 1
toast (*drink*) **brindar** *v.* 9
toast **pan** *m.* **tostado** 8
toasted **tostado/a** *adj.* 8
toaster **tostadora** *f.*
today **hoy** *adv.* 2
Today is . . . **Hoy es...** 2, 5
together **juntos/as** *adj.* 9
tomato **tomate** *m.* 8
tomorrow **mañana** *adv.* 1
See you tomorrow. **Hasta**
mañana. 1
tonight **esta noche** *adv.* 4
too **también** *adv.* 2
too much **demasiado** *adv.* 6;
en exceso 15
tooth **diente** *m.* 7; tooth **muela**
f. 10
tornado **tornado** *m.*
tortilla **tortilla** *f.* 8
touch **tocar** *v.* 13
tour an area **recorrer** *v.;* **excursión** *f.* 4
go on a tour **hacer** *v.* **una**
excursión 5
tourism **turismo** *m.* 5
tourist **turista** *m., f.* 1; **turístico/a** *adj.*
toward **hacia** *prep.* 14
towel **toalla** *f.* 7
town **pueblo** *m.* 4
trade **oficio** *m.* 16
traffic **circulación** *f.;* **tráfico** *m.* 11
traffic signal **semáforo** *m.* 11

tragedy **tragedia** *f.*
trail **sendero** *m.* 13
trailhead **sendero** *m.* 13
train **entrenarse** *v.* 15; **tren** *m.* 5
train station **estación** *f.* **(de)**
tren *m.* 5
trainer **monitor** *m., f.* 15
translate **traducir** *v.* 8
trash **basura** *f.* 12
travel **viajar** *v.* 2
travel agency **agencia** *f.*
de viajes 5
travel agent **agente** *m., f.*
de viajes 5
travel documents **documentos**
pl.; m. **de viaje**
traveler **viajero/a** *m., f.* 5
traveler's check **cheque** *m.* **de**
viajero 14
tree **árbol** *m.* 13
trillion **billón** *m.* 5
trimester **trimestre** *m.* 2
trip **viaje** *m.* 5
take, go on a trip **hacer** *v.* **un viaje** 5
tropical forest **bosque** *m.*
tropical 13
truck **camión** *m.*
true **cierto/a** *adj.* 13
trunk **baúl** *m.* 11
truth **verdad** *f.* 9
try **intentar** *v.* 8; **probar (o:ue)**
v. 8
try (*to do something*) **tratar** *v.* **de**
(+ inf.) 15
try on **probarse (o:ue)** *v.* 7
t-shirt **camiseta** *f.* 6
Tuesday **martes** *m., sing.* 2
tuna **atún** *m.*
turkey **pavo** *m.* 8
turn **doblar** *v.* 14, 9
turn off (*electricity/appliance*)
apagar *v.* 11
turn on (*electricity/appliance*)
poner *v.* 11; **prender** *v.* 11
twelve **doce** *adj., pron.* 1
twenty **veinte** *adj., pron.* 1
twenty-eight **veintiocho** *adj., pron.* 1
twenty-five **veinticinco** *adj., pron.* 1
twenty-four **veinticuatro** *adj., pron.* 1
twenty-nine **veintinueve** *adj., pron.* 1
twenty-one **veintiún, veintiuno/a** *adj.,*
pron. 1
twenty-seven **veintisiete** *adj., pron.* 1
twenty-six **veintiséis** *adj., pron.* 1
twenty-three **veintitrés** *adj., pron.* 1
twenty-two **veintidós** *adj., pron.* 1
twice **dos veces** 6
twisted **torcido/a** *adj.* 10; be twisted
estar *v.* **torcido/a** 10
two **dos** *adj., pron.* 1
two hundred **doscientos/as** *adj.,*
pron. 5
two times **doce veces** 1, 6

U

ugly **feo/a** *adj.* 3
uncle **tío** *m.* 3
under **bajo** *prep.* 7; **debajo de** *prep.* 2
understand **comprender** *v.* 3;
entender (e:ie) *v.* 4
underwear **ropa** *f.* **interior** 6
unemployment **desempleo** *m.*
United States **Estados Unidos** *m., pl.* 1
university **universidad** *f.* 2
unless **a menos que** *adv.* 13
unmarried **soltero/a** *adj.* 9
unpleasant **antipático/a** *adj.* 3
until **hasta** *prep.* 1; **hasta que** *conj.* 14
up **arriba** *adv.* 15
urgent **urgente** *adj.* 12
use **usar** *v.* 6
useful **útil** *adj.*

V

vacation **vacaciones** *f., pl.* 5
be on vacation **estar** *v.* **de**
vacaciones 5
go on vacation **ir** *v.* **de**
vacaciones 5
vacuum **pasar** *v.* **la aspiradora** 12
vacuum cleaner **aspiradora**
f. 12
valley **valle** *m.* 13
various **varios/as** *adj. m., f., pl.* 8
VCR **videocasetera** *f.* 11
vegetables **verduras** *f., pl.* 8
verb **verbo** *m.*
very **muy** *adv.* 1
very much **muchísimo** *adv.* 2
Very good, thank you. **Muy**
bien, gracias. 1
very well, thanks. **muy bien,**
gracias 1
vest **chaleco** *m.* 6
video **video** *m.* 11
video(cassette) **video(casete)**
m. 11
video conference
videoconferencia *f.* 16
videocamera **cámara** *f.* **de video** 11
vinegar **vinagre** *m.*
violence **violencia** *f.* 18
visit **visitar** *v.* 4
visit monuments **visitar**
monumentos 4
vitamin **vitamina** *f.* 15
volcano **volcán** *m.* 13
volleyball **voleibol** *m.* 4
vote **votar** *v.*

W

wait for **esperar** *v.* 2
waiter **camarero/a** *m., f.* 8
wake up **despertarse (e:ie)** *v.* 7

walk **caminar** v. 2
   take a walk **pasear** v. 4
Walkman **walkman** m.
wall **pared** f. 12
wallet **cartera** f. 6
want **querer (e:ie)** v. 4
war **guerra** f.
warm (oneself) up **calentarse**
   v. 15
wash **lavar** v. 12
   wash one's face/hands **lavarse** v.
   la cara/las manos 7
   wash oneself **lavarse** 7
washing machine **lavadora** f. 12
watch **mirar** v. 2; **reloj** m. 2
   watch television **mirar (la)**
   televisión 2
water **agua** f. 8
   water pollution **contaminación**
   del agua 13
   water-skiing **esquí** m.
   acuático 4
way **manera** f. 16
weak **débil** adj. m., f. 15
wear **llevar** v. 6; **usar** v. 6
weather **tiempo** m. 5
   It's bad weather. **Hace mal**
   tiempo. 5
   It's good weather. **Hace buen**
   tiempo. 5
weaving **tejido** m.
Web site **sitio** m. **Web** 11
wedding **boda** f. 9
Wednesday **miércoles** m., sing. 2
week **semana** f. 2
weekend **fin** m. **de semana** 4
weight **peso** m. 15
   lift weights **levantar** v. **pesas** f., pl.
   15
welcome **bienvenido/a(s)** adj. 12
well **pues** adv. 2; **bueno** adv. 2
well-being **bienestar** m. 15
well organized **ordenado/a** adj. 5
west **oeste** m. 14
   to the west **al oeste** 14
western (genre) **de vaqueros** adj.
what **lo que** 12
   what? adj., pron. **¿qué?** 1;
   At what time . . . ? **¿A qué**
   hora...? 1
   What a . . . ! **¡Qué...!** 1
   What a pleasure to . . . ! **¡Qué**
   gusto (+ inf.)...
   What a surprise! **¡Qué**
   sorpresa! 9
   What day is it? **¿Qué día es**
   hoy? 2
   What did you say? **¿Cómo?** 1
   What do you think? **¿Qué**
   le/les form. **parece?** 9
   What happened? **¿Qué**
   pasó? 11
   What is the date (today)? **¿Cuál**
   es la fecha (de hoy)? 5
   What is the price? **¿Qué precio**

tiene? 6
   What is today's date? **¿Cuál es la**
   fecha de hoy?
   What pain! **¡Qué dolor!** 10
   What pretty clothes! **¡Qué ropa**
   más bonita! 6
   What size do you take? **¿Qué**
   talla lleva (usa)? 6
   What time is it? **¿Qué hora**
   es? 1
   What's going on? **¿Qué**
   pasa? 1
   What's happening? **¿Qué**
   pasa? 1
   What's like? **¿Cómo es...?** 3
   What's new? **¿Qué hay de**
   nuevo? 1
   What's the weather like? **¿Qué**
   tiempo hace? 4
   What's wrong? **¿Qué pasó?** 11
   What's your name? **¿Cómo se**
   llama (usted)? form. 1
   What's your name? **¿Cómo te**
   llamas (tú)? fam. 1
when **cuando** conj. 7
   When? **¿Cuándo?** 2
where **donde** adj., conj.
   where? (destination) **¿adónde?**
   2; (location)**¿dónde?** 1
   Where are you from? **¿De**
   dónde eres (tú)? (fam.) 1;
   ¿De dónde es (Ud.)?
   (form.) 1
   Where is . . .? **¿Dónde**
   está...? 2
   (to) where? **¿adónde?** 2
which? **¿cuál(es)?** adj., pron.; **¿qué?**
   2
   which ones? **¿cuáles?** 2
while **mientras** adv. 10
white **blanco/a** adj. 6
   white wine **vino** m. **blanco** 8
who **quien** pron. 1; **que** pron. 12;
   quien(es) pron. 12
   who? **¿quién(es)?** 1
   Who is . . . ? **¿Quién es...?** 1
   Who is calling? (on telephone)
   ¿De parte de quién? 11
   Who is speaking? (on telephone)
   ¿Quién habla? 11
whole **todo/a** adj. 4
whose **¿de quién(es)?** 1
why? **¿por qué?** adv. 2
widower/widow **viudo/a** adj. 9
wife **esposa** f. 3
win **ganar** v. 4
wind **viento** m. 4
window **ventana** f. 2
windshield **parabrisas** m.,
   sing. 11
windy: It's (very) windy. **Hace**
   (mucho) viento. 5
wine **vino** m. 8
   red wine **vino tinto** 8
   white wine **vino blanco** 8

wineglass **copa** f. 12
winter **invierno** m. 5
wish **desear** v. 2; **esperar** v. 13
   I wish (that) **Ojalá que** 13
with **con** prep. 2
   with me **conmigo** 4, 8
   with you **contigo** fam. 8
within **dentro de** prep. 16
without **sin** prep. 13, 15; **sin que** conj.
   13
   without a doubt **sin duda**
woman **mujer** f. 1
wool **lana** f. 6
   (made of) wool **de lana** 6
word **palabra** f. 1
work **trabajar** v. 2; **funcionar** v. 11;
   trabajo m. 16
   work (of art, literature, music,
   etc.) **obra** f.
   work out **hacer** v. **gimnasia** 15
world **mundo** m. 11
worldwide **mundial** adj. m., f. 5
worried **preocupado/a** adj. 5
worry (about) **preocuparse** v. (por) 7
   Don't worry. **No se preocupe.**
   form. 7
worse **peor** adj. m., f. 8
worst **el/la peor, lo peor**
Would you like to? **¿Te**
   gustaría? 4
write **escribir** v. 3
   write a letter/post card/e-mail
   message **escribir una**
   carta/(tarjeta) postal/
   mensaje m. **electrónico** 4
writer **escritor(a)** m., f.
written **escrito/a** p.p. 14
wrong **equivocado/a** adj. 5
   be wrong **no tener** v. **razón** 3

X

X-ray **radiografía** f. 10

Y

yard **jardín** m. 12; **patio** m.
year **año** m. 2
   be . . . years old **tener** v. . . .
   años 3
yellow **amarillo/a** adj. 6
yes **sí** interj. 1
yesterday **ayer** adv. 6
yet **todavía** adv. 5
yogurt **yogur** m.
You don't say! **¡No me digas!** fam.;
   ¡No me diga! form. 11
You're welcome. **De nada.** 1; **No hay**
   de qué. 1
young **joven** adj. 3
   young person **joven** m., f. 1
   young woman **señorita** f. 2
younger **menor** adj. m., f. 3

younger: younger brother, sister
hermano/a menor *m., f.* 3
youngest **el/la menor** *m., f.* 8
your **su(s)** *poss., adj., form.* 3
your **tu(s)** *poss., adj., fam. sing.* 3
your **vuestro/a(s)** *poss., adj.*
form., pl.
your(s) *form.* **suyo/a(s)**
poss. pron., form. 11
your(s) **tuyo/a(s)** *poss.,*
fam., sing. 11
youth **juventud** *f.* 9; (young person)
joven *m., f.* 1

Z

zero **cero** *m.* 1

Índice

Text Credits

348-349 © Carlos Fuentes, un fragmento de *La Muerte de Artemio Cruz*, 1962, reprinted by permission of Carmen Ballcels Agencia Literaria.

374-375 © Cristina Peri Rossi, "14," de *Indicios Pánicos*, 1970, reprinted by permission of the author.

396-397 © Augusto Monterroso, *Imaginación y destino*, Santiago, Mosquito, 1999, reprinted by permission of International Editors' Co. Barcelona.

Fine Art

99 *Triptych of the Rains: Part 3, To Turn Green Again* by Tomás Sánchez. **102** (*Caña de azúcar*) by Diego Rivera. **155** *Las Meninas* by Diego Rodríguez de Silva y Velázquez.

Illustration Credits

Sophie Casson: 14, 16, 17, 18, 19, 40, 41, 64, 66, 80, 82, 110, 133, 134, 147, 161, 174, 185, 194, 198, 199, 220, 238, 262, 272, 285, 297, 320, 324, 366, 369, 395

Debra Spina Dixon: 3, 26, 27, 56, (r) 78, 79, 88, 106, 107, 118, 119, 130, 131, 141, 158, 159, 182, 183, 210, 234, 235, 260, 261, 282, 283, 308, 309, 330, 331, 356, 357, 378

Herman Mejia: 247

Sebastià Serra: 78 (bl)

Pere Virgili: 54, 56, 58, 70, 73, 116, 117, 120, 123, 124, 132, 146, 178, 179, 192, 211, 292, 359, 370

Yayo: 7, 31, 59, 83, 111, 135, 163, 187, 215, 239, 265, 287, 313, 326, 327, 335, 361, 383

Photography Credits

AGEfotostock: 300

Carlos Gaudier: 115 (l), 126, 127

Corbis Images: Cover (ml) Premium Stock. **16** tr of page: (tl, ml) Mitchell Gerber, (tmr) Yoshikazu Tsuno. **17** (bl) Reuters NewMedia, Inc. **29** (t) Bettmann, (b) Yann Arthus-Bertrand. **35** (tr) Jon Hicks. **43** Pierre-Philippe Marcon. **49** Schwarz, Shaul. **50** (tl) Buddy Mays, (tr) Patrick Ward, (bl) Mitchell Gerber, (bcl) Rufus F. Folkks, (bcr) Reuters NewMedia, Inc. Jim Ruymen, (br). **51** (tc) Nik Wheeler, (tl, br) Danny Lehman, (tr) Buddy Mays, (bl) Richard Cummins. **64** (tl) Reuters NewMedia, Inc., (bl) Catherine Karnow. **65** (tl) Wally McNamee, (ml) Mitchell Gerber, (bl) Mark E. Gibson, (tr) Ted Spiegel, (tmr), (bmr) Neal Preston, (br) Reuters NewMedia, Inc. **78** (b) Jeffrey L. Rotman. **79** (tl) Galen Rowell, (bl) David Samuel Robbins, (tr) Neal Preston. **87** (tl) Reuters NewMedia, Inc. Desmond Boylan, (tr) Reuters NewMedia, Inc. Lucas Nunez, (bl) Danny Lehman. **91** (tl, tr) Chris Trotman, (bl) Warren Morgan. **101** Bill Ross. **102** (t) Morton Beebe, (bl) Bettmann. **103** (bl) Brian A. Vikander. **115** (tr) Nik Wheeler. **119** (tl) Sergio Carmona, (ml, bmr) Steven E. Sutton, (bl) Henry Diltz, (tr) Chris Trotman, (tmr) Reuters NewMedia, Inc. Brian Snyder, (br) Reuters NewMedia, Inc.Gary Hershorn. **153** Elke Stolzenberg. **154** (t) Patrick Ward, (b) Heino Kalis. **155** (t) Jean-Pierre Lescourret, (br) Mark L. Stephenson. **182** (mr) Lois Ellen Frank. **183** (bl). **191** (tl) Owen Franken, (tr) Reuters NewMedia, Inc. Ricky Rogers. **197** (tr, ml), (tm) Peter Barrett. **205** Galen Rowell. **207** (tr) Francoise de Mulder, (bl) Rick Price, (br) Moshe Shai. **210** (bl). **219** (tr) Patrick Ward, (b) AFP. **249** Patrick Kovarik **255** William Sallaz. **256** (tl) Jeremy Horner, (tr) Javier Pierini. **257** (tl) Dave G. Houser, (tr) Miki Kratsman, (bl) Page Nicolas, (br) Owen Franken. **269** (m) Carlos Dominguez, (b) Carl Purcell. **278** Najlah Feanny-Hicks. **291** (tl) Owen Franken, (b) K. M. Westermann. **299** Tony Arruza. **303** Owen Franken. **304** (l) Dave G. Houser, (r) Craig Lovell. **305** (tl) Kevin Schafer, (tr) Tony Arruza, (bl) Buddy Mays, (br) Yann Arthus-Bertrand. **308** (tr) Kevin Schafer. **309** (tc) Buddy Mays. **310** (tr) Stephanie Maze, (br) Roger Tidman. **312** (l) Joel W. Rogers, (r) Stephanie Maze. **317** (tr), (br) Hubert Stadler. **325** Kennan Ward. **339** (tr) Patrick Ward. **344** (bl) R. W. Jones. **348** Randy Faris. **349** Keith Dannemiller. **351** Bettmann. **352** (t) Jaques M. Chenet, (bl), (br) Bettmann. **353** (t) Bernard Bisson, (b) Bill Gentile. **365** (tl) Joel W. Rogers, (b) Pablo San Juan. **367** (l) Todd Gipstein, (r) Westlake Stock-Oz Productions. **373** (b) Robert Weight. **387** (tl) Joyce Naltchayan, (tr) Steve Azzara, (b) Bill Gentile. **396** Catherine Karnow. **399** Dave G. Houser. **400** (tl) Tibor Bognar, (tr) Bob Krist, (bl) Stan Honda, (br) Ron J. Berard. **401** (t, br) Jeremy Horner, (tl) Steve Chenn.

Getty Images: Cover: (c) Stephen Simpson. **78** (tl) John Kelly. **98** (t) Phil Hunt, (b) Ghislain & Marie David de Lossy. **103** PhotoDisc. **182** (mr) Mitch Hrdlicka. **206** (b) Ken Fisher.

Latin Focus: 16 tr of page: (bl, tr) Jimmy Dorantes, (bm) Vince Bucci, (br) John Castillo. **196** Moises Castillo. **317** Scott Sady. **339** (tl) Jimmy Dorantes.

Diana Patiño de Gee: 191 (c)

About the Authors

Philip Redwine Donley received his M.A. in Hispanic Literature from the University of Texas at Austin in 1986 and his Ph.D. in Foreign Language Education from the University of Texas at Austin in 1997. Dr. Donley has taught Spanish at Austin Community College, Southwestern University, and the University of Texas at Austin. He has published articles and conducted workshops about language anxiety, language anxiety management, and the development of critical thinking skills, and is involved in research about teaching languages to the visually impaired. Dr. Donley is also the co-author of two other introductory college Spanish textbook programs published by Vista Higher Learning, **VISTAS** and **PANORAMA**.

José Luis Benavides received his Ph.D. in Interdisciplinary Studies at the University of Texas at Austin in 1997 and currently holds a dual appointment as Assistant Professor in the Department of Modern and Classical Languages and Literatures and the Department of Journalism at California State University, Northridge. In addition to teaching Spanish, journalism, and communications, Dr. Benavides has worked as a writer, editor, and translator for several major publishers in the United States.

Solivia Márquez is a Spanish Language and Literature instructor at Boston University. She received a degree in English Philology at the *Universidad de Alicante*, Spain, and her M.A. in Hispanic Language and Literatures at Boston University in 1997. She is currently working on her Ph.D. in Hispanic Language and Literatures at Boston University.

Mar Caribe

Barranquilla
Maracaibo
Caracas
Puerto España ★
Trinidad

Venezuela

Medellín
Colombia
Bogotá ★
Cali

R. Orinoco

Georgetown ★
Guyana
Paramaribo
Surinam
Cayena ★
Guayana
Francesa

Pasto

R. Magdalena

★ **Quito**
Ecuador
Guayaquil

R. Negro
R. Amazonas
• Belém

Manaus

Iquitos

Perú

R. Madeira

Recife •

Cordillera de los Andes

Lima ★
Cuzco •
Lago Titicaca

Brasil
★ **Brasilia**

Salvador •

Arequipa •
★ **La Paz**
Bolivia
Arica •
Sucre ★

R. Paraguay

Belo Horizonte •

Océano
Pacífico

Iquique •

R. Paraná

Antofagasta •

Paraguay
• Salta
Asunción ★
São Paulo •
Santos •
Río de Janeiro •

Chile

R. Paraná

R. Uruguay

Córdoba •
Porto Alegre •

Valparaíso •
Mendoza •
Rosario •

R. Paraná

Santiago
Buenos Aires ★
Uruguay
Montevideo ★

Concepción •

Argentina

Océano
Atlántico

• Bahía Blanca

Cordillera de los Andes

Puerto Montt •

N

O ← → E

S

Estrecho de
Magallanes
Islas Malvinas

• Punta Arenas

Tierra
del Fuego

América del Sur